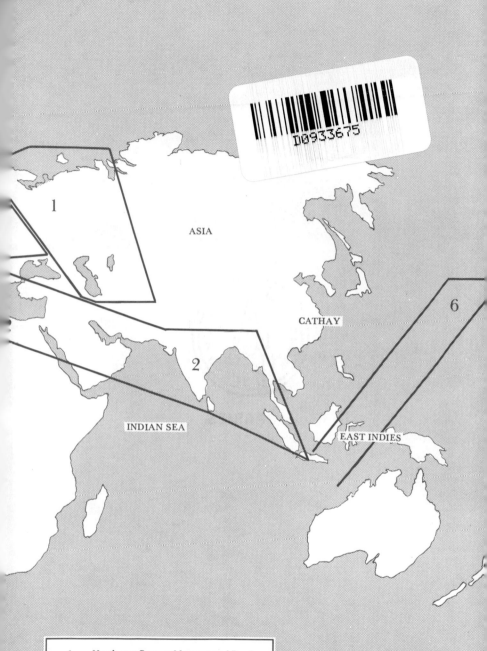

ASIA

CATHAY

INDIAN SEA

EAST INDIES

1

2

6

1. North-east Passage Muscovy and Persia
2. Mediterranean and the East
3. Guinea
4. Newfoundland and North-west Passage
5. Caribbean Virginia and Guiana
6. Straits of Magellan and beyond

HAKLUYT'S VOYAGES

A SELECTION

*1 Navigational instruments (1588).
At foot of page, on either side, are
magnetic compasses and dividers; at
top a quadrant and backstaff, with a
half-hour glass on the corner of the
canopy; in between mariners are
taking soundings with lead and line.*

HAKLUYT'S
VOYAGES

Selected and Edited by
RICHARD DAVID

Boston
HOUGHTON MIFFLIN COMPANY
1981

*Library of Congress Cataloging in
Publication Data*

Principall navigations, voiages, and discoveries
of the English nation. Selections.
Hakluyt's voyages.
Includes index.
1. America—Discovery and exploration—English.
2. Voyages and travels. I. Hakluyt, Richard, 1552?-
1616. II. David, Richard. III. Title.
E127.P752   910'.941   81-7013
ISBN 0-395-31556-5   AACR2

Contents

PART 5: THE CARIBBEAN, VIRGINIA, AND GUIANA

PART 6: THE STRAITS OF MAGELLAN AND BEYOND

Illustrations

Maps

Preface

"I do remember", wrote Richard Hakluyt to his first patron, Francis Walsingham, "that being a youth, and one of Her Majesty's scholars at Westminster, that fruitful nursery, it was my hap to visit the chamber of Master Richard Hakluyt, my cousin, a gentleman of the Middle Temple well known unto you, at a time when I found lying open upon his board certain books of cosmography, with a universal map; and he, seeing me somewhat curious in the view thereof, began to instruct my ignorance, by showing me the division of the earth into three parts after the old account and then, according to the later and better distribution, into more. He pointed with his wand to all the known seas, gulfs, bays, straits, capes, rivers, empires, kingdoms, dukedoms, and territories of each part, with declaration also of their special commodities, particular wants, which by the benefit of traffic and intercourse of merchants are plentifully supplied. From the map he brought me to the Bible, and turning to the 107th Psalm directed me to the 23rd and 24th verses, where I read that they which go down to the sea in ships, and occupy by the great waters, they see the works of the Lord, and his wonders in the deep." By this "hap" an Elizabethan schoolboy was initiated into a study of geography, and particularly human geography, that became his ruling passion throughout his subsequent career as scholar, diplomat, and clergyman, and inspired him to make the great collection of documents first published, in 1589, as *The Principall Navigations, Voiages and Discoveries of the English Nation*, and later enlarged, with the significant addition of the word *"Traffiques"* to the title (and only one l in *Principal*), into the three volumes issued between 1598 and 1600.

Hakluyt was an editor of skill and judgment as well as of enormous industry. The pieces that he printed were for the most part first-hand accounts of the actions described, with such supporting documents as are strictly relevant to them. Where he edits it is sensitively done: digressions are removed without distortion of the purpose of a narrative or of the personality of the narrator. The documents are arranged in a rational and coherent order. The whole, however, extends to one and a half million words; some of the papers are letters of state, legal documents, or "ruttiers" (what would now be called Pilots, or navigational guides to particular sea-passages); and the reader who is neither a naval nor an economic historian may find it hard to pick out those items that he would find of lasting interest. There is an obvious need of some selection.

For the non-professional reader the great glory of "Hakluyt" is likely to be that so much of it consists of eye-witness accounts of experiences that, whether tragic or triumphant, are generally testing and almost always extraordinary. The narrators, moreover, are almost as various as Chaucer's Canterbury pilgrims, except that Hakluyt's cast is all male. The man with a story to tell may be officer or seaman, merchant, gentleman-adventurer, servant, or curious tripper. Each tells his story in his own style, which may be polished or semi-literate, jocular or pious, critical or naïve. One voice counterpoints another. An early employee of the Muscovy Company writes a breezy account of life among the Samoyeds. Later his second-in-command hints, in a letter to his principals at home, that this breeziness goes too far and that their agent's fondness for the bottle is getting the Company a bad name. A year or two later, when the critic has succeeded to the headship of the trade mission to Persia, one of *his* juniors similarly hints that his boss is an old woman, too cautious and prim to succeed as an export sales manager. Such undercover rivalry is a permanent feature of human institutions; it is seldom so neatly and delicately exhibited as in these narratives of Hakluyt.

Because, in Hakluyt, what is projected with peculiar directness and vividness is human nature as revealed in reaction to experience, I have based my selection on the following principles:

(1) In general no narrative is included that is not written by an eye-witness and sharer in the enterprise described, but I have allowed myself three exceptions. I have included Hakluyt's own precis of his interview (to obtain which he made a 200-mile journey on horseback) with the last survivor of Hore's 1536 voyage to Newfoundland; and I have also accepted Richard Eden's histories of the first two voyages to Guinea, which are certainly based on first-hand evidence though padded out with much apocryphal (but still enjoyable) material from classical authors.

(2) Chosen narratives are printed in full without abridgment or editing: the human narrator is given at least as full a say as Hakluyt allowed him. He may at times be garrulous or monotonous. Nothing much happens on Steven Burrough's voyage towards the Ob, but I know no other writing that so instantly and authentically conveys the very feel of being at sea in a small ship; while the horrors of that north-east passage could not be more graphically conveyed than by Hugh Smith's patient logging of fog, fog, fog, and ice, ice, ice. Again there is an exception; I have omitted the first two chapters of Miles Philip's story, because his account of Hawkins' voyage up to the sinking of the *Jesus* in San Juan de Ulua closely duplicates Hawkins' own narrative and is probably borrowed from it.

(3) I have tended to concentrate on a few particular enterprises,

following them through their successive instalments. In this way the reader, becoming more and more familiar with the characters and the terrain, is likely to be more engrossed in the story. Such a panoramic view is not always practical. Barlow's "discovery" of Virginia and Raleigh's "discovery" of Guiana are both models of direct and detailed observation; but the story of Virginia thereafter becomes bogged down in intrigues with and among the natives and later narratives tell us nothing of what it was really like to be an English colonist, while the follow-up in Guiana was equally messy and abortive. Frobisher's expeditions to the north-west are too fully documented. I have preferred the three separate accounts here printed to George Best's considered history of the whole enterprise. He is fuller than the others, but I do not find his descriptions of events so precise or, at times, so lively.

(4) I have concentrated on Traffics and Discoveries and have included few or none of the many narratives of battles on land and sea. These are often stirring, and stirringly narrated, but they seem to me not so near the heart of Hakluyt's matter. The most painful exclusions under this head have been the account of the Spanish Armada, though this is no more than a translation, by Hakluyt himself, of a Latin history; and Ralcigh's brilliant, but not first-hand, report of the last fight of the *Revenge*.

I have followed Hakluyt's grouping of the narratives by geographical areas rather than adopt a strictly chronological arrangement. Geographical grouping helps the reader to become familiar with a region and its development, though it may mask some significant connections, as that the Charles Jackman who perished in a disastrous attempt on the north-east passage and the Andrew Dyer who was hanged in Tripoli through a miscarriage of justice were the two Master's Mates who had served Frobisher so brilliantly in the north-western ice.

The text printed is based on that of the MacLehose edition in 12 volumes, 1905; but spelling and punctuation have been modernised. This process necessarily entails a number of quite arbitrary decisions. In Elizabethan times many words were evolving, or being corrupted, from older into newer forms: examples within a single letter are "hale" and "haul", "harborough" and "harbour", "hoise" and "hoist". In all such cases I have adopted the later form for the sake of easier reading. On the same principle I have regularised the occasional "spake" to "spoke", "rid" to "rode", "holpen" to "helped". The older forms are preserved in the Authorised (King James) Version of the Bible, and if I were editing poetry I would keep them; but, in a narrative of action, immediacy and the avoidance of the merely quaint have seemed to me more important than the faithful preservation of actual word-forms. Yet a line must be drawn somewhere if the whole Elizabethan tone of the work is not to disintegrate, and I have baulked (again arbitrarily) at altering "speaketh" to "speaks", "doth" to "does", etc.

A few words give particular trouble. For the meanings that today we distinguish as "lose" and "loose", "travel" and "travail", the Elizabethans used either spelling indiscriminately. It is not always certain from the context which meaning is intended, and indeed the writer is sometimes punning on both.

It has not been easy to decide how far to modernise place-names. World-famous places must obviously appear in their familiar spelling, provided that this is not too far removed from what the Elizabethans wrote: thus "Mosco" becomes "Moscow". I have also adjusted differences in less common names where these differences are slight: "Shemmaki" and "Shamakhy" both become the modern "Shemakha". Where, however, the Elizabethans anglicised a foreign name I have left it as they wrote it, for it seems to me as pedantic to alter "Saint John de Ulua" to "San Juan" as to write "Felipe Segundo" for Philip II. Where modern names differ substantially from the Elizabethan I have left the originals but have glossed them in the Index (Prayag/Allahabad, Colmogro/Kholmogory).

Numerals pose a different, if minor problem. In the original text dates are most commonly given in the form "the 2. of Januarie", but "the 2. day", "the 2nd", and "the second" also occur, and all other figures are varied in the same ways. Probably these variations are no more than the vagaries of Elizabethan printers, but they help to emphasise the unstudied practicality of the narratives, and therefore, beyond amending "the 2." to "the 2nd", etc. and always using figures for degrees of latitude and longitude, I have left them as I found them. For the same reason I have not been too careful to tidy punctuation. The ship's company of the *Delight* in the Straits of Magellan were not particularly literate, and to put a high polish on their petition would be to destroy its urgency.

Every editor of Hakluyt owes an incalculable debt to the MacLehose edition, which not only established the text but provided, especially in its illustrations and the comments upon them, a wealth of background information. I would like also to render thanks to the Hakluyt Society whose publications, over more than a hundred years, have done so much to enrich our knowledge of the context in which Hakluyt wrote and his voyagers acted; and I am particularly indebted to the index, contributed by Alison Quinn to the fascimile of Hakluyt's first edition (1589) published by the Society in 1965, which embodies immense learning and enormously facilitates the indentification of places and persons.

I must also thank Dr A. P. McGowan, Deputy Keeper Department of Ships, National Maritime Museum, and Mr John Munday, Keeper of the Department of Weapons and Antiquities, for taking so much trouble to search for answers to questions, particularly questions about the ranges of Elizabethan guns, which in the event appear to be unanswerable.

The sources of illustrations are acknowledged in the list on pages 9–10.

Richard David
October 1980

Key Dates

1488	Portuguese (Dias) round the Cape of Good Hope
1492	Columbus discovers the Caribbean for Spain
1493	Pope Alexander VI divides the earth between Portugal and Spain
1497	The Cabots, in an English ship, explore Newfoundland
1506	Charles (Habsburg) inherits Burgundy and the Netherlands
1509	Henry VIII King of England; marries Catherine of Aragon
1517	Martin Luther attacks church abuses
1518	Charles becomes King of Aragon, Castile, and Sicily
1519	Charles elected Holy Roman Emperor
1521	Cortes conquers Mexico for Spain
1524	Francis I of France seizes Milan
1525	Francis at Milan taken prisoner by Charles
1529	Turks reach the walls of Vienna
1531	German Lutheran princes form the League of Schmalkalden
1532	Henry VIII divorces Catherine
1533	Piazarro conquers Peru for Spain
1536	Francis I concludes alliance with Turks
1547	Edward VI King of England; Charles defeats Lutheran princes at Mühlberg
1553	Mary Tudor Queen of England
1554	Mary Tudor marries Philip, Infante of Spain
1555	Charles abdicates in favour of his son, Philip II
1558	Elizabeth Queen of England
1559	Henry II of France killed jousting; protestant Huguenots in power
1565	Turks besiege Malta
1568	Spanish commander, Alba, disciplines rebellious Netherlanders
1571	Spain defeats Turks at sea-battle of Lepanto
1572	St Bartholomew's Day: Catholic Guises incite massacre of Huguenots
1580	Philip of Spain annexes Portugal
1558	English expeditionary force, under Leicester, aids Netherlanders
1587	Drake raids Cadiz to destroy Spanish invasion fleet
1588	Spanish Armada; Guises murdered; Henry III of France assassinated
1590	Spanish army saves Paris from Navarre, Huguenot heir to the throne
1593	Navarre embraces Catholic religion
1586	Dutch independence recognised by France and England
1598	France united under Navarre as King Henry IV; Philip of Spain dies

General Introduction

In 1488, as the climax to 75 years of Portuguese exploration of the west coast of Africa, Bartolomeu Dias rounded the Cape of Good Hope, and so opened a sea route to the East Indies, with which previous European contact had been only by devious journeys through Egypt or the Middle East. In 1492 Columbus, seeking, for Spain, a western access to this precious East, discovered a New World. In 1493 Pope Alexander VI divided the earth between Portugal and Spain, the boundary later negotiated between the parties being the meridian 370 leagues west of the Cape Verde Islands. All discoveries to the east of this line were declared the exclusive property of Portugal, all to the west of Spain.

These developments shifted the centre of gravity of the European civilisation. Hitherto its focus had been the Mediterranean. The great maritime powers of medieval times, the Venetians and the Genoese, were already facing incursions by the empire of the Osmanli Turks into their sea; they now found it to be no longer unique. It is significant that so many of the great explorers, Columbus, Cabot, Vespucci, Veruzzano, were Italians who migrated to the Atlantic seaboard in search of new fields of endeavour. Nations, such as England, which before had been on the fringes, were now in the front rank of progress; but the advantage gained by the Portuguese and Spanish initiatives and confirmed by the Pope were hard to overtake.

Further discoveries enormously increased this advantage. In 1521 Cortes, from a Spanish base in the newly consolidated Caribbean, conquered Mexico; and in 1533 the adventurer Pizarro against all expectation became master of Peru. From these new acquisitions, vigorously exploited, Spain received a huge addition of wealth which not only boosted the Spanish predominance but also helped to create an inflation that increasingly pinched the poorer nations. In seeking to compete with Spain, the French, the English, and later the Dutch, were as much actuated by the urge to self-preservation as by greed. Competition, however, was not direct or simple, for it was counterpointed by political, dynastic, and later religious rivalries, which in the course of the 16th century periodically altered the configuration of the nations, destroying old alignments and creating new.

The chief rivals were the House of Valois, Kings of France, and the

House of Habsburg, originally Austrian. The French kings, attempting from the middle of the 15th century to regain dominance after the punishing Hundred Years War with England, found themselves constantly harassed by the territorial ambitions of their eastern neighbours the Dukes of Burgundy, who had come to control not only part of eastern France but also the Netherlands. The potentiality of the Burgundians was further extended when in 1477 the orphaned daughter of the House married Maximilian, son of the Habsburg ruler of Austria who at that time was also Holy Roman Emperor, though that title now carried little political power. The son of that marriage, Philip the Handsome, brought further glory to Burgundy by marrying Juana, daughter of Ferdinand of Aragon and Isabella of Castile, for by this alliance his son, Charles V, was in 1518–19 to acquire dominion not only over Spain and the Netherlands but also over Sicily and Naples. The French therefore found themselves increasingly encircled by the Habsburg power, and rancour increased when, in 1519, Charles was elected Holy Roman Emperor in direct competition with the French King, Francis I.

The first French attempt to break the Habsburg ring was in Italy, whose fragmentation into a number of small states invited invasion and where France and Aragon had already clashed. For while Aragon ruled Sicily and, through a bastard branch, had a lien on Naples, France could make a claim to both Naples and Milan. In 1524 Francis succeeded in appropriating the latter, only to lose it again a year later when he rashly challenged a Spanish relief-force and was himself taken prisoner. Though ransomed, he had to leave two sons as hostages with Charles, and the experience did not improve relations between Habsburg and Valois. The next thirty years saw a continuing struggle, at times open, at times diplomatic, between France and Spain.

Two other elements complicated the political situation. The first was the continual pressure exerted upon the west by the Turks. The strength of the Osmanli empire depended on a caste of professional warriors who required a constant supply of adventure and plunder to keep them in health and loyalty. This was the trigger for a series of major expeditions, which overran much of Hungary and brought the Turks to the walls of Vienna in 1529. Charles went to the assistance of his brother Ferdinand, who had inherited the Austrian end of the Habsburg territories, but only the impossibility of supporting a large army 1,000 miles from its base, and fear of the Persians on their eastern frontier, held back the Turks from further penetration into Europe. Francis' main reprisal for his humiliation at Milan was an alliance (1536) with the Great Turk (Suleiman the Magnificent), which opened the western Mediterranean to Turkish influence. Certainly the need to stem Turkish inroads in eastern Europe, to protect Sicily, a vital granary for Spain, and Malta, and to keep control of Italy, distracted Charles' attention from the confrontation with France and constituted a continual drain on his resources. The second complication was religious. In 1517 Luther posted up his 95 objections to certain Catholic practices, notably the selling of indulgences and the papal claim to infallibility. It was Charles' duty as Holy Roman Emperor to maintain the faith. The Diet of Worms, convened at his order in 1521, condemned Luther, but Luther's prince, the Elector of Saxony, while himself remaining a Catholic, shielded his protégé from the consequences. Protest against Catholic abuses, allied with growing unrest among the peasant classes, led to the secession from Rome of a number of German principalities, not always from the purest of motives, for freedom to expropriate monastic wealth was a quick means of making up the deficit in a princely revenue. The seceding princes came together in 1531 to form an alliance, the League of Schmalkalden.

Henry II of France exploited the religious element as his father, Francis, had exploited that of the Turks. After the discomfiture of the League by Charles' army at Mühlberg (1547), an alliance between Saxony, Hesse, and the rest with (despite his title) the "Most Catholic Majesty of France" promised them French protection in return for the key fortresses of Metz, Toul, and Verdun. Charles, baulked of his ambition to consolidate the Holy Roman Empire under central control, took the surprising step of abdicating in 1555; and Henry was accidentally killed while jousting in 1559. The struggle between them had bankrupted both royal houses, but after an uneasy truce signalled by the Peace of Augsburg (1555) it was to be renewed by the next generation. But by now the religious struggle had become internal to both realms.

In France, Henry II had succeeded by rigorous persecution in stamping out Lutheranism, but another form of protestantism, preached by a banished Frenchman, Calvin, had penetrated the country from Switzerland and was favoured by several of the great families. French history for the next fifty years, until almost the turn of the century, was basically the contest between the Catholic Guises and the protestant Bourbon and Montmorency. In the Netherlands, too, Calvinism found adherents, especially in the north, now Holland. But it was Spanish insensitivity—perhaps that of Charles' successor, Philip II, himself—in seeking first to impose single, external government upon the native and very various councils of the towns and estates, and then to enforce religious unity and obedience by the Duke of Alba's campaign of military repression (1568), that drove the Netherlanders to extremes. Though more pacific commanders, notably Parma, succeeded in appeasing the Catholic south (Brabant, now Belgium), the protestant insurgents, commanding the sea and later associated with the House of Orange, progressively took control of the northern provinces and, with some losses and gains, held them from the early seventies onwards in a protracted stale-mate. In all these cross-currents the course steered by England was as erratic as any. When Henry VIII married Catherine of Aragon, he committed himself in anticipation to the Spanish party, for Charles V was Catherine's nephew; and the alliance became fact during Charles' first quarrel with Francis. When Henry divorced Catherine it was a double insult to Charles, head of the Catholic Empire, and in 1532 a common fear of Spain united England and France in a defensive alliance; yet by 1544 Henry was again giving aid to Charles by invading northern France. When Mary Tudor succeeded Edward VI, England again became a catholic state, and ties with Spain were confirmed by the Queen's marriage to Philip II, who in 1557 actively engaged England in his war with France. On Mary's death it was the French who most strongly campaigned against the succession of Elizabeth, for they had their own candidate for the English throne in Mary Queen of Scots, niece to the Guises and wife of Henry II's eldest son; while Philip, hoping to retain England by marriage to his deceased wife's half-sister, wooed Elizabeth. When plans to supplant Elizabeth and to marry her to Spain had equally failed, the French adopted Philip's tactics, and two French princes, Anjou (1572), and Alençon (1579 and again in 1581–2), successively sought the English Queen's hand. During this period England was at peace with France, while relations with Spain progressively worsened. English raids on Spanish territories in America increased in frequency and in seriousness; when in 1580, after the Portuguese royal line had failed, Spain annexed her neighbour, the English gave asylum and support to the Portuguese pretender, Dom Antonio; and in 1585 an English expeditionary force under the Earl of Leicester was sent to aid the protestant rebels in the Netherlands. Religious sympathy, again, aligned England with Henry of Navarre, the Huguenot claimant to the French throne after the assassination of Henry III in 1588. Thereafter the differences that had opposed nation to nation were overlaid by a new pattern of internal divisions. Spain and the French Catholics were for once on the same side, while England was linked with the Huguenots and with the Netherlanders. Small wonder that when Philip at last launched his Armada against England, Catholic and Huguenot strove the one to offer, the other to deny him, a supporting force on the Normandy coast; or that in 1590, the Netherlanders received a respite as Parma, the Spanish general opposed to them, was drawn off to bar Henry of Navarre from Paris.

The chapter of European history that concerns Hakluyt is rounded off by the politic volte-face of Navarre, who in 1593 declared his conversion to Rome and in 1598 was generally recognised as King of

France, by the death of Philip in the same year, and by virtual independence of the Dutch by 1596.

2. TO THE SEA IN SHIPS

The ships mentioned in Hakluyt's *Voyages* varied widely in size and structure, from the *San Felipe*, the giant Spaniard of 1,500 tons that first grappled with Grenville's *Revenge*, to the *Gabriel* and the *Michael*, of 25 and 20 tons, no bigger than an inshore fishing-trawler, with which Frobisher first set out to explore the north-west passage. Most of the bigger English ships were units of the Queen's navy, although this never mustered more than thirty capital ships throughout Elizabeth's reign. One of them might be lent as "admiral" or flagship to an expedition in which the Queen had an interest. The remainder were built and owned by private, and often very local and personal, enterprise.

Though English naval design was markedly improved, in the direction of greater speed, manoeuvrability, and power to maintain a stable platform for gunnery, while John Hawkins was Treasurer of the Navy (from 1578 onwards), many ships were of an antiquated pattern. The *Jesus of Lubeck*, a Queen's ship abandoned by Hawkins in the fight at San Juan de Ulua in 1568, had been bought for Henry VIII's navy in 1545 and had served the Hanseatic League in the Baltic before that. Such ships were carvel-built (the wooden planking set edge to edge and caulked between). They were squat and beamy. Below the main or "spar" deck there was a second, the gun-deck; and below that the two ends of the ship were often covered in, above the hold with its gravel ballast, with a third or half-deck, the orlop. The central space of the main deck (the "waist") was open, but before and abaft this the superstructure was built up, tier upon narrowing tier, into the forecastle and the poop, which might extend 20 feet beyond the sternpost. This enormous top-hamper made the ship unstable and difficult to bring to wind. It also caused them to pitch heavily in any sea, and for this reason the bows of the ship carried a heavy cut-water or beakhead.

Mainmast and foremast both ended in "tops", enclosed wooden platforms that served as look-out and firing posts, but above these were mounted the topmasts, separate spars that could be taken down in heavy weather. Each lower mast carried a large square-sail (fore course and main course) on yards almost as broad as the mast was high. The topmasts carried much smaller topsails narrowing sharply upwards to short upper yards. There was no system of reefing: in bad weather sails were simply taken in progressively. In light winds the area of the courses could be enlarged by lacing additional pieces of canvas ("bonnets" or "drablers") to the foot of the sail. A third mast, the mizen, abaft the mainmast, carried a lateen or fore-and-aft sail, and

was occasionally repeated in a fourth mast, the bonaventure mizen. The ends of the yards often carried shear-hooks, or iron sickles, intended to rip the rigging of any enemy vessel that came too close. From the bows another spar, the bow-sprit, projected upwards at a fairly sharp angle and on the underside of this was mounted a square spritsail. Jib and staysail, the headsails that so facilitate changing tack or "going about", were unknown to the Elizabethans.

Although one of these "great" or "tall" ships usually served as flagship of an expeditionary fleet, the actual work of exploration, in uncharted waters, was more easily performed by much smaller vessels, of shallow draft, flush-decked or with only a minimal poop, and therefore better sailers and more manoeuvrable. Indeed such work was frequently delegated to vessels even smaller than Frobisher's *Gabriel* and *Michael*, to the pinnaces that accompanied each fleet and were little more than decked ship's boats. These were sometimes clinker-built (with overlapping planking), and constructed in collapsible sections that could be stowed aboard the larger ships for the ocean passage and assembled at the point of destination. They could at a pinch be moved by oars, as were the regular ship's-boats, the "shallop" and the "cock".

Brief mention must be made of the foreign ships encountered by Hakluyt's voyagers: the "fusts" or "foists" of the Mediterranean, and the brigantines, light vessels which, like the English pinnace, could be propelled by either sails or oars; the fast-sailing lateen-rigged caravels of the Portuguese, and the Spanish (and Turkish) galleys and galleasses, vast hulks moved by several banks of oars with three or more galley-slaves chained to each oar.

Armament plays a large part in Hakluyt's narratives. The largest cannon in use in his time were the basilisk, with a bore of $8\frac{3}{4}$ inches, and the culverin, a muzzle-loading $5\frac{1}{2}$ inch gun, up to 15 feet in length, which threw an 18 pound metal cannon-ball a distance of a mile and a half; but these were too heavy, and in particular too long, for convenient use at sea. Most tall ships, however, carried a battery of demi-culverins ranged along either side of their gun-deck. These 8 to 10 foot, $4\frac{1}{2}$ inch bore, nine-pounder cannon were mounted on wheel carriages and secured to the side of the ship by tackles, with the aid of which they could be "run out" until their muzzles projected through the square gun-ports. The tackles also served to swivel and train them, while their elevation could be adjusted by inserting wooden wedges or

2 A tall ship (Ark Royal 1588). Note spritsail under bow-sprit, a second ("bonaventure") mizen, and on mainmast an extra sail (topgallant).

"quoins". A wire was passed through the touch-hole to pierce the cartridge (gunpowder sewn into a cloth or canvas pack) which had been rammed down the muzzle while it was inboard and followed by a wad and ball. The touch-hole was then filled with fine powder from the horn at the gunner's belt, and the "match", burning at the end of a wooden toasting-fork or "linstock", applied. The heat and the recoil generated on firing were enormous. The "run in" gun had then to be sponged out with a mop and cooled with water, and could not be fired again for at least five minutes. In continuing engagements much longer resting periods were often necessary. Missiles could be single metal or stone balls, or "chain-shot", several balls linked by chain, which scythed through the rigging or spars of the enemy ship, or again packages of nails that, flying in all directions like shrapnel, inflicted personal wounds on the crew. There were also bombards, or mortars of large bore, used to loft stones or fireballs onto the enemy.

Individual arms were arquebuses, a term including the heavier musket and the lighter caliver, muzzle-loaded hand-guns discharging a small bullet or arrow, the musket mounted on a staff to give support in aiming and firing; long-bows and cross-bows; and the pike, a spear with a broad cutting edge. These, with steel helmet ("morion") and "corselet", would be issued from the ship's stores to the fighting-man as his "furniture". He would provide his own knife or dagger, and perhaps a sword.

The complement of the 700 ton *Jesus of Lubeck* was 100 men and officers. Pet's 40 ton *George* carried, beside the captain, nine men; Jackman's 20 ton *William* five men and a boy. The crew of a Queen's ship would include volunteers, but also pressed men and occasionally prisoners drafted from the gaols (Frobisher preferred to dismiss all his "condemned men" before sailing). They were paid 10 shillings a month, and their keep. Though there were penalties for misdemeanours, including swearing, discipline was negligible by the standards of, say, Anson or Bligh. In the private ships the mariners were all independent volunteers, rewarded by a share of the takings and with a will of their own as to where the ship went and what it did. As Elizabethan voyages were undertaken as profitable speculations, the

3 a Caliver, b musket, c halberd, d pike.
The soldier with the caliver wears a corselet and Spanish morion and carries his match in his right hand. The musketeer's right hand holds his rest. The halberd was the distinctive weapon of a Sergeant. The pikeman wears a corselet and "comb" morion.

a

b

c

d

ships usually carried a varied supercargo of merchants, gentlemen-adventurers, soldiers, and owners' servants. On his third exploration of the north-west passage Frobisher took with him 30 miners who, with 30 soldiers to protect them, were to attempt to winter ashore in the arctic.

Living quarters were exceedingly cramped. The men were divided into messes of four or five, each reserving a tiny space, perhaps curtained off with canvas screens, on the gundeck or the orlop. Pairs of men from opposite watches shared a mattress or pile of gear, the one sleeping while the other was on watch. There was little room for possessions or spare clothes, and one of the agonies of bad weather was the difficulty of getting a "shift" of dry clothes. The junior officers shared primitive cabins on the orlop. The captain and the gentlemen were more roomily housed in the poop, where the captain's day-cabin, girdled with the stern-walk, was often a handsome room where the leader of the expedition dined in state from his own silver service and was entertained by his private musicians. The ship's trumpeter, however, had a more official function: it was he who often gave the signal to the fleet to close the admiral for orders, and for joining battle. It is curious that of Davis' crew of 23 for his second voyage to the north-west no fewer than four were musicians, presumably to "allure" the Eskimos.

The Captain was the executive head in each ship, and the Captain-General, carried in the admiral, the executive head of the whole expedition. The Captain might have an understudy, his Lieutenant. The Captain was by no means always a seaman; and while Hawkins, Drake and Frobisher personally supervised the navigation, Cumberland, Fenton, or Cavendish would have been incapable of this. The main responsibility for navigating and handling the ship rested with the Master, assisted in larger ships by a Master's Mate and possibly a specialist Pilot for the fleet. The Boatswain, with his Mate, had charge of the rigging and of the seaman's stores. He was also the ship's policeman and, if necessary, executioner. The Gunner kept the ordnance in good order and the Corporal did the same for the small arms. The Purser, assisted in larger ships by the Steward, oversaw the stowing and the issue of provisions and kept the ship's accounts. Four Quartermasters looked to the stowage and maintained good order in the hold. The Cook tended his wood fire (always to be dowsed at night) on a brick platform laid upon the ballast. Larger ships might carry a Chaplain, for divine service was regularly held, and a Surgeon; and there were two tradesmen, Carpenter and Cooper, whose great importance will be described later.

Before sailing, the ship would take in barrels of salted beef, pork, and fish, dried pease, cheese, butter, and sacks of meal for bread-making. A specimen allowance or "proportion" (Davis' first voyage), said to be generous on account of the arctic conditions, is, for a mess of five per day, 4 pounds of bread, 12 wine-quarts of beer, 6 Newfoundland fishes (probably cod), and on meat days (quantity of meat not stated) a gill of pease in addition. The beer tended to run out or became too acid to swallow and, as the ship might well be out of home waters for over a year and, on a long passage (e.g. from Guinea to the Caribbean), out of sight of land for 40 or 50 days, it was usually necessary to replenish stores during the voyage, either by purchase in any country touched on that was prepared to trade or by foraging. Fish was caught on passage; and in many voyages a party was sent ashore to massacre seals or penguins for fodder. As these did not preserve well the result, as in Cavendish's last voyage, could be disastrous. In this lay the importance of the Cooper who was shipped, with his staves and hoops, in order that any provisions so obtained could, after drying or salting, be cased up securely. The Cooper was also responsible for the water-butts; and narrative after narrative reveals how vital it was, especially in the later stages of a voyage, to find somewhere ashore where the water supplies could be conveniently replenished. The frequent refusal of the Spaniards or of the native peoples to allow this facility often forced the English commanders to take chances that sometimes led to disaster.

Another imperative need on a long voyage was to find a beach where the ship could be brought aground and hauled by tackles first on one side and then on the other so that the bottom could be careened or "trimmed" of clogging seaweeds and barnacles that had attached themselves to it. Then the bilges had to be "rummaged", or cleaned of any debris, especially food scraps, that might putrefy, and afterwards disinfected with plentiful vinegar. It was desirable also, in tropical waters, to make frequent inspection for damage by the dreaded boring-worm, the teredo, which could reduce the stoutest timbers to a crumbling honeycomb. No ship was metal-sheathed and the only preservative was an application of pitch. This, too, had to be provided; and the opportunity would no doubt be taken to carry out at the same time a certain amount of refitting. This might include the cutting of new spars to replace those sprung in bad weather. Here the Carpenter took charge. A major repair might require the setting up on shore of a portable forge for the making of nails and other ironmongery.

As already described, an Elizabethan ship, especially a large one with high "castles", was often not very handy. She could not lie closer to the wind than an angle of fifty degrees and tended to be blown to leeward of her course. Her tacks or "boards" were therefore shallow, and against a strong wind or tide she could make little headway. Her only recourse then was to anchor and wait for a change. This explains why it was so important to Elizabethan Masters to have plentiful and good ground-tackle and why they so often anchored in surprisingly

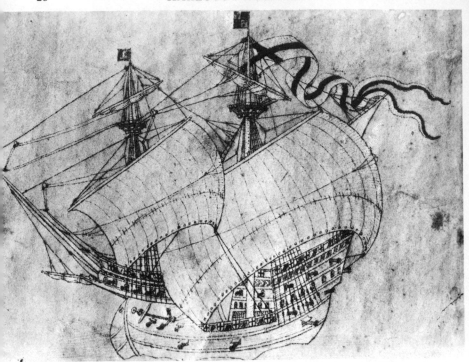

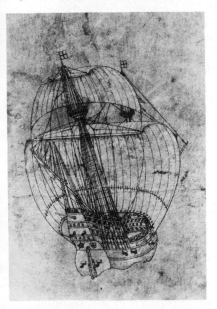

4 Ships on a wind and running free (1545). From the set of the sails on the first can be seen why Elizabethan ships made so little headway against the wind.

deep water. Because anchoring was frequently an emergency measure, the risk of getting the anchor fouled and of losing it was great; while without an anchor a ship would be completely at the mercy of the elements.

Changing tack or going about was a laborious process. The ship would "luff" or be brought head to wind, and would then be allowed to drift astern with rudder reversed until the courses had been reslanted and had filled with wind on the new tack. Backing the fore-and-aft mizen might help to kick the stern round; in any case this lateen sail had to be manhandled round the foreside of the mast. Often it was preferable to " go room", i.e. wear, or keep the ship's head falling away from the wind until it had turned the greater part of a circle and taken the wind on its other side. Occasionally such a manoeuvre was quite impossible. One of the most cliff-hanging accounts of Elizabethan seamanship is the description of how the *Desire*, separated from Cavendish on his last voyage and caught in a storm, succeeded against all expectation, with no time to luff and no room to wear, in clawing her way back from the South Sea into the comparative shelter of Magellan's Straits.

The Elizabethan navigator could, if the sun showed, fix his latitude each day at noon ("a south sun") by observing the angle between it and the horizon, or, at tabled times, by applying the same process to the pole-star. This he did with an astrolabe or the simple backstaff. But with only a half-hour glass to measure time between noon and noon he could not fix the moment for any other sights and so was unable to determine his longitude except by dead-reckoning, i.e. guessing the distance travelled along the ship's course and plotting each day's "run" on his "plat" or chart. When in sight of land he could take bearings of it with his compass, and, provided he had ascertained the size of the local compass-variation (and in some places the needle may wander as much as 30 degrees from true north), could fix his position from that—always supposing that the area in which he found himself had been charted and charted accurately. He also made much use of lead and line. These could at least warn him if he was standing into shoal water, and the tallow "arming" of the lead, bringing up samples of sand, mud, or shell from the bottom, might provide other evidence of locality. The value to the navigator of "ruttiers", today called "Pilots", containing descriptions of a coastline with bearings and depths of water, compiled by seamen who had passed that way before him, needs no stressing.

3. TRAFFIC AND INTERCOURSE OF MERCHANTS

In the 16th century England, unlike such Mediterranean powers as Venice which had to import quantities of grain, was virtually self-sufficient at least as regards the bare necessities of life. Nevertheless there were, quite apart from luxuries such as silk, furs, gold, ivory, jewels, and wine, many goods in common use that could only be obtained from abroad. These included spices, and especially pepper, to make food palatable at a time when, without freezers or even icehouses, many foodstuffs could not be preserved and tended to "go off"; leather (hides), principally from north Africa; and dye-stuffs for cloths manufactured by a vigorous weaving trade, particularly in East Anglia. These manufacturers, moreover, needed to export. To be able to "traffic" overseas had been, at least from the 13th century onwards, essential to the well-being of the nation.

The international trading was exercised through the companies set up to operate in specific areas, an early example being the Merchant Adventurers, founded in the middle of the 15th century to organise, mainly through Antwerp, the sale of English cloth to continental finishers. The companies might be either "regulated" or "joint stock" companies. The former were trade associations whose members accepted common regulations, and enjoyed some common privileges and services, but who traded each with his own capital and for his own profit. The members of the latter contributed to a common stock of capital and received a share of whatever profits were made from its use. Whereas in Spain and Portugal the organisation of overseas trade was largely in the hands of state agencies, which might nevertheless grant or lease monopolies for particular areas or goods to particular individuals and associations, in England the companies were private, although the Crown, as well as many an influential member of the Court, might be a sharer in them. In Hakluyt's lifetime were founded the Muscovy Company (1555), the Eastland Company (for the Baltic trade, 1579), the Levant Company (1581), the Africa Company (1588), and the East India Company (1600), besides ad hoc companies to fund Frobisher's expeditions to the north-west, Raleigh's enterprises in Virginia and Guiana, and a host of privateering expeditions that looked to make a profit from the plundering of Spanish and Portuguese shipping and colonies. Each sharer had his "bill of adventure", which recorded his stake and what would be his share of the profit struck after due deduction of the expenses of victualling, stores, and repairs. In privateering voyages a distinction was drawn between the bulk cargo of the prize, not to be broken up until, on arrival at a home port, it could be properly valued and his agreed share paid over to each sharer, including the members of the privateer's crew; and "pillage", that is the personal belongings of the complement of the prize, if less than forty shillings in value, which were by tradition the perquisite of the pillagers and were either privately pocketed or immediately shared out at a meeting by the mainmast.

The trading companies maintained a headquarters staff in the home town of their largest shareholders, whether London, Bristol, Southampton, or elsewhere; and, like the state offices of Spain and Portugal (the Casa de Contratacion, and the Casas de Guinea and dos Indias), they financed considerable research into navigation and into the commercial possibilities of the countries with which they were concerned. The two Richard Hakluyts (the author, and his elder cousin of the Middle Temple and Eyton in Herefordshire) were among those retained as consultants by the companies. In addition company agents or factors were often established overseas. Their duties included the maintainence of good relations with the potentates without whose permission and licence they could not trade at all, the active development of new markets through the planning, organisation, and equipment of exploratory expeditions, and attempts to obtain special concessions and the lowering of the often very high taxes and customs dues imposed on traders. These dues were levied by the "customer", either in cash or more often as a percentage of the goods carried. A special form of custom was exercised in Middle Eastern countries, where the local ruler (and often his roving competitors as well) would claim, for instance, "one ninth and two sevenths", meaning one each of nine different commodities and two each of seven others. The various activities of the agents are well illustrated, in the present collection, by the official reports made to the Muscovy Company. The companies also maintained an "English house" in many major ports overseas, providing accommodation and services for any visitor from England who carried the necessary introductions.

The prime commodity of English merchants was, as has already been mentioned, wool, generally in the form of rough weaves or "kerseys". Important markets were the eastern Mediterranean, Russia, and, through Russia, the countries round the Caspian Sea. Interesting lists of the goods sold, and taken in exchange, by English merchants in different markets are given by Arthur Edwards (for Persia, pp. 99–100 below) and William Towerson (for Guinea, pp. 263–4 below).

A very special trade was that in negro slaves. The Portuguese, in the course of their steady colonisation of Madeira, the Azores, the Cape Verde Islands, and Brazil had relied on slaves, obtained at first from North Africa and later from Senegal, the Gold Coast, and Benin, for the cultivation and development of their new territories and especially for the plantation of that highly profitable crop, the sugar cane. After the Spaniards had exhausted the native population of their Caribbean possessions, they were glad to replace the labour force with similar negro slaves, obligingly supplied to them by the Portuguese or by such English entrepreneurs as John Hawkins. This trade was, however, progressively discouraged by the Spanish authorities, not for humanitarian reasons but because it gave cover for the penetration, by substantial fleets, into the jealously guarded Caribbean empire.

While English traders operated largely by barter, exchanging their kerseys for silks, gold, or spices, the Portuguese, with nothing in the way of manufactured goods to export, were compelled to carry bullion to pay for their purchases abroad. The Dutch, on the other hand, despite their subjection to Spain, developed in the course of the century a major carrying trade between Spain and the Baltic and even farther afield, which well prepared them to become, with independence, the most enterprising of all the maritime powers.

Part 1

THE NORTH-EAST PASSAGE, MUSCOVY, AND PERSIA

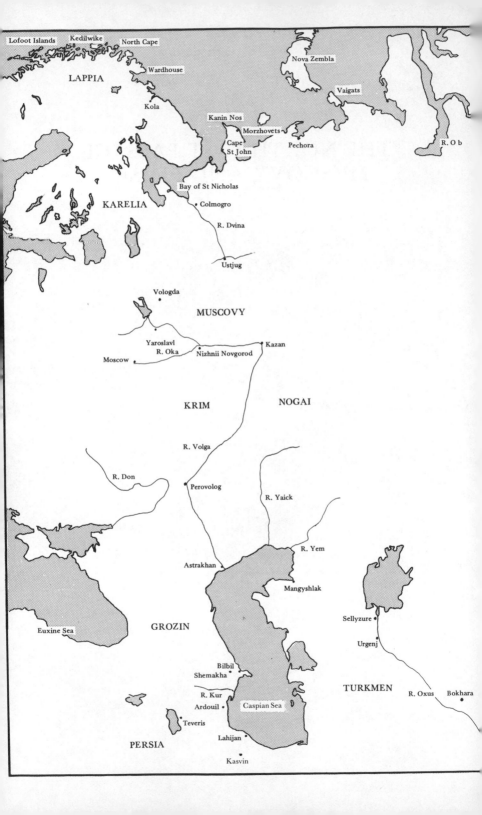

Of all possible routes to China and the fabulous East the most accessible to Englishmen appeared to be the passage between the northern coasts of Europe and Asia and the pole. Even the greatest geographer of the age, Mercator, opined that it was "very easy and short". In 1553 a Company of Merchant Adventurers was set up for the exploration of these regions, with the veteran discoverer Sebastian Cabot as its Governor or president. The first expedition was a dismal failure, two of the three ships being caught in the ice and only discovered several years later with the frozen bodies of the leader, Sir Hugh Willoughby, and all his company. Equally unsuccessful, though not fatal, was the dogged attempt of Steven Burrough, Master of the one survivor from Willoughby's fleet, to probe the passage farther with a single pinnace (1556); and in 1580 Pet and Jackman, the second of whom had already served Frobisher well in the north-west passage, were again defeated by arctic conditions, despite the expectations of their backers, who saw them entering the tropical harbours of Cathay, and some fine seamanship.

There was, however, a useful by-product of these enterprises. Willoughby's Pilot Major, Richard Chancellor, arrived near Archangel in the surviving ship. From there he travelled to Moscow and succeeded in obtaining from the Tsar, Ivan the Terrible, a licence for the English to trade direct with Russia, thus by-passing the normal route through the Baltic where the Danes imposed penal tolls. A Muscovy company was set up, with three depots in Russia, and the link between the two countries was strengthened by an exchange of ambassadors and by the efforts of an astute diplomat, Anthony Jenkinson. From the depots trade missions were sent out (the first under Jenkinson), and these penetrated via the Volga and the Caspian Sea as far south as Bokhara and Persia, where they made a side-entry into the East Indian traffic in silks, spices, and precious stones. The development of this trade is illustrated in reports sent home to the Company by a succession of its agents (the rakish Johnson, the over-cautious Edwards, the insinuating Chapman), who incidentally present a tragi-comedy of office rivalries.

Towards the end of the century the initiative in north-eastern exploration passed to the Dutch who, despite the achievement of Barents, made little better progress. The north-east passage does indeed exist, but was finally traversed only in 1878–9 by Baron Nordenskiöld in the Vega: and that voyage involved wintering for six months and more in the Arctic.

The navigation and discovery toward the River of Ob, made by Master Steven Burrough, Master of the pinnace called the *Searchthrift,* with divers things, worth the noting, passed in the year 1556.

April

23 We departed from Ratcliffe to Blackwall the 23rd of April. Saturday, being St Mark's Day, we departed from Blackwall to Grays.

27 The 27th, being Monday, the right worshipful Sebastian Cabota came aboard our pinnace at Gravesend, accompanied with divers gentlemen and gentlewomen who, after that they had viewed our pinnace and tasted of such cheer as we could make them aboard, they went on shore, giving to our mariners right liberal rewards; and the good old gentleman, Master Cabota, gave to the poor most liberal alms, wishing them to pray for the good fortune and prosperous success of the *Searchthrift,* our pinnace. And then at the sign of the Christopher he and his friends banqueted, and made me, and them that were in the company, great cheer; and for very joy that he had to see the towardness of our intended discovery he entered into the dance himself amongst the rest of the young and lusty company. Which being ended, he and his friends departed most gently, commending us to the governance of Almighty God.

28 Tuesday we rode still at Gravesend, making provision for such things as we wanted.

29 Wednesday in the morning we departed from Gravesend, the wind being at south-west: that night we came to an anchor thwart Our Lady of Hollands.

30 Thursday at three of the clock in the morning we weighed, and by eight of the clock we were at an anchor in Orwell Wands; and then incontinent I went aboard the *Edward Bonaventure,* where the worshipful company of merchants appointed me to be until the said good ship arrived at Wardhouse. Then I returned again to the pinnace.

May

15 Friday the 15 of May we were within 7 leagues of the shore on the coast of Norway, the latitude at a south sun 58 degrees and a half, when we saw three sails beside our own company; and thus we followed the shore or land which lieth north-north-west, north and by west, and north-west by north as it doth appear by the plat.

16 Saturday at an east sun we came to St Dunstan's Island, which

island I so named. It was off us east two leagues and a half, the wind being at south-east, the latitude this day at a south sun 59 degrees 42 minutes. Also the high round mountain bore east of us at a south sun; and when this hill is east of you, and being bound to the northward, the land lieth north and half a point westerly from this said south sun unto a north sun twenty leagues north-west along the shore.

17   Upon Sunday at six of the clock in the morning the farthest land that we could see that lay north-north-west was east of us three leagues, and then it trended to the northwards and to the eastwards of the north, which headland I judged to be Scoutsness. At seven of the clock we changed our course and went north, the wind being at south-south-east, and it waxed very thick and misty, and when it cleared we went north-north-east. At a south sun we lost sight of the *Searchthrift* because of the mist, making our way north; and when we lost sight of the shore and the pinnace we were within two leagues and a half of the shore. The last land that we saw when this mist came upon us, which is to the northwards of Scoutsness, lay north-north-east and south-south-west, and we made our way north until a west sun five leagues.

18   From that until Monday three o'clock in the morning ten leagues north-north-east; and then we went north and by east, because the wind came at the west-south-west with thick mist. The latitude this day at a south sun 63 degrees and a half, truly taken. At this season we had sight of our pinnace again.

19   From that until Tuesday a south sun, north-north-east forty-four leagues, and then north-east: from a south sun until eight of the clock, fifteen leagues north-east.

20   From that until Wednesday a south sun, north-north-east, except the first watch north-east. Then had we the latitude in 67 degrees 39 minutes. From that unto a north-west sun eighteen leagues north-east, and then we were within two leagues off the shore, and saw the high land to the southwards of Lofoot break out through the mist, and then we went north and by east.

21   From the said north-west sun until four of the clock in the morning north and by east ten leagues and a half, and then north-north-east until a south sun, the latitude being 69 degrees and a half. From that until half an hour past seven of the clock north-north-east eleven leagues and a half, and then we went north-east ten

22   leagues. From that 3 leagues and a half east-north-east, and then we saw the land through the clouds and haze thwart on the broadside of us, the wind being then at south-south-west.

23   From that until Saturday at eight of the clock in the morning east-north-east, and to the northwards forty-eight leagues, and then the wind came up at north, we being aboard the shore and

thwart of the chapel which I suppose is called Kedilwike. Then we cast the ship's head to the seawards, because the wind was very scant; and then I caused the pinnace to bear in with the shore to see whether she might find a harbour for the ships or not; and that she found, and saw two roaders ride in the sound, and also they saw houses. But notwithstanding, God be praised, the wind enlarged upon us, that we had not occasion to go into the harbour. And then the pinnace bore her mizen overboard with flag and all, and lost the flag. With the mast there fell two men overboard but, God be praised, they were saved. The flag was a token whereby we might understand whether there were a good harbour there or not.

At a north sun the North Cape (which I so named the first voyage) was thwart of us, which is nine leagues to the eastwards of the foresaid chapel from the easternmost point of it.

June

7 The Sunday we weighed in Corpus Christi Bay at a north-east and by east sun. The Bay is almost half a league deep; the headland which is Corpus Christi Point lieth south-east and by east one league from the head of the Bay, where we had a great tide, like a race, over the flood. The Bay is at the least two leagues over; so I do imagine, from the fair foreland to Corpus Christi Point ten leagues south-east and by east. It floweth in this Bay at a south and by west moon full sea. From that we went until seven o'clock at afternoon twenty leagues south-east and by south; and then we took in all our sails, because it was then very misty, and also we met with much ice that ran out of the Bay, and then we went south-south-east with our foresail. At eight of the clock we heard a piece of ordnance, which was out of the *Edward* which bade us farewell, and then we shot off another piece and bade her farewell. We could not one see the other because of the thick mist. At a north-west sun it began somewhat to clear, and then we saw a headland, and the shore trended to the south-westward, which I judged to be about Cross Island: it was off us, at a north-north-west sun, west-south-west.

8 From this north-north-west sun, until Monday, we went south-east, and this morning we came at anchor among the shoals that lie off Point Lookout at a north-east and by east sun, the wind being at east-south-east. At this Point Lookout a south moon maketh a full sea. Cape Good Fortune lieth from the Isle of Crosses south-east, and between them is ten leagues; Point Lookout lieth from Cape Good Fortune east-south-east and between them are six leagues. St Edmond's Point lieth from Point Lookout east-south-east and half a point to the southwards, and between them are six

leagues. There is between these two Points a bay that is half a league deep and is full of shoals and dangers. At a south-east sun we weighed and turned to the windwards, the wind being at east-south-east; and at a south-east sun we came to an anchor, being then a full sea, in five fathoms and a half water. It higheth at this place where we rode, and also at Point Lookout, four fathom water. At a west-north-west sun we weighed, and drove to the windwards until Tuesday a north-north-east sun, and then, being a high water, we came to an anchor open of the River Kola, in eight fathom water. Cape St Bernard lieth from St Edmond's Point south-east and by south, and betwixt them are six leagues; and also betwixt them is the River Kola, into which river we went this evening.

10 Wednesday we rode still in the said river, the wind being at the north. We sent our skiff aland to be dressed. The latitude of the mouth of the River Kola is 65 degrees 48 minutes.

11 Thursday at 6 of the clock in the morning there came aboard us one of the Russ *lodias*, rowing with twenty oars, and there were four and twenty men in her. The master of the boat presented me with a great loaf of bread and six rings of bread, which they call *colaches*, and four dried pikes and a peck of fine oatmeal; and I gave unto the master of the boat a comb and a small glass. And he declared unto me that he was bound to Pechora; and after that I made them to drink, the tide being somewhat broken, they gently departed. The master's name was Feodor.

Whereas the tenth day I sent our pinnace on shore to be mended, because she was leaky and weak, with the carpenter and three men more to help him, the weather chanced so that it was Sunday before they could get aboard our ship. All that time they were without provision of victuals, but only a little bread which they spent by Thursday at night, thinking to have come aboard when they had listed, but wind and weather denied them, insomuch that they were fain to eat grass and such weeds as they could find then above ground, but fresh water they had plenty; but the meat with some of them could scant frame by reason of their queasy stomachs.

14 From Thursday at afternoon until Sunday in the morning our bark did ride such a roadstead that it was to be marvelled, without the help of God, how she was able to abide it.

In the bight of the south-east shore of the River Kola there is a good road in five fathom or four fathom and a half at a low water; but you shall have no land north-north-east of you then. I proved with our pinnace that the depth goeth on the south-east shore.

15 Thursday we weighed our anchors in the River Kola and went into the sea seven or eight leagues, where we met with the wind far

5 *A Russian* Lodia, *or coasting vessel.*

northerly that of force it constrained us to go back into the said
river, where came aboard of us sundry of their boats which
declared unto me that they were also bound to the northwards
a-fishing for morse and salmon, and gave me liberally of their
white and wheaten bread. As we rode in this river we saw daily
coming down the river many of their *lodias*, and they that had least
had four and twenty men in them, and at the last they grew to
thirty sail of them; and amongst the rest there was one of them
whose name was Gabriel, who showed me very much friendship,
and he declared unto me that all they were bound to Pechora
a-fishing for salmon and morses. Insomuch that he showed me by
demonstrations that with a fair wind we had seven or eight days
sailing to the River Pechora, so that I was glad of their company.
This Gabriel promised to give me warning of shoals, as he did
indeed.

21 Sunday, being the one and twentieth day, Gabriel gave me a barrel of mead, and one of his special friends gave me a barrel of beer, which was carried upon men's backs at least 2 miles.

22 Monday we departed from the River Kola with all the rest of the said *lodias,* but sailing before the wind they were all too good for us; but according to promise this Gabriel and his friend did often strike their sails and tarried for us, forsaking their own company.

23 Tuesday at an east-north-east sun we were thwart of Cape St John. It is to be understood that from the Cape St John unto the river or bay that goeth to Mezen it is all sunk land, and full of shoals and dangers; you shall have scant two fathom water and see no land. And this present day we came to an anchor thwart of a creek which is 4 or 5 leagues to the northwards of the said Cape; into which creek Gabriel and his fellow rowed, but we could not get in. And before night there were above 20 sail that went into the said creek, the wind being at the north-east. We had indifferent good land-fang. This afternoon Gabriel came aboard with his skiff, and then I rewarded him for the good company that he kept with us over the shoals with two small ivory combs and a steel glass, with two or three trifles more, for which he was not ungrateful; but, notwithstanding, his first company had gotten farther to the northwards.

24 Wednesday, being midsummer day, we sent our skiff aland to sound the creek, where they found it almost dry at a low water, and all the *lodias* within were on ground. Although the harbour were evil, yet the stormy similitude of northerly winds tempted us to set our sails, and we let slip a cable and an anchor and bore with the harbour, for it was then near a high water; and, as always in such journeys varieties do chance, when we came upon the bar in the entrance the wind did shrink so suddenly upon us that we were not able to lead it in, and before we could have flatted the ship before the wind we should have been on ground on the lee shore, so that we were constrained to let fall an anchor under our sails and rode in a very breach, thinking to have warped in. Gabriel came out with his skiff, and so did sundry others also, showing their good will to help us, but all to no purpose, for they were likely to have been drowned for their labour; insomuch that I desired Gabriel to lend me his anchor, because our own anchors were too big for our skiff to lay out; who sent me his own, and borrowed another also and sent it us. Then we laid out one of those anchors with a hawser which he had of 140 fathom long, thinking to have warped in, but it would not be. For as we shorted upon the said warp the anchor came home, so that we were fain to bear the end of the warp, that we rushed in upon the other small anchor that Gabriel sent aboard and laid that anchor to seawards; and then between these two anchors we traversed the ship's head to

seawards, and set our foresail and mainsail, and when the bark had way we cut the hawser and so got the sea to our friend, and tried out all that day with our main course.

25 The Thursday we went room with Cape St John, where we found indifferent good road for a north-north-east wind and, for a need, for a north and by west wind.

26 Friday at afternoon we weighed and departed from thence, the weather being meetly fair and the wind at east-south-east, and plied for the place where we left our cable and anchor, and our hawser; and as soon as we were at an anchor the foresaid Gabriel came aboard of us with 3 or four more of their small boats, and brought with them of their aquavitae and mead, professing unto me very much friendship, and rejoiced to see us again, declaring that they earnestly thought we had been lost. This Gabriel declared unto me that they had saved both the anchors and our hawser; and after we had thus communed, I caused 4 or 5 of them to go into my cabin, where I gave them figs and made them such cheer as I could. While I was thus banqueting of them there came another of their skiffs aboard with one who was a Keril, whose name afterwards I learned and that he dwelt in Colmogro, and Gabriel dwelt in the town of Kola, which is not far from the river's mouth. This foresaid Keril said unto me that one of the anchors which I borrowed was his. I gave him thanks for the loan of it, thinking it had been sufficient. And as I continued in one accustomed manner, that, if the present which they brought were worth entertainment, they had it accordingly, he brought nothing with him and therefore I regarded him but little. And thus we ended, and they took their leave and went ashore. At their coming ashore Gabriel and Keril were at unconvenient words, and by the ears, as I understand. The cause was because the one had better entertainment than the other; but you shall understand that Gabriel was not able to make his party good, because there were 17 *lodias* of the Keril's company who took his part and but 2 of Gabriel's company.

The next high water Gabriel and his company departed from thence and rowed to their former company and neighbours, which were in number 28 at the least, and all of them belonging to the River Kola.

27 And as I understood, Keril made reckoning that the hawser which was fast in his anchor should have been his own, and at first would not deliver it to our boat, insomuch that I sent him word that I would complain upon him, whereupon he delivered the hawser to my company.

The next day, being Saturday, I sent our boat on shore to fetch fresh water and wood, and at their coming on shore this Keril welcomed our men most gently, and also banqueted them; and in the meantime caused some of his men to fill our barricoes with water, and to help our men to bear wood into the boat; and then he put on his best silk coat and his collar of pearls and came aboard again, and brought his present with him. And thus, having more respect to his present than to his person, because I perceived him to be vainglorious, I bade him welcome, and gave him a dish of figs; and then he declared unto me that his father was a gentleman, and that he was able to show me pleasure, and not Gabriel, who was but a priest's son.

28 After their departure from us we weighed and plied all the ebb to the windwards, the wind being northerly, and towards night it waxed very stormy so that of force we were constrained to go room with Cape St John again; in which storm we lost our skiff at our stern, that we bought at Wardhouse. And there we rode until the fourth of July. The latitude of Cape St John is 66 degrees 50 minutes; and it is to be noted that the land of Cape St John is of height from the full sea mark, as I judge, 10 fathoms, being clean without any trees growing, and also without stones or rocks, and consists only of black earth, which is so rotten that if any fall into the sea it will swim as though it were a piece of wood. In which place, about three leagues from the shore, you shall not have above 9 fathom water, and clay ground.

July

4 Saturday at a north-north-west sun the wind came at east-north-east, and then we weighed and plied to the northwards; and as we were two leagues shot past the cape we saw a house standing in a valley, which is dainty to be seen in those parts, and by and by I saw three men at the top of the hill. Then I judged them, as it afterwards proved, that they were men which came from some other place to set traps to take vermin for their furs, which traps we did perceive very thick along the shore as we went.

5 Sunday at an east sun we were thwart off the creek where the Russes lay, and there came to an anchor; and perceiving the most part of the *lodias* to be gone we thought it not good to tarry any longer there, but weighed and spent all the ebb plying to the windwards.

6 Monday at a south sun it was high water. All along the coast it floweth little, only a south moon makes a full sea. And as we were a-weighing we espied the Russ *lodias* which we first lost. They came out of a creek amongst the sandy hills, which hills begin 15

7 leagues north-north-east from Cape St John. Plying this ebb to an end we came to an anchor 6 leagues north-north-east from the place where we saw the Russes come out; and there the Russes

harboured themselves within a sunk bank, but there was not water enough for us. At a north sun we weighed and plied to the northwards, the land lying north-north-east and south-south-west, until a south sun, and then we were in the latitude of 68 degrees and a half; and in this latitude end those sandy hills, and the land beginneth to lie north and by west, south and by east, and north-north-west and to the westwards, and there the water beginneth to wax deep. At a north-west sun we came to an anchor within half a league of the shore, where we had good plenty of fish, both haddocks and cods, riding in 10 fathom water.

8 Wednesday we weighed and plied nearer the headland which is called Kanin Nos, the wind being at east and by north. Thursday,
9 the wind being scant, we turned to windwards the ebb, to get about Kanin Nos. The latitude this day at noon was 68 degrees 40 minutes.
10 Friday we turned to the windward of the ebb, but to no purpose; and as we rode at an anchor we saw the similitude of a storm rising at north-north-west, and could not tell where to get road nor succour for that wind, and harbour we knew none; and that land which we rode under with that wind was a lee shore. And as I was musing what was best to be done. I saw a sail come out of a creek under the foresaid Kanin Nos, which was my friend Gabriel, who forsook his harbour and company and came as near us as he might, and pointed us to the eastwards; and then we weighed and followed him, and went east and by south, the wind being at west-north-west, and very misty.
11 Saturday we went east-south-east and followed Gabriel, and he brought us into a harbour called Morzhovets, which is 30 leagues from Kanin Nos, and we had upon the bar going in two fathom and a fourth part; and after we were passed in over the bar it waxed deeper, for we had 5 fathoms, 4 and a half, and 3 fathom etc. Our bark being moored, I sent some of our men to shore to provide wood, where they had plenty of driftwood but none growing; and in this place we found plenty of young fowl, as gulls, sea-pies, and others, whereof the Russes would eat none, whereof we were nothing sorry for there came the more to our part.
12 Sunday our men cut wood on shore and brought it aboard, and we ballasted our ship with stones. This morning Gabriel saw a smoke on the way, who rowed into it with his skiff, which smoke was two leagues from the place where we rode. And at a north-west sun he came aboard again, and brought with him a Samoyed, which was but a young man. His apparel was then strange unto us; and he presented me with three young wild geese, and one young barnacle.

13 Monday I sent a man to the main in Gabriel's boat, and he brought us aboard 8 barricoes of fresh water. The latitude of the said Morzhovets is 68 degrees and a terce. It floweth there at a south-south-west moon full sea, and higheth two fathom and a half water.

14 At a west-north-west sun we departed from this place, and went east 25 leagues, and then saw an island north and by west of us eight leagues, which island is called Kolguyev; and from the easter-most part of this island there lieth a sand east and by south 7 leagues long.

15 Wednesday at a north and by east sun Svyatoi Nos was south of us 5 leagues. This day at afternoon we went in over the dangerous bar of Pechora, and had upon the bar but one fathom water.

16 Thursday we rode still.

17 Friday I went on shore and observed the variation of the compass, which was three degrees and a half from the north to the west. The latitude this day was 69 degrees 10 minutes. From two or three leagues to the eastward of Svyatoi Nos, until the entering of the River Pechora, it is all sandy hills, and towards Pechora the sandy hills are very low. It higheth on the bar of Pechora four foot water, and it floweth there at a south-west moon a full sea.

20 Monday, at a north and by east sun, we weighed and came out over the said dangerous bar, where we had but five foot water, insomuch that we found a foot less water coming out than we did going in. I think the reason was because when we went in the wind was off the sea, which caused the sands to break on either side of us and we kept in the smoothest between the breaches, which we durst not have done except we had seen the Russes to have gone in before us; and at our coming out the wind was off the shore, and fair weather, and then the sands did not appear with breaches as at our going in. We thank God that our ship did draw so little water.

When we were a-seaboard the bar the wind scanted upon us and was at east-south-east, insomuch that we stopped the ebbs, and plied all the floods to the windwards, and made our way east-north-east.

21 Tuesday at a north-west sun we thought that we had seen land at east or east and by north of us; which afterwards proved to be a monstrous heap of ice. Within a little more than half an hour after we first saw this ice we were enclosed within it before we were aware of it, which was a fearful sight to see. For, for the space of six hours, it was as much as we could do to keep our ship aloof from one heap of ice, and bear roomer from another, with as much wind as we might bear a course. And when we had passed from the danger of this ice we lay to the eastwards close by the wind.

22 The next day we were again troubled with the ice.

23 Thursday being calm we plied to the windwards, the wind being
northerly. We had the latitude this day at noon in 70 degrees 11
minutes. We had not run past two hours north-west, the wind
being at north-north-east and north-east and by north a good gale,
but we met again with another heap of ice. We weathered the
head of it, and lay a time to the seawards, and made way west 6
leagues.

24 Friday at a south-east sun we cast about to the eastwards, the wind
being at north-north-east. The latitude this day at noon was 70
degrees 15 minutes.

25 On St James' Day, bolting to the windwards, we had the latitude
at noon in 70 degrees 20 minutes. The same day at a south-west
sun there was a monstrous whale aboard of us, so near to our side
that we might have thrust a sword or any other weapon in him,
which we durst not for fear he should have overthrown our ship.
And then I called my company together, and all of us shouted, and
with the cry that we made he departed from us. There was as much
above water of his back as the breadth of our pinnace, and at his
falling down he made such a terrible noise in the water that a man
would greatly have marvelled except he had known the cause of it;
but, God be thanked, we were quietly delivered of him. And a
little while after we spied certain islands with which we bore, and
found good harbour in 15 or 18 fathom and black ooze. We came
to an anchor at a north-west sun, and named the island St James'

26 Island, where we found fresh water. Sunday, much wind blowing,
we lay still.

27 Monday I went on shore and took the latitude, which was 70
degrees 42 minutes. The variation of the compass was 7 degrees
and a half from the north to the west.

28 Tuesday we plied to the westwards along the shore, the wind
being at north-west and as I was about to come to anchor we saw a
sail coming about the point whereunder we thought to have
anchored. Then I sent a skiff aboard of him, and at their coming
aboard they took acquaintance of them, and the chief man said he
had been in our company in the River Kola, and also declared
unto them that we were past the way which should bring us to the
Ob. "This land", said he, "is called Nova Zembla, that is to say the
New Land"; and then he came aboard himself with his skiff, and
at his coming aboard he told me the like, and said further that in
this Nova Zembla is the highest mountain in the world, as he
thought, and that Camen Bolshoi, which is on the main of
Pechora, is not to be compared with this mountain; but I saw it
not. He made me also certain demonstrations of the way to the
Ob, and seemed to make haste on his own way, being very loth to
tarry, because the year was far past, and his neighbour had fetched

Pechora and not he. So I gave him a steel glass, two pewter spoons, and a pair of velvet-sheathed knives; and then he seemed somewhat the more willing to tarry, and showed me as much as he knew for our purpose. He also gave me 17 wild geese, and showed me that four of their *lodias* were driven perforce from Kamin Nos to this Nova Zembla. This man's name was Loshak.

29 Wednesday, as we plied to the eastwards, we espied another sail, which was one of this Loshak's company, and we bore room, and spoke with him, who in like sort told us of the Ob as the other had
30 done. Thursday we plied to the eastwards, the wind being at east-north-east.
31 Friday the gale of wind began to increase and came westerly withal, so that by a north-west sun we were at an anchor among the Islands of Vaigats, where we saw two small *lodias*. The one of them came aboard of us, and presented me with a great loaf of bread; and they told me that they were all of Colmogro, except one man that dwelt at Pechora, who seemed to be the chiefest among them in killing of the morse. There were some of their company on shore which did chase a white bear over the high cliffs into the water, which bear the *lodia* that was aboard of us killed in our sight. This day there was a great gale of wind at north, and we saw so much ice driving a-seaboard that it was then no going to sea.

August
1 Saturday I went ashore, and there I saw three morses that they had killed. They held one tooth of a morse, which was not great, at a rouble, and one white bearskin at three roubles and two roubles. They further told me that there were people called Samoyeds on the great Island, and that they would not abide them nor us; who have no houses, but only coverings made of deerskins set over them with stakes. They are men expert in shooting, and have great plenty of deer. This night there fell a cruel storm, the wind being at
2 west. Sunday we had very much wind, with plenty of snow, and we rode with two anchors ahead.
3 Monday we weighed, and went room with another island which was five leagues east-north-east from us. And there I met again with Loshak, and went on shore with him, and he brought me to a heap of the Samoyeds' idols, which were in number above 300, the worst and the most unartificial work that ever I saw. The eyes and mouths of sundry of them were bloody; they had the shape of men, women, and children, very grossly wrought, and that which they had made for other parts was also sprinkled with blood. Some of their idols were an old stick with two or three notches made with a knife in it. I saw much of the footing of the said Samoyeds, and of the sleds that they ride in. There was one of

their sleds broken and lay by the heap of idols, and there I saw a deerskin which the fowls had spoiled; and before certain of their idols blocks were made as high as their mouths, being all bloody. I thought that to be the table whereupon they offered their sacrifice. I saw also the instruments whereupon they had roasted flesh, and as far as I could perceive they make their fire directly under the spit. Loshak being there present told me that these Samoyeds were not so hurtful as they of Ob are, and that they have no houses, as indeed I saw none, but only tents made of deers' skins which they underprop with stakes and poles. Their boats are made of deers' skins, and when they come on shore they carry their boats with them upon their backs. For their carriages they have no other beasts to serve them but deer only. As for bread and corn they have none, except the Russes bring it to them. Their knowledge is very base, for they know no letter.

4   Tuesday we turned for the harbour where Loshak's bark lay, whereas before we rode under an island. And there he came aboard of us and said unto me, "If God send wind and weather to serve, I will go to the Ob with you, because the morses were scant at these Islands of Vaigats." But if he could not get to the river of Ob, then he said he would go to the river of Naramzay, where the people are not altogether so savage as the Samoyeds of the Ob are. He showed me that they will shoot at all men to the uttermost of their power that cannot speak their speech.

5   Wednesday we saw a terrible heap of ice approach near unto us, and therefore we thought good with all speed possible to depart from thence; and so I returned to the westwards again, to the island where we were the 31st of July.

6   Thursday I went ashore, and took the latitude which was 70 degrees 25 minutes; and the variation of the compass was 8 degrees from the north to the west. Loshak and the two small *lodias* of Pechora departed from this island while I was on shore taking the latitude and went to the southwards. I marvelled why he departed so suddenly, and went over the shoals amongst the islands where it was impossible for us to follow them; but after I perceived them to be weatherwise.

7   Friday we rode still, the wind being at north-north-east with a cruel storm. The ice came in so abundantly about us at both ends of the island that we rode under that it was a fearful sight to behold. The storm continued with snow, rain, and hail plenty.

8   Saturday we rode still also, the storm being somewhat abated, but it was altogether misty that we were not able to see a cable's length about us, the wind being at north-east and by east.

9   Sunday at four of the clock in the morning we departed from this island, the wind being at south-east; and as we were clear

a-seaboard the small islands and shoals, it came so thick with mists that we could not see a base-shot from us. Then we took in all our sails to make little way. At a south-east sun it waxed clear, and then we set our sails and lay close by the wind to the southwards along the Islands of Vaigats. At a west sun we took in our sail again because of the great mist and rain. We sounded at this place, and had five and twenty fathoms water and soft black ooze, being three leagues from the shore, the wind being at south and by east, but still misty.

10   Monday at an east sun we sounded and had 40 fathoms and ooze, still misty.

11   Tuesday at an east-north-east sun we let fall our anchor in three and twenty fathom, the mist still continuing.

12   Wednesday at three of the clock in the morning the mist broke up, the wind being at north-east and by east, and then we saw part of the Islands of Vaigats which we bore withal, and went east-south-east close by the wind. At a west sun we were at an anchor under the south-west part of the said Vaigats, and then I sent our skiff to shore with three men in her, to see if they might speak with any of the Samoyeds, but could not. All that day was rainy, but not windy.

13   Thursday the wind came westerly, so that we were fain to seek us another place to ride in because the wind came a-seaboard land; and although it were misty yet we followed the shore by our lead, and as we brought land in the wind of us we let fall our anchor. At a west sun the mist broke up so that we might see about us, and then we might perceive that we were entered into a sound. This afternoon we took in two or three skiff's lading of stones to ballast our ship withal. It higheth here four foot water, and floweth by fits, uncertain to be judged.

14   Friday we rode still in the sound, the wind at south-west with very much rain, and at the end of the rain it waxed again misty.

15   Saturday there was much wind at west, and much rain, and then
16   again misty. Sunday was very misty, and much wind; Monday very
17   misty, the wind at west-north-west. Tuesday was also misty,
18   except at noon. Then the sun broke out through the mist, so that we had the latitude in 70 degrees 10 minutes. The afternoon was misty again, the wind being at west-north-west.

19   Wednesday at three of the clock after noon the mist broke up and the wind came at east-north-east; and then we weighed, and went south and by east until seven of the clock, eight leagues, thinking to have had sight of the sandy hills that are to the eastwards of the River Pechora. At a north-west sun we took in our mainsail because the wind increased, and went with a foresail west-north-west, the wind being at east-north-east. At night there grew so terrible a storm that we saw not the like,

although we had endured many storms since we came out of
England. It was wonderful that our bark was able to brook such
monstrous and terrible seas, without the great help of God, who
never faileth them at need that put their sure trust in Him.

20 Thursday at a south-south-west sun, thanks be to God, the storm
was at the highest and then the wind began to slack, and came
northerly withal; and then I reckoned the westermost point of the
River Pechora to be south of us 15 leagues. At a west-south-west
sun we set our mainsail and lay close by the wind, the wind being
at north-east and by north, making but little way because the
billow went so high. At midnight we cast about, and the ship caped
north-north-east, making little way.

21 Friday at noon we had the latitude in 70 degrees 8 minutes; and
we sounded, and had 29 fathoms sand and in manner streamy
ground. At a west sun we cast about to the westwards, and a little
after the wind came up at west.

22 Saturday was calm. The latitude this day at noon was 70 degrees
and a tierce. We sounded here and had nine and forty fathoms and
ooze, which ooze signified that we drew towards Nova Zembla.

And thus, we being out of all hope to discover any more to the
eastward this year, we thought it best to return, and that for three
causes. The first, the continual north-east and northerly winds,
which have more power after a man is passed to the eastwards of
Kanin Nos than in any place that I do know in these northerly
regions. Second, because of great and terrible abundance of ice
which we saw with our eyes, and we doubt greater store abideth in
those parts. I adventured already somewhat too far in it, but I
thank God for my safe deliverance from it. Third, because the
nights waxed dark, and the winter began to draw on with his
storms. And therefore I resolved to take the first best wind that
God should send and ply towards the Bay of St Nicholas, and to
see if we might do any good there, if God would permit it.

This present Saturday we saw very much ice, and were within
two or three leagues of it. It showed unto us as though it had been
a firm land as far as we might see from north-west off us to the
eastwards; and this afternoon the Lord sent us a little gale of wind
at south, so that we bore clear off the westermost part of it, thanks
be to God. And then against night it waxed calm again, and the

24 wind was at south-west. We made our way until Sunday noon
north-west and by west, and then we had the latitude in 70 degrees
and a half, the wind at south-west. There was a billow, so that we
could not discern to take the latitude exactly, but by a reasonable
guess.

25 Monday there was a pretty gale of wind at south so that we went
west and by south. The latitude this day at noon was 70 degrees 10

minutes. We had little wind all day. At a west-north-west sun we sounded and had 29 fathoms black sandy ooze, and then were north-east 5 leagues from the north-east part of the island Kol-
26 guyev. Tuesday the wind all westerly we plied to the windwards.
27 Wednesday the wind was all westerly, and calm. We had the latitude this day in 70 degrees 10 minutes, we being within three
28 leagues of the north part of the island Kolguyev. Thursday we went room about the westermost part of the island, seeking where we might find a place to ride in for a north-west wind, but could find none; and then we cast about again to the seawards, and the wind came at west-south-west, and this morning we had plenty of
29 snow. Friday, the wind being at south-west and by west, we plied to the windwards.

Saturday, the wind being at south, we plied to the westwards, and at afternoon the mist broke up, and then we might see the land seven or eight leagues to the eastwards of Kanin Nos. We sounded a little before and had 35 fathoms and ooze. And a while after we sounded again and had 19 fathom and sand; then we were within three leagues and a half of the shore. And towards night there came down so much wind that we were fain to bring our ship a-try, and laid her head to the westwards.
30 Sunday the wind became more calm, and then it waxed very misty. At noon we cast about to the eastwards, the wind being at south, and ran eight hours on that board, and then we cast about and caped west-south-west. We sounded and had 32 fathoms and tough ooze like clay.
31 Monday we doubled about Kanin Nos, and came at an anchor there, to the intent that we might kill some fish if God would permit it; and there we got a great nurse, which nurses were there so plenty that they would scarcely suffer any other fish to come near the hooks. The said nurses carried away sundry of our hooks and leads. A little while after, at a west sun, the wind began to blow stormy at west-south-west, so that we were fain to weigh and forsake our fishing-ground, and went close by the wind south-west and south-west and by west, making our way south-south-west.

September

1 Tuesday at a west sun we sounded and had 20 fathoms and broken whelk-shells. I reckoned Kanin Nos to be 24 leagues north-north-east from us.
11 The eleventh day we arrived at Colmogro, and there we wintered, expecting the approach of the next summer to proceed further in our intended discovery for the Ob; which, by reason of our employments to Wardhouse the next spring for the search of some English ships, was not accordingly performed.

Certain notes imperfectly written by Richard Johnson, servant to
Master Richard Chancellor, which was in the discovery of
Vaigats and Nova Zembla with Steven Burrough in the *Searchthrift*, 1556, and afterward among the Samoyeds, whose devilish rites he describeth.

FIRST after we departed out of England we fell with Norway, and
on that coast lieth Northbern or Northbergen, and this people
are under the King of Denmark, but they differ in their speech
from the Danes, for they speak Norse. And north of Northbern lie the
Isles of Rost and Lofoot, and these islands pertain unto Finnmark, and
they keep the laws and speak the language of the Icelanders. And at the
eastermost part of that land is a castle which is called the Wardhouse,
and the King of Denmark doth fortify it with men of war; and the
Russes may not go to the westward of that castle.

And east-south-east from that castle is a land called Lappia, in which
land be two manner of people, that is to say the Lappians and the Scrik
Finns, which Scrik Finns are a wild people which neither know God nor
yet good order; and these people live in tents made of deers' skins, and
they have no certain habitations but continue in herds and companies
by one hundred and two hundred. And they are a people of small
stature, and are clothed in deers' skins, and drink nothing but water
and eat no bread but flesh all raw. And the Lappians be a people
adjoining to them and be much like to them in all conditions; but the
Emperor of Russia hath of late overcome many of them, and they are
in subjection to him. And this people will say that they believe in the
Russes' God; and they live in tents as the others do.

And south-east and by south from Lappia lieth a province called
Karelia, and these people are called Kerilli; and south-south-east from
Karelia lieth a country called Novogardia; and these three nations are
under the Emperor of Russia.

And the Russes keep the law of the Greeks in their churches, and
write somewhat like as the Greeks write, and they speak their own
language and they abhor the Latin tongue, neither have they to do with
the Pope of Rome; and they hold it not good to worship any carved
image, yet they will worship painted images on tables or boards. And in
Russia their churches, steeples, and houses are all of wood; and their
ships that they have are sewn with withies and have no nails. The
Kerils, Russians, and Moscovians be much alike in all conditions.

And south from the Moscovians lie the Tartarians, which be Mahometans, and live in tents and wagons and keep in herds and companies. And they hold it not good to abide long in one place, for they will say (when they will curse any of their children), "I would thou mightest tarry so long in a place that thou mightest smell thine own dung, as the Christians do"; and this is the greatest curse that they have. And east-north-east of Russia lieth Lampas, which is a place where the Russes, Tartars, and Samoyeds meet twice a year and make the fair to barter wares for wares.

And north-east from Lampas lieth the country of the Samoyeds which be about the river of Pechora, and these Samoyeds be in subjection to the Emperor of Russia: and they lie in tents made of deerskins, and they use much witchcraft, and shoot well in bows. And north-east from the River Pechora lieth Vaigats, and there are the wild Samoyeds which will not suffer the Russes to land out of the sea but they will kill them and eat them, as we are told by the Russes; and they live in herds, and have all their carriages with deer, for they have no horses. Beyond Vaigats lieth a land called Nova Zembla, which is a great land, but we saw no people; and there we had fowl enough, and there we saw white foxes and white bears.

And the said Samoyeds which are about the banks of Pechora (which are in subjection to the Emperor of Russia), when they will remove from one place to another, then they will make sacrifices in manner following. Every kindred doth sacrifice in their own tent, and he that is most ancient is their priest. And first the priest doth begin to play upon a thing like to a great sieve with a skin on the one end like a drum; and the stick that he playeth with is about a span long, and one end is round like a ball, covered with the skin of a hart. Also the priest hath upon his head a thing of white like a garland, and his face is covered with a piece of a shirt of mail, with many small ribs and teeth of fishes and wild beasts hanging on the same mail. Then he singeth as we use here in England to halloo, whoop, or shout at hounds, and the rest of the company answer him with this, "Owtis, Igha, Igha, Igha"; and then the priest replieth again with his voices. And they answer him with the selfsame words so many times that in the end he becometh as it were mad, and falling down as he were dead, having nothing on him but a shirt, lying upon his back I might perceive him to breathe. I asked them why he lay so, and they answered me, "Now doth our God tell him what we shall do and whither we shall go." And when he had lain still a little while they cried thus three times together, "Oghao, Oghao, Oghao"; and as they use these three calls he riseth with his head and lieth down again; and then he rose up and sang with like voices as he did before, and his audience answered him "Igha, Igha, Igha".

Then he commanded them to kill five *olens* or great deer, and continued singing both he and they as before. Then he took a sword of a cubit and a span long (I did mete it myself) and put it into his belly halfway and sometime less, but no wound was to be seen, they continuing in their sweet song still. Then he put the sword into the fire till it was warm, and so thrust it into the slit of his shirt and thrust it through his body, as I thought, in at his navel and out at his fundament; the point being out of his shirt behind, I laid my finger upon it. Then he pulled out the sword and sat down. This being done, they set a kettle of water over the fire to heat, and when the water doth seethe the priest beginneth to sing again, they answering him; for so long as the water was in heating they sat and sang not.

Then they made a thing being four-square, and in height and squareness of a chair, and covered with a gown very close the forepart thereof, for the hinder part stood to the tent's side (their tents are round and are called *chome* in their language). The water still seething on the fire, and this square seat being ready, the priest put off his shirt, and the thing like a garland which was on his head with those things which covered his face, and he had on yet all this while a pair of hose of deers' skins with the hair on, which came up to his buttocks. So he went into the square seat, and sat down like a tailor and sang with a strong voice or hallooing. Then they took a small line made of deers' skins, of four fathoms long, and with a small knot the priest made it fast about his neck and under his left arm, and gave it unto two men standing on both sides of him, which held the ends together. Then the kettle of hot water was set before him in the square seat. All this time the square seat was not covered, and then it was covered with a gown of broadcloth without lining, such as the Russes do wear. Then the two men which did hold the ends of the line, still standing there, began to draw, and drew till they had drawn the ends of the line stiff and together; and then I heard a thing fall into the kettle of water which was before him in the tent. Thereupon I asked them that sat by me what it was that fell into the water that stood before him; and they answered me that it was his head, his shoulder, and left arm, which the line had cut off, I mean the knot which I saw afterward drawn hard together. Then I rose up and would have looked whether it were so or not, but they laid hold on me, and said that if they should see him with their bodily eyes they should live no longer. And the most part of them can speak the Russ tongue to be understood; and they took me to be a Russian.

Then they began to halloo with these words, "Oghaoo, Oghaoo, Oghaoo", many times together. And as they were thus singing and out-calling I saw a thing like a finger of a man two times together thrust through the gown from the priest. I asked them that sat next to me what it was that I saw, and they said, not his finger, for he was yet dead; and that which I saw appear through the gown was a beast, but what beast they knew not nor would not tell. And I looked upon the gown and there was no hole to be seen. And then at the last the priest lifted up his head with his shoulder and arm and all his body, and came forth to the fire.

Thus far of their service which I saw during the space of certain hours; but how they do worship their idols, that I saw not, for they put up their stuff for to remove from that place where they lay. And I went to him that served the priest and asked him what their God said to him when he lay as dead. He answered that his own people doth not know; neither is it for them to know, for they must do as he commanded. This I saw the fifth day of January in the year of Our Lord 1556 after the English account.

The voyage wherein Ossip Nyepeya, the Muscovite ambassador, returned home into his country, with his entertainment at his arrival at Colmogro; and a large description of the manners of the country.

THE twelfth of May in the year of Our Lord 1557 there departed from Gravesend four good ships well appointed for merchants, which were presently bound into the Bay of St Nicholas in Russia; with which ships was transported, or carried home, one Ossip Grigorievitch Nyepeya, who was sent Messenger from the Emperor and Great Duke of Moscovia. The four ships were these whose names follow, viz. the *Primrose*, admiral, the *John Evangelist*, vice-admiral, the *Anne* and the *Trinity*, attendants.

The 13th of July the foresaid four ships came to an anchor in the Bay of St Nicholas before an abbey called the Abbey of St Nicholas, whereas the said Messenger, Ossip Grigorievitch Nyepeya, went ashore, and as many Englishmen as came to serve the Emperor remained with him at the Abbey for the space of six days until he had gotten all his things ashore and laden the same in barks to go up the River Dwina to Vologda, which is by water 1,000 versts and every verst is about three quarters of an English mile.

The 20th of July we departed from St Nicholas, and the 24th of the same we came to Colmogro, where we remained eight days; and the said Messenger was there of all his acquaintance welcomed home, and had presents innumerable sent unto him but it was nothing but meat and drink. Some sent white bread, some rye bread, and some buttered bread and pancakes, beef, mutton, bacon, eggs, butter, fishes, swans, geese, ducks, hens, and all manner of victuals, both fish and flesh, in the best manner that the rude people could devise. For among them these presents are highly esteemed.

The 29th of July we departed from Colmogro and the 14th of August we came to Ustyug, where we remained one day and changed our barks or boats. The 27th of August we came to Vologda, where we remained 4 days unloading the barks and loading our chests and things in small wagons, with one horse in apiece, which in their tongue are called *telegas*, and with these *telegas* they carried our stuff from Vologda unto the Moscow, which is 500 versts; and we were upon the same way 14 days, for we went no faster than the *telegas*.

There are three great towns between the Moscow and Vologda, that is to say Yaroslavl, Rostov, and Pereyaslavl. Upon one side of Yaroslavl, runneth a famous river which is called Volga. It runneth into the Caspian Sea, and it divideth itself, before it come into the Mare Caspium, in 50 parts or more; and near unto the same Sea there stands a great city called Bokhara, the inhabitants of the which are called by the same name. The people of the said city do traffic unto the city of Moscow. Their commodities are spices, musk, ambergris, rhubarb, with other drugs. They bring also many furs, which they buy in Siberia coming towards the Moscow. The said people are of the sect of Mahomet.

The 12th of September we came unto the city of Moscow, where we were brought by Nyepeya and two of the Emperor's gentlemen unto a large house where every one of us had his chamber appointed. The 14th of September we were commanded to come unto the Emperor, and immediately after our coming we were brought into his presence, unto whom each of us did his duty accordingly and kissed his right hand, His Majesty sitting in his chair of state with his crown on his head and a staff of goldsmith's work in his left hand well garnished with rich and costly stones. And when we had all kissed his hand and done our duties His Majesty did declare by his interpreter that we were all welcome unto him and into his country, and thereupon willed us to dine with him. That day we gave thanks unto His Majesty, and so departed until the dinner was ready.

When dinner-time approached, we were brought again into the Emperor's dining chamber, where we were set on one side of a table that stood over against the Emperor's table, to the end that he might well behold us all. And when we came into the foresaid chamber we found there ready set these tables following. First, at the upper end of one table were set the Emperor's Majesty, his brother, and the Emperor of Kazan, which is prisoner. About two yards lower sat the Emperor of Kazan's son, being a child of five years of age, and beneath him sat the most part of the Emperor's noblemen. And at another table, near unto the Emperor's table, there was set a monk all alone, which was in all points as well served as the Emperor. At another table sat another kind of people called *Chirkasses*, which the Emperor entertaineth for men of war to serve against his enemies; of which people and of their country I will hereafter make mention.

All the tables aforesaid were covered only with salt and bread, and after that we had sat awhile the Emperor sent unto every one of us a piece of bread, which were given and delivered unto every man severally by these words, "The Emperor and Great Duke giveth the bread this day"; and in like manner three or four times before dinner was ended he sent unto every man drink, which was given by these words, "The Emperor and Great Duke giveth thee to drink". All the tables aforesaid were served in vessels of pure and fine gold, as well basins and ewers, platters, dishes, and saucers as also of great pots, with an innumerable sort of small drinking pots of divers fashions, whereof a great number were set with stone. As for costly meats I have many times seen better; but for change of wines, and divers sorts of meads it was wonderful. For there was not left at any time so much void room on the table that one more cup might have been set, and as far as I could perceive all the rest were in the like manner served.

In the dinner time there came in six singers which stood in the midst of the chamber and their faces towards the Emperor, who sang there before dinner was ended three several times; whose songs or voices delighted our ears little or nothing.

The Emperor never putteth morsel of meat in his mouth but he first blesseth it himself, and in like manner as often as he drinketh; for after his manner he is very religious, and he esteemeth his religious men above his noblemen.

The dinner continued about the space of five hours, which being ended, and the tables taken up, we came into the midst of the chamber, where we did reverence unto the Emperor's Majesty; and then he delivered unto every one of us with his own hands a cup of mead, which when every man had received and drunk a quantity thereof we were licensed to depart, and so ended that dinner. And because the Emperor would have us to be merry, he sent to our lodging the same evening three barrels of mead of sundry sorts, of the quantity in all of one hogshead. The 16th day of September the Emperor sent home unto our lodging for every of us a Tartary horse to ride from place to place as we had occasion, for that the streets of Moscow are very foul and miry in the summer. The 18th of September there were given unto Master Standish, doctor in physic, and the rest of our men of our occupations certain furred gowns of branched velvet and gold, and some of red damask, of which Master Doctor's gown was furred with sables and the rest were furred some with white ermine and some with grey squirrel, and all faced and edged round about with black beaver.

The 1st of October in the morning we were commanded to come unto the Emperor's court, and when we came thither we were brought unto the Emperor, unto whom we did our duties accordingly; whereupon he willed us to dine with him that day. And so with thanks unto His Majesty we departed until dinner-time, at which time we came and found the tables covered with bread and salt as at the first; and after that we were all set upon one side of the table the Emperor's Majesty according to his accustomed manner sent unto every man a piece of bread by some of the Dukes which attended on His Highness. And whereas the 14th of September we were served in vessels of gold, we were now served in vessels of silver, and yet not so abundantly as was the first of gold. They brought drink unto the table in silver bowls which contained at the least six gallons apiece, and every man had a small silver cup to drink in and another to dip or to take his drink out of the great bowl withal. The dinner being ended, the Emperor gave unto every one of us a cup of mead, which when we had received we gave thanks and departed.

Moreover, whensoever the Emperor's pleasure is that any stranger shall dine with him, he doth send for them in the morning, and when they come before him he with his own mouth biddeth them to dinner, and this order he always observeth.

The 10th of October the Emperor gave unto Master Standish 70 roubles in money, and to the rest of our men of occupations 30 roubles apiece. The 3rd of November we dined again with the Emperor, where we were served as before. The 6th of December, being St Nicholas' Day, we dined again at the Emperor's, for that is one of the principal feasts which the Moscovites hold. We were served in silver vessels and ordered in all points as before, and it was past 7 of the clock at night before dinner was ended.

The Emperor's Majesty useth every year, in the month of December, to have all his ordnance that is in the city of Moscow carried into the field which is without the suburbs of the city, and there to have it planted and bent upon two houses of wood filled within with earth; against which two houses there were two fair white marks set up, at which marks they discharge all their ordnance to the end the Emperor may see what his gunners can do. They have fair ordnance of brass of all sorts, bases, falcons, minions, sakers, culverins, cannons double and royal, basilisks long and large. They have six great pieces whose shot is a yard of height, which shot a man may easily discern as they fly. They have also a great many of mortar pieces or pot-guns, out of which pieces they shoot wildfire.

The 12th of December the Emperor's Majesty and all his nobility came into the field on horseback, in most goodly order, having very fine jennets and Turkey horses garnished with gold and silver abundantly. The Emperor's Majesty having on him a gown of rich tissue, and a cap of scarlet on his head set not only with pearls but also with a great number of rich and costly stones, his noblemen were all in gowns of cloth of gold, which did ride before him in good order by 3 and 3, and before them there went 5,000 arquebusiers, which went 5 and 5 in a rank in very good order, every of them carrying his gun upon his left shoulder and his match in his right hand; and in this order they marched into the field whereas the foresaid ordnance was planted. And before the Emperor's Majesty came into the field, there was a certain stage made of small poles, which was a quarter of a mile long, and about threescore yards off from the stage of poles were certain pieces of ice of two foot thick and six foot high set up, which rank of ice was as long as the stage of poles; and as soon as the Emperor's Majesty came into the field, the arquebusiers went upon the stage of poles where they settled themselves in order. And when the Emperor's Majesty was settled where he would be, and where he might see all the ordnance discharged and shot off, the arquebusiers began to shoot off at the bank of ice, as though it had been in any skirmish or battle, who ceased not shooting until they had beaten all the ice flat on the ground.

After the handguns, they shot off their wildfire up into the air, which was a goodly sight to behold. And after this they began to discharge the small pieces of brass, beginning with the smallest and so orderly bigger and bigger until the last and biggest. When they had shot them all off they began to charge them again, and so shot them all off 3 times after the first order, beginning with the smallest and ending with the greatest. And note that before they had ended their shooting the 2 houses that they shot unto were beaten in pieces, and yet they were very strongly made of wood and filled with earth, being at the least 30 foot thick. This triumph being ended, the Emperor departed and rode home in the same order that he came forth into the field. The ordnance is discharged every year in the month of December according to the order before mentioned.

On Christmas Day we were all willed to dine with the Emperor's Majesty, where for bread, meat, and drink we were served as at other times before; but for goodly and rich plate we never saw the like or so much before. There dined that day in the Emperor's presence above 500 strangers and two hundred Russes, and all they were served in vessels of gold, and that as much as could stand one by another upon the tables. Besides this there were four cupboards garnished with goodly plate both of gold and silver. Among the which there were 12 barrels of silver containing above 12 gallons apiece, and at each end of every barrel were 6 hoops of fine gold. This dinner continued about six hours.

Every year upon the Twelfth Day they use to bless or sanctify the River Moskva, which runneth through the city of Moscow, after this manner. First they make a square hole in the ice about 3 fathoms large every way, which is trimmed about the sides and edges with white boards. Then about 9 of the clock they come out of the church with procession towards the river in this wise. First and foremost there go certain young men with wax tapers burning, and one carrying a great lantern. Then follow certain banners, then the cross, then the images of

Our Lady, of St Nicholas, and of other saints, which images men carry upon their shoulders. After the images follow certain priests to the number of 100 or more; after them the Metropolitan, who is led between two priests; and after the Metropolitan came the Emperor, with his crown upon his head, and after His Majesty all his noblemen orderly. Thus they followed the procession unto the water, and when they came unto the hole that was made, the priests set themselves in order round about it. And at one side of the same pool there was a scaffold of boards made upon which stood a fair chair in which the Metropolitan was set, but the Emperor's Majesty stood upon the ice.

After this the priests began to sing, to bless, and to cense, and did their service, and so by that time that they had done the water was holy; which being sanctified, the Metropolitan took a little thereof in his hands and cast it on the Emperor, likewise upon certain of the Dukes, and then they returned again to the church with the priests that sat about the water. But that press that there was about the water when the Emperor was gone was wonderful to behold, for there came above 5,000 pots to be filled of that water; for that Moscovite which hath no part of that water thinks himself unhappy. And very many went naked into the water, both men and women and children. After the press was a little gone, the Emperor's jennets and horses were brought to drink of the same water, and likewise many other men brought their horses thither to drink, and by that means they make their horses as holy as themselves.

All these ceremonies being ended, we went to the Emperor to dinner, where we were served in vessels of silver, and in all other points as we had been beforetime.

The Russes begin their Lent always 8 weeks before Easter. The first week they eat eggs, milk, cheese, and butter, and make great cheer with pancakes and such other things, one friend visiting another; and from the same Sunday until our Shrove Sunday there are but few Russes sober, but they are drunk day by day and it is accounted for no reproach or shame among them. The next week, being our first week of Lent, or our cleansing week, beginning our Shrove Sunday, they make and keep a great fast. It is reported, and the people do verily believe, that the Metropolitan neither eateth nor drinketh any manner of thing for the space of seven days, and they say that there are many religious men which do the like. The Emperor's Majesty eateth but one morsel of bread and drinketh but one draught of drink once in the day during that week, and all men that are of any reputation come not out of their houses during that time, so that the streets are almost void of company saving a few poor folks which wander to and fro. The other six weeks they keep as we do ours, but not one of them will eat either butter, cheese, eggs, or milk.

On Palm Sunday they have a very solemn procession in this manner following. First they have a tree of a good bigness which is made fast upon two sleds as though it were growing there, and it is hung with apples, raisins, figs, and dates, and with many other fruits abundantly. In the midst of the same tree stand 5 boys in white vestures, which sing in the tree before the procession. After this there followed certain young men with wax tapers in their hands burning, and a great lantern that all the light should not go out. After them followed two with long banners and six with round plates set upon long staves; the plates were of copper very full of holes and thin. Then followed 6 carrying painted images upon their shoulders; after the images followed certain priests to the number of 100 or more, with goodly vestures, whereof 10 or 12 are of white damask set and embroidered round about with fair and orient pearls as great as pease, and among them certain sapphires and other stones. After them followed the one half of the Emperor's noblemen. Then cometh the Emperor's Majesty and the Metropolitan after this manner. First there is a horse covered with white linen cloth down to the ground, his ears being made long with the same cloth like to an ass' ears. Upon this horse the Metropolitan sitteth sidelong like a woman. In his lap lieth a fair book, with a crucifix of goldsmith's work upon the cover, which he holdeth fast with his left hand, and in his right he hath a cross of gold, with which cross he ceaseth not to bless the people as he rideth. There are to the number of 30 men which spread abroad their garments before the horse, and as soon as the horse is passed over any of them they take them up again, and run before and spread them again, so that the horse doth always go on some of them. They which spread the garments are all priests' sons, and for their labours the Emperor giveth unto them new garments.

One of the Emperor's noblemen leadeth the horse by the head, but the Emperor himself, going on foot, leadeth the horse by the end of the rein of his bridle with one of his hands, and in the other of his hands he had a branch of a palm tree. After this followed the rest of the Emperor's noblemen and gentlemen with a great number of other people. In this order they went from one church to another within the castle, about the distance of two flight's-shot; and so returned again to the Emperor's church, where they made an end of their service. Which being done, the Emperor's Majesty and certain of his noblemen went to the Metropolitan's house to dinner, where of delicate fishes and good drinks there was no lack.

The rest of this week until Easter Day they kept very solemnly, continuing in their houses for the most part, and upon Monday or Thursday the Emperor doth always use to receive the sacrament, and so do most of his nobles. Upon Good Friday they continue all day in contemplation and prayers, and they use every year on Good Friday to let loose a prisoner in the stead of Barabbas. The night following they go to the church, where they sleep until the next morning, and at Easter they have the resurrection, and after every of the Lents they eat flesh the next week following, Friday, Saturday, and all.

They have an order at Easter which they always observe, and that is this: every year against Easter to dye or colour red with brazil a great number of eggs, of which every man and woman giveth one unto the priest of their parish upon Easter Day in the morning. And moreover the common people use to carry in their hands one of their red eggs, not only upon Easter Day but also three or four days after, and gentlemen and gentlewomen have eggs gilded which they carry in like manner. They use it, as they say, for a great love, and in token of the resurrection whereof they rejoice. For when two friends meet during the Easter holy days, they come and take one another by the hand; the one of them saith, "The Lord, or Christ, is risen", the other answereth, "It is so of a truth", and then they kiss and exchange their eggs, both men and women, continuing in kissing 4 days together.

The 12th of April, being Tuesday in the Easter week, Master Jenkinson and Master Gray and certain other of us Englishmen dined with the Emperor, where we were served as we had been beforetime. And after dinner the Emperor's Majesty gave unto Master Jenkinson and unto Master Gray, and so orderly unto every one of us, a cup of mead according to his accustomed manner; which when every man had received and given thanks, Master Jenkinson stepped into the midst of the chamber before the Emperor's Majesty and gave thanks to His Highness for his goodness unto him extended, desiring His Grace to license him to depart, and in like manner did Master Gray. His Majesty did not only license them to depart, but also granted unto Master Jenkinson his letters under his great seal unto all princes through whose dominions Master Jenkinson should have occasion to pass, that he might the sooner and quietlier pass by means thereof. Which being granted, Master Jenkinson and Gray lowly submitted themselves, thanking His Majesty. So the Emperor gave unto either a cup of mead to drink, and willed them to depart at their pleasure in God's peace.

The 14th of April in the morning, when Master Gray and I were ready to depart towards England, the Chancellors sent unto us and willed us to come to their office in the Chancery, where at our coming they showed us a great number of the Emperor's jewels and rich robes, willing us to mark and behold them well, to the end that at our arrival into England we might make report what we had seen there.

The chiefest was His Majesty's crown, being close under the top very fair wrought; in my opinion the workmanship of so much gold few men can amend. It was adorned and decked with rich and precious stones abundantly, among the which one was a ruby which stood a handful higher than the top of the crown upon a small wire; it was as big as a good bean. The same crown was lined with a fair black sable, worth by report 40 roubles.

We saw all His Majesty's robes which were very richly set with stones. They showed us many other great stones of divers kinds, but the most part of them were uneven, in manner as they came out of the work; for they do more esteem the greatness of stones than the proportion of them. We saw two goodly gowns which were as heavy as a man could easily carry, all set with pearls over and over; the guards or borders round about them were garnished with sapphires and other good stones abundantly. One of the same gowns was very rich, for the pearls were very large, round, and orient. As for the rest of his gowns and garments they were of rich tissue and cloth of gold and all furred with very black sables.

When we had sufficiently perused all these things, they willed Master Gray, at his arrival in England, to provide, if he could, such jewels and rich clothes as he had seen there, and better if he could, declaring that the Emperor would gladly bestow his money upon such things. So we took our leave the same time and departed towards Vologda immediately.

The manners, usages, and ceremonies of the Russes.

OF THE EMPEROR

The Emperor's name in their tongue is Ivan Vasilievitch, that is as much to say as John the son of Vasili; and by his princely state he is called *Otesara*, as his predecessors have been before, which, to interpret, is a king that giveth not tribute to any man. And this word *Otesara* His Majesty's interpreters have of late days interpreted to be emperor, so that now he is called Emperor and Great Duke of all Russia, etc. Before his father they were neither called emperors nor kings but only *Russe Velike*, that is to say Great Duke. And as this Emperor which now is, Ivan Vasilievitch, doth exceed his predecessors in name, that is from a duke to an emperor, even so much by report he doth exceed them in stoutness of courage and valiantness and a great deal more; for he is no more afraid of his enemies, which are not few, than the hobby of the larks. His enemies with whom he hath wars for the most part are these: Litto, Poland, Sweden, Denmark, Lifland, the Krims, Nogaians, and the whole nation of the Tartarians, which are a stout and a hardy people as any under the sun.

The Emperor useth great familiarity, as well unto all his nobles and subjects as also unto strangers which serve him either in his wars or in occupations. For his pleasure is that they shall dine oftentimes in the year in his presence, and besides that he is oftentimes abroad, either at one church or another and walking with his noblemen abroad. And by this means he is not only beloved of his nobles and commons but also had in great dread and fear through all his dominions, so that I think no prince in Christendom is more feared of his own than he is, nor yet better beloved. For if he bid any of his Dukes go, they will run. If he give any evil or angry words to any of them, the party will not come into His Majesty's presence again of a long time if he be not sent for, but will feign him to be very sick, and will let the hair of his head grow very long, without either cutting or shaving, which is an evident token that he is in the Emperor's displeasure; for when they be in prosperity they account it a shame to wear long hair, in consideration whereof they use to have their heads shaven.

His Majesty heareth all complaints himself, and with his own mouth giveth sentence and judgment of all matters, and that with expedition; but religious matters he meddleth not withal, but referreth them wholly unto the Metropolitan.

His Majesty retaineth and well rewardeth all strangers that come to serve him, and especially men of war.

He delighteth not greatly in hawking, hunting, or any other pastime, nor in hearing instruments or music, but setteth all his whole delight upon two things: first, to serve God, as undoubtedly he is very devout in his religion; and the second, how to subdue and conquer his enemies.

He hath abundance of gold and silver in his own hands or treasury; but the most part of his know not a crown from a counter, nor gold from copper, they are so much cumbered withal; and he that is worth 2, 3, or 4 groats is a rich man.

OF THEIR RELIGIOUS MEN

The Metropolitan is next unto God, Our Lady and St Nicholas excepted; for the Emperor's Majesty judgeth and affirmeth him to be of higher dignity than himself, "for that", saith he, "he is God's spiritual officer and I the Emperor am his temporal officer". And therefore His Majesty submitteth himself unto him in many things concerning religious matters, as in leading the Metropolitan's horse upon Palm Sunday and giving him leave to sit on a chair upon the Twelfth Day, when the River Moscow was in blessing, His Majesty standing on the ice.

All matters of religion are reformed by the Metropolitan. He heareth the causes and giveth sentence as himself listeth and is authorised so to do, whether it be to whip, hang, or burn his will must be fulfilled.

They have both monks, friars, and nuns, with a great number of great and rich monasteries. They keep great hospitality and do relieve much poor people day by day. I have been in one of the monasteries called Troietes, which is walled about with brick very strongly like a castle, and much ordnance of brass upon the walls of the same. They told me themselves that there are seven hundred brethren of them which belong unto that house. The most part of the lands, towns, and villages which are within 40 miles of it belong unto the same. They showed me the church, wherein were as many images as could hang about, or upon the walls of the church round about, and even the roof of the church was painted full of images. The chief image was of Our Lady, which was garnished with gold, rubies, sapphires, and other rich stones abundantly. In the midst of the church stood 12 wax tapers of two yards long and a fathom about in bigness, and there stands a kettle full of wax with about a hundredweight, wherein there is always the wick of a candle burning, as it were a lamp which goeth not out day nor night.

They showed me a coffin covered with a cloth of gold which stood upon one side within their church, in which they told me lay a holy man, who never ate or drank, and yet that he liveth. And they told me (supposing that I had believed them) that he healeth many diseases, and giveth the blind their sight, with many other miracles, but I was hard of belief because I saw him work no miracle whilst I was there.

After this they brought me into their cellars and made me taste of divers kinds of drinks, both wine and beer, mead and kvass, of sundry colours and kinds. Such abundance of drink as they have in their cellars I do suppose few princes have more, or so much at once. Their barrels or vessels are of an immeasurable bigness and size: some of them are 3 yards long and more, and 2 yards and more broad in their heads. They contain 6 or 7 tuns apiece—they have none in their cellars of their own making that are less than a tun. They have 9 or 10 great vaults which are full of those barrels, which are seldom removed; for they have trunks which come down through the roof of the vaults in sundry places, through which they pour drink down, having the cask right under it to receive the same, for it should be a great trouble to bring it all down the stairs.

They give bread, meat, and drink unto all men that come to them, not only while they are at their abbey but also when they depart, to serve them by the way.

There are a great number of such monasteries in the realm, and the Emperor's Majesty rideth oftentimes from one to another of them, and lieth at them 3 or 4 days together.

The same monks are as great merchants as any in the land of Russia, and do occupy buying and selling as much as any other men, and have boats which pass to and fro in the rivers with merchandise from place to place where any of their country do traffic.

They eat no flesh during their lives as it is reported; but upon Sunday, Monday, Tuesday, Thursday, and Saturday it is lawful for them to eat eggs, butter, cheese, and milk, and at all times to eat fish, and after this sort they lead their lives. They wear all black garments, and so do none other in all the land but at that abbey only.

They have no preachers, no, not one in all the land to instruct the people, so that there are many, and the most part of the poor in the country, who, if one ask them how many gods there be, they will say a great many, meaning that every image which they have is a god; for all the country, and the Emperor's Majesty himself, will bless and bow and knock their heads before their images, insomuch that they will cry earnestly unto their images to help them to the things which they need. All men are bound by their law to have those images in their houses, and over every gate in all their towns and cities are images set up, unto which the people bow and bend and knock their heads against the ground before them. As often as they come by any church or cross they do in like manner. And when they come to any house they bless themselves 3 or 4 times before they will salute any man in the house. They reckon and hold it for great sin to touch or handle any of their images within the circle of the board where the painting is, but they keep them very daintily; and rich men deck them over and about with gold, silver, and stones, and hang them over and about with cloth of gold.

The priests are married as other men are, and wear all their garments as other men do, except their nightcaps, which is cloth of some sad colour, being round, and reacheth unto the ears. Their crowns are shaven, but the rest of their hair they let grow as long as nature will permit, so that it hangeth beneath their ears upon their shoulders. Their beards they never shave. If his wife happen to die, it is not lawful for him to marry again during his life.

They minister the Communion with bread and wine after our order, but he breaketh the bread and putteth it into the cup unto the wine, and commonly some are partakers with them; and they take the bread out again with a spoon, together with part of the wine, and so take it themselves and give it to others that receive with them after the same manner. Their ceremonies are all, as they say, according to the Greek church used at this present day, and they allow no other religion but the Greeks' and their own; and will not permit any nation but the Greeks to be buried in their sacred burials or churchyards.

All their churches are full of images unto the which the people, when they assemble, do bow and knock their heads, as I have before said, that some will have knobs upon their foreheads, with knocking, as great as eggs. All their service is in the Russ tongue, and they and the common people have no other prayers but this: *Ghospodi Jesus Christos esine voze ponuloi nashe.* That is to say, O Lord Jesus Christ, son of God, have mercy on us; and this is their prayer, so that the most part of the unlearned know neither Pater noster, nor the Belief, nor Ten Commandments, nor scarcely understand the one half of their service which is read in their churches.

OF THEIR BAPTISM

When any child is born, it is not baptised until the next Sunday, and if it chance that it be not baptised then, it must tarry until the second Sunday after the birth; and it is lawful for them to take as many godfathers and godmothers as they will, the more the better.

When they go to the church, the midwife goeth foremost carrying the child, and the godfathers and godmothers follow into the midst of the church, where there is a small table ready set and on it an earthen pot full of warm water, about which the godfathers and godmothers, with the child, settle themselves. Then the clerk giveth unto every of them a small wax candle burning. Then cometh the priest and beginneth to say certain words, which the godfathers and godmothers must answer word for word; among which one is that the child shall forsake the devil, and as that name is pronounced they must all spit at the word as often as it is repeated. Then he blesseth the water which is in the pot and doth breathe over it. Then he taketh all the candles which the gossips have, and holding them all in one hand letteth part of them drop into the water, and then giveth every one his candle again; and when the water is sanctified he taketh the child and holdeth it in a small tub, and one of the godfathers taketh the pot with warm water and poureth it all upon the child's head.

After this he hath many more ceremonies, as anointing ears and eyes with spittle and making certain crosses with oil upon the back, head, and breast of the child; then, taking the child in his arms, carrieth it to the images of St Nicholas and Our Lady, etc. and speaketh unto the images, desiring them to take charge of the child, that he may live, and believe as a Christian man or woman ought to do, with many other words. Then coming back from the images, he taketh a pair of shears and clippeth the young and tender hairs of the child's head in three or four places, and then delivereth the child, whereunto every of the godfathers and godmothers lay a hand. Then the priest chargeth them that the child be brought up in the faith and fear of God or Christ, and that it be instructed to cling and bow to the images, and so they make an end. Then one of the godfathers must hang a cross about the neck of the child, which he must always wear; for that Russ which hath not a cross about his neck they esteem as no Christian man, and thereupon they say that we are no Christians because we do not wear crosses as they do.

OF THEIR MATRIMONY

Their matrimony is nothing solemnized, but rather in most points abominable, and as near as I can learn in this wise following.

First, when there is love between the parties, the man sendeth unto the woman a small chest or box, wherein is a whip, needles, thread, silk, linen cloth, shears, and such necessaries as she shall occupy when she is a wife, and perhaps sendeth therewithal raisins, figs, or some such things, giving her to understand that if she do offend she must be beaten with the whip, and by the needles, thread, cloth, etc. that she should apply herself diligently to sew and do such things as she could best do; and by the raisins or fruits he meaneth, if she do well, no good thing shall be withdrawn from her nor be too dear for her. And she sendeth unto him a shirt, handkerchiefs, and some such things of her own making. And now to the effect.

When they are agreed and the day of marriage appointed when they shall go towards the church the bride will in no wise consent to go out of the house, but resisteth and striveth with them that would have her out and feigneth herself to weep; yet in the end two women get her out and lead her towards the church, her face being covered close because of her dissimulation, that it should not be openly perceived. For she maketh a great noise, as though she were sobbing and weeping, until she come at the church, and then her face is uncovered. The man cometh after among other of his friends, and they carry with them to the church a great pot with wine or mead. Then the priest coupleth them together much after our order, one promising to love and serve the other during their lives together, etc. Which being done, they begin to drink, and first the woman drinketh to the man; and when he hath drunk he letteth the cup fall to the ground, hasting immediately to tread upon it, and so doth she, and whether of them tread first upon it must have the victory and be master at all times after; which commonly happeneth to the man, for he is readiest to set his foot on it because he letteth it fall himself. Then they go home again, the woman's face being uncovered. The boys in the streets cry out and make a noise in the meantime with very dishonest words.

When they come home the wife is set at the upper end of the table and the husband next unto her. They fall then to drinking till they be all drunk. They perchance have a minstrel or two, and two naked men, which led her from the church, dance naked a long time before all the company. When they are weary of drinking, the bride and the bridegroom get them to bed, for it is in the evening always when any of them are married; and when they are going to bed the bridegroom putteth certain money both gold and silver, if he have it, into one of his boots, and then sitteth down in the chamber, crossing his legs; and then the bride must pluck off one of his boots, which she will, and if she happen on the boot wherein the money is she hath not only the money for her labour but is also at such choice as she need not ever from that day forth to pull off his boots; but if she miss the boot wherein the money is she doth not only lose the money but is also bound from that day forwards to pull off his boots continually.

Then they continue in drinking and making good cheer three days following, being accompanied with certain of their friends, and during the same three days he is called a duke and she a duchess, although they be very poor persons; and this is as much as I have learned of their matrimony. But one common rule is amongst them: if the woman be not beaten with the whip once a week she will not be good; and therefore they look for it orderly, and the women say that if their husbands did not beat them they should not love them.

They use to marry there very young, their sons at 16 and 18 years old and the daughters at 12 or 13 years or younger. They use to keep their wives very closely, I mean those that be of any reputation, so that a man shall not see one of them but at a chance, when she goeth to church at Christmas or at Easter, or else going to visit some of her friends.

The most part of the women use to ride astride in saddles with stirrups, as men do, and some of them on sleds, which in summer is not commendable.

The husband is bound to find the wife colours to paint her withal, for they use ordinarily to paint themselves. It is such a common practice among them that it is counted for no shame. They grease their faces with such colours that a man may discern them hanging on their faces almost a flight-shot off. I cannot so well liken them as to a miller's wife, for they look as though they were beaten about the face with a bag of meal, but their eyebrows they colour as black as jet.

The best property that the women have is that they can sew well and embroider with silk and gold excellently.

OF THEIR BURIAL

When any man or woman dieth, they stretch him out, and put a new pair of shoes on his feet because he hath a great journey to go. Then do they wind him in a sheet, as we do, but they forget not to put a testimony in his right hand, which the priest giveth him, to testify unto St Nicholas that he died a Christian man or woman. And they put the corpse always in a coffin of wood, although the party be very poor; and when they go towards the church, the friends and kinsmen of the party departed carry in their hands small wax candles, and they weep and howl and make much lamentation.

They that be hanged or beheaded, or suchlike, have no testimony with them. How they are received into heaven it is a wonder, without their passport.

There are a great number of poor people among them which die daily for lack of sustenance, which is a pitiful case to behold. For there hath been buried in a small time, within these two years, above 80 persons young and old which have died only for lack of sustenance; for if they had had straw and water enough they would make shift to live, for a great many are forced in the winter to dry straw and stamp it, and to make bread thereof, or at the least they eat it instead of bread. In the summer they make good shift with grass, herbs, and roots; barks of trees are good meat with them at all times. There is no people in the world, as I suppose, that live so miserably as do the poverty in those parts; and the most part of them that have sufficient for themselves, and also to relieve others that need, are so unmerciful that they care not how many they see die of famine or hunger in the streets.

It is a country full of diseases, divers, and evil; and the best remedy is, for any of them (as they hold opinion), to go often unto the hot-houses, as in a manner every man hath one of his own which he heateth commonly twice every week, and all the household sweat, and wash themselves therein.

The names of certain sorts of drinks used in Russia and commonly drunk in the Emperor's court.

The first and principal mead is made of the juice or liquor taken from a berry called in Russia *malieno*, which is of a marvellous sweet taste and of a carmosant colour, which berry I have seen in Paris. The second mead is called *visnova*, because it is made of a berry so called and is like a black gooseberry; but it is like in colour and taste to the red wine of France. The third mead is called *amarodina*, or *smorodina* short, of a small berry much like to the small raisin and groweth in great plenty in Russia. The fourth mead is called *cherevnikina*, which is made of the wild black cherry. The fifth mead is made of honey and water, with other mixtures.

There is also a delicate drink drawn from the root of the birch tree, called in the Russ tongue *berozevites*, which drink the noblemen and others use in April, May, and June, which are the three months of the springtime; for after those months the sap of the tree dryeth, and then they cannot have it.

The voyage of Master Anthony Jenkinson, made from the city of
Moscow in Russia to the city of Bokhara in Bactria in the year
1558; written by himself to the Merchants of London in the
Muscovy Company.

THE 23rd day of April in the year 1558, having obtained the
Emperor of Russia's letters directed unto sundry kings and
princes by whose dominions I should pass, I departed from
Moscow by water, having with me two of your servants namely Richard
Johnson and Robert Johnson, and a Tartar *tolmach*, with divers
parcels of wares as by the inventory appeareth; and the 28th day we
came to a town called Collom, distant from the Moscow 20 leagues,
and passing one league beyond the said Collom we came unto a river
called Oka into the which the river Moskva falleth and loseth his name.
And passing down the said river Oka 8 leagues we came unto a castle
called Terrevettisko, which we left upon our right hand, and proceeding forward, the second day of May we came unto another castle called
Pereyaslavl, distant 8 leagues, leaving it also on our right hand. The
third day we came unto the place where old Ryazan was situated, being
now most of it ruined and overgrown, and distant from the said
Pereyaslavl 6 leagues. The 4th day we passed by a castle called
Terikhovo, from Ryazan 12 leagues, and the 6th day we came to
another castle called Kasimov, under the government of a Tartar
prince named Tzar Igorin, sometime Emperor of the worthy city of
Kazan and now subject unto the Emperor of Russia. But leaving
Kasimov on our left hand, the 8th day we came unto a fair town called
Morom, from Kasimov 20 leagues, where we took the sun and found
the latitude 56 degrees; and proceeding forward the 11th day we came
unto another fair town and castle called Nizhne Novgorod, situated at
the falling of the foresaid river Oka into the worthy river of Volga,
distant from the said Morom 25 leagues, in the latitude of 56 degrees
18 minutes.

From Ryazan to this Nizhne Novgorod, on both sides of the River
Oka, is raised the greatest store of wax and honey in all the land of
Russia. We tarried at the foresaid Nizhne Novgorod until the 19th
day for the coming of a captain which was sent by the Emperor
to rule at Astrakhan; who being arrived, and having the number
of 500 great boats under his conduct, some laden with victuals,
soldiers, and munition, and other some with merchandise, departed
all together the said 19th day from the said Nizhne Novgorod, and the
22nd we came unto a castle called Vasiliagorod distant 25 leagues,
which we left upon our right hand. This town or castle had his name

of this Emperor's father, who was called Vasilius, and *gorod* in the Russ tongue is as much to say as a castle, so that Vasiliagorod is to say Vasilius' castle; and it was the furthest place that the said Emperor conquered from the Tartars. But this present Emperor, his son, called Ivan Vasilievitch, hath had great good success in his wars both against the Christians and also the Mahometists and gentiles, but especially against the Tartars, enlarging his empire even to the Caspian Sea, having conquered the famous river of Volga with all the countries thereabout adjacent.

Thus proceeding on our journey the 25th day of May aforesaid we came to another castle called Sabowshare, which we left on our right hand, distant from Vasiliagorod 16 leagues. The country hereabout is called Mordovits, and the habitants did profess the law of the gentiles; but now being conquered by this Emperor of Russia most of them are christened, but lie in the woods and wilderness without town or habitation.

The 27th day we passed by another castle called Sviyazhsk, distant from Sabowshare aforesaid 25 leagues; we left it on our right hand and the 29th came unto an island one league from the city of Kazan, from which falleth down a river called Kazanka Reca and entereth into the foresaid Volga. Kazan is a fair town after the Russ or Tartar fashion, with a strong castle, situated upon a high hill, and was walled round about with timber and earth; but now the Emperor of Russia hath given order to pluck down the old walls and to build them again of freestone. It hath been a city of great wealth and riches, and being in the hands of the Tartars it was a kingdom of itself, and did more vex the Russes in their wars than any other nation, but 9 years past this Emperor of Russia conquered it, and took the king captive, who being but young is now baptised and brought up in his court with two other princes which were also kings of the said Kazan and, being each of them in time of their reigns in danger of their subjects through civil discord, came and rendered themselves at several times unto the said Emperor, so that at this present there are three princes in the court of Russia which had been Emperors of the said Kazan, whom the Emperor useth with great honour.

We remained at Kazan till the 13th day of June, and then departed from thence, and the same day passed by an island called the Island of Merchants, because it was wont to be a place where all merchants, as well Russes and Kazanites as Nogaians and Krims and divers other nations, did resort to keep mart for buying and selling; but now it is forsaken and standeth without any such resort thither, or at Kazan, or at any place about it from Moscow unto Mare Caspium.

Thus proceeding forward the 14th day we passed by a goodly river called Kama, which we left on our left hand. This river falleth out of the country of Permia into the river of Volga, and is from Kazan 15 leagues; and the country lying betwixt the said Kazan and the said River Kama on the left hand of Volga is called Vachen, and the inhabitants be gentiles and live in the wilderness without house or habitation; and the country on the other side of Volga over against the said River Kama is called the land of Cheremissi, half gentiles, half Tartars; and all the land on the left hand of the said Volga from the said river unto Astrakhan, and so following the north and north-east side of the Caspian Sea to a land of the Tartars called Turkmen, is called the country of Mangat or Nogai, whose inhabitants are of the law of Mahomet, and were all destroyed in the year 1558, at my being at Astrakhan, through civil wars among them, accompanied with famine, pestilence, and such plagues, in such sort that in the said year there were consumed of the people, in one sort and another, above one hundred thousand. The like plague was never seen in those parts, so that the said country of Nogai, being a country of great pasture, remaineth now unreplenished, to the great contention of the Russes who have had cruel wars a long time together.

The Nogaians, when they flourished, lived in this manner. They were divided into divers companies called *hords*, and every *hord* had a ruler, whom they obeyed as their king, and was called a *murse*. Town or house they had none, but lived in the open fields, every *murse*, or king, having his *hords* or people about him, with their wives, children, and cattle, who having consumed the pasture in one place removed unto another. And when they remove they have houses like tents set upon wagons or carts, which are drawn from place to place with camels, and therein their wives, children, and all their riches, which is very little, is carried about, and every man hath at the least four or five wives besides concubines. Use of money they have none, but do barter their cattle for apparel and other necessaries. They delight in no art nor science, except the wars, wherein they be expert, but for the most part they be pasturing people, and have great store of cattle, which is all their riches. They eat much flesh, and especially the horse, and they drink mares' milk, wherewith they be oftentimes drunk. They are seditious and inclined to theft and murder. Corn they sow not, neither do eat any bread, mocking the Christians for the same and disabling our strengths, saying we live by eating the top of a weed and drink a drink made of the same, allowing their great devouring of flesh and drinking of milk to be the increase of their strength. But now to proceed forward to my journey.

All the country upon our right hand the river Volga, from over against the River Kama unto the town of Astrakhan, is the land of Krim, whose inhabitants be also of the law of Mahomet and live for the most part according to the fashions of the Nogais, having continual wars with the Emperor of Russia, and are valiant in the field, having countenance and support from the Great Turk.

The 16th day of June we passed by certain fishermen's houses called Petowse twenty leagues from the River Kama, where is great fishing for sturgeon, so continuing our way until the 22nd day and passing by another great river called Samara, which falleth out of the aforesaid country and runneth through Nogai and entereth into the said river of Volga. The 28th day we came unto a great hill, where was in times past a castle made by the Krims, but now it is ruined, being the just midway between the said Kazan and Astrakhan (which is 200 leagues or thereabout) in the latitude of 51 degrees 47 minutes. Upon all this shore groweth abundance of liquorice, whose root runneth within the ground like a vine.

Thus going forward, the sixth day of July we came to a place called Perovolog, so named because in times past the Tartars carried their boats from Volga unto the river Tanais, otherwise called Don, by land, when they would rob such as passed down the said Volga to Astrakhan, and also such as passed down by the River Tanais to Azov, Kaffa, or any other town situated upon Mare Euxinum, into which sea Tanais falleth, who hath his springs in the country of Ryazan out of a plain ground. It is, at this strait of Perovolog, from the one river to the other two leagues by land, and is a dangerous place for thieves and robbers, but now it is not so evil as it hath been, by reason of the Emperor of Russia's conquests.

Departing from Perovolog, having the wilderness on both sides, we saw a great herd of Nogaians, pasturing, as is abovesaid, by estimation above a thousand camels drawing of carts with houses upon them like tents, of a strange fashion, seeming to be afar off a town. That *hord* was belonging to a great *murse* called Smille, the greatest prince in all Nogai, who hath slain and driven away all the rest, not sparing his own brethren and children, and having peace with this Emperor of Russia he hath what he needeth, and ruleth alone; so that now the Russes live in peace with the Nogaians, who were wont to have mortal wars together.

The 14th day of July, passing by an old castle, which was Old Astrakhan, and leaving it upon our right hand, we arrived at New Astrakhan, which this Emperor conquered six years past, in the year 1552. It is from the Moscow unto Astrakhan six hundred leagues or thereabout. The town of Astrakhan is situated in an island, upon a hillside, having a castle within the same, walled about with earth and timber, neither fair nor strong. The town is also walled about with earth; the buildings and houses, except it be the Captain's lodging and certain other gentlemen's, most base and simple. The island is most destitute and barren of wood and pasture, and the ground will bear no corn. The air is there most infected, by reason (as I suppose) of much fish, and specially sturgeon, by which only the inhabitants live, having great scarcity of flesh and bread. They hang up their fish in their streets and houses to dry for their provision, which causeth such abundance of flies to increase there as the like was never seen in any land, to their great plague. And at my being at the said Astrakhan there was a great famine and plague among the people, and specially among the Tartars called Nogaians, who the same time came thither in great numbers to render themselves to the Russes their enemies and to seek succour at their hands, their country being destroyed as I said before. But they were but ill entertained or relieved, for there died a great number of them for hunger, which lay all the island through in heaps dead and like to beasts unburied, very pitiful to behold. Many of them were also sold by the Russes, and the rest were banished from the island. At that time it had been an easy thing to have converted that wicked nation to the Christian faith if the Russes themselves had been good Christians; but how should they show compassion unto other nations when they are not merciful unto their own? At my being there I could have bought many goodly Tartars' children, if I would have had a thousand, of their own fathers and mothers, to say a boy or a wench for a loaf of bread worth sixpence in England; but we had more need of victuals at that time than of any such merchandise. This Astrakhan is the furthest hold that this Emperor of Russia hath conquered of the Tartars towards the Caspian Sea, which he keepeth very strong, sending thither every year provision of men and victuals and timber to build the castle.

There is a certain trade of merchandise there used, but as yet so small and beggarly that it is not worth the making mention, and yet there come merchants thither from divers places. The chiefest commodities that the Russes bring thither are red hides, red sheepskins, wooden vessels, bridles, and saddles, knives, and other trifles, with corn, bacon, and other victuals. The Tartars bring thither divers kinds of wares made of cotton-wool, with divers kinds of wrought silks; and they that come out of Persia, namely from Shemakha, do bring sewing-silk, which is the coarsest that they use in Russland, crasko, divers kinds of pied silks for girdles, shirts of mail, bows, swords, and suchlike things; and some years corn, and walnuts, but all such things in such small quantity, the merchants being so beggarly and poor that bring the same, that it is not worth the writing, neither is there any hope of trade in all those parts worth the following.

This foresaid island of Astrakhan is in length twelve leagues and in breadth three, and lieth east and west in the latitude of 47 degrees 9 minutes. We tarried there until the sixth day of August, and having bought and provided a boat in company with certain Tartars and Persians, we loaded our goods and embarked ourselves, and the same day departed, I, with the said two Johnsons, having the whole charge of the navigation down the said River Volga, being very crooked, and full of flats toward the mouth thereof. We entered into the Caspian Sea the tenth day of August at the easterly side of the said river, being twenty leagues from Astrakhan aforesaid, in the latitude of 46 degrees 27 minutes.

Volga hath seventy mouths or falls into the sea; and we having a large wind kept the north-east shore, and the eleventh day we sailed seven leagues east-north-east and came unto an island having a high hill therein, called Accurgar, a good mark in the sea. From thence east ten leagues we fell with another island called Bawhiata, much higher than the other. Within these two islands to the northwards is a great bay called the Blue Sea. From thence we sailed east and by north ten leagues, and having a contrary wind we came to an anchor in a fathom water, and so rode until the fifteenth day, having a great storm at south-east, being a most contrary wind, which we rode out. Then the wind came to the north, and we weighed and set our course south-east, and that day sailed eight leagues.

Thus proceeding forwards, the 17th day we lost sight of land, and the same day sailed thirty leagues, and the 18th day twenty leagues, winding east, and fell with a land called Baughleata, being 74 leagues from the mouth of the said Volga in the latitude of 46 degrees 54 minutes, the coast lying nearest east and by south and west and by north. At the point of this land lieth buried a holy prophet, as the Tartars call him, of their law, where great devotion is used of all such Mahometists as do pass that way.

The nineteenth day the wind being west and we winding east-south-east, we sailed ten leagues, and passed by a great river called Yaick, which hath his spring in the land of Siberia nigh unto the foresaid River Kama, and runneth through the land of Nogai falling into this Mare Caspium. And up this river one day's journey is a town called Saraychick, subject to the aforesaid Tartar prince called Murse Smille which is now in friendship with the Emperor of Russia. Here is no trade of merchandise used, for that the people have no use of money and are all men of war and pasturers of cattle, and given much to theft and murder. Thus being at an anchor against this River Yaick, and all our men being on land saving I, who lay sore sick, and five Tartars, whereof one was reputed a holy man because he came from Mecca, there came unto us a boat with thirty men well armed and appointed who boarded us, and began to enter into our bark; and our holy Tartar, called Azie, perceiving that, asked them what they would have, and withal made a prayer. With that these rovers stayed, declaring that they were gentlemen banished from their country, and out of living, and came to see if there were any Russes or other Christians (which they call *Caphars*) in our bark. To whom this Azie most stoutly answered that there were none, avowing the same by great oaths of their law (which lightly they will not break), whom the rovers believed, and upon his words departed. And so through the fidelity of that Tartar I with all my company and goods were saved; and our men being come on board, and the wind fair, we departed from that place, and winding east and south-east, that day being the 20th August, sailed 16 leagues.

The 21st day we passed over a bay of 6 leagues broad and fell with a cape of land having two islands at the south-east part thereof, being a good mark in the sea; and doubling that cape the land trended northeast, and maketh another bay into which falleth the great River Yem, springing out of the land of Kalmuk. The 22nd, 23rd, and 24th days we were at an anchor.

The 25th the wind came fair, and we sailed that day 20 leagues, and passed by an island of low land, and there about are many flats and sands. And to the northward of this island there goeth in a great bay, but we set off from this island and wound south to come into deep water, being much troubled with shoals and flats; and ran that course 10 leagues, then east-south-east 20 leagues, and fell with the mainland, being full of copped hills, and passing along the coast 20 leagues the further we sailed the higher was the land.

The 27th day we crossed over a bay, the south shore being the higher land, and fell with a high point of land; and being overthwart the cape, there rose such a storm at the east that we thought verily we should have perished. This storm continued 3 days. From this cape we passed to a port called Mangyshlak. The place where we should have arrived at the southermost part of the Caspian Sea is 12 leagues within a bay; but we, being sore tormented and tossed with this foresaid storm, were driven into another land on the other side of the bay, overthwart the said Mangyshlak being very low land, and a place, as well for the ill commodity of the haven as of those brute field people where never bark nor boat had before arrived, not liked of us. But yet here we sent certain of our men to land to talk with the governor and people, as well for our good usage at their hands as also for provision of camels to carry our goods from the said sea side to a place called Sellyzure, being from the place of our landing five and twenty days' journey. Our messengers returned with comfortable words and fair promises of all things.

Wherefore the 3rd day of September 1558 we discharged our bark, and I with my company were greatly entertained of the Prince and of his people. But before our departure from thence we found them to be very bad and brutish people, for they ceased not daily to molest us, either by fighting, stealing, or begging, raising the price of horse and camels and victuals double that it was wont to be, and forced us to buy the water that we did drink; which caused us to hasten away, and to conclude with them as well for the hire of camels as for the price of such as we bought, with other provision, according to their own demand. So that for every camel's lading, being but 4 hundredweight of ours, we agreed to give three hides of Russia and four wooden dishes, and to the Prince or governor of the said people one ninth and two sevenths, namely nine several things and twice seven several things, for money they use none.

And thus being ready, the fourteenth of September we departed from that place, being a caravan of a thousand camels. And having travelled five days' journey we came to another prince's dominion, and upon the way there came unto us certain Tartars on horseback, being well armed and servants unto the said prince called Timur Sultan, governor of the said country of Mangyshlak where we meant to have arrived and discharged our bark if the great storm aforesaid had not disappointed. These aforesaid Tartars stayed our caravan in the name of their prince, and opened our wares, and took such things as they thought best for their said prince without money. But for such things as they took from me, which was a ninth (after much dissension), I rode unto the same prince and presented myself before him, requesting his favour and passport to travel through his country, and not to be robbed nor spoiled of his people. Which request he granted me, and entertained me very gently, commanding me to be well feasted with flesh and mares' milk, for bread they use none, nor other drink except water; but money he had none to give me for such things as he took of me, which might be of the value in Russ money fifteen roubles, but he gave me his letter, and a horse worth seven roubles. And so I departed from him, being glad that I was gone; for he was reported to be a very tyrant, and, if I had not gone to him, I understood his commandment was that I should have been robbed and destroyed.

This Sultan lived in the fields without castle or town, and sat, at my being with him, in a little round house made of reeds covered without with felt and within with carpets. There was with him the Great Metropolitan of that wild country, esteemed of the people as the Bishop of Rome is in most parts of Europe, with divers other of his chief men. The Sultan with this Metropolitan demanded of me many questions, as well touching our kingdoms, laws, and religion as also the cause of my coming into those parts, with my further pretence. To whom I answered concerning all things as unto me seemed best, which they took in good part. So, having leave, I departed and overtook our caravan and proceeded on our journey, and travelled 20 days in the wilderness from the sea side without seeing town or habitation, carrying provision of victuals with us for the same time, and were driven by necessity to eat one of my camels and a horse for our part, as other did the like; and during the said 20 days we found no water but such as we drew out of old deep wells, being very brackish and salt, and yet sometimes passed two or three days without the same. And the 5th day of October ensuing we came unto a gulf of the Caspian Sea again, where we found the water very fresh and sweet. At this gulf the

6 *Caravan en route from Aleppo to Basra. In front is an escort of janissaries, or Turkish soldiers.*

customers of the King of Turkmen met us, who took custom of every 25 one, and 7 ninths for the said King and his brethren, which being received they departed and we remained there a day after to refresh ourselves.

Note that in times past there did fall into this gulf the great River Oxus, which hath his springs in the mountains of Paraponisus in India, and now cometh not so far but falleth into another river called Ardock, which runneth toward the north and consumeth himself in the ground, passing underground above 500 miles, and then issueth out again and falleth into the lake of Kithay.

We, having refreshed ourselves at the foresaid gulf, departed thence the 4th day of October, and the seventh day arrived at a castle called Sellyzure, where the King, called Azim Khan, remained with 3 other of his brethren. And the 9th day I was commanded to come before his presence, to whom I delivered the Emperor's letters of Russia, and I also gave him a present of a ninth; who entertained me very well, and caused me to eat in his presence as his brethren did, feasting me with flesh of a wild horse and mare's milk without bread. And the next day he sent for me again, and asked of me divers questions, as well touching the affairs of the Emperor of Russia as of our country and laws, to which I answered as I thought good, so that at my departure he gave me his letters of safe conduct.

This castle of Sellyzure is situated upon a high hill, where the King (called the Khan) lieth, whose palace is built of earth very basely, and not strong. The people are but poor, and have little trade of merchandise among them. The south part of this castle is low land but very fruitful, where grow many good fruits, among which is one called a *dynie*, of a great bigness and full of moisture, which the people do eat after meat instead of drink. Also there grows another fruit called a *carbuse*, of the bigness of a great cucumber, yellow and sweet as sugar; also a certain corn called *iegur*, whose stalk is much like a sugar cane, and as high, and the grain like rice, which groweth at the top of the cane like a cluster of grapes. The water that serveth all that country is drawn by ditches out of the River Oxus unto the great destruction of the said river, for which cause it falleth not into the Caspian Sea as it hath done in times past; and in short time all that land is like to be destroyed and to become a wilderness, for want of water when the river of Oxus shall fail.

The 14th day of the month we departed from this castle of Sellyzure, and the 16th of the same we arrived at a city called Urgenj, where we paid custom as well for our own heads as for our camels and horses. And having there sojourned one month, attending the time of our further travel, the king of that country, called Ali Sultan, brother to the forenamed Azim Khan, returned from a town called Khorasan, within the borders of Persia, which he lately had conquered from the Persians, with whom he and the rest of the kings of Tartaria have continual wars. Before this king also I was commanded to come, to whom I likewise presented the Emperor's letters of Russia, and he entertained me well and demanded of me divers questions, and at my departure gave me his letters of safe-conduct.

The city or town of Urgenj standeth in a plain ground, with walls of the earth by estimation 4 miles about it. The buildings within it are also of earth, but ruined and out of good order. It hath one long street that is covered above, which is the place of their market. It hath been won and lost 4 times within 7 years by civil wars, by means whereof there are but few merchants in it and they very poor, and in all that town I could not sell above 4 kerseys. The chiefest commodities there sold are such wares as come from Bokhara and out of Persia, but in most small quantity not worth the writing. All the land from the Caspian Sea to this city of Urgenj is called the land of Turkmen and is subject to the said Azim Khan and his brethren, which be five in number and one of them hath the name of the chief king called Khan, but he is little obeyed saving in his own dominion and where he dwelleth. For every one will be king of his own portion, and one brother seeketh always to destroy another, having no natural love among them by reason that they are begotten of divers women, and commonly they are the children of slaves, either Christians or gentiles, which the father doth keep as concubines; and every khan or sultan hath at the least 4 or 5 wives, besides young maidens and boys, living most viciously. And when there are wars betwixt these brethren (as they are seldom without) he that is overcome, if he be not slain flieth to the field with such company of men as will follow him, and there liveth in the wilderness resorting to watering places, and so robbeth and spoileth as many caravans of merchants and others as they be able to overcome, continuing in this sort his wicked life until such time as he may get power and aid to invade some of his brethren again. From the Caspian Sea unto the castle of Sellyzure aforesaid, and all the countries about the said sea, the people live without town or habitation in the wild fields, removing from one place to another in great companies with their cattle, whereof they have great store, as camels, horses, and sheep both tame and wild. Their sheep are of great stature with great buttocks, weighing 60 or 80 pound in weight. There are many wild horses which the Tartars do many times kill with their hawks, and that in this order.

The hawks are lured to seize upon the beasts' necks or heads, which with chafing of themselves and sore beating of the hawks are tired. Then the hunter following his game doth slay the horse with his arrow or sword. In all this land there groweth no grass but a certain brush or heath, whereon the cattle feeding become very fat.

The Tartars never ride without their bow, arrows, and sword, although it be on hawking or at any other pleasure; and they are good archers both on horseback and on foot also. These people have not the use of gold, silver, or any other coin, but when they lack apparel or other necessaries they barter their cattle for the same. Bread they have none, for they neither till nor sow. They be great devourers of flesh, which they cut in small pieces and eat it by handfuls most greedily, and especially the horseflesh. Their chiefest drink is mares' milk soured, as I have said before of the Nogaians, and they will be drunk with the same. They have no rivers nor places of water in this country until you come to the foresaid gulf distant from the place of our landing 20 days' journey, except it be in wells, the water whereof is saltish, and yet distant the one from the other two days' journey and more. They eat their meat upon the ground, sitting with their legs double under them, and so also when they pray. Art or science they have none, but live most idly, sitting round in great companies in the fields, devising and talking most vainly.

The 26th day of November we departed from the town of Urgenj, and having travelled by the River Oxus 100 mile we passed over another great river called Ardock, where we paid a certain petty custom. This River Ardock is great, and very swift, falling out of the foresaid Oxus, and passing about 1,000 mile to the northward it then consumeth itself in the ground, and passing under the same about 500 mile issueth out again and falleth into the lake of Kithay, as I have before declared.

The 7th of December following we arrived at a castle called Kait, subject to a sultan called Saramet Sultan, who meant to have robbed all the Christians in the caravan, had it not been for fear of his brother the King of Urgenj, as we were informed by one of his councillors who willed us to make him a present, which he took and delivered. Besides, we paid at the said castle, for custom, of every camel one red hide of Russia, besides petty gifts to his officers.

Thus proceeding in our journey, the tenth day at night, being at rest and our watch set, there came unto us four horsemen, which we took as spies, from whom we took their weapons, and bound them, and having well examined them they confessed that they had seen the track of many horsemen, and no footing of camels, and gave us to understand that there were rovers and thieves abroad; for there travel few people that are true and peaceable in that country but in company of caravan, where there be many camels, and horse-footing new without camels were to be doubted. Whereupon we consulted and determined amongst ourselves, and sent a post to the said Sultan of Kait, who immediately came himself with 300 men and met these four suspected men which we sent unto him, and examined them so straitly and threatened them in such sort that they confessed there was a banished prince with 40 men 3 days' journey forward, who lay in wait to destroy us if he could, and that they themselves were of his company.

The Sultan therefore understanding that the thieves were not many, appointed us 80 men well armed with a captain to go with us and conduct us in our way. And the Sultan himself returned back again, taking the four thieves with him. These soldiers travelled with us two days, consuming much of our victuals. And the third day in the morning very early they set out before our caravan, and having ranged the wilderness for the space of four hours they met us, coming towards us as fast as their horse could run, and declared that they had found the track of horses not far from us, perceiving well that we should meet with enemies; and therefore willed us to appoint ourselves for them, and asked us what we would give them to conduct us further, or else they would return. To whom we offered as we thought good, but they refused our offer and would have more; and so we not agreeing they departed from us and went back to their sultan who, as we conjectured, was privy to the conspiracy. But, they being gone, certain Tartars of our company called holy men (because they had been at Mecca) caused the whole caravan to stay, and would make their prayers and divine how we should prosper in our journey and whether we should meet with any ill company or no. To which our whole caravan did agree. And they took certain sheep and killed them, and took the blade bones of the same, and first sod them and then burnt them, and took of the blood of the said sheep and mingled it with the powder of the said bones, and wrote certain characters with the said blood, using many other ceremonies and words; and by the same divined and found that we should meet with enemies and thieves, to our great trouble, but should overcome them. To which sorcery I and my company gave no credit, but we found it true; for within 3 hours after that the soldiers departed from us, which was the 15th day of December in the morning, we escried far off divers horsemen which made towards us, and we, perceiving them to be rovers, gathered ourselves together, being 40 of us well appointed and able to fight, and we made our prayers together every one after his law, professing to live and die one with another, and so prepared ourselves. When the thieves were nigh unto us we perceived them to be in number 37 men well armed and appointed with bows, arrows, and swords, and the captain a prince banished from his country. They willed us to yield ourselves or else to be slain, but we defied them, wherewith they shot at us all at once, and we at them very hotly, and so continued our fight from morning until two hours within night, divers men, horses, and camels being wounded and slain on both parts; and had it not been for 4 handguns which I and my company had and used we had been overcome and destroyed, for the thieves were better armed and were also better archers than we. But after we had slain divers of their men and horses with our guns, they durst not approach so nigh, which caused them to come to a truce with us until the next morning. Which we accepted, and encamped ourselves upon a hill, and made the fashion of a castle, walling it about with packs of wares, and laid our horses and camels within the same to save them from the shot of arrows. And the thieves also encamped within an arrow-shot of us, but they were betwixt us and the water, which was to our great discomfort, because neither we nor our camels had drunk in 2 days before.

Thus keeping good watch, when half the night was spent the prince of the thieves sent a messenger half way unto us, requiring to talk with our captain (in their tongue the *caravan basha*); who answered the messenger, "I will not depart from my company to go into the half way to talk with thee; but if that thy prince with all his company will swear by our law to keep the truce, then will I send a man to talk with thee, or else not". Which the prince understanding as well himself as his company, swore so loud that we might all hear. And then we sent one of our company (reputed a holy man) to talk with the same messenger. The message was pronounced aloud in this order: "Our Prince demandeth of the Caravan Basha, and of all you that be Busormans" (that is to say circumcised), "not desiring your bloods, that you deliver into his hands as many Caphars" (that is unbelievers, meaning us Christians) "as are among you, with their goods; and in so doing he will suffer you to depart with your goods in quietness, and on the contrary you shall be handled with no less cruelty than the Caphars if he overcome you, as he doubteth not". To the which our Caravan Basha answered that he had no Christians in his company, nor other strangers but two Turks which were of their law, and, although he had, he would rather die than deliver them, and that we were not afraid of his threatenings, and that should he know when day appeared. And so passing in talk, the thieves, contrary to their oath, carried our holy man away to their prince, crying with a loud voice in token of victory, "Ollo, ollo". Wherewith we were much discomforted, fearing that that holy man betray us; but he, being cruelly handled and much examined, would not to death confess anything which was to us prejudicial, neither touching us, nor yet what men they had slain and wounded of ours the day before. When the night was spent, in the morning we prepared ourselves to battle again; which the thieves perceiving required to fall to agreement, and asked much of us. And to be brief, the most part of our company being loth to go to battle again, and having little to lose, and safe-conduct to pass, we were compelled to agree, and to give the thieves 20 ninths (that is to say 20 times 9 several things) and a camel to carry away the same; which being received, the thieves departed into the wilderness to their old habitation and we went on our way forward. And that night we came to the River Oxus, where we refreshed ourselves, having been 3 days without water and drink, and tarried there all the next day, making merry with our slain horses and camels, and then departed from that place; and for fear of meeting with the said thieves again or suchlike we left the highway which went along the said river and passed through a wilderness of sand, and travelled 4 days in the same before we came to water; and then came to a well, the water being very brackish, and we then as before were in need of water and of other victuals, being forced to kill our horses and camels to eat.

In this wilderness also we had almost fallen into the hands of thieves. For one night, being at rest, there came certain scouts and carried away certain of our men which lay a little separated from the caravan, wherewith there was a great shout and cry, and we immediately loaded our camels and departed, being about midnight and very dark, and drove sore till we came to the River Oxus again, and then we feared nothing, being walled with the said river. And whether it was for that we had gotten the water, or for that the same thieves were far from us when the scouts discovered us, we know not, but we escaped that danger.

So upon the 23rd day of December we arrived at the city of Bokhara in the land of Bactria. This Bokhara is situated in the lowest part of all the land, walled about with a high wall of earth, with divers gates into the same. It is divided into 3 partitions, whereof two parts are the King's and the 3rd part is for merchants and markets, and every science hath their dwelling and market by themselves. The city is very great and the houses for the most part of earth, but there are also many houses, temples, and monuments of stone sumptuously builded, and gilt, and specially bath-stoves so artificially built that the like thereof is not in the world, the manner whereof is too long to rehearse. There is a little river running through the midst of the said city, but the water thereof is most unwholesome, for it breedeth sometimes in men that drink thereof, and especially in them that be not there born, a worm of an ell long, which lieth commonly in the leg betwixt the flesh and the skin and is plucked out about the ankle with great art and cunning, the surgeons being much practised therein; and if she break in plucking out, the party dieth, and every day she cometh out about an inch, which is rolled up, and so worketh till she be all out. And yet it is there forbidden to drink any other thing than water and mares' milk, and whosoever is found to break that law is whipped and beaten most cruelly through the open markets, and there are officers appointed for the same, who have authority to go into any man's house to search if he have either aquavitae, wine, or brage, and finding the same do break the vessels, spoil the drink, and punish the masters of the house most cruelly, yea, and many times if they perceive but by the breath of a man that he hath drunk without further examination he shall not escape their hands.

There is a Metropolitan in this Bokhara who causeth this law to be so straitly kept; and he is more obeyed than the King, and will depose the King and place another at his will and pleasure, as he did by this King that reigned at our being there, and his predecessor, by means of the said Metropolitan. For he betrayed him, and in the night slew him in his chamber, who was a prince that loved all Christians well.

This country of Bokhara was sometime subject to the Persians, and do now speak the Persian tongue, but yet now it is a kingdom of itself and hath most cruel wars continually with the said Persians about their religion, although they be all Mahometists. One occasion of their wars is for that the Persians will not cut the hair of their upper lips, as the Bokharians and all other Tartars do, which they account great sin and call them Caphars, that is unbelievers, as they do the Christians.

The King of Bokhara hath no great power or riches, his revenues are but small, and he is most maintained by the city; for he taketh the tenth penny of all things that are there sold as well by the craftsmen as by the merchants, to the great impoverishment of the people, whom he keepeth in great subjection; and when he lacketh money he sendeth his officers to the shops of the said merchants to take their wares to pay his debts, and will have credit of force, as the like he did to pay me certain money that he owed me for 19 pieces of kersey. Their money is silver and copper, for gold there is none current. They have but one piece of silver and that is worth 12 pence English, and the copper money are called *poles*; and 120 of them goeth the value of the said 12 pence and is more common payment than the silver, which the King causeth to rise and fall to his most advantage every other month and sometimes twice a month, not caring to oppress his people for that he looketh not to reign above 2 or 3 years before he be either slain or driven away, to the great destruction of the country and merchants.

The 26th day of the month I was commanded to come before the said King, to whom I presented the Emperor of Russia's letters, who entertained us most gently and caused us to eat in his presence; and divers times he sent for me and devised with me familiarly in his secret chamber, as well of the power of the Emperor and the Great Turk as also of our countries, laws, and religion, and caused us to shoot in handguns before him and did himself practise the use thereof. But after all this great entertainment, before my departure he showed himself a very Tartar: for he went to the wars owing me money, and saw me not paid before his departure. And although indeed he gave order for the same, yet was I very ill satisfied, and forced to rebate part and to take wares as payment for the rest contrary to my expectation. But of a beggar better payment I could not have, and glad I was so to be paid and despatched.

But yet I must needs praise and commend this barbarous King who, immediately after my arrival at Bokhara, having understood our trouble with the thieves, sent 100 men well armed, and gave them great charge not to return before they had either slain or taken the said thieves. Who according to their commission ranged the wilderness in such sort that they met with the said company of thieves, and slew part, and part fled, and four they took and brought unto the King, and two of them were sore wounded in our skirmish with our guns. And after the King had sent for me to come to see them, he caused them all 4 to be hanged at his palace gate, because they were gentlemen, to the example of others. And of such goods as were gotten again I had part restored to me; and this good justice I found at his hands.

There is yearly great resort of merchants to this city of Bokhara, which travel in great caravans from the countries thereabout adjoining, as India, Persia, Balkh, Russia, with divers others, and in times past from Cathay when there were passage; but these merchants are so beggarly and poor, and bring so little quantity of wares, lying two or 3 years to sell the same, that there is no hope of any good trade there to be had worthy the following.

The chief commodities that are brought thither out of these foresaid countries are these following. The Indians do bring fine whites, which the Tartars do all roll about their heads, and all other kinds of whites, which serve for apparel made of cotton-wool and crasko; but gold, silver, precious stones, and spices they bring none. I enquired and perceived that all such trade passeth to the ocean sea, and the veins where all such things are gotten are in the subjection of the Portugals. The Indians carry from Bokhara again wrought silks, red hides, slaves, and horses, with suchlike, but of kerseys and other cloth they make little account. I offered to barter with merchants of those countries, which came from the furthest parts of India, even from the country of Bengala and the River Ganges, to give them kerseys for their commodities, but they would not barter for such commodity as cloth.

The Persians do bring thither crasko, woollen cloth, linen cloth, divers kinds of wrought pied silks, argomacks, with suchlike, and do carry from thence red hides with other Russian wares, and slaves, which are of divers countries, but cloth they will buy none, for that they bring thither themselves, and is brought unto them (as I have enquired) from Aleppo in Syria and the parts of Turkey. The Russes do carry unto Bokhara red hides, sheepskins, woollen cloth of divers sorts, wooden vessels, bridles, saddles, with suchlike, and do carry away from thence divers kinds of wares made of cotton-wool, divers kinds of silks, crasko, with other things, but there is but small utterance. From the countries of Cathay are brought thither, in time of peace and when the way is open, musk, rhubarb, satin, damask, with divers other things. At my being in Bokhara there came caravans out of all these foresaid countries, except from Cathay; and the cause why there came none from thence was the great wars that had dured 3 years before my coming thither and yet dured betwixt 2 great countries and cities of Tartars, that are directly in the way betwixt the said Bokhara and the said Cathay, and certain barbarous field people, as well gentiles as Mahometists, bordering to the said cities. The cities are called Tashkent and Kashgar, and the people that war against Tashkent are called Kazaks of the law of Mahomet, and they which war with the said country of Kashgar are called Kings, gentiles and idolaters. These 2 barbarous nations are of great force, living in the fields without house or town, and have almost subdued the foresaid cities, and so stopped up the way that it is impossible for any caravan to pass unspoiled; so that 3 years before our being there no caravan had gone, or used trade betwixt the countries of Cathay and Bokhara; and when the way is clear, it is 9 months journey.

To speak of the said country of Cathay, and of such news as I have heard thereof, I have thought it best to reserve it to our meeting. I

having made my solace at Bokhara in the winter time, and having
learned by much inquisition the trade thereof as also of all the other
countries thereto adjoining, and the time of the year being come for all
caravans to depart, and also the King being gone to the wars and news
come that he was fled, and I was advertised by the Metropolitan
himself that I should depart because the town was like to be besieged: I
thought it good and meet to take my journey some way, and determined to have gone from thence into Persia, and to have seen the trade
of that country, although I had informed myself sufficiently thereof as
well at Astrakhan as at Bokhara and perceived well the trades not to be
much unlike the trades of Tartaria. But when I should have taken my
journey that way, it was let by divers occasions. The one was the great
wars that did newly begin betwixt the Sophy and the kings of Tartaria,
whereby the ways were destroyed; and there was a caravan destroyed
with rovers and thieves, which came out of India and Persia by safe
conduct, and about ten days' journey from Bokhara they were robbed
and a great part slain. Also the Metropolitan of Bokhara, who is
greater than the King, took the Emperor's letters of Russia from me,
without which I should have been taken slave in every place. Also all
such wares as I had received in barter for cloth, and as I took perforce
of the King, and other his nobles, in payment of money due unto me,
were not vendible in Persia. For which causes, and divers others, I was
constrained to come back again to Mare Caspium the same way I went,
so that the eighth of March 1559 we departed out of the said city of
Bokhara, being a caravan of 600 camels; and if we had not departed
when we did, I and my company had been in danger to have lost life and
goods. For ten days after our departure the King of Samarkand came
with an army and besieged the said city of Bokhara, the King being
absent and gone to the wars against another prince, his kinsman, as the
like chanceth in those countries once in two or three years. For it is
marvel if a king reign there above three or four years, to the great
destruction of the country and merchants.

The 25th of March we came to the foresaid town of Urgenj, and
escaped the danger of 400 rovers which lay in wait for us back again,
being the most of them of kindred to that company of thieves which we
met with going forth, as we perceived by four spies which were taken.
There were in my company, and committed to my charge, two
ambassadors, the one from the King of Bokhara, the other from the
King of Balkh, and were sent unto the Emperor of Russia. And after
having tarried at Urgenj, and the castle of Sellyzure, eight days for the
assembling and making ready of our caravan, the second of April we
departed from thence, having four more ambassadors in our company,
sent from the King of Urgenj and other sultans, his brethren, unto the
Emperor of Russia with answer of such letters as I brought them. And
the same ambassadors were also committed unto my charge by the said

kings and princes; to whom I promised most faithfully, and swore by our law, that they should be well used in Russland and suffered to depart from thence again in safety, according as the Emperor had written also in his letters; for they somewhat doubted, because there had none gone out of Tartaria into Russia of long time before.

The 23rd of April we arrived at the Mare Caspium again, where we found our bark which we came in, but neither anchor, cable, cock, nor sail. Nevertheless we brought hemp with us and spun a cable ourselves, with the rest of our tackling, and made us a sail of cloth of cotton-wool, and rigged our bark as well as we could, but boat or anchor we had none. In the mean time being, devising to make an anchor of wood of a cartwheel, there arrived a bark, which came from Astrakhan with Tartars and Russes, which had 2 anchors, with whom I agreed for the one. And thus being in a readiness, we set sail and departed, I and the two Johnsons being Master and mariners ourselves, having in our bark the said six ambassadors, and 25 Russes which had been slaves a long time in Tartaria nor ever had, before my coming, liberty, or means to get home, and these slaves served to row when need was. Thus sailing sometimes along the coast, and sometimes out of sight of land, the 13th day of May, having a contrary wind, we came to an anchor being three leagues from the shore; and there rose a sore storm which continued 44 hours, and our cable being of our own spinning broke, and lost our anchor, and being off a lee shore, and having no boat to help us, we hoisted our sail and bore roomer with the said shore, looking for present death. But as God provided for us we ran into a creek full of ooze, and so saved ourselves with our bark, and lived in great discomfort for a time. For although we should have escaped the danger of the sea, yet, if our bark had perished, we knew we should have been either destroyed or taken slaves by the people of that country, who live wildly in the field, like beasts, without house or habitation. Thus, when the storm was ceased, we went out of the creek again, and having set the land with our compass and taken certain marks of the same, during the time of the tempest, whilst we rode at anchor, we went directly to the place where we rode with our bark again, and found our anchor which we lost; whereat the Tartars much marvelled how we did it. While we were in the creek we made an anchor of wood of cartwheels which we had in our bark, which we threw away when we had found our iron anchor again. Within two days after there arose another great storm, at the north-east, and we lay a-try, being driven far into the sea, and had much ado to keep our bark from sinking, the billow was so great. But at the last, having fair weather, we took the sun, and knowing how the land lay from us we fell with the River Yaick according to our desire, whereof the Tartars were very glad, fearing that we should have been driven to the coast of Persia, whose people were unto them great enemies.

Note that during the time of our navigation we set up the red cross of St George in our flags for honour of the Christians, which I suppose was never seen in the Caspian Sea before. We passed in this voyage divers fortunes. Notwithstanding, the 28th of May we arrived in safety at Astrakhan, and there remained till the tenth of June following, as well to prepare us small boats to go up against the stream of Volga, with our goods, as also for the company of the ambassadors of Tartary, committed unto me to be brought to the presence of the Emperor of Russia.

The Caspian Sea (to say something of it) is in length about two hundred leagues and in breadth 150, without any issue to other seas; to the east part whereof joineth the great desert country of the Tartars, called Turkmen, to the west the countries of the Chircasses, the mountains of Caucasus, and the Mare Euxinum, which is from the said Caspian Sea a hundred leagues. To the north is the River Volga and the land of Nogai, and to the south part join the countries of Media and Persia. This sea is fresh water in many places, and in other places as salt as our great ocean. It hath many goodly rivers falling into it, and it voideth not itself except it be underground. The notable rivers that fall into it are, first, the great river of Volga, called in the Tartar tongue Edell, which springeth out of a lake in a marsh or plain ground not far from the city of Novgorod in Russia, and it is from the spring to the Sea above two thousand English miles. It hath divers other goodly rivers falling into it as, out of Siberia, Yaick and Yem; also out of the mountains of Caucasus the rivers of Cyrus and Arash, and divers others.

As touching the trade of Shemakha in Media, and Teveris, with other towns in Persia, I have enquired, and do well understand that it is even like to the trades of Tartaria: that is, little utterance and small profit. And I have been advertised that the chief trade of Persia is into Syria, and so transported into the Levant Sea. The few ships upon the Caspian Seas, the want of mart and port towns, the poverty of the people, and the ice, maketh that trade naught.

At Astrakhan there were merchants of Shemakha, with whom I offered to barter and to give them kerseys for their wares, but they would not, saying they had them as good cheap in their country as I offered them, which was six roubles for a kersey that I asked; and while I was at Bokhara there were brought thither out of Persia, cloth, and divers commodities of our countries, which were sold as good cheap as I might sell ours.

The tenth day of June we departed from Astrakhan towards the Moscow, having a hundred gunners in our company at the Emperor's charges for the safe conduct of the Tartar ambassadors and me. And the eight and twentieth day of July following we arrived at the city of Kazan, having been upon the way from Astrakhan thither six weeks and more without any refreshing of victuals; for in all that way there is no habitation.

The seventh of August following we departed from Kazan, and transported our goods by water as far as the city of Morom, and then by land; so that the second of September we arrived at the city of Moscow, and the fourth day I came before the Emperor's Majesty, kissed his hand, and presented him a white cow's tail of Cathay and a drum of Tartaria, which he well accepted. Also I brought before him all the ambassadors committed to my charge, with all the Russ slaves; and that day I dined in His Majesty's presence, and at dinner His Grace sent me meat by a Duke, and asked me divers questions touching the lands and countries where I had been. And thus I remained at the Moscow about your affairs until the 17th day of February that your wares were sent down, and then, having licence of the Emperor's Majesty to depart, the 21st day I came to your house at Vologda, and there remained until the breaking up of the year; and then, having seen all your goods laden into your boats, I departed with the same, and arrived withal in safety at Colmogro the 9th of May 1560. And here I cease for this time, entreating you to bear with this my large discourse, which by reason of the variety of matter I could make no shorter; and I beseech God to prosper all your attempts.

The second voyage into Persia made by Tho. Alcock, who was slain there, and by George Wrenn and Ric. Cheyney, servants to the Worshipful Company of Muscovy Merchants in anno 1563. Written by the said Richard Cheyney.

IT may please your worships to understand that in the year 1563 I was appointed by Master Anthony Jenkinson and Master Thomas Glover, your agent in Russia, to go for Persia in your worships' affairs, one Thomas Alcock having the charge of the voyage committed to him, and I, one of your worships' servants, being joined with him in your business, having with us, as they said, 1,500 roubles. And if it shall please you, I cannot tell certainly what sum of money we had then of the Emperor's: for I received none, nor disbursed any of it in wares for the voyage. Also, God I take to record, I could not tell what stock your worships had there, for the books were kept so privily that a man could never see them.

The 10th of May, anno 1563, we departed from a town called Yaroslavl, upon our voyage toward Persia. The 24th of July we arrived at Astrakhan; and the second of August we departed from Astrakhan, and the 4th of the same month we came to the Caspian Sea, and the

11th day of the said month we arrived at our port in Media; and the 21st of the said August we arrived at Shemakha, whereas the King Abdullah Khan lay in the field. We were well entertained of heathen people, for the third day after our arrival at Shemakha we were called before the King. We gave him a present, and he entertained us very well.

At our coming to the court we were commanded to come before the King, who sat in his tent upon the ground with his legs a-cross, and all his dukes round about his tent, the ground being covered with carpets. We were commanded to sit down, the King appointing every man his place to sit. And the King commanded the Emperor of Russland's merchants to rise up and to give us the upper hand. The 20th of October Thomas Alcock departed from Shemakha towards Kasvin, leaving me at Shemakha to recover such debts as the dukes of Shemakha owed for wares which they took of him at his going to Kasvin. In the time I lay there I could recover but little. And at Thomas Alcock's coming from Kasvin, who arrived at a town called Leuvacta, whereas the King Abdullah Khan lay a day and a half's journey from the town whereas I lay, I, hearing of his arriving there, departed from Shemakha, finding him there in safety with all such goods as he had with him. During his abode there for seven days he made suit to the King for such money as the dukes owed him; but the King was displeased for that the Emperor of Russland's merchant had slain a *bosorman* at his going to Kasvin. Thomas Alcock, seeing the King would show us no favour, and also hearing from Shemakha that the Russes sent their goods to the sea side for that they feared that the King of Persia should have knowledge of the death of the *bosorman*, willed me to depart to Shemakha with all such goods as he had brought with him from Kasvin, I leaving him at the court.

The third day after my arrival at Shemakha I had news that Thomas Alcock was slain coming on his way towards me. Then the King Abdullah Khan, understanding of his death, demanded whether he had ever a brother. Some said I was, some said I was not his brother. When this fell out, your worships had no other servant there but me among those heathen people. Who, having such a sum of goods lying under my hands, and seeing how the Russes sent their goods with as much haste as they might to the sea side, and having but four men to send our wares to the sea side, I used such diligence that within two days after Thomas Alcock was slain I sent, in company with the Russes' goods, all your worships' goods with a mariner, William August, and a Sweden, for that they might the safer arrive at the sea side being safely laid in. All which goods afterwards arrived in Russland in good condition, Master Glover having the receipt of all things which I sent then out of those parts into Russland.

Concerning myself, I remained, after I had sent the goods into

Russland, six weeks in Shemakha for the recovery of such debts as were owing, and at last with much trouble recovered to the sum of fifteen hundred roubles or thereabout, which Master Glover received of me at my coming to Moscow, and all such goods as I brought with me out of Kisilbash, as by a note of hand that he hath shall appear. Also, he having the receipt of all such goods as I sent into Russland by these two above named, he then had that voyage in venture of his own better than a hundred roubles, one Richard Johnson twenty roubles, one Thomas Pet fifty roubles, one Ivan Chermisin, a Tartar, seventy roubles. All these had their return; Master Glover allowed himself God knoweth how, I then being in Persia in your worships' affairs. And whereas he saith the Emperor had but for his part a double, as far as I can see, knowing what the wares cost in those parts, he had treble; if they gave him so much wares, all charges turned to your worships as well of the Emperor's as of their own returns. I have sown the seed, and other men have gathered the harvest. I have travelled both by land and by water full many a time with a sorrowful heart, as well for the safeguard of their goods as yours, how to frame all things to the best; and they have reaped the fruits of my travail. But ever my prayer was to God to deliver me out of those miseries which I suffered for your service among those heathen people. Therefore, knowing my duty which I have done as a true servant ought to do, I beseech your worships, although I have but small recompense for my service, yet let me have no wrong, and God will prosper you the better.

Also, to inform your worships of your Persian voyage what I judge: it is a voyage to be followed. The King of Gilan, whereas yet you have had no traffic, liveth all by merchandise; and it is near Kasvin and not past six weeks travel from Ormuz, whither all the spices be brought; and here (I mean at Gilan) a trade may be established. But your worships must send such men as are no riotous livers, nor drunkards. For if such men go, it will be to your dishonour and great hindrance, as appeared by experience the year 1565 when as Richard Johnson went to Persia, whose journey had been better stayed than set forward. For whereas before we had the name among those heathen people to be such merchants as they thought none like in all respects, his vicious living there hath made us all to be counted worse than the Russes.

Again, if such men travail in your affairs in such a voyage, you shall never know what gain is to be gotten. For how can such men employ themselves to seek the trade that are inclined to such vices? or how can God prosper them in your affairs? But when a trade is established by wise and discreet men, then will it be for your worships to traffic there, and not before. For a voyage or market made evil at the first is the occasion that your worships shall never understand what gain is to be gotten thereby hereafter.

The third voyage into Persia, begun in the year 1565 by Richard
Johnson, Alexander Kitchin, and Arthur Edwards: a letter of
Arthur Edwards to Master Thomas Nichols, Secretary to the
Worshipful Company trading into Russia and other the north
parts, concerning the preparation of their voyage into Persia.

MASTER Nichols, my bounden duty remembered, with
desire of God for the preservation of you and yours!
You shall understand that the second of March I was sent by
Master Thomas Glover, your agent, unto Yaroslavl, appointed to
receive such goods as should come from Vologda, as also such kind of
wares as should be bought and sent from Moscow by your agent and
Master Edward Clarke thought meet for your voyage of Persia. And,
further, I was to provide for biscuit, beer, and beef and other victuals,
and things otherwise needful according to advice. Thus I remained
here until the coming of your agent, which was the 12th of May, who
tarried here three days to see us set forwards on our voyage, and then
he departed towards Colmogro, having appointed, as chief for your
voyage of Persia, Richard Johnson.

For my part I am willing, as also have been and shall be content, to
submit myself under him whom the agent shall appoint, although he
were such a one as you should think in some respects unmeet. Thirty-
two packs of kerseys are all of that kind of cloth that we shall have with
us. The other 18 packs that should have gone were sold in Moscow.
What other goods are shipped for our voyage you shall understand by
your agent's letters. Whereas Edward Clarke, being an honest man,
was appointed agent for Persia, as one for those parts more fit than any
I do know here, God hath taken him unto His mercy, who departed this
present life the 16th of March last year. I wished of God for my part he
had lived; for my desire was in his company to have travelled into
Persia.

Your bark or crayer made here for the river of Volga and the
Caspian Sea is very little, of the burden of 30 tons at the most. It is
handsomely made after the English fashion; but I think it too little for
your goods and provision of victuals. If the Worshipful Company
would send hither a shipwright, being skilful to make one of the burden
of 60 tons or more, drawing but six foot water at the most when it is
laden, I think it should be profitable. For if your own goods would not
lade the same, here be merchants that would be glad and fain to give
great freight to lade their goods with us, whereby your charges would
be much lessened; and so it may happen the wages of your men hired
here may be saved, and your servants and goods in far greater assurance, for their boats here are dangerous to sail with and to pass the

Caspian Sea. There be carpenters here that will do well enough having one to instruct them.

Your wares bought here, and orders taken for those that go for your voyage of Persia, are yet unknown unto me, wherefore I cannot, as I would at this present, write to you thereof. Yet, as you do know, it was the Governor's mind I should be acquainted with greater affairs than these. Howbeit, I doubt not but I shall be informed of them that are appointed, and all things shall be bought when they shall see time and have more leisure. Thus in haste (as appeareth) I commit you and yours into the hands of Almighty God: who preserve you in perfect health with increase of worship.

From Yaroslavl, the 15th of May 1565, by yours to command here or elsewhere during life,

Arthur Edwards

Another letter of the said Master Arthur Edwards, written the 26th of April 1566 in Shemakhá in Media, to the right worshipful Sir Thomas Lodge, knight and alderman; and in his absence to Master Thomas Nichols, Secretary to the Right Worshipful Company trading into Russia, Persia, and other the north and east parts, touching the success of Richard Johnson in the third voyage into Persia.

Worshipful Sir, my bounden duty remembered, with hearty prayer unto God for the preservation of you and yours in perfect health, with increase of worship.

It may please you that my last letter I sent you was from Astrakhan the 26th of July 1565, from whence Richard Johnson, myself, and Alexander Kitchin departed as the 30th of the same. And by means of contrary winds it was the 23rd of August before we came to our desired port named Nizovaya. There, after we had gotten your goods on land with much labour and strength of men, as also windlasses devised and made, we hauled your bark over a bar of beach or pebble-stones into a small river, sending your ship's apparel with other things to a house hired in a village thereby. And as soon as we might get camels, being the fifth of September, we departed thence and came to this town of Shemakha the 11th of the same; and the 17th day following we presented unto Abdullah Khan, the King of this country, one timber of sables, one tun or nest of silver cups parcel-gilt, three morse's teeth, 4 *areshines* of scarlet, 3 pieces of kerseys, with 40 red foxes.

He received our presents with giving us thanks for our goodwills, demanding if Master Jenkinson were in good health, and whether he would return into these parts again. He willed us also himself to sit down before him the distance of a quoit's cast from his tent where he sat with divers of his council and nobility, sending us from his table such meat as was before him. And after certain talk had with us, he said, if he might perceive or know any manner of person to do us any wrong, he would punish them in example of others, whereby we should live in quietness and have no cause to complain; giving us a little house for the time until a better might be provided in such place as we should think most meet, never willing us to rise or depart until such time as we of ourselves thought it convenient. At the taking of our leave he willed us to put our whole minds and requests in writing, that he might further understand our desires. But while we were about to do so, God took this good king, our friend, out of this present life the 2nd of October past. The want of him hath been the cause that as yet we cannot receive certain debts. Howbeit, we doubt not but we shall recover all such sums of money as are owing us for this voyage. As for Thomas Alcock's debts, they are past hope of recovery, which had not been lost if the King had lived. We trust in the place of him God will send as friendly a king towards us; who by report, and as we be credibly informed, shall be his son named the Mirza, who since the death of his father, at our being with him, promised to show us more friendship than ever we found. God grant the same!

Great troubles have chanced in these parts. Of those which were of the old King's council, or bore any rule about him in these quarters, some are in prison, some are pinched by the purse, and other sent for unto the Shah. These troubles have partly been the let that wares were not sold as they might, to more profit. Your agent Richard Johnson bought four horses, minding to have sent to Kasvin Alexander Kitchin, whom God took to His mercy the 23rd of October last; and before him departed Richard Davis, one of your mariners, whose souls I trust the Lord hath received to His mercy. We are now destitute of others to supply their rooms. Four mariners were few enough to sail your bark, whereof at this present we have but one, whose name is William Smith, an honest young man and one that doeth good service here. For want and lack of mariners that should know their labours we all were like to be cast away in a storm. For all the broadside of our bark lay in the water, and we had much ado to recover it, but God of His mercy delivered us. Mariners here may do you good service all the winter otherways; and merchants here will be gladder to ship their goods in us, giving good freight. One merchant at this present is content to pay 20 roubles for twenty camels lading freight to Astrakhan. Such barks as must pass these seas may not draw above five foot of water, because that in many places are very shallow waters. We mind hereafter to make the Russian boats more strong, and they shall serve our turns very well.

And whereas some in times past took great pains, travail, and care, and could not have their desire in the getting of the Shah's letters of privilege, now, I trust (with God's help) they may be obtained; which being had will be beneficial to the Company, and great quietness to those that shall remain here, although heretofore things have chanced ill, as the like in other countries hath been. But I doubt not, this privilege once gotten and obtained, we shall live in quietness and rest, and shall shortly grow into a great trade for silks both raw and wrought, with all kind of spices and drugs, and other commodities here, as to Master Anthony Jenkinson is well known, who, I doubt not, hath long ago thoughly advertised the company thereof.

The truth of the slaughter of Thomas Alcock, your servant, is not certainly known. Some think it was by the means of a nobleman, with whom your said servant was earnest in demanding of your debts, upon whose words he was so offended that he procured his death. But other do think verily that, in riding from the court without company, false knaves lay in wait, thinking he had much about him, and so slew him. I doubt not, though this misfortune hath chanced, that things shall come well to pass, and that we shall be better beloved when we shall be more known.

Honest merchants are glad of our being here and seek to grow in acquaintance with us, being glad to further us in that they may, and have spoken in our favours to the chiefest of this country, one being a nobleman, with whom your agent and I are entered into friendship, who is at this time in great favour with the Shah. He hath here and in other places of these parts set a good stay in things since the King's death. He is well known to Master Jenkinson; his name is Khoja Mohammed. Also another duke, named Ahmeddinbeck, is our great friend; and his sister is the Shah's wife. These two have promised your agent, by their law, not only to procure to get the Shah's privilege but also that I shall have the debts paid me of those that went from hence to Kasvin, if we would send one with them. In consideration whereof, I was upon short warning (for want of a better) appointed by your agent, Master Richard Johnson, all excuses laid apart, presently to put myself in readiness and to depart in company with these noblemen; with charge, when God should send me to Kasvin, to use my discretion, with their advice, for the recovering of your debts and privilege. I shall have with me one interpreter and two bought servants, one of which partly understandeth this tongue, and may be put in trust whatsoever should become of me. I have received 6 tumens in money (200 shahis is a tumen, reckoning every shahi for six pence Russian). I have further received two timbers of sables, one to be sold, the other to be given to Thomas the Shah; and have order further to give as I shall see good to those that shall further my suit, and as occasion serveth. And forasmuch as I am commanded to go, I shall willingly do my best, putting my trust in God that he will send me well to speed in this journey.

For all kind of wares bought or sold you shall thoroughly be advertised by your agent Richard Johnson, whose reckonings or accounts at no hands I might see or be privy unto. Your kerseys were good and well assorted; they are and will be sold from 150 shahis to 160 the piece. Two hundred pieces were sold under, but that needed not: one hundred pieces at 146 and 147 the piece, but more would have been given if circumspection had been used. They were sold to those noblemen aforesaid, when as yet it was not known that I should have gone with them. They may stand us much in stead, as they have promised us their goodwills in that they may do. Here is at this time bought for England 11 packs of raw silk, 25 and 26 batmans being in every pack, the batman being 7 pound, which may be 6 pound and a half of English weight, being bought here from 66 to 70 shahis the batman. It is fine and good; little coarse at this time was to be had, and where coarse silk might be had, being at Grozin, we could not send thither, for that time was neglected from the first. When we shall have liegers here to remain in summer we may buy it at first hand of the country people that bring it to sell hither and to other places. I would to God the Company could find the means to have a vent to make sales for the one half that we may buy here. The Company may have for 30 or 40 thousand pounds yearly. And, as appeareth by your agent's words being at Varas, he and others saw there so great abundance that, by report of divers, you may bestow (if it were not for the Turks) for a two hundred thousand pounds, besides silk of all colours dyed in grain, bound up in pound weights (I think 15 of our ounces to their pound weight) and here sold for 23 shahis, at 6 pence the shahi may be 11 shillings 6 pence.

From Astrakhan in 7 or 8 days we may sail with our bark to a place named Gilan, the which place in time to come, I think, shall serve our purpose best to go unto. Alum is there good cheap, being brought from thence hither to Shemakha and sold here for two bists their batman, which may be 5 pence in our money; and so I have bought to be sent home 223 batmans for example. And at Gilan there is raw silk enough for the Company's stock. I believe, if any great store of wares be sent from you, that must be the place; and from thence a man may travel in 4 days to Kasvin and there make quick and better sales, at which place your commodities are to be sold. For there be the chief and best merchants, and divers other cities round about, to wit Teveris, Ardouil, and Kashan, being the heart of the country, where there is more civility and merchants are better used. Concerning this point I have enquired of divers merchants, both Russes and others, who have been in those parts, and found them all agreeing in one tale, and perceive the same to be true and that all kind of wares come from thence into these parts. And from Kasvin to Ormuz is about 30 days' travelling with camels. I have written the prices of wares in my letter to the Governor, both for spices and some drugs which I do know.

Also you shall understand here is plenty of yew for bow-staves. I caused three horse loads to be bought for us to know the truth, but they were cut out of season this month of April, the sap being in them. Three months I never left speaking to the countrymen to bring some. Your agent will send some home for example.

This day, being the 26th of April, I departed towards Kasvin. God give me a good hour and well to speed, with a merry heart in returning again, as my hope is I shall. I have written my mind to Master Glover, your agent, what Russian wares I think best to be bought for this country, and to send someone hither that hath the Russ tongue, for we have need. And the Company shall do well hereafter, in taking of servants to be sent hither, to see that they be such as have discretion, and be something broken in the world and seen in the trade of merchandise; and one, if they can get some such, as can speak the Portugal tongue may do them as good service as those that shall be here two years before him. For then we may buy a slave that can speak this language and the Portugal tongue also, which shall then interpret unto us in all your secret doings, not making the Russes privy. For they are sorry that we do trade into these parts, for we are better beloved than they are; because they are given to be drunkards they are much hated of these people. It is to be wished that none should serve your worships in these parts that be given to that kind of vice: and that your chief agent and factor should be able to rule and govern himself, that no dishonesty should be imputed to him and to us. By his evil usage he paid here 24 roubles, being in this country 4 tumens, for a boy, that he was charged to have conveyed away from a *tesik*, one of this country men, who willed him to swear that he knew not where the boy was become and he should not pay it. If he were honest he might do your worships good service because of his Russian tongue.

Your London reds are not to be sent hither, for they will not give above 18 shahis their *areshine*. Here be reds of more orient colour, being Venice dye. The people are given much to wear cloth: the common people specially do wear kerseys, and the merchants of more wealth wear broadcloth. You shall do well to send five or six broadcloths, some blacks, pukes, or other sad colours, that may be afforded at 20 shahis the *areshine* and not above. It is here reported that King Philip hath given the Turks a great overthrow at Malta, and taken 70 or 80 of his chief captains.

Thus wishing I had more time to write, I pray you to bear with this my scribbled letter, and after you have read it that Master Nichols may have a sight thereof.

By your servant to command,
Arthur Edwards

Commodities to be carried out of England into Persia, with their prices there:

1. Kerseys are sold there for 180 shahis, so that a kersey is sold there in Persia for four pound ten shillings, for every shahi is six pence

English, and every bist is twopence halfpenny English, and in Russ money three pence.

2. Tin is sold in Persia for 14 and 18 shahis the batman, the batman containing as I have mentioned before.
3. Brazil is at 10 and 12 shahis the batman.
4. Red cloth, fine, at 25 and 30 shahis the yard.
5. Copper at 20 and 25 shahis the batman.

Commodities to be brought out of Persia for England:

1. Raw silk at 60 shahis the batman.
2. Pepper at 32 shahis the batman.
3. Ginger at 18 to 20 shahis the batman.
4. Nutmegs at 30 shahis the batman.
5. Brimstone at 4 shahis the great batman (the great batman is 12 pounds English).
6. Alum at 2 bists and a half the batman and less.
7. Rice at half a bist the batman.
8. Galls at half a bist the batman.
9. Cloves at 40 shahis the batman.
10. Yew for bow-staves at [blank].

The fourth voyage into Persia, made by Master Arthur Edwards, agent, John Sparke, Lawrence Chapman, Christopher Faucet, and Richard Pingle, in the year 1568, declared in this letter written from Kasvin in Persia by the foresaid Lawrence Chapman to a worshipful merchant of the Company of Russia in London; anno domini 1569, April 28.

WORSHIPFUL Sir, my duty always remembered, and your prosperous health and good success in all your affairs wished, to the glory of God, and your own heart's desire, etc. May it please you to understand that your agent, Master Arthur Edwards, and we departed from Yaroslavl in July 1568 and the 14 of August arrived at our port, called Bilbil, with your ship the *Grace of God* and the goods in her in good safety, God be thanked for it, finding there neither the people so ready to aid us for bringing of her in and unlading of the goods, nor yet so obedient to the Shah's privilege, as the Worshipful Company have been informed, Our goods brought upon land, we were compelled to open and sell as they would set the price, or otherwise it would have been worse for us. Being so satisfied to their contentment, we were speedily aided with camels by the Prince Erasbecke Sultan's appointment, to carry our goods to Shemakha, to which place we attained the first of September, finding it so thoroughly furnished with all manner of commodities by occasion of our late coming, and by such as came before us, that no man would ask to buy any one piece of kersey of us; and lying then the space of one whole month before your agent Arthur Edwards would disperse us abroad with the goods, such as came out of Russia afterwards had brought their goods to that and other places and spoiled those sales we might have made, being sent abroad in time convenient, being no little hindrance to the worshipful as also great grief unto us to see. To conclude, through our daily calling on him he bent himself for Kasvin, taking with him the greatest sum of the goods and two of the worshipfuls' servants, to wit John Sparke and myself, to help and procure the better sale of the same; and leaving at Shemakha Christopher Faucet and Richard Pingle with three hundred and fifty pieces of kerseys in their hands, supposed to be sold there or in Arrash before he should be able to make his return from Kasvin, which, so far forth as I can understand, lie for the greatest part unsold. And being upon our way, at a certain town called Ardouil we chanced to barter nine pieces of kerseys with those merchants for fourscore and four batmans of cinnamon, selling the kerseys at one hundred and fifty shahis the piece.

And being at that present not far from Teveris, called the principal place in this country for uttering of cloth or kerseys, by much entreaty I persuaded your agent to send thither to prove what might be done; and receiving from him four and fifty pieces of kerseys, as also his commission for the sale of the same, I proceeded on that voyage myself, and one *tolmach* in company with me, finding in that place great store of broadcloth and kerseys brought thither, some part by the Turks who be resident there, some by the Armenians who fetch them at Aleppo, and some by the townsmen, who travel unto Venice and there buy them, so that no man there offered me one penny more than a hundred and forty shahis for a kersey. And having special commission and charge from your agent not to stay there above the space of seven days after my arrival there, but to repair to Kasvin with all speed, and furthermore having regard to keep up the price of the worshipfuls' commodities according to their desire, I found means to barter them away for spices, such as were there to be had, neither in goodness nor yet in price to my content. Nevertheless, considering the cold sales which were there as well for your kerseys, as also the hot news that Ormuz way was shut up by occasion that the Indians do war against them, which is true indeed; and again the desire that the worshipful hath to have such commodities bought, I thought it necessary to buy them, the prices and weight whereof appeareth at large by my account sent to the worshipful, and is I think, the whole sum of spices bought at this time.

It chanced me in that place to meet with the Governor's merchant of

Grozin, who was not a little desirous to bargain with me for a hundred pieces of kerseys for his master, called Levontie, and offering me so good bonds for the payment of the money, or silk to the merchant's contentment upon the delivery of them, as in any place with in all this country is to be had: and offering me besides, his own letter in the behalf of his master that no custom should be demanded for the same, and the obtaining also at his master's hand as large a privilege for the worshipful to travel into all parts of his dominion as the Shah hath given them. And hearing good report made of him by the Armenians also, and that he was a Christian, I was much more the willing to bargain with him, and sold him a hundred pieces for a hundred and threescore shahis a piece, to be paid to the merchant in Grozin, either in money or silk to his contentment, within three days after the delivery of the kerseys there, having a bond of him made by the Metropolitan's own hand for the performance of the same, which is as sure as any here is to be devised. And upon the same I sent my *tolmach* from me back to Shemakha with such goods as I bought at Teveris, and to the end he might cause the worshipfuls' servants there to see this bargain accomplished. At whose arrival there, as I do perceive, the Captain would not accomplish his bargain to take them, but saith he hath no need of them. Such is the constancy of all men in this country, with whomsoever you shall bargain. If the ware be bought, and they do mislike it afterwards, they will bring it again, and compel you to deliver the money for it again, regarding the Shah's letters, which manifesteth the contrary, as a straw in the wind. By means whereof the worshipful may know whether all be true that hath been written of this country people or not.

I am informed by all the brokers in Teveris, that the way once open to Ormuz, from whence cometh no such store of spices as the worshipful doth look for, that here will be put away in Teveris, some for money and other some for barter, to the number of three hundred or four hundred pieces of kerseys, being in colours and goodness to the examples here sent you; the rest of the kerseys to make them up a thousand, and broadcloths to the sum of a hundred, be as many as will be put away yearly in this country, so far as yet I can perceive.

To break the trade betwixt the Venetians and the whole company of the Armenians it is not possible, unless the worshipful will find some means to receive of them yearly to the number of 100 catters' or mules' lading, and deliver them for the same one third part money, the rest cloth and kerseys fitted in colours meet for this country: the examples, as abovesaid, are sent unto you.

At Amadia, six days' journey from Teveris, grow abundance of galls, which are brought up yearly by the Venetians, and be sold there for two bists the Teveris batman, which as your agent here saith maketh six pound English weight, but I doubt it will not so be proved. Nevertheless it is supposed much good will be done by buying them; which might at this present have partly been proved, if so be that some could do but half that which hath been written.

Touching drugs, I find many as well at Teveris as also in Kasvin, but the goodness nothing like to such as be brought into England out of other places, and the price is so high that small gain will be had in buying of them, Albeit, if I had been furnished with money, as I might have been if some would, I would have bought some, to the end the goodness of them might have been seen in England. At my coming to Kasvin I found no manner of sales of any commodity made, but all lying there whole, and news given out (as your agent saith) that the Shah would buy all such commodities as he had, and give him silk and spices for the same; but by report the Shah never took cloth into his treasury all the days of his life, and will not now begin. His whole trade is in raw silk, which he selleth always for money to the Armenians and Turks, and such other as use to buy it. Thus hoping of that which is not like to be had he hath driven off the time, not sending to any other places; by means whereof the worshipfuls' goods lie unsold to this day, to their great hindrance, which I for my part am not a little sorry to see.

Babylon is from hence fifteen days' journey, whereas by true report be great store of dates, and sold for a bist the batman, the commodity fit for England, and the place so near unto us might easily have been known if he, whose deeds and sayings differ much, had been willing to the same. Kashan also is but seven days' journey from hence, and a place by report where most store of spices be at all times to be had, over and above any place in this country. It could not be granted by him to be seen and proved at this time. If this be loss to the worshipful, refer it to the want of one which can do that which he speaketh in words.

To travel in this country is not only miserable and uncomfortable for lack of towns and villages to harbour in when night cometh, and to refresh men with wholesome victuals in time of need, but also such scarcity of water that sometimes in three days' journey together is not to be found any drop fit for man or beast to drink; besides the great danger we stand in for robbing by these infidels, who do account it remission of sins to wash their hands in the blood of one of us. Better it is therefore in my opinion to continue a beggar in England during life than to remain a rich merchant seven years in this country, as some shall well find at their coming hither.

By commandment of the agent also I went to Gilan, as well to see what harbour was there for your ship as also to understand what commodity is there best sold, and for what quantity. I found the way from hence so dangerous and troublesome that with my pen I am not able to note it unto you. No man travelleth from hence thither but such poor people as need constraineth to buy rice for their relief to live upon, and they lay not above twenty batmans upon a catter and it lieth no lower than the skirts of the saddle, and he escapeth very hardly that cometh there with the same.

The town of Lahijan, which was the chiefest place in all that land, have I seen, and Langro and Rosar also, which be now overrun by the Shah and his power, and be so spoiled and the people so robbed that not one of them is able to buy one kersey. The best commodity there to be bought is raw silk, and is sold in the summertime for 38 shahis the Lahijan batman, which is little above 40 pounds weight, and for ready money; also there is to be had what store of alum you will, and sold there for one bist the Teveris batman.

In these parts be many Turkey merchants resident, which give an outward show as though they were glad of our coming hither, but secretly they be our mortal enemies, searching by all means to hinder our sales because we should the sooner give over our trade thither, which in process of time I hope will grow to better perfection. They wish us to go to Hallape with the rest of our commodities unsold, where they say we shall have good entertainment in spite of the great number of Venetians which be there resident, and the custom but two in the hundred, and our kerseys to be sold presently, had we never so many, for twelve ducats, which maketh of this money 165 shahis. But by such as know the place, market, and custom, it is reported to us credibly to the contrary, and that such kerseys as ours be are not sold for above 8 ducats there, the custom thirty in the hundred and more, that no place in the world is so well furnished with good cloth and kerseys and of so brave colour as that place is, supposing it to be craftily purposed of them to bring us into trouble, which God defend us from.

The price of spices be these, at this present enhanced by reason the way is shut to Ormuz, which when God shall send open I purpose, God willing, to see, and at my return to advertise the worshipful what benefit is there to be had in all points so near as I can learn. Pepper, 25 shahis the Teveris batman; cloves, 50 shahis; long pepper, 25 shahis; maces, large, 50 shahis; ginger, 24 shahis; ready money all, or else look not upon them. And the best sort of raw silk is sold for 60 shahis the Teveris batman.

Thus for want of further matter to enlarge, I end for this time, beseeching God to preserve you in continual health.

By your obedient servant,
Lawrence Chapman

The discovery made by Master Arthur Pet and Master Charles Jackman of the north-east parts beyond the Island of Vaigats, with two barks, the one called the *George*, and the other the *William*, in the year 1580. Written by Hugh Smith.

U PON Monday, the 30th of May, we departed from Harwich in the afternoon, the wind being at south, and to the eastward. The ebb being spent we could not double the Pole, and therefore were constrained to put in again until the next day in the morning, being the last of May; which day we weighed our anchors about 3 o'clock in the morning, the wind being west-south-west. The same day we passed Orfordness at an east sun and Stamford at a west sun and Yarmouth at a west-north-west sun, and so to Winterton, where we did anchor all night. It was then calm, and the flood was come.

The next day, being the first of June, we set sail at 3 o'clock in the morning, and set our course north, the wind at the south-west, and at south-south-west.

The 10th day, about one of the clock in the afternoon, we put into Norway to a place where one of the headlands of the sound is called Bottel; the other headland is called Moile. There is also an island called Kinn. Here I did find the pole to be elevated 62 degrees. It doth flow there south, and it higheth 7 or 8 foot, not above.

The 11th day in the morning the wind came to the south, and to the south-east; the same day at six in the afternoon we set sail and bore along the coast. It was very foul weather with rain and fog.

The 22nd day, the wind being at west, we did haul the coast east-north-east, and east. The same day at 6 in the morning we did double the North Cape. About 3 in the afternoon we past Skitesbearness, and hauled along the coast east, and east-south-east, and all the same night we hauled south-east, and south-east by east.

The 23rd day about 3 in the morning we came to Wardhouse, the wind at the north-west. The cause of our coming in was to seek the *William*, whose company we lost the 6th day of this month, and to send letters into England. About one of the clock in the afternoon the *William* also came into the Wardhouse to us in good safety, and all her company in good health. The 24th the wind came to the east-north-east. This day the *William* was hauled aground, because she was somewhat leaky, and to mend her steerage. This night about 12 of the clock she did haul afloat again.

The 25th day the wind was at east-north-east. The 26th day the *Toby* of Harwich departed from Wardhouse for London, Thomas Greene being master, to whom we delivered our letters. The 27th day the wind was at south-south-east, and the 28th also. The 29th day, about 6 in the afternoon, the wind came to the west-north-west for the space of one hour, and presently to the east again, and so was variable all the same night. The 30th, about six in the morning, the wind came to east-south-east, and continued so all the same day.

The first of July, about 5 in the afternoon, the wind was at north-north-west; and about 7 of the clock we set sail from Wardhouse east and by south. The second day, about 5 in the morning, the wind was east, and east-south-east, and we did lie to the shorewards. And about 10 in the morning the wind came to south-south-east, and we laid it to the eastward: sometime we lay east by south, sometime east-south-east, and sometimes east by north. About 5 in the afternoon we bore with the *William*, who was willing to go with Kegor, because we thought her to be out of try and sailed very ill, where we might mend her steerage. Whereupon Master Pet, not willing to go into harbour, said to Master Jackman that if he thought himself not able to keep the sea he should do as he thought best, and that he in the meantime would bear with Willoughby's Land, for that it was a parcel of our direction, and would meet him at Verove Ostrove, or Vaigats; and so we set our course east-north-east, the wind being at south-east.

The 3rd day, the wind at south-east, we found the pole to be elevated 70 degrees 46 minutes. The same night at 12 of the clock we sounded, but had no ground in 120 fathoms, being fifty leagues from the one side by our reckoning east-north-east from Kegor. The 4th day all the morning was calm. This day we found the pole to be elevated 71 degrees 38 minutes. This day at 9 in the afternoon, the wind at north-east with a gentle gale, we hauled along south-east by east. The 5th day, the wind at north-west, we hauled east and east by south. This day we saw land, but we could not make it, the wind being northerly so that we could not come near it.

The 6th day about 2 in the afternoon, the wind at north-north-west, we hauled east-south-east with a fair and gentle gale. This day we met with ice. About 6 in the afternoon it became calm. We with sail and oars laid it to the north-east part, hoping that way to clear us of it, for that we we did see the head part of it as we thought. Which done, about 12 of the clock at night we got clear of it. We did think it to be ice of the Bay of Saint Nicholas, but it was not, as we found afterwards.

The seventh day we met with more ice, at the east part of the other ice. We hauled along a-weather the ice to find some end thereof by east-north-east. This day there appeared more land north from us, being perfect land; the ice was between us and it, so that we could not come nearer to it.

The same morning at six of the clock we put into the ice to find some way through it; we continued in it all the same day and all the night following, the wind by the north-north-west. We were constrained to go many points of our compass, but we went most an easterly course.

The eighth day, the wind at north-north-west, we continued our course, and at five in the morning we sounded, and had 90 fathoms red ooze. This day at four in the afternoon we sounded again and had 84 fathoms, ooze as before. At six in the afternoon we cleared ourselves of the ice and hauled along south-east by south. We sounded again at 10 o'clock at night and had 43 fathom sandy ooze.

The 9th day at 2 in the morning we sounded again, and had 45 fathoms; then there appeared a shadow of land to us east-north-east, and so we ran with it the space of 2 hours and then, perceiving that it was but fog, we hauled along south-east. This day at 2 in the afternoon we sounded and had fifty fathoms black ooze. Our latitude was 70 degrees 3 minutes. At ten o'clock at night we sounded again, and had fifty fathoms black ooze.

The tenth day, the wind being at north-north-west, we hauled east and by north, which course we set because at ten of the clock afore noon we did see land; and then we sounded having 35 fathoms black ooze. All this day there was a great fog, so that we durst not bear with the land to make it and so we kept an outwardly course. This day at 6 in the afternoon we espied land, wherewith we hauled, and then it grew calm. We sounded, and had 120 fathoms black ooze; and then we sent our boat aland to sound and prove the land. The same night we came with our ship within an island, where we rode all the same night. The same night we went into a bay to ride near the land for wood and water.

The 11th day the wind came to the east-south-east. This day about a league from us to the eastwards we saw a very fair sound or river that passed very far into the country, with 2 or 3 branches with an island in the midst.

The 12th of July the wind was east-south-east. This day about 11 o'clock in the morning there came a great white bear down to the waterside, and took the water of his own accord. We chased him with our boat, but for all that we could do he got to land and escaped from us, where we named the bay Bear Bay. This day at 7 in the afternoon we set sail, for we had good hope that the wind would come westerly, and with sail and oars we got the sea. All the night it was calm with fog.

The 13th day in the morning the wind was very variable with fog, and as it cleared up we met with great store of ice, which at the first showed like land. This ice did us much trouble, and the more because of the fog, which continued until the 14th day, 12 of the clock.

The 14th day in the morning we were so embayed with ice that we were constrained to come out as we went in, which was by great good fortune, or rather by the goodness of God, otherwise it had been impossible; and at 12 of the clock we were clear of it, the wind being at south and south by west. The same day we found the pole to be elevated 70 degrees 26 minutes. We lay along the coast north-west, thinking it to be an island but, finding no end in rowing so long, we supposed it to be the mainland of Nova Zembla. About 2 in the afternoon we laid it to the southward to double the ice, which we could not do upon that board, so that we cast about again and lay west along under the ice. About seven in the afternoon we got about the greatest part thereof. About 11 o'clock at night we brought the ice south-east of us, and thus we were rid of this trouble at this time.

The 15th day, about 3 in the morning, the wind was at south-south-west. We cast about and lay to the eastwards. The wind did wester, so that we lay south-south-west with a flown sheet, and so we ran all the same day. About 8 in the afternoon we sounded, and had 23 fathoms small grey sand. This night at twelve of the clock we sounded again, and had 29 fathoms, sand as afore.

The 16th day unto 3 in the morning we hauled along east-south-east, where we found 18 fathoms red sand; then we hauled along north-east. In these soundings we had many overfalls. This day at 10 of the clock we met with more ice, which was very great, so that we could not tell which way to get clear of it. Then the wind came to the south-south-east, so that we lay to the northwards. We thought that way to clear ourselves of it, but that way we had more ice. About 6 in the afternoon the wind came to the east. Then we lay to the southwards, that we had 30 fathoms black ooze. This day we found the pole to be elevated 69 degrees 40 minutes, and this night at 12 o'clock we had 41 fathoms red sand.

The 17th day, at 3 in the morning, we had 12 fathoms. At 9 we had 8 and 7. All this day we ran south and south by west, at the depth aforesaid, red sand, being but shallow water. At eight in the afternoon the wind, with a shower and thunder, came to the south-west, and then we ran east-north-east. At 12 at night it came to the south and by east, and all this was in the Bay of Pechora.

The 18th day at 7 in the morning we bore with the headland of the bay, where we found two islands. There are also overfalls of water or tides. We went between the main and the island next to the head, where we had about 2 fathoms and a half. We found the pole elevated 69 degrees 13 minutes. This day we had sight of Vaigats. The land of the main of Pechora did trend south-east; we hauled east-south-east, and had 10 fathoms ooze all the same day until 4 in the afternoon. Then, being calm, we anchored in 10 fathoms all the same night.

The 19th day at two in the morning we set sail, and ran south and south-south-west all the same day at 8, 7, and 6 fathoms. This was off the south part of Vaigats; this part of the land lieth north and south. This day at 4 in the afternoon we found shallow water, sometime 4 fathoms, sometime 3 and 2 and a half, and one fathom and a half. There we anchored, and sent our boat away to sound, and all to leeward we had 4 foot and 3 foot and 2 foot; there was not water for the boat between Vaigats and the other side. Finding no more water, there was no other way but to go back as we came in, having the wind north-west; so at twelve at night we set sail. The 20th day we plied to the northwards, and got deep water again, 6 and 7 fathoms. The 21st day, the wind by the north-west, we hauled along the coast north and north-west. We had 8 and 9 and 10 fathoms. The 22nd day the wind came to the south-west. We bore along the coast of Vaigats as we found it to lie, north and by west, and north-north-west, and north. The wind blew very much, with great fog. We, lacking water and wood, bore within an island where we found great store of wood and water. There were three or four goodly sounds. Under two points there was a cross set up, and a man buried at the foot of it. Upon the said cross Master Pet did grave his name with the date of Our Lord, and likewise upon a stone at the foot of the cross; and so did I also, to the end that if the *William* did chance to come thither they might have knowledge that we had been there. At eight in the afternoon the wind came to the north-north-west; we set sail and turned out of the bay. The same night the wind came to the west, so that we lay north along the land.

The 23rd day, at five in the morning, the wind came to the south-west. A-seaboard we saw a great number of fair islands, to the number of six. A-seaboard of these islands there are many great overfalls, as great streams or tides. We hauled north-east and east-north-east as the land did trend. At eight afore noon the wind came to the south-east with very much wind, rain, and fog, and very great store of ice a-seaboard; so we lay to the south-west to attain to one of the islands to harbour us if the weather did so extremely continue, and to take in our boat, thinking it meet so to do and not to tow her in such weather. About twelve of the clock it became very calm upon the sudden, and came up to the west-north-west and north-west by west, and then we took in our boat; and this done, there came down so much wind as we were not able to steer afore it. With course and bonnets of each we hauled south with the land, for so the land did trend. This day all the afternoon we sailed under a great land of ice; we sailed between the land and it, being not able to cross it. About twelve at night we found the ice to stretch into the land, that we could not get clear to the eastward, so we laid it to the shore; and there we found it clear hard aboard the shore, and we found also a very fair island which makes a very good harbour, and within are 12 fathoms.

This island is to the eastwards of Vaigats 4 or 5 leagues. This land of the main doth trend south-east, and south-east by east. It is a very fair coast and even and plain, and not full of mountains nor rocks. You have but shallow water of 6 or 7 fathoms about a league from the shore. All this morning we hauled east-south-east. This day we found the pole to be elevated 69 degrees 14 minutes. About 12 o'clock we were constrained to put into the ice to seek some way to get to the northwards of it, hoping to have some clear passage that way, but there was nothing but whole ice.

About nine in the afternoon we had sight of the *William*, and when we saw her there was a great land of ice between her and us so that we could not come one to the other; but as we came near to her we sounded our trumpet and shot off two muskets, and she put out her flag upon her fore topmast in token that she did see us. All this time we did shorten our sails, and went with our foresail and main topsail, seeking the best way through the broken ice; she making a way the best that she could to follow us, we put out our flag to answer her again with the like. Thus we continued all the afternoon till about 12 o'clock at night, and then we moored our ship to a piece of ice to tarry for the *William*.

The 25th, about five in the morning, the *William* came to us, being both glad of our meeting. The *William* had her stern-post broken, that the rudder did hang clean besides the stern so that she could in no wise port her helm. With all hands she did lighten her stern and trim her head, and when we had brought her forward all that we could we brought a cable under her stern and with our capstan did wind up her stern, and so we made it as well as the place would give us leave, and in the end we brought her to steer again. We acknowledge this our meeting to be a great benefit of God for our mutual comfort, and so gave His majesty thanks for it. All the night after we took our rest, being made fast upon a piece of ice; the wind was at west-north-west, but we were so enclosed with ice that we could not tell which way to pass. Winds we have had at will, but ice and fog too much against our wills if it had pleased the Lord God otherwise.

The 26th day the wind was at west-north-west. We set sail to the northwards, to see if we could find any way clear to pass to the eastward; but the further we went that way the more and thicker was the ice, so that we could go no further. So about four in the afternoon we were constrained to moor upon another piece of ice. I think we sailed in all a league this day. Here we had 15 fathoms ooze, and this ooze is all the channel over. All the same day after four of the clock and all the night we tarried there, being without all good hope, or rather in despair. This day Master Jackman did see land east-north-east from us as he did think; whether it were land or no I cannot tell well, but it was very like land; but the fogs have many times deceived us.

The 27th day the wind was at north-west. This day at nine in the morning we set sail to seek the shore. Further into the ice we could not go, and at seven in the afternoon we moored to a piece of ice, and the *William* with us; here we had 14 fathoms ooze. At three in the afternoon we warped from one ice to another. At nine in the afternoon we moored again to a piece of ice until the next day. All this night it did snow, with much wind, being at west-north-west, and at north-west and by west.

The 28th day the wind came to the south-west, and south-south-west. This day was a very fair day. At one in the afternoon Master Pet and Master Jackman did confer together what was best to be done, considering that the winds were good for us, and we not able to pass for ice. They did agree to seek to the land again, and so to Vaigats, and there to confer further. At 3 in the afternoon we did warp from one piece of ice to another to get from them if it were possible. Here were pieces of ice so great that we could not see beyond them out of the top. Thus we warped until 9 in the afternoon, and then we moored both our ships to a great and high piece of ice until the next morning.

The nine and twentieth day the wind came to the south-west. We set sail at five in the morning to ply into the shore if it were possible. We made many turns among the ice to small purpose, for with the wind doth the current run. This day by misfortune a piece of ice struck off our gripe afore at two after noon, yet for all this we turned to do our best. The *William*, being encumbered with ice and perceiving that she did little good, took in all her sails and made herself fast to a piece of ice, and about four in the afternoon she set sail to follow us. We were afraid that she had taken some hurt, but she was well. At seven afore noon we took in all our sails to tarry for the *William*, and made our ship fast to a piece of ice. The *William* before she came to us took in all her sails and moored to another piece of ice, and thus we continued until the next morning.

The 30th day, the wind at south-east and by south, and at 9 in the morning we set sail, and sooner would have done if the *William* had been by us; but we did tarry for her to know whether all was well with her. But as soon as we made sail she did the like. All this day we did our best to seek our way as the ice would give us leave; sometime we lay south, sometime west, and sometime east, and thus we continued until eight at night; and then being calm, we made our ship fast to a piece of ice and went to supper. In the meantime the wind with a fair gentle gale came up to the east, and east by south, but there came down a shower of rain with it which continued the space of one hour. Which being done it became calm again, so that we could do no good all that night, but took our rest until the next day.

The 31st, the wind being at south-west, we set sail to turn to windward at three o'clock in the morning. In this turning we did little good, for the current would not give us leave. For as the wind is, so is the current. We did our best until ten of the clock and then, perceiving that we did no good, and being enclosed with ice, we made our ships fast to a piece of ice. All this day the *William* lay still, and did as much good as we that did labour all the forenoon. Thus we took our rest all the same day. In the afternoon we set sail, the wind being at south and by east; we lay to the westwards, as south-west and south-west and by south, and sometime to the westward, as we might. Thus we continued until 9 at night, and then we could go no further for ice. So we with the *William* were constrained to make our ship fast to a piece of ice all the same night. This day we found the pole elevated 69 degrees 20 minutes, and here we had 17 fathoms ooze.

The first day of August was very calm in the morning, the wind being at west-north-west. About twelve the wind came to the west, and continued so all the same night with great fog. The second day the wind was at south-west all the day with rain and fog. All this day we were enclosed with ice, so that we were forced to lie still. Here we had one and twenty fathoms ooze. At six in the afternoon the wind was at west with very much foul weather, and so continued all the same night. The third day the wind was at west, and west by north, and west-north-west. This day we lay still enclosed with ice, the weather being dark with fog. Thus abiding the Lord's leisure we continued with patience; and sounding we found 21 fathoms. The fourth day we lay still enclosed with ice, the wind being at west-north-west. This ice did every day increase upon us, yet, putting our trust in God, we hoped to be delivered out of it in good time.

The fifth day all the morning it rained, with very much wind, being at south-south-east. About 3 in the afternoon we set sail, and presently it became calm for the space of one hour; then the wind came to the north-north-east, and here we had 33 fathoms. Thus we made our way among the ice south-west, and south-south-west, and west, as we might find our way for the space of 3 hours. Then we met with a whole land of ice, so that we could go no further. Here we moored our ship to tarry for a further opening. Here we found 45 fathoms ooze; and all the night was very dark with fog.

The sixth day, having no opening of the ice, we lay still, the wind being at west, and west by south. Here we had sixty three fathoms ooze. All the same night the wind was at the west-north-west. The 7th day the wind was at west and west and by north all day. And all this day we lay still, being enclosed with ice that we could not stir, labouring only to defend the ice as it came upon us. Here we had 68 fathoms ooze. The 8th day was very fair and calm but foggy. This day towards night there was little wind by the south-south-west. Then the ice began a little to open, and here we had 70 fathoms ooze. All the night was foggy.

The 9th day the wind was at north-west and by west. All the afternoon we lay still because of the ice which did still enclose us. This day we found the pole elevated 70 degrees 4 minutes. We had 63 fathoms ooze. This night was a very fair night, but it froze; in the morning we had much ado to go through the same, and we were in doubt that, if it should have frozen so much the night following, we should hardly have passed out of it. This night there was one star that appeared to us.

The tenth day the wind was at east-north-east with a very small gale. We with sail and oars made way through the ice. About five in the morning we set sail: sometime we lay south-west, and sometime south, and sometime west, as we might best find the way. About three in the afternoon the gale began to fresh; about six in the afternoon the wind was at north-east with fog. Here we had eighty-eight fathoms. We bore sail all the same night, and it snowed very much.

The eleventh day we were much troubled with ice, and by great force we made our way through it, which we thought a thing impossible; but extremity doth cause men to do much, and in the weakness of man God's strength most appeareth. This day we had 95 fathoms. At three in the afternoon the wind came to the south-west; we were forced to make our ship fast to a piece of ice, for we were enclosed with it, and tarried the Lord's leisure. This night we had 97 fathoms. The 12th day the wind was at the south-east, not very much but in a manner calm. At 11 of the clock the wind came to the west-south-west. All the day was very dark with snow and fog. At 6 in the afternoon we set sail, the wind being at the north-north-east. All this night we bore away south-west and south-south-west, as well and as near as the ice would give us leave. All this night we found the ice somewhat favourable to us, more than it was before, whereupon we stood in good hope to get out of it.

The 13th day, at 7 in the morning, the wind was at the north-east, and north-east and by east. All this day we were much troubled with the ice, for with a blow against a piece of ice we broke the stock of our anchor, and many other great blows we had against the ice, that it was marvellous that the ship was able to abide them. The side of our boat was broken with our ship which did recoil back, the boat being betwixt a great piece of ice and the ship, and it perished the head of our rudder. This day was a very hard day with us. At night we found much broken ice, and all this night it blew very much wind, so that we lay in drift with the ice, and our drift was south, for the wind was at north all this night; and we had great store of snow. The 14th day in the morning we made our ship fast to a piece of ice and let her drive with it. In the meantime we mended our boat and our steerage. All this day the wind continued northerly, and here we had threescore and two fathoms. Thus we lay adrift all the same night.

The 15th day we set sail at 6 in the morning, the wind being at north-east. At 9 afore noon we entered into a clear sea without ice, whereof we were most glad and not without great cause, and gave God the praise. We had 19 fathoms water, and ran in south-west all the morning until we came to 14 fathoms, and thence we hauled west till we came to 10 fathoms, and then we went north-west, for so the land doth trend. At 12 of the clock we had sight of the land, which we might have had sooner, but it was dark and foggy all the same day; for when we had sight of the land we were not passing three leagues from it. This day we had the pole elevated 69 degrees 49 minutes. All day we ran along the coast in ten and nine fathoms, peppered sand. It is a very goodly coast and a bold, and fair soundings off it without sands or rocks.

The 16th day the wind was at east. This day we were troubled again with ice, but we made great shift with it: for we got between the shore and it. This day at twelve of the clock we were thwart of the south-east part of Vaigats, all along which part there was great store of ice, so that we stood in doubt of passage; yet by much ado we got betwixt the shore and it. About 6 in the afternoon was found a great white bear upon a piece of ice. All this day in the afternoon it was dark with fog. And all the night we hauled north and north by west, and sometime north and by east, for so doth the land trend.

The 17th day in the morning we hauled west, for so doth the land lie. The wind was at south-east, and it was very dark with fog; and in running along the shore we fell aground but, God be praised, without hurt, for we came presently off again. The *William* came to an anchor to stay for us, and sent some of their men to help us, but before they came we were under sail; and as we came to the *William* we did stow our boats, and made sail. We went within some of the islands, and hauled west-south-west.

About two of the clock in the afternoon we set our course south-west and by south; so we ran south-west until twelve at night the wind came to the north-north-east, and then we hauled west.

The 18th day at 6 in the morning we had 16 fathoms red sand; at 6 in the morning 13 fathoms. At 10, 14 fathoms, and we hauled west-north-west. At 12 o'clock the wind came to the east, and east by south; we hauled west and by north all the same day and night. At 6 in the afternoon we had 17 fathoms red sand. The 19th day the wind was at east-north-east. At 6 in the morning we had 19 fathoms red sand. At 12 of the clock the wind blew north and north by east, we had 17 fathoms, at 3 in the afternoon 15. The 20th day the wind was at north-east and north-north-east. At 7 in the morning we had 30 fathoms black ooze. At twelve of the clock we were upon the sudden in shoal water, among great sands, and could find no way out. By sounding and seeking about we came aground, and so did the *William*, but we had no hurt, for the wind was off the shore and the same night it was calm. All night we did our best, but we could not have her afloat. These shoals do lie off Kolguyev; it is very flat a great way off, and it doth not high above 2 or 3 foot water. It floweth north-east and south-west.

The 21st day the wind was at south-west, and being very fair weather we did lighten our ships as much as was possible for us to do by reason of the place. The same high water, by the help of God, we got both afloat, and the wind being at the south-west did help us, for it caused it to flow the more water. This day we found the pole to be elevated 68 degrees 40 minutes. In the afternoon we both set sail to seek way to get out of these sands, our boat ahead sounding, having 6, 7, and 8 fathoms all within the sand which was without us. We bore to the southward, and the *William* bore more to the eastwards, and night being at hand the wind came to the south-east, whereupon we laid it to the southwards, lying south-west and south and by west, and ran to 19 and 12 and 14 fathoms, and presently we had but six fathoms, which was off the sands' head which we were aground upon the day before. Then we cast about to the eastwards for deep water, which we presently had, as 10, 15, and 20, and so to 23 fathoms.

The 22nd day at 8 in the morning we cast about to the southward, and this day in the morning we saw the *William* under our lee as far as we could see her; and with a great fog we lost the sight of her, and since we have not seen her. Thus we ran till we came to thirty fathoms black ooze, which we had at twelve of the clock, and at three in the afternoon we had twenty and three fathoms; and then we ran west-north-west, and west by north, all the same night following.

The 23rd day we had at 6 in the morning 27 fathoms, at 8 o'clock 28 fathoms. At 9, the wind being at east-south-east, we hauled west-north-west. This day we had sight of the land of Hugriside. At twelve of the clock we had thirty two fathoms sand. This day we ran west and by north, and came to five fathoms off the Bay of Morzhovets. Then we laid it to the northwards, so that we lay north-north-east off. The wind after came to the north and north by east, and we lay east and east by north; then we laid it to the westward again. And thus we lay till we came to forty fathoms, and then we went north-west till we came to fourteen fathoms and so to ten fathoms. Then we cast about to the eastwards and lay east and east by north all the same night.

The 24th day at 8 in the morning we had 32 fathoms. We ran north-west till we came to 11 fathoms, then we lay to the northwards till 12 at night, and then we came to forty fathoms; then, the wind at north-east, we lay to the westwards, and hauled north-west along. The 25th at 4 in the morning we had 17 fathoms; we ran north-west, the wind at north-north-east very much. The 26th day we ran with the same wind, and found the pole to be elevated 70 degrees 40 minutes. The 27th at 7 in the morning we saw land, which we made to be Kegor; then we hauled north-west and north by west to double the North Cape. The 28th day at 3 in the morning we ran north-west, and so all day. At night the wind came to the south-west and we ran north-west all that night.

The 29th day we put into a sound called Tana, and the town is called Hungon. We came to anchor at 5 in the afternoon, at 25 fathoms very fair sand. This sound is very large and good; and the same night we got water aboard.

The 30th day in the morning, the wind at north-east, and but little, we set sail, and with our boat on head we got the sea about 12 of the clock. The wind with a fair gale came to the east-south-east, and all this day and night we ran west-north-west. The 31st day at 12 of the clock we doubled the North Cape; the wind being at east-south-east we hauled west all the same day, and at night we ran west-south-west. The 1st day of September the wind was at north-east with very much fog. All this day we ran west-south-west. At 2 in the afternoon the wind came north.

The second day at 3 in the morning we doubled Fowlness, and the wind was this day variable at all parts of the compass. In the afternoon we made but little way. At 6 o'clock the wind came to the south-west, and we went north-west. At 9 in the night there came down so much wind by the west-south-west that we were fain to lay it a-hull. We hauled it to northwards for the space of 2 hours, and then we laid her head to the southwards; and at the break of day we saw land, which is very high, and is called by the men of the country Fowlness. It is within full of small islands, and without full of rocks very far out, and within the rocks you have fair sand at 20 fathoms.

The 3rd day in the morning we bore with the sound aforesaid. Within it is but shoal-water, 4, 5, and 3 fathoms, sandy ground. The land is very high, and the church that is seen is called Helike Kirke. It doth high here not above 8 or 9 foot.

The 12th day at 3 in the afternoon we put into a sound by Lofoot, where it doth flow south-west and by south, and doth high 7 or 8 foot water.

The 13th day much wind at west. We had a ledge of rocks in the wind of us, but the road was reasonable good for all southerly and westerly winds. We had the mainland in the wind of us. This day was stormy with rain.

The 23rd day at four of the clock in the afternoon we put into Norway, into a sound called Romesal, where it floweth south-south-east, and doth high 8 foot water. This place is full of low islands, and many good sounds without the high mountain land. Here is great store of wood growing, as fir, birch, oak, and hazel. All this night the wind was at the south, very much wind, with rain and fog. The 28th day in the morning, the wind being at east-north-east, we set sail at 8 of the clock and hauled out of the bay west-south-west, and south-west, having a goodly gale until one of the clock, and then the wind came to south-east and to the south with rain and fog and very much wind. At six of the clock we came into a very good road where we did ride all the same night in good safety. The 29th day we put into a good sound, the wind by the south-west. At three in the afternoon there came down very much wind by the south, and all night with vehement blasts and rain. The 30th day all day the wind was at west-south-west. And in this sound the pole is elevated 63 degrees 10 minutes.

The first day of October the wind was at south with very much wind and vehement blasts. The 7th day we set sail; for from the first of this month until this 7th day we had very foul weather, but specially the fourth day when the wind was so great that our cables broke with the very storm, and I do not think that it is possible that any more wind than that was should blow. For after the breaking of our cable we did drive a league before our anchors would take any hold; but, God be thanked, the storm began to slack, otherwise we had been in ill case.

The 7th day at night we came to an anchor until the next day, which was the 8th day of the month, whenas the wind grew great again, with rain. Whereupon we set sail and returned into the sound again. And at our first coming to an anchor, presently there blew so much wind that, although our best anchor was out, yet the extremity of the storm drove us upon a ledge of rocks and did bruise our ship in such sort that we were constrained to lighten her to save her; and by this means (by the help of God) we got off our ship and stopped our leaks and moored her in good safety, abiding for a wind. We rode from this day, by reason of contrary winds with fog and rain, until the 24th day, which day in the morning the wind came to the north-east, and at 8 of the clock we set sail. This sound is called Moor Sound, where it higheth about 5 foot water and floweth south-south-east. The next day, being the 25th day, we put into a sound which is called Ultar Sound, where was a ship of the King of Denmark put into another sound there by, being 2 leagues to the southwards of us, that came out of Iceland. The wind was contrary for us at south-south-west.

The 12th day of November we set sail, the wind being at the east-south-east, and passed through the sound where the King's ship did lie, which sound is called Slour Sound. But as we did open the sound we found the wind at the south-west so that we could do no good; so that we moored our ship between 2 islands until the 18th day, and then the weather being fair and calm we set sail and went to sea, hoping to find a fair wind. But in the sea we found the wind at the south-west and south-south-west, so that we were constrained to return into the same sound. The next day, being the 19th, the King's ship came out also because she saw us put to sea, and came as far out as we, and moored where we did moor afore. And at our return back again we moored our ship in an outer sound called Skorpa Sound, because the King's ship was without victuals, and we did not greatly desire her company, although they desired ours. In this sound the pole is elevated 62 degrees 47 minutes. Thus we lay still for a wind until the 1st of December, which day we set sail at 6 o'clock in the morning, and at 4 in the afternoon we laid it to the inwards.

The 9th day we had sight of the coast of Scotland, which was Buchan Ness. The 10th day we were open off the Firth. The 11th day at 4 in the morning we were thwart of Berwick; at 6 we were thwart of Bamburgh; the same day at 10 at night we were shot as far as Hollyfoot. Then the wind came to the south and south-east, so that we lay still until the next day in the morning, and then we were constrained to put with Tynemouth. The same day at night we hauled aground to stop a leak, which we found to be in the scarf afore. The wind continued by the south-east and south-south-east until the 20th day, and then we set sail about 12 at night, bearing along the coast.

The 22nd day by reason of a south-east wind we thought we should have been put into Humber, but the wind came to the west, so that we hauled south-east; and at 3 in the afternoon we hauled a-seaboard the sands, and had shoal water off Lymery and Ower, and were in 4 fathoms off them. The next day we hauled as we might to seize Orfordness. The 24th day we came thwart of the Naze about 8 in the morning. The 25th day, being the Nativity of Christ, we came to an anchor between Oldhaven and Tilbury Hope. The same day we turned as high as Porshet. The 26th day we turned as high as Ratcliffe, and praised God for our safe return. And thus I end, 1580.

The *William*, with Charles Jackman, arrived at a port in Norway between Trondheim and Rostock in October 1580, and there did winter; and from thence departed again in February following, and went in company of a ship of the King of Denmark toward Iceland; and since that time he was never heard of.

Part 2

THE MEDITERRANEAN
AND THE EAST

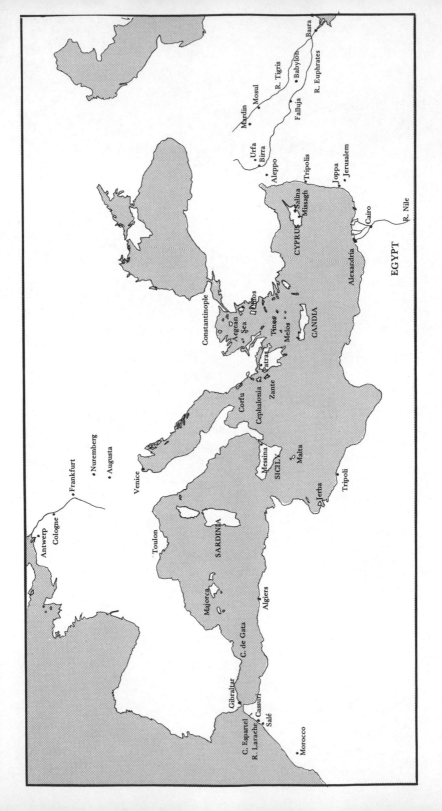

Despite the opening up of the Atlantic and the intrusion of the new Turkish empire into the Levant, the Mediterranean remained, throughout the sixteenth century, a main artery of travel and trade. And not only European trade; for the primary means of access to India and the East continued to be, as in the middle ages, either through Aleppo and along the middle-eastern caravan routes or through Egypt and with the Arab traders across the Red and Indian Seas.

Within the Mediterranean the chief carriers had been, in the fifteenth century, the Genoese and the Venetians. The Turks soon ousted the Genoese from their trading-posts in the Black Sea and Aegean. After capturing Aleppo in 1516 and overrunning Egypt two years later they imposed heavy customs duties on all goods passing through these vital entrepots. Yet the Venetians were still able to make a good living as middlemen in the transmission of the eastern products to Europe, and the trade was sufficiently attractive to warrant the establishment of an English Levant Company in 1581. There were also pilgrims and sight-seers, like Laurence Aldersey, to be transported on their tours.

Nevertheless, any voyage in the Mediterranean was subject to a variety of hazards. Not only were the Turks masters of the Aegean and Levant but, when in 1536 the French accepted them as allies, they were allowed to use French ports and so gained access to the western Mediterranean, where their position was quickly strengthened by ties with the Islamic principalities of the Barbary coast. Even when they were not actually on the warpath they resented interference in the areas that they controlled, and sought to impound or castigate intruders, while the Barbary pirates, encouraged by Turkish protection, pursued their traditional occupation with increasing boldness. As the stories of the Aucher *and the* Jesus *confirm, English ships trading in the Mediterranean needed to be in constant readiness for battle, and the penalty for defeat was likely to be slavery or the Turkish galleys until and unless luck brought ransom or rescue. It is almost a relief to read of the loss of the* Toby, *for this occurred through wholly natural causes.*

Thomas Stevens, an English Jesuit who elected to work in Goa, the Portuguese outpost on the west coast of India, travelled thither by the new route round the Cape of Good Hope, and his letter describing the journey is included by Hakluyt in his African section. It is transferred here because Stevens also figures in the story of Ralph Fitch, who reached India by the traditional route overland through Aleppo and Babylon to Ormuz, and from Goa proceeded right across northern India to Pegu (Burma), Malacca, and Ceylon. There is no reason to doubt that he made the journey, though for some of his descriptions he has plagiarised the account of the Italian, Cesare Federici, who had travelled much of the route twenty years earlier.

The voyage of Master Roger Bodenham with the great bark *Aucher* to Candia and Chios, in the year 1550. (Written by himself.)

IN the year 1550, the 13th of November, I, Roger Bodenham, captain of the bark *Aucher*, entered the said ship at Gravesend for my voyage to the islands of Candia and Chios in the Levant. The master of my ship was one William Sherwood. From thence we departed to Tilbury Hope, and there remained with contrary winds until the 6th of January 1551. The 6th of January the Master came to Tilbury, and I had provided a skilful pilot to carry me over the land's end, whose name was Master Wood, and with all speed I vailed down that night 10 miles to take the tide in the morning; which happily I did, and that night came to Dover and there came to an anchor, and there remained until Tuesday, meeting with the worthy knight Sir Anthony Aucher, owner of the said ship.

The 11th day we arrived in Plymouth, and the 13th in the morning we set forward on our voyage with a prosperous wind, and the 16th we had sight of Cape Finisterre on the coast of Spain. The 30th we arrived at Cadiz, and there discharged certain merchandise and took others aboard.

The 20th of February we departed from Cadiz and passed the Straits of Gibraltar that night, and the 25th we came to the Isle of Majorca, and stayed there five days with contrary winds. The first of March we had sight of Sardinia, and the fifth of the said month we arrived at Messina in Sicily, and there discharged much goods, and remained there until Good Friday in Lent.

The chief merchant that laded the said bark *Aucher* was a merchant stranger called Anselm Salvago, and because the time was then very dangerous, and no going into Levant, especially to Chios, without a safe conduct from the Turk, the said Anselm promised the owner, Sir Anthony Aucher, that we should receive the same at Messina. But I was posted from thence to Candia, and there I was answered that I should send to Chios, and there I should have my safe conduct. I was forced to send one, and he had his answer that the Turk would give none, willing me to look what was best for me to do; which was no small trouble to me, considering I was bound to deliver the goods that were in the ship at Chios or send them at my adventure. The merchants, without care of the loss of the ship, would have compelled me to go or send their goods at my adventure, the which I denied, and said plainly I would not go, because the Turk's galleys were come forth to go against Malta; but by the French King's means he was persuaded to leave Malta and to go to Tripoli in Barbary, which by the French he won.

In this time there were in Candia certain Turks' vessels called *skyrasas*, which had brought wheat thither to sell and were ready to depart for Turkey; and they departed in the morning betimes, carrying news that I would not go forth. The same night I prepared beforehand what I thought good, without making any man privy until I saw time. Then I had no small business to cause my mariners to venture with the ship in such a manifest danger. Nevertheless I won them all to go with me, except three which I set on land, and with all diligence I was ready to set forth about eight of the clock at night, being a fair moonshine night, and went out. Then my 3 mariners made such requests unto the rest of my men to come aboard as I was constrained to take them in. And so with good wind we put into the archipelago and, being among the islands, the wind scanted and I was forced to anchor at an island called Myconos, where I tarried 10 or 12 days, having a Greek pilot to carry the ship to Chios.

In this mean season there came many small boats with mizen sails to go for Chios with divers goods to sell, and the pilot requested me that I would let them go in my company, to which I yielded. After the said days expired, I weighed and set sail for the island of Chios, with which place I fell in the afternoon, whereupon I cast to seaward again to come with the island in the morning betimes. The foresaid small vessels, which came in my company, departed from me to win the shore to get in the night, but upon a sudden they espied 3 foists of Turks coming upon them to spoil them. My pilot, having a son in one of those small vessels, entreated me to cast about towards them, which at his request I did, and being something far from them I caused my gunner to shoot a demi-culverin at a foist that was ready to enter one of the boats. This was so happy a shot that it made the Turk to fall astern of the boat and to leave him, by the which means he escaped. Then they all came to me and requested that they might hang at my stern until daylight, by which time I came before the mole at Chios, and sent my boat on land to the merchants of that place to send for their goods out of hand, or else I would return back with all to Candia and they should fetch their goods there. But in fine, what by persuasion of my merchants, Englishmen and those of Chios, I was entreated to come into the harbour, and had a safe assurance for 20 days against the Turk's army with a bond of the city in the sum of 12,000 ducats.

So I made haste and sold such goods as I had to Turks that came thither, and put all in order with as much speed as I could, fearing the coming of the Turk's navy, of the which the chief of the city knew right well. So upon the sudden they called me, of great friendship, and in secret told me I had no way to save myself but to be gone. "For", said they, "we be not able to defend you that are not able to help ourselves, for the Turk where he cometh taketh what he will and leaveth what he lists but the chief of the Turks set order that none shall do any harm to the people or to their goods".

This was such news to me that indeed I was at my wits' end, and was brought into many imaginations how to do, for that the wind was contrary. In fine, I determined to go forth. But the merchants, Englishmen and other, regarding more their gains than the ship, hindered me very much in my purpose of going forth, and made the mariners to come to me to demand their wages to be paid them out of hand and to have a time to employ the same there. But God provided so for me that I paid them their money that night, and then charged them that, if they would not set the ship forth, I would make them to answer the same in England with danger of their heads. Many were married in England and had somewhat to lose: those did stick to me. I had twelve gunners. The Master Gunner, who was a mad-brained fellow, and the owner's servant had a parliament between themselves, and he upon the same came up to me with his sword drawn, swearing that he had promised the owner, Sir Anthony Aucher, to live and die in the said ship against all who should offer any harm to the ship, and that he would fight with the whole army of the Turks and never yield. With this fellow I had much to do, but at the last I made him confess his fault and follow my advice.

Thus with much labour I got out of the mole of Chios into the sea, by warping forth with the help of Genoeses' boats and a French boat that was in the mole; and being out God sent me a special gale of wind to go my way. Then I caused a piece to be shot off for some of my men that were yet in the town, and with much ado they came aboard; and then I set sail a little before one of the clock and I made all the sail I could. And about half an hour past two of the clock there came seven galleys into Chios to stay the ship; and the Admiral of them was in a great rage because she was gone. Whereupon they put some of the best in prison, and took all the men of the three ships which I left in the port and put them into the galleys. They would have followed after me, but that the townsmen found means they did not. The next day came thither a hundred more of galleys and there tarried for their whole company, which being together were about two hundred and 50 sail taking their voyage for to surprise the island of Malta.

The next day after I departed I had the sight of Candia, but I was two days after ere ever I could get in where I thought myself out of their danger. There I continued until the Turk's army was past, who came within the sight of the town. There was preparation made as though the Turks had come thither. There be in that island of Candia many banished men, that live continually in the mountains. They came down to serve, to the number of four or five thousand. They are good archers, every one with his bow and arrows, a sword and a dagger, with long hair, and boots that reach up to their groin, and a shirt of mail hanging the one half before and the other half behind. These were sent away again as soon as the army was past. They would drink wine out of all measure. Then, the army being past, I laded my ship with wines and other things; and so, after I had that which I left in Chios, I departed for Messina. In this way I found, about Zante, certain galliots of Turks laying aboard of certain vessels of Venice laden with muscatels. I rescued them, and had but a barrel of wine for my powder and shot; and within a few days after I came to Messina.

I had in my ship a Spanish pilot called Noblezia, which I took in at Cadiz at my coming forth. He went with me all this voyage into the Levant without wages, of good will that he bore me and the ship. He stood me in good stead until I came back again to Cadiz, and then I needed no pilot. And so from thence I came to London with the ship and goods in safety, God be praised. And all those mariners that were in my said ship, which were, besides boys, threescore and ten, for the most part were within five or six years after able to take charge, and did. Richard Chancellor, who first discovered Russia, was with me in that voyage, and Matthew Baker, who afterward became the Queen's Majesty's chief shipwright.

A letter written from Goa, the principal city of all the East Indies, by one Thomas Stevens, an Englishman, and sent to his father, Master Thomas Stevens: anno 1579.

AFTER most humble commendations, these shall be to crave your daily blessing, with like commendations unto my mother; and withal, to certify you of my being, according to your will and my duty. I wrote unto you, taking my journey from Italy to Portugal, which letters I think are come to your hands, so that, presuming thereupon, I think I have the less need at this time to tell you the cause of my departing, which nevertheless in one word I may conclude if I do but name obedience.

I came to Lisbon toward the end of March, eight days before the departure of the ships, so late that if they had not been stayed about some weighty matters they had been long gone before our coming, insomuch that there were others ordained to go in our places that the kings's provision and ours also might not be in vain. Nevertheless our sudden coming took place, and the fourth of April five ships departed for Goa, wherein, besides shipmen and soldiers, there were a great number of children which in the seas bear out better than men, and no marvel when that many women also pass very well. The setting forth from the port I need not to tell how solemn it is, with trumpets and shooting of ordnance, you may easily imagine it considering that they go in the manner of war. The tenth of the foresaid month we came to the sight of Porto Santo near unto Madeira, where an English ship set upon ours (which was then also alone) with a few shots, which did no harm, but after that our ship had laid out her greatest ordnance they straight departed as they came. The English ship was very fair and great, which I was sorry to see so ill occupied, for she went roving about so that we saw her again at the Canary Isles, unto the which we came the thirteenth of the said month, and good leisure we had to wonder at the high mountain of the Island Tenerife, for we wandered between that and Grand Canary four days by reason of contrary winds: and briefly, such evil weather we had until the fourteenth of May that they despaired to compass the Cape of Good Hope that year.

Nevertheless, taking our voyage between Guinea and the Islands of Cape Verde, without seeing of any land at all, we arrived at length unto the coast of Guinea, which the Portuguese so call chiefly that part of the burning zone which is from the sixth degree unto the equinoctial, in which parts they suffered so many inconveniences of heats and lack of winds that they think themselves happy when they have passed it; for sometimes the ship standeth there almost by the space of many days, sometime she goeth, but in such order that it were almost as good to stand still. And the greatest part of this coast not clear, but thick and cloudy, full of thunder and lightning, and rain so unwholesome that if the water stand a little while all is full of worms, and falling on the meat, which is hanged up, it maketh it straight full of worms.

Along all that coast we often times saw a thing swimming upon the water like a cockscomb (which they call a ship of Guinea) but the colour much fairer; which comb standeth upon a thing almost like the swimmer of a fish in colour and bigness, and beareth underneath in the water strings which save it from turning over. This thing is so poisonous that a man cannot touch it without great peril.

In this coast, that is to say from the sixth degree unto the equinoctial, we spent no less than thirty days, partly with contrary winds, partly with calm. The thirtieth of May we passed the equinoctial with contentation, directing our course as well as we could to pass the promontory, but in all that gulf, and in all the way beside, we found so often calms that the expertest mariners wondered at it. And in places where are always wont to be most horrible tempests we found most quiet calms, which was very troublesome to those ships which be the greatest of all other and cannot go without good winds. Insomuch, that when it is tempest almost intolerable for other ships and maketh them maine all their sails, these hoist up and sail excellent well, unless the waters be too furious, which seldom happened in our navigation.

You shall understand that, being past the line, they cannot straightway go the next way to the promontory; but, according to the wind, they draw always as near south as they can to put themselves in the latitude of the point, which is 35 degrees and a half, and then they take their course towards the east and so compass the point. But the wind served us so that at 33 degrees we did direct our course toward the point or promontory of Good Hope.

You know that it is hard to sail from east to west, or contrary, because there is no fixed point in all the sky whereby they may direct their course, wherefore I shall tell you what helps God provided for these men. There is not a fowl that appeareth, or sign in the air, or in the sea, which they have not written which have made the voyages heretofore. Wherefore, partly by their own experience, and pondering withal what space the ship was able to make with such a wind, and such direction, and partly the experience of others whose books and navigations they have, they guess whereabouts they be touching degrees of longitude, for of latitude they be always sure. But the greatest and best industry of all is to mark the variation of the needle or compass, which in the meridian of the Island of St Michael, which is one of the Azores in the latitude of Lisbon, is just north, and thence swerveth towards the east so much that betwixt the meridian aforesaid and the point of Africa it carrieth three or four quarters of 32. And again in the point of Africa, a little beyond the point that is called Cape das Agulhas (in English the needles) it returneth again unto the north, and that place passed it swerveth again toward the west, as it did before proportionally.

As touching our first signs, the nearer we came to the people of Africa the more strange kinds of fowls appeared, insomuch that when we came within no less than thirty leagues (almost an hundred miles) and six hundred miles as we thought from any island, as good as three thousand fowls of sundry kinds followed our ship, some of them so great that their wings being opened from one point to the other contained seven spans, as the mariners said. A marvellous thing to see how God provided so that in so wide a sea these fowls are all fat, and nothing wanteth them. The Portugals have named them all according to some propriety which they have: some they call Rushtails because their tails be not proportionable to their bodies but long and small like a rush, some Forked Tails because they be very broad and forked, some Velvet Sleeves because they have wings of the colour of velvet and bow them as a man boweth his elbow. This bird is always welcome, for he appeareth nearest the Cape. I should never make an end if I should tell all particulars; but it shall suffice briefly to touch a few, which yet shall be sufficient, if you mark them, to give occasion to glorify Almighty God in his wonderful works, and such variety in his creatures. And to speak somewhat of fishes, in all places of calm, especially in the burning zone, near the line (for without we never saw any) there waited on our ship fishes as long as a man, which they call *tuberones*. They come to eat such things as from the ship fall into the sea, not refusing men themselves if they light upon them. And if they find any meat tied in the sea they take it for theirs. These have waiting on them six or seven small fishes (which never depart) with guards blue and green round about their bodies, like comely serving men, and they go two or three before him, and some on every side. Moreover, they have other fishes which cleave always unto their body, and seem to take such superfluities as grow about them, and they are said to enter into their bodies also to purge them if they need. The mariners in time past have eaten of them, but since they have seen them eat men their stomachs abhor them. Nevertheless, they draw them up with great hooks and kill of them as many as they can, thinking that they have made a great revenge.

There is another kind of fish, as big almost as a herring, which hath wings and flieth, and they are together in great number. These have two enemies, the one in the sea, the other in the air. In the sea the fish which is called albacore, as big as a salmon, followeth them with great swiftness to take them. This poor fish not being able swim fast, for he hath no fins but swimmeth with moving of his tail, shutting his wings, lifteth himself above the water and flieth not very high. The albacore seeing that, although he have no wings, yet he giveth a great leap out of the water and sometimes catcheth him, or else he keepeth himself under the water going that way on as fast as he flieth. And when the fish, being weary of the air or thinking himself out of danger, returneth into the water, the albacore meeteth with him; but sometimes his other enemy, the sea-crow, catcheth him before he falleth.

With these and like sights, but always making our supplications to God for good weather and salvation of the ship, we came at length unto the point, so famous and feared of all men, but we found there no tempest, only great waves, where our pilot was a little overseen. For whereas commonly all other never come within sight of land, but seeing signs ordinary and finding bottom go their way sure and safe, he, thinking himself to have wind at will, shot so nigh the land that the wind, turning into the south, and the waves being exceeding great, rolled us so near the land that the ship stood in less than 14 fathoms of water, no more than six miles from the cape which is called Das Agulhas. And there we stood as utterly cast away; for under us were rocks of main stone so sharp and cutting that no anchor could hold the ship, the shore so evil that nothing could take land, and the land itself so full of tigers, and people that are savage and killers of all strangers, that we had no hope of life nor comfort, but only in God and a good conscience. Notwithstanding, after we had lost anchors, hoisting up the sails for to get the ship a-coast in some safer place, or when it should please God, it pleased His mercy suddenly, where no man looked for help, to fill our sails with wind from the land, and so we escaped, thanks be to God.

And the day following, being in the place where they are always wont to catch fish, we also fell a-fishing, and so many they took that they served all the ship for that day, and part of the next. And one of them pulled up a coral of great bigness and price. For there they say (as we saw by experience) that the corals do grow in the manner of stalks upon the rocks in the bottom, and wax hard and red.

The day of peril was the nine and twentieth of July. And you shall understand that, the Cape passed, there be two ways to India: one within the Isle of St Laurence, which they take willingly because they refresh themselves at Mozambique a fortnight or a month, not without great need, and thence in a month more land in Goa. The other is without the Isle of St Laurence, which they take when they set forth so late, and come so late to the point that they have no time to take the foresaid Mozambique, and then they go heavily because in this way they take no port. And by reason of the long navigation, and want of food and water, they fall into sundry diseases, their gums wax great and swell and they are fain to cut them away; their legs swell, and all the body becometh sore and so benumbed that they cannot stir hand nor foot, and so they die for weakness. Others fall into fluxes and agues and die thereby. And this way it was our chance to make. Yet, though we had more than one hundred and fifty sick, there died not past seven and twenty; which loss they esteemed not much in respect of other times. Though some of ours were diseased in this sort, yet, thanks be to God, I had my health all the way, contrary to the expectation of many. God send me my health so well in the land, if it may be to His honour and service.

This way is full of privy rocks and quicksands so that sometimes we durst not sail by night, but by the providence of God we saw nothing, nor never found bottom until we came to the coast of India. When we had passed again the line, and were come to the third degree or somewhat more, we saw crabs swimming on the water that were red as though they had been sodden; but this was no sign of land. After, about the eleventh degree, the space of many days more than ten thousand fishes by estimation followed round about our ship, whereof we caught

so many that for fifteen days we did eat nothing else, and they served
our turn very well; for at this time we had neither meat nor almost
anything else to eat, our navigation growing so long that it drew near to
seven months, whereas commonly they go it in five, I mean when they
sail the inner way. But these fishes were not sign of land but rather of
deep sea.

At length we took a couple of birds, which were a kind of hawks,
whereof they joyed much thinking that they had been of India, but
indeed they were of Arabia as we found afterward. And we that
thought we had been near India were in the same latitude near Socotra,
an isle in the mouth of the Red Sea. But there God sent us great winds
from the north-east or north-north-east, whereupon unwillingly they
bore up towards the east, and thus we went ten days without seeing sign
of land, whereby they perceived their error. For they had directed their
course before always north-east, coveting to multiply degrees of
latitude, but partly the difference of the needle, and most of all the
running seas, which at that time ran north-west, had drawn us to this
other danger, had not God sent us this wind, which at length waxed
larger and restored us to our right course. These running seas be so
perilous that they deceive the most part of the governors, and some be
so little curious, contenting themselves with ordinary experience, that
they care not to seek out any means to know when they swerve, neither
by the compass nor by any other trial.

The first sign of land were certain fowls which they knew to be of
India; the second, boughs of palms and sedges; the third, snakes
swimming on the water, and a substance which they call by the name of
a coin of money, as broad and as round as a groat, wonderfully printed
and stamped of nature like unto some coin. And these two last signs be
so certain that the next day after, if the wind serve, they see land, which
we did to our great joy, when all our water (for you know they make no
beer in those parts) and victuals began to fail us. And to Goa we came
the four and twentieth day of October, there being received with
passing great charity.

The people be tawny, but not disfigured in their lips and noses as the
Moors and Kaffirs of Ethiopia. They that be not of reputation, or at
least the most part, go naked, saving an apron of a span long, and as
much in breadth before them, and a lace two fingers broad before
them, girded about with a string and no more: and thus they think
them as well as we with all our trimming. Of the fruits and trees that be
here I cannot now speak for I should make another letter as long as
this. For hitherto I have not seen a tree here whose like I have seen in
Europe, the vine excepted, which nevertheless here is to no purpose, so
that all the wines are brought out of Portugal. The drink of this country
is good water, or wine of the palm-tree, or of a fruit called cocos. And
this shall suffice for this time.

If God send me my health I shall have opportunity to write to you once again. Now the length of my letter compelleth me to take my leave; and thus I wish your most prosperous health.

From Goa the tenth of November, 1579.
Your loving son,
Thomas Stevens.

The first voyage or journey made by Master Laurence Aldersey, merchant of London, to the cities of Jerusalem and Tripolis, etc. in the year 1581. Penned and set down by himself.

I departed from London the first day of April in the year of Our Lord 1581, passing through the Netherland and up the River Rhine by Cologne and other cities of Germany; and upon Thursday the third day of May I came to Augusta, where I delivered the letter I had to Master Jenise and Master Castler, whom I found very willing to pleasure me in anything that I could or would reasonably demand. He first furnished me with a horse to Venice for my money, and then took me with him a-walking to show me the city, for that I had a day to tarry there for him that was to be my guide. He showed me first the State-house, which is very fair and beautiful; then he brought me to the finest garden and orchard that ever I saw in my life. For there was in it a place for canary-birds as large as a fair chamber, trimmed with wire both above and beneath, with fine little branches of trees for them to sit in, which was full of those canary-birds. There was such another for turtle-doves; also there were two pigeon-houses joining to them, having in them store of turtle-doves and pigeons. In the same garden also were six or seven fishponds, all railed about and full of very good fish; also seven or eight fine fountains or water springs of divers fashions. As for fruit, there wanted none of all sorts, as oranges, figs, raisins, walnuts, grapes, besides apples, pears, filberts, small nuts, and such other fruit as we have in England.

Then did he bring me to the water tower of the same city, that by a sleight and device hath the water brought up as high as any church in the town; and to tell you the strange devices of all it passeth my capacity. Then he brought me to another fair garden called the Shooters' House, where are butts for the long-bow, the cross-bow, the stone-bow, the long piece, and for divers other exercises more. After this we walked about the walls of the city, where is a great, broad, and deep ditch upon one side of the town, so full of fish as ever I saw any pond in my life, and it is reserved only for the States of the city. And upon the other side of the city is also a deep place, all green, wherein deer are kept, and when it pleaseth the States to hunt for their pleasure thither they resort, and have their courses with greyhounds which are kept for that purpose.

The fifth of May I departed from Augusta towards Venice, and came thither upon Whitsunday, the thirteenth of the same month. It is needless to speak of the height of the mountains that I passed over and of the danger thereof, it is so well-known already to the world. The height of them is marvellous, and I was the space of six days in passing them. I came to Venice at the time of a fair, which lasted fourteen days, wherein I saw very many and fair shows of wares. I came thither too short for the first passage, which went away from Venice about the seventh or eighth of May, and with them about three score pilgrims, which ship was cast away at a town called Istria two miles from Venice, and all the men in her, saving thirty or thereabout, lost.

Within eight days after fell Corpus Christi Day, which was a day amongst them of procession, in which was shown the plate and treasure of Venice which is esteemed to be worth two millions of pounds; but I do not account it worth half a quarter of that money, except there be more than I saw. To speak of the sumptuousness of the copes and vestments of the Church I leave, but the truth is they be very sumptuous, many of them set all over with pearl and made of cloth of gold. And for the Jesuits, I think there be as many at Venice as there be in Cologne.

The number of Jews is there thought to be 1000, who dwell in a certain place of the city, and have also a place to which they resort to pray which is called the Jews' Synagogue. They all and their offspring use to wear red caps, for so they are commanded because they may thereby be known from other men. For my further knowledge of these people I went into their Synagogue upon a Saturday, which is their Sabbath day, and I found them in their service or prayers very devout. They receive the five books of Moses, and honour them by carrying them about their church as the Papists do their cross. Their Synagogue is in form round, and the people sit round about it, and in the midst there is a place for him that readeth to the rest. As for their apparel, all of them wear a large white lawn over their garments, which reacheth from their head down to the ground. The Psalms they sing as we do, having no image nor using any manner of idolatry; their error is that they believe not in Christ, nor yet receive the New Testament.

This city of Venice is very fair and greatly to be commended, wherein is good order for all things; and also it is very strong and populous. It standeth upon the main sea and hath many islands about it that belong to it. To tell you of the Duke of Venice and of the Signory: there is one chosen that ever beareth the name of a duke, but in truth he is but servant to the Signory for of himself he can do little. It is no otherwise with him than with a priest that is at mass upon a festival day, which putting on his golden garment seemeth to be a great man, but if any man come unto him and crave some friendship at his hands he will say "You must go to the masters of the parish, for I cannot pleasure you otherwise than by preferring of your suit"; and so it is with the Duke of Venice. If any man having a suit come to him, and make his complaint and deliver his supplication, it is not in him to help him, but he will tell him "You must come this day or that day and then I will prefer your suit to the Signory and do you the best friendship that I may". Furthermore, if any man bring a letter unto him, he may not open it but in the presence of the Signory, and they are to see it first; which being read, perhaps they will deliver it to him, perhaps not. Of the Signory there be about three hundred, and about forty of the Privy Council of Venice, who usually are arrayed in gowns of crimson satin or crimson damask when they sit in council.

In the city of Venice no man may wear a weapon except he be a soldier for the Signory, or a scholar of Padua, or a gentleman of great countenance; and yet he may not do that without licence.

As for the women of Venice, they be rather monsters than women. Every shoemaker's or tailor's wife will have a gown of silk and one to carry up her train, wearing their shoes very near half a yard high from the ground. If a stranger meet one of them he will surely think, by the state that she goeth with, that he meeteth a lady.

I departed from this city of Venice upon Midsummer Day, being the four and twentieth of June; and thinking that the ship would the next day depart I stayed, and lay a-shipboard all night, and we were made believe from time to time that we should this day and that day depart. But we tarried still till the fourteenth of July, and then with scant wind we set sail and sailed that day and that night not above fifty Italian miles. And upon the sixteenth day at night the wind turned flat contrary so that the Master knew not what to do; and about the fifth hour of the night, which we reckon to be about one of the clock after midnight, the pilot descried a sail, and at last perceived it to be a galley of the Turks, whereupon we were in great fear.

The Master, being a wise fellow and a good sailor, began to devise how to escape the danger and to lose little of our way; and while both he and all of us were in our dumps, God sent us a merry gale of wind, that we ran threescore and ten leagues before it was twelve o'clock next day, and in six days after we were seven leagues past Zante. And upon Monday morning, being the three and twentieth of the same month, we came in the sight of Candia, which day the wind came contrary, with great blasts and storms, until the eight and twentieth of the same month; in which time the mariners cried out upon me, because I was an Englishman, and said I was no good Christian, and wished that I were in the midst of the sea, saying that they and the ship were the worse for me. I answered, "Truly, it may well be, for I think myself the worst creature in the world; and consider you yourselves also, as I do myself, and then use your discretion". The Friar preached, and the sermon being done I was demanded whether I did understand him. I answered yea, and told the Friar himself, "Thus you said in your sermon, that we were not all good Christians, or else it were not possible for us to have such weather"; to which I answered, "Be you well assured that we are not indeed all good Christians, for there are in the ship some that hold very unchristian opinions". So for that time I satisfied him, although they said that I would not see, when they said the procession and honoured their images and prayed to Our Lady and St Mark.

There was also a gentleman, an Italian, which was a passenger in the ship, and he told me what they said of me because I would not sing Salve Regina and Ave Maria as they did. I told them that they that prayed to so many, or sought help of any other than of God the Father or of Jesus Christ His only son, go a wrong way to work, and robbed God of His honour and wrought their own destructions. All this was told the friars, but I heard nothing of it in three days after; and then at evening prayer they sent the purser about with the image of Our Lady to every one to kiss, and I perceiving it went another way from him and would not see it. Yet at last he fetched his course about so that he came to me, and offered it to me as he did to others but I refused it, whereupon there was a great stir. The patron and all the friars were told of it, and everyone said I was a Lutheran, and so called me. But two of the friars that were of greatest authority seemed to bear me better good will than the rest, and travailed to the patron in my behalf, and made all well again.

The second day of August we arrived in Cyprus, at a town called Missagh. The people there be very rude, and like beasts and no better. They eat their meat sitting upon the ground, with their legs a-cross, like tailors; their beds for the most part be hard stones, but yet some of them have fair mattresses to lie upon.

Upon Thursday the eighth of August we came to Joppa in a small bark which we hired between Missagh and Salina, and could not be suffered to come on land till noon the next day, and then we were permitted by the great Basha, who sat upon the top of a hill to see us sent away. Being come on land, we might not enter into any house for victuals, but were to content ourselves with our own provision, and that which we brought to carry with us was taken from us. I had a pair of stirrups which I bought in Venice to serve me in my journey, and, trying to make them fit for me, when the Basha saw me up before the rest of the company he sent one to dismount me and to strike me; whereupon I turned me to the Basha, and made a long leg, saying "Grand merci, signor". And after a while we were horsed upon little asses, and sent away, with about fifty light horsemen to be our conduct through the wilderness, called Deserta Felix, who made us good sport by the way with their pikes, guns, and falchions. That day, being St Laurence Day, we came to Rama, which is ten Italian miles from Joppa, and there we stayed that night, and paid to the captain of the castle every man a *chekin*, which is seven shillings and twopence sterling. So then we had a new guard of soldiers and left the other.

The house we lodged in at Rama had a door so low to enter into that I was fain to creep in, as it were upon my knees, and within it are three rooms to lodge travellers that come that way. There are no beds, except a man buy a mat and lay it on the ground; that is all the provision, without stools or benches to sit upon. Our victuals were brought us out of the town, as hens, eggs, bread, great store of fruit, as pomegranates, figs, grapes, oranges, and suchlike, and drink we drew out of the well. The town itself is so ruinated that I take it rather to be a heap of stones than a town.

Then the next morning we thought to have gone away, but we could not be permitted that day; so we stayed there till two of the clock the next morning, and then with a fresh guard of soldiers we departed toward Jerusalem. We had not ridden five English miles but we were encountered with a great number of the Arabians, who stayed us, and would not suffer us to pass till they had somewhat, so it cost us for all our guard above twenty shillings a man betwixt Joppa and Jerusalem. These Arabians troubled us oftentimes. Our dragoman that paid the money for us was struck down and had his head broken because he would not give them as much as they asked, and they that should have rescued both him and us stood still, and durst do nothing, which was to our cost.

Being come within sight of Jerusalem, the manner is to kneel down and give God thanks that it hath pleased Him to bring us to that holy place where He Himself had been; and there we leave our horses, and go on foot to the town. And being come to the gates, there they took our names and our fathers' names, and so we were permitted to go to our lodgings.

The governor of the house met us a mile out of the town, and very courteously bade us all welcome and brought us to the monastery. The gates of the city are all covered with iron. The entrance into the house of the Christians is a very low and narrow door, barred or plated with iron, and then come we into a very dark entry. The place is a monastery. There we lay and, dieted of free cost, we fared reasonable well; the bread and wine was excellent good, the chambers clean, and all the meat well served in, with clean linen.

We lay at the monastery two days, Friday and Saturday; and then we went to Bethlehem with two or three of the friars of the house with us. In the way thither we saw many monuments, as the mountain where the angel took up Habakkuk by the hair and brought him to Daniel in the lions' den; the fountain of the prophet Jeremiah; the place where the Wise Men met that went to Bethlehem to worship Christ, where is a fountain of stone.

Being come to Bethlehem we saw the place where Christ was born, which is now a chapel with two altars whereupon they say mass. The place is built with grey marble, and hath been beautiful, but now it is partly decayed. Near thereto is the sepulchre of the Innocents slain by Herod, the sepulchres of Paul, of Jerome, and of Eusebius. Also a little from this monastery is a place under the ground where the Virgin Mary abode with Christ when Herod sought Him to destroy Him.

We stayed at Bethlehem that night, and the next day we went from thence to the mountains of Judaea, which are about eight miles from Jerusalem, where are the ruins of an old monastery. In the mid way from the monastery to Jerusalem is the place where John Baptist was born, being now an old monastery, and cattle kept in it. Also a mile from Jerusalem is a place called Inventio Sanctae Crucis, where the wood was found that made the cross.

In the city of Jerusalem we saw the hall where Pilate sat in judgment when Christ was condemned, the stairs whereof are at Rome as they told us. A little from thence is the house where the Virgin Mary was born. There is also the piscina or fish-pool where the sick folks were healed, which is by the walls of Jerusalem; but the pool is now dry.

The Mount of Calvary is a great church, and within the door thereof, which is little and barred with iron, and five great holes in it to look in like the holes of tavern doors in London, they sit that are appointed to receive our money, with a carpet under them upon a bench of stone and their legs across like tailors. Having paid our money we are permitted to go into the church. Right against the church door is the grave where Christ was buried, with a great long stone of white marble over it, and railed about. The outside of the sepulchre is very foul, by means that every man scrapes his name and mark upon it, and is ill kept. Within the sepulchre is a partition, and in the further part thereof is the stone whereupon the angel sat when he said to Mary "He is risen", which stone was also rolled to the door of the sepulchre. The altar stone within the sepulchre is of white marble, the place able to contain but four persons. Right over the sepulchre is a device or lantern for light, and over that a great louvre such as are in England in ancient houses. There is also the chapel of the sepulchre, and in the midst thereof is a canopy, as it were a bed, with a great sort of ostrich eggs hanging at it, with tassels of silk and lamps. Behind the sepulchre is a little chapel for the Chaldeans and Syrians.

Upon the right hand coming into the church is the tomb of Baldwin, King of France, and of his son; and in the same place the tomb of Melchisedec.

There is a chapel also in the same church erected to St Helen, through which we go up to the place where Christ was crucified. The stairs are fifty steps high. There are two altars in it: before the high altar is the place where the cross stood, the hole whereof is trimmed about with silver, and the depth of it is half a man's arm deep. The rent also of the mountain is there to be seen in the crevice, wherein a man may put his arm.

Upon the other side of the Mount of Calvary is the place where Abraham would have sacrificed his son, where also is a chapel, and the place paved with stones of divers colours. There is also the house of Annas the high priest, and the olive tree whereunto Christ was bound when he was whipped; also the house of Caiaphas, and by it the prison where Christ was kept, which is but the room of one man and hath no light but the opening of the door.

Without Jerusalem in the valley of Jehoshaphat is a church under the ground, like to the shrouds in St Paul's, where the sepulchre of the Virgin Mary is. The stairs be very broad, and upon the stairs going down are two sepulchres: upon the left hand lieth Jehoshaphat, and upon the right hand lieth Joachim and Anna, the father and mother of the Virgin Mary. Going out of the valley of Jehoshaphat we came to Mount Olivet, where Christ prayed unto His Father before His death; and there is to be seen (as they told me) the water and blood that fell from the eyes of Christ. A little higher upon the same Mount is the place where the apostles slept and watched not. At the foot of the Mount is the place where Christ was imprisoned. Upon the mountain also is the place where Christ stood when He wept over Jerusalem, and where He ascended into heaven.

Now, having seen all these monuments, I with my company set from Jerusalem the 20th day of August, and came again to Joppa the 22nd of the same month, where we took shipping presently for Tripolis, and in four days we came to Mccina, the place where the ships lie that come for Tripolis.

The city of Tripolis is a mile and a half within the land, so that no ship can come further than Mecina; so that night I came thither, where I lay nine days for passage, and at last we embarked ourselves in a good ship of Venice called the new *Nave Ragasona*. We entered the ship the second of September, the fourth we set sail, the seventh we came to Salina, which is 140 miles from Tripolis. There we stayed four days to take in more lading, in which meantime I fell sick of an ague, but recovered again, I praise God. Salina is a ruinated city, and was destroyed by the Turk ten years past. There are in it now but seventeen persons, women and children. A little from this city of Salina is a salt piece of ground, where the water groweth salt that raineth upon it.

Thursday, the 21st of September, we came to Missagh, and there we stayed eight days for our lading. The 18th of September, before we came to Missagh and within ten miles of the town, as we lay at an anchor because the wind was contrary, there came a great boat full of men to board us. They made an excuse to seek for four men which, they said, our ship had taken from theirs about Tripolis, but our Captain would not suffer any of them to come in to us. The next morning they came to us again with a great galley manned with 500 men at the least, whereupon our Captain sent the boat to them with twelve men to know their pleasure. They said they sought for 4 men, and therefore would talk with our Master. So then the Master's Mate was sent them, and him they kept, and went their way. The next morning they came again with him, and with three other galleys, and then would needs speak with our Captain, who went to them in a gown of crimson damask and other very brave apparel, and five or six other gentlemen richly apparelled also. They, having the Turk's safe conduct, showed it to the Captain of the galleys, and laid it upon his head, charging him to obey it. So, with much ado, and with the gift of 100 pieces of gold, we were quit of them, and had our man again.

That day, as aforesaid, we came to Missagh, and there stayed eight days and at last departed towards Candy with a scant wind. The 11th day of October we were boarded with four galleys manned with 1200 men, which also made a sleeveless errand, and troubled us very much; but our Captain's passport, and the gift of 100 *chekins*, discharged all.

The 27th of October we passed by Zante with a merry wind, the 29th by Corfu, and the third of November we arrived at Istria, and there we left our great ship and took small boats to bring us to Venice. The 9th of November I arrived again at Venice in good health, where I stayed nine days; and the 25th of the same month I came to Augusta, and stayed there but one day.

The 27th of November I set towards Nuremberg where I came the 29th, and there stayed till the 9th of December, and was very well entertained of the English merchants there; and the governors of the town sent me and my company sixteen gallons of excellent good wine. From thence I went to Frankfurt, from Frankfurt to Cologne, from Cologne to Arnhem, from Arnhem to Utrecht, from Utrecht to Dort, from Dort to Antwerp, from Antwerp to Flushing, from Flushing to London, where I arrived upon Twelfth Eve in safety and gave thanks to God, having finished my journey to Jerusalem and home again in the space of nine months and five days.

7 *A Galley. Galley-slaves are chained*
five to an oar.

Durch Ioseph Furttenbach.

The voyage made to Tripoli in Barbary, in the year 1583, with a ship called the *Jesus*, wherein the adventures and distresses of some Englishmen are truly reported and other necessary circumstances observed. Written by Thomas Sanders.

THIS voyage was set forth by the right worshipful Sir Edward Osborne, Knight, chief merchant of all the Turkish Company, and one Master Richard Staper, the ship being of the burden of one hundred tons, called the *Jesus*. She was built at Fareham, a river by Portsmouth. The owners were Master Thomas Thomson, Nicholas Carnaby, and John Gilman. The master was one Zacheus Hellier of Blackwall, and his mate was one Richard Morris of that place; their pilot was one Anthony Jerado, a Frenchman, of the province of Marseilles. The purser was one William Thomson, our owner's son. The merchants' factors were Romaine Sonnings, a Frenchman, and Richard Skegs, servant unto the said Master Staper.

The owners were bound unto the merchants by charter party thereupon, in one thousand marks, that the ship by God's permission should go for Tripoli in Barbary: that is to say, first from Portsmouth to Newhaven in Normandy, from thence to San Lucar, otherwise called Saint Lucas in Andalusia, and from thence to Tripoli, which is in the east part of Africa, and so to return unto London. But here ought every man to note and consider the works of our God, that many times what man doth determine God doth disappoint. The said master, having some occasion to go to Fareham, took with him the pilot and the purser and, returning again, by means of a perry of wind the boat wherein they were was drowned with the said master, the purser, and all the company; only the said pilot by experience in swimming saved himself.

These were the beginnings of our sorrows. After which the said master's mate would not proceed in that voyage, and the owner, hearing of this misfortune, and the unwillingness of the master's mate, did send down one Richard Deimond, and shipped him for master, who did choose for his mate one Andrew Dyer, and so the said ship departed on her voyage accordingly: that is to say, about the 16th of October in anno 1583 she made sail from Portsmouth, and the 18th day then next following she arrived at Newhaven, where our said last master Deimond by a surfeit died. The factors then appointed the said Andrew Dyer, being then master's mate, to be their master for that voyage, who did choose to be his mates the two quartermasters of the same ship, to wit Peter Austin and Shillabey; and for purser was shipped one Richard Burges. Afterward about the 8th day of November we made sail forthward, and by force of weather we were driven back again into Portsmouth, where we renewed our victuals and other necessaries, and then the wind came fair. About the 29th day then next following we departed thence, and the first day of December by means of a contrary wind we were driven to Plymouth. The 18th day then next following we made forthward again, and by force of weather we were driven to Falmouth, where we remained until the first day of January; at which time the wind coming fair, we departed thence and about the 20th day of the said month we arrived safely at San Lucar.

And about the 9th day of March next following we made sail from thence, and about the 18th day of the said month we came to Tripoli in Barbary, where we were very well entertained by the King of that country, and also of the commons. The commodities of that place are sweet oils. The King there is a merchant, and the rather (willing to prefer himself before his commons) requested our said factors to traffic with him, and promised them that if they would take his oils at his own price they should pay no manner of custom, and they took of him certain tuns of oil and afterward perceiving that they might have far better cheap, notwithstanding the custom free, they desired the King to license them to take the oils at the pleasure of his commons, for that his price did exceed theirs. Whereupon the King would not agree, but was rather contented to abate his price, insomuch that the factors bought all their oils of the King custom-free, and so laded the same aboard.

In the meantime there came to the place one Miles Dickenson in a ship of Bristol, who together with our factors took a house to themselves there. Our French factor, Romaine Sonnings, desired to buy a commodity in the market and, wanting money, desired the said Miles Dickenson to lend him a hundred *chikinos* until he came to his lodging, which he did; and afterward the same Sonnings met with Miles Dickenson in the street, and delivered him money bound up in a napkin, saying "Master Dickenson, there is the money I borrowed of you", and so thanked him for the same. He doubted nothing less than falsehood, which is seldom known among merchants, and specially being together in one house, and is the more detestable among Christians, they being in Turkey among the heathen. The said Dickenson did not tell the money presently until he came to his lodging, and then finding nine *chikinos* lacking of his hundred, which was about three pounds for that every *chikino* is worth seven shillings of English money, he came to the said Romaine Sonnings and delivered him his handkerchief, and asked him how many *chikinos* he had delivered him. Sonnings answered a hundred; Dickenson said no; and so they protested and swore on both parts. But in the end the said Romaine Sonnings did swear deeply with detestable oaths and curses, and prayed God that he might show his works on him that other might take example thereby, and that he might be hanged like a dog and never come into England again, if he did not deliver unto the said Dickenson a hundred *chikinos*. And here behold a notable example of all blasphemers, cursers, and swearers, how God rewarded them accordingly: for many times it cometh to pass that God showeth His miracles upon such monstrous blasphemers, to the example of others, as now hereafter you shall hear what befell to this Romaine Sonnings.

There was a man in the said town, a pledge, whose name was Patrone Norado, who the year before had done this Sonnings some pleasure there. The foresaid Patrone Norado was indebted unto a Turk of that town in the sum of four hundred and fifty crowns, for certain goods sent by him into Christendom in a ship of his own, and by his own brother, and himself remained in Tripoli as pledge until his said brother's return; and, as the report went there, after his brother's arrival into Christendom he came among lewd company, and lost his brother's said ship and goods at dice and never returned to him again. The said Patrone Norado being void of all hope, and finding now opportunity, consulted with the said Sonnings for to swim a-seaboard the islands, and the ship being then out of danger should take him in (as after was confessed) and so to go to Toulon in the province of Marseilles with this Patrone Norado, and there to take in his lading.

The ship being ready the first day of May and having her sails all aboard, our said factors did take their leave of the King, who very courteously bade them farewell; and when they came aboard they commanded the Master and the company hastily to get out the ship. The Master answered that it was impossible, for that the wind was contrary and overblown. And he required us, upon forfeiture of our bonds, that we should do our endeavour to get her forth. Then went we to warp out the ship, and presently the King sent a boat aboard of us, with three men in her, commanding the said Sonnings to come ashore; at whose coming the King demanded of him custom for the oils. Sonnings answered him that His Highness had promised to deliver them custom-free. But, notwithstanding, the King weighed not the said promise, and as an infidel that hath not the fear of God before his eyes, nor regard of his word, albeit he was a king, he caused the said Sonnings to pay the custom to the uttermost penny, and afterward willed him to make haste away, saying that the janissaries would have the oil ashore again. (These janissaries are soldiers there under the Great Turk, and their power is above the King's.) And so the said factor departed from the King, and came to the waterside and called for a boat to come aboard, and he brought with him the foresaid Patrone Norado. The company, inquisitive to know what man that was, Sonnings answered that he was his countryman, a passenger. "I pray God", said the company, "that we come not into trouble by this man". Then said Sonnings angrily, "What have you to do with any matters of mine? If anything chance otherwise than well I must answer for all".

Now the Turk unto whom this Patrone Norado was indebted, missing him (supposed to be aboard of our ship), presently went unto the King and told him that he thought that his pledge Patrone Norado was aboard of the English ship. Whereupon the King presently sent a boat aboard of us, with three men in her, commanding the said Sonnings to come ashore, and not speaking anything as touching the man. He said that he would come presently in his own boat; but as soon as they were gone he willed us to warp forth the ship, and said that he would see the knaves hanged before he would go ashore. And when the King saw that he came not ashore, but still continued warping away the ship, he straight commanded the gunner of the bulwark next unto us to shoot three shots without ball. Then we came all to the said Sonnings and asked of him what the matter was that we were shot at. He said that it was the janissaries who would have the oil ashore again, and willed us to make haste away.

And after that he had discharged three shots without ball, he commanded all the gunners in the town to do their endeavour to sink us, but the Turkish gunners could not once strike us. Wherefore the King sent presently to the Bagnio (this Bagnio is the prison whereas all the captives lay at night), and promised, if that there were any that could either sink us or else cause us to come in again, he should have a hundred crowns and his liberty. With that came forth a Spaniard called Sebastian, which had been an old servitor in Flanders, and he said that, upon the performance of that promise, he would undertake either to sink us or to cause us to come in again, and thereto he would gage his life. And at the first shot he split our rudder's head in pieces, and the second shot he struck us under the water and the third shot he shot us through our foremast with a culverin shot; and thus he having rent both our rudder and mast, and shot us under water, we were enforced to go in again.

This Sebastian, for all his diligence herein, had neither his liberty nor a hundred crowns so promised by the said King, but after his service done was committed again to prison, whereby may appear the regard that the Turk or infidel hath of his word, although he be able to perform it, yea more, though he be a king.

Then our merchants seeing no remedy, they together with five of our company went ashore, and then they ceased shooting. They shot unto us in the whole nine and thirty shots, without the hurt of any man. And when our merchants came ashore, the King commanded presently that they, with the rest of our company that were with them, should be chained four and four to a hundredweight of iron. And when we came in with the ship, there came presently above a hundred Turks aboard of us, and they searched us, and stripped our very clothes from our backs, and broke open our chests, and made a spoil of all that we had; and the Christian caitiffs likewise that came aboard of us made spoil of our goods, and used us as ill as the Turks did.

And our master's mate having a Geneva Bible in his hand, there came the King's chief gunner and took it out from him, who showed me of it; and I, having the language, went presently to the King's Treasurer and told him of it, saying that sith it was the will of God that we should fall into their hands, yet that they should grant us to use our consciences to our own discretion, as they suffered the Spaniards and other nations to use theirs. And he granted us. Then I told him that the master gunner had taken away a Bible from one of our men. The Treasurer went presently and commanded him to deliver up the Bible again, which he did; and within a little after he took it from the man again, and I showed the Treasurer of it and presently he commanded him to deliver it again, saying "Thou villain, wilt thou turn to Christianity again?" For he was a renegado, which is one that first was a Christian and afterwards becometh a Turk; and so he delivered me the Bible the second time. And then, I having it in my hand, the gunner came to me and spoke these words, saying "Thou dog, I will have the book in despite of thee", and took it from me, saying "If thou tell the King's Treasurer of it any more, by Mahomet I will be revenged of thee". Notwithstanding, I went the third time unto the King's Treasurer and told him of it, and he came with me, saying thus to the gunner, "By the head of the Great Turk, if thou take it from him again thou shalt have a hundred bastinadoes". And forthwith he delivered me the book, saying he had not the value of a pin of the spoil of the ship, which was the better for him, as hereafter you shall hear. For there was none, neither Christian nor Turk, that took the value of a pennyworth of our goods from us, but perished both body and goods within seventeen months following, as hereafter shall plainly appear.

Then came the Guardian Basha, which is the keeper of the King's captives, to fetch us all ashore. And then I, remembering the miserable estate of poor distressed captives in the time of their bondage to those infidels, went to my own chest and took out thereof a jar of oil, and filled a basket full of white rusk to carry ashore with me, but before I came to the Bagnio the Turkish boys had taken away almost all my bread, and the Keeper said "Deliver me the jar of oil, and when thou comest to the Bagnio thou shalt have it again"; but I never had it of him any more.

But when I came to the Bagnio, and saw our merchants and all the rest of our company in chains, and we all ready to receive the same reward, what heart in the world is so hard but would have pitied our cause, hearing or seeing the lamentable greeting there was betwixt us. All this happened the first of May 1584.

And the second day of the same month the King with all his council sat in judgment upon us. The first that were had forth to be arraigned were the factors and the masters, and the King asked them wherefore they came not ashore when he sent for them. And Romaine Sonnings answered that though he were king on shore and might command there, so was he as touching those that were under him; and therefore said, "If any offence be, the fault is wholly in myself and in no other".

Then forthwith the King gave judgment, that the said Romaine Sonnings should be hanged over the north-east bulwark from whence he conveyed the forenamed Patrone Norado; and then he called for our master, Andrew Dyer, and used few words to him and so condemned him to be hanged over the walls of the westermost bulwark.

Then fell our other factor, named Richard Skegs, upon his knees before the King, and said "I beseech Your Highness either to pardon our Master or else suffer me to die for him, for he is ignorant of this cause". And then the people of that country, favouring the said Richard Skegs, besought the King to pardon them both. So then the King spoke these words, "Behold, for thy sake I pardon the Master". Then presently the Turks shouted and cried, saying "Away with the Master from the presence of the King". And then he came into the Bagnio whereas we were and told us what had happened, and we all rejoiced at the good hap of Master Skegs, that he was saved, and our Master for his sake.

But afterward our joy was turned to double sorrow, for in the meantime the King's mind was altered, for that one of his council had advised him that, unless the master died also, by the law they could not confiscate the ship nor goods, neither captive any of the men. Whereupon the King sent for our Master again and gave him another judgment after his pardon for one cause, which was that he should be hanged. Here all true Christians may see what trust a Christian man may put in an infidel's promise, who, being a king, pardoned a man now, as you have heard, and within an hour after hanged him for the same cause before a whole multitude; and also promised our factors their oils custom-free and at their going away made them pay the uttermost penny for the custom thereof.

And when that Romaine Sonnings saw no remedy but that he should die, he protested to turn Turk, hoping thereby to have saved his life. Then said the Turk, "If thou wilt turn Turk, speak the words that thereunto belong"; and he did so. Then said they unto him, "Now thou shalt die in the faith of a Turk", and so he did, as the Turks reported that were at his execution. And the forenamed Patrone Norado, whereas before he had liberty and did nothing, he then was condemned slave perpetual except there were payment made of the foresaid sum of money.

Then the King condemned us all, who were in number six and twenty: of the which, two were hanged as you have heard, and one died the first day we came on shore by the visitation of Almighty God; and the other three and twenty he condemned slaves perpetually unto the Great Turk, and the ship and goods were confiscated to the use of the Great Turk. And then we all fell down upon our knees, giving God thanks for this sorrowful visitation and giving ourselves wholly to the almighty power of God, unto whom all secrets are known, that He of His goodness would vouchsafe to look on us.

Here may all true Christian hearts see the wonderful works of God shown upon such infidels, blasphemers, whoremasters, and renegade Christians; and so you shall read, in the end of this book, of the like upon the unfaithful King and all his children, and of as many as took any portion of the said goods.

But first to show our miserable bondage and slavery, and unto what small pittance and allowance we were tied: for every five men had allowance but five *aspers* of bread in a day, which is but twopence English; and our lodging was to lie on the bare boards with a very simple cape to cover us. We were also forcibly and most violently shaven, head and beard. And within three days after I and six more of my fellows, together with fourscore Italians and Spaniards, were sent forth in a galliot to take a Greekish caramoussal, which came into Africa to steal negroes; and went out of Tripoli unto that place, which was two hundred and forty leagues thence. But we were chained three and three to an oar, and we rowed naked above the girdle; and the boatswain of the galley walked abaft the mast and his mate afore the mast, and each of them a bull's pizzle dried in their hands, and when their devilish choler rose they would strike the Christians for no cause. And they allowed us but half a pound of bread a man in a day without any other kind of sustenance, water excepted. And when we came to the place whereas we saw the caramoussal, we were not suffered to have neither needle, bodkin, knife, or any other weapon about us, nor at any other time in the night, upon pain of one hundred bastinadoes. We were then also cruelly manacled in such sort that we could not put our hands the length of one foot asunder the one from the other, and every night they searched our chains three times to see if they were fast riveted. We continued fight with the caramoussal three hours, and then we took it, and lost but two of our men in that fight; but there were slain of the Greeks five, and fourteen were cruelly hurt, and they that were sound were presently made slaves and chained to the oars; and within fifteen days after we returned again into Tripoli, and then we were put to all manner of slavery. I was put to hew stones and other to carry stones, and some to draw the cart with earth, and some to make mortar and some to draw stones, for at that time the Turks built a church; and thus we were put to all kind of slavery that was to be done. And in the time of our being there the Moors that are the husbandmen of the country rebelled against the King, because he would have constrained them to pay greater tribute than heretofore they had done, so that the soldiers of Tripoli marched forth of the town to have joined battle against the Moors for their rebellion; and the King sent with them four pieces of ordnance, which were drawn by the captives twenty miles into the country after them, and at the sight thereof the Moors fled and then the captains returned back again. Then I and certain Christians more were sent twelve miles into the country with a cart to load timber, and we returned again the same day.

Now the King had 18 captives which three times a week went to fetch wood thirty miles from the town; and on a time he appointed me for one of the 18, and we departed at eight of the clock in the night. And upon the way, as we rode upon the camels, I demanded of one of our company who did direct us the way. He said that there was a Moor in our company which was our guide. And I demanded of them how Tripoli and the wood bore one off the other; and he said east-north-east and west-south-west. And at midnight or near thereabouts, as I was riding upon my camel I fell asleep, and the guide and all the rest rode away from me, not thinking but I had been among them. When I awoke, and finding myself alone durst not call nor halloo for fear lest the wild Moors should hear me (because they hold this opinion that in killing a Christian they do God good service); and musing with myself what were best for me to do (if I should go forth and the wild Moors should hap to meet with me they would kill me; and, on the other side, if I should return back to Tripoli without any wood or company I should be most miserably used): therefore, of two evils, rather I had to go forth to the losing of my life than to turn back and trust to their mercy, fearing to be used as before I had seen others. For understanding by some of my company before how Tripoli and the said wood did lie one off another, by the north star I went forth at adventure and, as God would have it, I came right to the place where they were even about an hour before day. There all together we rested and gave our camels provender, and as soon as the day appeared we rode all into the wood; and I seeing no wood there but a stick here and a stick there, about the bigness of a man's arm, growing in the sand, it caused me to marvel how so many camels should be loaded in that place. The wood was juniper; we needed no axe nor edge-tool to cut it, but plucked it up by strength of hands roots and all, which a man might easily do, and so gathered it together, a little at one place and so at another, and laded our camels and came home about seven of the clock that night following. Because I fell lame, and my camel was tired, I left my wood in the way.

There was in Tripoli that time a Venetian, whose name was Benedetto Venetiano, and seventeen captives more of his company, which ran away from Tripoli in a boat and came in sight of an island called Malta, which lieth forty leagues from Tripoli right north. And being within a mile of the shore, and very fair weather, one of their company said "In dispetto di Dio adesso venio a pigliar terra", which is as much to say "In the despite of God I shall now fetch the shore". And presently there arose a mighty storm, with thunder and rain and the wind at north, their boat being very small, so that they were enforced to bear up room and to shear right afore the wind over against the coast of Barbary from whence they came; and rowing up and down the coast, their victuals being spent, the 21st day after their departure they were enforced through the want of food to come ashore, thinking to have stolen some sheep. But the Moors of the country, very craftily perceiving their intent, gathered together a threescore horsemen and hid themselves behind a sandy hill; and when the Christians were come all ashore and passed up half a mile into the country, the Moors rode betwixt them and their boat and some of them pursued the Christians, and so they were all taken and brought to Tripoli from whence they had before escaped. And presently the King commanded that the foresaid Benedetto with one more of his company should lose their ears and the rest should be most cruelly beaten, which was presently done.

This King had a son which was a ruler in an island called Jerba, whereunto arrived an English ship called the *Green Dragon,* of the which was master one Master Blonket, who having a very unhappy boy in that ship and understanding that whosoever would turn Turk should be well entertained of the King's son, this boy did run ashore and voluntarily turned Turk. Shortly after the King's son came to Tripoli to visit his father and, seeing our company, he greatly fancied Richard Burges, our purser, and James Smith. They were both young men, therefore he was very desirous to have them to turn Turks, but they would not yield to his desire, saying "We are your father's slaves, and as slaves we will serve him". Then his father the King sent for them and asked them if they would turn Turks. And they said, "If it please Your Highness, Christians we were born, and so we will remain", and besought the King that they might not be enforced thereto. The King had there before in his house a son of a yeoman of our Queen's Guard, whom the King's son had enforced to turn Turk. His name was John Nelson. Him the King caused to be brought to these young men, and then said unto them, "Will not you bear this your countryman company, and be Turk as he is?" And they said that they would not yield thereto during life. But it fell out that within a month after the King's son went home to Jerba again, being six score miles from Tripoli, and carried our two foresaid young men with him, which were Richard Burges and James Smith; and after their departure they sent us a letter, signifying that there was no violence showed unto them as yet. But within three days after they were violently used, for that the King's son demanded of them again if that they would turn Turk. Then answered Richard Burges, "A Christian I am, and so I will remain". Then the King's son very angrily said unto him, "By Mahomet, thou shalt presently be made Turk". Then called he for his men and commanded them to make him Turk, and they did so, and circumcised him, and would have had him speak the words that thereunto belonged, but he answered them stoutly that he would not; and although they had put on him the habit of a Turk, yet said he, "A Christian I was born and so I will remain, though you force me to do otherwise". And then he called for the other, and commanded him to be made Turk perforce also. But he was very strong, for it was so much as eight of the King's son's men could do to hold him; so in the end they circumcised him and made him Turk. Now to pass over a little, and so to show the manner of our deliverance out of that miserable captivity.

In May aforesaid, shortly after our apprehension, I wrote a letter into England unto my father dwelling in Tavistock in Devonshire, signifying unto him the whole estate of our calamities; and I wrote also to Constantinople, to the English ambassador, both which letters were faithfully delivered. But when my father had received my letter, and understood the truth of our mishap and the occasion thereof, and what had happened to the offenders, he certified the Right Honourable the Earl of Bedford thereof, who in short space acquainted Her Highness with the whole cause thereof; and Her Majesty, like a most merciful princess tendering her subjects, presently took order for our deliverance. Whereupon the Right Worshipful Sir Edward Osborne, knight, directed his letters with all speed to the English ambassador in Constantinople to procure our delivery; and he obtained the Great Turk's commission, and sent it forthwith to Tripoli by one Master Edward Barton, together with a justice of the Great Turk's, and one soldier, and another Turk, and a Greek which was his interpreter, which could speak, besides Greek, Turkish, Italian, Spanish, and English. And when they came to Tripoli they were well entertained. And the first night they did lie in a captain's house in the town. All our company that were in Tripoli came that night for joy to Master Barton and the other commissioners to see them. Then Master Barton said unto us, "Welcome, my good countymen", and lovingly entertained us, and at our departure from him he gave us two shillings and said, "Serve God, for tomorrow I hope you shall be as free as ever you were". We all gave him thanks and so departed.

The next day in the morning very early the King, having intelligence of their coming, sent word to the keeper that none of the Englishmen, meaning our company, should go to work. Then he sent for Master Barton and the other commissioners and demanded of the said Master Barton his message. The justice answered that the Great Turk his sovereign had sent them unto him, signifying that he was informed that a certain English ship, called the *Jesus*, was by him the said King confiscated about twelve months since, "and now my said Sovereign hath here sent his especial commission by us unto you for the deliverance of the said ship and goods, and also the free liberty and deliverance of the Englishmen of the same ship whom you have taken and kept in captivity". And further the same justice said, "I am authorised by my said sovereign, the Great Turk, to see it done; and therefore I command you, by virtue of this commission, presently to make restitution of the premisses or the value thereof"; and so did the justices deliver unto the King the Great Turk's commission to the effect aforesaid, which commission the King with all obedience received. And after the perusing of the same he forthwith commanded all the English captives to be brought before him, and then willed the keeper to strike off all our irons. Which done, the King said, "You Englishmen, for that you did offend the laws of this place, by the same laws therefore some of your company were condemned to die, as you know, and you to be perpetual captives during your lives. Notwithstanding, seeing it hath pleased my sovereign lord the Great Turk to pardon your said offences and to give you your freedom and liberty, behold, here I make delivery of you to this English gentleman". So he delivered us all that were there, being thirteen in number, to Master Barton, who required also those two young men which the King's son had taken with him. Then the King answered that it was against their law to deliver them, for that they were turned Turks; and touching the ship and goods, the King said that he had sold her, but would make restitution of the value, and as much of the goods as came into his hands. And so the King arose and went to dinner, and commanded a Jew to go with Master Barton and the other commissioners, to show them their lodging, which was a house provided and appointed them by the said King. And because I had the Italian and Spanish tongues, by which their most traffic in that country is, Master Barton made me his caterer to buy his victuals for him and his company, and delivered me money needful for the same. Thus were we set at liberty the 28th day of April 1585.

Now to return to the King's plagues and punishments, which Almighty God at His will and pleasure sendeth upon men in the sight of the world, and likewise of the plagues that befell his children and others aforesaid. First when we were made bondmen, being the second day of May 1584, the King had 300 captives, and before the month was expired there died of them of the plague 150. And whereas there were 26 men of our company, of whom two were hanged and one died the same day that we were made bondslaves, that present month there died nine more of our company of the plague, and other two were forced to turn Turks as before is rehearsed; and on the fourth day of June next following the King lost 150 camels which were taken from him by the wild Moors; and on the 28th day of the said month of June one Geoffrey Maltese, a renegado of Malta, ran away to his country, and stole a brigantine which the King had built for to take the Christians withal, and carried with him twelve Christians more which were the King's captives. Afterwards about the tenth day of July next following, the King rode forth upon the greatest and fairest mare that might be seen, as white as any swan. He had not ridden forty paces from his house but on a sudden the same mare fell down under him stark dead, and I with six more were commanded to bury her, skin, shoes, and all, which we did.

And about three months after our delivery, Master Barton, with all the residue of his company, departed from Tripoli to Zante in a vessel, called a *settea*, of one Marcus Segoorus who dwelt in Zante; and after our arrival in Zante we remained fifteen days there aboard our vessel before we could have *platego* (that is, leave to come ashore), because the plague was in that place from whence we came. And about three days after we came ashore thither came another *settea* of Marseilles bound for Constantinople. Then did Master Barton and his company, with two more of our company, ship themselves as passengers in the same *settea* and went to Constantinople. But the other nine of us, that remained in Zante, about three months after shipped ourselves in a ship of the said Marcus Segoorus, which came to Zante and was bound for England. In which three months the soldiers of Tripoli killed the said King. And then the King's son, according to the custom there, went to Constantinople to surrender up all his father's treasure, goods, captives, and concubines unto the Great Turk, and took with him our said purser Richard Burges, and James Smith, and also the other two Englishmen which he, the said King's son, had enforced to become Turks as is aforesaid. And they, the said Englishmen, finding now some opportunity, concluded with the Christian captives which were going with them unto Constantinople, being in number about one hundred and fifty, to kill the King's son and all the Turks which were aboard of the galley; and privily the said Englishmen conveyed unto the said Christian captives weapons for that purpose. And when they came into the main sea toward Constantinople, upon the faithful promise of the said Christian captives these four Englishmen leapt suddenly into the *crossia*, that is into the midst of the galley, where the cannon lieth, and with their swords drawn did fight against all the foresaid Turks; and for want of help of the said Christian captives, who falsely broke their promises, the said Master Blonket's boy was killed and the said James Smith, and our purser Richard Burges and the other Englishman were taken and bound into chains, to be hanged at their arrival in Constantinople.

And as the Lord's will was, about two days after, passing through the Gulf of Venice, at an island called Cephalonia, they met with two of the Duke of Venice's galleys, which took that galley, and killed the King's son and his mother, and all the Turks that were there, in number 150; and they saved the Christian captives, and would have killed the two Englishmen because they were circumcised and become Turks, had not the other Christian captives excused them, saying that they were enforced to be Turks by the King's son, and showed the Venetians also how they did enterprise at sea to fight against all the Turks, and that their two fellows were slain in that fight. Then the Venetians saved them, and they, with all the residue of the said captives, had their liberty, which were in number 150 or thereabouts; and the said galley and all the Turks' treasure was confiscated to the use of the state of Venice.

And from thence our two Englishmen travelled homeward by land; and in this meantime we had one more of our company which died in Zante, and afterward the other eight shipped themselves at Zante in a ship of the said Marcus Segoorus which was bound for England. And before we departed thence there arrived the *Ascension* and the *George Bonaventure* of London in Cephalonia, in a harbour there called Argostoli, whose merchants agreed with the merchants of our ship, and so laded all the merchandise of our ship into the said ships of London, who took us eight in as passengers, and so we came home; and within two months after our arrival at London, our said purser Richard Burges and his fellow came home also. For the which we are bound to praise Almighty God during our lives, and as duty bindeth us to pray for the preservation of our most gracious Queen, for the great care Her Majesty had over us, her poor subjects, in seeking and procuring of our deliverance aforesaid, and also for her honourable Privy Council; and I especial for the prosperity and good estate of the house of the late deceased the Right Honourable the Earl of Bedford, whose honour, I must confess, most diligently at the suit of my father, now departed, travailed herein. For the which I rest continually bound to him, whose soul I doubt not but is already in the heavens in joy with the Almighty; unto which place He vouchsafe to bring us all, that for our sins suffered most vile and shameful death upon the cross, there to live perpetually world without end, Amen.

The voyage of Master Ralph Fitch, merchant of London, by the way of Tripolis in Syria to Ormuz, and so to Goa in the East India, to Cambaia, and all the kingdom of Zelabdim Akbar the Great Mogul to the mighty River Ganges and down to Bengala, to Bacola, and Chondery, to Pegu, to Jamahey in the kingdom of Siam, and back to Pegu, and from thence to Malacca, Ceylon, Cochin, and all the coast of the East India, begun in the year of Our Lord 1583 and ended 1591; wherein the strange rites, manners, and customs of those people, and the exceeding rich trade and commodities of those countries are faithfully set down and diligently described by the aforesaid Master Ralph Fitch.

IN the year of Our Lord 1583 I, Ralph Fitch of London, merchant, being desirous to see the countries of the East India in the company of Master John Newbery, merchant, which had been at Ormuz once before, of William Leeds, jeweller, and James Story, painter, being chiefly set forth by the Right Worshipful Sir Edward Osborne, knight, and Master Richard Staper, citizens and merchants of London, did ship myself in a ship of London called the *Tiger*, wherein we went for Tripolis in Syria; and from thence we took the way for Aleppo, which we went in seven days with the caravan. Being in Aleppo, and finding good company, we went from thence to Birra, which is two days and a half travel with camels.

Birra is a little town, but very plentiful of victuals; and near to the wall of the town runneth the river of Euphrates. Here we bought a boat, and agreed with a master and bargemen, for to go to Babylon. These boats be but for one voyage; for the stream doth run so fast downwards that they cannot return. They carry you to a town which they call Falluja, and there you sell the boat for a little money, for that which cost you fifty at Birra you sell there for seven or eight. From Birra to Falluja is sixteen days' journey; it is not good that one boat go alone, for if it should chance to break you should have much ado to save your goods from the Arabians which be always there abouts robbing, and in the night, when your boats be made fast, it is necessary that you keep good watch. For the Arabians that be thieves will come swimming and steal your goods and flee away, against which a gun is very good, for they do fear it very much. In the river of Euphrates from Birra to Falluja there be certain places where you pay custom, so many *medines* for a *some*, or camel's lading, and certain raisins and soap which is for the sons of Abu Rish, which is lord of the Arabians and all that great desert, and hath some villages upon the river. Falluja, where you unlade your goods which come from Birra, is a little village, from whence you go to Babylon in a day.

Babylon is a town not very great but very populous and of great traffic of strangers, for that it is the way to Persia, Turkia, and Arabia, and from thence do go caravans for these and other places. Here are great store of victuals, which come from Armenia down the river of Tigris. They are brought upon rafts made of goats' skins blown full of wind and boards laid upon them; and thereupon they lade their goods which are brought down to Babylon, which being discharged they open their skins, and carry them back by camels to serve another time. Babylon in times past did belong to the kingdom of Persia, but now is subject to the Turk. Over against Babylon there is a very fair village from whence you pass to Babylon upon a long bridge made of boats and tied to a great chain of iron which is made fast on either side of the river. When any boats are to pass up or down the river they take away certain of the boats until they be past.

The tower of Babel is built on this side the River Tigris, towards Arabia from the town seven or eight miles, which tower is ruinated on all sides, and with the fall thereof hath made as it were a little mountain, so that it hath no shape at all. It was made of bricks dried in the sun, and certain canes and leaves of the palm tree laid betwixt the bricks. There is no entrance to be seen to go into it. It doth stand upon a great plain betwixt the rivers of Euphrates and Tigris.

By the River Euphrates two days' journey from Babylon at a place called Heit, in a field near unto it, is a strange thing to see: a mouth that doth continually throw forth against the air boiling pitch with a filthy smoke, which pitch doth run abroad into a great field which is always full thereof. The Moors say that it is the mouth of hell. By reason of the great quantity of it the men of that country do pitch their boats two or three inches thick on the outside, so that no water doth enter into them. Their boats be called *danec*. When there is great store of water in Tigris you may go from Babylon to Basra in 8 or 9 days; if there be small store it will cost you the more days.

Basra in times past was under the Arabians but now is subject to the Turk. But some of them the Turk cannot subdue, for that they hold certain islands in the River Euphrates which the Turk cannot win of them. They be thieves all and have no settled dwelling, but remove from place to place with their camels, goats, and horses, wives and children and all. They have large blue gowns, their wives' ears and noses are ringed very full of rings of copper and silver, and they wear rings of copper about their legs.

Basra standeth near the Gulf of Persia, and is a town of great trade of spices and drugs which come from Ormuz. Also there is great store of wheat, rice, and dates growing thereabout, wherewith they serve Babylon and all the country, Ormuz, and all the parts of India. I went from Basra to Ormuz down the Gulf of Persia in a certain ship made of boards and sewn together with *cayro*, which is thread made of the husks of cocos, and certain canes or straw leaves sewn upon the seams of the boards, which is the cause that they leak very much. And so, having Persia always on the left hand and the coast of Arabia on the right hand, we passed many islands, and among others the famous island Bahrein from whence come the best pearls, which be round and orient.

Ormuz is an island in circuit about five and twenty or thirty miles, and is the driest island in the world, for there is nothing growing in it but only salt. For their water, wood, or victuals, and all things necessary, come out of Persia, which is about twelve miles from thence. All the islands thereabout be very fruitful, from whence all kind of victuals are sent unto Ormuz. The Portugals have a castle here which standeth near unto the sea, wherein there is a captain for the King of Portugal having under him a convenient number of soldiers, whereof some part remain in the castle and some in the town. In this town are merchants of all nations, and many Moors and gentiles. Here is very great trade of all sorts of spices, drugs, silk, cloth of silk, fine tapestry of Persia, great store of pearls which come from the Isle of Bahrein and are the best pearls of all others, and many horses of Persia which serve all India. They have a Moor to their king, which is chosen and governed by the Portugals. Their women are very strangely attired, wearing on their noses, ears, necks, arms, and legs many rings set with jewels, and locks of silver and gold in their ears, and a long bar of gold upon the side of their noses. Their ears with the weight of their jewels be worn so wide that a man may thrust three of his fingers into them.

Here very shortly after our arrival we were put in prison, and had part of our goods taken from us by the Captain of the castle, whose name was Don Mathias de Albuquerque; and from hence the eleventh of October he shipped us and sent us for Goa unto the Viceroy, which at that time was Don Francisco de Mascarenhas. The ship wherein we were embarked for Goa belonged to the Captain, and carried one hundred twenty and four horses in it. All merchandise carried to Goa in a ship wherein are horses pay no custom to Goa. The horses pay custom, the goods pay nothing; but if you come in a ship which bringeth no horses you are then to pay eight in the hundred for your goods.

The first city of India that we arrived at, upon the fifth of November, after we had passed the coast of Sind, is called Diu, which standeth in an island in the kingdom of Cambaia and is the strongest town that the Portugals have in those parts. It is but little, but well stored with merchandise; for here they lade many great ships with divers commodities for the Straits of Mecca, for Ormuz, and other places, and these be ships of the Moors and of Christians, but the Moors cannot pass except they have a passport from the Portugals. Cambaietta is the chief city of that province, which is great and very populous, and fairly built for a town of the gentiles; but if there happen any famine the people will sell their children for very little. The last king of Cambaia was Sultan Badu, which was killed at the siege of Diu, and shortly after his city was taken by the Great Mogul, which is the king of Agra and of Delhi which are forty days' journey from the country of Cambaia. Here the women wear upon their arms infinite numbers of rings made of elephants' teeth, wherein they take so much delight that they had rather be without their meat than without their bracelets.

Going from Diu we come to Daman, the second town of the Portugals in the country of Cambaia, which is distant from Diu forty leagues. Here is no trade but of corn and rice. They have many villages under them which they quietly possess in time of peace, but in time of war the enemy is master of them. From thence we passed by Bassein, and from Bassein to Thana, at both which places is small trade but only of corn and rice. The tenth of November we arrived at Chaul, which standeth in the firm land. There be two towns, the one belonging to the Portugals and the other to the Moors. That of the Portugals is nearest to the sea and commandeth the bay, and is walled round about. A little above that is the town of the Moors, which is governed by a Moor king called Zamaluco. Here is great traffic for all sorts of spices and drugs, silk and cloth of silk, sandals, elephants' teeth, and much China work, and much sugar which is made of the nut called *gagara*. The tree is called the palmer, which is the profitablest tree in the world. It doth always bear fruit, and doth yield wine, oil, sugar, vinegar, cords, coals; of the leaves are made thatch for the houses, sails for ships, mats to sit or lie on; of the branches they make their houses and brooms to sweep, of the tree wood for ships. The wine doth issue out of the top of the tree. They cut a branch of a bough, and bind it hard, and hang an earthen pot upon it which they empty every morning and every evening, and still it and put in certain dried raisins, and it becometh very strong wine in short time. Hither many ships come from all parts of India, Ormuz, and many from Mecca. Here be many Moors and gentiles. They have a very strange order among them: they worship a cow, and esteem much of the cow's dung to paint the walls of their houses. They will kill nothing, not so much as a louse; for they hold it a sin to kill anything. They eat no flesh, but live by roots and rice and milk. And when the husband dieth his wife is burned with him if she be alive; if she will not, her head is shaven and then is never any account made of her after. They say if they should be buried it were a great sin, for of their bodies would come many worms and other vermin, and when their bodies were consumed those worms would lack sustenance, which were a sin, therefore they will be burned. In Cambaia they will kill nothing, nor have anything killed. In the town they have hospitals to keep lame dogs and cats, and for birds. They will give meat to the ants.

Goa is the most principal city which the Portugals have in India, wherein the Viceroy remaineth with his court. It standeth in an island, which may be 25 or 30 miles about. It is a fine city, and for an Indian town very fair. The island is very fair, full of orchards and gardens and many palmer trees, and hath some villages. Here be many merchants of all nations; and the fleet which cometh every year from Portugal, which be four, five, or six great ships, cometh first hither. And they come for the most part in September, and remain there forty or fifty days, and then go to Cochin, where they lade their pepper for Portugal. Oftentimes they lade one in Goa, the rest go to Cochin which is from Goa a hundred leagues southward. Goa standeth in the country of Hidalcan, who lieth in the country six or seven days' journey. His chief city is called Bijapur.

At our coming we were cast into the prison, and examined before the Justice and demanded for letters, and were charged to be spies, but they could prove nothing by us. We continued in prison until the two and twentieth of December, and then we were set at liberty, putting in sureties for two thousand ducats not to depart the town; which sureties Father Stevens, an English Jesuit which we found there, and another religious man, a friend of his, procured for us. Our surety's name was Andreas Taborer, to whom we paid 2150 ducats, and still he demanded more; whereupon we made suit to the Viceroy and Justice to have our money again, considering that they had had it in their hands near five months and could prove nothing against us. The Viceroy made us a very sharp answer, and said we should be better sifted before it were long and that they had further matter against us. Whereupon we presently determined rather to seek our liberties than to be in danger for ever to be slaves in the country, for it was told us we should have the strappado. Whereupon presently, the fifth day of April 1585 in the morning, we ran from thence; and being set over the river we went two days on foot, not without fear, not knowing the way nor having any guide, for we durst trust none.

One of the first towns which we came unto is called Belgaum, where there is a great market kept of diamonds, rubies, sapphires, and many other soft stones. From Belgaum we went to Bijapur, which is a very great town where the King doth keep his court. He hath many gentiles in his court and they be great idolaters; and they have their idols standing in the woods which they call pagodas. Some be like a cow, some like a monkey, some like buffaloes, some like peacocks, and some like the devil. Here be very many elephants which they go to war withal. Here they have good store of gold and silver; their houses are of stone, very fair and high. From hence we went for Golconda, the King whereof is called Cutup-de-lashach. Here, and in the kingdom of Hidalcan and in the country of the King of Deccan, be the diamonds found of the old water. It is a very fair town, pleasant, with fair houses of brick and timber. It aboundeth with great store of fruits and fresh water. Here the men and the women do go with a cloth bound

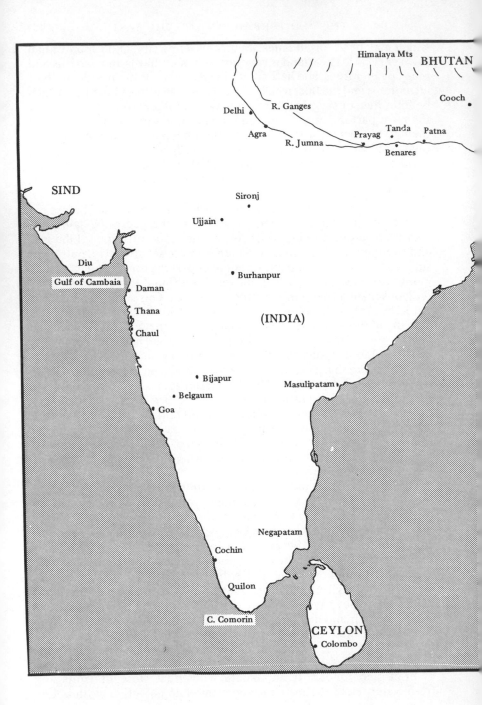

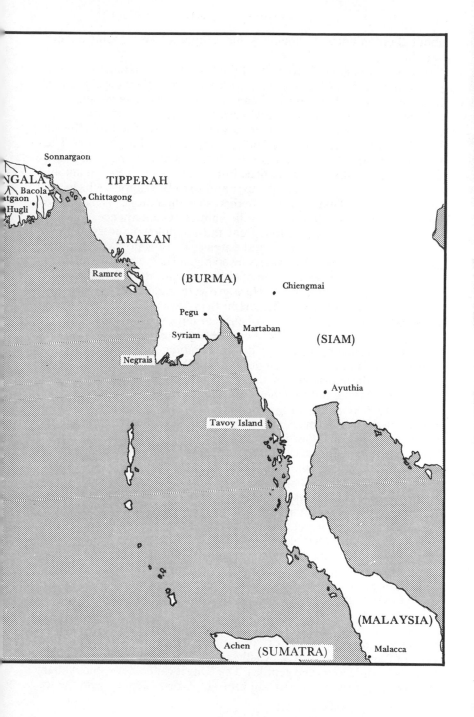

about their middles without any more apparel. We found it here very hot.

The winter beginneth here about the last of May. In these parts is a port or haven called Masulipatam, which standeth eight days' journey from hence toward the Gulf of Bengala, whither come many ships out of India, Pegu, and Sumatra, very richly laden with pepper, spices, and other commodities. The country is very good and fruitful. From thence I went to Servidore, which is a fine country, and the king is called The King of Bread. The houses here be all thatched and made of loam. Here be many Moors and gentiles, but there is small religion among them. From thence I went to Balapur and so to Burhanpur, which is in the country of Zelabdim Akbar. In this place their money is made of a kind of silver round and thick, to the value of twenty pence, which is very good silver. It is marvellous great and a populous country. In their winter, which is in June, July, and August, there is no passing in the streets but with horses, the waters be so high. The houses are made of loam and thatched. Here is great store of cotton cloth made, and painted cloths of cotton-wool. Here groweth great store of corn and rice. We found marriages great store both in towns and villages in many places where we passed, of boys of eight or ten years and girls of five or six years old. They both do ride upon one horse very trimly decked, and are carried through the town with great piping and playing, and so return home and eat of a banquet made of rice and fruits, and there they dance the most part of the night and so make an end of the marriage. They lie not together until they be ten years old. They say they marry their children so young because it is an order that when the man dieth the woman must be burned with him; so that if the father die, yet they may have a father-in-law to help to bring up the children which be married; and also that they will not leave their sons without wives nor their daughters without husbands.

From thence we went to Mandoway, which is a very strong town. It was besieged twelve years by Zelabdim Akbar before he could win it. It standeth upon a very great high rock, as the most part of their castles do, and was of a very great circuit. From hence we went to Ujjain and Sironj, where we overtook the ambassador of Zelabdim Akbar with a marvellous great company of men, elephants and camels. Here is great trade of cotton and cloth made of cotton, and great store of drugs. From thence we went to Agra, passing many rivers, which by reason of the rain were so swollen that we waded and swam oftentimes for our lives.

Agra is a very great city and populous, built with stone, having fair and large streets, with a fair river running by it which falleth into the Gulf of Bengala. It hath a fair castle and a strong, with a very fair ditch. Here be many Moors and gentiles. The King is called Zelabdim Akbar; the people for the most part call him The Great Mogul. From thence we went for Fatehpur, which is the place where the King kept his court. The town is greater than Agra, but the houses and streets be not so fair. Here dwell many people, both Moors and gentiles. The King hath in Agra and Fatehpur as they do credibly report 1000 elephants, thirty thousand horses, 1400 tame deer, 800 concubines; such store of ounces, tigers, buffaloes, cocks, and hawks that is very strange to see. He keepeth a great court, which they call *dericcan*. Agra and Fatehpur are two very great cities, either of them much greater than London and very populous. Between Agra and Fatehpur are 12 miles, and all the way is a market of victuals and other things, as full as though a man were still in a town and so many people as if a man were in a market. They have many fine carts, and many of them carved and gilded with gold, with two wheels, which be drawn with two little bulls about the bigness of our great dogs in England, and they will run with any horse and carry two or three men in one of these carts. They are covered with silk or very fine cloth, and be used here as our coaches be in England. Hither is great resort of merchants from Persia and out of India, and very much merchandise of silk and cloth and of precious stones, both rubies, diamonds, and pearls. The King is apparelled in a white *cabie* made like a shirt tied with strings on the one side, and a little cloth on his head coloured oftentimes with red or yellow. None come into the house but his eunuchs which keep his women.

Here in Fatehpur we stayed all three until the 28th of September 1585, and then Master John Newbery took his journey toward the city of Lahore, determining from thence to go for Persia and then for Aleppo or Constantinople, whether he could get soonest passage to, and directed me to go for Bengala and for Pegu, and did promise me, if it pleased God, to meet me in Bengala within two years with a ship out of England. I left William Leeds the jeweller in service with the King Zelabdim Akbar in Fatehpur, who did entertain him very well, and gave him a house and five slaves, a horse, and every day six shillings in money. I went from Agra to Satgaon in Bengala in the company of one hundred and fourscore boats laden with salt, opium, hing, lead, carpets, and divers other commodities, down the River Jumna. The chief merchants are Moors and gentiles. In these countries they have many strange ceremonies. The Brahmins, which are their priests, come to the water, and have a string about their necks made with great ceremonies, and lade up water with both their hands, and turn the string first with both their hands within and then one arm after the other out. Though it be never so cold they will wash themselves in cold water or in warm. These gentiles will eat no flesh nor kill anything. They live with rice, butter, milk, and fruits. They pray in the water naked, and dress their meat and eat it naked, and for their penance they lie flat upon the earth and rise up and turn themselves about 30 or 40 times, and use to heave up their hands to the sun, and to kiss the earth with their arms and legs stretched along out, and their right leg always before the left. Every time they lie down they make a score on the ground with their finger to know when their stint is finished. The Brahmins mark themselves in the foreheads, ears, and throats with a kind of yellow gear which they grind, and every morning they do it; and they have some old men which go in the streets with a box of yellow powder, and mark men on their heads and necks as they meet them. And their wives do come by 10, 20, and 30 together to the waterside singing, and there do wash themselves, and then use their ceremonies, and mark themselves in their foreheads and faces, and carry some with them and so depart singing. Their daughters be married at or before the age of 10 years. The men may have 7 wives. They be a kind of crafty people, worse than the Jews. When they salute one another they heave up their hands to their heads and say "Rame, rame".

From Agra I came to Prayag, where the River Jumna entereth into the mighty River Ganges and Jumna loseth his name. Ganges cometh out of the north-west and runneth east into the Gulf of Bengala. In those parts there are many tigers, and many partridges and turtle-doves, and much other fowl. Here be many beggars in these countries which go naked, and the people make great account of them; they call them *schesche*. Here I saw one which was a monster among the rest. He would have nothing upon him, his beard was very long, and with the hair of his head he covered his privities. The nails of some of his fingers were two inches long, for he would cut nothing from him, neither would he speak. He was accompanied with eight or ten, and they spoke for him. When any man spoke to him, he would lay his hand upon his breast and bow himself, but would not speak. He would not speak to the King.

We went from Prayag down Ganges, the which is here very broad. Here is great store of fish of sundry sorts and of wild fowl, as of swans, geese, cranes, and many other things. The country is very fruitful and populous. The men for the most part have their faces shaven and their heads very long, except some which be all shaven save the crown; and some of them are as though a man should set a dish on their heads and shave them round, all but the crown. In this river of Ganges are many islands. His water is very sweet and pleasant, and the country adjoining very fruitful.

From thence we went to Benares, which is a great town, and great store of cloth is made there of cotton, and sashes for the Moors. In this place they be all gentiles, and be the greatest idolaters that ever I saw. To this town come the gentiles on pilgrimage out of far countries. Here along the water's side be very many fair houses, and in all of them, or for the most part, they have their images standing, which be evil-favoured, made of stone and wood, some like lions, leopards, and monkeys, some like men and women, and peacocks, and some like the devil with four arms and 4 hands. They sit cross-legged, some with one thing in their hands and some another; and by break of day and before there are men and women which come out of the town and wash themselves in Ganges. And there are divers old men which, upon places of earth made for the purpose, sit praying, and they give the people three or four straws, which they take and hold them between their fingers when they wash themselves. And some sit to mark them in the foreheads, and they have in a cloth a little rice, barley, or money, which, when they have washed themselves, they give to the old men which sit there praying. Afterwards they go to divers of their images and give them of their sacrifices; and when they give, the old men say certain prayers and then is all holy. And in divers places there standeth a kind of image which in their language they call *Ada*. And they have divers great stones carved, whereon they pour water, and throw thereupon some rice, wheat, barley, and some other things. This *Ada* hath four hands with claws. Moreover they have a great place made of stone like to a well with steps to go down, wherein the water standeth very foul and stinketh; for the great quantity of flowers, which continually they throw into it, do make it stink. There be always many people in it; for they say, when they wash themselves in it that their sins be forgiven them, because God, as they say, did wash himself in that place. They gather up the sand in the bottom of it, and say it is holy. They never pray but in the water, and they wash themselves overhead, and lade up water with both their hands, and turn themselves about; and then they drink a little of the water three times, and so go to their gods which stand in those houses. Some of them will wash a place which is their length, and then will pray upon the earth with their arms and legs at length out, and will rise up and lie down and kiss the ground twenty or thirty times, but they will not stir their right foot. And some of them will make their ceremonies with fifteen or sixteen pots little and great, and ring a little bell when they make their mixtures ten or twelve times. And they make a circle of water round about their pots and pray, and divers sit by them, and one that reacheth them their pots; and they say divers things over their pots many times, and when they have done they go to their gods and strew their sacrifices which they think are very holy, and mark many of them which sit by in the foreheads, which they take as a great gift. There come fifty and sometime a hundred together to wash them in this well and to offer to these idols.

They have in some of these houses their idols standing, and one sitteth by them in warm weather with a fan to blow wind upon them. And when they see any company coming they ring a little bell which hangeth by them, and many give them their alms but especially those which come out of the country. Many of them are black and have claws of brass with long nails, and some ride upon peacocks and other fowls which be evil-favoured, with long hawks' bills, and some like one thing and some another but none with a good face. Among the rest there is one which they make great account of, for they say he giveth them all things, both food and apparel, and one sitteth always by him with a fan to make wind towards him. Here some be burned to ashes, some scorched in the fire and thrown into the water and dogs and foxes do presently eat them. The wives here do burn with their husbands when they die; if they will not, their heads be shaven and never any account is made of them afterward.

The people go all naked save a little cloth bound about their middle. Their women have their necks, arms, and ears decked with rings of silver, copper, tin, and with round hoops made of ivory adorned with amber stones and with many agates, and they are marked with a great spot of red in their foreheads and a stroke of red up to the crown, and so it runneth three manner of ways. In their winter, which is our May, the men wear quilted gowns of cotton like to our mattresses and quilted caps like to our great grocers' mortars, with a slit to look out at and so tied down beneath their ears.

If a man or woman be sick and like to die, they will lay him before their idols all night, and that shall help him or make an end of him. And if he do not mend that night, his friends will come and sit with him a little and cry, and afterwards will carry him to the water's side and set him upon a little raft made of reeds, and so let him go down the river.

When they be married, the man and the woman come to the water side, and there is an old man which they call a Brahmin, that is a priest, a cow, and a calf, or a cow with calf. Then the man and the woman, cow and calf, and the old man go into the water together, and they give the old man a white cloth of four yards long, and a basket cross-bound with divers things in it. The cloth he layeth upon the back of the cow, and then he taketh the cow by the end of the tail and sayeth certain words. And she hath a copper or a brass pot full of water, and the man doth hold his hand by the old man's hand and the wife's hand by her husband's, and all have the cow by the tail, and they pour water out of the pot upon the cow's tail and it runneth through all their hands, and they lade up water with their hands; and then the old man doth tie him and her together by their clothes. Which done, they go round about the cow and calf, and then they give somewhat to the poor which be always there, and to the Brahmin or priest they give the cow and calf; and afterward go to divers of their idols and offer money, and lie down flat upon the ground and kiss it divers times, and then go their way. Their chief idols be black and evil-favoured, their mouths monstrous, their ears gilded and full of jewels, their teeth and eyes of gold, silver, and glass, some having one thing in their hands and some another. You may not come into the houses where they stand with your shoes on. They have continually lamps burning before them.

From Benares I went to Patna down the river of Ganges, where in the way we passed many fair towns, and a country very fruitful; and many very great rivers do enter into Ganges, and some of them as great as Ganges, which cause Ganges to be of a great breadth, and so broad that in the time of rain you cannot see from one side to the other. These Indians, when they be scorched and thrown into the water, the men swim with their faces downwards, the women with their faces upwards. I thought they tied something to them to cause them to do so; but they say no. There be very many thieves in this country which be like to the Arabians; for they have no certain abode, but are sometime in one place and sometime in another. Here the women be so decked with silver and copper that it is strange to see. They use no shoes by reason of the rings of silver and copper which they wear on their toes.

Here at Patna they find gold in this manner. They dig deep pits in the earth, and wash the earth in great bowls, and therein they find the gold; and they make the pits round about with brick that the earth fall not in. Patna is a very long and a great town. In times past it was a kingdom, but now it is under Zelabdim Akbar, the Great Mogul. The men are tall and slender, and have many old folks among them. The houses are simple, made of earth and covered with straw; the streets are very large. In this town there is a trade of cotton and cloth of cotton, much sugar, which they carry from hence to Bengala and India, very much opium, and other commodities. He that is chief here under the King is called Tipperdas, and is of great account among the people. Here in Patna I saw a dissembling prophet which sat upon a horse in the market-place and made as though he slept, and many of the people came and touched his feet with their hands, and then kissed their hands. They took him for a great man, but sure he was a lazy lubber. I left him there sleeping. The people of these countries be much given to such prating and dissembling hypocrites.

From Patna I went to Tanda, which is in the land of Gaur. It hath in times past been a kingdom, but now is subdued by Zelabdim Akbar. Great trade and traffic is here of cotton and cloth of cotton. The people go naked with a little cloth bound about their waist. It standeth in the country of Bengala. Here be many tigers, wild buffs, and great store of wild fowl. They are very great idolaters. Tanda standeth from the River Ganges a league, because in times past the river, flowing over the banks, in time of rain did drown the country and many villages, and so they do remain. And the old way which the River Ganges was wont to run remaineth dry, which is the occasion that the city doth stand so far from the water. From Agra down the River Jumna and down the River Ganges I was five months coming to Bengala, but it may be sailed in much shorter time.

I went from Bengala into the country of Cooch, which lieth 25 days' journey northwards from Tanda. The King is a gentile; his name is Suckel Counse. His country is great, and lieth not far from Cochin

China; for they say they have pepper from thence. The port is called Cacchegat. All the country is set with bamboos and canes made sharp at both the ends and driven into the earth, and they can let in the water and drown the ground above knee-deep, so that men nor horses can pass. They poison all the waters if any wars be. Here they have much silk and musk and cloth made of cotton. The people have ears which be marvellous great of a span long, which they draw out in length by devices when they be young. Here they be all gentiles, and they will kill nothing. They have hospitals for sheep, goats, dogs, cats, birds, and for all other living creatures. When they be old and lame they keep them until they die. If a man catch or buy any quick thing in other places and bring it thither, they will give him money for it or other victuals, and keep it in their hospitals or let it go. They will give meat to the ants. Their small money is almonds, which oftentimes they use to eat.

From thence I returned to Hugli, which is the place where the Portugals keep in the country of Bengala, which standeth in 23 degrees of northerly latitude, and standeth a league from Satgaon; they call it Porto Pequeno. We went through the wilderness, because the right way was full of thieves, where we passed the country of Gaur where we found but few villages but almost all wilderness, and saw many buffs, swine, and deer, grass longer than a man, and very many tigers. Not far from Porto Pequeno south-westward standeth a haven which is called Angeli, in the country of Orissa. It was a kingdom of itself, and the King was a great friend to strangers. Afterwards it was taken by the King of Patan, which was their neighbour; but he did not enjoy it long, but was taken by Zelabdim Akbar which is King of Agra, Delhi, and Cambaia. Orissa standeth 6 days' journey from Satgaon south-westward. In this place is very much rice, and cloth made of cotton, and great store of cloth which is made of grass, which they call *yerva*; it is like a silk. They make good cloth of it, which they send for India and divers other places. To this haven of Angeli come every year many ships out of India, Negapatam, Sumatra, Malacca, and divers other places, and lade from thence great store of rice, and much cloth of cotton-wool, much sugar, and long pepper, great store of butter, and other victuals for India. Satgaon is a fair city for a city of the Moors, and very plentiful of all things. Here in Bengala they have every day in one place or other a great market which they call *chandeau*, and they have many great boats which they call *pericose*, wherewithal they go from place to place and buy rice and many other things. These boats have 24 or 26 oars to row them, they be great of burden, but have no coverture. Here the gentiles have the water of Ganges in great estimation, for having good water near them yet they will fetch the water of Ganges a great way off; and if they have not sufficient to drink they will sprinkle a little on them, and then they think themselves well. From Satgaon I travelled by the country of the King of Tipperah or Porto Grande, with whom the Moguls or Mogen have almost continual wars. The Mogen, which be of the kingdom of Arakan or Ramree, be stronger than the King of Tipperah, so that Chittagong or Porto Grande is oftentimes under the King of Arakan.

There is a country 4 days' journey from Cooch or Quicheu before mentioned which is called Bottanter, and the city Bhotia (the King is called Dermain), the people whereof are very tall and strong, and there are merchants which come out of China, and they say out of Muscovia or Tartary. And they come to buy musk, cambals, agates, silk, pepper, and saffron like the saffron of Persia. The country is very great, 3 months' journey. There are very high mountains in this country, and one of them so steep that when a man is 6 days' journey off it he may see it perfectly. Upon these mountains are people which have ears of a span long; if their ears be not long they call them apes. They say that when they be upon the mountains they see ships in the sea sailing to and fro, but they know not from whence they come nor whither they go. There are merchants which come out of the east, they say, from under the sun, which is from China, which have no beards, and they say there it is something warm. But those which come from the other side of the mountains, which is from the north, say there it is very cold. These northern merchants are apparelled with woollen cloth and hats, white hose close, and boots which be of Moscovia or Tartary. They report that in their country they have very good horses, but they be little. Some men have four, five, or six hundred horses and kine; they live with milk and flesh. They cut the tails of their kine, and sell them very dear, for they be in great request and much esteemed in those parts. The hair of them is a yard long, the rump is above a span long. They use to hang them for bravery upon the heads of their elephants; they be much used in Pegu and China. They buy and sell by scores upon the ground. The people be very swift on foot.

From Chittagong in Bengala I came to Bacola, the King whereof is a gentile, a man very well disposed and delighteth much to shoot in a gun. His country is very great and fruitful, and hath store of rice, much cotton cloth, and cloth of silk. The houses be very fair and high-built, the streets large, the people naked except a little cloth about their waist. The women wear great store of silver hoops about their necks and arms, and their legs are ringed with silver and copper and rings made of elephants' teeth. From Bacola I went to Sripur, which standeth upon the river of Ganges; the King is called Chondery. They be all hereabout rebels against their King, Zelabdim Akbar; for here are so many rivers and islands that they flee from one to another, whereby his horsemen cannot prevail against them. Great store of cotton cloth is made here.

Sonnargaon is a town six leagues from Sripur, where there is the best and finest cloth made of cotton that is in all India. The chief king of all these countries is called Isa Khan, and he is chief of all the other kings, and is a great friend to all Christians. The houses here, as they be in the most part of India, are very little, and covered with straw, and have a few mats round about the walls, and the door to keep out the tigers and the foxes. Many of the people are very rich. Here they will eat no flesh, nor kill no beast. They live of rice, milk, and fruits. They go with a little cloth before them, and all the rest of their bodies is naked. Great store of cotton cloth goeth from hence, and much rice, wherewith they serve all India, Ceylon, Pegu, Malacca, Sumatra, and many other places.

I went from Sripur the 28th of November 1586 for Pegu in a small ship or foist of one Albert Caravalhos; and so, passing down Ganges and passing by the Island of Sundiva, Porto Grande, or the country of Tipperah, the kingdom of Arakan and Mogen, leaving them on our left side with a fair wind at north-west, our course was south and by east which brought us to the bar of Negrais in Pegu. If any contrary wind had come, we had thrown many of our things overboard; for we were so pestered with people and goods that there was scant place to lie in. From Bengala to Pegu is 90 leagues. We entered the bar of Negrais, which is a brave bar and hath 4 fathoms water where it hath least. Three days after we came to Cosmin, which is a very pretty town and standeth very pleasantly, very well furnished with all things. The people be very tall and well disposed: the women white, round-faced, with little eyes. The houses are high-built, set upon great high posts, and they go up to them with long ladders for fear of the tigers, which be very many. The country is very fruitful of all things. Here are very great figs, oranges, cocos, and other fruits. The land is very high that we fall withal, but after we be entered the bar it is very low and full of rivers, for they go all to and fro in boats which they call *paroes*, and keep their houses with wife and children in them.

From the bar of Negrais to the city of Pegu is ten days' journey by the rivers. We went from Cosmin to Pegu in *paroes,* or boats, and passing up the rivers we came to Medon, which is a pretty town where there be a wonderful number of *paroes,* for they keep their houses and their markets in them all upon the water. They row to and fro, and have all their merchandises in their boats with a great sombrero or shadow over their heads to keep the sun from them, which is as broad as a great cart-wheel, made of the leaves of the coco-trees and fig-trees, and is very light.

From Medon we went to Dalla, which is a very fair town, and hath a fair port into the sea, from whence go many ships to Malacca, Mecca, and many other places. Here are 18 or 20 very great and long houses, where they tame and keep many elephants of the king's; for thereabout in the wilderness they catch the wild elephants. It is a very fruitful country. From Dalla we went to Syriam, which is a good town, and hath a fair port into the sea, whither come many ships from Mecca, Malacca, Sumatra, and from divers other places. And there the ships stay and discharge, and send up their goods in *paroes* to Pegu. From Syriam we went to Makhau, which is a pretty town, where we left our boats or *paroes,* and in the morning taking *delingeges,* which are a kind of coaches made of cords and cloth quilted, and carried upon a stang between 3 or 4 men, we came to Pegu the same day.

Pegu is a city very great, strong and very fair, with walls of stone, and great ditches round about it. There are two towns, the old town and the new. In the old town are all the merchants-strangers, and very many merchants of the country. All the goods are sold in the old town, which is very great, and hath many suburbs round about it and all the houses are made of canes which they call bamboos, and be covered with straw. In your house you have a warehouse, which they call *godon,* which is made of brick, to put your goods in, for oftentimes they take fire and burn in an hour four or five hundred houses; so that if the *godon* were not, you should be in danger to have all burned, if any wind should rise, at a trice.

In the new town is the King, and all his nobility and gentry. It is a city very great and populous, and is made square and with very fair walls, and a great ditch round about it full of water, with many crocodiles in it. It hath twenty gates, and they be made of stone, for every square five gates. There are also many turrets for sentinels to watch, made of wood, and gilded with gold very fair.

The streets are the fairest that ever I saw, as straight as a line from one gate to the other, and so broad that ten or twelve men may ride afront through them. On both sides of them, at every man's door, is set a palmer tree, which is the nut tree; which make a very fair show and a very commodious shadow, so that a man may walk in the shade all day. The houses be made of wood, and covered with tiles.

The King's house is in the middle of the city, and is walled and ditched round about; and the buildings within are made of wood very sumptuously gilded, and great workmanship is upon the forefront, which is likewise very costly gilded. And the house wherein his pagoda or idol standeth is covered with tiles of silver, and all the walls are gilded with gold. Within the first gate of the King's house is a great large room, on both sides whereof are houses made for the King's elephants, which be marvellous great, and fair, and are brought up to wars and in service of the King. And among the rest he hath four white elephants, which are very strange and rare: for there is none other king which hath them but he. If any other king hath one, he will send unto him for it. When any of these white elephants is brought unto the King, all the merchants in the city are commanded to see them, and to give him a present of half a ducat, which doth come to a great sum, for that there are many merchants in the city. After that you have given your present, you may come and see them at your pleasure, although they stand in the King's house.

This King in his title is called The King of the White Elephants. If any other king have one, and will not send it him, he will make war with him for it, for he had rather lose a great part of his kingdom than not to conquer him. They do very great service unto these white elephants; every one of them standeth in a house gilded with gold and they do feed in vessels of silver and gilt. One of them when he doth go to the river to be washed, as every day they do, goeth under a canopy of cloth of gold or of silk carried over him by six or eight men, and eight or ten men go before him playing on drums, shawms or other instruments; and when he is washed and cometh out of the river, there is a gentleman which doth wash his feet in a silver basin which is his office given him by the King. There is no such account made of any black elephant, be he never so great. And surely there be wonderful fair and great, and some be nine cubits in height. And they do report that the King hath about five thousand elephants of war, besides many other which be not taught to fight.

This King hath a very large place wherein he taketh the wild elephants. It standeth about a mile from Pegu, built with a fair court within, and is in a great grove or wood. And there be many huntsmen, which go into the wilderness with she elephants: for without the she they are not to be taken, and they be taught for that purpose, and every hunter hath five or six of them and they say that they anoint the she-elephants with a certain ointment, which when the wild elephant doth smell, he will not leave her. When they have brought the wild elephant near unto the place, they send word unto the town, and many horsemen and footmen come out and cause the she-elephant to enter into a strait way which doth go to the palace, and the she and he do run in; for it is like a wood, and when they be in the gate doth shut. Afterward they get out the female, and when the male seeth that he is left alone, he weepeth and crieth, and runneth against the walls, which be made of so strong trees that some of them do break their teeth with running against them.

Then they prick him with sharp canes, and cause him to go into a strait house, and there they put a rope about his middle and about his feet, and let him stand there three or four days, without eating or drinking; and then they bring a female to him, with meat and drink, and within few days he becometh tame.

The chief force of the King is in these elephants. And when they go into the wars, they set a frame of wood upon their backs, bound with great cords, wherein sit four or six men, which fight with guns, bows and arrows, darts, and other weapons. And they say that their skins are so thick that a pellet of an arquebus will scarce pierce them, except it be in some tender place. Their weapons be very bad. They have guns, but shoot very badly in them, darts, and swords, short without points.

The King keepeth a very great state; when he sitteth abroad, as he doth every day twice, all his noblemen, which they call *shemines*, sit on each side, a good distance off, and a great guard without them. The court yard is very great. If any man will speak with the King, he is to kneel down, to heave up his hands to his head, and put his head to the ground three times, when he entereth, in the middle way, and when he cometh near to the King; and then he sitteth down and talketh with the King. If the King like well of him, he sitteth near him within three or four paces; if he think not well of him, he sitteth further off.

When he goeth to war, he goeth very strong. At my being there he went to Odia in the country of Siam with three hundred thousand men and five thousand elephants. Thirty thousand men were his guard.

These people do eat roots, herbs, leaves, dogs, cats, rats, serpents and snakes; they refuse almost nothing. When the King rideth abroad, he rideth with a great guard, and many noblemen, oftentimes upon an elephant with a fine castle upon him, very fairly gilded with gold; and sometimes upon a great frame like a horse-litter, which hath a little house upon it, covered overhead, but open on the sides, which is all gilded with gold and set with many rubies and sapphires, whereof he hath infinite store in his country, and is carried upon sixteen or eighteen men's shoulders. This coach in their language is called *serrion*. Very great feasting and triumphing is many times before the King, both of men and women.

This King hath little force by sea, because he hath but very few ships. He hath houses full of gold and silver, and bringeth in often, but spendeth very little, and hath the mines of rubies and sapphires and spinels. Near unto the palace of the King there is a treasure wonderful rich, the which, because it is so near, he doth not account of it, and it standeth open for all men to see, in a great walled court with two gates which be always open.

There are four houses gilded very richly, and covered with lead. In every one of them are pagodas or images of huge stature and great value. In the first is the picture of a king in gold, with a crown of gold on his head full of great rubies and sapphires, and about him there stand four children of gold. In the second house is the picture of a man in silver, wonderful great, as high as a house; his foot is as long as a man, and he is made sitting, with a crown on his head, very rich in stones. In the third house is the picture of a man greater than the other, made of brass, with a rich crown on his head. In the fourth and last house doth stand another, made of brass, greater than the other, with a crown also on his head very rich with stones. In another court, not far from this, stand four other pagodas or idols, marvellous great, of copper, made in the same place where they do stand, for they be so great that they be not to be removed. They stand in four houses gilded very fair, and are themselves gilded all over save their heads, and they shew like a black Morian. Their expenses in gilding of their images are wonderful. The King hath one wife and above three hundred concubines, by which they say he hath fourscore or fourscore and ten children. He sitteth in judgment almost every day. They use no speech, but give up their supplications written in the leaves of a tree with the point of an iron bigger than a bodkin. These leaves are an ell long and about two inches broad; they are also double. He which giveth in his supplication doth stand in a place a little distance off with a present. If his matter be liked of, the King accepteth of his present and granteth his request; if his suit be not liked of he returneth with his present, for the King will not take it.

In India there are few commodities which serve for Pegu except opium of Cambaia, painted cloth of St Thomé or of Masulipatam, and white cloth of Bengala, which is spent there in great quantity. They bring thither also much cotton, yarn red coloured with a root which they call *saia*, which will never lose his colour. It is very well sold here, and very much of it cometh yearly to Pegu. By your money you lose much. The ships which come from Bengala, St Thomé, and Masulipatam, come to the bar of Negrais and to Cosmin. To Martaban, a port of the sea in the Kingdom of Pegu, come many ships from Malacca laden with sandal, porcelains, and other wares of China, and with camphor of Borneo and pepper from Achen in Sumatra. To Syriam, a port of Pegu, come ships from Mecca with woollen cloth, scarlets, velvets, opium, and suchlike. There are in Pegu eight brokers, whom they call *tareghe*, which are bound to sell your goods at the price which they be worth, and you give them for their labour two in the hundred; and they be bound to make your debt good because you sell your merchandises upon their word. If the broker pay you not at his day, you may take him home and keep him in your house, which is a great shame for him. And if he pay you not presently, you may take his wife and children and his slaves, and bind them at your door and set them in the sun; for that is the law of the country.

Their current money in these parts is a kind of brass which they call *gansa*, wherewith you may buy gold, silver, rubies, musk, and all other things. The gold and silver is merchandise, and is worth sometimes more and sometimes less, as other wares be. This brazen money doth go by a weight which they call a *biza*; and commonly this *biza* after our account is worth about half-a-crown or somewhat less. The merchandise which be in Pegu are gold, silver, rubies, sapphires, spinels, musk, benjamin or frankincense, long pepper, tin, lead, copper, laccha whereof they make hard wax, rice, and wine made of rice, and some sugar. The elephants do eat the sugar-canes, or else they would make very much; and they consume many canes likewise in making of their *varellas* or idol-temples, which are in great number both great and small. They be made round like a sugar-loaf; some are as high as a church, very broad beneath, some a quarter of a mile in compass. Within they be all earth done about with stone. They consume in these *varellas* great quantity of gold, for that they be all gilded aloft, and many of them from the top to the bottom; and every ten or twelve years they must be new gilded, because the rain consumeth off the gold, for they stand open abroad. If they did not consume their gold in these vanities it would be very plentiful and good cheap in Pegu.

About two days' journey from Pegu there is a *varella* or pagoda which is the pilgrimage of the Peguese. It is called Dagon, and is of a wonderful bigness, and all gilded from the foot to the top; and there is a house by it wherein the *tallipoys*, which are their priests, do preach. This house is five and fifty paces in length, and hath three pawns or walks in it, and forty great pillars gilded which stand between the walks; and it is open on all sides with a number of small pillars which be likewise gilded. It is gilded with gold within and without. There are houses very fair round about for the pilgrims to lie in, and many goodly houses for the *tallipoys* to preach in, which are full of images both of men and women which are all gilded over with gold. It is the fairest place, as I suppose, that is in the world. It standeth very high, and there are four ways to it, which all along are set with trees of fruits, in such wise that a man may go in the shade above two miles in length. And when their feast-day is, a man can hardly pass by water or by land for the great press of people, for they come from all places of the kingdom of Pegu thither at their feast.

In Pegu they have many *tallipoys* or priests which preach against all abuses. Many men resort unto them. When they enter into their *kiack*, that is to say their holy place or temple, at the door there is a great jar of water with a cock or a ladle in it, and there they wash their feet; and then they enter in, and lift up their hands to their heads, first to their preacher, and then to the sun, and so sit down. The *tallipoys* go very strangely apparelled with one cameline or thin cloth next to their body, of a brown colour, another of yellow doubled many times upon their shoulder, and those two be girded to them with a broad girdle. And they have a skin of leather hanging on a string about their necks, whereupon they sit, bare-headed and bare-footed (for none of them weareth shoes), with their right arms bare and a great broad sombrero or shadow in their hands to defend them in the summer from the sun and in the winter from the rain.

When the *tallipoys* or priests take their orders, first they go to school until they be twenty years old or more, and then they come before a *tallipoy* appointed for that purpose whom they call *rowli*. He is of the chiefest and most learned, and he opposeth them, and afterward examineth them many times whether they will leave their friends and the company of all women and take upon them the habit of a *tallipoy*. If any be content, then he rideth upon a horse about the streets very richly apparelled, with drums and pipes, to show that he leaveth the riches of the world to be a *tallipoy*. In a few days after he is carried upon a thing like a horse-litter, which they call a *serion*, upon ten or twelve men's shoulders, in the apparel of a *tallipoy*, with pipes and drums, and many *tallipoys* with him and all his friends, and so they go with him to his house which standeth without the town, and there they leave him.

Every one of them hath his house, which is very little, set upon six or eight posts, and they go up to them with a ladder of twelve or fourteen staves. Their houses be for the most part by the highway's side, and among the trees and in the woods. And they go with a great pot made of wood or fine earth, and covered, tied with a broad girdle upon their shoulder, which cometh under their arm, wherewith they go to beg their victuals which they eat, which is rice, fish, and herbs. They demand nothing, but come to the door, and people presently do give them some one thing and some another; and they put all together in their pot for they say they must eat of their alms and therewith content themselves. They keep their feasts by the moon, and when it is new moon they keep their greatest feast; and then the people send rice and other things to that *kiack* or church of which they be, and there all the *tallipoys* do meet which be of that church and eat the victuals which are sent them. When the *tallipoys* do preach, many of the people carry them gifts into the pulpit where they sit and preach, and there is one which sitteth by them to take that which the people bring. It is divided among them. They have none other ceremonies nor service that I could see but only preaching.

I went from Pegu to Jamahey, which is in the country of the Langeiannes, whom we call Jangomes. It is five and twenty days' journey north-east from Pegu, in which journey I passed many fruitful and pleasant countries. The country is very low, and hath many fair rivers. The houses are very bad, made of canes and covered with straw. Here are many wild buffs and elephants. Jamahey is a very fair and great town with fair houses of stone, well peopled; the streets are very large, the men very well set and strong, with a cloth about them, bare-headed and bare-footed, for in all these countries they wear no shoes. The women be much fairer than those of Pegu. Here in all these countries they have no wheat. They make some cakes of rice. Hither to Jamahey come many merchants out of China and bring great store of musk, gold, silver, and many other things of China work. Here is great store of victuals; they have such plenty that they will not milk the buffaloes, as they do in all other places. Here is great store of copper and benjamin.

In these countries when the people be sick they make a vow to offer meat unto the devil if they escape; and when they be recovered they make a banquet, with many pipes and drums and other instruments, and dancing all the night, and their friends come and bring gifts, cocos, figs, arecas, and other fruits, and with great dancing and rejoicing they offer to the devil, and say they give the devil to eat and drive him out. When they be dancing and playing they will cry and halloo very loud, and in this sort they say they drive him away. And when they be sick a *tallipoy* or two every night doth sit by them and sing, to please the devil that he should not hurt them. And if any die, he is carried upon a great frame made like a tower, with a covering, all gilded with gold, made of canes, carried with fourteen or sixteen men, with drums and pipes and other instruments playing before him to a place out of the town, and there is burned. He is accompanied with all his friends and neighbours, all men, and they give to the *tallipoys* or priests many mats and cloth, and then they return to the house and there make a feast for two days; and then the wife with all the neighbours' wives and her friends go to the place where he was burned, and there they sit a certain time and cry and gather the pieces of bones which be left unburned and bury them, and then return to their houses and make an end of all mourning. And the men and women which be near of kin do shave their heads, which they do not use except it be for the death of a friend; for they much esteem of their hair.

Caplan is the place where they find the rubies, sapphires, and spinels. It standeth six days' journey from Ava in the kingdom of Pegu. There are many great high hills out of which they dig them. None may go to the pits but only those which dig them.

In Pegu, and in all the countries of Ava, Langeiannes, Siam, and the Bramas, the men wear bunches or little round balls in their privy members. Some of them wear two and some three. They cut the skin and so put them in, one into one side and another into the other side, which they do when they be 25 or 30 years old; and at their pleasure they take one or more of them out as they think good. When they be married the husband is, for every child which his wife hath, to put in one until he come to three, and then no more; for they say the women do desire them. They were invented because they should not abuse the male sex. For in times past all those countries were so given to that villainy that they were very scarce of people. It was also ordained that the women should not have past three cubits of cloth in their nether clothes, which they bind about them; which are so strait that when they go in the streets they show one side of the leg bare above the knee. The bunches aforesaid be of divers sorts: the least be as big as a little walnut, and very round; the greatest are as big as a little hen's egg. Some are of brass and some of silver, but those of silver be for the King and his noblemen. These are gilded and made with great cunning, and ring like a little bell. There are some made of lead, which they call *selwy* because they ring but little; and these be of lesser price for the poorer sort. The King sometimes taketh his out and giveth them to his noblemen as a great gift; and because he hath used them they esteem them greatly. They will put one in and heal up the place in seven or eight days.

The Bramas which be of the King's country (for the King is a Brama) have their legs or bellies, or some part of their body as they think good themselves, made black with certain things which they have. They use to prick the skin and to put on a kind of anil or blacking which doth continue always; and this is counted an honour among them, but none may have it but the Bramas which are of the King's kindred.

These people wear no beards. They pull out the hair on their faces with little pincers made for that purpose. Some of them will let 16 or 20 hairs grow together, some in one place of his face and some in another, and pulleth out all the rest; for he carrieth the pincers always with him to pull the hairs out as soon as they appear. If they see a man with a beard they wonder at him. They have their teeth blacked, both men and women, for they say a dog hath his teeth white, therefore they will black theirs.

The Peguese, if they have a suit in the law which is so doubtful that they cannot well determine it, put two long canes into the water where it is very deep; and both the parties go into the water by the poles, and there sit men to judge, and they both do dive under the water and he which remaineth longest under the water doth win the suit.

The 10th of January I went from Pegu to Malacca, passing by many of the ports of Pegu, as Martaban, the Island of Tavoy, from whence cometh great store of tin which serveth all India, the Islands of Tenasserim, Junkseylon, and many others, and so came to Malacca the 8th of February, where the Portugals have a castle which standeth near the sea; and the country fast without the town belongeth to the Malays, which is a kind of proud people. They go naked with a cloth about their middle and a little roll of cloth about their heads. Hither come many ships from China and from the Moluccas, Banda, Timor, and from many other islands of the Javas, which bring great store of spices and drugs, and diamonds and other jewels. The voyages into many of these islands belong unto the Captain of Malacca; so that none may go thither without his licence, which yield him great sums of money every year. The Portugals here have oftentimes wars with the King of Achen which standeth in the Island of Sumatra, from whence cometh great store of pepper and other spices every year to Pegu and Mecca within the Red Sea, and other places.

When the Portugals go from Macao in China to Japan they carry much white silk, gold, musk, and porcelains, and they bring from thence nothing but silver. They have a great carrack which goeth thither every year, and she bringeth from thence every year above six hundred thousand crusadoes; and all this silver of Japan, and two hundred thousand crusadoes more in silver which they bring yearly out of India, they employ to their great advantage in China, and they bring from thence gold, musk, silk, copper, porcelains, and many other things very costly and gilded. When the Portugals come to Canton in China to traffic, they must remain there but certain days; and when they come in at the gate of the city they must enter their names in a book, and when they go out at night they must put out their names. They may not lie in the town all night, but must lie in their boats without the town. And their days being expired, if any man remain there, they are evil used and imprisoned.

The Chinians are very suspicious and do not trust strangers. It is thought that the King doth not know that any strangers come into his country. And further it is credibly reported that the common people see their king very seldom or not at all, nor may not look up to that place where he sitteth; and when he rideth abroad he is carried upon a great chair or *serrion* gilded very fair, wherein there is made a little house with a lattice to look out at, so that he may see them but they may not look up at him, and all the time that he passeth by them they heave up their hands to their heads and lay their heads on the ground and look not up until he be past.

The order of China is, when they mourn, that they wear white thread shoes and hats of straw. The man doth mourn for his wife two years, the wife for her husband three years, the son for his father a year, and for his mother two years. And all the time which they mourn they keep the dead in the house, the bowels being taken out and filled with *chownam* or lime, and coffined. And when the time is expired they carry them out playing and piping and burn them; and when they return they pull off their mourning weeds and marry at their pleasure. A man may keep as many concubines as he will, but one wife only. All the Chinians, Japonians, and Cochin Chinians do write right downwards, and they do write with a fine pencil made of dog's or cat's hair.

Labuan is an island among the Javas, from whence come the diamonds of the new water; and they find them in the rivers, for the King will not suffer them to dig the rock. Jambe is an island among the Javas also, from whence come diamonds. And the King hath a mass of earth which is gold; it groweth in the middle of a river, and when the King doth lack gold they cut part of the earth and melt it, whereof cometh gold. This mass of earth doth appear but once in a year, which is when the water is low; and this is in the month of April. Bima is another island among the Javas, where the women travail and labour as our men do in England, and the men keep house and go where they will.

The 29th of March 1588 I returned from Malacca to Martaban and so to Pegu, where I remained the second time until the 17th of September, and then I went to Cosmin and there took shipping; and

passing many dangers by reason of contrary winds, it pleased God that
we arrived in Bengala in November following, where I stayed for want
of passage until the third of February 1589 and then I shipped myself
for Cochin. In which voyage we endured great extremity for lack of
fresh water, for the weather was extreme hot, and we were many
merchants and passengers, and we had very many calms and hot
weather. Yet it pleased God that we arrived in Ceylon the sixth of
March, where we stayed five days to water and to furnish ourselves
with other necessary provision.

This Ceylon is a brave island, very fruitful and fair; but by reason of
continued wars with the king thereof all things are very dear, for he will
not suffer anything to be brought to the castle where the Portugals be,
wherefore oftentimes they have great want of victuals. Their provision
of victuals cometh out of Bengala every year. The King is called Raja,
and is of great force; for he cometh to Colombo, which is the place
where the Portugals have their fort, with a hundred thousand men and
many elephants. But they be naked people all of them, yet many of
them be good with their pieces, which be muskets. When the King
talketh with any man, he standeth upon one leg and setteth the other
foot upon his knee, with his sword in his hand. It is not their order for
the King to sit, but to stand. His apparel is a fine painted cloth made of
cotton-wool about his middle. His hair is long and bound up with a little
fine cloth about his head. All the rest of his body is naked. His guard are
a thousand men, which stand round about him, and he in the middle;
and when he marcheth many of them go before him and the rest come
after him. They are of the race of the Cingalese, which they say are the
best kind of all Malabars. Their ears are very large, for the greater they
are the more honourable they are accounted. Some of them are a span
long. The wood which they burn is cinnamon wood, and it smelleth
very sweet. There is great store of rubies, sapphires, and spinels in this
island. The best kind of all be here, but the King will not suffer the
inhabitants to dig for them lest his enemies should know of them, and
make wars against him, and so drive him out of his country for them.
They have no horses in all the country. The elephants be not so great as
those of Pegu, which be monstrous huge; but they say all other
elephants do fear them, and none dare fight with them though they be
very small. Their women have a cloth bound about them from their
middle to their knee, and all the rest is bare. All of them be black and
but little, both men and women. Their houses are very little, made of
the branches of the palmer or coco-tree, and covered with the leaves of
the same tree.

The eleventh of March we sailed from Ceylon, and so doubled
the Cape of Comorin. Not far from thence, between Ceylon and the
mainland of Negapatam, they fish for pearls, and there is fished every
year much which doth serve all India, Cambaia, and Bengala. It is not

so orient as the pearl of Bahrein in the Gulf of Persia. From Cape de Comorin we passed by Quilon, which is a fort of the Portugals, from whence cometh great store of pepper which cometh to Portugal, for oftentimes there ladeth one of the carracks of Portugal. Thus passing the coast we arrived at Cochin the 22nd of March, where we found the weather warm, but scarcity of victuals; for here groweth neither corn nor rice, and the greatest part cometh from Bengala. They have here very bad water, for the river is far off. This bad water causeth many of the people to be like lepers, and many of them have their legs swollen as big as a man in the waist, and many of them are scant able to go. These people here be Malabars, and of the race of the Naires of Calicut; and they differ much from the other Malabars. These have their heads very full of hair and bound up with a string, and there doth appear a bush without the band wherewith it is bound. The men be tall and strong, and good archers with a long-bow and a long arrow, which is their best weapon; yet there be some calivers among them, but they handle them badly.

Here groweth the pepper, and it springeth up by a tree or pole, and is like our ivy berry but something longer, like the wheat ear; and at the first the bunches are green, and as they wax ripe they cut them off and dry them. The leaf is much lesser than the ivy leaf and thinner. All the inhabitants here have very little houses covered with the leaves of the coco-trees. The men be of a reasonable stature, the women little, all black, with a cloth bound about their middle hanging down to their hams. All the rest of their bodies be naked. They have horrible great ears with many rings set with pearls and stones in them. The King goeth encoached, as do they all. He doth not remain in a place above five or six days; he hath many houses, but they be but little. His guard is but small. He removeth from one house to another according to their order. All the pepper of Calicut and coarse cinnamon groweth here in this country. The best cinnamon doth come from Ceylon, and is peeled from fine young trees. Here are very many palmer or coco trees, which is their chief food, for it is their meat and drink, and yieldeth many other necessary things as I have declared before.

The Naires which be under the King of Zamorin, which be Malabars, have always wars with the Portugals. The King hath always peace with them; but his people go to sea to rob and steal. Their chief captain is called Cogi Ali; he hath three castles under him. When the Portugals complain to the King he saith he doth not send them out; but he consenteth that they go. They range all the coast from Ceylon to Goa, and go by four or five *paroes* or boats together, and have in every one of them fifty or threescore men, and board presently. They do much harm on that coast, and take every year many foists and boats of the Portugals. Many of these people be Moors. This King's country beginneth twelve leagues from Cochin and reacheth near unto Goa. I remained in Cochin until the second of November, which was eight months, for that there was no passage that went away in all that time. If I had come two days sooner I had found a passage presently. From Cochin I went to Goa, where I remained three days. From Cochin to Goa is a hundred leagues. From Goa I went to Chaul, which is three-score leagues, where I remained three and twenty days, and, there making my provision of things necessary for the ship, from thence I departed to Ormuz, where I stayed for a passage to Basra fifty days. From Goa to Ormuz is four hundred leagues.

Here I thought good, before I make an end of this my book, to declare some things which India and the country further eastward do bring forth. The pepper groweth in many parts of India, especially about Cochin, and much of it doth grow in the fields among the bushes without any labour, and when it is ripe they go and gather it. The shrub is like unto our ivy-tree, and if it did not run about some tree or pole it would fall down and rot. When they first gather it, it is green, and then they lay it in the sun and it becometh black. The ginger groweth like unto our garlic, and the root is the ginger. It is to be found in many parts of India. The cloves do come from the Isles of the Moluccas, which be divers islands. Their tree is like to our bay tree. The nutmegs and maces grow together, and come from the Isle of Banda. The tree is like to our walnut tree, but somewhat lesser. The white sandal is wood very sweet and in great request among the Indians; for they grind it with a little water and anoint their bodies therewith. It cometh from the Isle of Timor.

Camphor is a precious thing among the Indians, and is sold dearer than gold. I think none of it cometh for Christendom. That which is compounded cometh from China, but that which groweth in canes, and is the best, cometh from the great Isle of Borneo. Lignum aloes cometh from Cochin China. The benjamin cometh out of the countries of Siam and Jangomes. The long pepper groweth in Bengala, in Pegu, and in the Islands of the Javas.

The musk cometh out of Tartary, and is made after this order, by report of the merchants which bring it to Pegu to sell. In Tartary there is a little beast like unto a young roe, which they take in snares and beat him to death with the blood. After that they cut out the bones, and beat the flesh with the blood very small, and fill the skin with it; and hereof cometh the musk.

Of the amber they hold divers opinions; but most men say it cometh out of the sea and that they find it upon the shore's side. The rubies, sapphires, and spinels are found in Pegu. The diamonds are found in divers places, as in Bisnagar, in Agra, in Delhi, and in the Islands of the Javas. The best pearls come from the Island of Bahrein in the Persian Sea, the worser from the piscary near the Isle of Ceylon, and from Ayman, a great island on the southernmost coast of China.

Spodium and many other kinds of drugs come from Cambaia. Now to return to my voyage. From Ormuz I went to Balsara or Basra, and from Basra to Babylon; and we passed the most part of the way by the strength of men by hauling the boat up the river with a long cord. From Babylon I came by land to Mosul, which standeth near to Nineveh, which is all ruinated and destroyed. It standeth fast by the river of Tigris. From Mosul I went to Mardin, which is in the country of the Armenians, but now there dwell in that place a people which they call Cordies or Kurdi. From Mardin I went to Urfa, which is a very fair town and it hath a goodly fountain full of fish; where the Moors hold many great ceremonies and opinions concerning Abraham, for they say he did once dwell there. From thence I went to Birra, and so passed the river of Euphrates. From Birra I went to Aleppo, where I stayed certain months for company, and then I went to Tripolis; where finding English shipping I came with a prosperous voyage to London, where by God's assistance I safely arrived the 29th of April 1591, having been eight years out of my native country.

The second voyage of Master Laurence Aldersey, to the cities of Alexandria and Cairo in Egypt, anno 1586.

I embarked myself at Bristol in the *Hercules*, a good ship of London, and set sail the 21st day of February about ten of the clock in the morning, having a merry wind; but the 23rd day there arose a very great storm, and in the midst of it we descried a small boat of the burden of ten tons, with four men in her, in very great danger, who called amain for our help. Whereupon our Master made towards them, and took them into our ship, and let the boat, which was laden with timber and appertained to Chepstow, to run adrift. The same night about midnight arose another great storm, but the wind was large with us until the 27th of the same month, which then grew somewhat contrary. Yet notwithstanding we held on our course, and the tenth day of March we descried a sail about Cape Sprat, which is a little on this side the Strait of Gibraltar, but we spoke not with her. The next day we descried twelve sail more, with whom we thought to have spoken to have learned what they were, but they made very fast away and we gave over.

Thursday, the 16th of March, we had sight of the Straits and of the coast of Barbary. The 18th day we passed them, and sailed towards Patras. Upon the 23rd of March we met with the *Centurion* of London, which came from Genoa, by whom we sent letters to England, and the four men also which we took in upon the coast of England, beforementioned. The 29th of March we came to Goletta, a small island, and had sight of two ships which we judged to be of England. Tuesday the fourth of April we were before Malta, and being there becalmed our Master caused the two ship-boats to be had out, and they towed the ship till we were out of sight of the castle of Malta. The 9th day of April we came to Zante and, being before the town, William Aldridge, servant to Master Thomas Cordall of London, came aboard us, with whom our Master and twelve more of our company thought to have gone on shore, but they could not be permitted. So we all came aboard again and went to Patras, where we arrived upon Good Friday and lay there with good entertainment at the English house, where was the consul, Master Grimes, Ralph Ashley, and John Doddington, who very kindly went with us and showed us the pleasures of the town.

They brought us to the house of the Cadi, who was made then to understand of the 20 Turks that we had aboard, which were to go to Constantinople, being redeemed out of captivity by Sir Francis Drake in the West Indies and brought with him into England, and by order of the Queen's Majesty sent now into their country. Whereupon the Cadi commanded them to be brought before him that he might see them; and when he had talked with them and understood how strangely they were delivered, he marvelled much, and admired the Queen's Majesty of England who, being but a woman, is notwithstanding of such power and renown amongst all the princes of Christendom, with many other honourable words of commending Her Majesty. So he took the names of those 20 Turks, and recorded them in their great books to remain in perpetual memory. After this our foresaid countrymen brought me to the Chapel of St Andrew, where his tomb or sepulchre is, and the board upon which he was beheaded; which board is now so rotten that if any man offer to cut it, it falleth to powder, yet I brought some of it away with me.

Upon Tuesday in Easter week we set out towards Zante again, and the 24th of April with much ado we were all permitted to come on shore, and I was carried to the English house in Zante, where I was very well entertained. The commodities of Zante are currants and oil. The situation of the town is under a very great hill, upon which standeth a very strong castle which commandeth the town. At Zante we took in a captain and 16 soldiers, with other passengers. We departed from Zante upon Tuesday the 15th of April, and the next day we anchored at a small island called Strivalia, which is desolate of people, saving a few religious men who entertained us well without taking any money; but of courtesy we bestowed somewhat upon them for their maintenance, and then they gave us a couple of lean sheep which we carried aboard. The last day of April we arrived at Candy, at a castle called Suda, where we set the captain, soldiers, and mariners ashore which we took in at Zante, with all their carriage.

The second day of May we set sail again, and the fourth day came to the Islands of Melos, where we anchored, and found the people there very courteous, and took in such necessaries as we wanted. The Islands are in my judgment a hundred in number, and all within the compass of a hundred miles. The 11th day the Choush, which is the greatest man there in authority, for certain offences done in a little chapel by the waterside, which they said one of our ship had done, and imputed it to me because I was seen to go into it three days before, came to us and made much ado, so that we were fain to come out of our ship armed; but by three pieces of gold the brabbling was ended, and we came to our ship. This day we also set sail, and the next day passed by the Castle of Serpeto, which is an old ruinated thing, and standeth under a hill's side.

The 13th day we passed by the Island of Paros, and the island of the banks of Helicon, and the Island called Ditter, where are many boars, and the women be witches. The same day also we passed by the Castle of Tinos, standing upon a very high mountain, and near unto it is the island of Diana.

The 15th of May we came to Chios, where I stayed thirty and three days. In it is a very proper town after the building of that country, and the people are civil; and while we were here there came in six galleys which had been at Alexandria, and one of them, which was the admiral, had a prince of the Moors prisoner whom they took about Alexandria, and they meant to present him to the Turk. The town standeth in a valley and along the waterside pleasantly. There are about 26 windmills about it, and the commodities of it are cotton-wool, cotton yarn, mastic, and some other drugs.

As we remained at Chios, there grew a great controversy between the mariners of the *Hercules* and the Greeks of the town of Chios about the bringing home of the Turks, which the Greeks took in ill part, and the boys cried out "Vive el re Felipe". Whereupon our men beat the boys, and threw stones, and so a broil began and some of our men were hurt; but the Greeks were fetched out of their houses and manacled together with irons and threatened to the galleys. About forty of them were sent to prison, and what became of them when we were gone we know not, for we went thence within two days after, which was the 19th of June.

The 20th day we passed by the Island of Singonina, an island risen by the casting of stones in that place. The substance of the ground there is brimstone, and burneth sometimes so much that it bloweth up the rocks. The 24th of June we came to Cyprus, and had sight in the way of the aforesaid six galleys that came from Alexandria, one whereof came unto us and required a present for himself and for two of the other galleys, which we for quietness' sake gave them.

The 27th of June we came to Tripolis, where I stayed till the fifth of July and then took passage in a small bark called a caramoussal, which was a passage-boat and was bound for Bichier, thirteen miles on this side Alexandria, which boat was freighted with Turks, Moors, and Jews. The 20th day of July this bark which I passed in ran upon a rock, and was in very great danger, so that we all began some to be ready to swim, some to leap into the ship-boat; but it pleased God to set us quickly off the rock and without much harm.

The 28th of July I came to Bichier, where I was well entertained of a Jew which was the customer there, giving me muscadine and drinking water himself. Having broken my fast with him, he provided me a camel for my carriage and a mule for me to ride upon and a Moor to run by me to the city of Alexandria, who had charge to see me safe in the English house, whither I came, but found no Englishmen there. But then my guide brought me aboard a ship of Alderman Martin's called the *Tiger* of London, where I was well received of the Master of the said ship, whose name was Thomas Rickman, and of all the company.

The said Master, having made me good cheer and made me also to drink of the water of Nilus, having the keys of the English house went thither with me himself and appointed me a fair chamber, and left a man with me to provide me all things that I needed; and every day came himself to me and carried me into the city, and showed me the monuments thereof, which be these. He brought me first to Pompey's pillar, which is a mighty thing of grey marble, and all of one stone in height by estimation above 52 yards and the compass about six fathom. The city hath three gates, one called the gate of Barbaria, the other of Merina, and the third of Rosetta. He brought me to a stone in the street of the city whereupon St Mark was beheaded; to the place where St Catherine died, having there hid herself because she would not marry; also to the Bath of St Catherine. I saw there also Pharaoh's Needle, which is a thing in height almost equal with Pompey's pillar, and is in compass five fathom and a half and all of one stone. I was brought also to a most brave and dainty bath, where we washed ourselves, the bath being of marble and of very curious workmanship.

The city standeth upon great arches or vaults, like unto churches, with mighty pillars of marble to hold up the foundation, which arches are built to receive the water of the river of Nilus which is for the use of the city. It hath three castles and a hundred churches, but the part that is destroyed of it is six times more than that part which standeth.

The last day of July I departed from Alexandria towards Cairo in a passage-boat, wherein first I went to Rosetta, standing by the riverside, having 13 or 14 great churches in it. Their building there is of stone and brick, but as for lodging there is little except we bring it with us. From Rosetta we passed along the river of Nilus which is so famous in the world, twice as broad as the Thames at London. On both sides grow date trees in great abundance. The people be rude, insomuch that a man cannot travel without a janissary to conduct him.

The time that I stayed in Egypt was the Turks' and Moors' Lent, in all which time they burn lamps in their churches as many as may hang in them. Their Lent endureth 40 days, and they have three Lents in the year, during which time they neither eat nor drink in the day time, but all the night they do nothing else.

Betwixt Rosetta and Cairo there are along the waterside three hundred cities and towns, and the length of the way is not above three hundred miles.

To this famous city of Cairo I came the fifth day of August, where I found Master William Alday and William Caesar, who entertained me in very good sort. Master Caesar brought me to see the Pyramids, which are three in number, one whereof King Pharaoh made for his own tomb. The tomb itself is almost in the top of it. The monuments be high and in form 4-square, and every of the squares is as long as a man may shoot a roving arrow, and as high as a church. I saw also the ruins of the city of Memphis hard by those Pyramids. The house of Joseph is yet standing in Cairo, which is a sumptuous thing, having a place to walk in of 56 mighty pillars all gilt with gold; but I saw it not, being then lame.

The 11th day of August the land was cut at Cairo to let in the water of the river of Nilus, which was done with great joy and triumph. The 12th of August I set from Cairo towards Alexandria again, and came thither the 14th of August. The 26th day there was kept a great feast of the Turks and Moors, which lasted two days, and for a day they never ceased shooting off of great ordnance.

From Alexandria I sailed to Algiers, where I lay with Master Tipton, consul of the English nation, who used me most kindly and at his own charge. He brought me to the King's court, and into the presence of the King to see him and the manners of the court. The King doth only bear the name of a king, but the greatest government is in the hands of the soldiers.

The King of Potanca is prisoner in Algiers who, coming to Constantinople to acknowledge a duty to the Great Turk, was betrayed by his own nephew, who wrote to the Turk that he went only as a spy, by that means to get his kingdom. I heard at Algiers of seven galleys that were at that time cast away at a town called Formentera; three of them were of Algiers, the other four were the Christians'. We found here also 13 Englishmen, which were by force of weather put into the Bay of Tunis, where they were very ill used by the Moors, who forced them to leave their bark; whereupon they went to the Council of Algiers to require a redress and remedy for the injury. They were all belonging to the ship called the *Golden Noble* of London, whereof Master Bird is owner. The Master was Stephen Haslewood and the Captain Edmund Bence.

The third day of December the pinnace called the *Moonshine* of

London came to Algiers, with a prize which they took upon the coast of Spain laden with sugar, hides, and ginger, the pinnace also belonging to the *Golden Noble*. And at Algiers they made sale both of ship and goods, where we left them at our coming away, which was the seventh day of January; and the first day of February I landed at Dartmouth and the seventh day came to London, with humble thanks to Almighty God for my safe arrival.

The casting away of the *Toby* near Cape Espartel, corruptly called Cape Sprat, without the Strait of Gibraltar on the coast of Barbary, 1593.

THE *Toby* of London, a ship of 250 tons, manned with fifty men, the owner whereof was the worshipful Master Richard Staper, being bound for Livorno, Zante, and Patras in Morea, being laden with merchandise to the value of 11 or 12 thousand pounds sterling, set sail from Blackwall the 16th of August 1593, and we went thence to Portsmouth, where we took in great quantity of wheat, and set sail forth of Stokes Bay in the Isle of Wight the 6th day of October, the wind being fair. And the 16th of the same month we were in the height of Cape St Vincent, where on the next morning we descried a sail which lay in try right ahead off us, to which we gave chase, with very much wind, the sail being a Spaniard, which we found in fine so good of sail that we were fain to leave her and give her over.

Two days after this we sighted Mount Chiego, which is the first high land which we descry on the Spanish coast at the entrance of the Strait of Gibraltar, where we had very foul weather, and the wind scant two days together. Here we lay off to the sea. The Master, whose name was George Goodley, being a young man, and one which never took charge before for those parts, was very proud of that charge which he was little able to discharge, neither would take any counsel of any of his company, but did as he thought best himself, and in the end of the two days of foul weather, cast about, and the wind being fair, bore in with the Strait's mouth.

The 19th day at night, he, thinking that he was farther off the land than he was, bore sail all that night, and an hour and a half before day had run our ship upon the ground on the coast of Barbary without the Strait, four leagues to the south of Cape Espartel. Whereupon, being all not a little astonished, the Master said unto us, "I pray you forgive me; for this is my fault and no man's else."

The company asked him whether they should cut off the mainmast.

THE MEDITERRANEAN AND THE EAST

"No," said the master, "we will hoist out our boat." But one of our men coming speedily up said, "Sirs, the ship is full of water." "Well," said the master, "then cut the mainmast over-board"; which thing we did with all speed. But the after part suddenly split asunder in such sort that no man was able to stand upon it, but all fled upon the foremast up into the shrouds thereof, and hung there for a time. But seeing nothing but present death approach (being so suddenly taken that we could not make a raft which we had determined) we committed ourselves unto the Lord, and began with doleful tune and heavy hearts to sing the 12th Psalm, "Help Lord, for good and godly men, &c." Howbeit before we had finished four verses the waves of the sea had stopped the breaths of most of our men. For the foremast, with the weight of our men and the force of the sea, fell down into the water, and upon the fall thereof there were 38 drowned, and only 12, by God's providence, partly by swimming and other by means of chests, got on shore, which was about a quarter of a mile from the wreck of the ship. The Master, called George Goodley, and William Palmer his mate, both perished. Master Caesar also, being Captain and owner, was likewise drowned. None of the officers were saved but the carpenter.

We twelve, which the Lord had delivered from extreme danger of the sea, at our coming ashore fell in a manner into as great distress. At our first coming ashore we all fell down on our knees, praying the Lord most humbly for His merciful goodness. Our prayers being done, we consulted together what course to take, seeing we were fallen into a desert place, and we travelled all that day until night, sometimes one way and sometimes another, and could find no inhabitants. Only we saw where wild beasts had been, and places where there had been houses, which afterwards we perceived to have been burnt by the Portugals. So at night, falling into certain groves of olive trees, we climbed up and sat in them to avoid the danger of lions and other wild beasts, whereof we saw many the next morning.

The next day we travelled until three of the clock in the afternoon without any food but water and wild date roots; then going over a mountain, we had sight of Cape Espartel, whereby we knew somewhat better which way to travel, and then we went forward until we came to a hedgerow made with great long canes. We spied and looked over it, and beheld a number of men, as well horsemen as footmen, to the number of some five thousand, in skirmish together with small shot and other weapons.

And after consultation what we were best to do, we concluded to yield ourselves unto them, being destitute of all means of resistance. So rising up, we marched towards them, who espying us, forthwith some hundred of them with their javelins in their hands came running towards us, as though they would have run us through. Howbeit they only struck us flatling with their weapons, and said that we were

Spaniards; and we told them that we were Englishmen, which they would not believe yet.

By and by, the conflict being ended, and night approaching, the captain of the Moors, a man of some 56 years old, came himself unto us, and by his interpreter, which spoke Italian, asked what we were, and from whence we came. One Thomas Henmore of our company, which could speak Italian, declared unto him that we were merchants, and how by great misfortune our ship, merchandise and the greatest part of our company were pitifully cast away upon their coast. But he, void of humanity and all manhood, for all this, caused his men to strip us out of our apparel, even to our shirts, to see what money and jewels we had about us, which when they had found to the value of some 200 pounds in gold and pearls, they gave us some of our apparel again, and bread and water only to comfort us.

The next morning they carried us down to the shore where our ship was cast away, which was some sixteen miles from that place, in which journey they used us like their slaves, making us (being extreme weak) to carry their stuff, and offering to beat us if we went not so fast as they. We asked them why they used us so, and they replied that we were their captives. We said we were their friends, and that there was never an Englishman captive to the King of Morocco. So we came down to the ship and lay there with them seven days, while they had gotten all the goods they could, and then they parted it amongst them.

After the end of these seven days the captain appointed twenty of his men, well armed, to bring us up into the country; and the first night we came to the side of a river called Larache, where we lay on the grass all that night. So the next day we went over the river in a frigate of nine oars on a side, the river being in that place above a quarter of a mile broad, and that day we went to a town of thirty houses, called Totteon. There we lay four days, having nothing to feed on but bread and water; and then we went to a town called Cassuri, and there we were delivered by those twenty soldiers unto the *alcaide*, which examined us what we were, and we told him. He gave us a good answer, and sent us to the Jew's house, where we lay seven days. In the meanwhile that we lay here there were brought thither twenty Spaniards and twenty Frenchmen which Spaniards were taken in a conflict on land, but the Frenchmen were by foul weather cast on land within the Straits about Cape de Gata, and so made captives.

Thus at the seven days' end we twelve Englishmen, the twelve French, and the twenty Spaniards were all conducted toward Morocco, with nine hundred soldiers, horsemen and footmen, and in two days' journey we came to the river of Fez, where we lodged all night, being provided of tents. The next day we went to a town called Salé, and lay without the town in tents. From thence we travelled almost a hundred miles without finding any town, but every night we came to fresh water, which was partly running water and sometime rain water. So we came at last within three miles of the city of Morocco, where we pitched our tents; and there we met with a carrier which did travel in the country for the English merchants; and by him we sent word unto them of our estate. And they returned the next day unto us a Moor, which brought us victuals, being at that instant very feeble and hungry; and withal sent us a letter, with pen, ink and paper, willing us to write unto them what ship it was that was cast away, and how many and what men were alive. "For", said they, "we would know with speed, for tomorrow is the King's court; and therefore we would know, for that you should come into the city like captives."

But for all that, we were carried in as captives and with ropes about our necks, as well English as the French and Spaniards. And so we were carried before the King; and when we came before him, he did commit us all to ward, where we lay 15 days in close prison. And in the end we were cleared by the English merchants, to their great charges, for our deliverance cost them 700 ounces, every ounce in that country containing two shillings.

And when we came out of prison, we went to the Alfandica, where we continued eight weeks with the English merchants. At the end of which time, being well apparelled by the bounty of our merchants, we were conveyed down by the space of eight days' journey to Santa Cruz, where the English ships rode; where we took shipping about the 20th of March, two in the *Anne Francis* of London, and five more of us five days after in the *Expedition* of London, and two more in a Flemish flyboat, and one in the *Mary Edward*, also of London.

Other two of our number died in the country of the bloody flux: the one at our first imprisonment at Morocco, whose name was George Hancock, and the other at Santa Cruz, whose name was Robert Swancon, whose death was hastened by eating of roots and other unnatural things to slake their raging hunger in our travel, and by our hard and cold lodging in the open fields without tents.

Thus of fifty persons, through the rashness of an unskilful master, ten only survived of us, and after a thousand miseries returned home poor, sick, and feeble, into our country.

Richard Johnson	Thomas Henmore
William Williams, carpenter	John Silvester
John Durham	Thomas Whiting
Abraham Rouse	William Church
John Matthews	John Fox

Part 3

GUINEA

The West African coast, or "Guinea" as it was known to the Elizabethans, was the trial-ground in which the Portuguese, in the century before Hakluyt's, exercised their growing skill in navigation. This initiative was sponsored and monitored by a younger son of King John I of Portugal. With the express object of reclaiming Africa from the heathen, Henrique ("Prince Henry the Navigator", 1394–1460) devoted himself to the improvement of charts, of instruments, and of navigational technique, especially the fixing of latitude by taking the altitude of the pole-star. With his encouragement Portuguese navigators pushed further and further afield, discovering or rediscovering Madeira in 1419, in 1434 daring to round Cabo de Não (Cape Nun, reputedly the point of no return because of prevailing northerly winds), and in 1446 reaching the Cape Verde Islands. In 1455 Pope Nicholas V granted Portugal exclusive jurisdiction over Guinea "and past that southern shore all the way to the Indians"; and the process culminated in the passing of the Cape of Good Hope in 1488 and the establishment, by Vasco da Gama in 1498, of direct communications by that route with India and the East Indies.

The more northerly territories, and the Azores (1448), were cultivated by the Portuguese who, having long employed Moorish slaves in their home economy, imported negro labourers, mostly prisoners in the wars of the West African tribes. They also sought the products that gave the Ivory and Gold Coasts their names. These enterprises were protected by forts at key points, such as São Jorge da Mina (called by English sailors "the Mine") in what is now Ghana; but the mainland was then too unhealthy for long residence by Europeans.

The English and the French soon challenged the Portuguese monopoly, particularly of gold, ivory, and "grains of paradise" or pepper. (The slave-trade, which developed later, is here, as in Hakluyt's original, treated in the section relating to the Caribbean, where the slaves were sold.) The first English voyage came to grief through the intemperate behaviour of its Captain, Wyndham; but Locke's and Towerson's voyages yielded promising results. Then Portuguese resistance to the intruders stiffened, and in addition the English had to face growing competition from the French and later, when the Queen's husband, Philip of Spain, had in March 1557 brought England into his war with France, open hostilities. Locke's letter of 1561 suggests, despite his disclaimer, that the difficulties of the Guinea voyage were proving a deterrent. Nevertheless the Company for African trade, set up for the first voyage in 1555, was reactivated in 1588.

Narratives of English voyages that proceeded further on the Portuguese route round the Cape are mostly rather flat. The jewel among them (Thomas Stevens) has already been given in Part 2.

The first voyage to Guinea and Benin. (Compiled by Richard Eden from collected reports and investigations.)

IN the year of our Lord 1553, the twelfth day of August, sailed from Portsmouth two goodly ships, the *Primrose* and the *Lion*, with a pinnace called the *Moon*, being all well furnished as well with men of the lustiest sort to the number of seven score as also with ordnance and victuals requisite to such a voyage; having also two captains, the one a stranger called Anthony Anes Pinteado, a Portugal born in a town named the Port of Portugal, a wise, discreet and sober man, who for his cunning in sailing, being as well an expert pilot as a politic captain, was sometime in great favour with the King of Portugal, and to whom the coasts of Brazil and Guinea were committed to be kept from the Frenchmen, to whom he was a terror on the sea in those parts, and was furthermore a gentleman of the King his master's house. But as fortune in manner never favoureth but flattereth, never promiseth but deceiveth, never raiseth but casteth down again, and as great wealth and favour have always companions, emulation and envy, he was after many adversities and quarrels made against him enforced to come into England, where in this golden voyage he was evil matched with an unequal companion, an unlike match of most sundry qualities and conditions, with virtues few or none adorned.

Thus departed these noble ships under sail on their voyage; but first Captain Wyndham, putting forth of his ship at Portsmouth a kinsman of one of the head merchants, and showing herein a muster of the tragical parts he had conceived in his brain, and with such small beginnings nourished so monstrous a birth that more happy, yea, and blessed was that young man being left behind than if he had been taken with them, as some do wish he had done the like by theirs.

Thus sailed they on their voyage until they came to the island of Madeira, where they took in certain wines for the store of their ships and paid for them as they agreed of the price. At these islands they met with a great galleon of the King of Portugal, full of men and ordnance, yet such as could not have prevailed if it had attempted to withstand or resist our ships, for the which cause it was set forth not only to let and interrupt these our ships of their purposed voyage but all other that should attempt the like; yet chiefly to frustrate our voyage. For the King of Portugal was sinisterly informed that our ships were armed to his castle of Mina in those parts, whereas nothing less was meant.

After that our ships departed from the island of Madeira forward on their voyage began this worthy Captain Pinteado's sorrow, as a man tormented with the company of a terrible hydra who hitherto flattered with him and made him a fair countenance and show of love. Then did he take upon him to command all alone, setting nought both by Captain Pinteado and the rest of the merchants' factors, sometimes with opprobrious words and sometimes with threatenings most shamefully abusing them, taking from Pinteado the service of the boys and certain mariners that were assigned him by the order and direction of the worshipful merchants, and leaving him as a common mariner, which is the greatest despite and grief that can be to a Portugal or Spaniard, to be diminished of their honour, which they esteem above all riches.

Thus sailing forward on their voyage they came to the Islands of Canary, continuing their course from thence until they arrived at the island of St Nicholas, where they victualled themselves with fresh meat of the flesh of wild goats, whereof is great plenty in that island and in manner of nothing else. From hence, following on their course and tarrying here and there at the desert islands in the way, because they would not come too timely to the country of Guinea for the heat, and tarrying somewhat too long (for what can be well ministered in a commonwealth where inequality with tyranny will rule alone?) they came at the length to the first land of the country of Guinea, where they fell with the great river of Cestos, where they might for their merchandises have laden their ships with the grains of that country, which is a very hot fruit and much like unto a fig as it groweth on the tree. For as the figs are full of small seeds, so is the said fruit full of grains which are loose within the cod, having in the midst thereof a hole on every side. This kind of spice is much used in cold countries and may there be sold for great advantage for exchange of other wares. But our men, by the persuasion or rather enforcement of this tragical Captain, not regarding and setting light by that commodity in comparison of the fine gold they thirsted, sailed a hundred leagues further until they came to the golden land; where, not attempting to come near the castle pertaining to the King of Portugal, which was within the river of Mina, they made sale of their ware only on this side and beyond it for the gold of that country to the quantity of a hundred and fifty pounds weight, there being in case that they might have despatched all their ware for gold if the untame brain of Wyndham had or could have given ear to the counsel and experience of Pinteado. For when that Wyndham, not satisfied with the gold which he had, and more might have had if he had tarried about the Mina, commanding the said Pinteado (for so he took upon him) to lead the ships to Benin, being under the equinoctial line and a hundred and fifty leagues beyond the Mina, where he looked to have their ships laden with pepper; and being counselled of the said Pinteado considering the late time of the year for that time to go no further, but to make sale of their wares such as they had for gold, whereby they might have been great gainers, Wyndham not assenting hereunto fell into a sudden rage, reviling the said Pinteado, calling him Jew, with other opprobrious words, saying, "This whoreson Jew hath promised to bring us to such places as are not, or as he cannot bring us unto; but if he do not I will cut off his ears and nail them to the mast."

Pinteado gave the foresaid counsel to go no further for the safeguard of the men and their lives, which they should put in danger if they came too late for the *rossia*, which is their winter, not for cold but for smothering heat, with close and cloudy air and storming weather of such putrifying quality that it rotted the coats off their backs; or else for coming too soon for the scorching heat of the sun, which caused them to linger in the way. But of force and not of will brought he the ships before the river of Benin, where, riding at an anchor, they sent their pinnace up into the river 50 or 60 leagues, from whence certain of the merchants with Captain Pinteado, Francisco, a Portugal, Nicholas Lambert, gentleman, and other merchants were conducted to the court where the king remained, ten leagues from the riverside; whither when they came they were brought with a great company to the presence of the king, who, being a black Moor (although not so black as the rest), sat in a great huge hall, long and wide, the walls made of earth, without windows, the roof of thin boards, open in sundry places like unto louvres to let in the air.

And here to speak of the great reverence they give to their king, it is such that if we would give as much to Our Saviour Christ we should remove from our heads many plagues which we daily deserve for our contempt and impiety. So it is, therefore, that when his noblemen are in his presence they never look him in the face, but sit cowering, as we upon our knees, so they upon their buttocks, with their elbows upon their knees and their hands before their faces, not looking up until the king command them. And when they are coming toward the king as far as they do see him they do show such reverence, sitting on the ground with their faces covered as before. Likewise, when they depart from him they turn not their backs toward him but go creeping backward with like reverence.

And now to speak somewhat of the communication that was between the King and our men, you shall first understand that he himself could speak the Portugal tongue which he had learned of a child. Therefore after he had commanded our men to stand up and demanded of them the cause of their coming into that country, they answered by Pinteado that they were merchants travelling into those parts for the commodities of his country for exchange of wares which they had brought from their countries, being such as should be no less commodious for him and his people. The King then having of old lying in a certain storehouse 30 or 40 quintals of pepper (every quintal being a hundredweight) willed them to look upon the same, and again to bring him a sight of such merchandises as they had brought with them.

And thereupon sent with the Captain and the merchants certain of his men to conduct them to the water's side, with other to bring the ware from the pinnace to the Court; who when they were returned and the wares seen, the King grew to this end with the merchants to provide in 30 days the lading of all their ships with pepper. And in case their merchandises would not extend to the value of so much pepper he promised to credit them to their next return, and thereupon sent the country round about to gather pepper, causing the same to be brought to the court, so that within the space of thirty days they had gathered fourscore ton of pepper.

In the mean season our men, partly having no rule of themselves, but eating without measure of the fruits of the country and drinking the wine of the palm trees that droppeth in the night from the cut of the branches of the same, and in such extreme heat running continually into the water, not used before to such sudden and vehement alterations (than the which nothing is more dangerous) were thereby brought into swellings and agues; insomuch that the later time of the year coming on, caused them to die sometimes three and sometimes four or five in a day.

Then Wyndham, perceiving the time of the 30 days to be expired and his men dying so fast, sent to the court in post to Captain Pinteado and the rest to come away and to tarry no longer. But Pinteado with the rest wrote back to him again, certifying him of the great quantity of pepper they had already gathered, and looked daily for much more; desiring him furthermore to remember the great praise and name they should win if they came home prosperously, and what shame of the contrary. With which answer Wyndham not satisfied, and many of their men dying daily, willed and commanded them again either to come away forthwith or else threatened to leave them behind. When Pinteado heard this answer, thinking to persuade him with reason, he took his way from the court toward the ships, being conducted thither with men by the King's commandment.

In the mean season Wyndham, all raging, broke up Pinteado's cabin, broke open his chests, spoiled such provision of cold stilled waters and suckets as he had provided for his health, and left him nothing, neither of his instruments to sail by nor yet of his apparel; and in the meantime falling sick himself died also. Whose death Pinteado, coming aboard, lamented as much as if he had been the dearest friend he had in the world. But certain of the mariners and other officers did spit in his face, some calling him Jew, saying that he had brought them thither to kill them, and some drawing their swords at him making a show to slay him.

Then he perceiving that they would needs away desired them to tarry that he might fetch the rest of the merchants that were left at the court, but they would not grant this request. Then desired he them to give him the ship-boat, with as much of an old sail as might serve for the same, promising them therewith to bring Nicholas Lambert and the rest into England, but all was in vain. Then wrote he a letter to the court to the merchants informing them of all the matter, and promising them if God would lend him life to return with all haste to fetch them. And thus was Pinteado kept a-shipboard against his will, thrust among the boys of the ship, not used like a man nor yet like an honest boy, but glad to find favour at the cook's hand. Then departed they, leaving one of their ships behind them, which they sunk for lack of men to carry her.

After this, within six or seven days sailing, died also Pinteado for very pensiveness and thought that struck him to the heart; a man worthy to serve any prince, and most vilely used. And of sevenscore men came home to Plymouth scarcely forty, and of them many died. And that no man should suspect these words, which I have said in commendation of Pinteado, to be spoken upon favour otherwise than truth, I have thought good to add hereunto the copy of the letters which the King of Portugal and the Infante, his brother, wrote unto him to reconcile him, at such time as upon the King his master's displeasure (and not for any other crime or offence as may appear by the said letters) he was only for poverty enforced to come into England, where he first persuaded our merchants to attempt the said voyages to Guinea.

But as the King of Portugal too late repented him that he had so punished Pinteado upon malicious informations of such as envied the man's good fortune; even so may it hereby appear that in some cases even lions themselves may either be hindered by the contempt, or aided by the help of the poor mice, according unto the fable of Aesop.

The copy of Anthony Anes Pinteado's letters patents, whereby the King of Portugal made him Knight of his house, after all his troubles and imprisonment which, by wrong information to the King, he had sustained of long time, being at the last delivered, his cause known and manifested to the King, by a Grey Friar, the King's confessor.

I the King do give you to understand, Lord Francis Desseaso, one of my council and overseer of my house, that, in consideration of the good service which Anthony Anes Pinteado, the son of John Anes, dwelling in the town called the Port, hath done unto me, my will and pleasure is to make him Knight of my house, allowing to him in pension seven hundred reis monthly, and every day one alcair of barley as long as he keepeth a horse, and to be paid according to the ordinance of my house. Providing always that he shall reccive but one marriage gift; and this also in such condition, that the time which is accepted in our ordinance, forbidding such men to marry for getting such children as might succeed them in this allowance, which is 6 years after the making of this patent, shall be first expired before he do marry. I therefore command you to cause this to be entered in the book called the Matricula of our household, under the title of Knights. And when it is so entered, let the clerk of the Matricula, for the certainty thereof, write in the backside of this alvala or patent the number of the leaf wherein this our grant is entered. Which done, let him return this writing unto the said Anthony Anes Pinteado for his warrant.

I Diego Henriques have written this in Almarin the two and twentieth day of September in the year of Our Lord 1551. And this benevolence the King gave unto Anthony Anes Pinteado the five and twentieth day of July this present year.

Rey.

The Secretary's declaration written under the King's grant:

Your Majesty hath vouchsafed, in respect and consideration of the good service of Anthony Anes Pinteado, dwelling in the Port, and son of John Anes, to make him Knight of your house, with ordinary allowance of seven hundred reis pension by the month, and one alcair of barley by the day as long as he keepeth a horse; and to be paid according to the ordinance of your house, with condition that he shall have but one marriage gift, and that not within the space of six years after the making of these letters patents. The Secretary's note; entered in the book of the Matricula, folio 683.

Francisco de Siquera

The copy of the letter of Don Lewis, the Infante and brother to the King of Portugal, sent into England to Anthony Anes Pinteado.

Anthony Anes Pinteado, I, the Infante, brother to the King, have me heartily commended unto you. Peter Gonsalves is gone to seek you, desiring to bring you home again into your country. And for that purpose he hath with him a safe-conduct for you, granted by the King, that thereby you may freely and without all fear come home. And although the weather be foul and stormy, yet fail not to come. For in the time that His Majesty hath given you you may do many things to your contentation and gratifying the King, whereof I would be right glad; and to bring the same to pass I will do all that lieth in me for your profit. But forasmuch as Peter Gonsalves will make further declaration hereof unto you, I say no more at this present.

Written in Lisbon, the eighth day of December, anno 1552.

The Infante, Don Lewis

All these foresaid writings I saw under seal in the house of my friend Nicholas Liese, with whom Pinteado left them at his unfortunate departing to Guinea. But notwithstanding all these friendly letters and fair promises Pinteado durst not attempt to go home, neither to keep company with the Portugals his countrymen without the presence of other; forasmuch as he had secret admonitions that they intended to slay him, if time and place might have served their wicked intent.

The second voyage to Guinea set out by Sir George Barne, Sir John York, Thomas Locke, Anthony Hickman, and Edward Castelin in the year 1554; the Captain whereof was Master John Locke. (Compiled by Richard Eden, largely from notes supplied by Robert Gainsh, master of the *John Evangelist*.)

AS in the first voyage I have declared rather the order of the history than the course of the navigation, whereof at that time I could have no perfect information, so in the description of this second voyage my chief intent hath been to show the course of the same according to the observation and ordinary custom of the mariners and as I received it at the hands of an expert pilot, being one of the chief in this voyage; who also with his own hands wrote a brief declaration of the same as he found and tried all things, not by conjecture but by the art of sailing and instruments pertaining to the mariner's faculty. Not therefore assuming to myself the commendations due unto other, neither so bold as in any part to change or otherwise dispose the order of this voyage so well observed by art and experience, I have thought good to set forth the same in such sort and phrase of speech as is commonly used among them, and as I received it of the said pilot, as I have said. Take it therefore as followeth.

In the year of Our Lord 1554, the eleventh day of October, we departed the river of Thames with three goodly ships, the one called the *Trinity*, a ship of the burden of seven score ton, the other called the *Bartholomew*, a ship of the burden of ninety, the third was the *John Evangelist*, a ship of seven score ton. With the said ships and two pinnaces (whereof the one was drowned on the coast of England) we went forward on our voyage, and stayed at Dover fourteen days. We stayed also at Rye three or four days; moreover last of all we touched at Dartmouth.

The first day of November at nine of the clock at night, departing from the coast of England we set off the Start, bearing south-west all that night in the sea, and the next day all day and the next night after, until the third day of the said month about noon, making our way good, did run threescore leagues.

The 17th day in the morning we had sight of the Isle of Madeira, which doth rise, to him that cometh, in the north-north-east part upright land in the west part of it and very high; and to the south-south-east a low long land, and a long point, with a saddle through the midst of it, standing in 32 degrees; and in the west part many springs of water running down from the mountain, and many white fields like unto cornfields, and some white houses to the south-east part of it. And the top of the mountain showeth very ragged, if you may see it, and in the north-east part there is a bight or bay as though it were a harbour. Also in the said part there is a rock a little distance from the shore, and over the said bight you shall see a great gap in the mountain.

The 19th day at twelve of the clock we had sight of the Isle of Palma and Tenerife and the Canaries. The Isle of Palma riseth round, and lieth south-east and north-west, and the north-west part is lowest. In the south is a round hill over the headland and another round hill above that in the land. There are between the south-east part of the Isle of Madeira and the north-west part of the Isle of Palma seven and fifty leagues. This Isle of Palma lieth in 28 degrees; and our course from Madeira to the Isle of Palma was south and south by west, so that we had sight of Tenerife and of the Canaries. The south-east part of the Isle of Palma and the north-north-east of Tenerife lie south-east and north-west and between them are 20 leagues. Tenerife and the Great Canary (called Gran Canaria) and the west part of Fuerteventura stand in 27 degrees and a half. Gomera is a fair island but very ragged, and lieth west-south-west off Tenerife. And whosoever will come between them two islands must come south and by east; and in the south part of Gomera is a town and a good road in the said part of the island, and it standeth in 27 degrees and three [sic] tierces. Tenerife is a high land, with a great high peak like a sugar-loaf, and upon the said peak is snow throughout the whole year; and by reason of that peak it may be known above all other islands. And there we were becalmed the twentieth day of November from six of the clock in the morning until four of the clock at afternoon.

The two and twentieth day of November under the Tropic of Cancer the sun goeth down west and by south. Upon the coast of Barbary, five and twenty leagues by north Cape Blank, at three leagues off the main there are fifteen fathoms and good shelly ground, and sand among and no streams, and two small islands standing in 22 degrees and a tierce.

From Gomera to Cape de las Barbas is a hundred leagues, and our course was south and by east. The said Cape standeth in 22 and a half; and all that coast is flat, sixteen or seventeen fathom deep. Seven or eight leagues off from the Rio do Ouro to Cape de las Barbas there use many Spaniards and Portugals to trade for fishing during the month of November; and all that coast is very low lands. Also we went from Cape de las Barbas south-south-west and south-west and by south till we brought ourselves in 20 degrees and a half, reckoning ourselves seven leagues off; and there were the least shoals off Cape Blank. Then we went south until we brought ourselves in 13 degrees, reckoning ourselves five and twenty leagues off; and in 15 degrees we did rear the Crosiers, and we might have reared them sooner if we had looked for them. They are not right a cross in the month of November by reason that the nights are short there; nevertheless we had the sight of them the 29th day of the said month at night.

The first of December, being in 13 degrees, we set our course south and by east until the fourth day of December at 12 of the clock the same day. Then we were in 9 degrees and a tierce, reckoning ourselves 30 leagues off the shoals of the river called Rio Grande, being west-south-west off them, the which shoals be 30 leagues long. The fourth of December we began to set our course south-east, we being in 6 degrees and a half. The ninth day of December we set our course east-south-east; the fourteenth day of the said month we set our course east, we being in 5 degrees and a half, reckoning ourselves thirty and six leagues from the coast of Guinea.

The nineteenth of the said month we set our course east and by north, reckoning ourselves seventeen leagues distant from Cape Mesurado, the said Cape being east-north-east of us and the river of Cestos being east. The one and twentieth of the said month we fell with Cape Mesurado to the south-east about two leagues off. This Cape may be easily known by reason that the rising of it is like a porpoise-head. Also toward the south-east there are three trees, whereof the eastermost tree is the highest, and the middlemost is like a haystack, and the southermost like unto a gibbet; and upon the main are four or five high hills rising one after another like round hummocks or hillocks. And the south-east of the three trees brand-iron-wise, and all the coast along is white sand. The said Cape standeth within a little in 6 degrees. The two and twentieth of December we came to the river of Cestos, and remained there until the nine and twentieth day of the said month. Here we thought it best to send before us the pinnace to the River Dulce, called Rio Dulce, that they might have the beginning of the market before the coming of the *John Evangelist*.

At the river of Cestos we had a tun of grains. This river standeth in 6 degrees lacking a tierce. From the river of Cestos to Rio Dulce are five and twenty leagues. Rio Dulce standeth in 5 degrees and a half. The river of Cestos is easy to be known by reason there is a ledge of rocks on the south-east part of the road, and at the entering into the haven are five or six trees that bear no leaves. This is a good harbour, but very narrow at the entrance into the river. There is also a rock in the haven's mouth right as you enter. And all that coast between Cape de Monte and Cape de las Palmas lieth south-east and by east, north-west and by west, being three leagues off the shore. And you shall have in some places rocks two leagues off, and that between the river of Cestos and Cape de las Palmas.

Between the river of Cestos and the River Dulce are five and twenty leagues, and the high land that is between them both is called Cakeado, being eight leagues from the river of Cestos. And to the south-eastward of it is a place called Shawgro and another called Shyawe or Shavo, where you may get fresh water. Off this Shyawe lieth a ledge of rocks, and to the south-eastward lieth a headland called Croke. Between Cakeado and Croke are nine or ten leagues. To the south-eastward off is a harbour called St Vincent. Right over against St Vincent is a rock under the water, two leagues and a half off the shore. To the south-eastward of that rock you shall see an island about three or four leagues off; this island is not past a league off the shore. To the east-south-east of the island is a rock that lieth above the water, and by that rock goeth in the River Dulce which you shall know by the said river and rock. The north-west side of the haven is flat sand and the south-east side thereof is like an island, and a bare plot without any trees; and so is it not in any other place. In the road you shall ride in thirteen or fourteen fathoms, good ooze and sand, being the marks of the road to bring the island and the north-east land together; and here we anchored the last of December.

The third day of January we came from the River Dulce. Note that Cape de las Palmas is a fair high land, but some low places thereof by the waterside look like red cliffs with white streaks like highways, a cable-length apiece, and this is the east part of the Cape. This Cape is the southermost land in all the coast of Guinea, and standeth in 4 degrees and a tierce. The coast from Cape de las Palmas to Cape Trepointes or das Tres Pontas is fair and clear without rock or other danger.

Twenty and five leagues from Cape de las Palmas the land is higher than in any place until we come to Cape Trepointes; and about ten leagues before you come to Cape Trepointes the land riseth still higher and higher until you come to Cape Trepointes. Also before you come to the said Cape, after other 5 leagues to the north-west part of it, there is certain broken ground with two great rocks, and within them in the bight of a bay is a castle called Arra pertaining to the King of Portugal. You shall know it by the said rocks that lie off it, for there is none such from Cape de las Palmas to Cape Trepointes. This coast lieth east and by north, west and by south. From Cape de las Palmas to the said castle is fourscore and fifteen leagues; and the coast lieth from the said castle to the westermost point of Trepointes south-east and by south, north-west and by north. Also the westermost point of Trepointes is a low land, lying half a mile out in the sea, and upon the innermost neck, to the landward, is a tuft of trees; and there we arrived the eleventh day of January.

The 12th day of January we came to a town called Shama or Samva, being 8 leagues from Cape Trepointes toward east-north-east. Between Cape Trepointes and the town of Samva is a great ledge of rocks a great way out in the sea. We continued four days at that town, and the captain thereof would needs have a pledge ashore; but when they received the pledge they kept him still and would traffic no more, but shot off their ordnance at us. They have two or three pieces of ordnance and no more.

The sixteenth day of the said month we made reckoning to come to a place called Cape Corea, where Captain Don John dwelleth, whose men entertained us friendly. This Cape Corea is four leagues eastward of the castle of Mina, otherwise called La Mina, or Castello de Mina, where we arrived the 18th day of the month. Here we made sale of all our cloth saving two or three packs.

The 26th day of the same month we weighed anchor and departed from thence to the *Trinity*, which was seven leagues eastward of us where she sold her wares. Then they of the *Trinity* willed us to go eastward of that eight or nine leagues to sell part of their wares in a place called Beraku and another place named Beraku Grande, being the eastermost place of both these, which you shall know by a great round hill near unto it named Monte Rodondo, lying westward from it; and by the waterside are many high palm trees. From hence did we set forth homeward the thirteenth day of February and plied up alongst till we came within seven or eight leagues to Cape Trepointes. About eight of the clock, the 15th day at afternoon, we did cast about to seaward. And beware of the currents, for they will deceive you sore. Whosoever shall come from the coast of Mina homeward, let him be sure to make his way good west until he reckon himself as far as Cape de las Palmas, where the current setteth always to the eastward; and within twenty leagues eastward of Cape de las Palmas is a river called De los Potos, where you may have fresh water and ballast enough, and plenty of ivory or elephants' teeth. This river standeth in 4 degrees and almost two tierces. And when you reckon yourself as far shot as Cape de las Palmas, being in 1 degree or 1 degree and a half, you may go west, and west by north, until you come in 3 degrees; and then you may go west-north-west and north-west and by west until you come in 5 degrees, and then north-west. And in 6 degrees we met northerly winds, and great ruffling of tides; and, as we could judge, the currents went to the north-north-west. Furthermore, between Cape de Monte and Cape Verde go great currents, which deceive many men.

The 22nd day of April we were in 8 degrees and two tierces; and so we ran to the north-west, having the wind at north-east and east-north-east and sometimes at east, until we were at 18 degrees and a tierce, which was on May Day. And so from 18 and two tierces we had the wind at east and east-north-east, and sometimes at east-south-east; and then we reckoned the Islands of Cape Verde east-south-east of us, we judging ourselves to be 48 leagues off. And in 20 and 21 degrees we had the wind more easterly to the southward than before. And so we ran to the north-west and north-north-west, and sometimes north and by west and north, until we came into 31 degrees, where we reckoned ourselves a hundred and fourscore leagues south-west and by south of the Island de los Flores; and there we met with the wind at south-south-east, and set our course north-east.

In 23 degrees we had the wind at the south and south-west, and then we set our course north-north-east, and so we ran to 40 degrees; and then we set our course north-east, the wind being at the south-west, and having the Isle de Flores east of us and 17 leagues off. In the 41 degrees we met with the wind at north-east, and so we ran north-westward; then we met with the wind west-north-west, and at the west within 6 leagues running towards the north-west, and then we cast about and lay north-east until we came in 42 degrees where we set our course east-north-east, judging the Isle of Corvo south and by west of us and six and thirty leagues distant from us.

A remembrance, that the 21st of May we communed with John Ralph, and he thought it best to go north-east, and judged himself 25 leagues eastward to the Isle of Flores, and in 39 degrees and a half.

Note that on the fourth day of September, under 9 degrees, we lost the sight of the north star. Note also that in 45 degrees the compass is varied 8 degrees to the west; item, in 40 degrees the compass did vary 15 degrees in the whole; item, in 30 degrees and a half the compass is varied 5 degrees to the west.

Be it also in memory that two or three days before we came to Cape das Tres Pontas the pinnace went along the shore, thinking to sell some of our wares, and so we came to anchor three or four leagues west and by south of the Cape das Tres Pontas, where we left the *Trinity*. Then our pinnace came aboard with all our men; the pinnace also took in more wares. They told me, moreover, that they would go to a place where the *Primrose* was and had received much gold at the first voyage to these parts, and told me furthermore that it was a good place. But I, fearing a brigantine that was there upon the coast, did weigh and follow them, and left the *Trinity* about four leagues off from us, and there we rode against that town four days. So that Martin, by his own desire, and assent of some of the commissioners that were in the pinnace, went ashore to the town; and there John Berin went to traffic from us, being three miles off trafficking at another town. The town is called Shama or Samva, for Shama and Sammaterra are the names of the two first towns where we did traffic for gold to the north-east of Cape das Tres Pontas. Hitherto continueth the course of the voyage as it was described by the said pilot. Now therefore I will speak somewhat of the country and people, and of such things as are brought from thence.

They brought from thence at the last voyage four hundred pound weight and odd of gold, of two and twenty carats and one grain in fineness, also six and thirty butts of grains, and about two hundred and fifty elephants' teeth of all quantities. Of these I saw and measured some of nine spans in length, as they were crooked. Some of them were as big as a man's thigh above the knee, and weighed about fourscore and ten pound weight apiece. They say that some one hath been seen of a hundred and five and twenty pound weight. Other there were which they call the teeth of calves, of one or two or three years, whereof some were a foot and a half, some two foot and some three or more, according to the age of the beast.

These great teeth or tusks grow in the upper jaw downward, and not in the nether jaw upward, wherein the painters and arras-workers are deceived. At this last voyage was brought from Guinea the head of an elephant, of such huge bigness that only the bones or cranium thereof, beside the nether jaw and great tusks, weighed about two hundred weight, and was as much as I could well lift from the ground; insomuch that considering also herewith the weight of two such great teeth, the nether jaw with the less teeth, the tongue, the great hanging ears, the big and long snout or trunk, with all the flesh, brains and skin with all other parts belonging to the whole head, in my judgment it could weigh little less than five hundredweight. This head divers have seen in the house of the worthy merchant Sir Andrew Judd, where also I saw it, and beheld it not only with my bodily eyes, but much more with the eyes of my mind and spirit, considering by the work the cunning and wisdom of the workmaster; without which consideration, the sight of such strange and wonderful things may rather seem curiosities than profitable contemplations.

The elephant (which some call an oliphant) is the biggest of all four-footed beasts. His forelegs are longer than his hinder, he hath ankles in the lower part of his hinder legs, and five toes on his feet undivided. His snout or trunk is so long, and in such form, that it is to him in the stead of a hand; for he neither eateth nor drinketh but by bringing his trunk to his mouth. Therewith he helpeth up his master or keeper; therewith he overthroweth trees. Beside his two great tusks, he hath on each side of his mouth four teeth, wherewith he eateth and grindeth his meat. Either of these teeth is almost a span in length, as they grow along in the jaw, and are about two inches in height, and almost as much in thickness. The tusks of the male are greater than of the female. His tongue is very little and so far in his mouth, that it cannot be seen. Of all beasts they arc most gentle and tractable; for by many sundry ways they are taught, and do understand; insomuch that they learn to do due honour to a king, and arc of quick sense and sharpness of wit.

When the male hath once seasoned the female he never after toucheth her.

The male elephant liveth two hundred years, or at the least one hundred and twenty; the female almost as long, but the flower of their age is but threescore years, as some write. They cannot suffer winter or cold. They love rivers, and will often go into them up to the snout, wherewith they blow and snuff, and play in the water, but swim they cannot, for the weight of their bodies. Pliny and Soline write that they use no adultery.

If they happen to meet with a man in the wilderness, being out of the way, gently they will go before him, and bring him into the plain way. Joined in battle they have no small respect unto them that be wounded, for they bring them that are hurt or weary into the middle of the army to be defended. They are made tame by drinking the juice of barley.

They have continual war against dragons, which desire their blood, because it is very cold; and therefore the dragon, lying await as the elephant passeth by, windeth his tail (being of exceeding length) about the hinder legs of the elephant, and so staying him, thrusteth his head into his trunk and exhausteth his breath, or else biteth him in the ear, whereunto he cannot reach with his trunk. And when the elephant waxeth faint, he falleth down on the serpent, being now full of blood, and with the poise of his body breaketh him so that his own blood with the blood of the elephant runneth out of him mingled together, which being cold, is congealed into that substance which the apothecaries call *sanguis draconis*, that is, dragon's blood, otherwise called *cinnabaris*, although there be another kind of *cinnabaris*, commonly called cinnabar or vermilion, which the painters use in certain colours.

They are also of three kinds, as of the marshes, the plains, and the mountains, no less differing in conditions. Philostratus writeth that as much as the elephant of Libya in bigness passeth the horse of Nysea, so much do the elephants of India exceed them of Libya: for the elephants of India, some have been seen of the height of nine cubits. The other do so greatly fear these that they dare not abide the sight of them. Of the Indian elephants only the males have tusks, but of them of Ethiopia and Libya both kinds are tusked. They are of divers heights, as of twelve, thirteen and fourteen dodrants, every dodrant being a measure of nine inches. Some write that an elephant is bigger than three wild oxen or buffs. They of India are black, or of the colour of a mouse, but those of Ethiopia or Guinea are brown. The hide or skin of them all is very hard, and without hair or bristles. Their ears are two dodrants broad, and their eyes very little. Our men saw one drinking at a river in Guinea, as they sailed into the land.

Of other properties and conditions of the elephant, as of their marvellous docility, of their fight and use in the wars, of their generation and chastity, when they were first seen in the theatres and triumphs of the Romans, how they are taken and tamed, and when they cast their tusks, with the use of the same in medicine, whoso desireth to know, let him read Pliny, in the eighth book of his *Natural History*. He also writeth in his twelfth book that in old time they made many goodly works of ivory or elephants' teeth: as tables, trestles, posts of houses, rails, lattices for windows, images of their gods, and divers other things of ivory, both coloured and uncoloured, and intermixed with sundry kinds of precious woods, as at this day are made of certain chairs, lutes, and virginals. They had such plenty thereof in old time, that (as far as I remember) Josephus writeth that one of the gates of Jerusalem was called Porta Eburnea, that is the Ivory Gate. The whiteness thereof was so much esteemed that it was thought to represent the natural fairness of man's skin: insomuch that such as went about to set forth (or rather corrupt) natural beauty with colours and painting, were reproved by this proverb, *Ebur atramento candefacere*, that is, To make ivory white with ink. The poets also, describing the fair necks of beautiful virgins, call them *eburnea colla*, that is, ivory necks. And to have said thus much of elephants and ivory, it may suffice.

Now therefore I will speak somewhat of the people and their manners and manner of living, with another brief description of Africa also. It is to be understood that the people which now inhabit the regions of the coast of Guinea and the middle parts of Africa, as Libya the Inner and Nubia, with divers other great and large regions about the same, were in old time called Ethiops and Nigritae, which we now call Moors, Morians, or negroes: a people of beastly living, without a god, law, religion, or commonwealth, and so scorched and vexed with the heat of the sun that in many places they curse it when it riseth. Of the regions and people about the Inner Libya (called Libya Interior) Gemma Frisius writeth thus.

Libya Interior is very large and desolate, in the which are many horrible wildernesses and mountains replenished with divers kinds of wild and monstrous beasts and serpents. First from Mauritania or Barbary toward the south is Getulia, a rough and savage region whose inhabitants are wild and wandering people. After these follow the people called Melanogetuli and Pharusii, which wander in the wilderness, carrying with them great gourds of water. The Ethiopians called Nigritae occupy a great part of Africa and are extended to the West Ocean. Southward also they reach to the River Nigritis, whose nature agreeth with the river of Nilus forasmuch as it is increased and diminished at the same time and bringeth forth the like beasts, as the crocodile. By reason whereof I think this to be the same river which the Portugals call Senegal, for this river is also of the same nature. It is furthermore marvellous and very strange that is said of this river; and this is, that on the one side thereof the inhabitants are of high stature and black, and on the other side of brown or tawny colour and low stature, which thing also our men confirm to be true.

There are also other people of Libya called Garamantes, whose women are common: for they contract no matrimony, neither have respect to chastity. After these are the nations of the people called Pyrei, Saphiodaphnitae, Odrangi, Mimaces, Lynxamatae, Dolopes, Aganginae, Leuci Ethiopes, Xilicei Ethiopes, Calcei Ethiopes, and Nubi. These have the same situation in Ptolemy that they now give to the kingdom of Nubia. Here are certain Christians under the dominion of the great Emperor of Ethiopia called Prester John. From these toward the west is a great nation of people called Aphricerones, whose region, as far as may be gathered by conjecture, is the same that is now called Regnum Orguene, confining upon the east parts of Guinea. From hence westward, and somewhat toward the north, are the kingdoms of Gambra and Budomel, not far from the river of Senegal; and from hence toward the inland regions and along by the sea coast are the regions of Ginoia or Guinea which we commonly call Ginnee. On the west side of these regions, toward the Ocean, is the cape or point called Cabo Verde, or Caput Viride, that is the green cape, to the which the Portugals first direct their course when they sail to America or the land of Brazil. Then, departing from hence, they turn to the right hand toward the quarter of the wind called *garbino*, which is between the west and the south.

But to speak somewhat more of Ethiopia. Although there are many nations of people so named, yet is Ethiopia chiefly divided into two parts, whereof the one is called Ethiopia under Egypt, a great and rich region. To this pertaineth the island Meroe, embraced round about with the streams of the River Nilus. In this island women reigned in old time. Josephus writeth that it was sometime called Sabea; and that the Queen of Saba came from thence to Jerusalem to hear the wisdom of Solomon. From hence toward the east reigneth the said Christian Emperor Prester John, whom some call Papa Johannes, and other say that he is called Pean Juan, that is Great John; whose empire reacheth far beyond Nilus and is extended to the coasts of the Red Sea and Indian Sea. The middle of the region is almost in 66 degrees of longitude and 12 degrees of latitude. About this region inhabit the people called Clodi, Risophagi, Babylonii, Axiunitae, Molili, and Molibae. After these is the region called Trogloditica, whose inhabitants dwell in caves and dens; for these are their houses, and the flesh of serpents their meat, as writeth Pliny and Diodorus Siculus. They have no speech, but rather a grinning and chattering. There are also people without heads, called Blemines, having their eyes and mouth in their breasts. Likewise Strucophagi, and naked Ganphasantes; Satyrs also, which have nothing of men but only shape; moreover Oripei, great hunters, Mennones also, and the region of Smyrnophora, which bringeth forth myrrh. After these is the region of Azania, in the which many elephants are found. A great part of the other regions of Africa that are beyond the equinoctial line are now ascribed to the kingdom of Malindi, whose inhabitants are accustomed to traffic with the nations of Arabia, and their King is joined in friendship with the King of Portugal, and payeth tribute to Prester John.

The other Ethiopia, called Ethiopia Interior, that is the Inner Ethiopia, is not yet known, for the greatness thereof, but only by the sea coasts; yet it is described in this manner. First, from the equinoctial toward the south, is a great region of Ethiopians which bringeth forth white elephants, tigers, and the beasts called rhinoceroses; also a region that bringeth forth plenty of cinnamon, lying between the branches of Nilus. Also the kingdom of Habech or Habasia, a region of Christian men lying both on this side and beyond Nilus. Here are also the Ethiopians called Ichthyophagi, that is such as live only by fish, and were sometimes subdued by the wars of great Alexander. Furthermore the Ethiopians called Rhapsii and Anthropophagi, that are accustomed to eat man's flesh, inhabit the regions near unto the mountains called Montes Lunae, that is the mountains of the moon. Gazatia is under the Tropic of Capricorn. After this followeth the front of Africa, the Cape of Buena Speranza or Caput Bonae Spei, that is the Cape of Good Hope, by which they pass that sail from Lisbon to Calicut; but by what names the capes and gulfs are called, forasmuch as the same are in every globe and card, it were here superfluous to rehearse them.

Some write that Africa was so named by the Grecians because it is without cold; for the Greek letter Alpha or A signifieth privation, void, or without, and Phrike signifieth cold. For indeed, although in the stead of winter they have a cloudy and tempestuous season, yet it is not cold, but rather smothering hot, with hot showers of rain also, and somewhere such scorching winds, that what by one means and other they seem at certain times to live as it were in furnaces and in manner already half way in Purgatory or hell. Gemma Frisius writeth that in certain parts of Africa, as in Atlas the Greater, the air in the night season is seen shining, with many strange fires and flames rising in manner as high as the moon; and that in the element are sometime heard as it were the sound of pipes, trumpets, and drums; which noises may perhaps be caused by the vehement and sundry motions of such fiery exhalations in the air, as we see the like in many experiences wrought by fire, air, and wind. The hollowness also, and divers reflexions and breaking of the clouds, may be great causes hereof, beside the vehement cold of the middle region of the air, whereby the said fiery exhalations, ascending thither, are suddenly struck back with great force. For even common and daily experience teacheth us, by the hissing of a burning torch, what noise fire maketh in the air, and much more where it striveth when it is enclosed with air, as appeareth in guns, and as the like is seen in only air enclosed, as in organ pipes and such other instruments that go by wind. For wind, as say the philosophers, is none other than air vehemently moved, as we see in a pair of bellows and such other.

Some of our men of good credit that were in this last voyage to Guinea affirm earnestly that in the night season they felt a sensible heat to come from the beams of the moon. The which thing, although it be strange and insensible to us that inhabit cold regions, yet doth it stand with good reason that it may so be, forasmuch as the nature of stars and planets, as writeth Pliny, consisteth of fire and containeth in it a spirit of life, which cannot be without heat. And that the moon giveth heat upon the earth the prophet David seemeth to confirm in his 121st Psalm where, speaking of such men as are defended from evils by God's protection, he saith thus: *per diem sol non exuret te, nec luna per noctem*, that is to say, in the day the sun shall not burn thee nor the moon by night.

They say furthermore that in certain places of the sea they saw certain streams of water, which they call spouts, falling out of the air into the sea, and that some of these are as big as the great pillars of churches; insomuch that sometimes they fall into ships and put them in great danger of drowning. Some feign that these should be the cataracts of heaven, which were all opened at Noah's flood; but I think them rather to be such fluxions and eruptions as Aristotle in his book *De Mundo* saith to chance in the sea. For speaking of such strange things as are seen oftentimes in the sea he writeth thus: Oftentimes also even in the sea are seen evaporations of fire, and such eruptions and breaking forth of springs that the mouths of rivers are opened; whirlpools and fluxions are caused of such other vehement motions, not only in the midst of the sea but also in creeks and straits; at certain times also a great quantity of water is suddenly lifted up and carried about with the moon, etc. By which words of Aristotle it doth appear that such waters be lifted up in one place at one time and suddenly fall down in another place at another time. And hereunto perhaps pertaineth it that Richard Chancellor told me that he heard Sebastian Cabot report that, as far as I remember either about the coasts of Brazil or Rio de Plata, his ship or pinnace was suddenly lifted from the sea and cast upon land, I wot not how far. The which thing and such other like wonderful and strange works of nature while I consider, and call to remembrance the narrowness of man's understanding and knowledge in comparison of her mighty power, I can but cease to marvel, and confess with Pliny that nothing is to her impossible, the least part of whose power is not yet known to men.

Many things more our men saw and considered in this voyage worthy to be noted, whereof I have thought good to put some in memory, that the reader may as well take pleasure in the variety of things as knowledge of the history. Among other things, therefore, touching the manners and nature of the people, this may seem strange, that their princes and noblemen use to pounce and race their skins with pretty knots in divers forms, as it were branched damask, thinking that to be a decent ornament. And albeit they go in manner all naked, yet are many of them, and especially their women, in manner laden with collars, bracelets, hoops, and chains, either of gold, copper, or ivory. I myself have one of their bracelets of ivory, weighing two pound and six ounces of troy weight, which make eight and thirty ounces; this one of their women did wear upon her arm. It is made of one whole piece of the biggest part of the tooth, turned and somewhat carved, with a hole in the midst wherein they put their hands to wear it on their arm. Some have on every arm one, and as many on their legs, wherewith some of them are so galled that, although they are in manner made lame thereby, yet will they by no means leave them off. Some wear also on their legs great shackles of bright copper which they think to be no less comely. They wear also collars, bracelets, garlands, and girdles of certain blue stones like beads. Likewise some of their women wear on their bare arms certain foresleeves made of the plates of beaten gold. On their fingers also they wear rings made of golden wires, with a knot or wreath, like to that which children make in a ring of a rush. Among other things of gold that our men bought of them for exchange of their wares were certain dog-chains and collars.

They are very wary people in their bargaining, and will not lose one spark of gold of any value. They use weights and measures, and are very circumspect in occupying the same. They that shall have to do with them must use them gently; for they will not traffic or bring in any wares if they be evil used. At the first voyage that our men had into these parts it so chanced that, at their departure from the first place where they did traffic, one of them either stole a musk cat or took her away by force, not mistrusting that that should have hindered their bargaining in another place whither they intended to go. But for all the haste they could make with full sails, the fame of their misusage so prevented them that the people of that place also, offended thereby, would bring in no wares; insomuch that they were enforced either to restore the cat or pay for her at their price before they could traffic there.

Their houses are made of four posts or trees, and covered with boughs. Their common feeding is of roots, and such fishes as they take, whereof they have great plenty. There are also such flying fishes as are seen in the sea of the West Indies. Our men salted of their fishes, hoping to provide store thereof; but they would take no salt, and must therefore be eaten forthwith, as some say. Howbeit, other affirm that if they be salted immediately after they be taken they will last uncorrupted ten or twelve days. But this is more strange, that part of such flesh as they carried with them out of England, which putrefied there, became sweet again at their return to the clime of temperate regions. They use also a strange making of bread in this manner. They grind between two stones with their hands as much corn as they think may suffice their family, and when they have thus brought it to flour they put thereto a certain quantity of water, and make thereof very thin dough, which they stick upon some post of their houses, where it is baked by the heat of the sun. So that when the master of the house or any of his family will eat thereof, they take it down and eat it.

They have very fair wheat, the ear whereof is two handfuls in length, and as big as a Great Bulrush and almost four inches about where it is biggest. The stem or straw seemeth to be almost as big as the little finger of a man's hand, or little less. The grains of this wheat are as big as our pease, round also, and very white and somewhat shining, like pearls that have lost their colour. Almost all the substance of them turneth into flour, and maketh little bran or none. I told in one ear two hundred and threescore grains. The ear is enclosed in three blades longer than itself, and of two inches broad apiece. And by this fruitfulness the sun seemeth partly to recompense such griefs and molestations as they otherwise receive by the fervent heat thereof. It is doubtless a worthy contemplation to consider the contrary effects of the sun, or rather the contrary passions of such things as receive the influence of his beams, either to their hurt or benefit.

Their drink is either water or the juice that droppeth from the cut branches of the barren date-trees, called *palmitos*. For either they hang great gourds at the said branches every evening, and let them so hang all night, or else they set them on the ground under the trees that the drops may fall therein. They say that this kind of drink is in taste much like unto whey, but somewhat sweeter and more pleasant. They cut the branches every evening, because they are seared up in the day by the heat of the sun. They have also great beans as big as chestnuts, and very hard, with a shell in the stead of a husk.

Many more things might be said of the manners of the people, and of the wonders and monstrous things that are engendered in Africa; but it shall suffice to have said thus much of such things as our men partly saw and partly brought with them. And whereas before, speaking of the fruit of grains, I described the same to have holes by the side, as indeed it hath as it is brought hither, yet was I afterward informed that those holes were made to put strings or twigs through the fruit, thereby to hang them up to dry at the sun. They grow not past a foot and a half or two foot from the ground, and are as red as blood when they are gathered. The grains themselves are called of the physicians *grana paradisi*.

At their coming home the keels of their ships were marvellously overgrown with certain shells of two inches length and more, as thick as they could stand, and of such bigness that a man might put his thumb in the mouths of them. They certainly affirm that in these there groweth a certain slimy substance which, at the length slipping out of the shell and falling in the sea, becometh those fowls which we call barnacles. The like shells have been seen in ships returning from Iceland, but these shells were not past half an inch in length. Of the other that came from Guinea, I saw the *Primrose* lying in the dock and in manner covered with the said shells, which in my judgment should greatly hinder her sailing. Their ships were also in many places eaten with the worms called *bromas* or *bissas*, whereof mention is made in the *Decades*. These creep between the planks, which they eat through in many places.

Among other things that chanced to them in this voyage, this is worthy to be noted, that whereas they sailed thither in seven weeks they could return in no less space than twenty weeks. The cause whereof they say to be this: that about the coast of Cabo Verde the wind is ever at the east, by reason whereof they were enforced to sail far out of their course into the main ocean to find the wind at west to bring them home. There died of our men at this last voyage about twenty and four, whereof many died at their return into the clime of the cold regions, as between the Islands of Azores and England. They brought with them certain black slaves, whereof some were tall and strong men and could well agree with our meats and drinks. The cold and moist air doth somewhat offend them. Yet doubtless men that are born in hot regions may better abide cold than men that are born in cold regions may abide heat, forasmuch as vehement heat resolveth the radical moisture of men's bodies, as cold constraineth and preserveth the same.

This is also to be considered as a secret work of nature, that throughout all Africa under the equinoctial line, and near about the same on both sides, the regions are extremely hot and the people very black. Whereas contrarily such regions of the West Indies as are under the same line are very temperate, and the people neither black nor with curled and short wool on their heads, as they of Africa have, but of the colour of an olive with long and black hair on their heads; the cause of which variety is declared in divers places in the *Decades*.

It is also worthy to be noted that some of them that were at this voyage told me: that is, that they overtook the course of the sun, so that they had it north of them at noon the 14th day of March. And to have said thus much of these voyages, it may suffice.

The first voyage made by Master William Towerson, merchant of
London, to the coast of Guinea, with two ships, in the year 1555.

UPON Monday, the thirtieth day of September, we departed
from the Isle of Wight out of the haven of Newport, with two
good ships, the one called the *Hart* the other the *Hind*, both of
London, and the masters of them were John Ralph and William Carter,
for a voyage to be made unto the River dos Cestos in Guinea and to
other havens thereabout.

It fell out by the variety of winds that it was the fourteenth day of
October before we could fetch Dartmouth; and being there arrived we
continued in the road six days, and the 20th of October we warped out
of the haven and set sail, directing our course towards the south-west,
and the next morning we were run by estimation thirty leagues.

The first of November we found ourselves to be 31 degrees of
latitude by the reckoning of our Master. This day we ran about 40
leagues also. The second day we ran 36 leagues.

The third day we had sight of Porto Santo, which is a small island
lying in the sea, about three leagues long and a league and a half broad,
and is possessed by Portugals. It riseth as we came from the north-
north-west like two small hills near together. The east end of the same
island is a high land like a saddle with a valley, which makes it to bear
that form. The west end of it is lower, with certain small round hillocks.
This island lieth in 33 degrees. The same day at 11 of the clock we
raised the Isle of Madeira, which lieth 12 leagues from Porto Santo
towards the south-west. That island is a fair island and fruitful, and is
inhabited by Portugals; it riseth afar off like a great whole land and
high. By three of the clock this day at afternoon we were thwart of
Porto Santo, and we set our course south-west to leave the Isle of
Madeira to the eastward, as we did Porto Santo. These two islands
were the first land that we saw since we left the coast of England. About
three of the clock after midnight we were thwart of Madeira, within
three leagues of the west end of it, and by means of the high hills there
we were becalmed. We suppose we ran this day and night 30 leagues.

The fourth day we lay becalmed under the Isle of Madeira until one
of the clock at afternoon, and then, the wind coming into the east, we
went our course, and ran that day fifteen leagues. The 5th day we ran
15 leagues more.

The 6th day in the morning we raised the Isle of Tenerife, otherwise
called the Pike, because it is a very high island with a pike upon the top
like a loaf of sugar. The same night we raised the Isle of Palma, which is
a high land also, and to the westward of the Isle of Tenerife.

The 7th day we perceived the Isle of Gomera, which is an island standing betwixt Tenerife and Palma about 12 leagues eastward from Palma and 8 leagues westward from Tenerife; and for fear of being becalmed with the Isle of Tenerife we left both it and Gomera to the eastward of us, and went betwixt Palma and Gomera. We ran this day and night 30 leagues. Note that these islands be 60 leagues from Madeira, and that there are 3 islands more to the westward of Tenerife, named the Grand Canaria, Fuerteventura, and Lancerota, of which islands we came not in sight. They be inhabited by Spaniards.

This day also we had sight of the Isle of Ferro, which is to the southwards 13 leagues from the other islands, and is possessed by Spaniards. All this day and night by reason of the wind we could not double the point of the Isle of Ferro except we would have gone to the westward of it, which had been much out of our course. Therefore we kept about, and ran back five hours east-north-east to the end we might double it upon the next board, the wind continuing south-east which hath not been often seen upon that coast by any travellers; for the wind continueth there for the most part north-east, and east-north-east. So upon the other board by the next morning we were in a manner with the island and had room enough to double the same.

The 8th day we kept our course as near the wind as we could, because that our due course to fetch the coast of Barbary was south-east and by east; but by the scant wind we could not go our due course but went as near it as we could, and ran this day and night 25 leagues. The 9th day we ran 30 leagues, the 10th 25 leagues, the 12th 24.

The 12th day we saw a sail under our lee, which was, as we thought, a fisherman, so that we went room to have spoken with him; but within one hour there fell such a fog that we could not see the ship, nor one of us the other. We shot off divers pieces to the *Hind*, but she heard them not. At afternoon she shot off a piece which we heard and made her answer with another; and within one half hour after the fog broke up, and we were within 4 leagues of the shore upon the coast of Barbary, and we sounded and had 14 fathom water. The bark also came room with us, and there anchored by reason of the contrary wind. When we fell with the land, we could not judge justly what part of the land it was, because the most part of that coast is low land and no part to be judged of it but the forepart of the shore, which is white, like chalk or sand, and very deep unto the hard shore. There immediately we began to fish, and found great store of a kind of fish which the Portugals commonly fish for upon that coast, which they call *pergosses*; the Frenchmen call them *saders*, and our men salt-water bream. Before the clearing up of the fog the ship which we followed shaped us such a course that we could see her no more, by reason of our shooting off to find the *Hind* again. This part of the coast of Barbary, by our pilot's reckoning, is about 16 leagues to the eastwards the River do Ouro.

The 13th day in the afternoon we spied a sail coming towards us which we judged to be the sail that we saw the day before; and as soon as we spied him we caused the *Hind* to weigh her anchor and to go towards him, and manned out our skiff in like case to lay him aboard or to discern what he was, and we ourselves within half an hour after weighed also. But after the sail had espied us he kept about and turned back again, and shortly after there fell such another fog that we could not see him, which fogs continued all that night so that we were constrained to leave the chase. This afternoon the wind came about, and we went our course south-west and by west to go clear of the coast; we ran that night sixteen leagues.

The fourteenth day in the morning was very foggy; but about twelve o'clock we espied a caravel of 60 ton which was fishing, and we sent our skiff to him with five men, and all without any weapon saving their oars. The caravel for haste let slip her anchor and set sail; and they, seeing that, fearing that they should not fetch her, would tarry for no weapons, and in the end overtook the caravel, and made her to strike sail and brought her away, although they had fourteen or fifteen men aboard and every man his weapon, but they had not the hearts to resist our men. After they were come to us they let fall their anchor, for we had cast anchor because the wind was not good. I caused then the skiff to come for me, and I went aboard of them to see that no harm should be done to them, nor to take anything but that which they might spare us for our money. So we took of them 3 topnets of figs, two small pots of oil, two pipes of water, four hogsheads of salt-fish which they had taken upon the coast, and certain fresh fish which they did not esteem, because there is such store upon that coast that in an hour and sometime less a man may take as much fish as will serve twenty men a day. For these things, and for some wine which we drank aboard of them, and three or four great cans which they sent aboard of our ships, I paid them twenty and seven pistolets, which was twice as much as they willingly would have taken; and so let them go to their anchor and cable which they had let slip, and got it again by our help. After this we set sail, but the wind caused us to anchor again about twelve leagues off the River do Ouro, as the Portugals told us. There were five caravels more in this place, but when they saw us they made all away for fear of us.

The 15th day we rode still because of the wind. The 16th day we set sail and ran our course 40 leagues. This day, by the reckoning of our pilots, we were right under the Tropic of Cancer. The 17th day we ran 25 leagues within sight for the most part of the coast of Barbary. The 18th day we ran thirty leagues, and at twelve of the clock by the reckoning of our pilots we were thwart of Cape Blank. The 22nd day our pilots reckoned us to be thwart of Cape Verde.

The 12th day of December we had sight of land of Guinea, which as soon as we saw we hauled into the land north-east, and about 12 of the clock at night we were near the shore within less than 2 leagues; and then we kept about and sounded, and found 18 fathom water. Afterwards we saw a light towards the shore, which we thought to have been a ship, and thereby judged it to be the River dos Cestos; which light as soon as we espied, we came to an anchor, and armed our tops and made all things ready to fight, because we doubted that it might be some Portugal or Frenchman. This night we remained at an anchor, but in the morning we saw no man, only we espied 4 rocks about 2 English miles from us, one great rock and the 3 other small ones, which when we saw we supposed that the light came from the shore, and so weighed and set sail east-south-east along the shore, because the Master did not well know the place but thought that we were not so far to the east as the River dos Cestos.

This land all along is a low land, and full of very high trees all along the shore so that it is not possible to know the place that a man doth fall withal except it be by the latitude. In these 24 hours I think we ran 16 leagues, for all the night we had a great gale as we were under sail, and had withal store of thunder and lightnings.

The 13th day for the most part we ran east-south-east all along the shore, within two leagues always of the same, and found the land all as at the first, full of woods and great rocks hard aboard the shore, and the billow beating so sore that the seas broke upon the shore as white as snow and the water mounted so high that a man might easily discern it 4 leagues off, in such wise that no boat could land there. Thus we ran until 12 of the clock, and then they took the sun and after judged themselves to be 24 leagues past the River dos Cestos to the eastwards; by reason whereof we hauled into the shore within two English miles, and there anchored and found fifteen fathom water, and all off from the shore the sea so smooth that we might well have rid by a hawser. All that afternoon we trimmed our boat and made her a sail, to the end that she might go along by the shore to seek some place to water in. For we could not go back again to the River dos Castos because the wind blows always contrary, and the current runneth always to the eastwards, which was also against us.

The 14th day we set sail and went back again along the coast, and sent our boats hard aboard the shore to seek a watering-place, which they found about 12 of the clock; and we being far into the sea met with divers boats of the country, small, long, and narrow, and in every boat one man and no more. We gave them bread, which they did eat and were very glad of it. About 4 of the clock our boats came to us with fresh water, and this night we anchored against a river.

The 15th day we weighed and set sail to go near the shore, and with our lead we sounded all the way and found sometimes rocks and sometimes fair ground, and at the shallowest found 7 fathoms always at the least. So in fine we found 7 fathom and a half within an English mile of the shore, and there we anchored in a manner before the mouth of the river; and then we sent our boats into the river for water, which went about a mile within the river, where they had very good water. This river lieth by estimation 8 leagues beyond the River dos Cestos and is called in the card River St Vincent, but it is so hard to find that a boat being within half a mile of it shall not be able to discern that it is a river, by reason that directly before the mouth of it there lieth a ledge of rocks which is much broader than the river, so that a boat must run in along the shore a good way betwixt the rocks and the shore before it come to the mouth of the river; and being within it, it is a great river and divers other rivers fall into it. The going into it is somewhat ill, because that in entering the seas do go somewhat high, but being once within it, it is as calm as the Thames.

There are near to the sea upon this river divers inhabitants, which are mighty big men and go all naked except some thing before their privy parts, which is like a clout, about a quarter of a yard long, made of the bark of trees; and yet it is like a cloth, for the bark is of that nature, that it will spin small after the manner of linen. Some of them also wear the like upon their heads, being painted with divers colours, but the most part of them go bare-headed, and their heads are clipped and shorn of divers sorts, and the most part of them have the skin of their bodies raced with divers works, in manner of a leather jerkin. The men and women go so alike that one cannot know a man from a woman but by their breasts, which in the most part be very foul and long, hanging down low like the udder of a goat.

The same morning we went into the river with our skiff, and carried certain basins, manillas, etc. And there we took that day one hogshead and one hundred pounds weight of grains and two elephants' teeth at a reasonable good reckoning. We sold them both basins and manillas and margarites, but they desired most to have basins. For the most part of our basins we had by estimation about thirty pounds for a piece, and for an elephant's tooth of thirty pounds weight we gave them six.

The 16th day in the morning we went into the river with our skiff, and took some of every sort of our merchandise with us, and showed it to the negroes, but they esteemed it not, but made light of it, and also of the basins, manillas and margarites which yesterday they did buy. Howbeit for the basins they would have given us some grains, but to no purpose, so that this day we took not by estimation above one hundred pound weight of grains, by means of their captain, who would suffer no man to sell anything but through his hands and at his price. He was so subtle, that for a basin he would not give fifteen pound weight of grains, and sometimes would offer us small dishfuls, whereas before we had baskets full; and when he saw that we would not take them in contentment, the captain departed, and caused all the rest of the boats to depart, thinking belike that we would have followed them, and have given them their own askings. But after that we perceived their fetch, we weighed our grapnel and went away, and then went on land into a small town to see the fashions of the country. And there came a threescore of them about us, and at first they were afraid of us, but in the end, perceiving that we did no hurt, they would come to us and take us by the hand, and be familiar with us.

And then we went into their towns, which were like to twenty small hovels, all covered over with great leaves and baggage, and all the sides open, and a scaffold under the house about a yard high, where they work many pretty things of the barks of trees, and there they lie also.

In some of their houses they work iron and make fair darts, and divers other things to work their boats, and other things withal, and the women work as well as the men. But when we were there divers women, to show us pleasure, danced and sang after their manner, full ill to our ears. Their song was thus: "Sakere, sakere, ho! ho! Sakere, sakere ho! ho!" And with these words, they leap, dance, and clap their hands.

Beasts we could see none that they had, but two goats, small dogs, and small hens; other beasts we saw none.

After that we had well marked all things, we departed and went aboard our ships: which thing the captain of the other town perceiving, sent two of his servants in a boat with a basket of grains, and made us signs that if when we had slept we would come again into their river we should have store of grains, and so showed us his grains and departed.

The 17th day in the morning, as we thought that the negroes would have done something because the captain sent for us, I required the Master to go on shore, and sent the rest of our merchants with him, and tarried aboard myself by reason that the last day he esteemed our things so little. So when the Master and the rest came into the river, the captain with divers others came to them, and brought grains with them, and after he saw that I was not there, he made signs to know where I was, and they made signs to him again that I was in the ships. Then he made signs to know who was captain, by the name of *Diago*, for so they call their captain, and they pointed to the Master of the ship. Then he began to show his grains, but he held them so unreasonably that there was no profit to be made of them; which things the Master perceiving, and seeing they had no store of grains, came away, and took not above fifty pound weight of grains.

Then he went ashore to the little town where we were the day before, and one of them plucked a gourd, wherewith the negroes were offended, and came many of them to our men with their darts and great targets, and made signs to them to depart; which our men did, having but one bow and two or three swords, and went aboard the boat and came away from them. And as soon as they were come aboard we weighed and set sail, but the wind was off the sea, so that we could not get out clear of certain rocks, and therefore we came to an anchor again.

This river is called River St Vincent, standing in 4 degrees and a half, and it ebbeth and floweth there every 12 hours, but not much water when it ebbeth the most. While we were there, it ebbcd one fathom and a half water.

This country as far as we could perceive is altogether woody, and all strange trees, whereof we knew none, and they were of many sorts, with great leaves like great docks, which be higher than any man is able to reach the top of them. There are certain pease by the sea-side, which grow upon great and very long stalks; one of the stalks I measured, and found it 27 paces long, and they grow upon the sand like to trees, and that so near the sea that sometimes the sea floweth into the woods, as we might perceive by the water marks. The trees and all things in this place grow continually green.

Divers of the women have such exceeding long breasts that some of them will lay the same upon the ground and lie down by them; but all the women have not such breasts.

At this place all the day the wind bloweth off the sea and all the night off the land, but we found it to differ sometimes, which our Master marvelled at.

This night at 9 of the clock the wind came up at east, which ordinarily about that time was wont to come out of the north-north-west off the shore. Yet we weighed and hauled off south with that wind all night into the sea, but the next morning we hauled in again to the land, and took in 6 tuns of water for our ship, and I think the *Hind* took in as much. I could not perceive that here was any gold, or any other good thing, for the people be so wild and idle that they give themselves to seek out nothing. If they would take pains they might gather great store of grains, but in this place I could not perceive two tun. There are many fowls in the country, but the people will not take the pains to take them.

I observed some of their words of speech, which I thought good here to set down:

> Bezow, bezow, is their salutation.
> Manegete afoy, grains enough.
> Crocow afoy, hens enough
> Zeramme afoy, have you enough?
> Begge sack, give me a knife.
> Begge come, give me bread.
> Borke, hold your peace.
> Coutrecke, you lie.
> Veede, put forth, or empty.
> Brekeke, row.
> Diago, their captain, and some call him Dabo.

These and other words they speak very thick, and oftentimes recite one word three times together, and at the last time longer than at the two first.

The 18th day towards night, as we were sailing along the coast, we met with certain boats in the sea, and the men showed us that there was a river thwart of us where there were grains to be sold; but we thought it not good to tarry there lest the other ships should get before us. This river hath lying before it three great rocks and 5 small rocks, one great tree, and a little tree right by the river which in height exceeded all the rest. We hauled this night along the coast 10 leagues. The 19th day, as we coasted the shore, about twelve of the clock there came out to us 3 boats to tell us that they had grains, and brought some with them for a show, but we could not tarry there. We proceeded along the coast, and anchored by the shore all the night, and ran this day 10 leagues.

The 20th day the *Hind*, having anchored by us amongst rocks and foul ground, lost a small anchor. At noon, as we passed along the coast, there came forth a negro to us, making signs that if we would go ashore we should have grains; and where we anchored at night there came another to us, and brought grains and showed us them, and made signs that we should tarry; and made a fire upon the land in the night, meaning thereby to tell us where we should land. And so they did in divers other places upon the coast where they saw us to anchor.

In the places where we have anchored since we came from our watering-place, we have found the tide always running to the westwards, and all along the coast many rocks hard aboard the shore, and many of them a league off the shore or more. We ran this day 12 leagues.

The 21st day, although we ran all day with a good gale of wind, yet the tides came so sore out of the coast that we were not able to run above six leagues; and this day there came some negroes to us as there had done other times. The 22nd day we ran all day and night to double a point called Das Palmas, and ran sixteen leagues.

The 23rd day about 3 of the clock we were thwart of the point, and before we came to the westermost part of it we saw a great ledge of rocks which lie west from the Cape about 3 leagues and a league or more from the land. Shortly after we had sight of the eastermost part of the Cape, which lieth 4 leagues from the westermost part, and upon the very corner thereof lie two green places, as it were closes, and to the westwards of the Cape the land parted from the Cape, as it were closes, and to the westwards of the Cape the land parted from the Cape, as it were a bay, whereby it may well be known. Four leagues more beyond that there lieth a headland in the sea, and about two leagues beyond the headland there goeth in a great bay, as it were a river, before which place we anchored all that night, which we did lest in the night we should overrun a river where the last year they had all their elephants' teeth.

This Cape das Palmas lieth under 4 degrees and a half, and betwixt the said Cape and the River dos Cestos is the greatest store of grains to be had; and being past the said Cape there is no great store elsewhere. When we anchored this night we found that the tide, which before ran always to the westward, from this Cape runneth all to the eastward. This day we ran some 16 leagues.

The 24th day, running our course, about eight of the clock there came forth to us certain boats which brought with them small eggs, which were soft without shells; and they made us signs that there was within the land fresh water and goats. And the Master, thinking that it was the river which we sought, cast anchor and sent the boat on shore with one that knew the river; and coming near the shore he perceived that it was not the river, and so came back again and went along the shore with their oars and sail, and we weighed and ran along the shore also. And being thirteen leagues beyond the Cape the Master perceived a place which he judged to be the river when we were indeed two miles shot past it; yet the boat came from the shore and they that were in her said that there was no river. Notwithstanding, we came to an anchor, and the Master and I took five men with us in the boat, and when he came near the shore he perceived that it was the same river which he did seek. So we rowed in, and found the entrance very ill by reason that the sea goeth so high. And being entered, divers boats came to us, and showed us that they had elephants' teeth, and they brought us one of about eight pound, and a little one of a pound, which we bought. Then they brought certain teeth to the riverside, making signs that if the next day we would come again they would sell us them. So we gave unto two captains to either of them a manilla, and so we departed and came aboard, and sent out the other boat to another place where certain boats that came into the sea made us signs that there was fresh water. And being come thither they found a town, but no river; yet the people brought them fresh water, and showed them an elephant's tooth, making signs that the next day they would sell them teeth. And so they came aboard.

This river lieth by the card thirteen leagues from the Cape das Palmas, and there lieth to the westwards of the same a rock about a league in the sea, and the river itself hath a point of land coming out into the sea, whereupon grow five trees, which may well be discerned two or three leagues off coming from the westward; but the river cannot be perceived until such time as a man be hard by it, and then a man may perceive a little town on each side the river, and to each town belongeth a captain. The river is but small, but the water is good and fresh.

Two miles beyond the river, where the other town is, there lieth another point into the sea which is green like a close, and not above six trees upon it, which grow one of them from the other, whereby the coast may well be known. For along all the coast that we have hitherto sailed by I have not seen so much bare land.

In this place, and three or four leagues to the westward of it, there grow many palm trees, whereof they make their wine *De Palma*. These trees may easily be known almost two leagues off, for they be very high and white-bodied and straight, and be biggest in the midst. They have no boughs, but only a round bush in the top of them; and at the top of the same trees they bore a hole, and there they hang a bottle, and the juice of the tree runneth out of the said hole into the bottle, and that is their wine.

From the Cape das Palmas to the Cape Tres Pontas there are 100 leagues; and to the port where we purpose to make sales of our cloth beyond the Cape Tres Pontas 40 leagues. Note that betwixt the River dos Cestos and the Cape das Palmas is the place where all the grains be gathered.

The language of the people of this place, as far as I could perceive, differeth not much from the language of those which dwell where we watered before; but the people of this place be more gentle in nature than the other, and goodlier men. Their building and apparel is all one with the others'. Their desire in this place was most of all to have manillas and margarites; as for the rest of our things, they did little esteem them.

About nine of the clock there came boats to us forth, from both of the places aforesaid, and brought with them certain teeth; and after they had caused me to swear by the water of the sea that I would not hurt them, they came aboard our ship, three or four of them, and we gave them to eat of all such things as we had, and they did eat and drink of all things as well as we ourselves. Afterwards we bought all their teeth, which were in number 14; and of those 14 there were 10 small. Afterwards they departed, making us signs that the next day we should come to their towns.

The 26th day, because we would not trifle long at this place, I required the Master to go unto one of the towns and to take two of our merchants with him, and I myself went to the other and took one with me, because these two towns stand three miles asunder. To these places we carried somewhat of every kind of merchandise that we had; and he had at the one town nine teeth, which were but small, and at the other town where I was I had eleven, which were also not big; and we left aboard with the Master certain manillas, wherewith he bought 12 teeth aboard the ship in our absence. And having bought these of them we perceived that they had no more teeth. So in that place where I was one brought to me a small goat, which I bought, and to the Master at the other place they brought five small hens, which he bought also; and after that we saw there was nothing else to be had we departed, and by one of the clock we met aboard, and then weighed and went east, our course, 18 leagues still within sight of land.

The 28th the wind varied, and we ran into the sea; and the wind coming again off the sea we fell with the land again, and the first of the land which we raised showed as a great red cliff round, but not very high, and to the eastward of that another smaller red cliff, and right above that into the land a round hummock and green, which we took to be trees. We ran in these 24 hours not above four leagues.

The 29th day, coming near to the shore, we perceived the red cliff aforesaid to have right upon the top of it a great heap of trees, and all to the westwards of it full of red cliffs as far as we could see, and all along the shore, as well upon the cliffs as otherwise, full of wood. Within a mile of the said great cliff there is a river to the eastwards, and no cliffs that we could see except one small cliff which is hard by it. We ran this day and night 12 leagues. The winds that we had in this place, by the reports of the people and of those that have been there, have not been usual, but in the night at north off the land, and in the day south off the sea, and most commonly north-west and south-west.

The 31st day we went our course by the shore northwards. This land is all along a low shore and full of wood, as all the coast is for the most part, and no rocks. This morning came out many boats which went a-fishing, which be greater boats than those which we saw before, so that in some of them there sat 5 men; but the fashion of the boats is all one. In the afternoon about three of the clock we had sight of a town by the sea side, which our pilots judged to be 25 leagues to the westwards of the Cape Tres Pontas.

The third of January in the morning we fell with the Cape Tres Pontas, and in the night passed, as our pilots said, by one of the Portugals' castles which is 8 leagues to the westwards of the Cape. Upon the first sight of the Cape we discerned it a very high land, and all grown over with trees; and coming near to it we perceived two headlands, as it were two bays betwixt them which opened right to the westward, and the uttermost of them is the western cape. There we perceived the middle cape and the eastermost cape. The middle cape standeth not above a league from the west cape, although the card showeth them to be 3 leagues one from the other; and that middle cape hath right before the point of it a small rock so near to it that it cannot be discerned from the cape except a man be near to the shore. And upon the same cape standeth a great heap of trees; and when a man is thwart the same cape to the eastward there riseth hard by it a round green hummock which cometh out of the main. The third cape is about a league beyond the middle cape, and is a high land like to the other capes; and betwixt the middle and the third cometh out a little head or point of a land out of the main, and divers rocks hard aboard the shore.

Before we came to the capes, being about 8 leagues off them, we had the land south-east and by east, and being past the capes the land runneth in again east-north-east.

About two leagues beyond the farthest cape there is a low glade about two miles long, and then the land riseth high again, and divers headlands rise one beyond another, and divers rocks lie at the point of the first headland. The middest of these capes is the nearest to the southwards, I mean farther into the sea than any of the other, so that, being to the eastward of it, it may be discerned far off, and, being so to the eastward, it riseth with two small rocks.

This day we anchored for fear of overshooting a town called St John's. We ran this day not above 8 leagues. In the afternoon this day there came a boat of the country from the shore, with five men in her, and went along by us, as we thought to discern our flags, but they would not come near us, and when they had well looked upon us they departed.

The fourth day in the morning, sailing by the coast, we espied a ledge of rocks by the shore, and to the westwards of them two great green hills joining together, so that between them it was hollow like a saddle, and within the said rocks the Master thought the aforenamed town had stood; and therefore we manned our boats, and took with us cloth and other merchandise and rowed ashore. But going along by the coast we saw that there was no town, therefore we went aboard again. From these two hills aforesaid about two leagues to the eastward lie out into the sea almost two miles a ledge of rocks, and beyond that a great bay, which runneth into the north-north-westward, and the land in this place lieth north-north-east along the shore. But the uttermost point of land in that place that we could see lay north-east and by east from us.

After that we were with a small gale of wind run past that uttermost headland, we saw a great red cliff, which the Master again judged to be the town of St John's; and then we took our boat with merchandise and went thither, and when we came thither we perceived that there was a town upon the top of the hill, and so we went toward it. And when we were hard by it, the people of the town came together a great sort of them, and waved us to come in with a piece of cloth, and so we went into a very fair bay which lieth to the eastward of the cliff whereupon the town standeth; and being within the cliff we let fall our grapnel. And after that we had tarried there a good space, they sent a boat aboard of us, to show us that they had gold; and they showed us a piece about half a crown weight, and required to know our measure and our weight, that they might show their captain thereof. And we gave them a measure of two ells and a weight of two angels to show unto him, which they took, and went on shore, and showed it unto their captain; and then they brought us a measure of two ells, one quarter and a half, and one crusado-weight of gold, making us signs that so much they would give for the like measure and less they would not have. After this we tarried there about an hour, and when we saw that they would do no otherwise, and withal understood that all the best places were before us, we departed to our ships and weighed, and ran along the shore, and went before with our boat; and having sailed about a league we came to a point where there lay forth a ledge of rocks like to the others before spoken of. And being past that people, the Master spied a place which he said plainly was the town of Don John; and the night was come upon us, so that we could not well discern it, but we anchored as near unto the place as we could.

The fifth day in the morning we perceived it to be the same town indeed, and we manned our boats and went thither; and because that the last year the Portugals at that place took away a man from them, and after shot at them with great bases, and did beat them from the place, we let fall our grapnel almost a base-shot off the shore, and there we lay about two hours and no boats came to us. Then certain of our men, with the *Hind*'s boat, went into the bay which lieth to the eastward of the town, and within that bay they found a goodly fresh river; and afterwards they came and waved to us also to come in, because they perceived the negroes to come down to that place. Which we did; and immediately the negroes came to us, and made us signs that they had gold. But none of them would come aboard our boats, neither could we perceive any boats that they had to come withal, so that we judged that the Portugals had spoiled their boats, because we saw half of their town destroyed.

We having stayed there a good space, and seeing that they would not come to us, thrust our boats' heads ashore, being both well appointed. And then the captain of the town came down, being a grave man; and he came with his dart in his hand, and six tall men after him, every one with his dart and his target, and their darts were all of iron, fair and sharp. And there came another after them which carried the captain's stool. We saluted him, and put off our caps, and bowed ourselves; and he, like one that thought well of himself, did not move his cap nor scant bowed his body, and sat himself down very solemnly upon his stool. But all his men put off their caps to us, and bowed down themselves.

He was clothed from the loins down with a cloth of that country making, wrapped about him and made fast about his loins with a girdle, and his cap of a certain cloth of the country also, and bare-legged, and bare-footed, and all bare above the loins except his head. His servants, some of them had cloth about their loins, and some nothing but a cloth betwixt their legs and made fast before and behind to their girdles, and caps of their own making, some like a basket and some like a great wide purse of beasts' skins.

All their cloth, cords, girdles, fishing-lines and all suchlike things which they have, they make of the bark of certain trees, and thereof they can work things very prettily; and iron work they can make very fine of all such things as they do occupy, as darts, fish-hooks, hooking irons, iron heads, and great daggers, some of them as long as a wood-knife, which be on both sides exceeding sharp, and bended after the manner of Turkey blades; and the most part of them have hanging at their left side one of those great daggers. Their targets be made of such peels as their cloth is made of, and very closely wrought; and they be in form four-square, and very great, and somewhat longer than they be broad, so that kneeling down they make their targets to cover their whole body. Their bows be short, and of a pretty strength, as much as a man is able to draw with one of his fingers; and the string is of the bark of a tree made flat, and about a quarter of an inch broad. As for their arrows, I have not as yet seen any of them, for they had wrapped them up close, and because I was busy I could not stand about it to have them open them. Their gold also they work very well.

When the captain was set, I sent him two ells of cloth and two basins, and gave them unto him, and he sent again for a weight of the same measure, and I sent him a weight of two angels, which he would not take, neither would he suffer the town to buy anything but the basins of brass. So that we sold that day 74 basins unto the men of the town for about half an angel weight, one with another, and nine white basins which we sold for a quarter of an angel apiece or thereabouts. We showed them all our other things which we had, but they did not esteem them.

About two of the clock the captain, who did depart in the morning from us, came again, and brought with him, to present me withal, a hen and two great roots, which I received, and after made me signs that the country would come to his town that night and bring great store of gold, which indeed about 4 of the clock they did. For there came about 100 men under 3 captains, well appointed with their darts and bows; and when they came to us every man stuck down his dart upon the shore, and the captains had stools brought them and they sat down, and sent a young man aboard of us which brought a measure with him of an ell and one fourth part and one sixteenth part, and he would have that four times for a weight of one angel and twelve grains. I offered him two ells, as I had done before, for two angels' weight, which he esteemed nothing but still stuck at his four measures aforesaid; yet in the end, when it grew very late and I made him signs that I would depart, he came to four ells for the weight abovesaid and otherwise he would not deal, and so we departed. This day we took for basins six ounces and a half and one eighth part.

The sixth day in the morning we manned our boats and the skiff well, for fear of the Portugals, which the last year had taken away a man from the other ships, and went on shore and landed, because they had no boats to come to us. And so the young man which was with us the night before was sent aboard, who seemed to have dealt and bargained before with the Portugals, for he could speak a little Portuguese and was perfect in weights and measures. At his coming he offered us, as he had done before, one angel and twelve grains for four ells, and more he would not give, and made signs that if we would not take that we should depart, which we did; but before we did indeed depart I offered him of some rotten cloth three ells for his weight of an angel and twelve grains, which he would not take, and then we departed, making signs to him that we would go away, as indeed we would have done rather than have given that measure, although the cloth was ill, seeing we were so near to the places which we judged to be better for sale. Then we went aboard our ships, which lay about a league off, and came back again to the shore for sand and ballast; and then the captain, perceiving that the boats had brought no merchandise but came only for water and sand, and seeing that we would depart, came unto them, making signs again to know whether we would not give the four ells, and they made signs again that we would give them but three; and when they saw that the boats were ready to depart they came unto them and gave them the weight of our angel and twelve grains, which we required before, and made signs that if we would come again they would take three ells. So when the boats came aboard we laid wares in them both, and for the speedier despatch I and John Savill went in one boat and the Master, John Makeworth, and Richard Curligin in the other, and went on shore; and that night I took for my part fifty and two ounces and in the other boat they took eight ounces and a quarter, all by one weight and measure; and so, being very late, we departed and went aboard, and took in all this day three pound.

The seventh day we went ashore again, and that day I took in our boat three pound 19 ounces, so that we despatched almost all the cloth that we carried with us before noon. And then many of the people were departed, and those that remained had little gold; yet they made us signs to fetch them some latten basins, which I would not, because I purposed not to trifle out the time but go thence with speed to Don John's town. But John Savill and John Makeworth were desirous to go again; and I, loth to hinder them of any profit, consented but went not myself; so they took eighteen ounces of gold and came away, seeing that the people, at a certain cry made, were departed.

While they were at the shore, there came a young fellow which could speak a little Portuguese, with three more with him, and to him I sold 39 basins and two small white saucers for three ounces etc., which was the best reckoning that we did make of any basins; and in the forenoon, when I was at the shore, the Master sold five basins unto the same fellow for half an ounce of gold. This fellow, so far as we could perceive, had been taken into the Castle by the Portugals and was gotten away from them, for he told us that the Portugals were bad men, and that they made them slaves if they could take them, and would put irons upon their legs; and besides he told us that as many Frenchmen or Englishmen as they could take (for he could name these two very well) they would hang them. He told us further that there were 60 men in the Castle, and that every year there came thither two ships, one great, and one small caravel, and further that Don John had wars with the Portugals, which gave me the better courage to go to his town, which lieth but four leagues from the Castle, wherehence our men were beaten the last year.

This fellow came aboard our ship without fear, and as soon as he came he demanded why we had not brought again their men which the last year we took away, and could tell us that there were five taken away by Englishmen. We made him answer that they were in England, well used, and were there kept till they could speak the language, and then they should be brought again to be a help to Englishmen in this country; and then he spoke no more of that matter.

Our boats being come aboard, we weighed and set sail, and a little after spied a great fire upon the shore, and by the light of the fire we might discern a white thing which they took to be the Castle; and for fear of overshooting the town of Don John we there anchored two leagues off the shore, for it is hard to fetch up a town here if a ship overshoot it. This day we took seven pound and five ounces of gold.

This town lieth in a great bay, which is very deep. The people in this place desired most to have basins and cloth. They would buy some of them also many trifles, as knives, horsetails, horns; and some of our men going ashore sold a cap, a dagger, a hat, etc. They showed us a certain coarse cloth which I think to be made in France, for it was coarse wool and a small thread, and as thick as worsted, and striped with stripes of green, white, yellow, etc. Divers of the people did wear about their necks great beads of glass of divers colours. Here also I learned some of their language, as followeth:

> Mattea, mattea is their salutation.
> Dassee, dassee, I thank you.
> Sheke, gold.
> Cowrt, cut.
> Cracca, knives.
> Bassina, basins.
> Foco, foco, cloth.
> Molta, much, or great store.

The eighth day in the morning we had sight of the Castle, but by reason of a mist that then fell we could not have the perfect sight of it till we were almost at the town of Don John; and then it cleared up, and we saw it and a white house, as it were a chapel, upon the hill about it. Then we hauled into the shore within two miles of Don John's town, and there anchored in seven fathom water. Here, as in many other places before, we perceived that the current went with the wind. The land here is in some places low and in some high, and full of wood altogether.

The town of Don John is but little, of about twenty houses, and the most part of the town is walled in with a wall of a man's height made with reed or sedge or some such thing. Here we stayed two or three hours after we had anchored, to see if any man would come unto us; and seeing that none did come we manned our boats and put in merchandise, and went and anchored with our boats near to the shore. Then they sent out a man to us who made us signs that that was the town of Don John, and that he himself was in the country, and would be at home at the going down of the sun; and when he had done he required a reward, as the most part of them will do which first come aboard, and I gave him one ell of cloth and he departed, and that night we heard no more of him.

The ninth day in the morning we went again with our boats to the shore, and there came forth a boat to us, who made signs that Don John was not come home but would be at home this day; and to that place also came another boat from the other town a mile from this, which is called Don Devi's, and brought with him gold to show us, making signs that we should come thither. I then left in this place John Savill and John Makeworth, and took the *Hind* and went to the other town and there anchored and took cloth and went to shore with the boat; and by and by the boats came to us and brought a measure of four yards long and a half, and showed us a weight of an angel and twelve grains which they would give for so much and not otherwise. So I stayed and made no bargain; and all this day the bark lay at Don John's town and did nothing, having answer that he was not come home.

The tenth day we went again to the shore, and there came out a boat with good store of gold; and having driven the matter off a long time, and having brought the measure to a nail less than three ells and their weight to an angel and twenty grains, and could not bring them to more, I did conclude with them and sold, and within one quarter of an hour I took one pound and a quarter of an ounce of gold. And then they made me signs to tarry till they had parted their cloth upon the shore, as their manner is, and they would come again; and so they went away and laid the cloth all abroad upon the sand piece by piece, and by and by one came running down from the town to them and spoke unto them, and forthwith every man made as much haste as he could away, and went into the wood to hide his gold and his cloth.

We mistrusted some knavery, and being waved by them to come ashore yet we would not, but went aboard the *Hind*, and perceived upon the hill 30 men which we judged to be Portugals; and they went up to the top of the hill and there mustered and showed themselves, having a flag with them. Then I, being desirous to know what the *Hart* did, took the *Hind*'s boat and went towards her; and when I came near to them they shot off two pieces of ordnance, which I marvelled at. I made as much haste as I could to her, and met her boat and skiff coming from the shore in all haste, and we met aboard together. They showed me that they had been ashore all that day, and had given to the two sons of Don John to either of them three yards and a half of cloth, and three basins betwixt them, and had delivered him 3 yards of cloth more and the weight of an angel and twelve grains, and being on land did tarry for his answer. And in the meantime the Portugals came running from the hill upon them, whereof the negroes a little before had given them warning and bade them to go away, but they perceived it not. The son of Don John conspired with the Portugals against them, so that they were almost upon them, but yet they recovered their boat and set off from the shore, and the Portugals shot their calivers at them but hurt no man; and then the ship perceiving it shot off the two pieces aforesaid among them. Hereupon we laid bases in both the boats and in the skiff, and manned them well, and went ashore again. But because of the wind we could not land, but lay off in the sea about ten score and shot at them, but the hill succoured them, and they from the rocks and from the hills shot at us with their half-hakes, and the negroes more for fear than for love stood by them to help them. And when we saw that the negroes were in such subjection unto them that they durst not sell us anything for fear of them, we went aboard, and that night the wind kept at the east so that we could not with our ship fetch the *Hind*; but I took the boat in the night and went aboard the bark to see what was there to be done, and in the morning we perceived the town to be in like case laid with Portugals so we weighed and went along the coast.

This town of John de Viso standeth upon a hill like the town of Don John, but it hath been burned, so that there are not passing six houses in it. The most part of the gold that comes thither comes out of the country, and no doubt if the people durst for fear of the Portugals bring forth their gold there would be had good store; but they dare not sell anything, their subjection is so great to the Portugals. The 11th day, running by the shore, we had sight of a little town four leagues from the last town that we came from, and, about half a league from that, of another town upon a hill, and half a league from that also of another great town upon the shore, whither we went to see what could there be done: if we could do nothing, then to return to the other town, because we thought that the Portugals would leave the town upon our departure. Along from the Castle unto this place are very high hills, which may be seen above all other hills, but they are full of wood, and great red cliffs by the sea side. The boats of these places are somewhat large and big, for one of them will carry twelve men; but their form is alike with the former boats of the coast. There are about these towns few rivers. Their language differeth not from the language used at Don John's town; but everyone can speak three or four words of Portuguese, which they used altogether to us.

We saw this night, about 5 of the clock, 22 boats running along the shore to the westward, whereupon we suspected some knavery intended against us. The 12th day therefore we set sail and went further along the coast, and descried more towns wherein were greater houses than in the other towns, and the people came out of the towns to look upon us but we could see no boats. Two mile beyond the eastermost town are black rocks, which black rocks continue to the uttermost cape of the land which is about a league off; and then the land runs in east-north-east and a sandy shore again. Upon these black rocks came down certain negroes, which waved us with a white flag; but we, perceiving the principal place to be near, would not stay, but bore still along the shore, and as soon as we had opened the point of the land we raised another headland about a league off the point, which had a rock lying off it into the sea, and that they thought to be the place which we sought. When we came thwart the place they knew it, and we put wares into our boat, and the ship being within half a mile of the place anchored in five fathom water and fair ground.

We went on shore with our boat, and anchored about ten of the clock in the forenoon. We saw many boats lying upon the shore, and divers came by us, but none of them would come near us, being, as we judged, afraid of us because that four men were taken perforce the last year from this place, so that no man came to us. Whereupon we went aboard again and thought here to have made no sale. Yet towards night a great sort came down to the water side and waved us on shore with a white flag. And afterward their captain came down, and many men with him, and sat him down by the shore under a tree; which when I perceived I took things with me to give him. At last he sent a boat to call to us, which would not come near us but made signs to come again the next day. But in fine I got them to come aboard in offering them things to give to their captain, which were two ells of cloth, one latten basin, one white basin, a bottle, a great piece of beef, and six biscuit cakes, which they received, making us signs to come again the next day saying that their captain was Gran Capitan, as appeared by those that attended upon him with their darts and targets and other weapons.

This town is very great, and stands upon a hill among trees so that it cannot well be seen except a man be near it. To the eastward of it upon the hill hard by the town stand 2 high trees, which is a good mark to know the town, and under the town lieth another hill lower than it, whereupon the sea beats; and that end next the sea is all great black rocks, and beyond the town in a bay lieth another small town.

The 13th day in the morning we took our boat and went to shore, and stayed till ten o'clock and no man came to us. We went about therefore to return aboard, and when the negroes saw that they came running down with a flag to wave us again; so we anchored again, and then one showed us that the captain would come down by and by. We saw a sail in the meantime pass by us, but it was small and we regarded it not. Being on shore we made a tilt with our oars and sail, and then there came a boat to us with five men in her, who brought us again our bottle and brought me a hen, making signs by the sun that within two hours the merchants of the country would come down and buy all that we had. So I gave them six manillas to carry to their captain, and they made signs to have a pledge of us and they would leave us another man; and we, willing to do so, put one of our men in their boat, but they would not give us one of theirs, so we took our man again and there tarried for the merchants. And shortly after one came down arrayed like their captain, with a great train after him, who saluted us friendly, and one of the chiefest of them went and sat down under a tree where the last year the captain was wont to sit. And at last we perceived a great many of them to stand at the end of a hollow way, and behind them the Portugals had planted a base, who suddenly shot at us but overshot us, and yet we were in a manner hard by them, and they shot at us again before we could ship our oars to get away but did no hurt. Then the negroes came to the rocks hard by us and discharged calivers at us, and again the Portugals shot off their base twice more; and then our ship shot at them, but the rocks and hills defended them.

Then we went aboard to go from this place, seeing the negroes bent against us because that the last year Master Gainsh did take away the captain's son and three others from this place with their gold and all that they had about them; which was the cause that they became friends with the Portugals, whom before they hated, as did appear the last year by the courteous entertainment which the *Trinity* had there, when the captain came aboard the ship, and brought them to his town, and offered them ground to build a castle in, and there they had good sales.

The 14th day we weighed and plied back again to seek the *Hind*, which in the morning we met, and so we turned both back to the eastwards to see what we could do at that place where the *Trinity* did sell her eight friezes the last year. The *Hind* had taken eighteen ounces and a half more of gold of other negroes the day after that we left them. This day about one of the clock we espied certain boats upon the sand and men by them, and went to them with merchandises and took three ounces of gold for 18 fuffs of cloth, every fuff three yards and a half after one angel and 12 grains the fuff; and then they made me signs that the next day I should have gold enough. So the Master took the *Hind* with John Savill and John Makeworth and went to seek the place aforesaid, and I with Richard Pakeman remained in this place to see what we could do the next day. And when the negroes perceived our ship to go away they feared that the other would follow, and so sent forth 2 boats to us with 4 men in them, requiring us to tarry and to give them one man for a pledge and 2 of them should tarry with us for him. So Edward, Master Morley's servant, seeing these men so earnest therein, offered himself to be pledge, and we let him go for two of them, one whereof had his weights and scales, and a chain of gold about his neck and another about his arm. They did eat of such things as we had and were well contented. In the night the negroes kept a light upon the shore thwart of us, and about one of the clock we heard and saw the light of a base which shot off twice at the said light, and by and by discharged two calivers, which in the end we perceived to be the Portugals' brigantine which followed us from place to place, to give warning to the people of the country that they should not deal with us.

The 15th day in the morning the captain came down with 100 men with him, and brought his wife, and many others brought their wives also, because their town was 8 miles up in the country and they determined to lie by the sea side till they had bought what they would. When he was come he sent our man aboard and required to have two men pledges and he himself would come aboard; and I sent him two, of whom he took but one and so came aboard us, he and his wife with divers of his friends, and brought me a goat and two great roots, and I gave him again a latten basin, a white basin, 6 manillas, and a bottle of malmsey, and to his wife a small casket. After this we began to make our measure and weight; and he had a weight of his own which held one angel and 14 grains, and required a measure of 4 ells and a half. In fine we concluded the 8th part for one angel and 20 grains, and before we had done they took my own weight and measure.

The 16th day I took 8 pound 1 ounce of gold; and since the departure of the *Hind* I heard not of her, but when our pledge went into the country the first night he said he saw her cast anchor about five leagues from this place. The 17th day I sold about 17 pieces of cloth and took 4 pounds 4 ounces and a half of gold. The 18th day the captain desired to have some of our wine, and offered half a ducat of gold for a bottle; but I gave it him freely, and made him and his train drink besides. And this day also I took 5 pound 5 ounces of gold. The 19th day we sold about 18 cloths and took 4 pound 4 ounces and one quarter of gold. The 20th day we took 3 pound six ounces and a quarter of gold. The 21st we took 8 pound 7 ounces and a quarter; the 22nd 3 pound 8 ounces and a quarter. And this night about 4 of the clock the captain, who had lain all this while upon the shore, went away with all the rest of the people with him.

The 23rd day we were waved ashore by other negroes, and sold them cloth, caskets, knives, and a dozen of bells, and took 1 pound 10 ounces of gold. The 24th likewise we sold bells, sheets, and thimbles, and took two pound one ounce and a quarter of gold. The 25th day we sold 7 dozen of small bells and other things, and then, perceiving their gold to be done, we weighed and set sail and went to leeward to seek the *Hind*; and about 5 of the clock at night we had sight of her and bore with her, and understood that she had made some sales. The 26th day we received out of the *Hind* 48 pounds 3 ounces and one eighth part of gold, which they had taken in the time that we were from them. And this day upon the request of a negro that came unto us from a captain we went to shore with our merchandise and took 7 pound and 1 ounce of gold. At this place they required no gages of us, but at night they sent a man aboard us which lay with us all night because we might know that they would also come to us the next day. The 27th day in both our ships we took 8 pound 1 ounce three quarters and half a quarter gold. The 28th we made sales for the company and took one pound and half an ounce of gold. The 29th day in the morning we heard two calivers shot off upon the shore, which we judged to be either by the Portugals or by the negroes of the Portugals. We manned our boats and armed ourselves and went to shore, but could find nothing, for they were gone. The 30th day we made more sales for the company and for the Masters.

The 31st we sent our boat to shore to take in sand for ballast, and there our men met the negroes, with whom they had made sale the day before, a-fishing, which did help them to fill sand, and having no gold sold fish to our men for their handkerchiefs and night-kerchiefs.

The 1st day of February we weighed and went to another place, and took 1 pound 9 ounces 3 quarters of gold. The 2nd day we made more sales; but having viewed our victuals we determined to tarry no long time upon the coast, because the most part of our drink was spent, and that which remained grew sour. The 3rd and 4th day we made some sales, though not great, and finding the wind this 4th day to come off the shore we set sail and ran along the shore to the westwards. Upon this coast we found by experience that ordinarily about 2 of the clock in the night the wind comes off the shore at north-north-east, and so continueth until eight of the clock in the morning, and all the rest of the day and night it comes out of the south-west; and as for the tide or current upon this shore, it goeth continually with the wind. The 5th day we continued sailing and thought to have met with some English ships, but found none.

The sixth day we went our course south-west to fetch under the line, and ran by estimation 24 leagues. The 13th day we thought ourselves by our reckoning to be clear off the Cape das Palmas, and ran 12 leagues. The 22nd day we were thwart of the Cape de Monte, which is to the westward of the River dos Cestos about 30 leagues.

The first day of March in a tornado we lost the *Hind*, whereupon we set up a light and shot off a piece, but could not hear of her; so that then we struck our sail and tarried for her, and in the morning had sight of her again three leagues astern of us. Upon the 22nd day we found ourselves to be in the height of Cape Verde, which stands in 14 degrees and a half. From this day till the 29th day we continued our course, and then we found ourselves to be in 22 degrees. This day one of our men, called William King, who had been long sick, died in his sleep. His apparel was distributed to those that lacked it, and his money was kept for his friends, to be delivered them at his coming home.

The 30th day we found ourselves to be under the Tropic. The 31st day we went our course, and made way 18 leagues. From the first day of April to the 20th we went our course, and then found ourselves to be in the height of the Azores.

The seventh day of May we fell with the south part of Ireland, and going on shore with our boat had fresh drink and two sheep of the country people, which were wild kerns, and we gave them gold for them, and bought further such victuals as we had need of and thought would serve us till we arrived in England.

The 14th day with the afternoon tide we went into the port of Bristol called Hungrode, and there anchored in safety and gave thanks to God for our safe arrival.

The second voyage made by Master William Towerson to the coast of Guinea and the Castle of Mina, in the year 1556, with the *Tiger* of London, a ship of 120 tons, the *Hart* of London of 60 tons, and a pinnace of sixteen tons.

THE fourteenth day of September, the year abovesaid, we departed from Harwich and directed our course for the Isle of Scilly, to meet there with the *Hart* and the pinnace which were rigged and victualled at Bristol; but arriving there the eight and twentieth day we found them not, and therefore after long lying at hull to tarry for them, but not espying them, we turned back to Plymouth the 12th day of October. And being there, the *Hart* and the pinnace came to us, so that the 15th of November we all departed together from Plymouth at one of the clock in the afternoon, and the 28th day we had sight of the Isle of Porto Santo and the next day in the morning of Madeira. The third day of December we fell with the Isle of Palma, and the 9th we were thwart of Cape Blank, and found there certain caravels fishing for pargoes.

The 19th we found ourselves in the height of Sierra Leone, and all this day we ran thwart of certain currents which did set to the west-south-westward so fast as if it had been the overfall of a sand, making a great noise like unto a stream or tide-gate when the water is shoal; and to prove whether we could find ground in this place we sounded, and had 150 fathom and no ground, and so departed.

The 30th of December we fell with the coast of Guinea, and had first sight of it about 4 leagues off. The best mark that we could take of the place to know it was three hills, which lay north-east and by east from us; betwixt the northermost two hills there are two high and great trees standing in sight as it were a sail's breadth one from another, and a little more to the north-westwards are certain hummocks. Having sailed somewhat into the shore we took ourselves to be shot somewhat past the River dos Cestos, so that we kept about to fetch it. And a little after we had sight of three sails of ships and two pinnaces which were in the weather of us, and having sight of them we made ourselves ready to meet them and hauled off our ships to fetch the wind as near as we could. And having sailed about an hour or two, they also went about, and went as we went to make themselves ready, and when we had them in chase they went away from us; but when they had made themselves ready they kept about again, and came with us, very finely appointed with their streamers and pendants and ensigns and noise of trumpets very bravely. So when we met they had the weather of us, and we, being determined to fight if they had been Portugals, waved them to come under our lee, which they denied stoutly. Then we demanded of them whence they were, and they said of France; we told them again that we were of London in England. They asked us of what Portugals we had seen; we answered none but fishermen. Then they told us that there were certain Portugal ships gone to the Mina to defend it, and that they met with another at the River dos Cestos which was a ship of two hundred, which they had burned, and had saved none but the master and two or three negroes and certain others which were sore burned which they left ashore there.

Then they desired to come aboard of us with their boats to talk with us, and we gave them leave. Then the captain of the admiral and divers others came aboard very friendly, desiring us to keep them company because of the Portugals, and to go to the Mina with them. We told them that we had not watered, and that we were but now fallen with the coast; and they showed us that we were fifty leagues past the River dos Cestos. Notwithstanding, there was water enough to be had, and they would help us to water with their own boats because they would have our company; and told us further that they had been six weeks upon the coast and had gotten but three tuns of grains amongst them all. And when we had heard them we made our reckoning that, although the Mina were clear, yet if they did go before us they would mar our market; and if it were not clear, then if the Portugals were there and did take them they would understand that we were behind, and so would wait for us. And further we made account that if we went with them we should do as well as they if the coast were clear; if it were not clear, then by them we were assured to be the stronger. Therefore, having considered thus much of their gentle offers, we told them that the next day we would confer more largely of the matter. Whereupon they desired me to come the next day to dinner to them, and to bring the masters of our ships with me and such merchants as I thought good, promising to give us water out of their own ships if we would take it, or else to tarry with us and help us to water with their own boats and pinnaces.

The 31st day in the morning the Admiral sent his boat aboard for me, and I took our masters and certain of our merchants and went to him, who had provided a notable banquet for us and entreated us very friendly, desiring us still to keep his company, promising that what victuals were in his ships, or other things that might do us pleasure until the end, we should have the one half of it, offering us if we would to furl his flags and to be at our commandment in all things. In the end we agreed to come to an anchor, and to send our boat on shore with the Admiral's boat and one of his pinnaces, and an *almaine* which they had brought out of France, to seek water. As for our pinnace, she came to anchor to seaward of us all, and would not come at us. All this night the boats continued on shore.

The first day of January our boats came to us again and had found no river, whereupon we weighed and set sail, and anchored again at another river. The 2nd day we went into the river and bargained, and took 5 small elephants' teeth. The 3rd day we took 5 more. The fourth day the French admiral and we took fifteen small teeth. This day we took thirty men with us and went to seek elephants, our men being all well armed with arquebuses, pikes, long-bows, cross-bows, partisans, long-swords, and swords and bucklers. We found two elephants which we struck divers times with arquebuses and long-bows, but they went away from us, and hurt one of our men.

The fifth day we set sail and ran along the coast. The 6th day we fell with the River de St André, at which place the land is somewhat high to the westward of the river, and a fair bay also to the westward of it; but to the eastward of it is low land. The 7th day we went into the river and found no village, but certain wild negroes not accustomed to trade. It is a very great river and 7 fathom water in some places at the entering. Here we filled water, and after set sail. The 8th day we sailed along the shore and came to the red cliffs, and went forward in sailing the 9th day also.

The 10th day we came together to confer with Captain Blundel, Admiral of the French ships, Jerome Baudet, his Vice-admiral, and John de Orleans, master of a ship of 70 ton, and with their merchants, and agreed that when God should send us to any place where we might make sale that we should be of one accord and not one of us hurt the market of the other, but certain of our boats to make the price for all the rest and then one boat to make sale for every ship. This night our boats going to the shore met with certain negroes who said that they had gold, and therefore we here cast anchor.

The 11th day all the day we took but one half angel weight of 4 grains, which we took by hand, for the people of this place had no weight. The negroes called this place Allow. The 12th day we ran along the coast and found but one town, but no boats would come out to us and therefore we went our course.

The 13th day I took my boat and went along the shore, and passed by divers small towns, and was waved to come on shore at 3 places, but the sea went so high upon the shore that it was not possible for us to land; neither could they come to us if they had had boats, as I could see none but at one place where there was one that would have come to us but the land-wash went so sore that it overthrew his boat, and one of the men was drowned, which the people lamented and cried so sore that we might easily hear them; and they got his body out of the sea and carried it amongst them to their town.

The 14th day we came within saker-shot of the Castle, and straightway they sent forth an *almade* to descry us, and when they perceived that we were no Portugals they ran within the town again; for there is a great town by the Castle which is called by the negroes Dondow. Without this there lieth two great rocks like islands, and the castle standeth upon a point which showeth almost like an island. Before we came at this castle we found the land for five or six leagues to be high land, and about seven leagues before we came to the castle low land until we came at the castle, and then we found the land high again. This castle standeth about five leagues to the east of Cape das Tres Pontas. Here I took the boat with our negroes and ran along the shore till I came to the Cape and found two small towns, but no boats at them, neither any traffic to be had. At these places our negroes did understand them well, and one of them went ashore at all the places and was well received of them. This night we anchored at the Cape das Tres Pontas.

The 15th day I took our boat and went along the shore, and about 3 leagues beyond the eastermost part of the Cape we found a fair bay, where we ran in and found a small town and certain boats which belonged to the same town; but the negroes in a long time would not come to us. But at the last, by the persuasion of our own negroes, one boat came to us, and with him we sent George our negro ashore, and after he had talked with them they came aboard our boats without fear, and I gave to their captain a basin and two strings of margarites, and they showed us about 5 ducats weight of gold. But they required so much for it that we would not take it, because the Frenchmen and we had agreed to make price of our goods all in one boat, and the price being made then every man to sell in his own boat and no man to give more than the price which should be set by us all. This place is called

Bulle, and here the negroes were very glad of our negroes, and showed them all the friendship they could, when they had told them that they were the men that were taken away being now again brought by us.

The negroes here showed us that a month since there were 3 ships that fought together, and the two ships put the other to flight. And before that at the Castle of Mina there were 4 ships of the Portugals which met with one Frenchman, which Frenchman caused them all to flee, which ship we took to be the *Roebarge*; for the Frenchmen of our company judged her to be thereabout that time with her pinnace also, and, further, that after her went a ship of twelve score named the *Shaudet* all alone, and after her a ship of fourscore, and both for the Mina. And there were two others also which they left, one at Cape Verde called the *Levriere* of Dieppe, and another at the River dos Cestos, besides these 3 which all this time be in our company, whose names be these:

The *Espoir* of Havre, which is the admiral, whose captain is Denis Blundel.

The *Levriere* of Rouen, vice-admiral, whose master is Jerome Baudet.

The other is of Honfleur, whose master is called John de Orleans.

The sixteenth day I went along the shore with two pinnaces of the Frenchmen and found a bay and a fresh river, and after that went to a town called Ahanta, twelve leagues beyond the Cape. At this town our negroes were well known, and the men of the town wept for joy when they saw them, and demanded of them where Anthony and Binny had been; and they told them that they had been at London in England, and should be brought home the next voyage. So after this our negroes came aboard, with other negroes which brought a weight with them, which was so small that we could not give them the half of that which they demanded for it. The negroes here told us that there were five Portugal ships at the Castle, and one pinnace, and that the Portugals did much harm to their country, and that they lived in fear of them; and we told them again that we would defend them from Portugals, whereof they were very glad.

The 17th day we went ashore and the Frenchmen with us, but did no great good, the negroes were so unreasonable; we sold 80 manillas for one ounce of gold. Then we departed and went to Shama, and went into the river with five boats well appointed with men and ordnance, and with our noises of trumpets and drums, for we thought here to have found some Portugals, but there were none. So we sent our negroes on shore, and after them went divers of us and were very well received, and the people were very glad of our negroes, specially one of their brothers' wives and one of their aunts, which received them with much joy, and so did all the rest of the people, as if they had been their natural brethren. We comforted the captain, and told him that he should not fear the Portugals, for we would defend him from them; whereupon we caused our boats to shoot off their bases and arquebuses, and caused our men to come on shore with their long-bows and they shot before the captain, which he, with all the rest of the people, wondered much at, specially to see them shoot so far as they did, and essayed to draw their bows but could not. When it grew to be late we departed to our ships, for we looked every hour for the Portugals. And here the negroes showed us that there was an English ship at the Mina, which had brought one of the negroes again which Robert Gainsh took away.

The 18th day we went into the river with no less strength than before, and concluded with the negroes to give them for every fuff two yards and three nails of cloth and to take for it one angel-ducat; so that we took in all 70 ducats, whereof the Frenchmen had forty and we thirty. The nineteenth day we went ashore every man for himself, and took a good quantity of gold; and I for my part took four pound and two ounces and a half of gold, and our *Hart*'s boat took one and twenty ounces. At night the negroes showed us that the next day the Portugals would be with us by land or by sea; and when we were ready to depart we heard divers arquebuses shoot off in the woods by us which we knew to be Portugals, which durst come no nearer to us, but shot off in the woods to see if they could fear us and so make us to leave our traffic.

The 20th day we manned our five boats, and also a great boat of the Frenchmen's, with our men and the admiral's, 12 of them in their morions and corselets and the rest all well appointed, with four trumpets, a drum and a fife, and the boat all hung with streamers of silk and pendants very fair, and went into the river and trafficked, our man-of-war lying off and on in the river to waft us, but we heard no more of the Portugals. This day the negroes told us that there were certain ships come into Ahanta, which town is about 2 leagues to the westward of this place. This 21st day we manned our boats again and went to a place a league from this to the westwards, and there found many negroes with another captain, and sold at the same rate that we had done with the others. The 22nd day we went ashore again and trafficked in like sort quietly, and I took 4 pound and six ounces of gold.

The 23rd day about night the negroes with their captain came to us and told us that the King of Portugal's ships were departed from the Castle, meaning the next day to ply to the windward to come to us, giving us warning to take heed to ourselves. We told them again that we were very glad of their coming and would be ready at all times to meet them; and to assure them that we were glad of it we sounded our trumpets and shot off certain bases, whereof the negroes were very glad and requested us that if the Portugals sought to hinder our traffic to show them all the extremity that we could, promising us that if they came by land they would advertise us thereof.

The 24th we went ashore with our trumpets and drums, and trafficked, and I bade the captain of the town to dinner.

The 25th day, we being ashore, our ships had descried five sails of the King of Portugal's, and our ships shot off ordnance to call us away; and we threw every man his cask ashore for water, and went to our ships, and by that time that we had weighed and given order one to another what to do it was night, so that night nothing was done. We set sail and lay close all night to get the wind if we could. We were near some of them, and one shot off a piece, which we judged to be the admiral of the Portugals to cause the rest to come and speak with him. So all this night we made ourselves ready for fight.

The 26th we came in with the shore and had sight of the Portugals where they rode at anchor, and we bore with them; and we gave all our men white scarves, to the end that the Frenchmen might know one the other if we came to boarding. But the night came upon us that we could not fetch them, but we anchored within demi-culverin shot of them.

The 27th day we weighed, and so did the Portugals, and about eleven of the clock we had the wind of them and then we went room with them; which when they perceived they kept about to the shore again and we after them. And when they were so near the shore that they could not well run any further on that board they kept about again and lay to the seaward, and then we kept about with them and were ahead of them, and took in our topsails and tarried for them. And the first that came up was a small bark which sailed so well that she cared not for any of us, and carried good ordnance; and as soon as she came up she shot at us, and overshot us, and then she shot at the admiral of the Frenchmen and shot him through in two or three places, and went forth ahead of us because we were in our fighting sails. Then came up another caravel under our lee in like case, which shot at us and at the Frenchman, and hurt two of his men and shot him through the main-mast. And after them came up the admiral under our lee also, but he was not able to do us so much harm as the small ships, because he carried ordnance higher than they, neither were we able to make a good shot at any of them because our ship was so weak in the side that she laid all her ordnance in the sea, wherefore we thought to lay the great ship aboard. And as soon as the French admiral went room with him he fell astern and could not fetch him, and after he fell astern of the two caravels more and could fetch none of them but fell to leeward of them all; and when he was to leeward he kept about to the shoreward and left us. And then we put out our topsails and gave them chase; and both the other Frenchmen kept the wind and would not come near us, and our own ship was astern so that she could not come to us.

And after we had followed them about two hours to the seaward they kept about again towards the shore, thinking to pay us as they

8 The castle of Mina, with one tall ship and two caravels in the roadstead.

went along by, and to have the wind of the French admiral which
before ran in towards the shore; and we kept about with them and kept
still the wind of them, thinking that our vice-admiral and the other
would have followed us as we willed them to do. But after that the
Portugal was passed by them, and every one had shot at us and our
vice-admiral, both our vice-admiral and the two Frenchmen and our
own pinnace left us in the lapse and ran to seaward; and we ran still
along, and kept the wind of them, to succour the French admiral, who
was under all their lees. And when they met with him every one went
room with him and gave him the broadside, and after they cast about
again and durst not board him, because they saw us in the weather of
them, or else without doubt they had taken or sunk them. For three of
them, which were the smallest, went so fast that it was not possible for a
ship to board them, and carried such ordnance that if they had had the
weather of us they would have troubled 3 of the best ships that we had;

and as for their admiral and vice-admiral they were both notably appointed.

When the Frenchman was clear of them he lay as near the wind as he could, and we followed them still towards the shore, and then the admiral ran to sea after the rest and left us all alone. And when the Portugals perceived that we were alone, and gave them chase, they kept about with us and we with them to keep the wind of them, and we ran still within base-shot of them, but they shot not at us, because we had the weather of them, and saw that they could do us no hurt. And thus we followed one another until night, and in the night we lost them; but as for all the rest of our ships, they packed on all sails that they could and ran to sea, and, as they themselves confess, they prayed for us, but as for help at their hands we could have none.

The 28th day we met with our vice-admiral, our pinnace, and two of the Frenchmen, and the third was fled, which was a ship of fourscore ton and belonged to Rouen. And when I had the sight of the rest of our ships I took our skiff and went to them to know why they lost us in such a case; and John Kire made me answer that his ship would neither rear nor steer, and as for the pinnace John Davis made me answer that she would do nothing and that he could carry her no further, for her rudder was broken, so that the *Hart* was glad to tow her. Then I went to the French Admiral, and found himself to be a man of good stomach, but the one half of his men were sick and dead; and then I talked with the smaller Frenchman, and he made me answer that he could do nothing, saying that his ship would bear no sail and had 16 of his men dead and sick, so he made us plain answer that he was able to do nothing. After this the Frenchmen durst not anchor for fear of the Portugals.

The 29th day the master of the pinnace came to us and said that they were not able to keep her any longer; and then we viewed her, and seeing there was no remedy, her rudder with all the iron work being broken both aloft and below, we agreed to break her up and put the men into the *Hart*. So we took out of her four bases, one anchor, and certain firewood, and set her on fire, and afterwards ran along the shore.

The thirtieth day we went in to the shore, and spoke with certain negroes who told us that some French ships had been there; but we could not bargain with them, they were so unreasonable. The 31st day I went on shore but did not traffic. The 1st day of February we weighed, seeing we could not bring the negroes to any reason, and came to another place, which standeth upon a hill.

The third day I went to a town four leagues from us, and shot off two pieces and the captain came to us. And I sent Thomas Rippen aland, who knew the captain; and as soon as he came on shore the captain knew him, and divers of the negroes, who then began to ask for me; and having told the captain that I was in the boat, he made no longer tarrying but by and by caused two boats to be put to the sea and came to me himself, and when he saw me he cried to me before he came to the boat and seemed to be the gladdest man alive, and so did all the company that knew me. And I gave him a reward, as the manner of the country is, and caused the Frenchmen to give another, promising the next day to give him wine; and that night, because it was late, he would not talk of any price, but left me a pledge, and took another of me, and so departed.

The 4th day, going on shore, I found that the ships of France which had been there had done much hurt to our markets, but yet I took five ounces and a half of gold. The fifth day I took eight ounces and one eighth part of gold; but I saw that the negroes perceived the difference in cloth betwixt ours and that which the Frenchmen had, which was better and broader than ours. And then I told Captain Blundel that I would go to the leeward because I perceived that being there where his cloth was sold I should do no good, whereof he was sorry.

The 6th day there came an *almade* and negroes aboard me, requesting me to come to their town for they had much gold and many merchants, and so I went, and found their old captain gone and another in his place; but this night we did no good because the merchants were not come down, so he required a pledge which I let him have and took another of him. The 7th day George our negro came to us, who had followed us at the least 30 leagues in a small boat, and when he came the negroes and we soon concluded of price. I took this day five pound and one ounce and 3 quarters of gold. This negro we had left at Shama at the time of the fight, who said that he saw the fight, being on shore, and that when we were gone from the Portugals the Portugals came into their river, and told them that the Englishmen had slain two Portugals with a piece, which was indeed out of our ship, and they required harbour there, but the captain of Shama would not suffer them.

The 8th day we took nineteen pound three ounces and a half. The 9th day we took two pound six ounces and a half; the 10th day three pound.

The 11th day came to us Jerome Baudet, the Vice-admiral of the Frenchmen, and his pinnace, and he showed us that where we left him there was no good to be done, and said he would go to the eastward; but we told him he should not, and thereupon commanded him to go to his company which he was appointed to be with, which he refused to do until we had shot three or four pieces at their pinnace. And when the ship saw that she kept about and ran to seaward, and durst come no nearer to us, so the pinnace went after her. We took this day one pound five ounces. The 12th day there came one of the Frenchmen's pinnaces to us laden with cloth, and would have made sale, but I would not suffer him, and therefore took him and sent him aboard of our ship and caused him to ride there all day. We took five pound six ounces and a half. The 14th day we took of some negroes 4 ounces of gold.

The 16th we came to another town. The 17th day I went ashore, and understood that 3 of the Portugal ships were at the Castle and the other two at Shama. The captain of this town was gone to the principal town to speak with their king, and would return shortly, as they told me, and so he did, and brought me a weight and measure, and I sent a man to see that principal town and their king. The Portugal ships rode so near us that within 3 hours they might be with us, yet were all contented to tarry for sales.

The 18th day certain of the King's servants came to us, and we took one pound two ounces and one eighth part of gold. The 10th day we took five pound one ounce; the 20th day one pound and four ounces. The 21st I took four pound and one ounce; and the negroes enquired for fine cloth, and I opened two pieces which were not fine enough, as they said, but seeing that we had no other they bought of them. At night I provided a gift or present, and sent one merchant and a mariner with it to the King, to certify him of our want of victuals, by reason whereof we could not stay long. For indeed we searched our ship, and the most part of our beer was leaked out of all our barrels.

The 22nd day we took three ounces and a half. The 23rd our men came from the King, Abaan, and told us that he had received them very friendly, but he had little gold, but promised, if we would tarry, to send into all his country for gold for us; and he willed our men at their coming home to speak to our King to send men and provision into his country to build a castle, and to bring tailors with them to make them apparel, and good wares and they should be sure to sell them; but for that present the Frenchmen had filled them full of cloth.

This town standeth about four leagues up in the land and is, by the estimation of our men, as big in circuit as London, but the building is like to the rest of the country. They have about this town great store of the wheat of the country, and they judge that on one side of the town there were one thousand ricks of wheat and another sort of corn which is called mill, which is much used in Spain. About this town they keep good watch every night, and have to warn the watchmen certain cords made fast over their ways which lead into the town, and certain bells upon them, so that if any man touch the cords the bells ring, and then the watchmen run forth of their watch-houses to see what they be. And if they be enemies, if they pass the cord they have provision with certain nets hanged over the ways, where they must pass, to let fall upon them and so take them; and otherwise than by the ways it is not possible to enter the town by reason of the thickets and bushes which are about the same, and the town is also walled round about with long cords and bound together with sedge and certain barks of trees.

When our men came to the town it was about five of the clock in the morning, for there they travel always in the night by reason of the heat of the day. And about nine of the clock the King sent for them, for there may no man come to him before he be sent for, and then they would have carried their present with them. But the negroes told them that they must be three times brought before him before they might offer their gift. And when they came to him he talked with them, and received them very friendly, and kept them about half an hour and then they departed, and after that sent for them again three times; and last of all they brought him their present, which he received thankfully, and then caused a pot of wine of palm to be brought forth and made them drink. And before they drink, both here and in all the country, they use certain ceremonies. First they bring forth their pot of drink, and then they make a hole in the ground and put some of the drink into it, and they cast the earth upon it which they digged forth before, and then they set the pot upon the same. Then they take a little thing made of a gourd, and with that they take out of the same drink and put it upon the ground in three places; and in divers places they have certain bunches of the peels of palm trees set in the ground before them, and there they put in some drink, doing great reverence in all places to the same palm trees.

All these ceremonies first done, the King took up a cup of gold, and they put him in wine and he drank of it; and when he drank the people cried all with one voice "Abaan, Abaan", with certain other words, like as they cry commonly in Flanders upon the Twelfth Night "The *Kinning* drinks". And when he had drunk, then they gave drink to everyone, and that done the King licensed them to depart. And everyone that departeth from him boweth 3 times towards him, and waveth with both hands together as they bow, and then do depart. The King hath commonly sitting by him 8 or 10 ancient men with grey beards.

This day we took one pound and 10 ounces of gold. The 24th day we took 3 pound and 7 ounces. The 25th we took 3 ounces and 3 quarters. The 26th we took 2 pound and 10 ounces; the 27th two pound and five ounces; the 28th four pound; and then, seeing that there was no more gold to be had, we weighed and went forth.

The first day of March we came to a town called Moree, but we found no boats nor people there. But being ready to depart, there came two *almades* to us from another town of whom we took two ounces and a half of gold, and they told us that the negroes that dwelt at Moree were gone to dwell at Laguy.

The second day we came thwart of the Castle and about two leagues off, and there saw all the five Portugal ships at anchor, and this day by night we fetched Shama. The third day we had sight of one tall ship, of about two hundred tons, in the weather of us and within less than two leagues of our ships, and then we saw two more astern of her, the one a ship of five hundred or more and the other a pinnace; and these were a new fleet at that present arrived out of Portugal. Whereupon we weighed, and made shift to double out of the land; and then the wind coming to the south-south-west, the *Hart*, going room with them, fell three leagues to the leewards of us. These Portugals gave us the chase from nine of the clock in the morning till five at night, but did no good against us. At last we, perceiving the admiral to be far astern of his company, because his main topmast was spent, determined to cast about with them again, because we were sure to weather them and the wind being as it was it was our best course. But the *Hart* was so far to the leeward that we could not do it except we would lose her company, so that we took in some of our sails and went room with him; which when he perceived he luffed to and was able to lie as near as he did before. At night, when we came to him, he would not speak to us. Then we asked of his company why he went so room, and they made excuse that they were able to bear no sail by, for fear of bearing their fore-topmast overboard; but this was a simple excuse.

The fourth day, being put from our watering place, we began to seethe our meat in salt water and to rebate our allowance of drink to make it endure the longer; and so concluded to set our course thence for our own country.

The 12th of March I found myself thwart of Cape das Palmas. The 16th day we fell with the land, which we judged to be the Cape Mesurado, about which place is very much high land. The 18th day we lost sight of the *Hart*, and I think the wilful Master ran in with the shore of purpose to lose us, being offended I told him of his own folly.

The 27th day we fell in sight of two small islands, which lie by our reckoning six leagues off the headland of Sierra Leone; and before we came in sight of the same islands we made our reckoning to be forty or thirty leagues at the least off them. Therefore all they that sail this way are to regard the currents which set north-north-west, or else they may be much deceived.

The 14th of April we met with two great ships of Portugal, which although they were in the weather of us yet came not room with us, whereby we judged that they were bound for Calicut.

The 18th day we were in the height of Cape Verde. The 24th we were directly under the Tropic of Cancer. The first day of May Henry Wilson, our steward, died; and the next day died John Underwood. The fifth day we were in the height of St Michael.

The 23rd we had sight of a ship in the weather of us which was a Frenchman of 90 ton, who came with us as stoutly and as desperately as might be, and coming near us perceived that we had been upon a long voyage, and judging us to be weak, as indeed we were, came nearer us and thought to have laid us aboard; and there stepped up some of his men in armour and commanded us to strike sail. Whereupon we sent them some of our stuff, cross-bars, and chain-shot, and arrows so thick that it made the upper works of their ship fly about their ears, and we spoiled him with all his men and tore his ship miserably with our great ordnance, and then he began to fall astern of us and to pack on his sails and get away; and we, seeing that, gave him four or five good pieces more for his farewell, and thus we were rid of this Frenchman, who did us no harm at all. We had aboard us a Frenchman, a trumpeter, who, being sick and lying in his bed, took his trumpet notwithstanding, and sounded till he could sound no more, and so died.

The 28th we conferred together, and agreed to go into Severn and so to Bristol; but the same night we had sight of the Lizard, and by reason of the wind we were not able to double the Land's End to go into Severn, but were forced to bear in with the Lizard. The 29th day, about nine of the clock in the morning, we arrived safely in Plymouth, and praised God for our good arrival.

The third and last voyage of Master William Towerson to the coast of Guinea and the Castle of Mina, in the year 1557.

THE thirtieth day of January the year abovesaid we departed out of the Sound of Plymouth with three ships and a pinnace, whereof the names are these: 1, the *Minion*, admiral of the fleet; 2, the *Christopher*, vice-admiral; 3, the *Tiger*; 4, a pinnace called the *Unicorn*; being all bound for the Canaries, and from thence, by the grace of God, to the coast of Guinea.

The next day, being the last of this month, we met with two hulks of Danzig, the one called the *Rose*, a ship of four hundred tons, and the other called the *Unicorn*, of a hundred and fifty tons; the master of the *Rose* was called Nicholas Masse and the master of the *Unicorn* Melchior White; both laden at Bordeaux, and for the most part with wines. When we came to them we caused them to hoist forth their boats and to come and speak with us, and we examined every one of them apart what Frenchmen's goods they had in their ships, and they said they had none. But by the contrarieties of their tales, and by the suspicion which we gathered of their false charter-parties, we perceived that they had Frenchmen's goods in them. We therefore caused one of them to fetch up his bills of lading, and because he denied that he had any we sent certain with him, who caused him to go to the place where he had hid them, and by the differences of his bills of lading and his talk we gathered, as before, that they had Frenchmen's goods.

Whereupon we examined them straitly, and first the purser of the *Unicorn*, which was the smaller ship, confessed that they had two and thirty tuns and a hogshead of a Frenchman's. Then we examined the master in like case, and he acknowledged the same to be true. Then we examined also the master of the great ship, and he confessed that he had a hundred and eight and twenty tuns of the same Frenchman's, and more they would not confess, but said that all the rest was laden by Peter Leugues of Hamburg to be delivered to one Henry Summer of Camphire, notwithstanding all their letters were directed to Hamburg, and written in Dutch without and within in French.

When they had confessed that they had thus much Frenchmen's goods within their ships we conferred together what was best to be done with them. William Cretton and Edward Selman were of the opinion that it should be good either to carry them into Spain, and there make sale of the goods, or else into Ireland, or to return back again into England with them if the wind would permit it. But I, weighing what charge we had of our masters, first by mouth and afterwards by writing, that for no such matter we should in any case prolong the time for fear of losing the voyage, and considering that the time of the year was very far spent, and the money that we should make of the wines not very much in respect of the commodity which we hoped for by the voyage, persuaded them that to go into Ireland, the wind being easterly as it was, might be an occasion that we should be locked in there with that wind, and so lose our voyage; and to carry them into Spain, seeing they sailed so ill that having all their sails abroad we kept them company only with our foresails and without any topsails abroad, so that in every two days sailing they would have hindered us more than one; and, besides that, the wind being easterly we should not be able to seize the coast with them; besides all this the loss of time when we came thither was to be considered, whereupon I thought it not good to carry them any further. And as for carrying them into England, although the wind had been good, as it was not, considering what charge we had of our masters to shift us out of the way for fear of a stay by reason of the wars, I held it not in any wise convenient.

But notwithstanding all this, certain of our company not being herewith satisfied went to our Master to know his opinion therein, who made them a plain answer, that to carry them into any place it was not the best way nor the profit of their masters. And he told them further that if the time were prolonged one month longer before they passed the Cape but a few men would go the voyage. All these things considered, we all paused, and determined at the last that every man should take out of the hulks so much as he could well bestow for necessaries, and the next morning to conclude what should be further done with them. So we took out of them for us fourteen tuns and a half of wine, and one tun we put into the pinnace. More, we took out one hogshead of aquavitae; six cakes of rosin, a small hawser for ties; and certain chestnuts. The *Christopher* took out ten tuns of wine, and one hogshead; a quantity of aquavitae; shall-lines; chestnuts; six double bases with their chambers; and their men broke up the hulks' chests, and took out their compasses and running glasses, the sounding-lead and line, and candles, and cast some of their beef overboard, and spoiled them so much that of very pity we gave them a compass, a running-glass, a lead and a line, certain bread and candles, and what apparel of theirs we could find in their ship we gave them again, and some money also of that which William Crompton took for the ransom of a poor Frenchman who, being their pilot down the river of Bordeaux, they were not able to set him ashore again by reason of the foul weather. The *Tiger* also took out of the smaller hulk six or seven tuns of wine, one hogshead of aquavitae, and certain rosin, and two bases he took out of the great hulk.

The first day of February in the morning we all came together again, saving W. Crompton who sent us word that he was contented to agree to that order which we should take. Now Edward Selman was of this opinion, that it was not best to let the ships depart, but put men into them to carry them into England, which thing neither we nor our Master would agree unto, because we thought it not good to unman our ships going outward, considering how dangerous the time was. So that in fine we agreed to let them depart, and give them the rest of the wine which they had in their ships of the Frenchmen's, for the freight of that which we had taken and for their ordnance, rosin, aquavitae, chestnuts, and other things which the company had taken from them. So we received a bill of their hands that they confessed how much Frenchmen's goods they had, and then we let them depart.

The 10th day we reckoned ourselves to be 25 leagues from the Grand Canary, and this day about nine of the clock the pinnace broke her rudder, so that we were forced to tow her at the stern of the *Minion*, which we were able to do and yet kept company with the rest of our ships. About eleven of the clock this day we had sight of the Grand Canary. The 11th day when we came to the island we perceived that it was the Isle of Tenerife, and then indeed we had sight of the Grand Canary, which lieth 12 leagues to the eastwards of Tenerife; and because the road of Tenerife is foul ground, and nothing was there to be gotten for the helping of our pinnace, having the wind large we agreed to go with the Grand Canary.

The 12th day we came into the road of the town of Canary, which lieth one league from the same town; and after we had shot off divers pieces of ordnance to salute the town and the castle, the Governor and captains of the island sent to us which were the captains of the ships, requiring us to come ashore. And when we came to them they received us very friendly, offering us their own jennets to ride to the town, and what other friendship they could show us; and we went to the town with two English merchants which lay there and remained in their house that day. The second day following we came aboard to deliver our merchandise and to get our pinnace mended.

The 14th day came into the road the Spanish fleet which was bound to the Emperor's Indies, which were in number nineteen sail, whereof six were ships of four hundred and five hundred apiece; the rest were of two hundred, a hundred and fifty, and of a hundred. When they were come to an anchor they saluted us with ordnance, and so we did them in like case; and afterwards the Admiral, who was a knight, sent his pinnace to desire me to come to him. And when I came to him he received me friendly, and was desirous to hear somewhat of the state of England and Flanders. And after he had made me a banquet I departed; and I being gone into the boat he caused one of his gentlemen to desire Francisco the Portugal, which was my interpreter, to require me to furl my flag, declaring that he was General of the Emperor's fleet. Which thing, being come aboard, Francisco showed me; and because I refused to furl it, and kept it forth still, certain of the soldiers in the ships shot divers arquebus-shot about the ship and over the flag; and at the same time there came certain gentlemen aboard our ship to see her, to whom I said that if they would not cause their men to leave shooting I would shoot the best ordnance I had through their sides. And when they perceived that I was offended they departed, and caused their men of war and soldiers to shoot no more, and afterwards they came to me again and told me that they had punished their men. That done, I showed them the ship, and made them such cheer as I could, which they received very thankfully. And the day following they sent for me to dine with them, and sent me word that their General was very sorry that any man should require me to furl my flag, and that it was without his consent; and therefore he requested me not to think any ungentleness to be in him, promising that no man of his should misdemean himself.

The 17th day we set sail in the road of Grand Canary, and proceeded on our voyage. The 20th in the morning we had sight of the coast of Barbary, and running along the shore we had sight of Rio do Ouro, which lieth almost under the Tropic of Cancer. The 21st day we found ourselves to be in 20 degrees and a half, which is the height of Cape Blank. The 25th we had sight of the land in the bay to the northward of Cape Verde.

The 26th I took Francisco and Francis Castelin with me and went into the pinnace, and so went to the *Tiger*, which was nearer the shore than the other ships, and went aboard her; and with her and the other ships we ran west and by south and west-south-west until about four of the clock, at which time we were hard aboard the Cape, and then we ran in south-west. And beyond the Cape about four leagues we found a fair island, and besides that two or three islands which were of very high rocks, being full of divers sorts of sea-fowl and of pigeons with other sorts of land-fowls, and so many that the whole island was covered with the dung thereof and seemed so white as if the whole island had been of chalk. And within those islands was a very fair bay, and hard aboard the rocks eighteen fathom water and fair ground. And when we perceived the bay, and understanding that the French had a great trade there which we were desirous to know, we came to an anchor with the *Tiger*, and after that the *Minion* and the *Christopher* anchored in like case. Then we caused the pinnace to run beyond another cape of land to see if there were any place to trade in there.

It being near night I took our cock and the *Tiger's* skiff and went to the island, where we got certain fowls like unto gannets; and then I came aboard again and took two of the gannets which we had taken and carried them to the Captain of the *Christopher*. And when I had talked with him I found him not willing to tarry there, neither was I desirous to spend any long time there but only to attempt what was to be done. The Master of the *Christopher* told me he would not tarry being not bound for that place.

The 27th the Captain of the *Tiger* and Edward Selman came to me, and John Makeworth from the *Christopher*; and then we agreed to take the pinnace and to come along the shore, because that where we rode no negroes came to us, and the night before our pinnace brought us word that there was a very fair island. And when I came beyond the point I found it so, and withal a goodly bay, and we saw upon the main certain negroes which waved us on shore; and then we came to an anchor with the pinnace, and went ashore with our cock, and they showed us where their trade was, and that they had elephants' teeth, musk, and hides, and offered us to fetch down their captain if we would send a man with them, and they would leave a pledge for him. Then we asked them when any ship had been there; and some of them said not in eight months, others in six months, and others in four, and that they were Frenchmen. Then we perceiving the *Christopher* not willing to tarry departed from them, and set sail with the pinnace and went aboard the *Tiger*.

The 10th day of March we fell with the coast of Guinea five leagues to the eastward of Cape de Monte, beside a river called Rio das Palmas. The 11th we went to the shore and found one man that could speak some Portuguese, who told us that there were three French ships passed by, one of them two months past and the other one month past. At this place I received nineteen elephants' teeth, and two ounces and a half a quarter of gold.

The 12th we set sail to go to the River dos Cestos. The 13th at night we fell with the same river. The 14th we sent in our boats to take water, and rummaged our ships, and delivered such wares to the *Christopher* and *Tiger* as they had need of.

The 15th we came together and agreed to send the *Tiger* to another river to take in her water and to see what she could do for grains. After that we took merchandise with us and went into the river, and there we found a negro which was born in Lisbon, left there by a ship of Portugal which was burned the last year at this river in fighting with three Frenchmen; and he told us further that two months past there were three Frenchmen at this place, and six weeks past there were two French ships at the river, and fifteen days past there was one, all which ships were gone towards the Mina. This day we took but few grains.

The 19th day, considering that the Frenchmen were gone before us, and that by reason of the unwholesome airs of this place fourteen of our men in the *Minion* were fallen sick, we determined to depart, and with all speed to go to the Mina. The 21st we came to the River de los Potos, where some of our boats went in for water, and I went in with our cock and took 12 small elephants' teeth. The 23rd day, after we had taken as many teeth as we could get, about nine of the clock we set sail to go towards the Mina. The 31st we came to Ahanta, and made sale of certain manillas.

The first April we had sight of five sail of Portugals, whereupon we set sail and went off to sea to get the wind of them, which we should have had if the wind had kept his ordinary course, which is all the day at the south-west and west-south-west. But this day with a flaw it kept all the day at the east and east-south-east, so that the Portugals had the wind of us, and came room with the *Tiger* and us until night, and brought themselves, all save one which sailed not so well as the rest, within shot of us. Then it fell calm, and the wind came up to the south-west; howbeit it was near night, and the *Christopher*, by means of her boat, was about four leagues to the leewards of us. We tacked and ran into the weather of the admiral and three more of his company, and when we were near him we spoke to him, but he would not answer. Then we cast about and lay in the weather of him; and casting about he shot at us, and we shot at him, and shot him four or five times through. They shot divers times through our sails, but hurt no man. The *Tiger* and the pinnace, because it was night, kept out their sails and would not meddle with them. After we had thus fought together 2 hours or more, and would not lay him aboard because it was night, we left shooting one at the other, and kept still the weather of them. Then the *Tiger* and the pinnace kept about and came to us, and afterward, being near the shore, we three kept about and lay to the sea, and shot off a piece to give warning to the *Christopher*.

This night about 12 of the clock, being very little wind, and the Master of the *Tiger* asleep, by the ill work of his men the ship fell aboard of us, and with her shear-hooks cut our mainsail, and her boat, being betwixt us, was broken and sunk, with certain merchandise in her, and the ship's wales were broken with her outligger; yet in the end we cleared her without any more hurt, but she was in hazard to be broken down to the water.

The second day we had sight of the *Christopher*, and were near unto her, so that I took our boat and went to her. And when I came thither they showed me that after the Portugals had left us they went all room with him, and about twelve o'clock at night met him and shot at him, and he at them, and they shot him through the sails in divers places and did no other great hurt. And when we had understood that they had been with him as well as with us we agreed altogether to seek them, if we might find them, and keep a-weather our places of traffic.

The third day we ran all day to the south-westwards to seek the Portugals, but could have no sight of them, and hauled into the shore. The fourth day, when we had sight of land, we found that the current had set us thirty leagues to the eastwards of our reckoning, which we wondered at: for the first land we made was Laguy. Then I caused our boat to be manned, and the *Christopher*'s also, and went to the shore and took our negro with us. And on shore we learned that there were four French ships upon the coast: one at Perinnen, which is six leagues to the westward of Laguy, another at Weamba, which is four leagues to the eastward of Laguy, a third at Beraku, which is four leagues to the eastward of Weamba, and the fourth at Egrand, which is four leagues to the eastward of Beraku. When we had intelligence of these news we agreed to go to the eastwards with the Frenchmen to put them from their traffic, and shot off two or three pieces in our boats to cause the ships to weigh; and having been about one hour under sail we had sight of one of the Frenchmen under sail, hauling off from Weamba; to whom we gave chase, and agreed in the night, for fear of overshooting them, that the *Minion* should first come to anchor, and after that about three hours the *Tiger*, and the *Christopher* to bear along all night.

The 5th day we found three of the French ships at anchor: one called *La Foi de Honfleur*, a ship of 220 tons, another called the *Ventureuse* or small *Roebarge* of Honfleur, of 100 tons, both appertaining to Shaudet of Honfleur; the third was called the *Mulet de Batville*, a ship of 120 tons, and this ship belonged to certain merchants of Rouen.

When we came to them, we determined to lay the admiral aboard, the *Christopher* the vice-admiral, and the *Tiger* the smallest; but when we came near them they weighed, and the *Christopher*, being the headmost and the weathermost man, went room with the admiral. The *Roebarge* went so fast that we could not fetch her. The first that we came to was the *Mulet*, and her we laid aboard, and our men entered and took her, which ship was the richest except the admiral. For the admiral had taken about 80 pound of gold, and the *Roebarge* had taken but 22 pound; and all this we learned of the Frenchmen, who knew it very well for they were all in consort together, and had been upon the coast of Mina two months and odd days. Howbeit the *Roebarge* had been there before with another ship of Dieppe and a caravel, which had beaten all the coast, and were departed one month before our arriving there, and they three had taken about 700 pound of gold.

As soon as we had laid the ship aboard, and left certain men in her to keep her, we set sail and gave chase to the other two ships, and chased them all day and night and the next day until three o'clock in the afternoon, but we could not fetch them; and therefore, seeing that we brought ourselves very far to leeward of our place, we left the chase and kept about again to go with the shore.

The 7th day I sent for the captain, merchants, and masters of the other ships, and when they came we weighed the gold which we had from the Frenchmen, which weighed fifty pound and five ounces of gold. This done, we agreed to put men out of every ship into the prize to keep her.

The 12th day we came to the further place of the Mina called Egrand and, being come to an anchor, discharged all the merchants' goods out of the prize, and would have sold the ship with the victuals to the Frenchmen; but because she was leaky they would not take her, but desired us to save their lives in taking them into our own ships. Then we agreed to take out the victuals and sink the ship, and divide the men among our ships. The 15th at night we made an end of discharging the prize, and divided all the Frenchmen except four which were sick and not able to help themselves; which four both the *Christopher* and the *Tiger* refused to take, leaving them in their ship alone in the night, so that about midnight I was forced to fetch them into our ship.

The 15th of April, moving our company for the voyage to Benin, the most part of them all refused it. The 16th, seeing the unwillingness of the company to go thither, we determined to spend as much time upon the coast as we could, to the end we might make our voyage; and agreed to leave the *Minion* here at Egrand, the *Tiger* to go to Beraku which is four leagues off, and the *Christopher* to go to Weamba, which is ten leagues to the weatherward of this place. And if any of them both should have sight of more sails than they thought good to meddle withal, to come room with their fellows, to wit first the *Christopher* to come with the *Tiger* and then both they to come with us.

We remained in this place called Egrand until the last day of April, in which time many of our men fell sick, and six of them died. And here we could have no traffic with the negroes but three or four days in the week, and all the rest of the week they would not come at us. The 3rd of May, not having the pinnace sent us with cloth from the other ships as they promised, we sold French cloth, and gave but three yards thereof to every fuff. The 5th day the negroes departed, and told us they would come to us again within four days, which we determined there to tarry although we had divers of our men sick. The 8th day, all our cloth in the *Minion* being sold, I called the company together to know whether they would tarry the sale of the cloth taken in the prize at this place or no. They answered that, in respect of the death of some of their men and the present sickness of twenty more, they would not tarry, but repair to the other ships, of whom they had heard nothing since the 27th of April, and yet they had our pinnace with them only to carry news from one to another.

The 9th day we determined to depart hence to our fellows, to see what they had done, and to attempt what was to be done at the town of Don John. The 10th day in the morning we set sail to seek the *Christopher* and the *Tiger*. The 11th day the Captain of the *Christopher* came to us and told us that they could find small doings at the places where they had been. The 12th William Crompton and I in our small pinnace went to the *Tiger* and the *Christopher* at Perinnen. The 13th we sent away the *Tiger* to Egrand, because we found nothing to do at Perinnen worth the tarrying for.

The 14th our great pinnace came to us, and presently we put cloth into her and sent her back to Weamba, where she had been before and had taken there ten pound of gold. The 15th the *Minion* came to us, and the next day we went ashore with our boats, and took but one ounce of gold. The 19th day having set sail we came to an anchor before Moree, and there we tarried two days, but took not an ounce of gold. The 21st we came to an anchor before Don John's town.

The 22nd we manned our boats and went to shore, but the negroes would not come at us. Then the Captain of the *Christopher* and I took a skiff and eight men with us, and went and talked with the negroes, and they said that they would send a man to the great town where Don John himself lay, to advertise him of our coming. The 23rd we went ashore again, and the negroes told us that this day the merchants of Don John would come down. So we tarried there until night, and no man would come to us, but divers of the negroes made us signs to depart.

The 24th the Captain of the *Christopher* took his boat and went to Moree. And when he came thither certain negroes came to him to know the price of his wares; but in the end there came an *almade*, which he judged came from the Castle, and caused all the negroes to depart from him. And when he saw they would come no more to him, he went ashore and took certain men with him, and then the negroes cast stones at them and would not suffer them to come up to their town. And when they saw that, they took certain of the *almades* and put them to the sea, and afterwards departed. The same morning I went ashore at Don John's town, and took a white flag with me, but none of the negroes could come to me, which caused us to judge that the Portugals were in the town. After this our boat came to us well manned and I sent one man up to the town with a white flag in his hand; but when he was come thither all the negroes went away and would not speak with him. Then I sent one alone into the woods after them, but they in no case would come to us. When we saw that, we took twelve goats and fourteen hens which we found in the town, and went aboard without doing any further hurt to the town. And when I came aboard I found our pinnace come from Cormatin, which had taken there two pound and five ounces of gold. Then, after much ado with the froward mariners, we went thitherwards with our ship, and the *Christopher* went to Moree.

The 25th day the Master of the *Christopher* sent his boat to the shore for ballast, and the negroes would have beaten the company from the shore; whereupon the company resisted them, and slew and hurt divers of them, and having put them to flight burned their town and broke all their boats.

The 26th day our pinnace came to us from Cormatin, and had taken two pound and eleven ounces of gold; and John Shiriff told us that the negroes of that place were very desirous to have a ship come back again to their town. The 27th we weighed and went to Cormatin. The 28th the *Christopher* came to us from Moree, and trafficked there two days. The second day of June the *Tiger* came to us from Egrand and the pinnace from Weamba, and they two had taken about fifty pound of gold since they departed from us.

The 4th day we departed from Cormatin to ply up to Shama, being not able to tarry any longer upon the coast for lack of victuals, and specially of drink. The 7th day we had sight of five of the King of Portugal's ships, which came to an anchor besides the castle. The 8th day George and Binny came to us, and brought with them about two pound of gold.

The 10th day in the morning I took our small pinnace, and the Captain of the *Christopher* with me, and manned her well, and went to the Castle to view the Portugals' ships; and there we found one ship of about 300 ton, and four caravels. When we had well viewed them we returned back again to our ships, which we found seven leagues at sea.

The 11th day in the morning we found ourselves well shot toward Shama, and the *Tiger* with us, but the *Minion* and the pinnace had not weighed that night, so that we were out of sight of them; and having brought ourselves in the weather of the Portugals' ships, we came to an anchor to tarry for the *Minion*, or else we might have fetched Shama. At night the *Minion* and the pinnace came up to us, but could not fetch so far to the weatherward as we, and therefore they anchored about a league a-weather the Castle, and we weighed in the *Christopher* and went room with her.

The 12th day the *Tiger* came room with us, and she and the

Christopher, finding themselves to stand in great need of victuals, would have gone with the Portugals' ships to have fetched some of them forth. But our Master and company would in no case consent to go with them, for fear of hanging when we came home; and the other two ships being fully minded to have gone and fearing that their own company would accuse them, durst not go to them. After this, by reason of the want of victuals in the pinnace, which could receive no victuals from the other ships but from us only, we took out all our men and put twelve Frenchmen in her, and gave them victuals to bring them to Shama.

The 19th day the *Tiger* and *Minion* arrived at Shama, and the *Christopher* within two leagues off them, but could not fetch the wind by reason of the scantness of the wind, which hath been so scant that in fifteen days we have plied to the windwards but twelve leagues, which before we did in one day and a night.

The 20th day I took our pinnace and went to the town of Shama to speak with the captain, and he told me that there was no gold there to be had, nor so much as a hen to be bought, and all by reason of the accord which he had made with the Portugals; and I seeing that departed peaceably from him.

The 21st I put such things as we had into our small pinnace, and took one merchant of our ship and another of the *Tiger*, and sent her to Ahanta to attempt if she could do anything there. That night they could do nothing, but were promised to have gold the next day. The next day, which was the 22nd, being come, we sent our pinnace to Ahanta again, but there neither the captain nor the negroes durst traffic with us, but enticed us from place to place, and all to no purpose. This day we put away our pinnace, with five and twenty Frenchmen in her, and gave them such victuals as we could spare, putting fifteen of them to the ransom of six crowns a man. The 23rd of June our pinnace came to us from Ahanta, and told us that the negroes had dealt very ill with them, and would not traffic with them to any purpose.

The 24th we took our boat and pinnace and manned them well and went to the town of Shama; and because the captain thereof was become subject to the Portugals we burned the town. And our men seeking the spoil of such trifles as were there found a Portugal's chest, wherein was some of his apparel and his weights, and one letter sent to him from the Castle, whereby we gathered that the Portugal had been there of a long time.

The 25th day, about three of the clock at afternoon, we set sail and put into the sea for our return to England. The last day of this month we fell with the shore again, and made our reckoning to be eighteen leagues to the weatherward of the place where we set off. When we came to make the land, we found ourselves to be eighteen leagues to the leeward of the place where we set off, which came to pass by reason of the extreme current that runneth to the eastward. When we perceived ourselves so abused, we agreed to cast about again, and to lie as near the wind as we could, to fetch the line.

The seventh of July we had sight of the Isle of St Thomé, and thought to have sought the road to have anchored there; but the next morning the wind came about, and we kept our course. The ninth, the wind varying, we kept about again and fell with the Island of St Thomé, and seeking the road were becalmed near the Island, and with the current were put near the shore, but could have no ground to anchor; so that we were forced to hoist out our pinnace and the other ships their skiffs to tow from the Island, which did little good, but in the end the wind put us three leagues from shore.

The tenth day the *Christopher* and the *Tiger* cast about, whereby we judged them to have agreed together to go seek some ships in the road, and to leave us. Our men were not willing to go after them, for fear of running in with the Island again, and of putting ourselves into the same danger that we were in the night before. But we shot off a piece, and put out two lights, and they answered us with lights again. Whereupon we kept our course, and thought that they had followed us, but in the morning we could not see them, so that they left us willingly, and we determined to follow them no more. But the eleventh day we altered our opinion and course, and consented to cast about again for the Island to seek our ships; and about four of the clock in the afternoon we met with them.

The 13th we fell again with the Island of St Thomé, and the same night we found ourselves directly under the line. This Island is a very high island, and being upon the west side of it you shall see a very high pike, which is very small and strait, as it were the steeple of a church, which pike lieth directly under the line; and at the same south end of the Island, to the westward thereof, lieth a small island about a mile from the great island.

The third of August we departed from the Isle of St Thomé and met the wind at the south-west. The 12th day we were in the height of Cape Verde. The 22nd day we fell with one of the Isles of Cape Verde called the Isle of Salt, and being informed, by a Scottish man that we took among the Frenchmen upon the coast, that there were fresh victuals to be had, we came to an anchor there. The 23rd day in the morning we manned our skiff and went ashore, and found no houses, but we saw four men which kept themselves always far from us; as for cattle we could find none but great store of goats, and they were so wild that we could not take above three or four of them. But there we had good store of fish, and upon a small island which lay by the same we had great store of sea-birds.

At night the *Christopher* broke her cable and lost an anchor, so that she could tarry no longer; so we all weighed and set sail. Upon the same island we left the Scottish man which was the occasion of our going aland at that place, but how he was left we could not tell; but, as we judged, the people of the island found him sleeping and so carried him away for at night I went myself to the island to seek him but could hear nothing of him.

The 24th day the Master of the *Tiger* came aboard us and told us that his men were so weak and the ship so leaky that he was not able to keep her above the water, and therefore requested us to go back again to the island that we might discharge her and give her up. But we entreated him to take pain with her awhile, and we put a French carpenter into her to see if he could find the leak. This day we took a view of all our men, both those that were whole and the sick also, and we found that in all the three ships were not above thirty sound men.

The 25th we had sight of the Isle of St Nicholas and the day following of the other isles, St Lucia, St Vincent, and St Anthony, which four isles lie the one from the other north-west and by west, south-east and by east. The 26th we came again with the Island of St Anthony, and could not double the cape. This day Philip Jones, the master of the *Christopher*, came aboard us, who had been aboard the *Tiger*, and told us that they were not able to keep the *Tiger* because she was leaky, and the Master very weak; and said further, he had agreed with the Master and the company that if the next day we could double the island we should run to the leeward of it and there discharge her; but if we could not double it, then to put in betwixt the Island of St Vincent and St Anthony to see if we could discharge her.

The third day of September I went aboard the *Tiger*, with the Master and merchants with me, to view the ship and men; and we found the ship very leaky, and only six labouring men in her, whereof one was the Master Gunner. So that we, seeing that they were not able to keep the ship, agreed to take in the men, and of the goods that we could save, and then to put the ship away.

The fifth day we went to discharge the *Tiger*. The eighth day, having taken out the artillery, goods, victuals, and gold of the *Tiger*, we gave her up 25 degrees by north the line.

The 27th we had sight of two of the Isles of the Azores, St Mary and St Michael. The fourth of October we found ourselves to be 41 degrees and a half from the line.

The sixth day the *Christopher* came to us and willed us to put with the Cape, for they also were so weak that they were not able to keep the sea; and we, being weak also, agreed to go for Vigo, being a place which many Englishmen frequent.

The 10th day the *Christopher* went room with the Cape. But we, having a merry wind for England, and fearing the danger of the enemies which ordinarily lie about the Cape; besides, not knowing the state of our country and Spain, and although it were peace yet there was little hope of friendship at their hands considering the voyage that we had made; and we also being so weak that by force and violence we could come by nothing; and doubting also that the King of Portugal, knowing of our being there, might work some way with the Council of Spain to trouble us; and further, considering that, if we did put in with any harbour, we should not be able to come out again till we sent for more men into England, which would be a great charge and loss of time and means of many dangers: all these things pondered we agreed to shoot off two pieces of ordnance to warn the *Christopher*, and then we went our course for England. She, hearing our pieces, followed us, and we carried a light for her; but the next day in the morning it was thick, and we could not see her in the afternoon neither, so that we suspected that either she was gone with Spain, or else that she should put forth more sails than we in the night and was shot ahead of us. So that then we put forth our topsails and went our course with England. At the time when the *Christopher* left us we were within 120 leagues of England, and 45 leagues north-west and by west from Cape Finisterre; and at the same time in our ships we had not above six mariners and six merchants in health, which was but a weak company for such a ship to seek a foreign harbour.

The 16th day, about six of the clock at night, we met with a great storm at the west-south-west, and west, and our men being weak and not able to handle our sails we lost the same night our mainsail, foresail, and spritsail, and were forced to lie a-hulling until the eighteenth day. And then we made ready an old course of a foresail and put it to the yard, and therewith finding ourselves far shot into the Sleeve, we bore with our own coast. But that foresail continued not above two hours before it was blown from the yard with a fret, and then we were forced to lie a-hull again until the nineteenth day of October in the morning; and then we put an old bonnet to our foreyard which, by the good blessing and providence of God, brought us to the Isle of Wight, where we arrived the 20th of October in the afternoon.

The commodities and wares that are most desired in Guinea, betwixt Sierra Leone and the furthest place of the Mine:

> Manillas of brass, and some of lead.
> Basins of divers sorts, but the most latten.
> Pots of coarse tin, of a quart or more.
> Some wedges of iron.
> Margarites, and certain other slight beads.
> Some blue coral.
> Some horse-tails.
> Linen cloth principally.
> Basins of Flanders.

Some red cloth of low price, and some kersey.
Kettles of Dutchland with brazen handles.
Some great brass basins graved, such as in Flanders they set
upon cupboards.
Some great basins of pewter, and ewers graven.
Some lavers, such as be for water.
Great knives of a low price.
Slight Flanders caskets.
Chests of Rouen of a low price, or any other chests.
Great pins.
Coarse French coverings.
Packing sheets good store.
Swords, daggers, frieze mantles and gowns, cloaks, hats, red
caps, Spanish blankets, axe-heads, hammers, short pieces of
iron, slight bells, gloves of a low price, leather bags, and what
other trifles you will.

A letter of Master John Locke to the Worshipful Company of
Merchant Adventurers for Guinea, written 1561; showing
reasons for his not proceeding in a voyage then intended to the
foresaid country.

WORSHIPFUL Sirs,
Since the arrival of Master Pet and Buttoll Montjoy, as I
understand for the voyage it is concluded that the *Minion*
shall proceed on her voyage if within 20 days she may be repaired of
those hurts she hath received by the last storm; or in the month of
January also, if the wind will serve therefor. Wherefore, for that your
Worships shall not be ignorant of my determined purpose in the same,
with the reasons that have persuaded me thereunto, I have thought
good to advertise you thereof, trusting that your Worships will weigh
them as I uprightly and plainly mean them, and not for any fear or
discouragement that I have of myself by the raging of the storms of the
sea, for that (I thank the Lord) these have not been the first that I have
abidden, neither trust I they shall be the last.

First the state of the ship: in which, though I think not but Master Pet
can do more for her strengthening than I can conceive, yet for all that it
will neither mend her conditions nor yet make her so staunch that any
cabin in her shall be staunch for men to lie dry in: the which sore, what a
weakening it will be to the poor men, after their labour, that they
neither can have a shift of apparel dry nor yet a dry place to rest in, I
refer to your discretion. For though at Harwich she was both bound

and caulked as much as might be both within and without, yet for all that she left not, afore this flaw, in other weathers, being stressed to open those seams and become in the state she was before – I mean in wetting her men, notwithstanding her new work. And my judgment, with what little experience I have had, leadeth me to think that the ship whose water works and footings be spent and rotten cannot be but leaky for men.

Next, the unseasonable time of the year which is now present. And how only by means of the unseasonable times in the return from the voyage home, many thereby have decayed, to the great misery and calamity of the rest and also to the great slander of the voyage (which I much respect), the last and other voyages have declared; and what it is to make the voyage in unseasonable time, that hath the second voyage also declared. Wherefore weighing and foreseeing this, as I may well term it, calamity and inevitable danger of men, and that by men she must be brought home again (except that God will show an extraordinary miracle), I purpose not nor dare I venture with a safe conscience to tempt God herein.

Again, forasmuch as she is alone, and hath so little help of boat or pinnace in her trade and also for her watering, where a long time of force must be spent, my going, to the accomplishment of your expectations, will be to small effect for this time, because I shall want both vessel and men to accomplish it. And I would not gladly so spend my time and travail, to my great charges and pain, and after, for not falling out accordingly, to lose both pot and water as the proverb is.

As for the *Primrose*, if she be there, her trade will be ended or ever we come there, so that she of force, by want of provision, must return; yea, though we should carry with us a supply for her, yet is the meeting of her doubtful, and though we met her yet will the men not tarry, as no reason is they should. Howbeit, my opinion of her is that she is put into Ireland. The *Flowerdeluce* was in Milford.

Thus, for that your Worships might understand the whole cause why I do not proceed, I have troubled you at this time with this my long letter; and, as God is my judge, not for fear of the Portugals which there we shall meet, and yet alone without aid. As here is a ship which was in Lisbon, whose men say that there are in a readiness (only to meet us) four great ships, of the which one is accounted 700 tons, and other pinnaces. Yet not for fear of them, nor raging of the seas (whose rage God is above to rule), but only for the premises; the sequel whereof must by reason turn to a great misery to the men, the which I for my part, though it might turn me to as much gain as the whole cometh to, yet would I not be so tormented, as the sight thereof would be a corsive to my heart, and the more because, foreseeing the same, I should be so lewd as, yielding, to have run into the danger thereof; and therefore I have absolutely determined with myself not to go this voyage.

Howbeit, if in a seasonable time of the year I had but one ship sufficient, though much less by the half, I would not refuse, as trial being made thereof should appear, or if I had ability of myself to venture so much it should well be seen. And this I speak to give you to understand that I refuse not this for fear.

If you purpose to proceed therein, send someone whom you please, to whom I will not only deliver the articles which I have received, but also will give some particular notes which I have noted in the affairs which you have committed unto me, with the best help and counsel I can.

Thus the living God keep your Worships all.

Bristol, this 11th of December 1561,

Your Worships' to command to his power,

John Locke

Part 4

NEWFOUNDLAND AND THE
NORTH-WEST PASSAGE

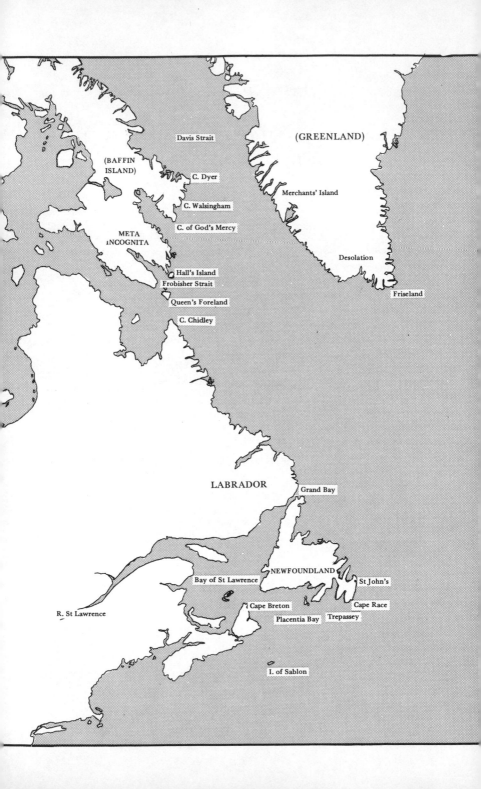

Davis Strait

(GREENLAND)

(BAFFIN ISLAND)

C. Dyer

Merchants' Island

C. Walsingham

C. of God's Mercy

META INCOGNITA

Desolation

Hall's Island
Frobisher Strait

Friseland

Queen's Foreland

C. Chidley

LABRADOR

Grand Bay

NEWFOUNDLAND

Bay of St Lawrence

St John's

R. St Lawrence

Cape Breton

Cape Race

Placentia Bay

Trepassey

I. of Sablon

In 1497 John Cabot, with his son Sebastian (whose map of the voyage, drawn up nearly fifty years later, appears to be highly misleading), discovered Newfoundland and claimed it for his sponsor, Henry VII of England. From this originated a series of explorations of the north-west, motivated partly by the urge to discover, partly by the richness of the cod-fisheries off Newfoundland, and, especially after attempts to find a north-east passage to Cathay had foundered, by the hope of tracing an alternative short-cut to the Pacific via the north-west.

Most of the credit for the opening up of mainland Canada belongs to the Portuguese and to the French. The English for their part developed Newfoundland with some success, although the principal voyages retailed by Hakluyt, Hore's in the William (Hakluyt's "Minion" is an error) and Humphrey Gilbert's, were almost unmitigated disasters. The English were also responsible for a succession of searches for a north-west passage. In the earlier of these, Frobisher's three voyages of 1576 to 1578, the discovery of what was thought to be gold ore, but in the end proved to be worthless pyrites, perverted the whole enterprise from exploration to treasure-seeking. The balance was restored by the three voyages (1585 to 1587) of John Davis, who was both the greatest of the Elizabethan navigators and a single-minded explorer.

The search was continued in the next generation, Hudson and Baffin being notable names; but, as in the north-east, all the would-be discoverers were defeated by never-ending fog and ice, and the puzzle of the north-west passage remained unsolved for even longer than the other. The way through was eventually found in 1905, by Roald Amundsen in the 47 ton Gjøa.

The interesting thing about the large new island south-east of Greenland, discovered, and described in some detail, by the Buss of Bridgewater in 1578, is that it does not exist. Whether what the crew saw was pack-ice, or fog-bank, or mirage, will never be known.

The voyage of Master Hore and divers other gentlemen to Newfoundland and Cape Breton, in the year 1536, and in the 28th year of King Henry the Eighth. (Compiled by the two Richard Hakluyts from the recollections of Oliver Daubeny and Thomas Butts.)

ONE, Master Hore of London, a man of goodly stature and of great courage and given to the study of cosmography, in the 28th year of King Henry the Eighth and in the year of Our Lord 1536, encouraged divers gentlemen and others, being assisted by the King's favour and good countenance, to accompany him in a voyage of discovery upon the north-west parts of America: wherein his persuasions took such effect that within short space many gentlemen of the Inns of Court, and of the Chancery, and divers others of good worship, desirous to see the strange things of the world, very willingly entered into the action with him, some of whose names were as followeth: Master Weeks, a gentleman of the west country of five hundred marks by the year living, Master Tuck, a gentleman of Kent, Master Tuckfield, Master Thomas Butts, the son of Sir William Butts, knight, of Norfolk, which was lately living and from whose mouth I wrote most of this relation, Master Hardy, Master Byron, Master Carter, Master Wright, Master Rastal, Sergeant Rastal's brother, Master Ridley, and divers other, which all were in the admiral called the *Trinity*, a ship of seven score tons, wherein Master Hore himself was embarked.

In the other ship, whose name was the *Minion*, went a very learned and virtuous gentleman, one Master Armigil Wade, afterwards Clerk of the Councils of King Henry the Eighth and King Edward the Sixth, father to the Worshipful Master William Wade, now Clerk of the Privy Council, Master Oliver Daubeny, merchant of London, Master Joy, afterward Gentleman of the King's Chapel, with divers other of good account. The whole number that went in the two tall ships aforesaid, to wit, the *Trinity* and the *Minion*, were about six score persons, whereof thirty were gentlemen, which all we mustered in warlike manner at Gravesend, and after the receiving of the sacrament they embarked themselves in the end of April, 1536.

From the time of their setting out from Gravesend they were very long at sea, to wit, above two months, and never touched any land until they came to part of the West Indies about Cape Breton, shaping their course thence north-eastwards until they came to the island of Penguin, which is very full of rocks and stones, whereon they went and found it full of great fowls, white and grey, as big as geese, and they saw infinite numbers of their eggs. The drove a great number of the fowls into their boats upon their sails, and took up many of their eggs; the fowls they flayed and their skins were very like honeycombs full of holes being flayed off. They dressed and ate them and found them to be very good and nourishing meat. They saw also store of bears, both black and white, of whom they killed some and took them for no bad food.

Master Oliver Daubeny, which (as it is before mentioned) was in this voyage and in the *Minion*, told Master Richard Hakluyt of the Middle Temple these things following: to wit, that after their arrival in Newfoundland, and having been there certain days at anchor and not having yet seen any of the natural people of the country, the same Daubeny, walking one day on the hatches, spied a boat with savages of those parts rowing down the bay toward them to gaze upon the ship and our people, and taking view of their coming aloof, he called to such as were under the hatches and willed them to come up if they would see the natural people of the country that they had so long and so much desired to see. Whereupon they came up and took view of the savages rowing toward them and their ship, and upon the view they manned out a ship-boat to meet them and to take them. But they, spying our ship-boat making towards them, returned with main force and fled into an island that lay up in the bay or river there, and our men pursued them into the island and the savages fled and escaped; but our men found a fire and the side of a bear on a wooden spit left at the same by the savages that were fled.

There in the same place they found a boot of leather garnished on the outward side of the calf with certain brave trails, as it were of raw silk, and also found a certain great warm mitten; and these carried with them they returned to their ship, not finding the savages, nor seeing anything else besides the soil and the things growing in the same, which briefly were store of fir and pine trees.

And further, the said Master Daubeny told him that lying there they grew into great want of victuals and that there they found small relief, more than that they had from the nest of an osprey that brought hourly to her young great plenty of divers sorts of fishes. But such was the famine that increased amongst them from day to day that they were forced to seek to relieve themselves of raw herbs and roots that they sought on the main; but the famine increasing and the relief of herbs being to little purpose to satisfy their insatiable hunger, in the fields and deserts here and there the fellow killed his mate while he stopped to take up a root for his relief, and cutting out pieces of his body whom he had murdered broiled the same on the coals and greedily devoured them.

By this means the company decreased, and the officers knew not what was become of them. And it fortuned that one of the company driven with hunger to seek abroad for relief, found out in the fields the savour of broiled flesh, and fell out with one for that he would suffer him and his fellows to starve, enjoying plenty as he thought; and this matter growing to cruel speeches, he that had the broiled meat burst out into these words, "If thou would'st needs know, the broiled meat that I had was a piece of such a man's buttock".

The report of this brought to the ship, the Captain found what became of those that were missing and was persuaded that some of them were neither devoured with wild beasts nor yet destroyed with savages. And hereupon he stood up and made a notable oration, containing how much these dealings offended the Almighty, and vouched the Scriptures from first to last what God had in cases of distress done for them that called upon Him, and told them that the power of the Almighty was then no less than in all former time it had been; and added that if it had not pleased God to have helped them in that distress that it had been better to have perished in body, and to have lived everlastingly, than to have relieved for a poor time their mortal bodies, and to be condemned everlastingly both body and soul to the unquenchable fire of hell. And thus having ended to that effect he began to exhort to repentance, and besought all the company to pray that it might please God to look upon their miserable present state and for His own mercy to relieve the same.

The famine increasing, and the inconvenience of the men that were missing being found, they agreed amongst themselves rather than all should perish to cast lots who should be killed. And such was the mercy of God that the same night there arrived a French ship in that port, well furnished with victual, and such was the policy of the English that they became masters of the same, and changing ships and victualling them they set sail to come into England.

In their journey they were so far northwards that they saw mighty islands of ice in the summer season on which were hawks and other fowls to rest themselves, being weary of flying overfar from the main. They saw also certain great white fowls with red bills and red legs, somewhat bigger than herons, which they supposed to be storks. They arrived at St Ives in Cornwall about the end of October. From thence they departed unto a certain castle belonging to Sir John Luttrell, where Master Thomas Butts and Master Rastal and other gentlemen of the voyage were very friendly entertained. After that they came to the Earl of Bath at Bath, and thence to Bristol, so to London.

Master Butts was so changed in the voyage with hunger and misery that Sir William, his father, and my lady, his mother, knew him not to be their son until they found a secret mark which was a wart upon one of his knees, as he told me, Richard Hakluyt of Oxford, himself, to whom I rode 200 miles only to learn the whole truth of this voyage from his own mouth as being the only man now alive that was in this discovery.

Certain months after those Frenchmen came into England and made complaint to King Henry the Eighth. The King, causing the matter to be examined, and finding the great distress of his subjects and the causes of the dealing so with the French, was so moved with pity that he punished not his subjects, but of his own purse made full and royal recompense unto the French.

In this distress of famine the English did somewhat relieve their vital spirits by drinking at the springs the fresh water out of certain wooden cups out of which they had drunk their aqua composita before.

The first voyage of Master Martin Frobisher to the north-west, for the search of the strait or passage to China, written by Christopher Hall, master in the *Gabriel*, and made in the year of Our Lord 1576.

THE 7th of June, being Thursday, the two barks, viz. the *Gabriel* and the *Michael*, and our pinnace, set sail at Ratcliffe and bore down to Deptford, and there we anchored; the cause was that our pinnace burst her bowsprit and foremast aboard of a ship that rode at Deptford, else we meant to have passed that day by the Court then at Greenwich.

The 8th day, being Friday, about 12 of the clock we weighed at Deptford and set sail all three of us, and bore down by the Court, where we shot off our ordnance and made the best show we could. Her Majesty, beholding the same, commended it, and bade us farewell with shaking her hand at us out of the window. Afterward she sent a gentleman aboard of us, who declared that Her Majesty had good liking of our doings, and thanked us for it, and also willed our Captain to come the next day to the Court to take his leave of her. The same day towards night Master Secretary Wolley came aboard of us, and declared to the company that Her Majesty had appointed him to give them charge to be obedient and diligent to their Captain and governors in all things, and wished us happy success.

The 12th day, being over against Gravesend by the castle or blockhouse, we observed the latitude, which was 51 degrees 33 minutes; and in that place the variation of the compass is 11 degrees and a half.

The 24th day at 2 of the clock after noon I had sight of Fair Isle, being from us 6 leagues north and by east, and when I brought it north-west and by north it did rise at the southermost end with a little hummock, and swamp in the midst.

The 25th day, from 4 to 8 o'clock in the forenoon (the wind at north-west and by north a fresh gale) I cast about to the westward, the southermost head of Shetland called Swinborn Head north-north-west from me and the land of Fair Isle west-south-west from me. I sailed directly to the north head of that said land, sounding as I ran in, having 60, 50, and 40 fathoms, and grey-red shells. And within half a mile of that island there are 36 fathoms, for I sailed to that island to see whether there were any roadstead for a north-west wind, and I found by my sounding hard rocks and foul ground and deep water, within two cables length of the shore 28 fathom, and so did not anchor but plied to and fro with my foresail and mizen till it was a high water under the island. The tide setteth there north-west and south-east; the flood setteth south-east and the ebb north-west.

The 26th day, having the wind at south a fair gale sailing from Fair Isle to Swinborn Head, I did observe the latitude, the Island of Foula being west-north-west from me 6 leagues and Swinborn Head east-south-east from me. I found my elevation to be 37 degrees and my declination 22 degrees 46 minutes, so that my latitude was 59 degrees 46 minutes. At that present being near to Swinborn Head, having a leak which did trouble us, as also to take in fresh water, I plied room with a sound which is called St Tronions, and there did anchor in seven fathoms water, and fair sand. You have, coming in the sound's mouth, in the entering 17, 15, 12, 10, 9, 8, and 7 fathoms, and the sound lieth in north-north-west; and there we rode to a west sun, and stopped our leak, and having refreshed ourselves with water at a north-north-west sun I set sail from St Tronions, the wind at south-south-east, and turned out till we were clear of the sound, and so sailed west to go clear of the Island of Foula. And running off toward Foula I sounded, having fifty fathom and streamy ground; and also I sounded Foula being north from me, one league off the island, having fifty fathom at the south head and streamy ground like broken oatmeal, and one shell being red and white like mackerel.

The 27th day at a south sun I did observe the latitude, the Island of Foula being from me two leagues east-north-east. I found myself to be in latitude 59 degrees 59 minutes, truly observed. The wind at south-south-west I sailed west and by north. From 12 to four o'clock after noon, the wind at south a fair gale, the ship sailed west and by north 6 leagues; and at the end of this watch I sounded, having 60 fathom with little stones and shells, the Island from us 8 leagues east.

The first of July, from 4 to 8 o'clock, we sailed west 4 glasses 4 leagues, and at that present we had so much wind that we spooned afore the sea south-west 2 leagues. The 3rd day we found our compass to be varied one point to the westwards. This day from 4 to 8 o'clock we sailed west and by north 6 leagues, from 8 to 12 o'clock at noon west and by north 4 leagues. At that present I found our compass to be varied 11 degrees and one fourth part to the westwards, which is one point.

The 11th day at a south-east sun we had sight of the land of Friseland bearing from us west-north-west 16 leagues and rising like pinnacles of steeples and all covered with snow. I found myself in 61 degrees of latitude. We sailed to the shore and could find no ground at 150 fathoms. We hoisted out our boat, and the Captain with 4 men rowed to the shore to get on land, but the land lying full of ice they could not get on land, and so they came aboard again. We had much ado to get clear of the ice by reason of the fog. Yet from Thurdsay 8 o'clock in the morning to Friday at noon we sailed south-west 20 leagues.

The 18th day at a south-west sun I found the sun to be elevated 33 degrees and at a south-south-east sun 40 degrees; so I observed it till I found it at the highest, and then it was elevated 52 degrees. I judged the variation of the compass to be 2 points and a half to the westward.

The 21st day we had sight of a great drift of ice, seeming a firm land, and we cast westward to be clear of it. The 26th we had sight of a land of ice; the latitude was 62 degrees and 2 minutes. The 28th day in the morning was very foggy; but at the clearing up of the fog we had sight of land which I supposed to be Labrador, with great store of ice about the land. I ran in towards it and sounded but could get no ground at 100 fathom, and, the ice being so thick, I could not get to the shore, and so lay off and came clear of the ice. Upon Monday we came within a mile of the shore and sought a harbour. All the sound was full of ice, and our boat, rowing ashore, could get no ground at 100 fathom within a cable's length of the shore. The we sailed east-north-east along the shore, for so the land lieth, and the current is there great, setting north-east and south-west; and if we could have gotten anchor-ground we would have seen with what force it had run, but I judge a ship may drive a league and a half in one hour with that tide.

This day at 4 of the clock in the morning, being fair and clear, we had sight of a headland, as we judged, bearing from us north and by east, and we sailed north-east and by north to that land, and when we came thither we could not get to the land for ice. For the ice stretched along the coast, so that we could not come to the land, by five leagues.

Wednesday the first of August it calmed, and in the afternoon I caused my boat to be hoisted out, being hard by a great island of ice; and I and four men rowed to that ice, and sounded within two cables' length of it, and had sixteen fathom and little stones, and after that sounded again within a minion-shot and had ground at a hundred fathom and fair sand. We sounded the next day a quarter of a mile from it and had sixty fathom rough ground; and at that present, being aboard, that great island of ice fell one part from another, making a noise as if a great cliff had fallen into the sea. And at four of the clock I sounded again and had 90 fathom and small black stones and little white stones like pearls. The tide here did set to the shore.

The tenth I took four men, and myself, and rowed to shore to an island one league from the main, and there the flood setteth south-west along the shore, and it floweth, as near as I could judge, so too. I could not tarry to prove it, because the ship was a great way from me and I feared a fog; but when I came ashore it was a low water. I went to the top of the island, and before I came back it was highed a foot water, and so without tarrying I came aboard. The 11th we found our latitude to be 63 degrees and 8 minutes, and this day we entered the strait. The 12th we set sail towards an island, called the Gabriel's Island, which was 10 leagues then from us. We espied a sound, and bore with it, and came to a sandy bay where we came to an anchor, the land bearing east-south-east off us, and there we rode all night in 8 fathom water. It floweth there a south-east moon. We called it Prior's Sound, being from the Gabriel's Island ten leagues.

The 14th we weighed and ran into another sound, where we anchored in 8 fathom water, fair sand and black ooze, and there caulked our ship, being weak from the wales upward, and took in fresh water. The 15th day we weighed and sailed to Prior's Bay, being a mile from thence. The 16th day was calm, and we rode still, without ice, but presently within two hours it was frozen round about the ship a quarter of an inch thick, and that day very fair and calm. The 17th day we weighed and came to Thomas Williams Island. The 18th day we sailed north-north-west, and anchored again in 23 fathom and tough ooze under Burcher's Island, which is from the former island ten leagues.

The 19th day in the morning, being calm and no wind, the Captain and I took our boat, with eight men in her to row us ashore, to see if there were there any people or no. And going to the top of the island we had sight of seven boats which came rowing from the east side toward that island, whereupon we returned aboard again. At length we sent our boat with five men in her to see whither they rowed, and so with a white cloth brought one of their boats with their men along the shore, rowing after our boat, till such time as they saw our ship, and then they rowed ashore. Then I went on shore myself, and gave every of them a threaden point, and brought one of them aboard of me, where he did eat and drink, and then carried him on shore again. Whereupon all the rest came aboard with their boats, being nineteen persons, and they spoke, but we understood them not. They be like to Tartars, with long black hair, broad faces and flat noses, and tawny in colour, wearing seals' skins, and so do the women not differing in the fashion, but the women are marked in the face with blue streaks down the cheeks and round about the eyes. Their boats are made all of sealskins, with a keel of wood within the skin. The proportion of them is like a Spanish shallop, save only they be flat in the botton and sharp at both ends.

The twentieth day we weighed and went to the eastside of this island, and I and the Captain with four men more went on shore, and there we saw their houses; and the people espying us came rowing towards our boat. Whereupon we plied toward our boat; and we being in our boat and they ashore, they called to us, and we rowed to them, and one of their company came into our boat, and we carried him aboard and gave him a bell and a knife. So the Captain and I willed five of our men to set him ashore at a rock, and not among the company which they came from; but their wilfulness was such that they would go to them, and so were taken themselves and our boat lost.

The next day in the morning we stood in near the shore and shot off a falconet and sounded our trumpet, but we could hear nothing of our men. This sound we called the Five Men's Sound, and plied out of it but anchored again in thirty fathom and ooze; and riding there all night, in the morning the snow lay a foot thick upon our hatches.

The 22nd day in the morning we weighed and went again to the place where we lost our men and our boat. We had sight of fourteen boats, and some came near to us, but we could learn nothing of our men. Among the rest, we enticed one boat to our ship's side with a bell, and in giving him the bell we took him and his boat, and so kept him; and so rowed down to Thomas Williams Island and there anchored all night.

The 26th day we weighed, to come homeward, and by 12 of the clock at noon we were thwart of Trumpets Island. The next day we came thwart of Gabriel's Island and at 8 of the clock at night we had the Cape Labrador as we supposed west from us ten leagues. The 28th day we went our course south-east. We sailed south-east and by east 22 leagues.

The first day of September in the morning we had sight of the Island of Friseland being eight leagues from us, but we could not come nearer it for the monstrous ice that lay about it. From this day till the sixth of this month we ran along Iceland, and had the south part of it at eight of the clock east from us ten leagues.

The seventh day of this month we had a very terrible storm, by force whereof one of our men was blown into the sea out of our waist, but he caught hold of the foresail sheet, and there held till the Captain plucked him again into the ship. The 25th day of this month we had sight of the Island of Orkney, which was then east from us. The first day of October we had sight of the Scheldt, and so sailed about the coast and anchored at Yarmouth; and the next day we came into Harwich.

The language of the people of Meta Incognita:

Argoteyt, a hand	Attegay, a coat
Cangnawe, a nose	Pollevetagay, a knife
Arered, an eye	Accaskay, a ship
Keiotot, a tooth	Coblone, a thumb
Mutchatet, the head	Teckkere, the foremost finger
Chewat, an ear	Ketteckle, the middle finger
Comagaye, a leg	Mekellacane, the fourth finger
Ationiagay, a foot	Yacketrone, the little finger
Callagay, a pair of breeches	

The second voyage of Master Martin Frobisher, made to the west
and north-west regions in the year 1577, with a description of the
country and people. Written by Master Dionyse Settle.

ON Whitsunday, being the six and twentieth of May in the year
of Our Lord God 1577, Captain Frobisher departed from
Blackwall with one of the Queen's Majesty's ships called the
Aid, of nine score tons or thereabouts, and two other little barks
likewise, the one called the *Gabriel*, whereof Master Fenton, a gentleman of my Lord of Warwick's, was captain, and the other the *Michael*,
whereof Master York a gentleman of my Lord Admiral's, was captain;
accompanied with seven score gentlemen, soldiers, and sailors, well
furnished with victuals and other provision necessary for one half year,
on this his second voyage for the further discovering of the passage to
Cathay, and other countries thereunto adjacent, by west and north-
west navigations. Which passage or way is supposed to be on the north
and north-west part of America, and the said America to be an island
environed with the sea, where-through our merchants may have course
and recourse, with their merchandise, from these our northernmost
parts of Europe to those oriental coasts of Asia in much shorter time
and with greater benefit than any others, to their no little commodity
and profit that do or shall frequent the same. Our said Captain and
General of this present voyage and company having the year before,
with two little pinnaces, to his great danger and no small commendations, given a worthy attempt towards the performance thereof, is also
pressed, when occasion shall be ministered (to the benefit of his Prince
and native country), to adventure himself further therein. As for this
second voyage, it seemeth sufficient that he hath better explored and
searched the commodities of those people and countries which in his
first voyage the year before he had found out.

Upon which consideration, the day and year before expressed we
departed from Blackwall to Harwich, where making an accomplishment of things necessary, the last of May we hoisted up sails, and with a
merry wind the 7th of June we arrived at the islands called Orcades, or
vulgarly Orkney, being in number 30, subject and adjacent to
Scotland, where we made provision of fresh water; in the doing
whereof our General licensed the gentleman and soldiers for their
recreation to go on shore. At our landing the people fled from their
poor cottages with shrieks and alarms to warn their neighbours of
enemies, but by gentle persuasions we reclaimed them to their houses.
It seemeth they are often frighted with pirates or some other enemies
that move them to such sudden fear. Their houses are very simply built
with pebble-stone, without any chimneys, the fire being made in the

midst thereof. The goodman, wife, children, and other of their family eat and sleep on the one side of the house, and the cattle on the other, very beastly and rudely in respect of civility. They are destitute of wood; their fire is turfs and cowsherds. They have corn, bigg, and oats, with which they pay their King's rent, to the maintenance of his house. They take great quantity of fish, which they dry in the wind and sun. They dress their meat very filthily, and eat it without salt. Their apparel is after the rudest sort of Scotland. Their money is all base. Their church and religion is reformed according to the Scots. The fishermen of England can better declare the dispositions of those people than I; wherefore I remit other their usages to their reports as yearly repair thither in their course to and from Iceland for fish.

We departed here-hence the 8th of June, and followed our course between west and north-west until the 4th of July. All which time we had no night, but that easily and without any impediment we had, when we were so disposed, the fruition of our books and other pleasures to pass away the time: a thing of no small moment to such as wander in unknown seas and long navigations, especially when both the winds and raging surges do pass their common and wonted course. This benefit endureth in those parts not 6 weeks, while the sun is near the Tropic of Cancer; but where the pole is raised to 70 or 80 degrees it continueth much longer.

All along these seas, after we were six days sailing from Orkney, we met floating in the sea great fir trees which, as we judged, were with the fury of great floods rooted up, and so driven into the sea. Iceland hath almost no other wood nor fuel but such as they take up upon their coasts. It seemeth that these trees are driven from some part of the Newfoundland with the current that setteth from the west to the east.

The 4th of July we came within the making of Friseland. From this shore 10 or 12 leagues we met great islands of ice, of half a mile, some more, some less, in compass, showing above the sea 30 or 40 fathoms and, as we supposed, fast on ground where with our lead we could scarce sound the bottom for depth. Here, in place of odoriferous and fragrant smells of sweet gums, and pleasant notes of musical birds, which other countries in more temperate zones do yield, we tasted the most boisterous boreal blasts mixed with snow and hail, in the months of June and July, nothing inferior to our untemperate winter: a sudden alteration, and especially in a place or parallel where the pole is not elevated above 61 degrees, at which height other countries more to the north, yea, unto 70 degrees, show themselves more temperate than this doth.

All along this coast ice lieth, as a continual bulwark, and so defendeth the country that those that would land there incur great danger. Our General 3 days together attempted with the ship-boat to have gone on shore, which, for that without great danger he could not accomplish, he deferred it until a more convenient time. All along the coast lie very high mountains covered with snow, except in such places where through the steepness of the mountains of force it must need fall. Four days coasting along this land we found no sign of habitation. Little birds, which we judged to have lost the shore by reason of thick fogs which that country is much subject unto, came flying into our ships, which caused us to suppose that the country is both more tolerable, and also more habitable within, than the outward shore maketh show or signification.

From hence we departed the eighth of July; and the 16th of the same we came with the making of land, which land our General the year before had named the Queen's Foreland, being an island, as we judge, lying near the supposed continent with America; and on the other side, opposite to the same, one other island called Hall's Island, after the name of the master of the ship, near adjacent to the firm land supposed continent with Asia. Between the which two islands there is a large entrance or strait, called Frobisher's Strait after the name of our General, the first finder thereof. This said strait is supposed to have passage into the Sea of Sur, which I leave unknown as yet.

It seemeth that either here or not far hence the sea should have more large entrance than in other parts within the frozen or untemperate zone; and that some contrary tide, either from the east or west, with main force casteth out that great quantity of ice which cometh floating from this coast even unto Friseland, causing that country to seem more untemperate than others much more northerly than the same. I cannot judge that any temperature under the pole, the time of the sun's northern declination being half a year together, and one whole day, (considering that the sun's elevation surmounteth not 23 degrees and 30 minutes) can have power to dissolve such monstrous and huge ice comparable to great mountains, except by some other force, as by swift currents and tides, with the help of the said day of half a year.

Before we came within the making of these lands we tasted cold storms, insomuch that it seemed we had changed summer with winter if the length of the days had not removed us from that opinion.

At our first coming the straits seemed to be shut up with a long mure of ice, which gave no little cause of discomfort unto us all. But our General, to whose diligence imminent dangers and difficult attempts seemed nothing in respect of his willing mind for the commodity of his Prince and country, with two little pinnaces, prepared of purpose, passed twice through them to the east shore and the islands thereunto adjacent; and the ship with the two barks lay off and on something further into the sea from the danger of the ice. Whilst he was searching the country near the shore, some of the people of the country showed themselves leaping and dancing, with strange shrieks and cries, which gave no little admiration to our men. Our General, desirous to allure them unto him by fair means, caused knives and other things to be proffered unto them, which they would not take at our hands but, being laid on the ground and the party going away, they came and took up, leaving some thing of theirs to countervail the same. At the length two of them, leaving their weapons, came down to our General and Master, who did the like to them, commanding the company to stay, and went unto them; who, after certain dumb signs and mute congratulations, began to lay hands upon them, but they deliverly escaped and ran to their bows and arrows and came fiercely upon them, not respecting the rest of our company which were ready for their defence but with their arrows hurt divers of them. We took the one and the other escaped.

Whilst our General was busied in searching the country and those islands adjacent on the east shore, the ship and barks, having great care not to put far unto the sea from him, for that he had small store of victuals, were forced to abide, in a cruel tempest chancing in the night, amongst and in the thickest of the ice, which was so monstrous that even the least of a thousand had been of force sufficient to have shivered our ship and barks into small portions if God, who in all necessities hath care upon the infirmity of man, had not provided for this our extremity a sufficient remedy through the light of the night, whereby we might well discern to flee from such imminent dangers, which we avoided with 14 boards in one watch the space of 4 hours. If we had not incurred this danger amongst these monstrous islands of ice we should have lost our General and Master, and the most of our best sailors, which were on the shore destitute of victuals. But by the valour of our Master Gunner, Master Jackman and Andrew Dyer, the master's mates, men expert both in navigation and other good qualities, we were all content to incur the dangers afore rehearsed before we would, with our own safety, run into the seas to the destruction of our said General and his company.

The day following, being the 19th of July, our Captain returned to the ship, with report of supposed riches which showed itself in the bowels of those barren mountains, wherewith we were all satisfied.

Within four days after we had been at the entrance of the straits, the north-west and west winds dispersed the ice into the sea and made us a large entrance into the straits, so that without any impediment, on the 19th of July, we entered them; and the 20th thereof our General and Master with great diligence sought out and sounded the west shore and found out a fair harbour for the ship and barks to ride in and named it, after our Master's Mate, Jackman's Sound, and brought the ship, barks and all their company to safe anchor except one man which died by God's visitation.

At our first arrival, after the ship rode at anchor, our General, with such company as could well be spared from the ships, in marching order entered the land, having special care by exhortations that at our entrance thereinto we should all, with one voice, kneeling upon our knees, chiefly thank God for our safe arrival; secondly, beseech him that it would please His Divine Majesty long to continue our Queen, for whom he and all the rest of our company in this order took possession of the country; and thirdly, that by our Christian study and endeavour those barbarous people, trained up in paganism and infidelity, might be reduced to the knowledge of true religion and to the hope of salvation in Christ our redeemer; with other words very apt to signify his willing mind and affection toward his Prince and country, whereby all suspicion of an undutiful subject may credibly be judged to be utterly exempted from his mind. All the rest of the gentlemen and other deserve worthily herein their due praise and commendation. These things in this order accomplished, our General commanded all the company to be obedient, in things needful for our own safeguard, to Master Fenton, Master York, and Master Best, his lieutenant, while he was occupied in other necessary affairs concerning our coming thither.

After this order we marched through the country, with ensign displayed, as far as was thought needful, and now and then heaped up stones on high mountains and other places in token of possession, as likewise to signify unto such as hereafter may chance to arrive there that possession is taken in the behalf of some other prince by those who first found out the country.

Whoso maketh navigations to those countries hath not only extreme winds and furious seas to encounter withal, but also many monstrous and great islands of ice: a thing both rare, wonderful, and greatly to be regarded. We were forced sundry times, while the ship did ride here at anchor, to have continual watch, with boats and men ready with hawsers to knit fast unto such ice as with the ebb and flood were tossed to and fro in the harbour, and with force of oars to haul them away, for endangering the ship.

Our General certain days searched this supposed continent with America and, not finding the commodity to answer his expectation, after he had made trial thereof he departed thence with two little barks and men sufficient to the east shore, being the supposed continent of Asia, and left the ship with most of the gentlemen, soldiers, and sailors until such time as he either thought good to send or come for them.

The stones of this supposed continent with America be altogether sparkled, and glister in the sun like gold, so likewise doth the sand in the bright water; yet they verify the old proverb, all is not gold that glistereth. On this west shore we found a dead fish floating, which had in his nose a horn straight and torqued, of length two yards lacking two inches, being broken in the top where we might perceive it hollow, into the which some of our sailors putting spiders they presently died. I saw not the trial hereof, but it was reported unto me of a truth; by the virtue whereof we supposed it to be the sea-unicorn.

After our General had found out good harbour for the ship and barks to anchor in, and also such store of supposed gold ore as he thought himself satisfied withal, he returned to the *Michael*, whereof Master York aforesaid was captain, accompanied with our Master and his Mate. Who, coasting along the west shore not far from whence the ship rode, they perceived a fair harbour and, willing to sound the same, at the entrance thereof they espied two tents of seal skins, unto which the Captain, our said Master, and other company resorted. At the sight of our men the people fled into the mountains. Nevertheless they went to their tents, where leaving certain trifles of ours, as glasses, bells, knives, and suchlike things, they departed, not taking anything of theirs except one dog. They did in like manner leave behind them a letter, pen, ink, and paper whereby our men whom the Captain lost the year before, and in that people's custody, might, if any of them were alive, be advertised of our presence and being there.

On the same day, after consultation had, all the gentlemen and others likewise that could be spared from the ship, under the conduct and leading of Master Philpot (unto whom in our General's absence, and his lieutenant Master Best, all the rest were obedient) went ashore, determining to see if by fair means we could either allure them to familiarity, or otherwise take some of them and so attain to some knowledge of those men whom our General lost the year before. At our coming back again to the place where their tents were before, they had removed their tents further into the said bay or sound where they might, if they were driven from the land, flee with their boats into the sea. We, parting ourselves into two companies and compassing a mountain, came suddenly upon them by land, who, espying us, without any tarrying fled to their boats, leaving the most part of their oars behind them for haste, and rowed down the bay, where our two pinnaces met them and drove them to shore. But if they had had all their oars, so swift are they in rowing it had been lost time to have chased them.

When they were landed they fiercely assaulted our men with their bows and arrows, who wounded three of them with our arrows; and perceiving themselves thus hurt they desperately leapt off the rocks into the sea and drowned themselves. Which if they had not done, but had submitted themselves, or if by any means we could have taken them alive, being their enemies (as they judged) we would both have saved them and also have sought remedy to cure their wounds received at our hands. But they, altogether void of humanity and ignorant what mercy meaneth, in extremities look for no other than death; and, perceiving they should fall into our hands, thus miserably by drowning rather desired death than otherwise to be saved by us. The rest,

9 Frobisher's men in a skirmish with Eskimos.

perceiving their fellows in this distress, fled into the high mountains. Two women, not being so apt to escape as the men were, the one for her age, the other being encumbered with a young child, we took. The old wretch, whom divers of our sailors supposed to be either a devil or a witch, had her buskins plucked off to see if she were cloven-footed, and for her ugly hue and deformity we let her go. The young woman and the child we brought away. We named the place where they were slain Bloody Point, and the bay or harbour York's Sound after the name of one of the Captains of the two barks.

Having this knowledge both of their fierceness and cruelty, and perceiving that fair means as yet is not able to allure them to familiarity, we disposed ourselves, contrary to our inclination, something to be cruel, returned to their tents, and made a spoil of the same; where we found an old shirt, a doublet, a girdle, and also shoes of our men whom we lost the year before. On nothing else unto them belonging could we set our eyes.

Their riches are not gold, silver, or precious drapery, but their said tents and boats, made of the skins of red deer and seal skins; also dogs like unto wolves, but for the most part black, with other trifles more to be wondered at for their strangeness than for any other commodity needful for our use.

Thus returning to our ship the 3rd of August we departed from the west shore, supposed firm with America, after we had anchored there 13 days. And so the 4th thereof we came to our General on the east shore and anchored in a fair harbour named Anne Warwick's Sound, unto which is annexed an island, both named, after the Countess of Warwick, Anne Warwick's Sound and Isle. In this Isle our General thought good for this voyage to freight both the ship and barks with such stone or supposed gold mineral as he judged to countervail the charges of his first and this his second navigation to these countries.

In the meantime of our abode here some of the country people came to show themselves unto us sundry times on the main shore, near adjacent to the said Isle. Our General, desirous to have some news of his men whom he lost the year before, with some company with him repaired with the ship-boat to common or sign with them for familiarity, whereunto he is persuaded to bring them. They at the first show made tokens that three of his five men were alive, and desired pen, ink, and paper and that within three or four days they would return and, as we judged, bring those of our men which were living, with them. They also made signs or tokens of their king, whom they called *cacough*, and how he was carried on men's shoulders, and a man far surmounting any of our company in bigness and stature. With these tokens and signs of writing, pen, ink, and paper was delivered them, which they would not take at our hands, but being laid upon the shore and the party gone away they took up; which likeness they do when they desire anything

for change of theirs, laying for that which is left so much as they think
will countervail the same, and not coming near together. It seemeth
they have been used to this trade or traffic with some other people
adjoining or not far distant from their country.

After 4 days some of them showed themselves upon the firm land,
but not where they were before. Our General, very glad thereof,
supposing to hear of our men, went from the island, with the boat and
sufficient company with him. They seemed very glad, and allured him
about a certain point of the land, behind which they might perceive a
company of the crafty villains to lie lurking; whom our General would
not deal withal, for that he knew not what company they were, and so
with few signs dismissed them and returned to his company.

Another time, as our said General was coasting the country with two
little pinnaces whereby at our return he might make the better relation
thereof, three of the crafty villains with a white skin allured us to them.
Once again our General, for that he hoped to hear of his men, went
towards them. At our coming near the shore whereon they were, we
might perceive a number of them lie hidden behind great stones, and
those 3 in sight labouring by all means possible that some would come
on land; and perceiving we made no haste by words nor friendly signs,
which they used by clapping of their hands, and being without weapon
and but 3 in sight, they sought further means to provoke us thereunto.
One alone laid flesh on the shore, which we took up with the boat-
hook, as necessary victuals for the relieving of the man, woman, and
child whom we had taken, for that as yet they could not digest our
meat; whereby they perceived themselves deceived of their expectation for all their crafty allurements. Yet once again to make as it were a
full show of their crafty natures and subtle sleights, to the intent
thereby to have entrapped and taken some of our men, one of them
counterfeited himself impotent and lame of his legs, who seemed to
descend to the waterside with great difficulty; and to cover his craft the
more, one of his fellows came down with him, and in such places where
he seemed unable to pass he took him on his shoulders, set him by the
waterside, and departed from him, leaving him, as it should seem, all
alone; who, playing his counterfeit pageant very well, thought thereby
to provoke some of us to come on shore, not fearing but that one of us
might make our party good with a lame man.

Our General, having compassion of his impotency, thought good, if
it were possible, to cure him thereof; wherefore he caused a soldier to
shoot at him with his caliver, which grazed before his face. The counterfeit villain deliverly fled, without any impediment at all, and got him
to his bows and arrows, and the rest from their lurking-holes with their
weapons, bows, arrows, slings, and darts. Our General caused some
calivers to be shot off at them, whereby, some being hurt, they might
hereafter stand in more fear of us. This was all the answer for this time

we could have of our men or of our General's letter. Their craft dealing at these three several times being thus manifest unto us may plainly show their disposition in other things to be correspondent. We judged that they used these stratagems thereby to have caught some of us, for the delivering of the man, woman, and child whom we had taken.

They are men of a large corporature and good proportion. Their colour is not much unlike the sunburnt countryman, who laboureth daily in the sun for his living. They wear their hair something long, and cut before, either with stone or knife, very disorderly. Their women wear their hair long, and knit up with two loops showing forth on either side of their faces, and the rest folded upon a knot. Also some of their women race their faces proportionally, as chin, cheeks, and forehead, and the wrists of their hand, whereupon they lay a colour which continueth dark azurine.

They eat their meat all raw, both flesh, fish, and fowl, or something parboiled with blood and a little water, which they drink. For lack of water they will eat ice that is hard frozen as pleasantly as we will do sugar-candy or other sugar. If they for necessity's sake stand in need of the premisses, such grass as the country yieldeth they pluck up and eat, not daintily or salad-wise to allure their stomachs to appetite, but for necessity's sake, without either salt, oils, or washing, like brute beasts devouring the same. They neither use table, stool, or table-cloth for comeliness, but when they are embrued with blood knuckle-deep, and their knives in like sort, they use their tongues as apt instruments to lick them clean, in doing whereof they are assured to lose none of their victuals.

They frank or keep certain dogs not much unlike wolves, which they yoke together as we do oxen and horses, to a sled or trail, and so carry their necessities over the ice and snow from place to place; as the captive whom we have made perfect signs. And when those dogs are not apt for the same use, or when with hunger they are constrained for lack of other victuals, they eat them, so that they are as needful for them, in respect of their bigness, as our oxen are for us.

They apparel themselves in the skins of such beasts as they kill, sewn together with the sinews of them. All the fowl which they kill they skin, and make thereof one kind of garment or other to defend them from the cold. They make their apparel with hoods and tails, which tails they give when they think to gratify any friendship shown unto them: a great sign of friendship with them. The men have them not so side as the women.

The men and women wear their hose close to their legs, from the waist to the knee without any open before, as well the one kind as the other. Upon their legs they wear hose of leather with the fur side inward, two or three pair on at once, and especially the women. In those hose they put their knives, needles, and other things needful to bear about. They put a bone within their hose, which reacheth from the foot to the knee, whereupon they draw their said hose, and so in place of garters they are held from falling down about their feet. They dress their skins very soft and supple, with the hair on. In cold weather or winter they wear the fur side inward, and in summer outward. Other apparel they have none but the said skins.

Those beasts, fishes, and fowls which they kill are their meat, drink, apparel, houses, bedding, hose, shoes, thread, and sails for their boats, with many other necessaries whereof they stand in need and almost all their riches. Their houses are tents made of seal skins, pitched up with 4 fir quarters foursquare meeting at the top, and the skins sewn together with sinews and laid thereupon. They are so pitched up that the entrance into them is always south or against the sun. They have other sorts of houses which we found not to be inhabited, which are raised with stones and whale bones and a skin laid over them to withstand the rain or other weather, the entrance of them being not much unlike an oven's mouth; whereto I think they resort for a time to fish, hunt, and fowl, and so leave then until the next time they come thither again.

Their weapons are bows, arrows, darts, and slings. Their bows are of wood of a yard long, sinewed at the back with strong sinews, not glued to, but fast girded and tied on. Their bow-strings are likewise sinews. Their arrows are three pieces nocked with bone and ended with bone; with those two ends and the wood in the midst they pass not in length half a yard or little more. They are feathered with two feathers, the pen end being cut away and the feathers laid upon the arrow with the broad side to the wood, insomuch that they seem when they are tied on to have four feathers. They have also three sorts of heads to those arrows: one sort of stone or iron, proportioned like to a heart; the second sort of bone, much like unto a stopped head with a hook on the same; the third sort of bone likewise, made sharp at both sides and sharp-pointed. They are not made very fast, but lightly tied to, or else set in a nock, that upon small occasion the arrows leave these heads behind them; and they are of small force except they be very near when they shoot. Their darts are made of two sorts, the one with many forks of bones in the fore end and likewise in the midst; their proportions are not much unlike our toasting-irons, but longer. These they cast out of an instrument of wood, very readily. The other sort is greater than the first aforesaid, with a long bone made sharp on both sides not much unlike a rapier, which I take to be their most hurtful weapon.

They have two sorts of boats made of leather, set out on the inner side with quarters of wood artificially tied together with thongs of the same. The greater sort are not much unlike our wherries, wherein sixteen or twenty men may sit. They have for a sail dressed the guts of such beasts as they kill very fine and thin, which they sew together. The other boat is but for one man to sit and row in with one oar. Their order of fishing, hunting, and fowling are with these said weapons, but in what sort, or how they use them, we have no perfect knowledge as yet.

I can suppose their abode or habitation not to be here, for that neither their houses or apparel are of such force to withstand the extremity of cold that the country seemeth to be infected withal, neither do I see any sign likely to perform the same. Those houses or rather dens which stand there have no sign of footway or anything else trodden, which is one of the chiefest tokens of habitation. And those tents which they bring with them, when they have sufficiently hunted and fished they remove to other places; and when they have sufficiently stored them of such victuals as the country yieldeth or bringeth forth they return to their winter stations or habitations. This conjecture do I make for the infertility which I conjecture to be in the country.

They have some iron whereof they make arrow-heads, knives, and other little intruments. to work their boats, bows, arrows, and darts withal, which are very unapt to do anything withal but with great labour. It seemeth that they have conversation with some other people of whom for exchange they should receive the same. They are greatly delighted with anything that is bright, or giveth a sound.

What knowledge they have of God, or what idol they adore, we have no perfect intelligence. I think them rather anthropophagi, or devourers of man's flesh, than otherwise, for that there is no flesh or fish which they find dead, smell it never so filthily, but they will eat it as they find it without any other dressing; a loathsome thing, either to the beholders or hearers.

There is no manner of creeping beast hurtful except some spiders (which as many affirm are signs of great store of gold), and also certain stinging gnats, which bite fiercely that the place where they bite shortly after swelleth and itcheth very sore.

They make signs of certain people that wear bright plates of gold in their foreheads and other places of their bodies.

The countries on both sides the straits lie very high with rough stony mountains and great quantity of snow thereon. There is very little plain ground, and no grass, except a little which is much like unto moss that groweth on soft ground such as we get turfs in. There is no wood at all. To be brief, there is nothing fit or profitable for the use of man which that country with root yieldeth or bringeth forth. Howbeit there is great quantity of deer, whose skins are like unto asses'; their heads or horns do far exceed, as well in length as also in breadth, any in these our parts or countries. Their feet likewise are as great as our oxen's, which we measured to be seven or eight inches in breadth. There are also hares, wolves, fishing-bears, and sea-fowl of sundry sorts. As the country is barren and unfertile, so are they rude and of no capacity to culture the same to any perfection, but are contented by their hunting, fishing, and fowling, with raw flesh and warm blood to satisfy their greedy paunches, which is their only glory.

There is great likelihood of earthquakes or thunder, for that there are huge and monstrous mountains, whose greatest substance are stones, and those stones so shaken with some extraordinary means that one is separated from another, which is discordant from all other quarries.

There are no rivers or running springs but such as through the heat of the sun, with such water as descendeth from the mountains and hills whereon great drifts of snow do lie, are engendered. It argueth also that there should be none, for that the earth which, with the extremity of the winter, is so frozen within that that water which should have recourse within the same to maintain springs, hath not his motion; whereof great waters have their original, as by experience is seen otherwise. Such valleys as are capable to receive the water, that in the summer time by the operation of the sun descendeth from great abundance of snow which continually lieth on the mountains and hath no passage, sinketh into the earth and so vanisheth away without any runnel above the earth; by which occasion or continual standing of the said water, the earth is opened and the great frost yieldeth to the force thereof, which in other places, four or five fathoms within the ground, for lack of the said moisture the earth (even in the very summer time) is frozen, and so combineth the stones together that scarcely instruments with great force can unknit them. Also, where the water in those valleys can have no such passage away by the continuance of time, in such order as is before rehearsed, the yearly descent from the mountains filleth them full, that at the lowest bank of the same they fall into the valley and so continue as fishing-ponds or stagnes, in summer time full of water and in the winter hard frozen, as by scars that remain thereof in summer may easily be perceived. So that the heat of the summer is nothing comparable or of force to dissolve the extremity of cold that cometh in winter. Nevertheless I am assured that, below the force of the frost within the earth, the waters have recourse, and empty themselves out of sight into the sea, which through the extremity of the frost are constrained to do the same; by which occasion the earth within is kept the warmer, and springs have their recourse, which is the only nutriment of gold and minerals within the same.

There is much to be said of the commodities of these countries which are couched within the bowels of the earth, which I let pass till more perfect trial be made thereof.

The 24th of August, after we had satisfied our minds with freight sufficient for our vessels, though not our covetous desires with such knowledge of the country, people, and other commodities as are before rehearsed, we departed there-hence. The 17th of September we fell with the Land's End of England, and so sailed to Milford Haven, from whence our General rode to the Court for order to what port or haven to conduct the ship. We lost our two barks in the way homeward, the one the 29th of August, the other the 31st of the same month, by occasion of great tempest and fog. Howbeit God restored the one to Bristol, and the other made his course by Scotland to Yarmouth. In this voyage we lost two men, one in the way by God's visitation, and the other homeward, cast overboard with a surge of the sea.

I could declare unto the readers the latitude and longitude of such places and regions as we have been at, but not altogether so perfectly as our masters and others; with many circumstances of tempests and other accidents incident to seafaring men, which seem not altogether strange, but I let them pass to their reports as men most apt to set forth and declare the same. I have also left the names of the countries on both the shores untouched for lack of understanding the people's language, as also for sundry respects not needful as yet to be declared.

Countries new discovered, where commodity is to be looked for, do better accord with a new name given by the discoverers than an uncertain name by a doubtful author. Our General named sundry islands, mountains, capes, and harbours after the names of divers noblemen and other gentlemen, his friends, as well on the one shore as also on the other.

The third and last voyage unto Meta Incognita made by Master Martin Frobisher, in the year 1578. Written by Thomas Ellis.

THESE are to let you know that upon the 25th of May the *Thomas Allen*, being vice-admiral, whose captain was Master York, Master Gibbs master, Christopher Hall pilot, accompanied with the rear-admiral named the *Hopewell*, whose captain was Master Henry Carew, the master Andrew Dyer, and certain other ships, came to Gravesend, where we anchored and abode the coming of certain of our fleet which were not yet come.

The 27th of the same month, our fleet being now come together and all things prest in a readiness, the wind favouring and tide serving, we, being of sails in number eight, weighed anchor and hoisted our sails toward Harwich to meet with our admiral and the residue, which then and there abode our arrival; where we safely arrived the 28th thereof, finding there our admiral whom we with the discharge of certain pieces saluted according to order and duty, and were welcomed with the like courtesy. Which being finished we landed, where our General continued mustering his soldiers and miners, and setting things in order appertaining to the voyage, until the last of the said month of May;

which day we hoisted our sails, and committing ourselves to the conducting of Almighty God we set forward toward the west country in such lucky wise and good success that by the fifth of June we passed the Durseys, being the utmost part of Ireland to the westward.

And here it were not much amiss nor far from our purpose if I should a little discourse and speak of our adventures and chances by the way, as out landing at Plymouth, as also the meeting certain poor men which were robbed and spoiled of all that they had by pirates and rovers, amongst whom was a man of Bristol on whom our General used his liberality, and sent him away with letters into England. But because such things are impertinent to the matter, I will return (without any more mentioning the same) to that from the which I have digressed and swerved, I mean our ships now sailing on the surging seas, sometime passing at pleasure with a wished eastern wind, sometime hindered of our course again by the western blasts, until the 20th day of the foresaid month of June; on which day in the morning we fell with Friseland, which is a very high and cragged land and was almost clean covered with snow, so that we might see naught but craggy rocks and the tops of high and huge hills, sometimes (and for most part) all covered with foggy mists. There might we also perceive the great isles of ice lying on the seas, like mountains, some small, some big, of sundry kinds of shapes, and such a number of them that we could not come near the shore for them.

Thus sailing along the coast, at the last we saw a place somewhat void of ice, where our General, accompanied with certain other, went ashore; where they saw certain tents made of beasts' skins, and boats much the like unto theirs of Meta Incognita. The tents were furnished with flesh, fish, skins, and other trifles, amongst the which was found a box of nails; whereby we did conjecture that they had either artificers amongst them or else a traffic with some other nation. The men ran away, so that we could have no conference or communication with them. Our General, because he would have them no more to flee, but rather encouraged to stay through his courteous dealing, gave commandment that his men should take nothing away with them saving only a couple of white dogs, for the which he left pins, points, knives, and other trifling things, and departed without taking or hurting anything, and so came aboard and hoisted sails and passed forwards. But being scarce out of the sight thereof, there fell such a fog and hideous mist that we could not see one another. Whereupon we struck our drums and sounded our trumpets, to the end we might keep together, and so continued all that day and night till the next day that the mist broke up, so that we might easily perceive all the ships thus sailing together all that day until the next day, being the 22nd of the same; on which day we saw an infinite number of ice, from the which we cast about to shun the danger thereof.

But one of our small barks named the *Michael*, whose captain was Master Kindersley, the master Bartholomew Bull, lost our company, insomuch that we could not obtain the sight of her many days after, of whom I mean to speak further anon when occasion shall be ministered and opportunity serve. Thus we continued in our course until the second of July, on which day we fell with the Queen's Foreland, where we saw so much ice that we thought it impossible to get into the Straits. Yet at the last we gave the adventure and entered the ice. Being amongst it we saw the *Michael*, of whom I spoke before, accompanied with the *Judith*, whose captain was Master Fenton, the master Charles Jackman, bearing into the foresaid ice far distant from us, who in a storm that fell that present night (whereof I will at large, God willing, discourse hereafter) were severed from us and, being in, wandered up and down the Straits amongst the ice many days in great peril till at the last, by the providence of God, they came safely to harbour in their wished port in the Countess of Warwick's Sound the 20th of July aforesaid, ten days before any of the other ships, Who, going on shore, found where the people of the country had been, and had hid their provision in great heaps of stones, being both of flesh and fish which they had killed; whereof we also found great store in other places after our arrival. They also found divers engines, as bows, slings, and darts. They found likewise certain pieces of the pinnace which our General left there the year before, which pinnace he had sunk, minding to have it again the next year.

Now seeing I have entreated so much of the *Judith* and the *Michael*, I will return to the rest of the other ships, and will speak a little of the storm which fell, with the mishaps that we had, the night that we put into the ice, whereof I made mention before. At the first entering into the ice in the mouth of the Straits our passage was very narrow and difficult but, being once gotten in, we had a fair open place without any ice for the most part, being a league in compass, the ice being round about us and enclosing us as it were within the pales of a park. In which place, because it was almost night, we minded to take in our sails and lie a-hull all that night. But the storm so increased, and the waves began to mount aloft, which brought the ice so near us and coming on so fast upon us that we were fain to bear in and out where we might espy an open place. Thus, the ice coming on us so fast we were in great danger, looking every hour for death. And thus passed we on in that great danger, seeing both ourselves and the rest of our ships so troubled and tossed amongst the ice that it would make the strongest heart to relent. At the last the *Bark Dionyse*, being but a weak ship and bruised afore amongst the ice, being so leaky that no longer she could tarry above the water, sank, without saving any of the goods which were within her; which sight so abashed the whole fleet that we thought verily we should have tasted of the same sauce. But nevertheless we, seeing them in such danger, manned our boats and saved all the men in such wise that not one perished, God be thanked.

The storm still increased and the ice enclosed us, so that we were fain to take down top and topmasts, for the ice had so environed us that we could see neither land nor sea as far as we could ken. So that we were fain to cut our cables to hang overboard for fenders somewhat to ease the ships' sides from the great and dreary strokes of the ice, some with capstan bars, some fending off with oars, some with planks of two inches thick which were broken immediately with the force of the ice, some going out upon the ice to bear it off with their shoulders from the ships. But the rigorousness of the tempest was such and the force of the ice so great that not only they burst and spoiled the foresaid provision but likewise so razed the sides of the ships that it was pitiful to behold and caused the hearts of many to faint.

Thus we continued all that dismal and lamentable night plunged in this perplexity looking for instant death. But our God, who never leaveth them destitute which faithfully call upon Him although He often punisheth for amendment's sake, in the morning caused the winds to cease and the fog which all that night lay on the face of the water to clear, so that we might perceive about a mile from us a certain place clear from any ice, to which, with an easy breath of wind which our God sent us, we bent ourselves. And furthermore, He provided better for us than we deserved or hoped for: for when we were in the foresaid clear place He sent us a fresh gale at west or at south-west which set us clear without all the ice; and further He added more, for He sent us so pleasant a day as the like we had not of a long time before, as after punishment consolation.

Thus we joyful wights, being at liberty, took in all our sails and lay a-hull, praising God for our deliverance, and stayed to gather together our fleet; which once being done, we seeing that none of them had any great hurt, neither any of them wanted saving only they of whom I spoke before and the ship which was lost, then at the last we hoisted our sails and lay bolting off and on till such time as it would please God to take away the ice that we might get into the Straits. And as we thus lay off and on we came by a marvellous huge mountain of ice which surpassed all the rest that ever we saw; for we judged it to be near forescore fathoms above water, and we thought it to be aground for anything that we could perceive, being there nine score fathoms deep, and of compass about half a mile.

Also the fifth of July there fell a hideous fog and mist that continued till the nineteenth of the same, so that one ship could not see another. Therefore we were fain to bear a small sail and to observe the time, but there ran such a current of a tide that it set us to the north-west of the Queen's Foreland the backside of the Straits, where, through the contagious fog having no sight either of sun or star, we scarce knew where we were. In this fog the tenth of July we lost the company of the vice-admiral, the *Anne Francis*, the *Buss of Bridgwater*, and the *Francis* of Fowey.

The 16th day one of our small barks named the *Gabriel* was sent by our General to bear in with the land to descry it, where, being on land, they met with the people of the country, which seemed very humane and civil and offered to traffic with our men, proffering them fowls and skins for knives and other trifles; whose courtesy caused us to think that they had small conversation with other of the Straits.

Then we bore back again to go with the Queen's Foreland; and the eighteenth day we came by two islands whereon we went on shore, and found where the people had been but we saw none of them. This day we were again in the ice and like to be in as great peril as we were at the first. For through the darkness and obscurity of the foggy mist we were almost run on rocks and islands before we saw them; but God, even miraculously, provided for us, opening the fogs that we might see clearly both where and in what danger we presently were and also the way to escape, or else without fail we had ruinously run upon the rocks. When we knew perfectly our instant case we cast about to get again on seaboard, which, God be thanked, by night we obtained, and praised God. The clear continued scarce an hour but the fog fell again as thick as ever it was.

Then the rear-admiral and the *Bear* got themselves clear without danger of ice and rocks, struck their sails, and lay a-hull, staying to have the rest of the fleet come forth, which as yet had not found the right way to clear themselves from the danger of rocks and ice, until the next morning, at what time the rear-admiral discharged certain warning-pieces to give notice that she had escaped, and that the rest, by following her, might set themselves free, which they did that day. Then having gathered ourselves together we proceeded on our purposed voyage, bearing off and keeping ourselves distant from the coast till the 19th day of July, at which time the fogs broke up and dispersed, so that we might plainly and clearly behold the pleasant air which so long had been taken from us by the obscurity of the foggy mists; and after that time we were not much encumbered therewith until we had left the confines of the country.

Then we espying a fair sound supposed it to go into the Straits between the Queen's Foreland and Jackman's Sound, which proved as we imagined. For our General sent forth again the *Gabriel* to discover it, who passed through with much difficulty for there ran such an extreme current of a tide, with such a horrible gulf, that with a fresh gale of wind they were scarce able to stem it. Yet at the length with great travail they passed it and came to the Straits, where they met with the *Thomas Allen*, the *Thomas* of Ipswich, and the *Buss of Bridgwater*; who all together adventured to bear into the ice again to see if they could obtain their wished port. But they were so encumbered that with much difficulty they were able to get out again, yet, at the last they escaping, the *Thomas Allen* and the *Gabriel* bore in with the western shore, where they found harbour and there moored their ships until the fourth of August, at which time they came to us in the Countess of Warwick's Sound. The *Thomas* of Ipswich caught a great leak which caused her to cast again to seaboard and so was mended.

We sailed along still by the coast until we came to the Queen's Foreland, at the point whereof we met with part of the gulf aforesaid, which place or gulf, as some of our Masters do credibly report, doth flow nine hours and ebbs but three. At that point we discovered certain lands southward, which neither time nor opportunity would serve to search. Then, being come to the mouth of the Straits, we met with the *Anne Francis*, who had lain bolting up and down ever since her departure alone, never finding any of her company. We met then also the *Francis* of Fowey, with whom again we intended to venture and get in; but the ice was yet so thick that we were compelled again to retire and get us on seaboard. There fell also the same day, being the 26th of July, such a horrible snow that it lay a foot thick upon the hatches, which froze as it fell. We had also at other times divers cruel storms both of snow and hail, which manifestly declared the distemperature of the country. Yet for all that we were so many times repulsed and put back from our purpose, knowing that lingering delay was not profitable for us but hurtful to our voyage, we mutually consented to our valiant General once again to give the onset.

The 28th day therefore of the same July we assayed, and with little trouble (God be praised) we passed the dangers by daylight. Then, night falling on the face of the earth, we hulled in the clear till the cheerful light of the day had chased away the noisome darkness of the night, at which time we set forward towards our wished port. By the 30th day we obtained our expected desire, where we found the *Judith* and the *Michael*, which brought no small joy unto the General and great consolation to the heavy hearts of those wearied wights. The 30th day of July we brought our ships into the Countess of Warwick's Sound, and moored them, namely these ships: the admiral, the rear-admiral, the *Francis* of Fowey, the *Bear Armenel*, the *Salomon*, and the *Buss of Bridgwater*. Which being done, our General commanded us all to come ashore upon the Countess' Island, where he set his miners to work upon the mine, giving charge with expedition to despatch with their lading.

Our General himself, accompanied with his gentlemen, divers times made roads into sundry parts of the country, as well to find new mines as also to find out and see the people of the country. He found out one mine upon an island by Bear's Sound, and named it the Countess of Sussex Island. One other was found in Winter's Furnace, with divers others to which the ships were sent sundrily to be laden. In the same roads he met divers of the people of the country at sundry times, as once at a place called David's Sound; who shot at our men and very desperately gave them the onset, being not above three or four in number, there being of our countrymen above a dozen. But seeing themselves not able to prevail they took themselves to flight, whom our men pursued, but being not used to such craggy cliffs they soon lost sight of them and so in vain returned. We also saw of them at Bear's Sound, both by sea and land in great companies; but they would at all times keep the water between them and us. And if any of our ships chanced to be in the Sound (as they came divers times, because the harbour was not very good, the ship laded, and departed again), then so long as any ships were in sight the people would not be seen; but whenas they perceived the ships to be gone they would not only show themselves standing upon high cliffs, and call us to come over unto them, but also would come in their boats very near to us, as it were to brag at us. Whereof our General having advertisement, sent for the captains and gentlemen of the ships to accompany and attend upon him, with the Captain also of the *Anne Francis*, who was but the night before come unto us. For they and the flyboat, having lost us the 26th day in the great snow, put into a harbour in the Queen's Foreland, where they found good ore, wherewith they laded themselves and came to seek·the General. So that now we had all our ships, saving one bark which was lost and the *Thomas* of Ipswich who, compelled by what fury I know not, forsook our company and returned home without lading. Our General, accompanied with his gentlemen of whom I spoke, came all together to the Countess of Sussex Island, near to Bear's Sound, where he manned out certain pinnaces and went over to the people; who, perceiving his arrival, fled away with all speed and in haste left certain darts and other engines behind them, which we found, but the people we could not find.

The next morning our General, perceiving certain of them in boats upon the sea, gave chase to them in a pinnace under sail, with a fresh gale of wind, but could by no means come near unto them. For the longer he sailed the further off he was from them, which well showed their cunning and activity.

Thus, time wearing away and the day of our departure approaching, our General commanded us to lade with all expedition that we might be again on seaboard with our ships. For whilst we were in the country we were in continual danger of freezing in: for often snow and hail often falling, the water was so much frozen and congealed in the night that in the morning we could scarce row our boats or pinnaces, especially in Dyer's Sound which is a calm and still water; which caused our General to make the more haste, so that by the 30th day of August we were all laden, and made all things ready to depart.

But before I proceed any further herein to show what fortune befell at our departure, I will turn my pen a little to Master Captain Fenton and those gentlemen which should have inhabited all the year in those countries. Whose valiant minds were much to be commended; for doubtless they had done as they intended if luck had not withstood their willingness. For the bark *Dionyse*, which was lost, had in her much of their house which was prepared and should have been built for them, with many other implements. Also the *Thomas* of Ipswich, which had most of their provision in her, came not into the Straits at all, neither did we see her since the day we were separated in the great snow, of which I spoke before. For these causes, having not their house nor yet provision, they were disappointed of their pretence to tarry, and therefore laded their ships and so came away with us. But before we took shipping we built a little house in the Countess of Warwick's Island and garnished it with many kinds of trifles, as pins, points, laces, glasses, combs, babes on horseback and on foot, with innumerable other such fancies and toys, thereby to allure and entice the people to some familiarity against other years.

Thus having finished all things we departed the country as I said before; but because the *Buss* had not lading enough in her she put into Bear's Sound to take in a little more. In the meanwhile the admiral and the rest without at sea stayed for her. And that night fell such an outrageous tempest, beating on our ships with such vehement rigour, that anchor and cable availed naught; for we were driven on rocks and islands of ice, insomuch that, had not the great goodness of God been miraculously shown to us, we had been cast away every man. This danger was more doubtful and terrible than any that preceded or went before, for there was not any one ship, I think, that escaped without damage. Some lost anchor and also cables, some boats, some pinnaces, some anchor, cables, boats and pinnaces.

This boisterous storm so severed us from one another that one ship knew not what was become of another. The admiral knew not where to find the vice-admiral or rear-admiral or any other ship of our company. Our General, being on land in Bear's Sound, could not come to his ship but was compelled to go aboard the *Gabriel*, where he continued all the way homeward. For the boisterous blasts continued so extremely and so long a time that they sent us homeward (which was God's favour towards us) willy nilly in such haste as not any one of us were able to keep company with other, but were separated. And if by chance any one ship did overtake other by swiftness of sail, or met, as they often did, yet was the rigour of the wind so hideous that they could not continue company together the space of one whole night.

10 Frobisher in sea-going rig (1577)

MARTIN FROBISER MILES. EX DONO GVALTERI CHARLETON, M.D.

Thus our journey outward was not so pleasant but our coming thither, entering the coasts and country by narrow straits, perilous ice, and swift tides, our times of abode there in snow and storms, and our departure from thence the 31st of August with dangerous blustering winds and tempests which that night arose, was as uncomfortable; separating us so as we sailed that not any of us met together until the 28th of September, which day we fell on the English coasts between Scilly and the Land's End, and passed the Channel until our arrival in the river Thames.

The report of Thomas Wiars, passenger in the *Emmanuel*, otherwise called the *Buss* of *Bridgewater*, wherein James Leech was master, one of the ships in the last voyage of Master Martin Frobisher, 1578, concerning the discovery of a great island in their way homeward the 12th of September.

THE *Buss of Bridgewater* was left in Bear's Sound at Meta Incognita the second day of September behind the fleet, in some distress through much wind, riding near the lee shore and forced there to ride it out upon the hazard of her cables and anchors, which were all aground but two.

The third of September being fair weather and the wind north-north-west, she set sail and departed thence, and fell with Friseland on the 8th day of September at six of the clock at night; and then they set off from the south-west point of Friseland, the wind being at east and east-south-east, but that night the wind veered southerly, and shifted oftentimes that night. But on the tenth day in the morning, the wind at west-north-west fair weather, they steered south-east and by south, and continued that course until the 12th day of September, when about 11 o'clock before noon they described a land, which was from them about five leagues, and the southermost part of it was south-east by east from them and the northermost next north-north-east or north-east.

The Master accounted that the south-east point of Friseland was from him, at that instant when he first described this new island, north-west by north 50 leagues. They account this island to be 25 leagues long, and the longest way of it south-east and north-west. The southern part of it is in the latitude of 57 degrees and 1 second part, or thereabout. They continued in sight of it from the 12th day at 11 of the clock till the 13th day three of the clock in the afternoon, when they left it; and the last part they saw of it bore from them north-west by north.

There appeared two harbours upon that coast, the greatest of them seven leagues to the northwards of the southermost point, the other but four leagues. There was very much ice near the same land, and also twenty or thirty leagues from it, for they were not clear of ice till the 15th day of September after noon. They plied their voyage homewards, and fell with the west part of Ireland about Galway, and had first sight of it on the 25th day of September.

A report of the voyage, and success thereof, attempted in the year of our Lord 1583 by Sir Humphrey Gilbert, knight, with other gentlemen assisting him in that action, intended to discover and to plant Christian inhabitants in place convenient upon those large and ample countries extended northward from the Cape of Florida, lying under very temperate climes, esteemed fertile and rich in minerals, yet not in the actual possession of any Christian prince. Written by Master Edward Hayes, gentleman, and principal actor in the same voyage, who alone continued unto the end, and by God's special assistance returned home with his retinue safe and entire.

MANY voyages have been pretended, yet hitherto never any thoroughly accomplished by our nation, of exact discovery into the bowels of those main, ample, and vast countries extended infinitely into the north from 30 degrees, or rather from 25 degrees of septentrional latitude, neither hath a right way been taken of planting a Christian habitation and regiment upon the same, as well may appear both by the little we yet do actually possess therein, and by our ignorance of the riches and secrets within those lands, which unto this day we know chiefly by the travel and report of other nations, and most of the French, who albeit they cannot challenge such right and interest unto the said countries as we, neither these many years have had opportunity nor means so great to discover and to plant (being vexed with the calamities of intestine wars) as we have had by the inestimable benefit of our long and happy peace; yet have they both ways performed more, and had long since attained a sure possession and settled government of many provinces in those northerly parts of America, if their many attempts into those foreign and remote lands had not been impeached by their garboils at home.

The first discovery of these coasts (never heard of before) was well begun by John Cabot the father and Sebastian his son, an Englishman born, who were the first finders out of all that great tract of land stretching from the Cape of Florida unto those islands which we now call the Newfoundland; all which they brought and annexed unto the crown of England. Since when, if with like diligence the search of inland countries had been followed, as the discovery upon the coast and outparts thereof was performed by those two men, no doubt Her Majesty's territories and revenue had been mightily enlarged and advanced by this day. And, which is more, the seed of Christian religion had been sown amongst those pagans, which by this time might have brought forth a most plentiful harvest and copious congregation of Christians, which must be the chief intent of such as shall make any attempt that way. Or else whatsoever is builded upon other foundation shall never obtain happy success nor continuance.

And although we cannot precisely judge (which only belongeth to God) what have been the humours of men stirred up to great attempts of discovering and planting in those remote countries, yet the events do shew that either God's cause hath not been chiefly preferred by them, or else God hath not permitted so abundant grace as the light of His Word and knowledge of Him to be yet revealed unto those infidels before the appointed time. But most assuredly, the only cause of religion hitherto hath kept back, and will also bring forward at the time assigned by God, an effectual and complete discovery and possession by Christians both of those ample countries and the riches within them hitherto concealed; whereof notwithstanding God in His wisdom hath permitted to be revealed from time to time a certain obscure and misty knowledge, by little and little to allure the minds of men that way (which else will be dull enough in the zeal of His cause), and thereby to prepare us unto a readiness for the execution of His will against the due time ordained of calling those pagans unto Christianity.

In the meanwhile it behoveth every man of great calling, in whom is any instinct of inclination unto this attempt, to examine his own motions, which, if the same proceed of ambition or avarice, he may assure himself it cometh not of God, and therefore cannot have confidence of God's protection and assistance against the violence (else irresistible) both of sea and infinite perils upon the land, whom God yet may use as an instrument to further His cause and glory some way, but not to build upon so bad a foundation. Otherwise, if his motives be derived from a virtuous and heroical mind, preferring chiefly the honour of God, compassion of poor infidels captived by the devil, tyrannising in most wonderful and dreadful manner over their bodies and souls; advancement of his honest and well-disposed countrymen, willing to accompany him in such honourable actions; relief of sundry people within this realm distressed; all these be honourable purposes, imitating the nature of the munificent God, wherewith He is well pleased, who will assist such an actor beyond expectation of man. And the same, who feeleth this inclination in himself, by all likelihood may hope, or rather confidently repose in the preordinance of God, that in this last age of the world (or likely never) the time is complete of receiving also these gentiles into His mercy, and that God will raise him an instrument to effect the same; it seeming probable, by event of precedent attempts made by the Spaniards and French sundry times, that the countries lying north of Florida God hath reserved the same to be reduced unto Christian civility by the English nation. For not long after that Christopher Columbus had discovered the islands and continent of the West Indies for Spain, John and Sebastian Cabot made discovery also of the rest from Florida northwards to the behoof of England.

And whensoever afterwards the Spaniards (very prosperous in all their southern discoveries) did attempt anything into Florida and those regions inclining towards the north, they proved most unhappy, and were at length discouraged utterly by the hard and lamentable success of many both religious and valiant in arms, endeavouring to bring those northerly regions also under the Spanish jurisdiction; as if God had prescribed limits unto the Spanish nation which they might not exceed; as by their own gests recorded may be aptly gathered.

The French, as they can pretend less title unto these northern parts than the Spaniard, by how much the Spaniard made the first discovery of the same continent so far northward as unto Florida, and the French did but review that before discovered by the English nation, usurping upon our right, and imposing names upon countries, rivers, bays, capes, or headlands as if they had been the first finders of those coasts; which injury we offered not unto the Spaniards, but left off to discover when we approached the Spanish limits; even so God hath not hitherto permitted them to establish a possession permanent upon another's right, notwithstanding their manifold attempts, in which the issue hath been no less tragical than that of the Spaniards, as by their own reports is extant.

Then, seeing the English nation only hath right unto these countries of America from the Cape of Florida northwards by the privilege of first discovery, unto which Cabot was authorised by regal authority, and set forth by the expense of our late famous King Henry the Seventh, which right also seemeth strongly defended on our behalf by the powerful hand of Almighty God withstanding the enterprises of other nations, it may greatly encourage us upon so just ground, as is our right, and upon so sacred an intent, as to plant religion (our right and intent being meet foundations for the same), to prosecute effectually the full possession of those so ample and pleasant countries appertaining unto the Crown of England; the same (as is to be conjectured by infallible arguments of the world's end approaching) being now arrived unto the time by God prescribed of their vocation, if ever their calling unto the knowledge of God may be expected. Which also is very probable by the revolution and course of God's Word and religion, which from the beginning hath moved from the east towards, and at last unto, the west, where it is like to end, unless the same begin again where it did in the east, which were to expect a like world again. But we are assured of the contrary by the prophecy of Christ, whereby we gather that after His Word preached throughout the world shall be the end. And as the Gospel when it descended westward began in the south, and afterward spread into the north of Europe, even so, as the same hath begun in the south countries of America, no less hope may be gathered that it will also spread into the north.

These considerations may help to suppress all dreads rising of hard events in attempts made this way by other nations, as also of the heavy success and issue in the late enterprise made by a worthy gentleman our countryman, Sir Humphrey Gilbert, knight, who was the first of our nation that carried people to erect a habitation and government in those northerly countries of America. About which, albeit he had consumed much substance, and lost his life at last, his people also perishing for the most part; yet the mystery thereof we must leave unto God, and judge charitably both of the cause (which was just in all pretence) and of the person, who was very zealous in prosecuting the same, deserving honourable remembrance for his good mind and expense of life in so virtuous an enterprise. Whereby nevertheless, lest any man should be dismayed by example of other folks' calamity, and misdeem that God doth resist all attempts intended that way, I thought good, so far as myself was an eye-witness, to deliver the circumstance and manner of our proceedings in that action, in which the gentleman was so unfortunately encumbered with wants, and worse matched with many ill-disposed people, that his rare judgment and regiment premeditated for those affairs was subjected to tolerate abuses, and in sundry extremities to hold on a course more to uphold credit than likely in his own conceit happily to succeed.

The issue of such actions, being always miserable, not guided by God, who abhorreth confusion and disorder, hath left this for admonition (being the first attempt by our nation to plant) unto such as shall take the same cause in hand hereafter not to be discouraged from it; but to make men well advised how they handle His so high and excellent matters as the carriage is of His Word into those very mighty and vast countries. An action doubtless not to be intermeddled with base purposes; as many have made the same but a colour to shadow actions otherwise scarce justifiable, which doth excite God's heavy judgments in the end, to the terrifying of weak minds from the cause, without pondering His just proceedings; and doth also incense foreign princes against our attempts, how just soever, who cannot but deem the sequel very dangerous unto their state (if in those parts we should grow to strength), seeing the very beginnings are entered with spoil.

And with this admonition denounced upon zeal towards God's cause, also towards those in whom appeareth disposition honourable unto this action of planting Christian people and religion in those remote and barbarous nations of America (unto whom I wish all happiness), I will now proceed to make relation briefly, yet particularly, of our voyage undertaken with Sir Humphrey Gilbert, begun, continued, and ended adversely.

When first Sir Humphrey Gilbert undertook the western discovery of America, and had procured from Her Majesty a very large commission to inhabit and possess at his choice all remote and heathen lands not in the actual possession of any Christian prince, the same commission exemplified with many privileges, such as in his discretion he might demand, very many gentlemen of good estimation drew unto him, to associate him in so commendable an enterprise, so that the preparation was expected to grow unto a puissant fleet, able to encounter a king's power by sea. Nevertheless, amongst a multitude of voluntary men, their dispositions were diverse, which bred a jar, and made a division in the end, to the confusion of that attempt even before the same was begun. And when the shipping was in a manner prepared, and men ready upon the coast to go aboard, at that time some broke consort, and followed courses degenerating from the voyage before pretended. Others failed of their promises contracted, and the greater number were dispersed, leaving the General with few of his assured friends, with whom he adventured to sea, where, having tasted of no less misfortune, he was shortly driven to retire home with the loss of a tall ship and (more to his grief) of a valiant gentleman, Miles Morgan.

Having buried, only in a preparation, a great mass of substance, whereby his estate was impaired, his mind yet not dismayed he continued his former designment and purpose to revive this enterprise, good occasion serving. Upon which determination standing long without means to satisfy his desire, at last he granted certain assignments out of his commission to sundry persons of mean ability, desiring the privilege of his grant, to plant and fortify in the north parts of America about the river of Canada, to whom, if God gave good success in the north parts (where then no matter of moment was expected), the same (he thought) would greatly advance the hope of the south, and be a furtherance unto his determination that way. And the worst that might happen in that course might be excused without prejudice unto him by the former supposition, that those north regions were of no regard. But chiefly a possession taken in any parcel of those heathen countries, by virtue of his grant, did invest him of territories extending every way two hundred leagues, which induced Sir Humphrey Gilbert to make those assignments, desiring greatly their expedition, because his commission did expire after six years if in that space he had not gotten actual possession.

Time went away without anything done by his assignees, insomuch that at last he must resolve himself to take a voyage in person, for more assurance to keep his patent in force, which then almost was expired or within two years.

In furtherance of his determination, amongst others, Sir George Peckham, knight, showed himself very zealous to the action, greatly aiding him both by his advice and in the charge. Other gentlemen to their ability joined unto him, resolving to adventure their substance and lives in the same cause. Who beginning their preparation from that time, both of shipping, munition, victual, men, and things requisite, some of them continued the charge two years complete without intermission. Such were the difficulties and cross accidents opposing these proceedings, which took not end in less than two years, many of which circumstances I will omit.

The last place of our assembly, before we left the coast of England, was in Cawsand Bay, near unto Plymouth, then resolved to put unto the sea with shipping and provision, such as we had, before our store yet remaining, but chiefly the time and season of the year, were too far spent. Nevertheless, it seemed first very doubtful by what way to shape our course and to begin our intended discovery, either from the south northward or from the north southward. The first—that is, beginning south—without all controversy was the likeliest, wherein we were assured to have commodity of the current, which from the Cape of Florida setteth northward, and would have furthered greatly our navigation, discovering from the foresaid Cape along towards Cape Breton, and all those lands lying to the north. Also, the year being far spent, and arrived to the month of June, we were not to spend time in northerly courses, where we should be surprised with timely winter, but to covet the south, which we had space enough then to have attained, and there might with less detriment have wintered that season, being more mild and short in the south than in the north, where winter is both long and rigorous. These and other like reasons alleged in favour of the southern course first to be taken, to the contrary was inferred that, forasmuch as both our victuals and many other needful provisions were diminished and left insufficient for so long a voyage and for the wintering of so many men, we ought to shape a course most likely to minister supply; and that was to take the Newfoundland in our way, which was but seven hundred leagues from our English coast. Where, being usually at that time of the year and until the fine of August a multitude of ships repairing thither for fish, we should be relieved abundantly with many necessaries, which, after the fishing ended, they might well spare and freely impart unto us. Not staying long upon that Newland coast, we might proceed southward, and follow still the sun, until we arrived at places more temperate to our content.

By which reasons we were the rather induced to follow this northerly course, obeying unto necessity, which must be supplied. Otherwise we doubted that sudden approach of winter, bringing with it continual fog, and thick mists, tempest and rage of weather, also contrariety of currents descending from the Cape of Florida unto Cape Breton and Cape Race, would fall out to be great and irresistible impediments unto our further proceeding for that year, and compel us to winter in those north and cold regions.

Wherefore suppressing all objections to the contrary, we resolved to begin our course northward, and to follow directly as we might the trade way unto Newfoundland; from whence, after our refreshing and reparation of wants, we intended without delay (by God's permission) to proceed into the south, not omitting any river or bay which in all that large tract of land appeared to our view worthy of search. Immediately we agreed upon the manner of our course and orders to be observed in our voyage; which were delivered in writing unto the captains and masters of every ship a copy in manner following.

Every ship had delivered two billets or scrolls, the one sealed up in wax, the other left open; in both which were included several watchwords. That open, serving upon our own coast or the coast of Ireland; the other sealed, was promised on all hands not to be broken up until we should be clear of the Irish coast, which from thenceforth did serve until we arrived and met all together in such harbours of the Newfoundland as were agreed for our rendezvous. The said watchwords being requisite to know our consorts whensoever by night, either by fortune of weather, our fleet dispersed should come together again; or one should hail another; or if by ill watch and steerage one ship should chance to fall aboard of another in the dark.

The reason of the billet sealed was to keep secret that watchword while we were upon our own coast, lest any of the company stealing from the fleet might betray the same; which known to an enemy he might board us by night without mistrust, having our own watchword.

Orders agreed upon by the Captains and Masters to be observed by the fleet of Sir Humphrey Gilbert

First, the admiral to carry his flag by day, and his light by night.

2. Item, if the admiral shall shorten his sail by night, then to show two lights until he be answered again by every ship showing one light for a short time.

3. Item, if the admiral after his shortening of sail, as aforesaid, shall make more sail again; then he to show three lights one above another.

4. Item, if the admiral shall happen to hull in the night, then to make a wavering light over his other light, wavering the light upon a pole.

5. Item, if the fleet should happen to be scattered by weather, or other mishap, then so soon as one shall descry another, to hoist both topsails twice, if the weather will serve, and to strike them twice again;

but if the weather serve not, then to hoist the maintopsail twice, and forthwith to strike it twice again.

6. Item, if it shall happen a great fog to fall, then presently every ship to bear up with the admiral, if there be wind; but if it be a calm, then every ship to hull, and so to lie at hull till it clear. And if the fog do continue long, then the admiral to shoot off two pieces every evening, and every ship to answer it with one shot; and every man bearing to the ship that is to leeward so near as he may.

7. Item, every master to give charge unto the watch to look out well, for laying aboard one of another in the night, and in fogs.

8. Item, every evening every ship to hail the admiral, and so to fall astern him, sailing through the ocean; and being on the coast, every ship to hail him both morning and evening.

9. Item, if any ship be in danger in any way, by leak or otherwise, then she to shoot off a piece, and presently to hang out one light, whereupon every man to bear towards her, answering her with one light for a short time, and so to put it out again; thereby to give knowledge that they have seen her token.

10. Item, whensoever the admiral shall hang out her ensign in the main shrouds, then every man to come aboard her as a token of counsel.

11. Item, if there happen any storm or contrary wind to the fleet after the discovery, whereby they are separated, then every ship to repair unto their last good port, thereto meet again.

OUR COURSE AGREED UPON

The course first to be taken for the discovery is to bear directly to Cape Race, the most southerly cape of Newfoundland; and there to harbour ourselves either in Rogneux or Fermeuse, being the first places appointed for our rendezvous, and the next harbours unto the north-ward of Cape Race; and therefore every ship separated from the fleet to repair to that place so fast as God shall permit, whether you shall fall to the southward or to the northward of it, and there to stay for the meeting of the whole fleet the space of ten days, and when you shall depart to leave marks.

A DIRECTION OF OUR COURSE UNTO THE NEWFOUNDLAND

Beginning our course from Scilly, the nearest is by west-south-west (if the wind serve) until such time as we have brought ourselves in the latitude of 43 or 44 degrees, because the ocean is subject much to southerly winds in June and July. Then to take traverse from 45 to 47 degrees of latitude, if we be enforced by contrary winds; and not to go to the northward of the height of 47 degrees of septentrional latitude by no means, if God shall not enforce the contrary; but to do your endeavour to keep in the height of 46 degrees, so near as you can possibly, because Cape Race lieth about that height.

NOTES

If by contrary winds we be driven back upon the coast of England, then to repair unto Scilly for a place of our assembly or meeting.

If we be driven back by contrary winds that we cannot pass the coast of Ireland, then the place of our assembly to be at Bear Haven or Baltimore Haven.

If we shall not happen to meet at Cape Race, then the place of rendezvous to be at Cape Breton, or the nearest harbour unto the westward of Cape Breton.

If by means of other shipping we may not safely stay there, then to rest at the very next safe port to the westward; every ship leaving their marks behind them for the more certainty of the after comers to know where to find them.

The marks that every man ought to leave in such a case were of the General's private device written by himself, sealed also in close wax, and delivered unto every ship one scroll, which was not to be opened until occasion required, whereby every man was certified what to leave for instruction of after comers; that every of us coming into any harbour or river might know who had been there, or whether any were still there up higher into the river, or departed, and which way.

Orders thus determined, and promises mutually given to be observed, every man withdrew himself unto his charge. The anchors being already weighed, and our ships under sail, having a soft gale of wind, we began our voyage upon Tuesday, the 11th day of June, in the year of our Lord 1583, having in our fleet (at our departure from Cawsand Bay) these ships, whose names and burdens, with the names of the captains and masters of them, I have also inserted, as followeth: 1. The *Delight, alias* the *George*, of burden 120 tons, was admiral; in which went the General, and William Winter, captain in her and part owner, and Richard Clarke, master. 2. The bark *Raleigh*, set forth by Master Walter Raleigh, of the burden of 200 tons, was then vice-admiral; in which went Master Butler, captain, and Robert Davis, of Bristol, master. 3. The *Golden Hind*, of burden 40 tons, was then rear-admiral; in which went Edward Hayes, captain and owner, and William Cox, of Limehouse, master. 4. The *Swallow*, of burden 40 tons; in her was captain Maurice Browne. 5. The *Squirrel*, of burden 10 tons; in which went captain William Andrews, and one Cade, master. We were in number in all about 260 men, among whom we had of every faculty good choice, as shipwrights, masons, carpenters, smiths, and suchlike, requisite to such an action; also mineral men and refiners. Besides, for solace of our people and allurement of the savages, we were provided of music in good variety; not omitting the least toys, as Morris dancers, hobby-horse, and Maylike conceits to delight the savage people, whom we intended to win by all fair means possible. And to that end we were indifferently furnished of all petty haberdashery wares to barter with those simple people.

In this manner we set forward, departing (as hath been said) out of Cawsand Bay the 11th of June, being Tuesday, the weather and wind fair and good all day, but a great storm of thunder and wind fell the same night.

Thursday following, when we hailed one another in the evening (according to the order before specified) they signified unto us out of the vice-admiral, that both the Captain, and very many of the men were fallen sick; and about midnight the vice-admiral forsook us, notwithstanding we had the wind east, fair and good. But it was after credibly reported that they were infected with a contagious sickness, and arrived greatly distressed at Plymouth; the reason I could never understand. Sure I am, no cost was spared by their owner, Master Raleigh, in setting them forth; therefore I leave it unto God. By this time we were in 48 degrees of latitude, not a little grieved with the loss of the most puissant ship in our fleet, after whose departure the *Golden Hind* succeeded in the place of vice-admiral, and removed her flag from the mizen into the foretop.

From Saturday, the 15th of June, until the 28th, which was upon a Friday, we never had fair day without fog or rain, and winds bad, much to the west-north-west, whereby we were driven southward unto forty-one degrees scarce. About this time of the year the winds are commonly west towards the Newfoundland, keeping ordinarily within two points of west to the south or to the north, whereby the course thither falleth out to be long and tedious after June, which in March, April, and May, hath been performed out of England in 22 days and less. We had wind always so scant from west-north-west, and from west-south-west again, that our traverse was great, running south unto 41 degrees almost, and afterwards north into 51 degrees. Also we were encumbered with much fog and mists in manner palpable, in which we could not keep so well together, but were dissevered, losing the company of the *Swallow* and the *Squirrel* upon the 20th day of July, whom we met again at several places upon the Newfoundland coast the third of August, as shall be declared in place convenient. Saturday, the 27th July, we might descry, not far from us, as it were mountains of ice driven upon the sea, being then in 50 degrees, which were carried southward to the weather of us, whereby may be conjectured that some current doth set that way from the north.

Before we come to Newfoundland, about 50 leagues on this side, we pass the bank, which are high grounds rising within the sea and under water, yet deep enough and without danger, being commonly not less than 25 and 30 fathom water upon them; the same (as it were some vein of mountains within the sea) do run along, and from the Newfoundland, beginning northward about 52 or 53 degrees of latitude, and do extend into the south infinitely. The breadth of this bank is somewhere more, and somewhere less; but we found the same about 10 leagues over, having sounded both on this side thereof and the other towards Newfoundland, but found no ground with almost 200 fathom of line both before and after we had passed the bank. The Portugals, and French chiefly, have a notable trade of fishing upon this bank, where are sometimes a hundred or more sail of ships, who commonly begin the fishing in April, and have ended by July. That fish is large, always wet, having no land near to dry, and is called cod-fish.

During the time of fishing, a man shall know without sounding when he is upon the bank, by the incredible multitude of sea-fowl hovering over the same, to prey upon the offal and garbage of fish thrown out by fishermen and floating upon the sea.

Upon Tuesday, the 11th of June, we forsook the coast of England. So again Tuesday, the 30th of July (seven weeks after), we got sight of land, being immediately embayed in the Grand Bay, or some other great bay, the certainty whereof we could not judge, so great haze and fog did hang upon the coast as neither we might discern the land well, nor take the sun's height; but by our best computation we were then in the 51 degrees of latitude.

Forsaking this bay and uncomfortable coast (nothing appearing unto us but hideous rocks and mountains, bare of trees, and void of any green herb) we followed the coast to the south, with weather fair and clear. We had sight of an island named Penguin, of a fowl there breeding in abundance, almost incredible, which cannot fly, their wings not able to carry their body, being very large (not much less than a goose) and exceeding fat, which the Frenchmen use to take without difficulty upon that island, and to barrel them up with salt. But for lingering of time we had made us there the like provision.

Trending this coast, we came to the island called Baccaleu, being not past two leagues from the main; to the south thereof lieth Cape St Francis, 5 leagues distant from Baccaleu, between which goeth in a great bay, by the vulgar sort called the Bay of Conception. Here we met with the *Swallow* again, whom we had lost in the fog, and all her men altered into other apparel; whereof it seemed their store was so amended, that for joy and congratulation of our meeting they spared not to cast up into the air and overboard their caps and hats in good plenty. The Captain, albeit himself was very honest and religious, yet was he not appointed of men to his humour and desert; who for the most part were such as had been by us surprised upon the narrow seas of England, being pirates, and had taken at that instant certain

Frenchmen laden, one bark with wines, and another with salt, both which we rescued, and took the man-of-war with all her men, which was the same ship now called the *Swallow*, following still their kind so oft as (being separated from the General) they found opportunity to rob and spoil. And because God's justice did follow the same company, even to destruction, and to the overthrow also of the Captain (though not consenting to their misdemeanour) I will not conceal anything that maketh to the manifestation and approbation of His judgments, for examples of others, persuaded that God more sharply took revenge upon them, and hath tolerated longer as great outrage in others, by how much these went under protection of his cause and religion, which was then pretended.

Therefore upon further enquiry it was known how this company met with a bark returning home after the fishing with his freight, and because the men in the *Swallow* were very near scanted of victuals, and chiefly of apparel, doubtful withal where or when to find and meet with their admiral, they besought the Captain that they might go aboard this Newlander, only to borrow what might be spared, the rather because the same was bound homeward. Leave given, not without charge to deal favourably, they came aboard the fisherman, whom they rifled of tackle, sails, cables, victuals, and the men of the apparel, not sparing by torture (winding cords about their heads) to draw out else what they thought good. This done with expedition (like men skilful in such mischief), as they took their cock-boat to go aboard their own ship, it was overwhelmed in the sea, and certain of these men there drowned; the rest were preserved even by those silly souls whom they had before spoiled, who saved and delivered them aboard the *Swallow*. What became afterward of the poor Newlander, perhaps destitute of sails and furniture sufficient to carry them home (whither they had not less to run than 700 leagues) God alone knoweth, who took vengeance not long after of the rest that escaped at this instant, to reveal the fact, and justify to the world God's judgments inflicted upon them, as shall be declared in place convenient.

Thus after we had met with the *Swallow*, we held on our course southward until we came against the harbour called St John, about 5 leagues from the former Cape of St Francis, where before the entrance into the harbour we found also the frigate or *Squirrel* lying at anchor, whom the English merchants (that were and always be Admirals by turns interchangeably over the fleets of fishermen within the same harbour) would not permit to enter into the harbour. Glad of so happy meeting, both of the *Swallow* and frigate in one day (being Saturday, the 3rd of August), we made ready our fights, and prepared to enter the harbour, any resistance to the contrary notwithstanding, there being within of all nations to the number of 36 sails. But first the General despatched a boat to give them knowledge of his coming for no ill intent, having commission from Her Majesty for his voyage he had in hand; and immediately we followed with a slack gale, and in the very entrance (which is but narrow, not above two butts' length) the admiral fell upon a rock on the larboard side by great oversight, in that the weather was fair, the rock much above water fast by the shore, where neither went any sea-gate. But we found such readiness in the English merchants to help us in that danger that without delay there were brought a number of boats, which towed off the ship and cleared her of danger.

Having taken place convenient in the road, we let fall anchors, the Captains and Masters repairing aboard our admiral, whither also came immediately the masters and owners of the fishing fleet of Englishmen, to understand the General's intent and cause of our arrival there. They were all satisfied when the General had showed his commission and purpose to take possession of those lands to the behalf of the crown of England, and the advancement of the Christian religion in those pagan- ish regions, requiring but their lawful aid for repairing of his fleet, and supply of some necessaries, so far as conveniently might be afforded him, both out of that and other harbours adjoining. In lieu whereof he made offer to gratify them with any favour and privilege, which upon their better advice they should demand, the like being not to be obtained hereafter for greater price. So craving expedition of his demand, minding to proceed further south without long detention in those parts, he dismissed them, after promise given of their best endeavour to satisfy speedily his so reasonable request. The merchants with their masters departed, they caused forthwith to be discharged all the great ordnance of their fleet in token of our welcome.

It was further determined that every ship of our fleet should deliver unto the merchants and masters of that harbour a note of all their wants; which done, the ships, as well English as strangers, were taxed at an easy rate to make supply. And besides, commissioners were appointed, part of our own company and part of theirs, to go into other harbours adjoining (for our English merchants command all there) to levy our provision; whereunto the Portugals (above other nations) did most willingly and liberally contribute. In so much as we were presented (above our allowance) with wines, marmalades, most fine rusk or biscuit, sweet oils, and sundry delicacies. Also we wanted not of fresh salmon, trout, lobsters, and other fresh fish brought daily unto us. Moreover, as the manner is in their fishing every week to choose their Admiral anew, or rather they succeed in orderly course, and have weekly their Admiral's feast solemnized: even so the General, Cap- tains, and Masters of our fleet were continually invited and feasted. To grow short, in our abundance at home the entertainment had been delightful; but after our wants and tedious passage through the ocean it seemed more acceptable and of greater contentation by how much the same was unexpected in that desolate corner of the world, where at other times of the year wild beasts and birds have only the fruition of all those countries, which now seemed a place very populous and much frequented.

The next morning, being Sunday and the 4th of August, the General and his company were brought on land by English merchants, who showed unto us their accustomed walks unto a place they call the Garden. But nothing appeared more than nature itself without art, who confusedly hath brought forth roses abundantly, wild, but odoriferous, and to sense very comfortable. Also the like plenty of raspberries, which do grow in every place.

Monday following the General had his tent set up, who, being accompanied with his own followers, summoned the merchants and masters, both English and strangers, to be present at his taking possession of those countries. Before whom openly was read and interpreted unto the strangers his commission: by virtue whereof he took possession in the same harbour of St John, and 200 leagues every way, invested the Queen's Majesty with the title and dignity thereof, had delivered unto him (after the custom of England) a rod and a turf of the same soil, entering possession also for him, his heirs and assigns for ever; and signified unto all men that from that time forward they should take the same land as a territory appertaining to the Queen of England, and himself authorised under Her Majesty to possess and enjoy it and to ordain laws for the government thereof agreeable (so near as conveniently might be) unto the laws of England, under which all people coming thither hereafter, either to inhabit or by way of traffic, should be subjected and governed. And especially at the same time for a beginning, he proposed and delivered three laws to be in force immediately. That is to say: the first for religion, which in public exercise should be according to the Church of England; the second for maintenance of Her Majesty's right and possession of those territories, against which if any thing were attempted prejudicial, the party or parties offending should be adjudged and executed as in case of high treason, according to the laws of England; the third, if any person should utter words sounding to the dishonour of Her Majesty, he should lose his ears, and have his ship and goods confiscate.

These contents published, obedience was promised by general voice and consent of the multitude, as well of Englishmen as strangers, praying for continuance of this possession and government begun. After this, the assembly was dismissed; and afterward were erected not far from that place the arms of England engraved in lead, and infixed upon a pillar of wood. Yet further and actually to establish this possession taken in the right of Her Majesty, and to the behoof of Sir Humphrey Gilbert, knight, his heirs and assigns for ever, the General granted in fee farm divers parcels of land lying by the water side, both in this harbour of St John and elsewhere, which was to the owners a great commodity, being thereby assured (by their proper inheritance) of grounds convenient to dress and to dry their fish, whereof many times before they did fail, being prevented by them that came first into the harbour. For which grounds they did covenant to pay a certain rent and service unto Sir Humphrey Gilbert, his heirs or assigns for ever, and yearly to maintain possession of the same, by themselves or their assigns.

Now remained only to take in provision granted, according as every ship was taxed which did fish upon the coast adjoining. In the meanwhile the General appointed men unto their charge: some to repair and trim the ships, others to attend in gathering together our supply and provisions; others to search the commodities and singularities of the country, to be found by sea or land, and to make relation unto the General what either themselves could know by their own travail and experience, or by good intelligence of Englishmen or strangers who had longest frequented the same coast. Also some observed the elevation of the pole, and drew plats of the country exactly graded. And by that I could gather by each man's several relation, I have drawn a brief description of the Newfoundland, with the commodities by sea or land already made, and such also as are in possibility and great likelihood to be made. Nevertheless the cards and plats that were drawing, with the due gradation of the harbours, bays, and capes, did perish with the admiral; wherefore in the description following I must omit the particulars of such things.

A brief relation of the Newfoundland and the commodities thereof

That which we do call the Newfoundland, and the Frenchmen Baccaleu, is an island, or rather (after the opinion of some) it consisteth of sundry islands and broken lands situate in the north regions of America upon the gulf and entrance of a great river called St Lawrence in Canada; into the which navigation may be made both on the south and north side of this island. The land lieth south and north, containing in length between 300 and 400 miles, accounting from Cape Race (which is in 46 degrees 25 minutes) unto the Grand Bay in 52 degrees of septentrional latitude. The island round about hath very many goodly bays and harbours, safe roads for ships, the like not to be found in any part of the known world.

The common opinion that is had of intemperature and extreme cold that should be in this country, as of some part it may be verified, namely the north, where I grant it is more cold than in countries of Europe which are under the same elevation, even so it cannot stand with reason and nature of the clime that the south parts should be so intemperate as the bruit hath gone. For as the same do lie under the climes of Breton,

Anjou, Poitou in France, between 46 and 49 degrees, so can they not so much differ from the temperature of those countries unless upon the outcoast lying open unto the ocean and sharp winds it must indeed be subject to more cold than further within the land, where the mountains are interposed, as walls and bulwarks, to defend and to resist the asperity and rigour of the sea and weather. Some hold opinion that the Newfoundland might be the more subject to cold by how much it lieth high and near unto the middle region. I grant that not in Newfoundland alone, but in Germany, Italy and Africa, even under the equinoctial line, the mountains are extreme cold, and seldom uncovered of snow in their culm and highest tops, which cometh to pass by the same reason that they are extended towards the middle region; yet in the countries lying beneath them, it is found quite contrary. Even so all hills having their descents, the valleys also and low grounds must be likewise hot or temperate, as the clime doth give in Newfoundland; though I am of opinion that the sun's reflection is much cooled, and cannot be so forcible in Newfoundland, nor generally throughout America, as in Europe or Africa, by how much the sun, in his diurnal course from east to west, passeth over (for the most part) dry land and sandy countries before he arriveth at the west of Europe or Africa, whereby his motion increaseth heat, with little or no qualification by moist vapours; where, on the contrary, he passeth from Europe and Africa unto America over the ocean, from whence it draweth and carrieth with him abundance of moist vapours, which do qualify and enfeeble greatly the sun's reverberation upon this country chiefly of Newfoundland, being so much to the northward. Nevertheless (as I said before) the cold cannot be so intolerable under the latitude of 46, 47, and 48 (especially within land) that it should be unhabitable, as some do suppose, seeing also there are very many people more to the north by a great deal. And in these south parts there be certain beasts, ounces or leopards, and birds in like manner which in the summer we have seen, not heard of in countries of extreme and vehement coldness. Besides, as in the months of June, July, August and September the heat is somewhat more than in England at those seasons, so men remaining upon the south parts, near unto Cape Race, until after Hollantide have not found the cold so extreme, nor much differing from the temperature of England. Those which have arrived there after November and December have found the snow exceeding deep, whereat no marvel, considering the ground upon the coast is rough and uneven, and the snow is driven into the places most declining, as the like is to be seen with us. The like depth of snow happily shall not be found within land upon the plainer countries, which also are defended by the mountains, breaking off the violence of winds and weather. But admitting extraordinary cold in those south parts, above that with us here, it cannot be so great as in Swedeland, much less in Muscovia or Russia; yet are the same countries very populous, and the rigour of cold is dispensed with by the commodity of stoves, warm clothing, meats and drinks, all of which need not to be wanting in the Newfoundland, if we had intent there to inhabit.

In the south parts we found no inhabitants, which by all likelihood have abandoned those coasts, the same being so much frequented by Christians. But in the north are savages altogether harmless. Touching the commodities of this country, serving either for sustentation of inhabitants or for maintenance of traffic, there are and may be made divers; so that it seemeth that nature hath recompensed that only defect and incommodity of some sharp cold, by many benefits: viz., with incredible quantity and no less variety of kinds of fish in the sea and fresh waters, as trout, salmon, and other fish to us unknown; also cod, which alone draweth many nations thither, and is become the most famous fishing of the world. Abundance of whales, for which also is a very great trade in the bays of Placentia and the Grand Bay, where is made train oils of the whale; herring, the largest that have been heard of, and exceeding the Malstrond herring of Norway, but hitherto was never benefit taken of the herring fishing. There are sundry other fish very delicate, namely the bonito, lobsters, turbot, with others infinite not sought after; oysters having pearl but not orient in colour, I took it by reason they were not gathered in season.

Concerning the inland commodities, as well to be drawn from this land as from the exceeding large countries adjoining, there is nothing which our east and northerly countries of Europe do yield but the like also may be made in them as plentifully by time and industry: namely, rosin, pitch, tar, soap-ashes, deal-board, masts for ships, hides, furs, flax, hemp, corn, cables, cordage, linen cloth, metals, and many more. All which the countries will afford, and the soil is apt to yield. The trees for the most in those south parts are fir-trees, pine, and cypress, all yielding gum and turpentine; cherry trees bearing fruit no bigger than a small pea; also pear-trees, but fruitless; other trees of some sorts to us unknown. The soil along the coast is not deep of earth, bringing forth abundantly pease small, yet good feeding for cattle; roses passing sweet, like unto our musk roses in form; rasps; a berry which we call hurts, good and wholesome to eat. The grass and herb doth fat sheep in very short space, proved by English merchants which have carried sheep thither for fresh victual and had them raised exceeding fat in less than three weeks. Pease which our countrymen have sown in the time of May have come up fair, and been gathered in the beginning of August, of which our General had a present acceptable for the rareness, being the first fruits coming up by art and industry in that desolate and dishabited land. Lakes or pools of fresh water, both on the tops of mountains and in the valleys, in which are said to be mussels not unlike to have pearl; which I had put in trial, if by mischance falling unto me I had not been let from that and other good experiments I was minded to make. Fowl both of water and land in great plenty and diversity. All kind of green fowl; others as big as bustards, yet not the same. A great white fowl called of some a gaunt. Upon the land divers sorts of hawks, as falcons, and others by report. Partridges most plentiful, larger than ours, grey and white of colour, and rough-footed like doves, which our men after one flight did kill with cudgels, they were so fat and unable to fly. Birds some like blackbirds, linnets, canary birds, and other very small. Beasts of sundry kinds, red deer, buffaloes, or a beast as it seemeth by the track and foot very large, in manner of an ox. Bears, ounces or leopards, some greater and some lesser, wolves, foxes, which to the northward a little further are black, whose fur is esteemed in some countries of Europe very rich. Otters, beavers, martens. And in the opinion of most men that saw it, the General had brought unto him a sable alive, which he sent unto his brother, Sir John Gilbert, knight, of Devonshire, but it was never delivered, as after I understood. We could not observe the hundredth part of creatures in those unhabited lands, but these mentioned may induce us to glorify the magnificent God, who hath superabundantly replenished the earth with creatures serving for the use of man, though man hath not used a fifth part of the same, which the more doth aggravate the fault and foolish sloth in many of our nation, choosing rather to live indirectly, and very miserably to live and die within this realm pestered with inhabitants, than to adventure as becometh men, to obtain a habitation in those remote lands, in which nature very prodigally doth minister unto men's endeavours, and for art to work upon. For besides these already recounted and infinite more, the mountains generally make show of mineral substance; iron very common, lead, and somewhere copper. I will not aver of richer metals; albeit by the circumstances following more than hope may be conceived thereof.

For amongst other charges given to enquire out the singularities of this country, the General was most curious in the search of metals, commanding the mineral-man and refiner especially to be diligent. The same was a Saxon born, honest and religious, named Daniel, who after search brought at first some sort of ore, seeming rather to be iron than other metal. The next time he found ore, which with no small show of contentment he delivered unto the General, using protestation that, if silver were the thing which might satisfy the General and his followers, there it was, advising him to seek no further; the peril whereof he undertook upon his life (as dear unto him as the crown of England unto Her Majesty, that I may use his own words) if it fell not out accordingly.

Myself at this instant likelier to die than to live, by a mischance, could not follow this confident opinion of our refiner to my own satisfaction; but afterward demanding our General's opinion therein, and to have some part of the ore, he replied, "Content yourself, I have seen enough, and were it but to satisfy my private humour, I would proceed no further. The promise unto my friends, and necessity to bring also the south countries within compass of my patent near expired, as we have already done these north parts, do only persuade me further. And touching the ore, I have sent it aboard, whereof I would have no speech to be made so long as we remain within harbour; here being both Portugals, Biscayans, and Frenchmen not far off, from whom must be kept any bruit or muttering of such matter. When we are at sea proof shall be made; if it be our desire, we may return the sooner hither again." Whose answer I judged reasonable, and contenting me well; wherewith I will conclude this narration and description of the Newfoundland, and proceed to the rest of our voyage, which ended tragically.

While the better sort of us were seriously occupied in repairing our wants, and contriving of matters for the commodity of our voyage, others of another sort and disposition were plotting of mischief, some casting to steal away our shipping by night, watching opportunity by the Generals and Captains lying on the shore; whose conspiracies discovered, they were prevented. Others drew together in company, and carried away out of the harbours adjoining a ship laden with fish, setting the poor men on shore. A great many more of our people stole into the woods to hide themselves, attending time and means to return home by such shipping as daily departed from the coast. Some were sick of fluxes, and many dead; and in brief, by one means or other our company was diminished, and many by the General licensed to return home. Insomuch as after we had reviewed our people resolved to see an end of our voyage, we grew scant of men to furnish all our shipping; it seemed good therefore unto the General to leave the *Swallow* with such provision as might be spared for transporting home the sick people.

The Captain of the *Delight* or admiral returned into England, in whose stead was appointed captain Maurice Browne, before captain of the *Swallow*; who also brought with him into the *Delight* all his men of the *Swallow*, which before have been noted of outrage perpetrated and committed upon fishermen there met at sea.

The General made choice to go in his frigate the *Squirrel* (whereof the captain also was amongst them that returned into England), the same frigate being most convenient to discover upon the coast and to search into every harbour or creek, which a great ship could not do. Therefore the frigate was prepared with her nettings and fights, and overcharged with bases and such small ordnance, more to give a show than with judgment to foresee unto the safety of her and the men, which afterward was an occasion also of their overthrow.

Now having made ready our shipping, that is to say, the *Delight*, the *Golden Hind,* and the *Squirrel*, and put aboard our provision, which was wines, bread or rusk, fish wet and dry, sweet oils, besides many other, as marmalades, figs, lemons barrelled, and suchlike; also we had other necessary provisions for trimming our ships, nets and lines to fish withal, boats or pinnaces fit for discovery. In brief, we were supplied of our wants commodiously, as if we had been in a country or some city populous and plentiful of all things.

We departed from this harbour of St John's upon Tuesday, the twentieth of August, which we found by exact observation to be in 47 degrees 40 minutes; and the next day by night we were at Cape Race, 25 leagues from the same harbour. This Cape lieth south-south-west from St John's; it is a low land, being off from the Cape about half a league; within the sea riseth up a rock against the point of the Cape, which thereby is easily known. It is in latitude 46 degrees 25 minutes. Under this Cape we were becalmed a small time, during which we laid out hooks and lines to take cod, and drew in less than two hours fish so large and in such abundance that many days after we fed upon no other provision. From hence we shaped our course unto the island of Sablon, if conveniently it would so fall out, also directly to Cape Breton.

Sablon lieth to the seaward of Cape Breton about twenty-five leagues, whither we were determined to go upon intelligence we had of a Portugal (during our abode in St John's) who was himself present when the Portugals above thirty years past did put into the same island both neat and swine to breed, which were since exceedingly multiplied. This seemed unto us very happy tidings, to have in an island lying so near unto the main, which we intended to plant upon, such store of cattle, whereby we might at all times conveniently be relieved of victual and served of store for breed.

In this course we trended along the coast, which from Cape Race stretcheth into the north-west, making a bay which some called Trepassey. Then it goeth out again toward the west, and maketh a point, which with Cape Race lieth in manner east and west. But this point inclineth to the north, to the west of which goeth in the Bay of Placentia. We sent men on land to take view of the soil along this coast, whereof they made good report, and some of them had will to be planted there. They saw pease growing in great abundance everywhere.

The distance between Cape Race and Cape Breton is eighty-seven leagues; in which navigation we spent 8 days, having many times the wind indifferent good, yet could we never attain sight of any land all that time, seeing we were hindered by the current. At last we fell into such flats and dangers, that hardly any of us escaped; where nevertheless we lost our admiral with all the men and provision, not knowing certainly the place. Yet for inducing men of skill to make conjecture, by our course and way we held from Cape Race thither (that thereby the flats and dangers may be inserted in sea cards, for warning to others that may follow the same course hereafter), I have set down the best reckonings that were kept by expert men, William Cox, Master of the *Hind*, and John Paul, his mate, both of Limehouse.

Reckonings kept in our course from Cape Race towards Cape Breton and the Island of Sablon, to the time and place where we lost our admiral

August 22nd: West, 14 leagues; west and by south, 25; west-north-west, 25; west-north-west, 9; south-south-west, 10; south-west, 12; south-south-west, 10. August 29th: west-north-west, 12 (here we lost our admiral). Sum of these leagues, 117.

The reckoning of John Paul, Master's Mate, from Cape Race

August 22nd: west, 14 leagues. 23rd: north-west and by west, 9. 24th: south-west and by south, 5. 25th; west and by south, 40. 26th: west and by north, 7. 27th: south-west, 3. 28th: south-west, 9; south-west, 7; west-south-west, 7. 29th: north-west and by west, 20 (here we lost our admiral). Sum of all these leagues, 121. Our course we held in clearing us of these flats was east-south-east, and south-east, and south, fourteen leagues, with a marvellous scant wind.

The manner how our admiral was lost

Upon Tuesday, the 27th of August, toward the evening, our General caused them in his frigate to sound, who 'found white sand at 35 fathom, being then in latitude about 44 degrees. Wednesday toward night the wind came south, and we bore with the land all that night, west-north-west, contrary to the mind of Master Cox; nevertheless we followed the admiral, deprived of power to prevent a mischief, which by no contradiction could be brought to hold other course, alleging they could not make the ship to work better, nor to lie otherways. The evening was fair and pleasant, yet not without token of storm to ensue, and most part of this Wednesday night, like the swan that singeth before her death, they in the admiral, or *Delight*, continued in sounding of trumpets, with drums and fifes; also winding the cornets and hautboys, and in the end of their jollity left with the battle and ringing of doleful knells. Towards the evening also we caught in the *Golden Hind* a very mighty porpoise, with a harping iron, having first struck divers of them, and brought away part of their flesh sticking upon the iron, but could recover only that one. These also, passing through the ocean in herds, did portend storm. I omit to recite frivolous reports of them in the frigate of strange voices the same night, which scared some from the helm.

Thursday, the 29th of August, the wind rose, and blew vehemently at south and by east, bringing withal rain and thick mist, so that we could not see a cable's length before us; and betimes in the morning we were altogether run and folded in amongst flats and sands, amongst which we found shoal and deep in every three or four ship's length after we began to sound. But first we were upon them unawares, until Master Cox looking out, discerned, in his judgment, white cliffs, crying "Land" withal, though we could not afterward descry any land, it being very likely the breaking of the sea white, which seemed to be white cliffs through the haze and thick weather.

Immediately tokens were given unto the *Delight* to cast about to seaward, which, being the greater ship, and of burden 120 tons, was yet foremost upon the breach, keeping so ill watch that they knew not the danger before they felt the same, too late to recover it. For presently the admiral struck aground, and had soon after her stern and hinder parts beaten in pieces; whereupon the rest (that is to say the frigate, in which was the General, and the *Golden Hind*) cast about east-south-east, bearing to the south, even for our lives, into the wind's eye, because that way carried us to the seaward. Making out from this danger, we sounded one while seven fathom, then five fathom, then four fathom and less, again deeper, immediately four fathom, then but three fathom, the sea going mightily and high. At last we recovered (God be thanked), in some despair, to sea room enough.

In this distress we had vigilant eye unto the admiral, whom we saw cast away, without power to give the men succour, neither could we espy any of the men that leaped overboard to save themselves, either in the same pinnace, or cock, or upon rafters, and suchlike means presenting themselves to men in those extremities, for we desired to save the men by every possible means. But all in vain, sith God had determined their ruin; yet all that day, and part of the next, we beat up and down as near unto the wreck as was possible for us, looking out if by good hap we might espy any of them.

This was a heavy and grievous event, to lose at one blow our chief ship freighted with great provision, gathered together with much travail, care, long time, and difficulty. But more was the loss of our men, which perished to the number almost of a hundred souls. Amongst whom was drowned a learned man, a Hungarian, born in the city of Buda, called thereof Budæus, who of piety and zeal to good attempts adventured in this action, minding to record in the Latin tongue the gests and things worthy of remembrance happening in this discovery, to the honour of our nation, the same being adorned with the eloquent style of this orator and rare poet of our time.

Here also perished our Saxon refiner and discoverer of inestimable riches, as it was left amongst some of us in undoubted hope. No less heavy was the loss of the Captain, Maurice Browne, a virtuous, honest, and discreet gentleman, overseen only in liberty given late before to men that ought to have been restrained, who showed himself a man resolved, and never unprepared for death, as by his last act of this tragedy appeared, by report of them that escaped this wreck miraculously, as shall be hereafter declared. For when all hope was passed of recovering the ship, and that men began to give over, and to save themselves, the Captain was advised before to shift also for his life, by the pinnace at the stern of the ship; but refusing that counsel, he would not give example with the first to leave the ship, but used all means to exhort his people not to despair, nor so to leave off their labour, choosing rather to die than to incur infamy by forsaking his charge, which then might be thought to have perished through his default, showing an ill precedent unto his men by leaving the ship first himself. With this mind he mounted upon the highest deck, where he attended imminent death, and unavoidable; how long, I leave it to God, who withdraweth not His comfort from His servants at such times.

In the mean season, certain, to the number of fourteen persons, leaped into a small pinnace (the bigness of a Thames barge, which was made in the Newfoundland), cut off the rope wherewith it was towed, and committed themselves to God's mercy, amidst the storm and rage of sea and winds, destitute of food, not so much as a drop of fresh water. The boat seeming overcharged in foul weather with company, Edward Headly, a valiant soldier, and well reputed of his company, preferring the greater to the lesser, thought better that some of them perished than all, made this motion to cast lots, and them to be thrown overboard upon whom the lots fell, thereby to lighten the boat, which otherways seemed impossible to live, offered himself with the first, content to take his adventure gladly: which nevertheless Richard Clarke, that was master of the admiral, and one of this number, refused, advising to abide God's pleasure, who was able to save all as well as a few.

The boat was carried before the wind, continuing six days and nights in the ocean, and arrived at last with the men (alive, but weak) upon the Newfoundland, saving that the foresaid Headly (who had been late sick), and another called of us Brazil of his travel into those countries, died by the way, famished, and less able to hold out than those of better health. For such was these poor men's extremity, in cold and wet, to have no better sustenance than their own urine for six days together.

Thus whom God delivered from drowning He appointed to be famished, who doth give limits to man's times, and ordaineth the manner and circumstance of dying: whom again He will preserve, neither sea nor famine can confound. For those that arrived upon the Newfoundland were brought into France by certain Frenchmen then being upon that coast.

After this heavy chance we continued in beating the sea up and down, expecting when the weather would clear up, that we might yet bear in with the land which we judged not far off, either the continent or some island. For we many times and in sundry places found ground at 50, 45, 40 fathoms, and less; the ground coming upon our lead being sometimes oozy sand and otherwhile a broad shell, with a little sand about it.

Our people lost courage daily after this ill success, the weather continuing thick and blustering, with increase of cold, winter drawing on, which took from them all hope of amendment, settling an assurance of worse weather to grow upon us every day. The leeside of us lay full of flats and dangers inevitable if the wind blew hard at south. Some again doubted we were engulfed in the Bay of St Lawrence, the coast full of dangers, and unto us unknown. But above all, provision waxed scant, and hope of supply was gone with loss of our admiral.

Those in the frigate were already pinched with spare allowance, and want of clothes chiefly; whereupon they besought the General to return to England before they all perished. And to them of the *Golden Hind* they made signs of their distress, pointing to their mouths, and to their clothes thin and ragged; then immediately they also of the *Golden Hind* grew to be of the same opinion and desire to return home.

The former reasons having also moved the General to have compassion of his poor men, in whom he saw no want of good will, but of means fit to perform the action they came for, resolved upon retire; and calling the Captain and Master of the *Hind*, he yielded them many reasons enforcing this unexpected return, withal protesting himself greatly satisfied with that he had seen and knew already, reiterating these words, "Be content, we have seen enough, and take no care of expense past, I will set you forth royally the next spring, if God send us safe home. Therefore I pray you let us no longer strive here, where we fight against the elements."

Omitting circumstance, how unwillingly the Captain and Master of the *Hind* condescended to this motion his own company can testify; yet comforted with the General's promise of a speedy return at spring, and induced by other apparent reasons, proving an impossibility to accomplish the action at that time, it was concluded on all hands to retire.

So upon Saturday in the afternoon, the 31st of August, we changed our course, and returned back for England, at which very instant, even in winding about, there passed along between us and towards the land which we now forsook a very lion to our seeming, in shape, hair, and colour, not swimming after the manner of a beast by moving of his feet, but rather sliding upon the water with his whole body (excepting the legs) in sight, neither yet diving under, and again rising above the water, as the manner is of whales, dolphins, tunnies, porpoises, and all other fish, but confidently showing himself above water without hiding, notwithstanding we presented ourselves in open view and gesture to amaze him, as all creatures will be commonly at a sudden gaze and sight of men. Thus he passed along turning his head to and fro, yawning and gaping wide, with ugly demonstration of long teeth, and glaring eyes, and to bid us a farewell (coming right against the *Hind*) he sent forth a horrible voice, roaring or bellowing as doth a lion, which spectacle we all beheld so far as we were able to discern the same, as men prone to wonder at every strange thing, as this doubtless was, to see a lion in the ocean sea, or fish in shape of a lion. What opinion others had thereof, and chiefly the General himself, I forbear to deliver: But he took it for *bonum omen*, rejoicing that he was to war against such an enemy, if it were the devil. The wind was large for England at our return, but very high, and the sea rough, insomuch as the frigate wherein the General went was almost swallowed up.

Monday in the afternoon we passed in the sight of Cape Race, having made as much way in little more than two days and nights back again as before we had done in eight days from Cape Race unto the place where our ship perished. Which hindrance thitherward, and speed back again, is to be imputed unto the swift current, as well as to the winds, which we had more large in our return. This Monday the General came aboard the *Hind*, to have the surgeon of the *Hind* to dress his foot, which he hurt by treading upon a nail; at what time we comforted each other with hope of hard success to be all past, and of the good to come. So agreeing to carry out lights always by night, that we might keep together, he departed into his frigate, being by no means to be entreated to tarry in the *Hind*, which had been more for his security. Immediately after followed a sharp storm, which we overpassed for that time, praised be God.

The weather fair, the General came aboard the *Hind* again, to make merry together with the Captain, Master, and company, which was the last meeting, and continued there from morning until night. During which time there passed sundry discourses, touching affairs past, and to come, lamenting greatly the loss of his great ship, more of the men, but most of all his books and notes, and what else I know not, for which he was out of measure grieved, the same doubtless being some matter of more importance than his books, which I could not draw from him; yet by circumstances I gathered the same to be the ore which Daniel the Saxon had brought unto him in the Newfoundland. Whatsoever it was, the remembrance touched him so deep as, not able to contain himself, he beat his boy in great rage, even at the same time, so long after the miscarrying of the great ship, because upon a fair day, when we were becalmed upon the coast of the Newfoundland, near unto Cape Race, he sent his boy aboard the admiral to fetch certain things; amongst which, this being chief, was yet forgotten and left behind. After which time he could never conveniently send again aboard the great ship, much less he doubted her ruin so near at hand.

Herein my opinion was better confirmed diversely, and by sundry conjectures, which maketh me have the greater hope of this rich mine. For whereas the General had never before good conceit of these north parts of the world, now his mind was wholly fixed upon the Newfoundland. And as before he refused not to grant assignments liberally to them that required the same into these north parts, now he became contrarily affected, refusing to make any so large grants, especially of St John's, which certain English merchants made suit for, offering to employ their money and travail upon the same; yet neither by their own suit, nor of others of his own company, whom he seemed willing to pleasure, it could be obtained. Also laying down his determination in the spring following for disposing of his voyage then to be re-attempted, he assigned the Captain and Master of the *Golden Hind* unto the south discovery, and reserved unto himself the north, affirming that this voyage had won his heart from the south, and that he was now become a northern man altogether.

Last, being demanded what means he had at his arrival in England to compass the charges of so great preparation as he intended to make the next spring, having determined upon two fleets, one for the south, another for the north, "Leave that to me," he replied, "I will ask a penny of no man. I will bring good tidings unto Her Majesty, who will be so gracious to lend me 10,000 pounds," willing us therefore to be of good cheer; for he did thank God, he said, with all his heart for that he had seen, the same being enough for us all, and that we needed not to seek any further. And these last words he would often repeat, with demonstration of great fervency of mind, being himself very confident and settled in belief of inestimable good by this voyage, which the greater number of his followers nevertheless mistrusted altogether, not being made partakers of those secrets which the General kept unto himself. Yet all of them that are living may be witnesses of his words and protestations, which sparingly I have delivered.

Leaving the issue of this good hope unto God, who knoweth the truth only, and can at His good pleasure bring the same to light, I will hasten to the end of this tragedy, which must be knit up in the person of our General. And as it was God's ordinance upon him, even so the vehement persuasion and entreaty of his friends could nothing avail to divert him of a wilful resolution of going through in his frigate, which was overcharged upon their decks with fights, nettings, and small artillery, too cumbersome for so small a boat, that was to pass through the ocean sea at that season of the year, when by course we might expect much storm of foul weather, whereof, indeed, we had enough.

But when he was entreated by the Captain, Master, and other his well-willers of the *Hind* not to venture in the frigate, this was his answer: "I will not forsake my little company going homeward, with whom I have passed so many storms and perils." And in very truth he was urged to be so over hard by hard reports given of him that he was afraid of the sea, albeit this was rather rashness than advised resolution, to prefer the wind of a vain report to the weight of his own life. Seeing he would not bend to reason, he had provision out of the *Hind*, such as was wanting aboard his frigate. And so we committed him to God's protection, and set him aboard his pinnace, we being more than 300 leagues onward of our way home.

By that time we had brought the Islands of Azores south of us; yet we then keeping much to the north, until we had got into the height and elevation of England, we met with very foul weather and terrible seas, breaking short and high, pyramid-wise. The reason whereof seemed to proceed either of hilly grounds high and low within the sea (as we see hills and dales upon the land), upon which the seas do mount and fall, or else the cause proceedeth of diversity of winds, shifting often in sundry points, all which having power to move the great ocean, which again is not presently settled, so many seas do encounter together as there had been diversity of winds. Howsoever it cometh to pass, men which all their lifetime had occupied the sea never saw more outrageous seas. We had also upon our mainyard an apparition of a little fire by night, which seamen do call Castor and Pollux. But we had only one, which they take an evil sign of more tempest. The same is usual in storms.

Monday, the 9th of September, in the afternoon, the frigate was near cast away, oppressed by waves, yet at that time recovered; and giving forth signs of joy, the General, sitting abaft with a book in his hand, cried out to us in the *Hind* (so oft as we did approach within hearing), "We are as near to heaven by sea as by land," reiterating the same speech, well beseeming a soldier resolute in Jesus Christ, as I can testify he was.

The same Monday night, about twelve of the clock, or not long after, the frigate being ahead of us in the *Golden Hind*, suddenly her lights were out, whereof as it were in a moment we lost the sight, and withal our watch cried the General was cast away, which was too true; for in that moment the frigate was devoured and swallowed up of the sea. Yet still we looked out all that night and ever after, until we arrived upon the coast of England, omitting no small sail at sea, unto which we gave not the tokens between us agreed upon to have perfect knowledge of each other, if we should at any time be separated.

In great torment of weather and peril of drowning it pleased God to send safe home the *Golden Hind*, which arrived in Falmouth the 22nd day of September, being Sunday, not without as great danger escaped in a flaw, coming from the south-east, with such thick mist that we could not discern land to put in right with the haven.

From Falmouth we went to Dartmouth, and lay there at anchor before the Range, while the Captain went aland to enquire if there had been any news of the frigate, which, sailing well, might happily have been before us. Also to certify Sir John Gilbert, brother unto the General, of our hard success, whom the Captain desired (while his men were yet aboard him, and were witnesses of all occurrences in that voyage) it might please him to take the examination of every person particularly, in discharge of his and their faithful endeavour. Sir John Gilbert refused so to do, holding himself satisfied with report made by the Captain, and not altogether despairing of his brother's safety, offered friendship and courtesy to the Captain and his company, requiring to have his bark brought into the harbour; in furtherance whereof a boat was sent to help to tow her in.

Nevertheless, when the Captain returned aboard his ship, he found his men bent to depart every man to his home; and then the wind serving to proceed higher upon the coast, they demanded money to carry them home, some to London, others to Harwich, and elsewhere (if the bark should be carried into Dartmouth and they discharged so far from home), or else to take benefit of the wind, then serving to draw nearer home, which should be a less charge unto the Captain, and great ease unto the men, having else far to go.

Reason accompanied with necessity persuaded the Captain, who sent his lawful excuse and cause of this sudden departure unto Sir John Gilbert, by the boat of Dartmouth, and from thence the *Golden Hind* departed and took harbour at Weymouth; all the men tired with the tediousness of so unprofitable a voyage to their seeming, in which their long expense of time, much toil and labour, hard diet, and continual hazard of life was unrecompensed; their Captain nevertheless by his great charges impaired greatly thereby, yet comforted in the goodness of God, and His undoubted providence following him in all that voyage, as it doth always those at other times whosoever have confidence in Him alone. Yet have we more near feeling and perseverance of His powerful hand and protection when God doth bring us together with others into one same peril, in which He leaveth them and delivereth us, making us thereby the beholders, but not partakers of their ruin.

Even so, amongst very many difficulties, discontentments, mutinies, conspiracies, sicknesses, mortality, spoilings, and wrecks by sea, which were afflictions more than in so small a fleet or so short a time may be supposed, howbeit true in every particularity, as partly by the former relation may be collected, and some I suppressed with silence for their sakes living, it pleased God to support this company, of which only one man died of a malady inveterate and long infested, the rest kept together in reasonable contentment and concord, beginning, continuing, and ending the voyage, which none else did accomplish, either not pleased with the action, or impatient of wants, or prevented by death.

Thus have I delivered the contents of the enterprise and last action of Sir Humphrey Gilbert, knight, faithfully, for so much as I thought meet to be published, wherein may always appear (though he be extinguished) some sparks of his virtues, he remaining firm and resolute in a purpose by all pretence honest and godly, as was this, to discover, possess, and to reduce unto the service of God and Christian piety those remote and heathen countries of America not actually possessed by Christians, and most rightly appertaining unto the Crown of England; unto the which, as his zeal deserveth high commendation, even so he may justly be taxed of temerity and presumption (rather) in two respects.

First, when yet there was only probability, not a certain and determinate place of habitation selected, neither any demonstration of commodity there *in esse*, to induce his followers, nevertheless he both was too prodigal of his own patrimony and too careless of other men's expenses to employ both his and their substance upon a ground imagined good. The which falling, very like his associates were promised, and made it their best reckoning to be salved some other way, which pleased not God to prosper in his first and great preparation.

Secondly, when by his former preparation he was enfeebled of ability and credit to perform his designments, as it were impatient to abide in expectation better opportunity and means, which God might raise, he thrust himself again into the action, for which he was not fit, presuming the cause pretended on God's behalf would carry him to the desired end. Into which, having thus made re-entry, he could not yield again to withdraw, though he saw no encouragement to proceed, lest his credit, foiled in his first attempt, in a second should utterly be disgraced. Between extremities he made a right adventure, putting all to God and good fortune, and, which was worst, refused not to entertain every person and means whatsoever, to furnish out this expedition, the success whereof hath been declared.

But such is the infinite bounty of God, who from every evil deriveth good. For besides that fruit may grow in time of our travelling into those north-west lands, the crosses, turmoils, and afflictions, both in the preparation and execution of this voyage, did correct the intemperate humours which before we noted to be in this gentleman, and made unsavory and less delightful his other manifold virtues. Then as he was refined, and made nearer drawing unto the image of God, so it pleased the Divine Will to resume him unto Himself, whither both his and every other high and noble mind have always aspired.

A relation of Richard Clarke of Weymouth, master of the ship called the *Delight,* going for the discovery of Norembega with Sir Humphrey Gilbert, 1583. Written in excuse of that fault of casting away the ship and men, imputed to his oversight.

DEPARTING out of Saint John's harbour in the Newfoundland the 20th of August unto Cape Race, from thence we directed our course unto the Isle of Sablon or the Isle of Sand, which the General, Sir Humphrey Gilbert, would willingly have seen. But when we came within twenty leagues of the Isle of Sablon we fell to controversy of our course. The General came up in his frigate, and demanded of me, Richard Clarke, master of the admiral, what course was best to keep. I said that west-south-west was best, because the wind was at south and night at hand and unknown sands lay off a great way from the land. The General commanded me to go west-north-west. I told him again that the Isle of Sablon was west-north-west and but 15 leagues off, and that he should be upon the island before day if he went that course. The General said my reckoning was untrue, and charged me, in Her Majesty's name and as I would show myself in her country, to follow him that night.

I, fearing his threatenings because he presented Her Majesty's person, did follow his commandment, and about seven of the clock in the morning the ship struck on ground, where she was cast away. Then the General went off to sea, the course that I would have had them gone before, and saw the ship cast away, men and all, and was not able to save a man, for there was not water upon the sand for either of them, much less for the admiral that drew fourteen foot.

Now, as God would, the day before it was very calm, and a soldier of the ship had killed some fowl with his piece, and some of the company desired me that they might hoist out the boat to recover the fowl, which I granted them; and when they came aboard they did not hoist it in again that night. And when the ship was cast away the boat was astern, being in burden one ton and a half; there was left in the boat one oar and nothing else. Some of the company could swim, and recovered the boat and did haul in out of the water as many men as they could. Among the rest they had a care to watch for the Captain or the Master; they happened on myself, being the Master, but could never see the Captain. Then they hauled into the boat as many men as they could, in number 16 whose names hereafter I will rehearse. And when the 16 were in the boat, some had small remembrance and some had none; for they did not make account to live, but to prolong their lives as long as it pleased God, and looked every moment of an hour when the sea would eat them up, the boat being so little and so many men in her, and so foul weather that it was not possible for a ship to brook half a course of sail.

Thus while we remained two days and two nights, and that we saw it pleased God our boat lived in the sea (although we had nothing to help us withal but one oar, which we kept up the boat withal upon the sea and so went even as the sea would drive us), there was one in company, one Master Headly, that put forth this question to me, the Master. 'I do see that it doth please God that our boat liveth in the sea, and it may please God that some of us may come to the land if our boat were not overladen. Let us make sixteen lots, and those four that have the four shortest lots we will cast overboard, preserving the Master among us all'. I replied unto him, saying 'No, we will live and die together'. Master Headly asked me if my remembrance were good. I answered I gave God praise it was good, and knew how far I was off the land, and was in hope to come to the land within two or three days, and said they were but threescore leagues from the land (when they were seventy), all to put them in comfort. Thus we continued the third and fourth day without any sustenance, save only the weeds that swam in the sea and salt water to drink.

The fifth day Headly died and another moreover; then we desired all to die; for in all these five days and five nights we saw the sun but once and the star but one night, it was so foul weather. Thus we did remain the sixth day; then we were very weak and wished all to die saving only myself, which did comfort them and promised they should come soon to land by the help of God. But the company were very importunate, and were in doubt they should never come to land, but that I promised them the seventh day they should come to shore or else they should cast me overboard; which did happen true the seventh day, for at eleven of the clock we had sight of the land, and at 3 of the clock at afternoon we came on land.

All these seven days and seven nights the wind kept continually south. If the wind had in the meantime shifted upon any other point we had never come to land. We were no sooner come to the land but the wind came clean contrary at north within half an hour after our arrival. But we were so weak that one could scarcely help another of us out of the boat; yet, with much ado being come all on shore, we knelt down upon our knees and gave God praise that He had dealt so mercifully with us. Afterwards those which were strongest helped their fellows unto a fresh brook, where we satisfied ourselves with water and berries very well. There were of all sorts of berries plenty, and as goodly a country as ever I saw. We found a very fair plain, champaign ground, that a man might see very far every way. By the sea side was here and there a little wood with goodly trees as good as ever I saw any in Norway, able to mast any ship, of pine trees, spruce trees, fir, and very great birch trees.

Where we came on land we made a little house with boughs where we rested all that night. In the morning I divided the company three and three to go every way to see what food they could find to sustain themselves, and appointed them to meet there all again at noon with such food as they could get. As we went aboard we found great store of pease as good as any we have in England; a man would think they had been sown there. We rested there three days and three nights and lived very well with pease and berries. We named the place Saint Lawrence, because it was a very goodly river like the river of St Lawrence in Canada, and we found it very full of salmon. When we had well rested ourselves we rowed our boat along the shore, thinking to have gone to the Grand Bay to have come home with some Spaniards which are yearly there to kill the whale; and when we were hungry or athirst we put our boat on land and gathered pease and berries.

Thus we rowed our boat along the shore five days; about which time we came to a very goodly river that ran far up into the country, and saw very goodly grown trees of all sorts. There we happened upon a ship of Saint John de Luz, which ship brought us into Biscay to a harbour called The Passage. The Master of the ship was our great friend, or else we had been put to death if he had not kept our counsel. For when the Visitors came aboard, as it is the order in Spain, they demanding what we were he said we were poor fishermen that had cast away our ship in Newfoundland, and so the Visitors enquired no more of the matter at that time. As soon as night was come he put us on land and bade us shift for ourselves. Then had we but ten or twelve miles into France, which we went that night, and then cared not for the Spaniard. And so shortly after we came into England toward the end of the year 1583.

The first voyage of Master John Davis, undertaken in June 1585, for the discovery of the north-west passage. Written by Master John Janes, merchant, sometimes servant to the worshipful Master William Sanderson.

CERTAIN honourable personages and worthy gentlemen of the Court and country, with divers worshipful merchants of London and of the west country, moved with desire to advance God's glory and to seek the good of their native country, consulting together of the likelihood of the discovery of the north-west passage, which heretofore had been attempted but unhappily given over by accidents unlooked for which turned the enterprisers from their principal purpose, resolved, after good deliberation, to put down their adventures to provide for necessary shipping and a fit man to be chief conductor of this so hard an enterprise. The setting forth of this action was committed by the adventurers especially to the care of Master William Sanderson, merchant, of London, who was so forward therein that, besides his travail, which was not small, he became the greatest adventurer with his purse, and commended unto the rest of the company one Master John Davis, a man very well grounded in the principles of the art of navigation, for Captain and Chief Pilot of this exploit.

Thus therefore all things being put in a readiness, we departed from Dartmouth the seventh of June towards the discovery of the aforesaid north-west passage, with two barks, the one being of 50 tons, named the *Sunshine* of London, and the other being 35 tons, named the *Moonshine* of Dartmouth. In the *Sunshine* we had 23 persons, whose names are these following: Master John Davis, captain, William Easton, master, Richard Pope, master's mate, John Janes, merchant, Henry Davie, gunner, William Cross, boatswain, John Bagge, Walter Arthur, Luke Adams, Robert Coxworthy, John Ellis, John Kelly, Edward Helman, William Dick, Andrew Maddock, Thomas Hill, Robert Watts, carpenter, William Russell, Christopher Gurney, boy, James Cole, Francis Ridley, John Russell, Robert Cornish, musicians. The *Moonshine* had 19 persons, William Bruton, captain, John Ellis, master, the rest mariners.

The 7th of June the Captain and the Master drew out a proportion for the continuance of our victuals. The 8th day, the wind being at south-west and west-south-west, we put in for Falmouth, where we remained until the 13th. The 13th the wind blew at north and, being fair weather, we departed. The 14th with contrary wind we were forced to put into Scilly. The 15th we departed thence, having the wind north and by east, moderate, and fair weather. The 16th we were driven back again, and were constrained to arrive at New Grimsby in Scilly. Here the wind remained contrary 12 days, and in that space the Captain, the Master, and I went about all the islands, and the Captain did plat out and describe the situation of all the islands, rocks, and harbours to the exact use of navigation, with lines and scale thereunto convenient.

The 28th in God's name we departed, the wind being easterly but calm.

The first of July we saw great store of porpoises. The Master called for a harping iron, and shot twice or thrice. Sometimes he missed, and at last shot one and struck him in the side, and wound him into the ship. When we had him aboard the Master said it was a darley-head. The 2nd we had some of the fish sodden, and it did eat as sweet as any mutton. The 3rd we had more in sight, and the Master went to shoot at them, but they were so great that they burst our irons and we lost both fish, irons, pastime, and all. Yet nevertheless the Master shot at them with a pike, and had wellnigh gotten one, but he was so strong that he burst off the bars of the pike and went away. Then he took a boat-hook and hit one with that, but all would not prevail, so at length we let them alone.

The 6th we saw a very great whale, and every day we saw whales continually. The 16th, 17th, and 18th we saw great store of whales.

The 19th of July we fell into a great whirling and brustling of a tide, setting to the northwards; and sailing about half a league we came into a very calm sea, which bent to the south-south-west. Here we heard a mighty great roaring of the sea, as if it had been the breach of some shore, the air being so foggy and full of thick mist that we could not see the one ship from the other, being a very small distance asunder. So the Captain and the Master, being in distrust how the tide might set them, caused the *Moonshine* to hoist out her boat and to sound, but they could not find ground in 300 fathoms and better. Then the Captain, Master, and I went towards the breach to see what it should be, giving charge to our gunners that at every glass they should shoot off a musket-shot to the intent we might keep ourselves from losing them. Then, coming near to the breach, we met many islands of ice floating, which had quickly compassed us about; then we went upon some of them and did perceive that all the roaring which we heard was caused only by the rolling of this ice together. Our company, seeing us not to return according to our appointment, left off shooting muskets and began to shoot falconets, for they feared some mishap had befallen us; but before night we came aboard again with our boat laden with ice, which made very good fresh water. Then we bent our course toward the north, hoping by that means to double the land.

The 20th, as we sailed along the coast, the fog broke up and we discovered the land, which was the most deformed rocky and mountainous land that ever we saw: the first sight whereof did show as if it had been in form of a sugar-loaf, standing to our sight above the clouds, for that it did show over the fog like a white list in the sky, the tops altogether covered with snow, and the shore beset with ice a league off into the sea, making such irksome noise as that it seemed to be the true pattern of desolation; and after the same our Captain named it The Land of Desolation.

The 21st the wind came northerly and overblew, so that we were constrained to bend our course south again, for we perceived that we were run into a very deep bay, where we were almost compassed with ice, for we saw very much toward the north-north-east, west, and south-west; and this day and this night we cleared ourselves of the ice, running south-south-west along the shore.

Upon Thursday, being the 22nd of this month, about three of the clock in the morning we hoisted out our boat, and the Captain with six sailors went towards the shore, thinking to find a landing place; for the night before we did perceive the coast to be void of ice to our judgment, and the same night we were all persuaded that we had seen a canoe rowing along the shore, but afterwards we fell in some doubt of it but we had no great reason so to do. The Captain, rowing towards the shore, willed the Master to bear in with the land after him, and before he came near the shore by the space of a league or about two miles he found so much ice that he could not get to land by any means. Here our mariners put to their lines to see if they could get any fish, because there were so many seals upon the coast, and the birds did beat upon the water, but all was in vain. The water about this place was very black and thick like to a filthy standing pool. We sounded, and had ground in 120 fathoms. While the Captain was rowing to the shore, our men saw woods upon the rocks like to the rocks of Newfoundland, but I could not discern them, yet it might be so very well; for we had wood floating upon the coast every day, and the *Moonshine* took up a tree at sea not far from the coast being sixty foot of length and fourteen handfuls about, having the root upon it. After this the Captain came aboard; the weather being very calm and fair we bent our course toward the south with intent to double the land.

The 23rd we coasted the land, which did lie east-north-east and west-south-west. The 24th, the wind being very fair at east, we coasted the land, which did lie east and west, not being able to come near the shore by reason of the great quantity of ice. At this place, because the weather was somewhat cold by reason of the ice, and the better to encourage our men, their allowance was increased. The Captain and the Master took order that every mess, being five persons, should have half a pound of bread and a can of beer every morning to breakfast. The weather was not very cold, but the air was moderate like to our April weather in England; when the wind came from the land, or the ice, it was somewhat cold, but when it came off the sea it was very hot.

The 25th of this month we departed from sight of this land at six of the clock in the morning, directing our course to the north-westward, hoping in God's mercy to find our desired passage, and so continued above four days. The 29th of July we discovered land in 64 degrees 15 minutes of latitude, bearing north-east from us. The wind being contrary to go to the north-westwards, we bore in with this land to take some view of it, being utterly void of the pester of ice and very temperate. Coming near the coast we found many fair sounds and good roads for shipping, and many great inlets into the land, whereby we judged this land to be a great number of islands standing together. Here, having moored our bark in good order, we went on shore upon a small island to seek for water and wood. Upon this island we did perceive that there had been people: for we found a small shoe and pieces of leather sewn with sinews, and a piece of fur, and wool like to beaver. Then we went upon another island on the other side of our ships; and the Captain, the Master, and I being got up to the top of a high rock, the people of the country, having espied us, made a

lamentable noise, as we thought, with great outcries and screech-
ings. We, hearing them, thought it had been the howling of wolves.
At last I hallooed again, and they likewise cried. Then we perceiving
where they stood, some on the shore and one rowing in a canoe
about a small island fast by them, we made a great noise, partly to
allure them to us and partly to warn our company of them. Whereupon Master Bruton and the master of his ship, with others of their
company, made great haste towards us, and brought our musicians
from our ship, purposing either by force to rescue us if need should so
require, or with courtesy to allure the people. When they came unto
us we caused our musicians to play, ourselves dancing and making
many signs of friendship. At length there came ten canoes from the
other islands, and two of them came so near the shore where we were
that they talked with us, the other being in their boats a pretty way off.
Their pronunciation was very hollow through the throat, and their
speech such as we could not understand; only we allured them by
friendly embracings and signs of courtesy. At length one of them,
pointing up to the sun with his hand, would presently strike his breast
so hard that we might hear the blow. This he did many times before he
would any way trust us. Then John Ellis, the master of the *Moonshine*,
was appointed to use his best policy to gain their friendship; who struck
his breast and pointed to the sun after their order, which when he had
divers times done they began to trust him, and one of them came on
shore, to whom we threw our caps, stockings, and gloves, and such
other things as then we had about us, playing with our music and
making signs of joy and dancing. So, the night coming, we bade them
farewell and went aboard our barks.

The next morning, being the 30th of July, there came 37 canoes
rowing by our ships, calling to us to come on shore. We not making any
great haste unto them, one of them went up to the top of the rock and
leapt and danced, as they had done the day before, showing us a seal's
skin and another thing made like a timbrel which he did beat upon with
a stick, making a noise like a small drum. Whereupon we manned our
boats and came to them, they all staying in their canoes. We came to
the waterside where they were; and after we had sworn by the sun after
their fashion, they did trust us. So I shook hands with one of them, and
he kissed my hand, and we were very familiar with them. We were in so
great credit with them upon this single acquaintance that we could have
anything they had. We bought five canoes of them; we bought their
clothes from their backs, which were all made of seals' skins and birds'
skins, their buskins, their hose, their gloves all being commonly sewn
and well dressed so that we were fully persuaded that they have divers
artificers among them. We had a pair of buskins of them full of fine
wool like beaver. Their apparel for heat was made of birds' skins with
their feathers on them. We saw among them leather dressed like

glover's leather, and thick thongs like white leather of a good length. We had of their darts and oars, and found in them that they would by no means displease us but would give us whatsoever we asked of them and would be satisfied with whatsoever we gave them. They took great care one of another: for when we had bought their boats, then two other would come and carry him away between them that had sold us his. They are very tractable people, void of craft or double dealing, and easy to be brought to any civility or good order; but we judge them to be idolaters and to worship the sun.

During the time of our abode among these islands we found reasonable quantity of wood, both fir, spruce, and juniper which, whether it came floating any great distance to these places where we found it, or whether it grew in some great islands near the same place by us not yet discovered, we know not; but we judge that it groweth there further into the land than we were, because the people had great store of darts and oars which they made no account of but gave them to us for small trifles as points and pieces of paper. We saw about this coast marvellous great abundance of seals schooling together like schools of small fish. We found no fresh water among these islands but only snow water, whereof we found great pools. The cliffs were all of such ore as Master Frobisher brought from Meta Incognita. We had divers shows of stithy or Muscovy glass shining not altogether unlike to crystal. We found a herb growing upon the rocks whose fruit was sweet, full of red juice, and the ripe ones were like currants. We found also birch and willow growing like shrubs low to the ground. These people have great store of furs as we judge. They made shows unto us the 30th of this present, which was the second time of our being with them, after they perceived we would have skins and furs, that they would go into the country and come again the next day with such things as they had; but this night the wind coming fair, the Captain and the Master would by no means detract the purpose of our discovery. And so the last of this month, about four of the clock in the morning, in God's name we set sail, and were all that day becalmed upon the coast. The first of August we had a fair wind, and so proceeded towards the north-west for our discovery.

The sixth of August we discovered land in 66 degrees 40 minutes of latitude, altogether void from the pester of ice. We anchored in a very fair road under a brave mount, the cliffs whereof were as orient as gold. This mount was named Mount Raleigh. The road where our ships lay at anchor was called Totnes Road. The sound which did compass the mount was named Exeter Sound. The foreland towards the north was called Dyer's Cape; the foreland towards the south was named Cape Walsingham.

So soon as we were come to an anchor in Totnes Road under Mount Raleigh we espied four white bears at the foot of the mount. We, supposing them to be goats or wolves, manned our boats and went towards them; but when we came near the shore we found them to be white bears of a monstrous bigness. We, being desirous of fresh victual and the sport, began to assault them and, I being on land, one of them came down the hill right against me. My piece was charged with hail-shot and a bullet. I discharged my piece and shot him in the neck; he roared a little, and took the water straight, making small account of his hurt. Then we followed him with our boat and killed him with boar-spears, and two more that night. We found nothing in their maws; but we judged by their dung that they fed upon grass, because it appeared in all respects like the dung of a horse, wherein we might very plainly see the very straws.

The 7th we went on shore to another bear which lay all night upon the top of an island under Mount Raleigh, and when we came up to him he lay fast asleep. I levelled at his head, and the stone of my piece gave no fire. With that he looked up, and laid down his head again; then I shot, being charged with two bullets, and struck him in the head. He being but amazed fell backwards, whereupon we ran all upon him with boar-spears and thrust him in the body, yet for all that he gripped away our boar-spears and went towards the water; and as he was going down he came back again. Then our Master shot his boar-spear and struck him in the head, and made him to take the water and swim into a cove fast by, where we killed him, and brought him aboard. The breadth of his forefoot from one side to the other was fourteen inches over. They were very fat, so as we were constrained to cast the fat away. We saw a raven upon Mount Raleigh. We found withies also growing like low shrubs, and flowers like primroses in the said place. The coast is very mountainous, altogether without wood, grass, or earth, and is only huge mountains of stone, but the bravest stone that ever we saw. The air was very moderate in this country.

The 8th we departed from Mount Raleigh, coasting along the shore, which lieth south-south-west and east-north-east. The 9th our men fell in dislike of their allowance, because it was too small as they thought; whereupon we made a new proportion, every mess (being five to a mess) should have four pound of bread a day, twelve wine-quarts of beer, six Newland fishes, and the flesh days a gill of pease more. So we restrained them from their butter and cheese.

The 11th we came to the most southerly cape of this land, which we named the Cape of God's Mercy as being the place of our first entrance for the discovery. The weather being very foggy, we coasted this north land. At length, when it broke up, we perceived that we were shot into a very fair entrance or passage, being in some places twenty leagues broad and in some thirty, altogether void of any pester of ice, the weather very tolerable, and the water of the very colour, nature, and quality of the main ocean, which gave us the greater hope of our passage. Having sailed north-west sixty leagues in this entrance we discovered certain islands standing in the midst thereof, having open passage on both sides. Whereupon our ships divided themselves, the one sailing on the north side, the other on the south side of the said isles, where we stayed five days, having the wind at south-east, very foggy and foul weather.

The 14th we went on shore and found signs of people, for we found stones laid up together like a wall, and saw the skull of a man or a woman. The 15th we heard dogs howl on the shore, which we thought had been wolves and therefore we went on shore to kill them. When we came on land the dogs came presently to our boat very gently, yet we thought they came to prey upon us, and therefore we shot at them and killed two; and about the neck of one of them we found a leathern collar, whereupon we thought them to be tame dogs. There were twenty dogs, like mastiffs with pricked ears and long bush tails. We found a bone in the pizzles of their dogs. Then we went farther, and found two sleds made like ours in England: the one was of fir, spruce, and oaken boards sawn like inch boards, the other was made all of whalebone, and there hung on the tops of the sleds three heads of beasts which they had killed. We saw here larks, ravens, and partridges.

The 17th we went on shore, and in a little thing made like an oven with stones I found many small trifles, as a small canoe made of wood, a piece of wood made like an image, a bird made of bone, beads having small holes in one end of them to hang about their necks, and other small things. The coast was very barren without wood or grass; the rocks were very fair like marble, full of veins of divers colours. We found a seal which was killed not long before, being flayed, and hid under stones.

Our Captain and Master searched still for probabilities of the passage, and first found that this place was all islands with great sounds passing between them. Secondly, the water remained of one colour with the main ocean without altering. Thirdly, we saw to the west of those isles three or four whales in a school, which they judged to come from a westerly sea because to the eastward we saw not any whale. Also, as we were rowing into a very great sound lying south-west, from whence these whales came, upon the sudden there came a violent counter-check of a tide from the south-west against the flood which we came with, not knowing from whence it was maintained. Fifthly, in sailing twenty leagues within the mouth of this entrance we had sounding in 90 fathoms, fair grey oozy sand, and the further we ran into the westwards the deeper was the water, so that hard aboard the shore among these isles we could not have ground in 330 fathoms. Lastly, it did ebb and flow six or seven fathom up and down, the flood coming from divers parts so as we could not perceive the chief maintenance thereof.

The 18th and 19th our Captain and Master determined what was best to do, both for the safeguard of their credits and satisfying of the adventurers, and resolved, if the weather broke up, to make further search. The 20th the wind came directly against us; so they altered their purpose, and reasoned both for proceeding and returning. The 21st, the wind being north-west, we departed from these islands; and as we coasted the south shore we saw many fair sounds, whereby we were persuaded that it was no firm land but islands.

The 23rd of this month the wind came south-east, with very stormy and foul weather: so we were constrained to seek harbour upon the south coast of this entrance, where we fell into a very fair sound and anchored in 25 fathoms green oozy sand. Here we went on shore, where we had manifest signs of people where they had made their fire and laid stones like a wall. In this place we saw four very fair falcons, and Master Bruton took from one of them his prey, which we judged by the wings and legs to be a snipe, for the head was eaten off. The 24th in the afternoon, the wind coming somewhat fair, we departed from this road, purposing by God's grace to return for England. The 26th we departed from the sight of the north land of this entrance, directing our course homewards until the tenth of the next month.

The 10th of September we fell with the Land of Desolation, thinking to go on shore, but we could get never a good harbour. That night we put to sea again, thinking to search it the next day; but this night arose a very great storm, and separated our ships, so that we lost the sight of the *Moonshine*. The 13th about noon, having tried all the night before with a goose-wing, we set sail, and within two hours after we had sight of the *Moonshine* again. This day we departed from this land.

The 27th of this month we fell with sight of England. This night we had a marvellous storm and lost the *Moonshine*. The 30th of September we came into Dartmouth, where we found the *Moonshine*, being come in not two hours before.

The second voyage attempted by Master John Davis, with others, for the discovery of the north-west passage, in anno 1586. (Written by himself.)

THE 7th day of May I departed from the port of Dartmouth for the discovery of the north-west passage, with a ship of a hundred and twenty tons named the *Mermaid*, a bark of 60 tons named the *Sunshine*, a bark of 35 tons named the *Moonshine*, and a pinnace of ten tons named the *North Star*. And the 15th of June I discovered land in the latitude of 60 degrees and in longitude from the meridian of

London westward 47 degrees, mightily pestered with ice and snow so that there was no hope of landing. The ice lay in some places ten leagues, in some 20, and in some 50 leagues off the shore, so that we were constrained to bear into 57 degrees to double the same and to recover a free sea, which through God's favourable mercy we at length obtained.

The 29th of June, after many tempestuous storms, we again discovered land, in longitude from the meridian of London 58 degrees 30 minutes and in latitude 64, being east from us. Into which course sith it please God by contrary winds to force us, I thought it very necessary to bear in with it and there to set up our pinnace, provided in the *Mermaid* to be our scout for this discovery; and so much the rather because the year before I had been in the same place and found it very convenient for such a purpose, well stored with float wood and possessed by a people of tractable conversation. So that the 29th of this month we arrived within the isles which lay before this land, lying north-north-west and south-south-east we know not how far. This land is very high and mountainous, having before it on the west side a mighty company of isles full of fair sounds and harbours. This land is very little troubled with snow, and the sea altogether void of ice.

The ships being within the sounds, we sent out our boats to search for shoal water where we might anchor, which in this place is very hard to find; and as the boat went sounding and searching, the people of the country, having espied them, came in their canoes towards them with many shouts and cries. But after they had espied in the boat some of our company that were the year before here with us, they presently rowed to the boat and took hold on the oar, and hung about the boat with such comfortable joy as would require a long discourse to be uttered. They came with the boats to our ships, making signs that they knew all those that the year before had been with them. After I perceived their joy and small fear of us, myself with the merchants and others of the company went ashore, bearing with me 20 knives. I had no sooner landed but they leapt out of their canoes and came running to me and the rest, and embraced us with many signs of hearty welcome. At this present there were eighteen of them, and to each of them I gave a knife. They offered skins to me for reward, but I made signs that they were not sold but given them of courtesy, and so dismissed them for that time, with signs that they should return again after certain hours.

The next day with all possible speed the pinnace was landed upon an isle, there to be finished to serve our purpose for the discovery; which isle was so convenient for that purpose as that we were very well able to defend ourselves against many enemies. During the time that the pinnace was there setting up, the people came continually unto us, sometime a hundred canoes at a time, sometime forty, fifty, more and less as occasion served. They brought with them sealskins, stag skins, white hares, seal fish, salmon peal, small cod, dry capelin, with other fish and birds such as the country did yield.

Myself, still desirous to have a further search of this place, sent one of the ship-boats to one part of the land and myself went to another part to search for the habitation of this people, with straight commandment that there should be no injury offered to any of the people, neither any gun shot. The boats that went from me found the tents of the people made with sealskins set up upon timber, wherein they found great store of dried capelin, being a little fish no bigger than a pilchard. They found bags of train oil, many little images cut in wood, sealskins in tan-tubs, with many other trifles, whereof they diminished nothing. They also found, ten miles within the snowy mountains, a plain champaign country with earth and grass, such as our moory and waste grounds of England are. They went up into a river (which in the narrowest place is two leagues broad) about ten leagues, finding it still to continue they knew not how far. But I with my company took another river, which although at the first it offered a large inlet yet it proved but a deep bay, the end whereof in four hours I attained, and there leaving the boat well manned went with the rest of my company three or four miles into the country, but found nothing nor saw anything save only gripes, ravens, and small birds as larks and linnets.

The third of July I manned my boat and went with fifty canoes attending upon me up into another sound where the people by signs willed me to go, hoping to find their habitation. At length they made signs that I should go into a warm place to sleep, at which place I went on shore and ascended the top of a high hill to see into the country; but perceiving my labour vain I returned again to my boat, the people still following me and my company, very diligent to attend us and to help us up the rocks and likewise down. At length I was desirous to have our men leap with them, which was done, but our men did overleap them. From leaping they went to wrestling; we found them strong and nimble, and to have skill in wrestling, for they cast some of our men that were good wrestlers.

The fourth of July we launched our pinnace, and had forty of the people to help us, which they did very willingly. At this time our men again wrestled with them, and found them as before, strong and skilful. This fourth of July the Master of the *Mermaid* went to certain islands to store himself with wood, where he found a grave with divers buried in it, only covered with sealskins, having a cross laid over them. The people are of good stature, well in body proportioned, with small slender hands and feet, with broad visages and small eyes, wide mouths, the most part unbearded, great lips, and close-toothed. Their custom is, as often as they go from us, still at their return to make a new truce, in this sort: holding his hand up to the sun, with a loud voice he crieth "Ylyaoute", and striketh his breast; with like signs being promised safety, he giveth credit. These people are much given to bleed, and therefore stop their noses with deer's hair or the hair of an eland. They are idolaters and have images great store, which they wear about them and in their boats, which we suppose they worship. They are witches, and have many kinds of enchantments, which they often used but to small purpose, thanks be to God.

Being among them at shore the fourth of July, one of them, making a long oration, began to kindle a fire in this manner: he took a piece of board wherein was a hole half through; into that hole he puts the end of a round stick like unto a bedstaff, wetting the end thereof in train, and in fashion of a turner with a piece of leather by his violent motion doth very speedily produce fire. Which done, with turves he made a fire into which, with many words and strange gestures, he put divers things, which we supposed to be a sacrifice. Myself and divers of my company standing by, they were desirous to have me go into the smoke; I willed them likewise to stand in the smoke, which they by no means would do. I then took one of them and thrust him into the smoke, and willed one of my company to tread out the fire and to spurn it into the sea, which was done to show them that we did contemn their sorcery. These people are very simple in all their conversation, but marvellous thievish, especially for iron, which they have in great account. They began through our lenity to show their vile nature: they began to cut our cables, they cut away the *Moonlight*'s boat from her stern, they cut our cloth where it lay to air though we did carefully look unto it, they stole our oars, a caliver, a boar-spear, a sword, with divers other things. Whereat the company and masters being grieved, for our better security desired me to dissolve this new friendship and to leave the company of these thievish miscreants. Whereupon there was a caliver shot among them, and immediately upon the same a falcon, which strange noise did sore amaze them, so that with speed they departed. Notwithstanding, their simplicity is such that within ten hours after they came again to us to entreat peace; which being promised, we again fell into a great league. They brought us sealskins and salmon peal, but seeing iron they could in no wise forbear stealing. Which when I perceived, it did but minister unto me an occasion of laughter to see their simplicity, and I willed that in no case they should be any more hardly used, but that our own company should be the more vigilant to keep their things, supposing it to be very hard in so short time to make them know their evils.

They eat all their meat raw, they live most upon fish, they drink salt water, and eat grass and ice with delight. They are never out of the water, but live in the nature of fishes, save only when dead sleep taketh them, and then under a warm rock laying his boat upon the land he lieth down to sleep. Their weapons are all darts, but some of them have bow and arrows and slings. They make nets to take their fish of the fin of a whale. They do all things very artificially; and it should seem that these simple thievish islanders have war with those of the main, for many of them are sore wounded, which wounds they received upon the mainland, as by signs they gave us to understand. We had among them copper ore, black copper, and red copper. They pronounce their language very hollow and deep in the throat. These words following we learnt from them:

Kesinyoh, eat some	Paaotyck, an oar
Madlycoyte, music	Asanock, a dart
Aginyoh, go fetch	Sawygmeg, a knife
Yliaoute, I mean no harm	Uderah, a nose
Ponameg, a boat	Aoh, iron
Blete, an eye	Cocah, go to him
Unuicke, give it	Aba, fallen down
Tuckloak, a stag or eland	Icune, come hither
Panygmah, a needle	Awennye, yonder
Aob, the sea	Nugo, no
Mysacoah, wash it	Tucktodo, a fog
Lethicksaneg, a sealskin	Lechiksah, a skin
Canyglow, kiss me	Sugnacoon, a coat
Ugnera, my son	Gounah, come down
Acu, shot	Sasobneg, a bracelet
Conah, leap	Ugnake, a tongue
Maatuke, a fish	Ataneg, a seal
Sambah, below	Macuah, a beard
Maconmeg, will you have this?	Pignagogah, a thread
	Quoysah, give it to me

The 7th of July, being very desirous to search the habitation of this country, I went myself with our new pinnace into the body of the land, thinking it to be a firm continent; and passing up a very large river, a great flaw of wind took me, whereby we were constrained to seek succour for that night; which being had, I landed with the most part of my company and went to the top of a high mountain, hoping from thence to see into the country. But the mountains were so many and so mighty as that my purpose prevailed not. Whereupon I again returned to my pinnace, and willing divers of my company to gather mussels for my supper, whereof in this place there was great store, myself having espied a very strange sight, especially to me that never before saw the like: which was a mighty whirlwind taking up the water in very great quantity, furiously mounting it into the air, which whirlwind was not for a puff or blast, but continual for the space of three hours with very little intermission; which sith it was in the course that I should pass, we were constrained to take up our lodging under the rocks.

The next morning, the storm being broken up, we went forward in our attempt and sailed into a mighty great river directly into the body of the land, and in brief found it to be no firm land but huge, waste, and desert isles with mighty sounds and inlets passing between sea and sea. Whereupon we returned towards our ships, and landing to stop a flood we found the burial of these miscreants. We found of their fish in bags, plaice, and capelin dried, of which we took only one bag and departed.

The ninth of this month we came to our ships, where we found the people desirous, in their fashion, of friendship and barter. Our mariners complained heavily against the people, and said that my lenity and friendly using of them gave them stomach to mischief: "For they have stolen an anchor from us, they have cut our cable very dangerously, they have cut our boats from our stern, and now, since your departure, with slings they spare us not with stones of half a pound weight; and will you still endure these injuries? It is a shame to bear them." I desired them to be content, and said I doubted not but all should be well. The 10th of this month I went to the shore, the people following me in their canoes. I tolled them on shore, and used them with much courtesy, and then departed aboard, they following me and my company. I gave some of them bracelets, and caused seven or eight of them to come aboard, which they did willingly, and some of them went into the top of the ship; and thus courteously using them I let them depart. The sun was no sooner down but they began to practise their devilish nature, and with slings threw stones very fiercely into the *Moonlight*, and struck one of her men, then boatswain, that he overthrew withal. Whereat being moved, I changed my courtesy and grew to hatred. Myself in my own boat, well manned with shot, and the bark's boat likewise pursued them and gave them divers shot, but to small purpose by reason of their swift rowing; so smally content we returned.

The 11th of this month there came five of them to make a new truce. The Master of the admiral came to me to show me of their coming, and desired to have them taken and kept as prisoners until we had his anchor again; but when he saw that the chief ringleader and master of mischief was one of the five, he then was vehement to execute his purpose. So it was determined to take him. He came crying "Yliaout", and striking his breast offered a pair of gloves to sell. The Master offered him a knife for them, so two of them came to us; the one was not touched, but the other was soon captive among us. Then we pointed to him and his fellows for our anchor, which being had we made signs that he should be set at liberty. Within one hour after he came aboard the wind came fair, whereupon we weighed and set sail, and so brought the fellow with us. One of his fellows, still following our ship close aboard, talked with him and made a kind of lamentation, we still using him well with "Yliaout", which was the common course of courtesy. At length this fellow aboard us spoke four or five words unto the other and clapped his two hands upon his face, whereupon the other, doing the like, departed as we suppose with heavy cheer. We judged the covering of his face with his hands and bowing of his body down signified his death. At length he became a pleasant companion among us. I gave him a new suit of frieze after the English fashion, because I saw he could not endure the cold, of which he was very joyful. He trimmed up his darts, and all his fishing tools, and would make oakum and set his hand to a rope's end upon occasion. He lived with the dry capelin that I took when I was searching in the pinnace, and did eat dry Newland fish.

All this while, God be thanked, our people were in very good health, only one young man excepted, who died at sea the fourteenth of this month, and the fifteenth, according to the order of the sea, with praise given to God by service, was cast overboard.

The 17th of this month, being in the latitude of 63 degrees 8 minutes, we fell upon a most mighty and strange quantity of ice in one entire mass, so big as that we knew not the limits thereof, and being withal so very high, in form of a land with bays and capes and like high cliff-land, as that we supposed it to be land and therefore sent our pinnace off to discover it. But at her return we were certainly informed that it was only ice, which bred great admiration to us all considering the huge quantity thereof, incredible to be reported in truth as it was, and therefore I omit to speak any further thereof. This only I think, that the like before was never seen. And in this place we had very stickle and strong currents. We coasted this mighty mass of ice until the 30th of July, finding it a mighty bar to our purpose. The air in this time was so contagious and the sea so pestered with ice as that all hope was banished of proceeding. For the 24th of July all our shrouds, ropes, and sails were so frozen and compassed with ice, only by a gross fog, as seemed to me more than strange sith the last year I found this sea free and navigable without impediments.

Our men through this extremity began to grow sick and feeble, and withal hopeless of good success; whereupon very orderly, with good discretion, they entreated me to regard the state of this business, and withal advised me that in conscience I ought to regard the safety of my own life with the preservation of theirs, and that I should not through my overboldness leave their widows and fatherless children to give me bitter curses. This matter in conscience did greatly move me to regard their estates; yet considering the excellency of the business if it might be attained, the great hope of certainty by the last year's discovery, and that there was yet a third way not put in practice, I thought it would grow to my great disgrace if this action by my negligence should grow into discredit. Whereupon seeking help from God, the fountain of all mercies, it pleased His Divine Majesty to move my heart to prosecute that which I hope shall be to His glory and to the contentation of every Christian mind. Whereupon falling into consideration that the *Mermaid*, albeit a very strong and sufficient ship, yet by reason of her burden was not so convenient and nimble as a smaller bark, especially in such desperate hazards, further having in account her great charge to the adventurers, being at 100 pounds the month, and that in doubtful service; all the premises considered, with divers other things, I determined to furnish the *Moonlight* with revictualling and sufficient men and to proceed in this action as God should direct me. Whereupon I altered our course from the ice and bore east-south-east to recover the next shore where this thing might be performed. So, with favourable wind, it pleased God that the first of August we discovered the land in latitude 66 degrees 33 minutes and in longitude from the meridian of London 70 degrees, void of trouble without snow and ice.

The second of August we harboured ourselves in a very excellent good road, where with all speed we graved the *Moonlight* and revictualled her. We searched this country with our pinnace while the bark was trimming, which William Easton did. He found all this land to be only islands, with a sea on the east, a sea on the west, and a sea on the north. In this place we found it very hot, and we were very much troubled with a fly which is called mosquito, for they did sting grievously. The people of this place at our first coming in caught a seal, and with bladders fast tied to him sent him unto us with the flood so as he came right with our ships, which we took as a friendly present from them.

The fifth of August I went with the two Masters and others to the top of a hill, and by the way William Easton espied three canoes lying under a rock, and went unto them. There were in them skins, darts, with divers superstitious toys, whereof we diminished nothing, but left upon every boat a silk point, a bullet of lead, and a pin. The next day, being the sixth of August, the people came unto us without fear, and did barter with us for skins as the other people did. They differ not from the other, neither in their canoes nor apparel, yet is their pronunciation more plain than the others' and nothing hollow in the throat. Our savage aboard us kept himself close, and made show that he would fain have another companion. Thus being provided I departed from this land the twelfth of August at six of the clock in the morning, where I left the *Mermaid* at an anchor.

The fourteenth, sailing west about fifty leagues, we discovered land being in latitude 66 degrees 19 minutes; this land is 70 leagues from the other from which we came. This fourteenth day at nine o'clock at night till three o'clock in the morning we anchored by an island of ice twelve leagues off the shore, being moored to the ice. The fifteenth day at three o'clock in the morning we departed from this land to the south, and the eighteenth of August we discovered land north-west from us in the morning, being a very fair promontory in latitude 65 degrees, having no land on the south. Here we had great hope of a through passage.

This day at three o'clock in the afternoon we again discovered land south-west and by south from us, where at night we were becalmed. The nineteenth of this month at noon, by observation, we were in 64 degrees 20 minutes. From the eighteenth day at noon unto the nineteenth at noon by precise ordinary care we had sailed 15 leagues south and by west, yet by art and more exact observation we found our course to be south-west, so that we plainly perceived a great current striking to the west.

This land is nothing in sight but isles, which increaseth our hope. This nineteenth of August at six o'clock in the afternoon it began to snow and so continued all night with foul weather and much wind, so that we were constrained to lie at hull all night five leagues off the shore. In the morning, being the twentieth of August, the fog and storm breaking up, we bore in with the land, and at nine o'clock in the morning we anchored in a very fair and safe road and locked for all weathers. At ten of the clock I went on shore to the top of a very high hill, where I perceived that this land was islands. At four of the clock in the afternoon we weighed anchor, having a fair north-north-east wind with very fair weather. At six of the clock we were clear without the land, and so shaped our course to the south to discover the coast whereby the passage may be through God's mercy found.

We coasted this land till the eight and twentieth of August, finding it still to continue towards the south from the latitude of 67 to 57 degrees. We found marvellous great store of birds, gulls and mews, incredible to be reported; whereupon, being calm weather, we lay one glass upon the lee to prove for fish, in which space we caught 100 of cod, although we were but badly provided for fishing, not being our purpose. This eight and twentieth, having great distrust of the weather, we arrived in a very fair harbour in the latitude of 56 degrees, and sailed 10 leagues into the same, being two leagues broad, with very fair woods on both sides. In this place we continued until the first of September, in which time we had two very great storms. I landed, and went six miles by guess into the country, and found that the woods were fir, pineapple, alder, yew, withy, and birch. Here we saw a black bear. This place yieldeth great store of birds, as pheasant, partridge, Barbary hen or the like, wild geese, ducks, blackbirds, jays, thrushes, with other kinds of small birds. Of the partridge and pheasant we killed great store with bow and arrows. In this place at the harbour mouth we found great store of cod.

The first of September at ten o'clock we set sail and coasted the shore with very fair weather. The third day being calm, at noon we struck sail and let fall a kedge anchor, to prove whether we could take any fish, being in latitude 54 degrees 30 minutes, in which place we found great abundance of cod so that the hook was no sooner overboard but presently a fish was taken. It was the largest and the best-fed fish that ever I saw, and divers fishermen that were with me said that they never saw a more suavle or better school of fish in their lives, yet had they seen great abundance.

The fourth of September at five o'clock in the afternoon we anchored in a very good road among great store of isles, the country low land, pleasant, and very full of fair woods. To the north of this place eight leagues we had a perfect hope of the passage, finding a mighty great sea passing between two lands west. The south land to our judgment being nothing but isles, we greatly desired to go into this sea but the wind was directly against us. We anchored in four fathom fine sand. In this place is fowl and fish mighty store.

The sixth of September, having a fair north-north-west wind, having trimmed our bark we purposed to depart, and sent five of our sailors, young men, ashore to an island to fetch certain fish which we purposed to weather, and therefore left it all night covered upon the isle. The brutish people of this country lay secretly lurking in the wood, and upon the sudden assaulted our men; which when we perceived we presently let slip our cables upon the hawse and under our foresail bore into the shore, and with all expedition discharged a double musket upon them twice, at the noise whereof they fled. Notwithstanding, to our very great grief, two of our men were slain with their arrows and two grievously wounded, of whom at this present we stand in very great doubt. Only one escaped by swimming, with an arrow shot through his arm. These wicked miscreants never offered parley or speech, but presently executed their cursed fury.

This present evening it pleased God further to increase our sorrows with a mighty tempestuous storm, the wind being north-north-east, which lasted unto the tenth of this month very extreme. We unrigged our ship, and purposed to cut down our masts, the cable of our sheet-anchor broke, so that we only expected to be driven on shore among these cannibals for their prey. Yet in this deep distress the mighty mercy of God, when hope was past, gave us succour, and sent us a fair lee so as we recovered our anchor again and new-moored our ship; where we saw that God manifestly delivered us, for the strands of one of our old cables were broken and we only rode by an old junk. Thus being freshly moored, a new storm arose, the wind being west-north-west, very forcible, which lasted unto the tenth day at night.

The eleventh day with a fair west-north-west wind we departed with trust in God's mercy, shaping our course for England, and arrived in the west country in the beginning of October.

.   .   .   .   .

Master Davis, being arrived, wrote his letter to Master William Sanderson of London concerning his voyage, as followeth:

Sir,
The *Sunshine* came into Dartmouth the fourth of this month. She hath been at Iceland and from thence to Greenland, and so to Estotiland, from thence to Desolation, and to our Merchants', where she made trade with the people, staying in the country twenty days. They have brought home five hundred sealskins and a hundred and forty half-skins and pieces of skins. I stand in great doubt of the pinnace, God be merciful unto the poor men, and preserve them if it be His blessed will.

I have now experience of much of the north-west part of the world, and have brought the passage to that likelihood as that I am assured it must be in one of four places or else not at all. And further I can assure you upon the peril of my life that this voyage may be performed without further charge, nay, with certain profit to the adventurers, if I may have but your favour in the action. I hope I shall find favour with you to see your card. I pray God it be so true as the card shall be which I will bring you; and I hope in God that your skill in navigation shall be gainful unto you, although at the first it hath not proved so.

And thus with my humble commendations I commit you to God, desiring no longer to live than I shall be yours most faithfully to command.

Exon, this fourteenth of October, 1586,
Yours to command
John Davis

The third voyage north-westward, made by Master John Davis, gentleman, as chief Captain and Pilot-general, for the discovery of a passage to the Isles of the Moluccas or the coast of China, in the year 1587. Written by Master John Janes.

May
The nineteenth of this present month about midnight we weighed our anchors, set sail, and departed from Dartmouth with two barks and a clincher, the one named the *Elizabeth* of London, the other the *Sunshine* of London, and the clincher called the *Helen* of London. Thus in God's name we set forwards, with the wind at north-east a good fresh gale. About 3 hours after our departure, the night being somewhat thick with darkness, we had lost the pinnace. The Captain, imagining that the men had run away with her, willed the master of the *Sunshine*

to stand to seawards and see if we could descry them, we bearing in with the shore for Plymouth. At length we descried her, bore with her, and demanded what the cause was; they answered that the tiller of their helm was burst. So, shaping our course west-south-west, we went forward, hoping that a hard beginning would make a good ending, yet some of us were doubtful of it, falling in reckoning that she was a clincher; nevertheless we put our trust in God.

The 21st we met with the *Red Lion* of London which came from the coast of Spain, which was afraid that we had been men of war; but we hailed them, and after a little conference we desired the Master to carry our letters for London directed to my uncle Sanderson, who promised us a safe delivery. And after we had heaved them a lead and a line whereunto we had made fast our letters, before they could get them into the ship they fell into the sea, and so all our labour and theirs was lost; notwithstanding, they promised to certify our departure at London, and so we departed, and the same day we had sight of Scilly. The 22nd the wind was at north-east by east with fair weather, and so the 23rd and 24th the like. The 25th we laid our ships on the lee for the *Sunshine*, who was a-rummaging for a leak. They had 500 strokes at the pump in a watch, the wind at north-west.

The 26th and 27th we had fair weather, but this 27th the pinnace's foremast was blown overboard. The 28th the *Elizabeth* towed the pinnace, which was so much bragged off by the owners before we came out of England, but at sea she was like a cart drawn with oxen. Sometimes we towed her because she could not sail for scant wind.

The 31st day our Captain asked if the pinnace were staunch. Pearson answered that she was as sound and staunch as a cup. This made us something glad when we saw she would brook the sea and was not leaky.

June

The first 6 days we had fair weather; after that for 5 days we had fog and rain, the wind being south. The 12th we had clear weather. The mariners in the *Sunshine* and the Master could not agree: the mariners would go on their voyage a-fishing, because the year began to waste; the Master would not depart till he had the company of the *Elizabeth*. Whereupon the Master told our Captain that he was afraid his men would shape some contrary course while he was asleep, and so he should lose us. At length, after much talk and many threatenings, they were content to bring us to the land which we looked for daily.

The 14th day we discovered land at five of the clock in the morning, being very great and high mountains, the tops of the hills being covered with snow. Here the wind was variable, sometimes north-east, east-north-east, and east by north; but we imagined ourselves to be 16 or 17 leagues off from the shore.

The 16th we came to an anchor about 4 or 5 of the clock after noon. The people came presently to us after the old manner, with crying "Yliaoute" and showing us seals' skins. The 17th we began to set up the pinnace that Pearson framed at Dartmouth, with the boards which he brought from London. The 18th Pearson and the carpenters of the ships began to set on the planks. The 19th, as we went about an island, were found black pumice stones, and salt kerned on the rocks, very white and glistering. This day also the master of the *Sunshine* took of the people a very strong lusty young fellow.

The 20th, about twc of the clock in the morning, the savages came to the island where our pinnace was built ready to be launched, and tore the two upper strakes and carried them away, only for the love of the iron in the boards. While they were about this practice we manned the *Elizabeth*'s boat to go ashore to them. Our men, being either afraid or amazed, were so long before they came to shore that our Captain willed them to stay, and made the Gunner give fire to a saker, and laid the piece level with the boat, which the savages had turned on the one side because we should not hurt them with our arrows, and made the boat their bulwark against the arrows which we shot at them. Our Gunner, having made all things ready, gave fire to the piece; and, fearing to hurt any of the people and regarding the owners' profit, thought belike he would save a saker's shot, doubting we should have occasion to fight with men-of-war, and so shot off the saker without a bullet. We, looking still when the savages that were hurt should run away without legs, at length we could perceive never a man hurt, but all having their legs could carry away their bodies. We had no sooner shot off the piece but the master of the *Sunshine* manned his boat and came rowing toward the island, the very sight of whom made each of them take that he had gotten and flee away as fast as they could to another island about two miles off, where they took the nails out of the timber and left the wood on the isle. When we came on shore, and saw how they had spoiled the boat, after much debating of the matter we agreed that the *Elizabeth* should have her to fish withal; whereupon she was presently carried aboard and stowed.

Now, after this trouble, being resolved to depart with the first wind, there fell out another matter worse than all the rest, and that was in this manner. John Churchyard, one whom our Captain had appointed as pilot in the pinnace, came to our Captain and Master Bruton and told them that the good ship, which we must all hazard our lives in, had three hundred strokes at one time as she rode in the harbour. This disquieted us all greatly, and many doubted to go in her. At length our Captain, by whom we were all to be governed, determined rather to end his life with credit than to return with infamy and disgrace, and so, being all agreed, we purposed to live and die together and committed ourselves to the ship. Now the 21st having brought all our things aboard, about 11 or 12 of the clock at night, we set sail and departed from those isles, which lie in 64 degrees of latitude, our ships being all now at sea and we shaping our course to go coasting the land to the northwards upon the eastern shore, which we called the shore of our Merchants because there we met with people which trafficked with us. But here we were not without doubt of our ship.

The 24th, being in 67 degrees and 40 minutes, we had great store of whales, and a kind of sea-bird which the mariners call *cortinous*. This day about six of the clock at night we espied two of the country people at sea, thinking at the first they had been two great seals until we saw their oars glistering with the sun. They came rowing towards us as fast as they could, and when they came within hearing they held up their oars and cried "Yliaoute", making many signs; and at last they came to us, giving us birds for bracelets, and of them I had a dart with a bone in it, or a piece of unicorn's horn as I did judge. This dart he made store of, but when he saw a knife he let it go, being more desirous of the knife than of his dart. These people continued rowing after our ship the space of 3 hours.

The 25th in the morning at 7 of the clock we descried 30 savages rowing after us, being by judgment 10 leagues off from the shore. They brought us salmon peal, birds, and capelin, and we gave them pins, needles, bracelets, nails, knives, bells, looking glasses, and other small trifles; and for a knife, a nail, or a bracelet, which they call *ponigmah*, they would sell their boat, coats, or anything they had, although they were far from the shore. We had but few skins of them, about 20; but they made signs to us that if we would go to the shore we should have much store of *chichsanege*. They stayed with us till 11 of the clock, at which time we went to prayer and they departed from us.

The 28th and 29th were foggy with clouds. The 30th day we took the height, and found ourselves in 72 degrees and 12 minutes of latitude both at noon and at night, the sun being 5 degrees above the horizon. At midnight the compass set to the variation of 28 degrees to the westward. Now having coasted the land, which we called London Coast, from the 21st of this present till the 30th, the sea open all to the westwards and northwards, the land on starboard side east from us, the wind shifted to the north; whereupon we left that shore, naming the same Hope Sanderson, and shaped our course west, and ran 40 leagues and better without the sight of any land.

July

The second of July we fell with a mighty bank of ice west from us, lying north and south, which bank we would gladly have doubled out to the northwards but the wind would not suffer us; so that we were fain to coast it to the southwards, hoping to double it out, that we might have run so far west till we had found land, or else to have been thoroughly resolved of our pretended purpose.

The 3rd we fell with the ice again, and putting off from it we sought to the northwards, but the wind crossed us. The 4th was foggy; so was the 5th, also with much wind at the north. The 6th, being very clear, we put our bark with oars through a gap in the ice, seeing the sea free on the west side as we thought, which falling out otherwise caused us to return after we had stayed there between the ice. The 7th and the 8th about midnight by God's help we recovered the open sea, the weather being fair and calm, and so was the 9th. The 10th we coasted the ice. The 11th was foggy, but calm.

The 12th we coasted again the ice, having the wind at north-north-west. The 13th, bearing off from the ice, we determined to go with the shore and come to an anchor, and to stay 5 or 6 days for the dissolving of the ice, hoping that the sea continually beating it, and the sun with the extreme force of heat which it had always shining upon it, would make a quick despatch, that we might have a further search upon the western shore. Now when we were come to the eastern coast, the water something deep and some of our company fearful withal, we durst not come to an anchor but bore off into the sea again. The poor people, seeing us go away again, came rowing after us into the sea, the waves being somewhat lofty. We trucked with them for a few skins and darts, and gave them beads, nails, pins, needles, and cards, they pointing to the shore as though they would show us some great friendship, but we, little regarding their courtesy, gave them the gentle farewell and so departed.

The 14th we had the wind at south. The 15th there was some fault either in the bark or the set of some current, for we were driven six points beyond our course west. The 16th we fell with the bank of ice west from us. The 17th and 18th were foggy. The 19th, at one o'clock after noon, we had sight of the land which we called Mount Raleigh, and at 12 of the clock at night we were thwart the straits which we discovered the first year. The 20th we traversed in the mouth of the strait, the wind being at west with fair and clear weather. The 21st and 22nd we coasted the northern coast of the straits. The 23rd, having sailed threescore leagues north-west into the straits, at two o'clock after noon we anchored among many isles in the bottom of the gulf, naming the same the Earl of Cumberland's Isles; where, riding at anchor, a whale passed by our ship and went west in among the isles. Here the compass set at 30 degrees westward variation. The 23rd we departed, shaping our course south-east to recover the sea. The 25th we were becalmed in the bottom of the gulf, the air being ·xtreme hot. Master Bruton and some of the mariners went on shore to course dogs, where they found many graves, and train spilt on the ground; the dogs being so fat that they were scant able to run.

The 26th we had a pretty storm, the wind being at south-east. The 27th and 28th were fair. The 29th we were clear out of the straits, having coasted the south shore, and this day at noon we were in 62 degrees of latitude. The 30th in the afternoon we coasted a bank of ice which lay on the shore, and passed by a great bank or inlet which lay between 63 and 62 degrees of latitude, which we called Lumley's Inlet. We had oftentimes, as we sailed along the coast, great ruts, the water as it were whirling and overfalling as it were the fall of some great water through a bridge.

The 31st, as we sailed by a headland which we named Warwick's Foreland, we fell into one of those overfalls with a fresh gale of wind; and bearing all our sails, we, looking upon an island of ice between us and the shore, had thought that our bark did make no way, which caused us to take marks on the shore. At length we perceived ourselves to go very fast, and the island of ice which we saw before was carried very forcibly with the set of the current faster than our ship went. This day and night we passed by a very great gulf, the water whirling and roaring as it were the meetings of tides.

August
The first of August, having coasted a bank of ice which was driven out at the mouth of this gulf, we fell with the southermost cape of the gulf, which we named Chidley's Cape, which lay in 61 degrees and 10 minutes of latitude. The 2nd and 3rd were calm and foggy; so were the 4th, 5th, and 6th. The 7th was fair and calm, so was the 8th, with a little gale in the morning. The 9th was fair, and we had a little gale at night. The 10th we had a frisking gale at west-north-west, the 11th fair. The 12th we saw five deer on the top of an island, called by us Darcy's Island; and we hoisted out our boat and went ashore to them, thinking to have killed some of them. But when we came on shore and had coursed them twice about the island, they took the sea and swam towards islands distant from that three leagues. When we perceived that they had taken the sea we gave them over, because our boat was so small that it could not carry us and row after them, they swam so fast; but one of them was as big as a good pretty cow, and very fat, their feet as big as ox feet. Here upon this island I killed with my piece a grey hare.

The 13th in the morning we saw three or four white bears, but durst not go on shore to them for lack of a good boat. This day we struck a rock, seeking for a harbour, and received a leak; and this day we were in 54 degrees of latitude. The 14th we stopped our leak, in a storm not very outrageous, at noon.

The 15th, being almost in 52 degrees of latitude and not finding our ships, nor (according to their promise) any kind of mark, token, or beacon, which we willed them to set up, and they protested to do so, upon every headland, island, or cape within twenty leagues every way off from their fishing place, which our Captain appointed to be between 54 and 55 degrees: this 15th, I say, we shaped our course homewards for England, having in our ship but little wood and half a hogshead of fresh water. Our men were very willing to depart, and no man more forward than Pearson, for he feared to be put out of his office of stewardship. But because every man was so willing to depart, we consented to return for our own country; and so we had the 16th fair weather, with the wind at south-west.

The 17th we met a ship at sea, and as far as we could judge it was a Biscayan. We thought she went a-fishing for whales, for in 52 degrees or thereabout we saw very many. The 18th was fair, with a good gale at west; the 19th fair also, with much wind at west and by south. And thus after much variable weather and change of winds we arrived the 15th of September in Dartmouth anno 1587, giving thanks to God for our safe arrival.

A letter of the said Master John Davis, written to Master Sanderson of London concerning his forewritten voyage.

Good Master Sanderson,

With God's great mercy I have made my safe return, in health, with all my company, and have sailed threescore leagues further than my determination at my departure. I have been in 73 degrees, finding the sea all open and forty leagues between land and land. The passage is most probable, the execution easy, as at my coming you shall fully know.

Yesterday the 15th of September I landed all weary; therefore I pray you pardon my shortness.

Sandridge, this 16th of September anno 1587,

Yours equal as my own, which by trial you shall best know,

John Davis

Part 5

THE CARIBBEAN, VIRGINIA, AND GUIANA

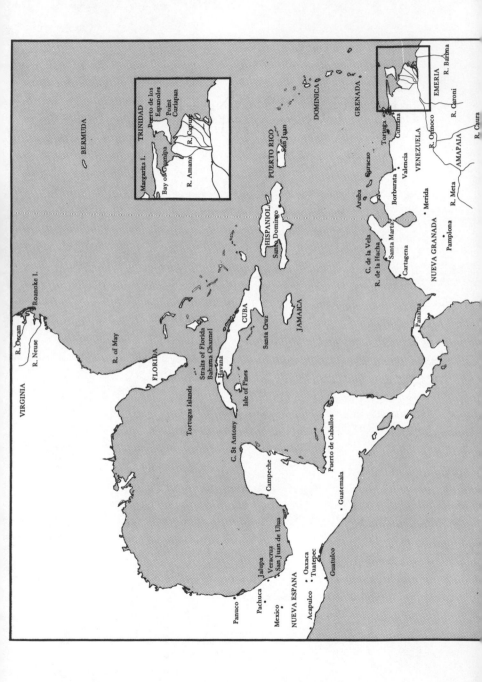

VIRGINIA

R. Decam

Roanoke I.

R. Neuse

BERMUDA

R. of May

FLORIDA

Tortugas Islands

Strait of Florida
Bahama Channel

Havana

Isle of Pines

CUBA

Santa Cruz

JAMAICA

C. St Antony

Campeche

Puerto de Caballos

Guatemala

Panuco

Pachuca

Jalupa

Mexico

Veracruz

San Juan de Ulua

Oaxaca

Tuatepec

NUEVA ESPANA

Acapulco

Guatulco

Guatemala

TRINIDAD

Margarita I.

Puerto de los
Espanoles

Point
Curiapan

Bay of Guanipa

R. Capuri

R. Amana

PUERTO RICO

San Juan

HISPANIOL

Santo Domingo

DOMINICA

GRENADA

Tortuga

Cumana

VENEZUELA

Curacao

Aruba

Valencia

Borburata

Merida

C. de la Vela

R. de la Hacha

Santa Marta

Cartagena

NUEVA GRANADA

Pamplona

Panama

EMERIA

R. Barima

R. Caroni

R. Orinoco

R. Caura

AMAPAIA

R. Meta

The Caribbean, where Columbus first encountered his new world, became its centre. The Spaniards rapidly colonised the larger islands of Haiti (Hispaniola) and Puerto Rico, and incidentally soon wiped out a large part of the native population by subjecting them to labours, especially in mining for gold, to which they were unaccustomed and unfitted. The Caribs of the outer islands and of the mainland were a fiercer people (the word "cannibal" derives, with reason, from their name) and proved almost impossible to subdue, but Spain nevertheless established garrison towns at strategic points around the Gulf of Mexico, in particular Cartagena and San Juan de Ulua. The Caribbean was the springboard for the conquest of Mexico and of Peru, and later the collecting-point from which the treasures of these dominions were shipped to Spain.

Other nations made tentative efforts to win a share of Spain's good fortune. The French, whose main holding was in Canada, prospected the American coast southward to Florida as early as 1524 (Verazzano), and in the sixties were the first to attempt a settlement in Virginia (Laudonnière). The Portuguese occupied Brazil which, as part of the eastern bulge of South America, lay on the Portuguese side of the meridian accepted by Spain as the boundary between the two empires.

The English at first sought the Caribbean for commercial reasons. They found that negro slaves, seized by force or procured by barter from West African chiefs, could be profitably sold as replacements, more durable than the originals, for the native labourers destroyed by the Spaniards. The trade was, however, frowned on by the authorities in Spain. Difficulties arose as early as John Hawkins' second voyage in 1564 (the account of the first is no more than a historian's precis of events and is not reprinted here); and matters reached a crisis during a third voyage when Hawkins came to blows with a Spanish fleet. The stories of two survivors of that engagement, Miles Philips and Job Hortop, are among the most extraordinary in Hakluyt.

The second reason for the English presence in the Caribbean was the hope of planting a colony there. In this Walter Raleigh was the great entrepreneur. His agents, Amadas and Barlow, reported in Virginia an earthly paradise from which their successors were soon expelled in consequence, it would seem, of a quite unnecessary tangling with the natives. Raleigh then turned to Guiana, with the rather different object of obtaining devious access to Peruvian gold; but this time he was chasing a will-of-the-wisp that eventually led him to the block.

After 1585 the English went to the Caribbean simply as privateers, to intercept and pillage the treasure-fleets in reprisal for Spanish seizure of English vessels and to "singe the beard" of a King who would shortly be a declared enemy of England.

The voyage made by Master John Hawkins, esquire and afterward knight, captain of the *Jesus of Lubeck*, one of Her Majesty's ships, and general of the *Salomon* and other two barks going in his company, to the coast of Guinea and the Indies of Nova Hispania, begun in A.D. 1564. (Written by John Sparke.)

MASTER John Hawkins, with the *Jesus of Lubeck*, a ship of 700, and the *Salomon*, a ship of 140, the *Tiger*, a bark of 50, and the *Swallow*, of 30 tons, being all well furnished with men to the number of one hundred threescore and ten, as also with ordnance and victuals requisite for such a voyage, departed out of Plymouth the 18th day of October in the year of our Lord 1564, with a prosperous wind; at which departing, in cutting the foresail, a marvellous misfortune happened to one of the officers in the ship, who by the pulley of the sheet was slain out of hand, being a sorrowful beginning to them all. And after their setting out ten leagues to sea, he met the same day with the *Minion*, a ship of the Queen's Majesty's, whereof was captain David Carlet, and also her consort, the *John Baptist*, of London, being bound to Guinea also, who hailed one another, after the custom of the sea, with certain pieces of ordnance for joy of their meeting; which done, the *Minion* departed from him to seek her other consort, the *Merlin*, of London, which was astern out of sight, leaving in Master Hawkins' company the *John Baptist*, her other consort.

Thus sailing forwards on their way with a prosperous wind until the 21st of the same month, at that time a great storm arose, the wind being at north-east about nine o'clock in the night, and continued so 23 hours together, in which storm Master Hawkins lost the company of the *John Baptist* aforesaid, and of his pinnace called the *Swallow*, his other 3 ships being sore beaten with a storm. The 23rd day, the *Swallow*, to his no small rejoicing, came to him again in the night, ten leagues to the northward of Cape Finisterre, he having put roomer, not being able to double the Cape, in that there rose a contrary wind at south-west. The 25th, the wind continuing contrary, he put into a place in Galicia called Ferrol, where he remained five days, and appointed all the masters of

ÆTATIS SVÆ LVIII
Anno Dñi 1591

his ships an order for the keeping of good company in this manner: The small ships to be always ahead and a-weather of the *Jesus*, and to speak twice a-day with the *Jesus* at least. If in the day the ensign be over the poop of the *Jesus*, or in the night two lights, then shall all the ships speak with her. If there be three lights aboard the *Jesus*, then doth she cast about. If the weather be extreme, that the small ships cannot keep company with the *Jesus*, then all to keep company with the *Salomon*, and forthwith to repair to the island of Tenerife, to the northward of the road of Sirroes. If any happen to any misfortune, then to show two lights, and to shoot off a piece of ordnance. If any lose company and come in sight again, to make three yaws and strike the mizen three times. Serve God daily, love one another, preserve your victuals, beware of fire, and keep good company.

The 26th day the *Minion* came in also where he was, for the rejoicing whereof he gave them certain pieces of ordnance, after the courtesy of the sea, for their welcome. But the *Minion*'s men had no mirth, because of their consort the *Merlin*, whom, at their departure from Master Hawkins upon the coast of England, they went to seek, and, having met with her, kept company two days together; and at last, by misfortune of fire (through the negligence of one of their gunners), the powder in the gunner's room was set on fire, which, with the first blast, struck out her poop, and therewithal lost three men, besides many sore burned (which escaped by the brigantine being at her stern), and immediately, to the great loss of the owners, and most horrible sight to the beholders, she sank before their eyes.

The 20th of the month Master Hawkins, with his consorts and company of the *Minion*, having now both the brigantines at her stern, weighed anchor, and set sail on their voyage, having a prosperous wind thereunto.

The fourth of November they had sight of the Island of Madeira, and, the sixth day, of Tenerife, which they thought to have been the Canary, in that they supposed themselves to have been to the eastward of Tenerife, and were not. But the *Minion*, being three or four leagues ahead of us, kept on her course to Tenerife, having better sight thereof than the other had, and by that means they parted company. For Master Hawkins and his company went more to the west, upon which course having sailed awhile, he espied another island, which he thought to be Tenerife; and being not able, by means of the fog upon the hills, to discern the same, nor yet to fetch it by night, went roomer until the morning, being the seventh of November, which as yet he could not discern, but sailed along the coast the space of two hours to perceive some certain mark of Tenerife, and found no likelihood thereof at all, accounting that to be, as it was indeed, the Isle of Palms; and so sailing forwards, espied another island called Gomera, and also Tenerife, with the which he made, and sailing all night, came in the morning the next day to the port of Adecia, where he found his pinnace which had departed from him the sixth of the month, being in the weather of him; and, espying the pike of Tenerife all a-high, bore thither. At his arrival, somewhat before he came to anchor, he hoisted out his ship's pinnace, rowing ashore, intending to have sent one with a letter to Peter de Ponte, one of the Governors of the island, who dwelt a league from the shore. But, as he pretended to have landed, suddenly there appeared upon the two points of the road men levelling of bases and arquebuses to them, with divers others, to the number of fourscore, with halberds, pikes, swords, and targets, which happened so contrary to his expectation that it did greatly amaze him; and the more because he was now in their danger, not knowing well how to avoid it without some mischief. Wherefore he determined to call to them for the better appeasing of the matter, declaring his name, and professing himself to be an especial friend to Peter de Ponte, and that he had sundry things for him which he greatly desired. And in the meantime, while he was thus talking with them, whereby he made them to hold their hands, he willed the mariners to row away, so that at last he got out of their danger. And then asking for Peter de Ponte, one of his sons, being Señor Nicolas de Ponte, came forth, whom he perceiving, desired to put his men aside, and he himself would leap ashore and commune with him, which they did. So that after communication had between them of sundry things, and of the fear they both had, Master Hawkins desired to have certain necessaries provided for him. In the mean space, while these things were providing, he trimmed the mainmast of the *Jesus*, which in the storm aforesaid was sprung. Here he sojourned 7 days, refreshing himself and his men. In which time Peter de Ponte, dwelling at Santa Cruz, a city 20 leagues off, came to him, and gave him as gentle entertainment as if he had been his own brother. To speak somewhat of these islands, being called in old time Insulæ Fortunatæ, by means of the flourishing thereof, the fruitfulness of them doth surely exceed far all other that I have heard of; for they make wine better than any in Spain, they have grapes of such bigness that they may be compared to damsons, and in taste inferior to none. For sugar, suckets, raisins of the sun, and many other fruits, abundance. For rosin and raw silk there is great store. They want neither corn, pullets, cattle, nor yet wild fowl. They have many camels also, which, being young, are eaten of the people for victuals, and, being old, they are used for the carriage of necessaries; whose property is as he is taught to kneel at the taking of his load and unlading again. His nature is to engender backward, contrary to other beasts; of understanding very good, but of shape very deformed, with a little belly, long misshapen legs, and feet very broad of flesh, without a hoof, all whole, saving the great toe, a back bearing up like a molehill, a large and thin neck, with a little head, with a bunch of hard flesh, which nature hath given him in his breast, to lean upon.

This beast liveth hardly, and is contented with straw and stubble, but of force strong, being well able to carry 5 hundredweight. In one of these islands, called Ferro, there is, by the report of the inhabitants, a certain tree that raineth continually, by the dropping whereof the inhabitants and cattle are satisfied with water, for other water have they none in all the island. And it raineth in such abundance that it were incredible unto a man to believe such a virtue to be in a tree; but it is known to be a divine matter and a thing ordained of God, at whose power therein we ought not to marvel, seeing He did by His providence, as we read in the Scriptures, when the children of Israel were going into the land of promise, feed them with manna from heaven for the space of 40 years. Of the trees aforesaid we saw in Guinea many, being of great height, dropping continually; but not so abundantly as the other, because the leaves are narrower, and are like the leaves of a pear-tree. About these islands are certain flitting islands, which have been oftentimes seen, and when men approached near them, they vanished. As the like hath been of these islands now known by the report of the inhabitants, which were not found of long time one after the other; and therefore it should seem he is not yet born to whom God hath appointed the finding of them. In this island of Tenerife there is a hill called The Pike, because it is piked, which is in height, by their reports, twenty leagues, having, both winter and summer, abundance of snow in the top of it. This Pike may be seen in a clear day fifty leagues off; but it showeth as though it were a black cloud a great height in the element. I have heard of none to be compared with this in height; but in the Indies I have seen many, and in my judgment not inferior to the Pike, and so the Spaniards write.

The 15th of November, at night, we departed from Tenerife, and the 20th of the same we had sight of ten caravels that were fishing at sea, with whom we would have spoken, but they, fearing us, fled into a place of Barbary, called Cape de las Barbas.

The twentieth the ship's pinnace, with two men in her, sailing by the ship, was overthrown by the oversight of them that went in her, the wind being so great that, before they were espied, and the ship had cast about for them, she was driven half a league to leeward of the pinnace, and had lost sight of her, so that there was small hope of recovery had not God's help and the Captain's diligence been, who, having well marked which way the pinnace was by the sun, appointed 24 of the lustiest rowers in the great boat to row to the windwards, and so recovered, contrary to all men's expectations, both the pinnace and the men sitting upon the keel of her.

The 25th he came to Cape Blanco, which is upon the coast of Africa, and a place where the Portugals do ride, that fish there in the month of November especially, and is a very good place of fishing for pargoes, mullet, and dog-fish. In this place the Portugals have no hold for their defence, but have rescue of the Barbarians, whom they entertain as their soldiers for the time of their being there and for their fishing upon that coast of Africa, paying a certain tribute to the King of the Moors. The people of that part of Africa are tawny, having long hair, without any apparel saving before their privy members. Their weapons in wars are bows and arrows.

The 26th we departed from St Avis Bay, within Cape Blanco, where we refreshed ourselves with fish and other necessaries; and the 29th we came to Cape Verde, which lieth in 14 degrees and a half. These people are all black, and are called negroes, without any apparel saving before their privities; of stature goodly men, and well liking by reason of their food, which passeth all other Guineans for kine, goats, pullets, rice, fruits, and fish. Here we took fishes with heads like conies, and teeth nothing varying, of a jolly thickness, but not past a foot long, and is not to be eaten without flaying or cutting off his head. To speak somewhat of the sundry sorts of these Guineans: the people of Cape Verde are called Leophares, and counted the goodliest men of all other, saving the Congoes, which do inhabit on this side the Cape de Buena Esperança. These Leophares have wars against the Jeloffes, which are borderers by them. Their weapons are bows and arrows, targets, and short daggers, darts also, but varying from other negroes'; for whereas the others use a long dart to fight with in their hands, they carry five or six small ones apiece, which they cast with. These men also are more civil than any other, because of their daily traffic with the Frenchmen, and are of nature very gentle and loving; for while we were there we took in a Frenchman, who was one of the 19 that, going to Brazil, in a bark of Dieppe, of 60 tons, and being a-seaboard of Cape Verde 200 leagues, the planks of their bark with a sea broke out upon them so suddenly, that much ado they had to save themselves in their boats. But, by God's providence, the wind being westerly, which is rarely seen there, they got to the shore, to the Isle Brava, and in great penury got to Cape Verde, where they remained six weeks, and had meat and drink of the same people. The said Frenchman having forsaken his fellows, which were three leagues off from the shore, and, wandering with the negroes to and fro, fortuned to come to the water's side; and, communing with certain of his countrymen which were in our ship, by their persuasions came away with us. But his entertainment amongst them was such that he desired it not; but, through the importunate request of his countrymen, consented at last. Here we stayed but one night and part of the day; for the 7th of December we came away, in that pretending to have taken negroes there perforce, the *Minion's* men gave them there to understand of our coming, and our pretence, wherefore they did avoid the snares we had laid for them.

The 8th of December we anchored by a small island called Alcatraça, wherein at our going ashore we found nothing but seabirds, as we call them gannets, but by the Portugals called *alcatrarses,* who for that cause gave the said island the same name. Herein half of our boats were laden with young and old fowl, who, not being used to the sight of men, flew so about us that we struck them down with poles. In this place the two ships riding, the two barks, with their boats, went into an island of the Sapis called La Formio, to see if they could take any of them, and there landed to the number of 80 in armour, and, espying certain, made to them; but they fled in such order into the woods, that it booted them not to follow. So, going on their way forward till they came to a river which they could not pass over, they espied on the other side two men, who with their bows and arrows shot terribly at them. Whereupon we discharged certain arquebuses to them again, but the ignorant people weighed it not, because they knew not the danger thereof; but used a marvellous crying in their fight, with leaping and turning their tails that it was most strange to see, and gave us great pleasure to behold them. At the last, one being hurt with an arquebus upon the thigh, looked upon his wound and wist not how it came, because he could not see the pellet. Here Master Hawkins perceiving no good to be done amongst them, because we could not find their towns, and also not knowing how to go into Rio Grande for want of a pilot, which was the very occasion of our coming thither; and finding so many shoals, feared with our great ships to go in, and therefore departed on our pretended way to the Idols.

The 10th of December we had a north-east wind, with rain and storm, which weather continuing two days together, was the occasion that the *Salomon* and *Tiger* lost our company. For whereas the *Jesus* and pinnace anchored at one of the islands called Sambula on the 12th day, the *Salomon* and *Tiger* came not thither till the 14th. In this island we stayed certain days, going every day on shore to take the inhabitants, with burning and spoiling their towns, who before were Sapis, and were conquered by the Samboses, inhabitants beyond Sierra Leone. These Samboses had inhabited there three years before our coming thither, and in so short space have so planted the ground that they had great plenty of mill, rice, roots, pumpkins, pullets, goats, of small fry dried; every house full of the country fruit planted by God's providence, as *palmito* trees, fruits like dates, and sundry other, in no place in all that country so abundantly, whereby they lived more deliciously than other. These inhabitants have divers of the Sapis which they took in the wars as their slaves, whom only they kept to till the ground, in that they neither have the knowledge thereof, nor yet will work themselves, of whom we took many in that place, but of the Samboses none at all, for they fled into the main. All the Samboses have white teeth as we have, far unlike to the Sapis which do inhabit about Rio Grande; for their teeth are all filed, which they do for a bravery, to set out themselves, and do jag their flesh, both legs, arms, and bodies, as workmanlike as a jerkinmaker with us pinketh a jerkin. These Sapis be more civil than the Samboses; for whereas the Samboses live most by the spoil of their enemies, both in taking their victuals and eating them also, the Sapis do not eat man's flesh, unless in the war they be driven by necessity thereunto, which they have not used but by the example of the Samboses, but live only with fruits and cattle, whereof they have great store. This plenty is the occasion that the Sapis desire not war, except they be thereunto provoked by the invasions of the Samboses, whereas the Samboses for want of food are enforced thereunto, and therefore are not wont only to take them that they kill, but also keep those that they take until such time as they want meat, and then they kill them. There is also another occasion that provoketh the Samboses to war against the Sapis, which is for covetousness of their riches. For whereas the Sapis have an order to bury their dead in certain places appointed for that purpose with their gold about them, the Samboses dig up the ground to have the same treasure. For the Samboses have not the like store of gold that the Sapis have. In this island of Sambula we found about fifty boats called *almades*, or canoes, which are made of one piece of wood, digged out like a trough, but of a good proportion, being about 8 yards long and one in breadth, having a beakhead and a stern very proportionably made, and on the outside artificially carved, and painted red and blue. They are able to carry twenty or thirty men; but they are about the coast able to carry three-score and upward. In these canoes they row standing upright, with an oar somewhat longer than a man, the end whereof is made about the breadth and length of a man's hand of the largest sort. They row very swift, and in some of them four rowers and one to steer make as much way as a pair of oars in the Thames of London.

Their towns are prettily divided with a main street at the entering in, that goeth through their town, and another overthwart street, which maketh their towns crossways. Their houses are built in a rank very orderly in the face of the street, and they are made round, like a dove-cot, with stakes set full of *palmito* leaves instead of a wall. They are not much more than a fathom large, and two of height, and thatched with *palmito* leaves very close, and other some with reed, and over the roof thereof, for the better garnishing of the same, there is a round bundle of reed, prettily contrived like a louvre. In the inner part they make a loft of sticks, whereupon they lay all their provision of victuals. A place they reserve at their entrance for the kitchen, and the place they lie in is divided with certain mats artificially made with the rind of *palmito* trees. Their bedsteads are of small staves laid along, and raised a foot from the ground, upon which is laid a mat, and another upon them when they list; for other covering they have none. In the middle of the town there is a house larger and higher than the other, but in form alike, adjoining unto the which there is a place made of four good stanchions of wood, and a round roof over it, the ground also raised round with clay a foot high, upon the which floor were strewed many fine mats. This is the Consultation-house, the like whereof is in all towns, as the Portugals affirm: in which place, when they sit in council, the king or captain sitteth in the midst, and the elders upon the floor by him (for they give reverence to their elders), and the common sort sit round about them. There they sit to examine matters of theft, which if a man be taken with, to steal but a Portugal cloth from another, he is sold to the Portugals for a slave. They consult, also, and take order what time they shall go to wars; and, as it is certainly reported by the Portugals, they take order in gathering of the fruits in the season of the year, and also of *palmito* wine, which is gathered by a hole cut in the top of a tree, and a gourd set for the receiving thereof, which falleth in by drops, and yieldeth fresh wine again within a month, and this divided part and portion-like to every man by the judgment of the captain and elders, every man holdeth himself contented. And this surely I judge to be a very good order; for otherwise, whereas scarcity of *palmito* is, every man would have the same, which might breed great strife. But of such things as every man doth plant for himself, the sower thereof reapeth it to his own use, so that nothing is common but that which is unset by man's hands. In their houses there is more common passage of lizards like evets, and other greater, of black and blue colour, of near a foot long, besides their tails, than there is with us of mice in great houses. The Sapis and Samboses also use in their wars bows, and arrows made of reeds, with heads of iron poisoned with the juice of a cucumber, whereof I had many in my hands. In their battles they have target-men, with broad wicker targets, and darts with heads at both ends of iron, the one in form of a two-edged sword, a foot and a half long, and at the other end, the iron long of the same length made to counterpoise it, that in casting it might fly level, rather than for any other purpose as I can judge. And when they espy the enemy, the captain, to cheer his men, crieth "Hungry," and they answer "Heygre," and with that every man placeth himself in order. For about every target-man three bowmen will cover themselves, and shoot as they see advantage. And when they give the onset, they make such terrible cries that they may be heard two miles off. For their belief, I can hear of none that they have, but in such as they themselves imagine to see in their dreams, and so worship the pictures, whereof we saw some like unto devils.

In this island aforesaid we sojourned unto the one and twentieth of December, where, having taken certain negroes and as much of their fruits, rice, and mill as we could well carry away (whereof there was such store that we might have laden one of our barks therewith), we departed. And at our departure, divers of our men being desirous to go on shore to fetch pumpkins, which, having proved, they found to be very good, certain of the *Tiger's* men went also. Amongst the which there was a carpenter, a young man, who, with his fellows, having fetched many and carried them down to their boats, as they were ready to depart, desired his fellow to tarry while he might go up to fetch a few which he had laid by for himself. Who, being more licorous than circumspect, went up without weapon, and, as he went up alone, possibly being marked of the negroes that were upon the trees, espying him what he did, perceiving him to be alone, and without weapon, dogged him. And finding him occupied in binding his pumpkins together, came behind him, overthrowing him, and straight cut his throat, as he afterwards was found by his fellows, who came to the place for him, and there found him naked.

The two and twentieth the Captain went into the river called Callousa, with the two barks, and the *John's* pinnace, and the *Salomon's* boat, leaving at anchor in the river's mouth the two ships, the river being twenty leagues in, where the Portugals rode. He came thither the five and twentieth, and despatched his business, and so returned with two caravels laden with negroes.

The 27th the Captain was advertised by the Portugals of a town of the negroes called Bymba, being in the way as they returned, where was not only great quantity of gold, but also that there were not above forty men and a hundred women and children in the town, so that if he would give the adventure upon the same, he might get a hundred slaves. With the which tidings he being glad, because the Portugals should not think him to be of so base a courage but that he durst give them that, and greater attempts; and being thereunto also the more provoked with the prosperous success he had in other islands adjacent, where he had put them all to flight and taken in one boat twenty together, determined to stay before the town three or four hours, to see what he could do; and thereupon prepared his men in armour and weapon together, to the number of forty men well appointed, having to their guides certain Portugals in a boat, who brought some of them to their death. We landing boat after boat, and divers of our men scattering themselves, contrary to the Captain's will, by one or two in a company, for the hope that they had to find gold in their houses, ransacking the same, in the meantime the negroes came upon them, and hurt many (being thus scattered), whereas if five or six had been together they had been able, as their companions did, to give the overthrow to 40 of them; and, being driven down to take their boats, were followed so hardly by a rout of negroes, who by that took courage to pursue them to their boats, that not only some of them, but others standing on shore, not looking for any such matter, by means that the negroes did flee at the first, and our company remained in the town, were suddenly so set upon that some with great hurt recovered their boats; other some, not able to recover the same, took the water, and perished by means of the ooze. While this was doing, the Captain, who, with a dozen men, went through the town, returned, finding 200 negroes at the water's side shooting at them in the boats, and cutting them in pieces which were drowned in the water; at whose coming they ran all away. So he entered his boats, and, before he could put off from the shore, they returned again, and shot very fiercely and hurt divers of them. Thus we returned back somewhat discomforted, although the Captain in a singular wise manner carried himself, with countenance very cheerful outwardly, as though he did little weigh the death of his men, nor yet the great hurt of the rest, although his heart inwardly was broken in pieces for it; done to this end, that the Portugals, being with him, should not presume to resist against him, nor take occasion to put him to further displeasure or hindrance for the death of our men; having gotten by our going ten negroes and lost seven of our best men, whereof Master Field, Captain of the *Salomon*, was one, and we had 27 of our men hurt. In the same hour while this was doing there happened at the same instant a marvellous miracle to them in the ships, who rode ten leagues to seaward, by many sharks, or *tuburones,* who came about the ships; among which one was taken by the *Jesus* and four by the *Salomon*, and one, very sore hurt, escaped. And so it fell out of our men, whereof one of the *Jesus'* men and four of the *Salomon*'s were killed, and the fifth, having twenty wounds, was rescued, and escaped with much ado.

The 28th they came to their ships, the *Jesus* and the *Salomon*, and the 30th departed from thence to Tanguarim.

The first of January the two barks and both the boats forsook the ships and went into a river called the Casserroes, and the 6th, having despatched their business, the two barks returned and came to Tanguarim, where the two ships were at anchor. Not two days after the coming of the two ships thither, they put their water-cask ashore, and filled it with water to season the same, thinking to have filled it with fresh water afterwards; and while their men were some on shore and some at their boats, the negroes set upon them in the boats and hurt divers of them, and came to the casks and cut off the hoops of twelve butts, which lost us 4 or 5 days' time, besides great want we had of the same. Sojourning at Tanguarim, the *Swallow* went up the river about her traffic, where they saw great towns of the negroes, and canoes that had threescore men in apiece. There they understood by the Portugals of a great battle between them of Sierra Leone side and them of Tanguarim. They of Sierra Leone had prepared three hundred canoes to invade the other. The time was appointed not past six days after our departure from thence, which we would have seen, to the intent we might have taken some of them, had it not been for the death and sickness of our men, which came by the contagiousness of the place, which made us to make haste away.

The 18th of January, at night, we departed from Tanguarim, being bound for the West Indies, before which departure certain of the *Salomon*'s men went on shore to fill water in the night. And as they came on shore with their boat, being ready to leap on land, one of them espied a negro in a white coat, standing upon a rock, being ready to have received them when they came on shore, having in sight of his fellows also eight or nine, some in one place leaping out and some in another, but they hid themselves straight again. Whereupon our men, doubting they had been a great company, and sought to have taken them at more advantage, as God would, departed to their ships, not thinking there had been such a mischief pretended toward them as then was indeed. Which the next day we understood of a Portugal that came down to us, who had trafficked with the negroes, by whom he understood that the King of Sierra Leone had made all the power he could to take some of us, partly for the desire he had to see what kind of people we were that had spoiled his people at the Idols, whereof he had news before our coming, and, as I judge also, upon other occasions provoked by the *tangomangoes*; but sure we were that the army was come down, by means that in the evening we saw such a monstrous fire, made by the watering place, that before was not seen, which fire is the only mark for the *tangomangoes* to know where their army is always. If these men had come down in the evening, they had done us great displeasure, for that we were on shore filling water; but God, who worketh all things for the best, would not have it so, and by Him we escaped without danger. His name be praised for it.

The 29th of this same month we departed with all our ships from Sierra Leone towards the West Indies, and for the space of eighteen days we were becalmed, having now and then contrary winds and some tornados amongst the same calm, which happened to us very ill, being but reasonably watered for so great a company of negroes and ourselves, which pinched us all, and that which was worst, put us in such fear that many never thought to have reached to the Indies without great death of negroes and of themselves; but the Almighty God, who never suffereth His elect to perish, sent us, the sixteenth of February, the ordinary breeze, which is the north-east wind, which never left us till we came to an island of the cannibals called Dominica, where we arrived the 9th of March, upon a Saturday. And because it was the most desolate place in all the island we could see no cannibals, but some of their houses where they dwelled, and, as it should seem, forsook the place for want of fresh water; for we could find none there but rain-water and such as fell from the hills and remained as a puddle in the dale, whereof we filled for our negroes. The cannibals of that island, and also others adjacent, are the most desperate warriors that are in the Indies by the Spaniards' report, who are never able to conquer them; and they are molested by them not a little when they are driven to water there in any of those islands. Of very late, not two months past, in the said island, a caravel, being driven to water, was in the night set upon by the inhabitants, who cut their cable in the hawse, whereby they were driven ashore, and so taken by them and eaten. The *Green Dragon* of Newhaven, whereof was captain one Bontemps, in March also, came to one of those islands called Grenada, and, being driven to water, could not do the same for the cannibals, who fought with him very desperately two days. For our part also, if we had not lighted upon the desertest place in all that island, we could not have missed but should have been greatly troubled by them, by all the Spaniards' reports, who make them devils in respect of men.

The 10th day at night we departed from thence, and the fifteenth had sight of nine islands called the Testigos; and the sixteenth of an island called Margarita, where we were entertained by the *alcalde*, and had both beeves and sheep given to us for the refreshing of our men. But the Governor of the island would neither come to speak with our Captain, neither yet give him any licence to traffic; and, to displease us the more, whereas we had hired a pilot to have gone with us, they would not only not suffer him to go with us, but also sent word by a caravel out of hand to Santo Domingo to the Viceroy, who doth represent the King's person, of our arrival in those parts, which had like to have turned us to great displeasure by the means that the same Viceroy did send word to Cape de la Vela, and to other places along the coast, commanding them that, by virtue of his authority and by the obedience that they owe to their Prince, no man should traffic with us, but should resist us with all the force they could. In this island, notwithstanding that we were not within four leagues of the town, yet were they so afraid that not only the Governor himself, but also all the inhabitants, forsook their town, assembling all the Indians to them, and fled into the mountains, as we were partly certified, and also saw the experience ourselves, by some of the Indians coming to see us, who, by three Spaniards on horseback passing hard by us, went unto the Indians, having every one of them their bows and arrows, procuring them away who before were conversant with us.

Here, perceiving no traffic to be had with them, nor yet water for the refreshing of our men, we were driven to depart the twentieth day, and the two and twentieth we came to a place in the main called Cumana, Cumana, whither the Captain going in his pinnace, spoke with certain Spaniards, of whom he demanded traffic; but they made him answer they were but soldiers newly come thither, and were not able to buy one negro. Whereupon he asked for a watering place, and they pointed him a place two leagues off called Santa Fé, where we found marvellously goodly watering, and commodious for the taking in thereof; for that the fresh water came into the sea, and so our ships had aboard the shore twenty fathom water. Near about this place inhabited certain

Indians, who the next day after we came thither came down to us, presenting mill and cakes of bread, which they had made of a kind of corn called maize, in bigness of a pease, the ear whereof is much like to a teasel, but a span in length, having thereon a number of grains. Also they brought down to us hens, potatoes, and pines, which we bought for beads, pewter whistles, glasses, knives, and other trifles.

These potatoes be the most delicate roots that may be eaten, and do far exceed our parsnips or carrots. Their pines be of the bigness of two fists, the outside whereof is of the making of a pine-apple, but it is soft like the rind of a cucumber, and the inside eateth like an apple; but it is more delicious than any sweet apple sugared. These Indians being of colour tawny like an olive, having every one of them, both men and women, hair all black, and no other colour, the women wearing the same hanging down to their shoulders, and the men rounded, and without beards, neither men nor women suffering any hair to grow in any part of their body, but daily pull it off as it groweth. They go all naked, the men covering no part of their body but their yard, upon the which they wear a gourd or piece of cane made fast with a thread about their loins, leaving the other parts of their members uncovered, whereof they take no shame. The women also are uncovered, saving with a cloth which they wear a hand-breadth, wherewith they cover their privities both before and behind.

These people be very small feeders; for travelling they carry but two small bottles of gourds, wherein they put in one the juice of sorrel, whereof they have great store, and in the other flour of their maize, which, being moist, they eat, taking sometime of the other. These men carry every man his bow and arrows, whereof some arrows are poisoned for wars, which they keep in a cane together, which cane is of the bigness of a man's arm, other some with broad heads of iron, wherewith they strike fish in the water; the experience whereof we saw not once or twice, but daily for the time we tarried there; for they are so good archers that the Spaniards for fear thereof arm themselves and their horses with quilted canvas of two inches thick, and leave no place of their body open to their enemies, saving their eyes, which they may not hide, and yet oftentimes are they hit in that so small a scantling. Their poison is of such a force that a man being stricken therewith dieth within four-and-twenty hours, as the Spaniards do affirm; and, in my judgment, it is like there can be no stronger poison as they make it, using thereunto apples which are very fair and red of colour, but are a strong poison, with the which, together with venomous bats, vipers, adders, and other serpents, they make a medley, and therewith anoint the same. The Indian women delight not when they are young in bearing of children, because it maketh them have hanging breasts which they account to be great deforming in them; and upon that occasion, while they be young, they destroy their seed, saying that it is fittest for old women. Moreover, when they are delivered of child they go straight to wash themselves, without making any further ceremony for it, not lying in bed as our women do. The beds which they have are made of Gossopine cotton, and wrought artificially of divers colours, which they carry about with them when they travel, and making the same fast to two trees, lie therein, they and their women. The people be surely gentle and tractable, and such as desire to live peaceably, or else had it been impossible for the Spaniards to have conquered them as they did, and the more to live now peaceably, they being so many in number and the Spaniards so few.

From hence we departed the eight and twenty, and the next day we passed between the mainland and the island called Tortuga, a very low island, in the year of our Lord God one thousand five hundred and sixty-five aforesaid, and sailed along the coast until the first of April, at which time the Captain sailed along in the *Jesus'* pinnace to discern the coast, and saw many Caribs on shore, and some also in their canoes, which made tokens unto him of friendship, and showed him gold, meaning thereby that they would traffic their wares. Whereupon he stayed to see the manners of them; and so for two or three trifles they gave such things as they had about them, and departed. But the Caribs were very importunate to have them come on shore, which, if it had not been for want of wares to traffic with them, he would not have denied them, because the Indians which we saw before were very gentle people, and such as do no man hurt. But, as God would have it, he wanted that thing, which if he had had would have been his confusion. For these were no such kind of people as we took them to be, but devilish a thousand parts, and are eaters and devourers of any man they can catch, as it was afterwards declared unto us at Borburata, by a caravel coming out of Spain with certain soldiers, and a captain-general sent by the King for those eastward parts of the Indians, who, sailing along in his pinnace, as our Captain did to descry the coast, was by the Caribs called ashore with sundry tokens made to him of friendship, and gold showed as though they desired traffic, with the which the Spaniard being moved, suspecting no deceit at all, went ashore amongst them. Who was no sooner ashore but, with four or five more, was taken. The rest of his company, being invaded by them, saved themselves by flight; but they that were taken paid their ransom with their lives, and were presently eaten. And this is their practice, to toll with their gold the ignorant to their snares. They are bloodsuckers both of Spaniards, Indians, and all that light in their laps, not sparing their own countrymen if they can conveniently come by them. Their policy in fight with the Spaniards is marvellous; for they choose for their refuge the mountains and woods, where the Spaniards with their horses cannot follow them. And if they fortune to be met in the plain, where one horseman may overrun 100 of them, they have a device of late practised by them to pitch stakes of wood in the ground and also small iron pikes to mischief their horses, wherein they show themselves politic warriors. They have more abundance of gold than all the Spaniards have, and live upon the mountains; where the mines are in such number that the Spaniards have much ado to get any of them from them; and yet sometimes by assembling a great number of them, which happeneth once in two years, they get a piece from them, which afterwards they keep sure enough.

Thus having escaped the danger of them, we kept our course along the coast, and came the third of April to a town called Borburata, where his ships came to an anchor, and he himself went ashore to speak with the Spaniards, to whom he declared himself to be an Englishman, and come thither to trade with them by the way of merchandise, and therefore required licence for the same. Unto whom they made answer that they were forbidden by the King to traffic with any foreign nation, upon penalty to forfeit their goods; therefore they desired him not to molest them any further, but to depart as he came, for other comfort he might not look for at their hands, because they were subjects and might not go beyond the law. But he replied that his necessity was such as he might not do so; for being in one of the Queen's Armadas of England, and having many soldiers in them, he had need both of some refreshing for them, and of victuals, and of money also, without the which he could not depart; and with much other talk persuaded them not to fear any dishonest part of his behalf towards them, for neither would he commit any such thing to the dishonour of his prince, nor yet for his honest reputation and estimation, unless he were too rigorously dealt withal, which he hoped not to find at their hands, in that it should as well redound to their profit as his own; and also he thought they might do it without danger, because their princes were in amity one with another; and for our parts we had free traffic in Spain and Flanders, which are in his dominions; and, therefore, he knew no reason why he should not have the like in all his dominions. To the which the Spaniards made answer that it lay not in them to give any licence, for that they had a governor to whom the government of those parts was committed; but if they would stay ten days, they would send to their governor, who was threescore leagues off, and would return answer, within the space appointed, of his mind.

In the meantime they were contented he should bring his ships into harbour, and there they would deliver him any victuals he would require. Whereupon the fourth day we went in, where being one day, and receiving all things according to promise, the Captain advised himself that to remain there ten days idle, spending victuals and men's wages, and perhaps in the end receive no good answer from the governor, it were mere folly; and therefore determined to make request to have licence for the sale of certain lean and sick negroes which he had in his ship like to die upon his hands if he kept them ten days, having little or no refreshing for them, whereas other men having them they would be recovered well enough. And this request he was forced to make, because he had not otherwise wherewith to pay for victuals and for necessaries which he should take. Which request being put in writing and presented, the officers and town-dwellers assembled together, and finding his request so reasonable, granted him licence for thirty negroes, which afterwards they caused the officers to view, to the intent that they should grant to nothing but that were very reasonable, for fear of answering thereunto afterwards. This being passed, our Captain, according to their licence, thought to have made sale, but the day passed and none came to buy, who before made show that they had great need of them, and therefore wist not what to surmise of them, whether they went about to prolong the time of the governor's answer, because they would keep themselves blameless, or for any other policy, he knew not; and for that purpose sent them word, marvelling what the matter was that none came to buy them. They answered because they had granted licence only to the poor to buy those negroes of small price, and their money was not so ready as other men's of more wealth. More than that, as soon as ever they saw the ships, they conveyed away their money by their wives, that went into the mountains for fear, and were not yet returned, and yet asked two days to seek their wives and fetch their money. Notwithstanding, the next day divers of them came to cheapen, but could not agree of price, because they thought the price too high. Whereupon the Captain, perceiving they went about to bring down the price, and meant to buy; and would not confess, if he had licence, that he might sell at any reasonable rate as they were worth in other places, did send for the principals of the town, and made a show he would depart, declaring himself to be very sorry that he had so much troubled them, and also that he had sent for the governor to come down, seeing now that his pretence was to depart; whereat they marvelled much, and asked him what cause moved him thereunto, seeing by their working he was in possibility to have his licence.

To the which he replied that it was not only a licence that he sought, but profit, which he perceived was not there to be had, and therefore would seek further; and withal showed them his writings what he paid for his negroes, declaring also the great charge he was at in his shipping and men's wages, and therefore, to countervail his charges, he must sell his negroes for a greater price than they offered. So they, doubting his departure, put him in comfort to sell better there than in any other place. And if it fell out that he had no licence, that he should not lose his labour in tarrying, for they would buy without licence. Whereupon the Captain being put in comfort promised them to stay, so that he might make sale of his lean negroes, which they granted unto. And the next day he did sell to some of them. Who having bought and paid for them, thinking to have had a discharge of the Customer for the custom of the negroes, being the King's duty, they gave it away to the poor for God's sake, and did refuse to give the discharge in writing; and the poor, not trusting their words, for fear lest hereafter it might be demanded of them, did refrain from buying any more; so that nothing else was done until the governor's coming down, which was the fourteenth day, and then the Captain made petition, declaring that he was come thither in a ship of the Queen's Majesty's of England, being bound to Guinea, and thither driven by wind and weather, so that being come thither he had need of sundry necessaries for the reparation of the said navy, and also great need of money for the payment of his soldiers, unto whom he had promised payment; and therefore, although he would, yet would not they depart without it, and for that purpose he requested licence for the sale of certain of his negroes, declaring that although they were forbidden to traffic with strangers, yet for that there was a great amity between their princes, and that the thing pertained to our Queen's Highness, he thought he might do their prince great service, and that it would be well taken at his hands to do it in this cause. The which allegations, with divers others put in request, were presented to the governor, who, sitting in council for that matter, granted his request for licence. But yet there fell out another thing, which was the abating of the King's custom, being upon every slave thirty ducats, which would not be granted unto.

Whereupon the Captain perceiving that they would neither come near his price he looked for by a great deal, nor yet would abate the King's custom of that they offered, so that either he must be a great loser by his wares, or else compel the officers to abate the same King's custom, which was too unreasonable, for to a higher price he could not bring the buyers; therefore the sixteenth of April he prepared one hundred men well armed with bows, arrows, arquebuses, and pikes, with which he marched to the townwards, and being perceived by the governor, he straight with all expedition sent messengers to know his request, desiring him to march no further forward until he had answer again, which incontinent he should have. So our Captain, declaring how unreasonable a thing the King's custom was, requested to have the same abated, and to pay seven and a half per cent, which is the ordinary custom for wares through his dominions there, and unto this if they would not grant he would displease them. And this word being carried to the governor, answer was returned that all things should be to his content; and thereupon he determined to depart, but the soldiers and mariners, finding so little credit in their promises, demanded gages for the performance of the premisses or else they would not depart. And thus they being constrained to send gages, we departed, beginning our traffic and ending the same without disturbance.

Thus having made traffic in the harbour until the 28th, our Captain with his ships intended to go out of the road, and purposed to make show of his departure; because now the common sort having employed their money, the rich men were come to town, who made no show that they were come to buy, so that they went about to bring down the price, and by this policy the Captain knew they would be made the more eager, for fear lest we departed and they should go without any at all.

The nine and twentieth, we being at anchor without the road, a French ship called the *Green Dragon*, of Newhaven, whereof was captain one Bontemps came in, who saluted us after the manner of the sea with certain pieces of ordnance, and we re-saluted him with the like again. With whom having communication, he declared that he had been at the Mine in Guinea, and was beaten off by the Portugals' galleys, and enforced to come thither to make sale of such wares as he had; and further, that the like was happened unto the *Minion*, besides the Captain Davie Carlet and a merchant with a dozen mariners betrayed by the negroes at their first arrival thither, and remaining prisoners with the Portugals; and besides other misadventures of the loss of their men, happened through the great lack of fresh water, with great doubts of bringing home the ships; which was most sorrowful for us to understand.

Thus having ended our traffic here the 4th of May, we departed, leaving the Frenchman behind us; the night before which the Caribs, whereof I have made mention before, being to the number of 200, came in their canoes to Borburata, intending by night to have burned the town and taken the Spaniards, who being more vigilant because of our being there than was their custom, perceiving them coming, raised the town, who in a moment were on horseback (by means their custom is for all doubts to keep their horses ready saddled), in the night set upon them and took one; but the rest making shift for themselves, escaped away. But this one, because he was their guide, and was the occasion that divers times they had made invasion upon them, had for his travail a stake thrust through his fundament, and so out at his neck.

The sixth of May aforesaid we came to an island called Curaçao, where we had thought to have anchored, but could not find ground, and having let fall an anchor with two cables, were fain to weigh it again; and the seventh, sailing along the coast to seek a harbour, and finding none, we came to an anchor where we rode open in the sea. In this place we had traffic for hides, and found great refreshing, both of beef, mutton, and lambs, whereof there was such plenty that, saving the skins, we had the flesh given us for nothing; the plenty whereof was so abundant that the worst in the ship thought scorn not only of mutton, but also of sodden lamb, which they disdained to eat unroasted.

The increase of cattle in this island is marvellous, which from a dozen of each sort brought thither by the governor, in 25 years he had a hundred thousand at the least and of other cattle was able to kill, without spoil of the increase, 1500 yearly, which he killeth for the skins, and of the flesh saveth only the tongues, the rest he leaveth to the fowl to devour. And this I am able to affirm, not only upon the governor's own report, who was the first that brought the increase thither which so remaineth unto this day, but also by that I saw myself in one field, where a hundred oxen lay one by another all whole, saving the skin and tongue taken away. And it is not so marvellous a thing why they do thus cast away the flesh in all the islands of the West Indies, seeing the land is great and more than they are able to inhabit, the people few, and having delicate fruits and meats enough besides to feed upon, which they rather desire, and the increase which passeth man's reason to believe, when they come to a great number. For in Santo Domingo, an island called by the finders thereof Hispaniola, is so great quantity of cattle, and such increase thereof, that notwithstanding the daily killing of them for their hides, it is not possible to assuage the number of them but they are devoured by wild dogs, whose number is such, by suffering them first to range the woods and mountains, that they eat and destroy 60,000 a year, and yet small lack found of them. And no marvel, for the said island is almost as big as all England, and being the first place that was found of all the Indies, and long time inhabited before the rest, it ought therefore of reason to be most populous; and to this hour, the Viceroy and Council Royal abideth there as in the chiefest place of all the Indies, to prescribe orders to the rest for the King's behalf; yet have they but one city and 13 villages in all the same island, whereby the spoil of them in respect of the increase is nothing.

The 15th of the foresaid month we departed from Curaçao, being not a little to the rejoicing of our Captain and us that we had there ended our traffic; but notwithstanding our sweet meat, we had sour sauce, for by reason of our riding so open at sea, what with blasts, whereby, our anchors being aground, three at once came home, and also with contrary winds blowing, whereby, for fear of the shore, we were fain to haul off to have anchor-hold, sometimes a whole day and a night we turned up and down; and this happened not once, but half a dozen times in the space of our being there.

The 16th we passed by an island called Aruba, and the 17th, at night, we anchored six hours at the west end of Cabo de la Vela, and in the morning, being the 18th, weighed again, keeping our course, in the which time the Captain, sailing by the shore in the pinnace, came to the Rancheria, a place where the Spaniards use to fish for pearls, and there spoke with a Spaniard, who told him how far off he was from Rio de la Hacha, which because he would not overshoot, he anchored that night again, and the 19th came thither. Where having talk with the King's Treasurer of the Indies resident there, he declared his quiet traffic in

Borburata, and showed a certificate of the same, made by the governor thereof, and therefore he desired to have the like there also. But the Treasurer made answer that they were forbidden by the Viceroy and Council of Santo Domingo, who having intelligence of our being on the coast, did send express commission to resist us with all the force they could, insomuch that they durst not traffic with us in no case, alleging that if they did they should lose all that they did traffic for, besides their bodies at the magistrate's commandment. Our Captain replied that he was in an armada of the Queen's Majesty's of England, and sent about other her affairs, but driven besides his pretended voyage, was enforced by contrary winds to come into those parts, where he hoped to find such friendship as he should do in Spain; to the contrary whereof he knew no reason, in that there was amity betwixt their princes. But seeing they would, contrary to all reason, go about to withstand his traffic, he would it should not be said by him that, having the force he hath, to be driven from his traffic perforce; but he would rather put it in adventure to try whether he or they should have the better, and therefore willed them to determine, either to give him licence to trade, or else to stand to their own harms. So upon this it was determined he should have licence to trade, but they would give him such a price as was the one half less than he had sold for before; and thus they sent word they would do, and none otherwise, and if it liked him not, he might do what he would, for they were determined not to deal otherwise with him. Whereupon the Captain, weighing their unconscionable request, wrote to them a letter, that they dealt too rigorously with him to go about to cut his throat in the price of his commodities, which were so reasonably rated as they could not by a great deal have the like at any other man's hands. But seeing they had sent him this to his supper, he would in the morning bring them as good a breakfast. And therefore in the morning, being the 21st of May, he shot off a whole culverin to summon the town, and preparing one hundred men in armour, went ashore, having in his great boat two falcons of brass, and in the other boats double bases in their noses, which being perceived by the townsmen, they incontinent in battle array, with their drum and ensign displayed, marched from the town to the sands, of footmen to the number of a hundred and fifty, making great brags with their cries, and waving us ashore, whereby they made a semblance to have fought with us indeed. But our Captain, perceiving them to brag, commanded the two falcons to be discharged at them, which put them in no small fear to see (as they afterward declared) such great pieces in a boat. At every shot they fell flat to the ground; and as we approached near unto them, they broke their array, and dispersed themselves so much for fear of the ordnance that at last they went all away with their ensign. The horsemen also, being about thirty, made as brave a show as might be, coursing up and down with their horses, their brave white leather targets in the one hand and their javelins in the other, as though they would have received us at our landing. But when we landed, they gave ground, and consulted what they should do, for little they thought we should have landed so boldly; and, therefore, as the Captain was putting his men in array, and marched forward to have encountered with them, they sent a messenger on horseback with a flag of truce to the Captain, who declared that the Treasurer marvelled what he meant to do to come ashore in that order, in consideration that they had granted to every reasonable request that he did demand. But the Captain, not well contented with this messenger, marched forwards. The messenger prayed him to stay his men, and said if he would come apart from his men, the Treasurer would come and speak with him, whereunto he did agree to commune together. The Captain only with his armour, without weapon, and the Treasurer on horseback with his javelin, was afraid to come near him for fear of his armour, which he said was worse than his weapon, and so keeping aloof communing together, granted in fine to all his requests. Which being declared by the Captain to the company, they desired to have pledges for the performance of all things, doubting that otherwise, when they had made themselves stronger, they would have been at defiance with us; and seeing that now they might have what they would request, they judged it to be more wisdom to be in assurance than to be forced to make any more labours about it. So upon this, gages were sent, and we made our traffic quietly with them.

In the meantime while we stayed here, we watered a good breadth off from the shore, where, by the strength of the fresh water running into the sea, the salt water was made fresh. In this river we saw many crocodiles of sundry bignesses, but some as big as a boat, with 4 feet, a long broad mouth, and a long tail, and whose skin is so hard that a sword will not pierce it. His nature is to live out of the water as a frog doth, but he is a great devourer, and spareth neither fish, which is his common food, nor beasts, nor men, if he take them, as the proof thereof was known by a negro who, as he was filling water in the river, was by one of them carried clean away and never seen after. His nature is ever when he would have his prey to cry and sob like a Christian body, to provoke them to come to him, and then he snatcheth at them, and thereupon came this proverb, that is applied unto women when they weep, *lacrimae crocodili*, the meaning whereof is, that as the crocodile when he crieth goeth then about most to deceive, so doth a woman most commonly when she weepeth. Of these the Master of the *Jesus* watched one, and by the bank's side struck him with a pike of a bill in the side, and after three or four times turning in sight, he sunk down, and was not afterward seen. In the time of our being in the rivers of Guinea we saw many of a monstrous bigness, amongst which the Captain, being in one of the barks coming down the same, shot a falcon at one, which very narrowly he missed, and with affear he plunged into the water, making a streak like the way of a boat.

Now while we were here, whether it were of a fear that the Spaniards doubted we would have done them some harm before we departed, or for any treason that they intended towards us, I am not able to say; but then came thither a captain from some of the other towns, with a dozen soldiers, upon a time when our Captain and the Treasurer cleared all things between them, and were in a communication of a debt of the governor of Borburata, which was to be paid by the said Treasurer, who would not answer the same by any means. Whereupon certain words of displeasure passed betwixt the Captain and him, and parting the one from the other, the Treasurer possibly doubting that our Captain would perforce have sought the same, did immediately command his men to arms, both horsemen and footmen; but because the Captain was in the river on the back-side of the town with his other boats, and all his men unarmed and without weapons, it was to be judged he meant him little good, having that advantage of him, that coming upon the sudden, he might have mischiefed many of his men. But the Captain having understanding thereof, not trusting to their gentleness if they might have the advantage, departed aboard his ships, and at night returned again, and demanded amongst other talk what they meant by assembling their men in that order, and they answered, that their captain being come to town did muster his men according to his accustomed manner. But it is to be judged to be a cloak, in that coming for that purpose he might have done it sooner, but the truth is, they were not of force until then whereby to enterprise any matter against us by means of pikes and arquebuses, whereof they have want, and were now furnished by our Captain, and also 3 falcons, which having got in other places, they had secretly conveyed thither, which made them the bolder, and also for that they saw now a convenient place to do such a feat, and time also serving thereunto, by the means that our men were not only unarmed and unprovided, as at no time before the like, but also were occupied in hewing of wood, and least thinking of any harm: these were occasions to provoke them thereunto. And I suppose they went about to bring it to effect, in that I, with another gentleman being in the town, thinking of no harm towards us, and seeing men assembling in armour to the Treasurer's house, whereof I marvelled, and revoking to mind the former talk between the Captain and him, and the unreadiness of our men, of whom advantage might have been taken, departed out of the town immediately to give knowledge thereof; but before we came to our men by a flight-shot, two horsemen riding a-gallop were come near us, being sent, as we did guess, to stay us lest we should carry news to our Captain. But seeing us so near our men they stayed their horses, coming together, and suffering us to pass, belike because we were so near that if they had gone about the same they would have been espied by some of our men which then immediately would have departed, whereby they should have been frustrate of their pretence; and so the two horsemen rode about the bushes to espy what we did, and seeing us gone, to the intent they might shadow their coming down in post, whereof suspicion might be had, feigned a simple excuse in asking whether he could sell any wine. But that seemed so simple to the Captain that, standing in doubt of their courtesy, he returned in the morning with his three boats, appointed with bases in their noses, and his men with weapons accordingly, whereas before he carried none; and thus dissembling all injuries conceived of both parts, the Captain went ashore, leaving pledges in the boats for himself, and cleared all things between the Treasurer and him, saving for the governor's debt, which the one by no means would answer, and the other, because it was not his due debt, would not molest him for it, but was content to remit it until another time, and therefore departed, causing the two barks which rode near the shore to weigh and go under sail, which was done because that our Captain, demanding a testimonial of his good behaviour there, could not have the same until he were under sail ready to depart. And therefore at night he went for the same again and received it at the Treasurer's hand, of whom very courteously he took his leave and departed, shooting off the bases of his boat for his farewell, and the townsmen also shot off four falcons and thirty arquebuses, and this was the first time that he knew of the conveyance of their falcons.

The 31st of May we departed, keeping our course to Hispaniola, and the fourth of June we had sight of an island, which we made to be Jamaica, marvelling that by the vehement course of the seas we should be driven so far to leeward; for setting our course to the west end of Hispaniola, we fell with the middle of Jamaica, notwithstanding that to all men's sight it showed a headland, but they were all deceived by the clouds that lay upon the land two days together, in such sort that we thought it to be the headland of the said island. And a Spaniard being in the ship, who was a merchant, and inhabitant in Jamaica, having occasion to go to Guinea, and being by treason taken by the negroes, and afterwards bought by the *tangomangoes*, was by our Captain brought from thence, and had his passage to go into his country, who, perceiving the land, made as though he knew every place thereof, and pointed to certain places which he named to be such a place, and such a man's ground, and that behind such a point was the harbour, but in the end he pointed so from one point to another that we were a-leeboard of all places, and found ourselves at the west end of Jamaica before we were aware of it, and being once to leeward, there was no getting up again; so that by trusting of the Spaniard's knowledge, our Captain sought not to speak with any of the inhabitants, which if he had not made himself sure of, he would have done as his custom was in other places. But this man was a plague not only to our captain, who made him lose by overshooting the place £2,000 by hides which he might have gotten, but also to himself, who being three years out of his country, and in great misery in Guinea, both among the negroes and *tangomangoes*, and in hope to come to his wife and friends, as he made sure account, in that at his going into the pinnace when he went to shore he put on his new clothes, and for joy flung away his old, could not afterwards find any habitation, neither there nor in all Cuba, which we sailed all along, but it fell out ever by one occasion or other that we were put beside the same, so that he was fain to be brought into England. And it happened to him as it did to a duke of Samaria, when the Israelites were besieged and were in great misery with hunger, and being told by the Prophet Elizæus that a bushel of flour should be sold for a shekel, would not believe him, but thought it impossible; and for that cause Elizæus prophesied he should see the same done, but he should not eat thereof. So this man being absent three years, and not ever thinking to have seen his own country, did see the same, went upon it, and yet was it not his fortune to come to it, or to any habitation whereby to remain with his friends according to his desire.

Thus having sailed along the coast two days, we departed the seventh of June, being made to believe by the Spaniard that it was not Jamaica, but rather Hispaniola. Of which opinion the Captain also was, because that which he made Jamaica seemed to be but a piece of the land, and thereby took it rather to be Hispaniola, by the lying of the coast; and also for that being ignorant of the force of the current, he could not believe he was so far driven to leeward, and therefore setting his course to Jamaica, and after certain days not finding the same, perceived then certainly that the island which he was at before was Jamaica, and that the clouds did deceive him, whereof he marvelled not a little. And this mistaking of the place came to as ill a pass as the overshooting of Jamaica. For by this did he also overpass a place in Cuba, called Santa Cruz, where, as he was informed, was great store of hides to be had. And thus being disappointed of two of his ports, where he thought to have raised great profit by his traffic, and also to have found great refreshing of victuals and water for his men, he was now disappointed greatly. And such want he had of fresh water, that he was forced to seek the shore to obtain the same, which he had sight of after certain days overpassed with storms and contrary winds, but yet not of the main of Cuba, but of certain islands in number two hundred, whereof the most part were desolate of inhabitants. By the which islands the Captain, passing in his pinnace, could find no fresh water until he came to an island bigger than all the rest, called the Isle of Pines, where we anchored with our ships the 16th of June, and found water, which although it were neither so toothsome as running water, by the means it is standing, and but the water of rain, and also being near the sea was brackish, yet did we not refuse it, but were more glad thereof, as the time then required, than we should have been another time with fine conduit water. Thus being reasonably watered we were desirous to depart, because the place was not very convenient for such ships of charge as they were, because there were many shoals to leeward, which also lay open to the sea for any wind that should blow, and therefore the Captain made the more haste away, which was not unneedful. For little sooner were their anchors weighed and foresail set, but there arose such a storm that they had not much to spare for doubling out the shoals; for one of the barks, not being fully ready as the rest, was fain for haste to cut the cable in the hawse, and lose both anchor and cable to save herself.

Thus the 17th of June we departed, and on the 20th we fell with the west end of Cuba, called Cape St Antony, where for the space of three days we doubled along, till we came beyond the shoals, which are 20 leagues beyond St Antony. And the ordinary breeze taking us, which is the north-east wind, put us the 24th from the shore, and therefore we went to the north-west to fetch wind, and also to the coast of Florida to have the help of the current, which was judged to have set to the eastward; so the 29th we found ourselves in 27 degrees and in the soundings of Florida, where we kept ourselves the space of four days, sailing along the coast as near as we could, in ten or twelve fathom water, having all the while no sight of land.

The 5th of July we had sight of certain islands of sand, called the Tortugas (which is low land) where the Captain went in with his pinnace, and found such a number of birds that in half-an-hour he laded her with them; and if they had been ten boats more they might have done the like. These islands bear the name of Tortoises because of the number of them which there do breed, whose nature is to live both in the water and upon land also, but breed only upon the shore, in making a great pit wherein they lay eggs, to the number of three or four hundred, and covering them with sand, they are hatched by the heat of the sun; and by this means cometh the great increase. Of these we took very great ones, which have both back and belly all of bone, of the thickness of an inch: the fish whereof we proved, eating much like veal; and finding a number of eggs in them, tasted also of them, but they did eat very sweetly. Here we anchored six hours, and then a fair gale of wind springing, we weighed anchor, and made sail toward Cuba, whither we came the sixth day, and weathered as far as the Table, being a hill so called because of the form thereof; here we lay off and on all night, to keep that we had gotten to windward, intending to have watered in the morning if we could have done it, or else, if the wind had come larger, to have plied to windward to Havana, which is a harbour whereunto all the fleet of the Spaniards come, and do there tarry to have one the company of another. This hill we thinking to have been the Table, made account (as it was indeed) that Havana was but eight leagues to windward, but by the persuasion of a Frenchman, who made the Captain believe he knew the Table very well and had been at Havana, said that it was not the Table, and that the Table was much higher, and nearer to the sea-side, and that there was no plain ground to the eastward, nor hills to the westward, but all was contrary, and that behind the hills to the westward was Havana. To which persuasion credit being given by some, and they not of the worst, the Captain was persuaded to go to leeward, and so sailed along on the seventh and eighth days, finding no habitation, nor no other Table; and then perceiving his folly to give ear to such praters, was not a little sorry, both because he did consider what time he should spend ere he could get so far to windward again, which would have been, with the weathering which we had, ten or twelve days' work, and what it would have been longer he knew not, and (that which was worst) he had not above a day's water, and therefore knew not what shift to make. But in fine, because the want was such that his men could not live with it, he determined to seek water, and to go farther to leeward, to a place (as it is set in the card) called Rio de los Puercos, which he was in doubt of, both whether it were inhabited, and whether there were water or not, and whether for the shoals he might have such access with his ships that he might conveniently take in the same. And while we were in these troubles, and kept our way to the place aforesaid, Almighty God our guide (who would not suffer us to run into any further danger, which we had been like to have incurred if we had ranged the coast of Florida along as we did before, which is so dangerous, by reports, that no ship escapeth which cometh thither, as the Spaniards have very well proved the same) sent us the eighth day at night a fair westerly wind, whereupon the Captain and company consulted, determining not to refuse God's gift, but every man was contented to pinch his own belly, whatsoever had happened; and taking the said wind, the 9th day of July got to the Table, and sailing the same night unawares overshot Havana; at which place we thought to have watered. But the next day, not knowing that we had overshot the same, sailed along the coast seeking it, and the eleventh day in the morning, by certain known marks, we understood that we had overshot it 20 leagues; in which coast ranging we found no convenient watering place, whereby there was no remedy but to disembogue, and to water upon the coast of Florida. For, to go further to the eastward we could not for the shoals, which are very dangerous; and because the current shooteth to the north-east, we doubted by the force thereof to be set upon them, and therefore durst not approach them. So making but reasonable way the day aforesaid and all the night, the twelfth day in the morning we fell with the islands upon the cape of Florida, which we could scant double, by the means that fearing the shoals to the eastwards, and doubting the current coming out of the west, which was not of that force we made account of, for we felt little or none till we fell with the cape, and then felt such a current that, bearing all sails against the same, yet were driven back again a great pace; the experience whereof we had by the *Jesus'* pinnace, and the *Salomon's* boat, which were sent the same day in the afternoon, whiles the ships were becalmed, to see if they could find any water upon the islands aforesaid, who spent a great part of the day in rowing thither, being further off than they deemed it to be; and in the meantime a fair gale of wind springing at sea, the ships departed, making a sign to them to come away, who, although they saw them depart, because they were so near the shore, would not lose all the labour they had taken, but determined to keep their way, and see if there were any water to be had, making no account but to find the ships well enough. But they spent so much time in filling the water which they had found, that the night was come before they could make an end. And having lost the sight of the ships, they rowed what they could, but were wholly ignorant which way they should seek them again; as indeed there was a more doubt than they knew of. For when they departed the ships were in no current, and sailing but a mile further they found one so strong that bearing all sails it could not prevail against the same, but were driven back. Whereupon the Captain sent the *Salomon* with the other two barks to bear near the shore all night, because the current was less there a great deal, and to bear light, with shooting off a piece now and then, to the intent the boats might better know how to come to them.

The *Jesus* also bore a light in her top-gallant, and shot off a piece also now and then, but the night passed, and the morning was come, being the thirteenth day, and no news could be heard of them; but the ships and bark ceased not to look still for them, yet they thought it was all in vain, by the means they heard not of them all the night past and therefore determined to tarry no longer, seeking for them till noon, and if they heard no news, then they would depart to the *Jesus*, who perforce (by the vehemency of the current) was carried almost out of sight. But as God would have it, now time being come, and they having tacked about in the pinnace's top had sight of them and took them up. They in the boats, being to the number of one-and-twenty, having sight of the ships and seeing them tacking about, whereas before at the first sight of them they did greatly rejoice, were now in a greater perplexity than ever they were; for by this they thought themselves utterly forsaken, whereas before they were in some hope to have found them. Truly God wrought marvellously for them, for they themselves having no victuals but water, and being sore oppressed with hunger, were not of opinion to bestow any further time in seeking the ships than that present noon-time; so that if they had not at that instant espied them, they had gone to the shore to have made provision for victuals and, with such things as they could have gotten, either to have gone for that part of Florida where the Frenchmen were planted (which would have been very hard for them to have done, because they wanted victuals to bring them thither, being a hundred and twenty leagues off), or else to have remained among the Floridians, at whose hands they were put in comfort by a Frenchman, who was with them, that had remained in Florida at the first finding thereof a whole year together, to receive victuals sufficient and gentle entertainment, if need were for a year or two, until which time God might have provided for them. But how contrary this would have fallen out to their expectations it is hard to judge, seeing those people of the Cape of Florida are of more savage and fierce nature, and more valiant than any of the rest; which the Spaniards well proved, who being five hundred men who intended there to land, returned few or none of them but were enforced to forsake the same. And of their cruelty mention is made in the book of *Decades*, of a friar, who taking upon him to persuade the people to subjection, was by them taken, and his skin cruelly pulled over his ears, and his flesh eaten.

In these islands they being ashore found a dead man, dried in a manner whole, with other heads and bodies of men; so that these sorts of men are eaters of the flesh of men as well as the cannibals. But to return to our purpose.

The fourteenth day the ship and barks came to the *Jesus*, bringing them news of the recovery of the men, which was not a little to the rejoicing of the Captain and the whole company; and so then altogether they kept on their way along the coast of Florida, and the fifteenth day came to an anchor, and so from 26 degrees to 30 degrees and a half, where the Frenchmen abode, ranging all the coast along, seeking for fresh water, anchoring every night because we would overshoot no place of fresh water, and in the day time the Captain in the ship's pinnace sailed along the shore, went into every creek, speaking with divers of the Floridians, because he would understand where the Frenchmen inhabited. And not finding them in 28 degrees, as it was declared unto him, marvelled thereat, and never left sailing along the coast till he found them, who inhabited in a river, by them called the River of May, and standing in 30 degrees and better. In ranging this coast along, the Captain found it to be all an island, and therefore it is all low land, and very scant of fresh water; but the country was marvellously sweet, with both marsh and meadow ground, and goodly woods among. There they found sorrel to grow as abundantly as grass, and where their houses were great store of maize and mill, and grapes of great bigness, but of taste much like our English grapes. Also deer great plenty, which came upon the sands before them. Their houses are not many together, for in one house a hundred of them do lodge; they being made much like a great barn, and in strength not inferior to ours, for they have stanchions and rafters of whole trees, and are covered with *palmito* leaves, having no place divided but one small room for their king and queen. In the midst of this house is a hearth, where they make great fires all night, and they sleep upon certain pieces of wood, hewn in for the bowing of their backs, and another place made high for their heads, which they put one by another all along the walls on both sides. In their houses they remain only in the nights, and in the day they desire the fields, where they dress their meat and make provision for victuals, which they provide only for a meal from hand to mouth. There is one thing to be marvelled at, for the making of their fire, and not only they, but also the negroes do the same, which is made only by two sticks, rubbing them one against another; and this they may do in any place they come, where they find sticks sufficient for the purpose. In their apparel the men only use deer skins, wherewith some only cover their privy member, other some use the same as garments to cover them before and behind; which skins are painted, some yellow and red, some black and russet, and every man according to his own fancy. They do not omit to paint their bodies also with curious knots, or antic work, as every man in his own fancy deviseth, which painting, to make it continue the better, they use with a thorn to prick their flesh and dent in the same, whereby the painting may have better hold. In their wars they use a slighter colour of painting their faces, thereby to make themselves show the more fierce; which after their wars ended they wash away again. In their wars they use bows and arrows, whereof their bows are made of a kind of yew, but blacker than ours, and for the most part passing the strength of the negroes', or Indians', for it is not greatly inferior to ours. Their arrows are also of a great length, but yet of reeds like other Indians', but varying in two points, both in length and also for nocks and feathers, which the other lack, whereby they shoot very steady. The heads of the same are vipers' teeth, bones of fishes, flint stones, piked points of knives, which they having gotten of the Frenchmen, broke the same, and put the points of them in their arrow-heads. Some of them have their heads of silver; other some that have want of these put in a kind of hard wood, notched, which pierceth as far as any of the rest. In their fight, being in the woods, they use a marvellous policy for their own safeguard, which is by clasping a tree in their arms, and yet shooting notwithstanding. This policy they used with the Frenchmen in their fight, whereby it appeareth that they are people of some policy; and although they are called by the Spaniards *gente triste*, that is to say "bad people," meaning thereby that they are not men of capacity, yet have the Frenchmen found them so witty in their answers that, by the captain's own report, a counsellor with us could not give a more profound reason.

The women also for their apparel use painted skins, but most of them gowns of moss, somewhat longer than our moss, which they sew together artificially, and make the same surplice-wise, wearing their hair down to their shoulders, like the Indians.

In this River of May aforesaid the Captain, entering with his pinnace, found a French ship of fourscore ton, and two pinnaces of fifteen ton apiece by her, and speaking with the keepers thereof, they told him of a fort two leagues up, which they had built, in which their captain Monsieur Laudonnière was, with certain soldiers therein. To whom our Captain sending to understand of a watering place, where he might conveniently take it in, and to have licence for the same, he straight, because there was no convenient place but up the river five leagues, where the water was fresh, did send him a pilot for the more expedition thereof, to bring in one of his barks, which, going in with other boats provided for the same purpose, anchored before the fort; into the which our Captain went, where he was by the General, with other captains and soldiers, very gently entertained, who declared unto him the time of their being there, which was fourteen months, with the extremity they were driven to for want of victuals, having brought very little with them. In which place they, being two hundred men at their first coming, had in short space eaten all the maize they could buy of the inhabitants about them, and therefore were driven certain of them to serve a king of the Floridians against other his enemies for mill and other victuals, which having gotten, could not serve them, being so many, so long a time; but want came upon them in such sort that they were fain to gather acorns, which, being stamped small and often washed to take away the bitterness of them, they did use for bread, eating withal sundry times roots, whereof they found many good and wholesome, and such as serve rather for medicines than for meats alone.

But this hardness not contenting some of them, who would not take the pains so much as to fish in the river before their doors, but would have all things put in their mouths, they did rebel against the captain, taking away first his armour, and afterwards imprisoning him; and so, to the number of fourscore of them, departed with a bark and a pinnace, spoiling their store of victuals, and taking away a great part thereof with them, and so went to the islands of Hispaniola and Jamaica a-roving, where they spoiled and pilled the Spaniards. And having taken two caravels laden with wine and cassava, which is a bread made of roots, and much other victuals and treasure, had not the grace to depart therewith, but were of such haughty stomachs that they thought their force to be such that no man durst meddle with them, and so kept harbour in Jamaica, going daily ashore at their pleasure. But God, who would not suffer such evil-doers unpunished, did indurate their hearts in such sort that they lingered the time so long that a ship and galleas being made out of Santo Domingo came thither into the harbour and took twenty of them, whereof the most part were hanged and the rest carried into Spain, and some (to the number of five-and-twenty) escaped in the pinnace and came to Florida, where, at their landing, they were put into prison; and incontinent four of the chiefest being condemned, at the request of the soldiers did pass the arquebusiers, and then were hanged upon a gibbet.

This lack of threescore men was a great discourage and weakening to the rest, for they were the best soldiers that they had. For they had now made the inhabitants weary of them by their daily craving of maize, having no wares left to content them withal, and therefore were enforced to rob them, and to take away their victual perforce, which was the occasion that the Floridians (not well contented therewith) did take certain of their company in the woods, and slew them; whereby there grew great wars betwixt them and the Frenchmen. And therefore they, being but a few in number, durst not venture abroad but at such times as they were enforced thereunto for want of food to do the same; and going, twenty arquebusiers in a company, were set upon by eighteen kings, having seven or eight hundred men, which with one of their bows slew one of their men, and hurt a dozen, and drove them all down to their boats. Whose policy in fight was to be marvelled at; for having shot at divers of their bodies which were armed, and perceiving that their arrows did not prevail against the same, they shot at their faces and legs, which were the places that the Frenchmen were hurt in. Thus the Frenchmen returned, being in ill case by the hurt of their men, having not above forty soldiers left unhurt, whereby they might ill make any more invasions upon the Floridians, and keep their fort withal, which they must have been driven unto had not God sent us thither for their succour; for they had not above ten days' victuals left before we came. In which perplexity our Captain seeing them, spared them out of his ship twenty barrels of meal and four pipes of beans, with divers other victuals and necessaries which he might conveniently spare; and to help them the better homewards, wither they were bound before our coming, at their request we spared them one of our barks of fifty ton.

Notwithstanding the great want that the Frenchemen had, the ground doth yield victuals sufficient if they would have taken pains to get the same; but they, being soldiers, desired to live by the sweat of other men's brows. For while they had peace with the Floridians they had fish sufficient by weirs which they made to catch the same; but when they grew to wars the Flordians took away the same again, and then would not the Frenchmen take the pains to make any more. The ground yieldeth naturally grapes in great store, for in the time that the Frenchmen were there they made 20 hogsheads of wine. Also it yieldeth roots passing good, deer marvellous store, with divers other beasts and fowl serviceable to the use of man. These be things wherewith a man may live, having corn or maize wherewith to make bread;

for maize maketh good savoury bread and cakes as fine as flour. Also it maketh good meal, beaten and sodden with water, and eateth like pap wherewith we feed children. It maketh also good beverage, sodden in water, and nourishable, which the Frenchmen did use to drink of in the morning, and it assuaged their thirst so that they had no need to drink all the day after. And this maize was the greatest lack they had, because they had no labourers to sow the same, and therefore to them that should inhabit the land it were requisite to have labourers to till and sow the ground; for they, having victuals of their own, whereby they neither rob nor spoil the inhabitants, may live not only quietly with them, who naturally are more desirous of peace than of wars, but also shall have abundance of victuals proffered to them for nothing. For it is with them as it is with one of us, when we see another man ever taking away from us, although we have enough besides, yet then wc think all too little for ourselves. For surely we have heard the Frenchmen report, and I know it by the Indians, that a very little contenteth them; for the Indians, with the head of maize roasted, will travel a whole day, and when they are at the Spaniards' finding, they give them nothing but sodden herbs and maize; and in this order I saw threescore of them feed, who were laden with wares, and came fifty leagues off.

The Floridans when they travel have a kind of herb dried, who, with a cane and an earthen cup in the end, with fire, and the dried herbs put together, do suck through the cane the smoke thereof, which smoke satisfieth their hunger, and therewith they live four or five days without meat or drink, and this all the Frenchmen used for this purpose. Yet do they hold opinion withal that it causeth water and steam to void from their stomachs.

The commodities of this land are more than are yet known to any man; for besides the land itself, whereof there is more than any king Christian is able to inhabit, it flourisheth with meadow, pasture-ground, with woods of cedar and cypress, and other sorts, as better cannot be in the world. They have for apothecary herbs, trees, roots, and gums great store, as *storax liquida*, turpentine, gum, myrrh, and frankincense, with many others whereof I know not the names. Colours, both red, black, yellow, and russet, very perfect, wherewith they so paint their bodies and deer-skins which they wear about them, that with water it neither fadeth away nor altereth colour. Gold and silver they want not; for at the Frenchmen's first coming thither they had the same offered them for little or nothing, for they received for a hatchet two pound weight of gold, because they knew not the estimation thereof. But the soldiers, being greedy of the same, did take it from them, giving them nothing for it, the which they perceiving, that both the Frenchmen did greatly esteem it, and also did rigorously deal with them by taking the same away from them, at last would not be known they had any more, neither durst they wear the same for fear of being taken away. So that, saving at their first coming, they could get none of them. And how they came by this gold and silver the Frenchmen know not as yet, but by guess, who, having travelled to the south-west of the cape, having found the same dangerous by means of sundry banks, as we also have found the same, and there finding masts which were wrecks of Spaniards coming from Mexico, judged that they had gotten treasure by them. For it is most true that divers wrecks have been made of Spaniards having much treasure. For the Frenchmen having travelled to the capeward a hundred and fifty miles, did find two Spaniards with the Floridians, which they brought afterward to their fort, whereof one was in a caravel coming from the Indies, which was cast away fourteen years ago, and the other twelve years, of whose fellows some escaped, other some were slain by the inhabitants. It seemeth they had estimation of their gold and silver, for it is wrought flat and graven, which they wear about their necks; other some made round like a pancake, with a hole in the midst, to bolster up their breasts withal, because they think it a deformity to have great breasts. As for mines, either of gold or silver, the Frenchmen can hear of none they have upon the island but of copper, whereof as yet also they have not made the proof, because they were but few men. But it is not unlike but that in the main, where are high hills, may be gold and silver as well as in Mexico, because it is all one main. The Frenchmen obtained pearls of them of great bigness, but they were black, by means of roasting of them; for they do not fish for them as the Spaniards do, but for their meat. For the Spaniards use to keep daily a-fishing some two or three hundred Indians, some of them that be of choice a thousand. And their order is to go in canoes, or rather great pinnaces, with thirty men in apiece, whereof the one half or most part be divers, the rest do open the same for the pearls. For it is not suffered that they should use dragging, for that would bring them out of estimation, and mar the beds of them. The oysters which have the smallest sorts of pearls are found in seven or eight fathom water; but the greatest, in eleven or twelve fathom.

The Floridians have pieces of unicorns' horns which they wear about their necks, whereof the Frenchmen obtained many pieces. Of those unicorns they have many; for that they do affirm it to be a beast with one horn, which, coming to the river to drink, putteth the same into the water before he drinketh. Of this unicorn's horn there are of our company that, having gotten the same of the Frenchmen, brought home thereof to show. It is therefore to be presupposed that there are more commodities as well as that, which, for want of time and people sufficient to inhabit the same, cannot yet come to light; but I trust God will reveal the same before it be long, to the great profit of them that shall take it in hand. Of beasts in this country besides deer, foxes, hares, polecats, coneys, ounces, and leopards, I am not able certainly to say; but it is thought that there are lions and tigers as well as unicorns—

lions especially, if it be true that is said of the enmity between them and
the unicorns; for there is no beast but hath his enemy, as the coney the
polecat, a sheep the wolf, the elephant the rhinoceros, and so of other
beasts the like, insomuch that whereas the one is the other cannot be
missing. And seeing I have made mention of the beasts of this country,
it shall not be from my purpose to speak also of the venomous beasts, as
crocodiles, whereof there is great abundance, adders of great bigness,
whereof our men killed some of a yard and a half long. Also I heard a
miracle of one of these adders, upon the which a falcon seizing, the said
adder did clasp her tail about her, which the French captain seeing,
came to the rescue of the falcon, and took her, slaying the adder; and
this falcon being wild did reclaim her, and kept her for the space of two
months, at which time for very want of meat he was fain to cast her off.
On these adders the Frenchmen did feed, to no little admiration of us,
and affirmed the same to be a delicate meat. And the captain of the
Frenchmen saw also a serpent with three heads and four feet, of the
bigness of a great spaniel, which for want of an arquebus he durst not
attempt to slay.

Of fish, also, they have in the river pike, roach, salmon, trout, and
divers other small fishes, and of great fish, some of the length of a man
and longer, being of bigness accordingly, having a snout much like a
sword of a yard long. There be also of sea-fishes, which we saw coming
along the coast, flying, which are of the bigness of a smelt, the biggest
sort whereof have four wings, but the others have but two. Of these
we saw coming out of Guinea a hundred in a company, which, being
chased by the gilt-heads, otherwise called the bonitos, do, to avoid
them the better, take their flight out of the water; but yet are they not
able to fly far, because of the drying of their wings, which serve them
not to fly but when they are moist, and therefore when they can fly no
further, they fall into the water, and having wet their wings, take a new
flight again. These bonitos be of bigness like a carp, and in colour like a
mackerel; but it is the swiftest fish in swimming that is, and followeth
her prey very fiercely, not only in the water, but also out of the water;
for as the flying-fish taketh her flight, so doth this bonito leap after
them, and taketh them sometimes above the water. There were some
of those bonitos which, being galled by a fizgig, did follow our ship
coming out of Guinea 500 leagues. There is a sea-fowl, also, that
chaseth this flying-fish as well as the bonito. For as the flying-fish taketh
her flight, so doth this fowl pursue to take her, which to behold is a
greater pleasure than hawking; for both the flights are as pleasant, and
also more often than a hundred times, for the fowl can fly no way but
one or other lighteth in her paws, the number of them are so abundant.
There is an innumerable young fry of these flying fishes, which commonly keep about the ship, and are not so big as butterflies, and yet by
flying do avoid the unsatiableness of the bonito. Of the bigger sort of

these fishes we took many, which both night and day flew into the sails of our ship, and there was not one of them which was not worth a bonito; for being put upon a hook drabbling in the water, the bonito would leap thereat, and so was taken. Also we took many with a white cloth made fast to a hook, which being tied so short in the water that it might leap out and in, the greedy bonito, thinking it to be a flying fish, leapeth thereat, and so is deceived. We took also dolphins, which are of very good colour and proportion to behold, and no less delicate in taste.

Fowls also there be many, both upon land and upon sea; but concerning them on the land I am not able to name them, because my abode was there so short. But for the fowl of the fresh rivers these two I noted to be the chief: whereof the flamingo is one, having all red feathers and long legs like a heron, a neck according to the bill, red, whereof the upper neb hangeth on inch over the nether; and an egret, which is all white as the swan, with legs like to a hernshaw, and of bigness accordingly; but it hath in her tail feathers of so fine a plume that it passeth the ostrich's feather. Of the sea-fowl above all other not common in England I noted the pelican, which is feigned to be the lovingest bird that is, which, rather than her young should want, will spare her heart's blood out of her belly; but for all this lovingness she is very deformed to behold, for she is of colour russet. Notwithstanding, in Guinea I have seen them as white as a swan, having legs like the same and a body like a heron, with a long neck and a thick long beak, from the nether jaw whereof down to the breast passeth a skin of such a bigness as is able to receive a fish as big as one's thigh, and this her big throat and long bill doth make her seem so ugly.

Here I have declared the estate of Florida and the commodities therein to this day known, which although it may seem unto some, by the means that the plenty of gold and silver is not so abundant as in other places, that the cost bestowed upon the same will not be able to quit the charges, yet am I of the opinion that, by that which I have seen in other islands of the Indians, where such increase of cattle hath been that of twelve head of beasts in five-and-twenty years did in the hides of them raise a thousand pounds profit yearly, that the increase of cattle only would raise profit sufficient for the same. For we may consider, if so small a portion did raise so much gains in such short time, what would a greater do in many years? And surely I may this affirm, that the ground of the Indians for the breed of cattle is not in any point to be compared to this of Florida, which all year long is so green as any time in the summer with us; which surely is not to be marvelled at, seeing the country standeth in so watery a climate. For once a day, without fail, they have a shower of rain, which, by means of the country itself, which is dry and more fervent hot than ours, doth make all things to flourish therein. And because there is not the thing we all seek for, being rather desirous of present gains, I do therefore affirm the attempt thereof to be more requisite for a prince, who is of power able to go through with the same, rather than for any subject.

From thence we departed the 28th day of July upon our voyage homewards, having there all things as might be most convenient for our purpose; and took leave of the Frenchmen that there still remained, who with diligence determined to make as great speed after as they could. Thus, by means of contrary winds oftentimes, we prolonged our voyage in such manner that victuals scanted with us, so that we were divers times (or rather the most part) in despair of ever coming home, had not God of His goodness better provided for us than our deserving. In which state of great misery we were provoked to call upon Him by fervent prayer, which moved Him to hear us, so that we had a prosperous wind, which did set us so far shot as to be upon the bank of Newfoundland on St Bartholomew's Eve, and we sounded thereupon, finding ground at a hundred-and-thirty fathoms, being that day somewhat becalmed, and took a great number of fresh cod-fish, which greatly relieved us; and being very glad thereof the next day we departed, and had lingering little gales for the space of four or five days, at the end of which we saw a couple of French ships, and had of them so much fish as would serve us plentifully for all the rest of the way, the Captain paying for the same both gold and silver, to the just value thereof, unto the chief owners of the said ships; but they, not looking for anything at all, were glad in themselves to meet with such good entertainment at sea as they had at our hands. After which departure from them with a good large wind the twentieth of September we came to Padstow, in Cornwall, God be thanked, in safety, with the loss of twenty persons in all the voyage, and with great profit to the venturers of the said voyage, as also to the whole realm, in bringing home both gold, silver, pearls, and other jewels great store. His name, therefore, be praised for evermore. Amen.

The names of certain gentlemen that were in this voyage:

Master John Hawkins	Master John Chester (Sir William
Master Anthony Parkhurst	Chester' son)
Master Thomas Woorley	Master Fitzwilliam
Master Edward Lacy	with divers others.

The register and true accounts of all herein expressed hath been approved by me, John Sparke the younger, who went upon the same voyage, and wrote the same.

The third troublesome voyage made with the *Jesus of Lubeck*, the *Minion*, and four other ships, to the parts of Guinea and the West Indies, in the years 1567 and 1568, by Master John Hawkins.

THE ships departed from Plymouth the second day of October, anno 1567, and had reasonable weather until the seventh day, at which time forty leagues north from Cape Finisterre there arose an extreme storm, which continued four days in such a sort that the fleet was dispersed and all our great boats lost, and the *Jesus* our chief ship in such case as not thought able to serve the voyage. Whereupon in the same storm we set our course homeward, determining to give over the voyage; but the eleventh day of the same month the wind changed with fair weather, whereby we were animated to follow our enterprise, and so did, directing our course with the islands of the Canaries, where according to an order before prescribed all our ships before dispersed met at one of those islands, called Gomera, where we took water, and departed from thence the fourth day of November towards the coast of Guinea, and arrived at Cape Verde the eighteenth of November, where we landed 150 men hoping to obtain some negroes, where we got but a few and those with great hurt and damage to our men, which chiefly proceeded of their envenomed arrows. And although in the beginning they seemed to be but small hurts yet there hardly escaped any that had blood drawn of them, but died in strange sort, with their mouths shut some ten days before they died and after their wounds were whole; where I myself had one of the greatest wounds yet, thanks be to God, escaped.

From thence we passed the time upon the coast of Guinea, searching with all diligence the rivers from Rio Grande unto Sierra Leone till the twelfth of January, in which time we had not gotten together a hundred and fifty negroes: yet, notwithstanding, the sickness of our men and the late time of the year commanded us away. And thus, having nothing wherewith to seek the coast of the West Indies, I was with the rest of our company in consultation to go to the coast of the Mine, hoping there to have obtained some gold for our wares and thereby to have defrayed our charge. But even in that present instant there came to us a negro, sent from a king oppressed by other kings his neighbours, desiring our aid, with promise that as many negroes as by these wars might be obtained, as well of his part as ours, should be at our pleasure. Whereupon we concluded to give aid and sent 120 of our men which, the 15th of January, assaulted a town of the negroes of our ally's adversaries which had in it 8,000 inhabitants, being very strongly impaled and fenced after their manner, but it was so well defended that our men prevailed not but lost six men and forty hurt; so that our men sent forthwith to me for more help. Whereupon, considering that the good success of this enterprise might highly further the commodity of our voyage, I went myself, and with the help of the king of our side assaulted the town, both by land and sea, and very hardly with fire (their houses being covered with dry palm leaves) obtained the town, put the inhabitants to flight, where we took 250 persons, men, women and children, and by our friend the king of our side there were taken 600 prisoners, whereof we hoped to have had our choice. But the negro (in which nation is seldom or never found truth) meant nothing less; for that night he removed his camp and prisoners so that we were fain to content us with those few which we had gotten ourselves.

Now had we obtained between four and five hundred negroes, wherewith we thought it somewhat reasonable to seek the coast of the West Indies, and there for our negroes and other our merchandise we hoped to obtain whereof to countervail our charges with some gains, whereunto we proceeded with all diligence, furnished our watering, took fuel, and departed the coast of Guinea the third of February, continuing at the sea with a passage more hard than before hath been accustomed till the 27th day of March, which day we had sight of an island, called Dominica, upon the coast of the West Indies in 14 degrees. From thence we coasted from place to place, making our traffic with the Spaniards as we might, somewhat hardly because the King had straitly commanded all his governors in those parts by no means to suffer any trade to be made with us.

Notwithstanding, we had reasonable trade and courteous entertainment from the isle of Margarita unto Cartagena without anything greatly worth the noting, saving at Capo de la Vela, in a town called Rio de la Hacha (from whence come all the pearls) the Treasurer, who had the charge there, would by no means agree to any trade or suffer us to take water. He had fortified his town with divers bulwarks in all places where it might be entered, and furnished himself with a hundred arquebusiers, so that he thought by famine to have enforced us to have put aland our negroes; of which purpose he had not greatly failed unless we had by force entered the town, which (after we could by no means obtain his favour) we were enforced to do, and so with two hundred men broke in upon their bulwarks and entered the town with the loss only of two men of our parts, and no hurt done to the Spaniards, because after their volley of shot discharged they all fled.

Thus having the town with some circumstances, as partly by the Spaniards' desire of negroes and partly by friendship of the Treasurer, we obtained a secret trade; whereupon the Spaniards resorted to us by night and bought of us to the number of 200 negroes. In all other places where we traded the Spaniards inhabitants were glad of us and traded willingly.

At Cartagena, the last town we thought to have seen on the coast, we could by no means obtain to deal with any Spaniard, the Governor was so strait. And because our trade was so near finished we thought not good either to adventure any landing or to detract further time, but in peace departed from thence the 24th of July hoping to have escaped the time of their storms, which then soon after began to reign, the which they call *furicanos*. But passing by the west end of Cuba towards the coast of Florida there happened to us the 12th day of August an extreme storm, which continued by the space of four days, which so beat the *Jesus* that we cut down all her higher buildings; her rudder also was sore shaken and withal was in so extreme a leak that we were rather upon the point to leave her than to keep her any longer, yet hoping to bring all to good pass we sought the coast of Florida, where we found no place nor haven for our ships because of the shallowness of the coast.

Thus, being in greater despair and taken with a new storm which continued other 3 days, we were enforced to take for our succour the port which serveth the city of Mexico, called Saint John de Ulua which standeth in 19 degrees; in seeking of which port we took in our way three ships which carried passengers to the number of a hundred, which passengers we hoped should be a mean to us the better to obtain victuals for our money and a quiet place for the repairing of our fleet. Shortly after this, the 16th of September, we entered the port of Saint John de Ulua and, in our entry the Spaniards thinking us to be the fleet of Spain, the chief officers of the country came aboard us, which being deceived of their expectation were greatly dismayed, but immediately when they saw our demand was nothing but victuals were recomforted.

I found also in the same port twelve ships which had in them by report two hundred thousand pound in gold and silver, all which (being in my possession, with the King's island, as also the passengers before in my way thitherward stayed) I set at liberty, without the taking from them the weight of a groat. Only because I would not be delayed of my despatch I stayed two men of estimation and sent post immediately to Mexico, which was two hundred miles from us, to the Presidents and Council there, showing them of our arrival there by the force of weather and the necessity of the repair of our ships and victuals, which wants we required as friends to King Philip to be furnished of for our money; and that the Presidents and Council there should with all convenient speed take order that at the arrival of the Spanish fleet, which was daily looked for, there might no cause of quarrel rise between us and them, but for the better maintenance of amity their commandment might be had in that behalf.

This message being sent away, the sixteenth day of September at night, being the very day of our arrival, in the next morning, which was the seventeenth day of the same month, we saw open of the haven

La çiudad, y castillo de la vera cruz

norueste norte
O. es le nordeste
sudueste leste
sur sueste

thirteen great ships; and understanding them to be the fleet of Spain I sent immediately to advertise the General of the Fleet of my being there, doing him to understand that before I would suffer them to enter the port there should some order of conditions pass between us for our safe being there and maintenance of peace.

Now it is to be understood that this port is made by a little island of stones not three foot above the water in the highest place and but a bow-shot of length any way. This island standeth from the mainland two bow-shots or more; also it is to be understood that there is not in all this coast any other place for ships to arrive in safety because the north wind hath there such violence that unless the ships be very safely moored with their anchors fastened upon this island there is not remedy for these north winds but death. Also the place of the haven was so little that of necessity the ships must ride one aboard the other, so that we could not give place to them nor they to us.

And here I began to bewail that which after followed, "For now," said I, "I am in two dangers, and forced to receive the one of them". That was, either I must have kept out the fleet from entering the port, the which with God's help I was very well able to do, or else suffer them to enter in with their accustomed treason, which they never fail to execute where they may have opportunity to compass it by any means. If I had kept them out then had there been present shipwreck of all the fleet which amounted in value to six millions, which was in value of our money 1,800,000 pounds, which I considered I was not able to answer, fearing the Queen's Majesty's indignation in so weighty a matter. Thus with myself revolving the doubts, I thought rather better to abide the jut of the uncertainty than the certainty. The uncertain doubt I account was their treason, which by good policy I hoped might be prevented, and therefore as choosing the least mischief I proceeded to conditions.

Now was our first messenger come and returned from the fleet with report of the arrival of a Viceroy, so that he had authority both in all this Province of Mexico (otherwise called *Nueva España*) and in the sea, who sent us word that we should send our conditions which of his part should (for the better maintenance of amity between the Princes) be both favourably granted and faithfully performed, with many fair

12   The Spanish treasure fleet arriving at San Juan de Ulua. This picture is dated c. 1614, by which time the town of Veracruz had been moved to the mainland opposite the island, on which a castle had been constructed; but the approaching fleet is very much as Hawkins, moored to the island, saw it.

words how passing the coast of the Indies he had understood of our honest behaviour towards the inhabitants where we had to do, as well elsewhere as in the same port, the which I let pass.

Thus following our demand we required victuals for our money and licence to sell as much ware as might furnish our wants, and that there might be of either part twelve gentlemen as hostages for the maintenance of peace; and that the island for our better safety might be in our own possession during our abode there, and such ordnance as was planted in the same island, which were eleven pieces of brass; and that no Spaniard might land in the island with any kind of weapon. These conditions at the first he somewhat misliked, chiefly the guard of the island to be in our own keeping, which if they had had we had soon known our fare, for with the first north wind they had cut our cables and our ships had gone ashore. But in the end he concluded to our request, bringing the twelve hostages to ten, which with all speed of either part were received, with a writing from the Viceroy signed with his hand and sealed with his seal of all the conditions concluded, and forthwith a trumpet blown with commandment that none of either part should be mean to violate the peace upon pain of death; and further it was concluded that the two Generals of the fleets should meet and give faith each to other for the performance of the premises, which was so done.

Thus at the end of 3 days all was concluded and the fleet entered the port, saluting one another as the manner of the sea doth require. Thus, as I said before, Thursday we entered the port, Friday we saw the fleet, and on Monday at night they entered the port. Then we laboured two days placing the English ships by themselves and the Spanish ships by themselves, the captains of each part and inferior men of their parts promising great amity of all sides; which even as with all fidelity it was meant on our part, so the Spaniards meant nothing less on their parts, but from the mainland had furnished themselves with a supply of men to the number of 1,000, and meant the next Thursday, being the 23rd of September, at dinner time to set upon us on all sides.

The same Thursday in the morning, the treason being at hand, some appearance showed, as shifting of weapon from ship to ship, planting and bending of ordnance from the ships to the island where our men warded, passing to and fro of companies of men more than required for their necessary business, and many other ill likelihoods which caused us to have a vehement suspicion, and therewithal sent to the Viceroy to enquire what was meant by it, which sent immediately strait commandment to unplant all things suspicious, and also sent word that he in the faith of a Viceroy would be our defence from all villainies. Yet we being not satisfied with this answer, because we suspected a great number of men to be hid in a great ship of 900 tons which was moored next unto the *Minion*, sent again to the Viceroy the Master of the *Jesus* which had the Spanish tongue, and required to be satisfied if any such thing were or not. The Viceroy, now seeing that the treason must be discovered, forthwith stayed our Master, blew the trumpet, and of all sides set upon us. Our men which warded ashore being stricken with sudden fear gave place, fled, and sought to recover succour of the ships. The Spaniards, being before provided for the purpose, landed in all places in multitudes from their ships, which they might easily do without boats, and slew all our men ashore without mercy; a few of then escaped aboard the *Jesus*. The great ship which had by the estimation three hundred men placed on her secretly immediately fell aboard the *Minion*, but by God's appointment in the time of the suspicion we had, which was only one half hour, the *Minion* was made ready to avoid, and so loosing her headfasts and hauling away by the sternfasts she was gotten out. Thus with God's help she defended the violence of the first brunt of these three hundred men.

The *Minion* being passed out, they came aboard the *Jesus*, which also with very much ado and the loss of many of our men were defended and kept out. Then there were also two other ships that assaulted the *Jesus* at the same instant so that she had hard getting loose, but yet with some time we had cut our headfasts and gotten out by the sternfasts. Now when the *Jesus* and the *Minion* were gotten about two ships' length from the Spanish fleet the fight began so hot on all sides that within one hour the admiral of the Spaniards was supposed to be sunk, their vice-admiral burned, and one other of their principal ships supposed to be sunk, so that the ships were little able to annoy us.

Then it is to be understood that all the ordnance upon the island was in the Spaniards' hands, which did us so great annoyance that it cut all the masts and yards of the *Jesus* in such sort that there was no hope to carry her away; also it sunk our small ships. Whereupon we determined to place the *Jesus* on that side of the *Minion* that she might abide all the battery from the land and so be a defence for the *Minion* till night, and then to take such relief of victual and other necessaries from the *Jesus* as the time would suffer us and to leave her.

As we were thus determining and had placed the *Minion* from the shot of the land, suddenly the Spaniards had fired two great ships which were coming directly with us, and having no means to avoid the fire it bred among our men a marvellous fear, so that some said, "Let us depart with the *Minion*," others said, "Let us see whither the wind will carry the fire from us". But to be short, the *Minion*'s men, which had always their sails in readiness, thought to make sure work, and so without either consent of the Captain or Master cut their sail, so that very hardly I was received into the *Minion*.

The most part of the men that were left alive in the *Jesus* made shift and followed the *Minion* in a small boat; the rest which the little boat was not able to receive were enforced to abide the mercy of the Spainards (which I doubt was very little). So with the *Minion* only and the *Judith* (a small bark of 50 ton) we escaped, which bark the same night forsook us in our great misery. We were now removed with the *Minion* from the Spanish ships two bowshots, and there rode all that night. The next morning we recovered an island a mile from the Spaniards where there took us a north wind, and being left only with two anchors and two cables (for in this conflict we lost three cables and two anchors) we thought always upon death which ever was present, but God preserved us to a longer time.

The weather waxed reasonable and the Saturday we set sail, and having a great number of men and little victuals our hope of life waxed less and less. Some desired to yield to the Spaniards, some rather desired to obtain a place where they might give themselves to the infidels, and some had rather abide with a little pittance the mercy of God at sea. So thus with many sorrowful hearts we wandered in an unknown sea by the space of 14 days till hunger enforced us to seek the land, for hides were thought very good meat, rats, cats, mice and dogs, none escaped that might be gotten, parrots and monkeys that were had in great price were thought there very profitable if they served the turn one dinner. Thus in the end the 8th day of October we came to the land in the bottom of the same Bay of Mexico, in 23 degrees and a half, where we hoped to have found inhabitants of the Spaniards, relief of victuals, and place for the repair of our ship, which was so sore beaten with shot from our enemies and bruised with shooting off our own ordnance, that our weary and weak arms were scarce able to defend and keep out water. But all things happened to the contrary, for we found neither people, victual, nor haven of relief, but a place where having fair weather with some peril we might land a boat. Our people being forced with hunger desired to be set on land, whereunto I consented.

And such as were willing to land I put them apart, and such as were desirious to go homewards I put apart, so that they were indifferently parted a hundred of one side and a hundred of the other side. These hundred men we set aland with all diligence in this little place beforesaid, which being landed, we determined there to take in fresh water, and so with our little remain of victuals to take the sea.

The next day, having aland with me fifty of our hundred men that remained, for the speedier preparing of our water aboard, there arose an extreme storm so that in three days we could by no means repair aboard our ship. The ship also was in such peril that every hour we looked for shipwreck.

But yet God again had mercy on us and sent fair weather. We had aboard our water, and departed the 16th day of October, after which day we had fair and prosperous weather till the 16th day of November, which day, God be praised, we were clear from the coast of the Indies and out of the channel and Gulf of Bahama, which is between Cape of Florida and the islands of Lucaios.

After this, growing near to the cold country, our men being oppressed with famine died continually, and they that were left grew into such weakness that we were scantly able to manage our ship, and the wind being always ill for us to recover England we determined to go with Galicia in Spain, with intent there to relieve our company and other extreme wants. And being arrived the last day of December in a place near unto Vigo, called Pontevedra, our men with excess of fresh meat grew into miserable diseases and died a great part of them. This matter was borne out as long as it might be, but in the end although there were none of our men suffered to go aland, yet by access of the Spaniards our feebleness was known to them. Whereupon they ceased not to seek by all means to betray us, but with all speed possible we departed to Vigo, where we had some help of certain English ships and twelve fresh men, wherewith we repaired our wants as we might, and departing the 20th day of January, 1568, arrived in Mounts Bay in Cornwall the 25th of the same month, praised be God therefore.

If all the miseries and troublesome affairs of this sorrowful voyage should be perfectly and thoroughly written there should need a painful man with his pen and as great a time as he had that wrote the lives and deaths of the *Martyrs*.

John Hawkins

A discourse written by one Miles Philips, Englishman, one of the
company put on shore northward of Panuco in the West Indies by
Master John Hawkins, 1568; containing many special things of
that country and of the Spanish government, but specially of their
cruelties used to our Englishmen, and amongst the rest to himself
for the space of 15 or 16 years together, until by good and happy
means he was delivered from their bloody hands, and returned
into his own country, anno 1582.

[Philip's first two chapters closely duplicate, and are almost certainly
borrowed from, Hawkins' own account of the voyage out and the battle
in San Juan de Ulua. They are therefore omitted here.]

Chapter 3

Wherein is showed how, after we were escaped from the Spaniards, we
were like to perish with famine at the sea, and how our General for the
avoiding thereof was constrained to put half of his men on land; and
what miseries we after that sustained among the savage people, and
how again we fell into the hands of the Spaniards.

After that the Viceroy, Don Martin Henriques, had thus contrary to
his faith and promise most cruelly dealt with our General, Master
Hawkins, at Saint John de Ulua, where most of his men were by the
Spaniards slain and drowned, and all his ships sunk and burned saving
the *Minion* and the *Judith* (which was a small bark of fifty ton, wherein
was then captain Master Francis Drake aforesaid), the same night the
said bark lost us, we being in great necessity and enforced to remove
with the *Minion* two bow-shot from the Spanish fleet, where we
anchored all that night. And the next morning we weighed anchor, and
recovered an island a mile from the Spaniards, where a storm took us
with a north wind, in which we were greatly distressed, having but two
cables and two anchors left; for in the conflict before we had lost three
cables and two anchors. The morrow after, the storm being ceased and
the weather fair, we weighed and set sail, being many men in number
and but small store of victuals to suffice us for any long time; by means
whereof we were in despair and fear that we should perish through
famine, so that some were in mind to yield themselves to the mercy of
the Spaniards, other some to the savages or infidels. And wandering
thus certain days in these unknown seas, hunger constrained us to eat
hides, cats and dogs, mice, rats, parrots and monkeys. To be short, our
hunger was so great that we thought it savoury and sweet whatsoever
we could get to eat.

And on the eighth of October we came to land again in the bottom of the Bay of Mexico, where we hoped to have found some inhabitants, that we might have had some relief of victuals and a place where to repair our ship, which was so greatly bruised that we were scarce able with our weary arms to keep forth the water. Being thus oppressed with famine on the one side and danger of drowning on the other, not knowing where to find relief, we began to be in wonderful despair, and we were of many minds; amongst whom there were a great many that did desire our General to set them on land, making their choice rather to submit themselves to the mercy of the savages or infidels than longer to hazard themselves at sea, where they very well saw that, if they should remain together, if they perished not by drowning yet hunger would enforce them in the end to eat one another. To which request our General did very willingly agree, considering with himself that it was necessary for him to lessen his number, both for the safety of himself and the rest; and thereupon being resolved to set half his people ashore that he had then left alive, it was a world to see how suddenly men's minds were altered, for they which a little before desired to be set on land were now of another opinion, and requested rather to stay. By means whereof our General was enforced for the more contentation of all men's minds, and to take away all occasions of offence, to take this order: first he made choice of such persons of service and account as were needful to stay; and that being done, of those which were willing to go he appointed such as he thought might be best spared, and presently appointed that by the boat they should be set on shore, our General promising us that the next year he would either come himself or else send to fetch us home. Here again it would have caused any stony heart to have relented to hear the pitiful moan that many did make, and how loth they were to depart. The weather was then somewhat stormy and tempestuous and therefore we were to pass with great danger; yet, notwithstanding, there was no remedy but we that were appointed to go away must of necessity do so.

Howbeit, those that went in the first boat were safely set on shore, but of them which went in the second boat, of which number I myself was one, the seas wrought so high that we could not attain the shore, and therefore we were constrained through the cruel dealing of John Hampton, Captain of the *Minion*, and John Sanders, boatswain of the *Jesus*, and Thomas Pollard, his mate, to leap out of the boat into the main sea, having more than a mile to shore, and so to shift for ourselves and either to sink or swim. And of those that so were, as it were, thrown out and compelled to leap into the sea there were two drowned, which were of Captain Bland's men.

In the evening of the same day, it being Monday the eighth of October 1568, when we were all come to shore, we found fresh water, whereof some of our men drunk so much that they had almost cast themselves away, for we could scarce get life of them for the space of two or three hours after. Other some were so cruelly swollen, what with the drinking in of the salt water and what with the eating of the fruit which we found on land, having a stone in it much like an almond (which fruit is called *capule*), that they were all in very ill case, so that we were in a manner all of us both feeble, faint, and weak.

The next morning, being Tuesday the ninth of October, we thought it best to travel along by the sea coast to seek out some place of habitation. Whether they were Christians or savages we were indifferent, so that we might have wherewithal to sustain our hungry bodies. And so, departing from a hill where we had rested all night, not having any dry thread about us, for those that were not wet being not thrown into the sea were thoroughly wet with rain, for all the night it rained cruelly—as we went from the hill and were come into the plain we were greatly troubled to pass for the grass and weeds that grew there higher than any man. On the left hand we had the sea and upon the right hand great woods, so that of necessity we must needs pass on our way westward through those marshes; and going thus, suddenly we were assaulted by the Indians, a warlike kind of people, which are in a manner as cannibals although they do not feed upon man's flesh as cannibals do.

These people are called Chichemici, and they use to wear their hair long, even down to their knees. They do also colour their faces green, yellow, red, and blue, which maketh them seem very ugly and terrible to behold. These people do keep wars against the Spaniards, of whom they have been oftentimes very cruelly handled, for with the Spaniards there is no mercy. They, perceiving us at our first coming on land, supposed us to have been their enemies, the bordering Spaniards, and having by their forerunners descried what number we were, and how feeble and weak without armour or weapon, they suddenly, according to their accustomed manner when they encounter with any people in warlike sort, raised a terrible and huge cry and so came running fiercely upon us, shooting off their arrows as thick as hail; unto whose mercy we were constrained to yield, not having amongst us any kind of armour, nor yet weapon saving one caliver and two old rusty swords, whereby to make any resistance or to save ourselves. Which, when they perceived that we sought not any other than favour and mercy at their hands, and that we were not their enemies the Spaniards, they had compassion on us, and came and caused us all to sit down. And when they had a while surveyed and taken a perfect view of us, they came to all such as had any coloured clothes amongst us, and those they did strip stark naked and took their clothes away with them, but those that were apparelled in black they did not meddle withal; and so went their ways, and left us without doing us any further hurt, only in the first brunt they killed eight of our men. And at our departure, they perceiving in what weak case we were pointed us with their hands which way we should go to come to a town of the Spaniards, which, as we afterwards perceived, was not past ten leagues from thence, using these words: Tampice, Tampice, Christiano, Tampice Christiano, which is as much (we think) as to say in English "at Tampice you shall find the Christians". The weapons that they use are no other but bows and arrows, and their arm is so good that they very seldom miss to hit anything that they shoot at.

Shortly after they had left us stripped as aforesaid, we thought it best to divide ourselves into two companies. And so being separated, half of us went under the leading of one Anthony Goddard, who is a man yet alive and dwelleth at this instant in the town of Plymouth, whom before we chose to be captain over us all; and those which went under his leading, of which number I, Miles Philips, was one, travelled westward that way which the Indians with their hands had before pointed us to go. The other half went under the leading of one John Hooper, whom they did choose for their captain, and with the company that went with him David Ingram was one, and they took their way and travelled northward. And shortly after, within the space of two days, they were again encountered with the savage people and their captain Hooper and two more of his company were slain. Then again they divided themselves, and some held on their way still northward, and other some, knowing that we were gone westward, sought to meet with us again; as in truth there was about the number of 25 or 26 of them that met with us in the space of four days again. And then we began to reckon amongst ourselves how many we were that were set on shore, and we found the number to be a hundred and fourteen, whereof two were drowned in the sea and eight were slain at the first encounter, so that there remained a hundred and four, of which 25 went westward with us and 52 to the north with Hooper and Ingram. And as Ingram since hath often told me, there were not past three of their company slain, and there were but six and twenty of them that came again to us, so that of the company that went northward there is yet lacking, and not certainly heard of, the number of three and twenty men. And verily I do think that there are some of them yet alive and married in the said country at Cibola, as hereafter I purpose (God willing) to discourse of more particularly, with the reason and causes that make me so to think of them that were lacking, which were David Ingram, Twide, Browne, and sundry others whose names we could not remember.

And being thus met again together, we travelled on still westward, sometime through such thick woods that we were enforced with cudgels to break away the brambles and bushes from tearing our naked bodies. Other sometimes we should travel through the plains in such high grass that we could scarce see one another, and as we passed in some places we should have of our men slain, and fall down suddenly, being struck by the Indians, which stood behind trees and bushes, in secret places, and so killed our men as they went by, for we went scatteringly in seeking of friuts to relieve ourselves. We were also oftentimes greatly annoyed with a kind of fly which in the Indian tongue is called *tequani* and the Spaniards call them mosquitoes. There are also in the said country a number of other kind of flies, but none so noisome as these *tequanis* be. You shall hardly see them they be so small, for they are scarce so big as a gnat. They will suck one's blood marvellously, and if you kill them while they are sucking they are so venomous that the place will swell extremely, even as one that is stung with a wasp or bee; but if you let them suck their fill and to go away of themselves, then they do no other hurt but leave behind them a red spot somewhat bigger than a flea-biting. At the first we were terribly troubled with these kind of flies, not knowing their qualities; and resistance we could make none against them, being naked. As for cold, we feared not any, the country there is always so warm.

And as we travelled thus for the space of ten or twelve days, our captain did oftentimes cause certain to go up into the tops of high trees to see if they could descry any town or place of inhabitants, but they could not perceive any; and using often the same order to climb up into high trees, at the length they descried a great river that fell from the north-west into the main sea. And presently after we heard an arquebus shot off, which did greatly encourage us, for thereby we knew that we were near to some Christians, and did therefore hope shortly to find some succour and comfort. And within the space of one hour after, as we travelled we heard a cock crow, which was also no small joy unto us, and so we came to the north side of the river of Panuco, where the Spaniards have certain salines, at which place it was that the arquebus was shot off which before we heard. To which place we went not directly, but missing thereof we left it about a bow-shot upon our left hand. Of this river we drank very greedily, for we had not met with any water in six days before. And as we were here by the river-side resting ourselves and longing to come to the place where the cock did crow and where the arquebus was shot off, we perceived many Spaniards upon the other side of the river, riding up and down on horseback; and they, perceiving us, did suppose that we had been of the Indians their bordering enemies, the Chichemici. The river was not past half a bow-shot over; and presently one of the Spaniards took an Indian boat called a canoe and so came over, being rowed by two Indians, and having taken the view of us did presently row over back again to the Spaniards. Who without any delay made out about the number of twenty horsemen and, embarking themselves in the canoes, they led their horses by the reins swimming over after them and, being come over to that side of the river where we were, they saddled their horses and, being mounted upon them with their lances charged, they came very fiercely running at us.

Our captain Anthony Goddard, seeing them come in that order, did persuade us to submit and yield ourselves unto them, for being naked, as we at this time were, and without weapon, we could not make any resistance; whose bidding we obeyed. And upon the yielding of ourselves they perceived us to be Christians, and did call for more canoes and carried us over by four and four in a boat. And being come on the other side, they understanding by our captain how long we had been without meat imparted between two and two a loaf of bread made of that country wheat which the Spaniards call maize, of the bigness of our halfpenny loaves, which bread is named in the indian tongue *clashacally*. This bread was very sweet and pleasant unto us, for we had not eaten any in a long time before; and what is it that hunger doth not make to have a savoury and a delicate taste? And having thus parted the bread amongst us, those which were men they sent afore to the town, having also many Indians, inhabitants of that place, to guard them; they which were young, as boys, and some such also as were feeble they took up upon their horses behind them, and so carried us to the town where they dwelt, which was very near distant a mile from the place where we came over.

This town is well situated, and well replenished with all kinds of fruits, as oranges, lemons, pomegranates, apricots, and peaches, and sundry others; and is inhabited with a great number of tame Indians, or Mexicans, and had in it also at that time about the number of two hundred Spaniards, men, women, and children, besides negroes. Of their salines, which lie upon the west side of the river, more than a mile distant from thence, they make a great profit, for it is an excellent good merchandise there. The Indians do buy much thereof and carry it up into the country, and there sell it to their own country people in doubling the price. Also much of the salt made in this place is transported from thence by sea to sundry other places, as to Cuba, Saint John de Ulua, and the other ports of Tamiago and Tamachos, which are two barred havens west and by south above threescore leagues from Saint John de Ulua. When we were all come into the town, the Governor there showed himself very severe unto us, and threatened to hang us all; and then he demanded what money we had, which in truth was very little, for the Indians which we first met withal had in a manner taken all from us, and of that which they left the Spaniards which brought us over took away a good part also. Howbeit, from Anthony Goddard the Governor here had a chain of gold, which was given unto him at Cartagena by the Governor there, and from others he had some small store of money; so that we accounted that amongst us all he had the number of five hundred pesos, besides the chain of gold.

And having thus satisfied himself, when he had taken all that we had, he caused us to be put into a little house much like a hog-sty, where we were almost smothered; and before we were thus shut up into that little cote, they gave us some of the country wheat called maize, sodden, which they feed their hogs withal. But many of our men which had been hurt by the Indians at our first coming on land, whose wounds were very sore and grievous, desired to have the help of their surgeons to cure their wounds. The Governor, and most of them all, answered that we should have none other surgeon but the hangman, which should sufficiently heal us of all our griefs; and thus reviling us, and calling us English dogs and Lutheran heretics, we remained the space of three days in this miserable state, not knowing what should become of us, waiting every hour to be bereaved of our lives.

Chapter 4

Wherein is showed how we were used in Panuco and in what fear of death we were there, and how we were carried to Mexico to the Viceroy, and of our imprisonment there and at Tezcoco, with the courtesies and cruelties we received during that time; and how in the end we were by proclamation given to serve as slaves to sundry gentlemen Spaniards.

Upon the fourth day after our coming thither, and there remaining in a perplexity, looking every hour when we should suffer death, there came a great number of Indians and Spaniards weaponed to fetch us out of the house, and amongst them we espied one that brought a great many of new halters, at the sight whereof we were greatly amazed and made no other account but that we should presently have suffered death, and so crying and calling to God for mercy and forgiveness of our sins we prepared ourselves, making us ready to die. Yet in the end, as the sequel showed, their meaning was not so. For when we were come out of the house, with those halters they bound our arms behind us, and so coupling us two and two together they commanded us to march on through the town, and so along the country from place to place toward the city of Mexico, which is distant from Panuco west and by south the space of ninety leagues, having only but two Spaniards to conduct us, they being accompanied with a great number of Indians warding on either side with bows and arrows lest we should escape from them. And travelling in this order, upon the second day at night we came unto a town which the Indians call Nohele and the Spaniards call it Santa Maria. In which town there is a house of White Friars, which did very courteously use us, and gave us hot meat, as mutton and broth, and garments also to cover ourselves withal, made of white baize. We fed very greedily of the meat and of the Indian fruit, called *nochole*, which fruit is long and small, much like in fashion to a little cucumber. Our greedy feeding caused us to fall sick of hot burning agues. And here at this place one Thomas Baker one of our men died of a hurt; for he had been before shot with an arrow into the throat at the first encounter.

The next morrow, about ten of the clock, we departed from thence, bound two and two together and guarded as before, and so travelled on our way toward Mexico till we came to a town within forty leagues of Mexico, named Metztitlan, where is a house of Black Friars; and in this town there are about the number of three hundred Spaniards, both men, women, and children. The friars sent us meat from the house ready dressed, and the friars and the men and women used us very courteously and gave us some shirts and other such things as we lacked. Here our men were very sick of their agues, and with eating of another fruit called in the Indian tongue *guiaccos*, which fruit did bind us so sore that for the space of ten or twelve days we could not ease ourselves. The next morning we departed from thence with our two Spaniards and Indian guard as aforesaid. Of these two Spaniards the one was an aged man who all the way did very courteously entreat us, and would carefully go before to provide for us both meat and things necessary to the uttermost of his power. The other was a young man who all the way travelled with us and never departed from us, who was a very cruel caitiff; and he carried a javelin in his hand and sometimes, when as our men with very feebleness and faintness were not able to go so fast as he required them, he would take his javelin in both his hands and strike them with the same between the neck and the shoulders so violently that he would strike them down. Then he would cry and say "Marchad, marchad Ingleses perros, Luterianos, enemigos de Dios"; which is as much to say in English as "March, march on you English dogs, Lutherans, enemies to God". And the next day we came to a town called Pachuca. And there are two places of that name, as this town of Pachuca and the mines of Pachuca, which are mines of silver and are about six leagues distant from this town of Pachuca towards the north-west.

Here at this town the good old man, our governor, suffered us to stay two days and two nights, having compassion of our sick and weak men; full sore against the mind of the young man, his companion. From thence we took our journey and travelled four or five days by little villages and *estancias*, which are farms or dairy houses of the Spaniards, and ever as we had need the good man would still provide us sufficient of meats, fruits, and water to sustain us. At the end of which five days we came to a town within five leagues of Mexico, which is called Quoghliclan, where we also stayed one whole day and two nights, where was a fair house of Grey Friars; howbeit we saw none of them. Here we were told by the Spaniards in the town that we had not past fifteen English miles from thence to Mexico, whereof we were all very joyful and glad, hoping that when we came thither we should either be relieved and set free out of bonds, or else be quickly despatched out of our lives. For seeing ourselves thus carried bound from place to place, although some used us courteously, yet could we never joy nor be merry till we might perceive ourselves set free from that bondage either by death or otherwise.

The next morning we departed from thence on our journey towards Mexico, and so travelled till we came within two leagues of it, where there was built by the Spaniards a very fair church, called Our Lady's church, in which there is an image of Our Lady of silver and gilt, being as high and as large as a tall woman, in which church, and before this image, there are as many lamps of silver as there be days in the year, which upon high days are all lighted. Whensoever any Spaniards pass by this church, although they be on horseback, they will alight, and come into the church, and kneel before the image and pray to Our Lady to defend them from all evil, so that whether he be horseman or footman he will not pass by, but first go into the church and pray as aforesaid, which if they do not, they think and believe that they shall never prosper; which image they call in the Spanish tongue Nuestra Senora de Guadalupe.

At this place there are certain cold baths which arise, springing up as though the water did seethe; the water whereof is somewhat brackish in taste, but very good for any that have a sore or wound to wash themselves therewith, for as they say it healeth many. And every year once, upon Our Lady Day, the people use to repair thither to offer, and to pray in that church before the image; and they say that Our Lady of Guadalupe doth work a number of miracles. About this church there is not any town of Spaniards that is inhabited, but certain Indians do dwell there in houses of their own country building.

Here we were met with a great number of Spaniards on horseback which came from Mexico to see us, both gentlemen and men of occupations, and they came as people to see a wonder. We were still called upon to march on; and so about four of the clock in the afternoon of the said day we entered into the city of Mexico by the way or street called La Calle Santa Catherina; and we stayed not in any place till we came to the house or palace of the Viceroy, Don Martin Henriques, which standeth in the midst of the city hard by the market place called La Plaça del Marquese. We had not stayed any long time at this place but there was brought us by the Spaniards from the market place great store of meat, sufficient to have satisfied five times so many as we were. Some also gave us hats, and some gave us money. In which place we stayed for the space of two hours, and from thence we were conveyed by water in two large canoes to a hospital where as certain of our men were lodged which were taken before the fight at Saint John de Ulua. We should have gone to Our Lady's Hospital, but that there were also so many of our men taken before at that fight that there was no room for us. After our coming thither, many of the company that came with me from Panuco died within the space of fourteen days; soon after which we were taken forth from that place and put together into Our Lady's Hospital, in which place we were courteously used, and visited oftentimes by virtuous gentlemen and gentlewomen of the city, who brought us divers things to comfort us withal, as suckets and marmalades and such other things, and would also many times give us many things, and that very liberally. In which hospital we remained for the space of six months, until we were all whole and sound of body, and then we were appointed by the Viceroy to be carried unto the town of Tezcoco, which is from Mexico south-west, distant eight leagues; in which town there are certain houses of correction and punishment for ill people called *obraches*, like to Bridewell here in London, into which place divers Indians are sold for slaves, some for ten years and some for twelve.

It was no small grief unto us when we understood that we should be carried thither, and to be used as slaves we had rather be put to death. Howbeit, there was no remedy but we were carried to the prison of Tezcoco, where we were not put to any labour but were very straitly kept, and almost famished. Yet by the good providence of our merciful God we happened there to meet with one Robert Sweeting, who was the son of an Englishman born of a Spanish woman. This man could speak very good English, and by his means we were helped very much with victuals from the Indians, as mutton, hens, and bread. And if we had not been so relieved we had surely perished; and yet all the provision that we had gotten that way was but slender. And continuing thus straitly kept in prison there for the space of two months, at the length we agreed amongst ourselves to break forth of prison, come of it what would, for we were minded rather to suffer death than longer to live in that miserable state. And so, having escaped out of prison, we knew not what way to fly for the safety of ourselves. The night was dark, and it rained terribly, and not having any guide we went we knew not whither; and in the morning, at the appearing of the day, we perceived ourselves to be come hard to the city of Mexico, which is 24 English miles from Tezcoco. The day being come we were espied by the Spaniards, and pursued and taken and brought before the Viceroy and head justices, who threated to hang us for breaking the King's prison. Yet in the end they sent us into a garden belonging to the Viceroy, and coming thither we found there our English gentlemen which were delivered as hostages whenas our General was betrayed at Saint John de Ulua as is aforesaid, and with them we also found Robert Barrett, the Master of the *Jesus*. In which place we remained, labouring and doing such things as we were commanded, for the space of 4 months, having but two sheep a day allowed to suffice us all, being very near a hundred men; and for bread we had every man two loaves a day of the quantity of one halfpenny loaf. At the end of which four months, they having removed our gentlemen hostages and the Master of the *Jesus* to a prison in the Viceroy's own house did cause it to be proclaimed that, what gentleman Spaniard soever was willing or would have any Englishman to serve him, and be bound to keep him forthcoming to appear before the justices within one month after notice given, that they should repair to the said garden and there take their choice; which proclamation was no sooner made but the gentlemen came and repaired to the garden amain, so that happy was he that could soonest get one of us.

Chapter 5

Wherein is showed in what good sort and how wealthily we lived with our masters until the coming of the Inquisition, whenas again our sorrows began afresh; of our imprisonment in the Holy House, and of the severe judgment and sentences given against us, and with what rigour and cruelty the same were executed.

The gentlemen that thus took us for their servants or slaves did new-apparel us throughout, with whom we abode, doing such service as they appointed us unto, which was for the most part to attend upon them at the table, and to be as their chamberlains, and to wait upon them when they went abroad, which they greatly accounted of. For in that country no Spaniard will serve one another, but they are all of them attended and served by Indians weekly, and by negroes which be their slaves during their life. In this sort we remained and served in the said city of Mexico and thereabouts for the space of a year and somewhat longer. Afterwards many of us were by our masters appointed to go to sundry of their mines where they had to do, and to be as overseers of the negroes and Indians that laboured there. In which mines many of us did profit and gain greatly: for, first, we were allowed three hundred pesos a man for a year, which is threescore pound sterling; and besides that, the Indians and negroes which wrought under our charge, upon our well using and entreating of them, would at times (as upon Saturdays when they had left work) labour for us, and blow as much silver as should be worth unto us 3 marks or thereabouts, every mark being worth 6 pesos and a half of their money, which 19 pesos and a half is worth £4 10s. of our money. Sundry weeks we did gain so much by this means, besides our wages, that many of us became very rich and were worth three thousand or four thousand pesos, for we lived and gained thus in those mines some three or four years.

As concerning those gentlemen which were delivered as hostages, and that were kept in prison in the Viceroy's house, after that we were gone from out the garden to serve sundry gentlemen as aforesaid they remained prisoners in the said house for the space of 4 months after their coming thither, at the end whereof, the fleet being ready to depart from Saint John de Ulua to go for Spain, the said gentlemen were sent away into Spain with the fleet, whereas I have heard it credibly reported many of then died with the cruel handling of the Spaniards in the Inquisition House, as those which have been delivered home after they had suffered the persecution of that House can more perfectly declare. Robert Barrett also, Master of the *Jesus*, was sent away with the fleet into Spain the next year following, where afterwards he suffered persecution in the Inquisition and at the last was condemned to be burnt, and with him one more of our men whose name was John Gilbert.

Now after that six years were fully expired since our first coming into the Indies, in which time we had been imprisoned and served in the said countries as is before truly declared, in the year of Our Lord one thousand five hundred seventy four the Inquisition began to be established in the Indies, very much against the minds of many of the Spaniards themselves; for never until this time since their first conquering and planting in the Indies were they subject to that bloody and cruel Inquisition. The chief Inquisitor was named Don Pedro Moya de Contreres, and John de Bovilla his companion, and John Sanchez the Fiscal, and Pedro de los Rios the Secretary. They, being come and settled, and placed in a very fair house near unto the White Friars, considering with themselves that they must make an entrance and beginning of that their most detestable Inquisition here in Mexico, to the terror of the whole country, thought it best to call us that were Englishmen first in question, and so much the rather for that they had perfect knowledge and intelligence that many of us were become very rich as hath been already declared, and therefore we were a very good booty and prey to the Inquisitors. So that now again began our sorrows afresh, for we were sent for, and sought out in all places of the country, and proclamation made, upon pain of losing of goods and excommunication, that no man should hide or keep secret any Englishman or any part of their goods. By means whereof we were all soon apprehended in all places, and all our goods seized and taken for the Inquisitors' use; and so from all parts of the country we were conveyed and sent as prisoners to the city of Mexico, and there committed to prison in sundry dark dungeons, where we could not see but by candlelight, and were never past two together in one place so that we saw not one another, neither could one of us tell what was become of another.

Thus we remained close imprisoned for the space of a year and a half, and others for some less time, for they came to prison ever as they were apprehended. During which time of our imprisonment, at the first beginning we were often called before the Inquisitors alone and there severely examined of our faith and commanded to say the Pater Noster, the Ave Maria, and the Creed in Latin, which God knoweth a great number of us could not say otherwise than in the English tongue. And having the said Robert Sweeting who was our friend at Tezcoco always present with them for an interpreter, he made report for us that in our own country speech we could say them perfectly, although not word for word as they were in Latin. Then did they proceed to demand of us upon our oaths what we did believe of the sacrament, and whether there did remain any bread or wine after the words of consecration, yea or no, and whether we did not believe that the host of bread which the priest did hold up over his head and the wine that was in the chalice was the very true and perfect body and blood of our Saviour Christ, yea or no. To which if we answered not yea, then was there no way but death. Then they would demand of us what we did remember of ourselves, what opinions we had held, or had been taught to hold, contrary to the same while we were in England; to which we for the safety of our lives were constrained to say that we never did believe nor had been taught otherwise than as before we had said. Then would they charge us that we did not tell them the truth, that they knew the contrary, and therefore we should call ourselves to remembrance and make them a better answer at the next time, or else we should be racked, and made to confess the truth whether we would or no. And so coming again before them the next time we were still demanded of our belief while we were in England, and how we had been taught, and also what we thought or did know of such of our own company as they did name unto us, so that we could never be free from such demands. And at other times they would promise us that if we would tell them truth then should we have favour and be set at liberty, although we very well knew their fair speeches were but means to entrap us, to the hazard and loss of our lives. Howbeit, God so mercifully wrought for us by a secret means that we had, that we kept us still to our first answer, and would still say that we had told the truth unto them, and knew no more by ourselves nor any other of our fellows than as we had declared; and that for our sins and offences in England against God and Our Lady or any of His blessed Saints we were heartily sorry for the same, and did cry God mercy, and besought the Inquisitors for God's sake, considering that we came into those countries by force of weather and against our wills, and that never in all our lives we had either spoken or done anything contrary to their laws, and therefore they would have mercy upon us. Yet all this would not serve; for still from time to time we were called upon to confess, and about the space of 3 months before they proceeded to their severe judgment we were all racked, and some enforced to utter that against themselves which afterwards cost them their lives.

And thus having gotten from our own mouths matter sufficient for them to proceed in judgment against us, they caused a large scaffold to be made in the midst of the market-place in Mexico right over against the head church, and 14 or 15 days before the day of their judgment, with the sound of a trumpet and the noise of their *attabalies*, which are a kind of drums, they did assemble the people in all parts of the city; before whom it was then solemnly proclaimed that whosoever would upon such a day repair to the market-place, they should hear the sentence of the Holy Inquisition against the English heretics, Lutherans, and also see the same put in execution. Which being done, and the time approaching of this cruel judgment, the night before they came to the prison where we were with certain officers of that holy hellish house, bringing with them certain fools' coats which they had prepared for us, being called in their language San Benitos, which coats were made of yellow cotton and red crosses upon them both before and behind. They were so busied in putting on their coats about us, and bringing us out into a large yard, and placing and pointing us in what order we should go to the scaffold or place of judgment upon the morrow, that they did not once suffer us to sleep all that night long. The next morning being come, there was given to every one of us for our breakfast a cup of wine and a slice of bread fried in honey; and so about eight of the clock in the morning we set forth of the prison, every man alone in his yellow coat and a rope about his neck and a great green wax candle in his hand unlighted, having a Spaniard appointed to go upon either side of every one of us. And so, marching in this order and manner towards the scaffold in the market-place, which was a bow-shot distant or thereabouts, we found a great assembly of people all the way, and such a throng that certain of the Inquisitors' officers on horseback were constrained to make way; and so coming to the scaffold we went up by a pair of stairs and found seats ready made and prepared for us to sit down on, every man in order as he should be called to receive his judgment. We being thus set down as we were appointed, presently the Inquisitors came up another pair of stairs and the Viceroy and all the chief justices with them. When they were set down and placed under the cloth of state agreeing to their degrees and calling, then came up also a great number of friars, White, Black, and Grey, about the number of 300 persons, they being set in the places for them appointed. Then was there a solemn Oyez made and silence commanded, and then presently began their severe and cruel judgment.

The first man that was called was one Roger, the chief armourer of the *Jesus*, and he had judgment to have three hundred stripes on horseback, and after condemned to the galleys as a slave for 10 years.

After him was called John Gray, John Browne, John Rider, John

Moon, James Collier, and one Thomas Browne; these were adjudged to have 200 stripes on horseback and after to be committed to the galleys for the space of 8 years.

Then was called John Keyes, and was adjudged to have 100 stripes on horseback and condemned to serve in the galleys for the space of 6 years.

Then were severally called the number of 53 one after another, and every man had his several judgment, some to have 200 stripes on horseback and some 100, and condemned for slaves to the galleys, some for 6 years, some for 8, and some for 10.

And then was I, Miles Philips, called, and was adjudged to serve in a monastery for 5 years, without any stripes, and to wear a fool's coat or San Benito during all that time.

Then were called John Story, Richard Williams, David Alexander, Robert Cooke, Paul Horsewell, and Thomas Hull; the six were condemned to serve in monasteries, without stripes, some for 3 years and some for four, and to wear the San Benito during all the said time. Which being done, and it now drawing toward night, George Rively, Peter Momfry, and Cornelius the Irishman were called and had their judgment to be burnt to ashes, and so were presently sent away to the place of execution in the market-place but a little from the scaffold, where they were quickly burnt and consumed. And as for us that had received our judgment, being 68 in number, we were carried back that night to prison again.

And the next day in the morning, being Good Friday, the year of Our Lord 1575, we were all brought into a court of the Inquisitors' palace, where we found a horse in readiness for every one of our men which were condemned to have stripes and to be committed to the galleys, which were in number 60. And so they, being enforced to mount up on horseback, naked from the middle upward, were carried to be shown as a spectacle for all the people to behold throughout the chief and principal streets of the city, and had the number of stripes to every one of them appointed most cruelly laid upon their naked bodies with long whips by sundry men appointed to be the executioners thereof; and before our men went a couple of criers which cried as they went "Behold these English dogs, Lutherans, enemies to God", and all the way as they went there were some of the Inquisitors themselves, and of the familiars of that rakehell order that cried to the executioners "Strike, lay on those English heretics, Lutherans, God's enemies". And so this horrible spectacle being shown round about the city, they returned to the Inquisitors' house, with their backs all gore blood and swollen with great bumps, and were then taken from their horses and carried again to prison, where they remained until they were sent into Spain to the galleys, there to receive the rest of their martyrdom. And I and the six other with me which had judgment and were condemned amongst the rest to serve an apprenticeship in the monastery, were taken presently and sent to certain religious houses appointed for the purpose.

Chapter 6

Wherein is showed how we were used in the religious houses, and that, when the time was expired that we were adjudged to serve in them, there came news to Mexico of Master Francis Drake being in the South Sea, and what preparation was made to take him; and how I, seeking to escape, was again taken and put in prison at Vera Cruz, and how again I made my escape from thence.

I, Miles Philips, and William Lowe were appointed to the Black Friars, where I was appointed to be an overseer of Indian workmen who wrought there in building of a new church; amongst which Indians I learned their language or Mexican tongue very perfectly, and had great familiarity with many of them, whom I found to be a courteous and loving kind of people, ingenious, and of great understanding; and they hate and abhor the Spaniards with all their hearts, they have used such horrible cruelties against them, and do still keep them in such subjection and servitude that they and the negroes also do daily lie in wait to practise their deliverance out of that thraldom and bondage that the Spaniards do keep them in. William Lowe, he was appointed to serve the cook in the kitchen, Richard Williams and David Alexander were appointed to the Grey Friars, John Story and Robert Cooke to the White Friars; Paul Horsewell the Secretary took as his servant; Thomas Hull was sent to a monastery of priests, where afterward he died. Thus we served out the years that we were condemned for, with the use of our fools' coats, and we must needs confess that the friars did use us very courteously. For every one of us had his chamber, with bedding and diet and all things clean and neat; yea, many of the Spaniards and friars themselves do utterly abhor and mislike of that cruel Inquisition, and would as they durst bewail our miseries and comfort us the best they could, although they stood in such fear of that devilish Inquisition that they durst not let the left hand know what the right doth.

Now after that the time was expired for which we were condemned to serve in those religious houses, we were then brought again before the chief Inquisitor and had all our fools' coats pulled off and hanged up in the head church, called Ecclesia Major, and every man's name and judgment written thereupon with this addition, "A heretic Lutheran reconciled". And there are also all their coats hanged up which were condemned to the galleys, with their names and judgments, and underneath his coat "Heretic Lutheran reconciled"; and also the coats and names of the three that were burned, whereupon was written "an

obstinate heretic Lutheran burnt". Then were we suffered to go up and
down the country, and to place ourselves as we could, and yet not so
free but that we very well knew that there was good espial always
attending us and all our actions, so that we durst not once speak or look
awry. David Alexander and Robert Cooke returned to serve the
Inquisitor, who shortly after married them both to two of his negro
women. Richard Williams married a rich widow of Biscay with 4000
pesos. Paul Horsewell is married to a *mestiza*, as they name those whose
fathers were Spaniards and their mothers Indians; and this woman
which Paul Horsewell hath married is said to be the daughter of one
that came in with Hernando Cortes the conqueror; who had with her
4000 pesos and a fair house. John Story is married to a negro woman.
William Lowe had leave and licence to go into Spain where he is now
married. For my own part I could never thoroughly settle myself to
marry in that country, although many fair offers were made unto me of
such as were of great ability and wealth, but I could have no liking to
live in that place, where I must everywhere see and know such horrible
idolatry committed and durst not for my life speak against it; and
therefore I had always a longing and desire to this my native country.
And to return and serve again in the mines, where I might have
gathered great riches and wealth, I very well saw that at one time or
another I should fall again into the danger of that devilish Inquisition,
and so be stripped of all, with loss of life also. And therefore I made my
choice rather to learn to weave grosgrains and taffetas, and so, com-
pounding with a silk-weaver, I bound myself for three years to serve
him, and gave him a hundred and fifty pesos to teach me the science,
otherwise he would not have taught me under seven years' apprenticeship; and by this means I lived the more quiet and free from suspicion.
Howbeit, I should many times be charged by familiars of that devilish
House that I had a meaning to run away into England and to be a
heretic Lutheran again. To whom I would answer that they had no
need to suspect any such thing in me, for that they knew all very well
that it was impossible for me to escape by any manner of means. Yet
notwithstanding I was called before the Inquisitor, and demanded why
I did not marry. I answered that I had bound myself at an occupation.
"Well," said the Inquisitor, "I know thou meanest to run away, and
therefore I charge thee here upon pain of burning as a heretic relapsed
that thou depart not out of this city, nor come near to the port of Saint
John de Ulua nor to any other port." To the which I answered that I
would willingly obey. "Yea," said he, "see thou do so, and thy fellows
also, they shall have the like charge."

So I remained at my science the full time and learned the art. At the
end whereof there came news to Mexico that there were certain
Englishmen landed with a great power at the port of Acapulco upon
the South Sea, and that they were coming to Mexico to take the spoil

thereof; which wrought a marvellous great fear amongst them, and many of those that were rich began to shift for themselves, their wives, and children. Upon which hurly-burly the Viceroy caused a general muster to be made of all the Spaniards in Mexico, and there were found to be the number of 7000 and odd householders of Spaniards in the city and suburbs, and of single men unmarried the number of 3000, and of *mestizos*, which are counted to be the sons of Spaniards born of Indian women, twenty thousand persons. And then was Paul Horsewell and I, Miles Philips, sent for before the Viceroy, and were examined if we did know an Englishman named Francis Drake, which was brother to Captain Hawkins. To which we answered that Captain Hawkins had not any brother but one, which was a man of the age of threescore years or thereabouts, and was now governor of Plymouth in England. And then he demanded of us if we knew one Francis Drake, and we answered no.

While these things were in doing, there came news that all the Englishmen were gone, yet were there eight hundred men made out under the leading of several captains, whereof two hundred were sent to the port of Saint John de Ulua upon the North Sea under the conduct of Don Luys Suares, two hundred were sent to Guatemala in the South Sea, who had for their captain John Cortes, two hundred more were sent to Guatulco, a port of the South Sea, over whom went for captain Don Pedro de Robles, and two hundred more were sent to Acapulco, the port where it was said that Captain Drake had been. And they had for captain Doctor Robles Alcalde de Corte, with whom I, Miles Philips, went as interpreter, having licence given by the Inquisitors. When we were come to Acapulco we found that Captain Drake was departed from thence more than a month before we came thither; but yet our Captain, Alcalde de Corte, there presently embarked himself in a small ship of threescore ton or thereabout, having also in company with him two other small barks, and not past two hundred men in all, with whom I went as interpreter in his own ship; which God knoweth was but weak and ill appointed, so that for certain, if we had met with Captain Drake, he might easily have taken us all. We being embarked kept our course and ran southward towards Panama, keeping still as nigh the shore as we could and leaving the land upon our left hand; and having coasted thus for the space of eighteen or twenty days we met at last with other ships which came from Panama, of whom we were certainly informed that he was clean gone off the coast more than a month before. And so we returned back to Acapulco again and there landed, our Captain being thereunto forced, because his men were very sore sea-sick.

All the while that I was at sea with them I was a glad man, for I hoped that if we met Master Drake we should all be taken, so that then I should have been freed out of danger and misery wherein I lived and

should return to my own country of England again. But missing
thereof, when I saw there was no remedy but that we must needs come
on land again, little doth any man know the sorrow and grief that
inwardly I felt, although outwardly I was constrained to make fair
weather of it. And so being landed, the next morrow after we began our
journey towards Mexico and passed these towns of name in our way, as
first the town of Tuatepec, 50 leagues from Mexico, from thence to
Oaxhaca, 40 leagues from Mexico, from thence to Tepeyac, 24 leagues
from Mexico, and from thence to Puebla de los Angeles, where is a
high hill which casteth out fire three times a day, which hill is 18 leagues
in manner directly west from Mexico. From thence we went to
Stapelapa, 8 leagues from Mexico, and there our Captain and most of
his men took boat and came to Mexico again, having been forth about
the space of seven weeks or thereabouts.

Our Captain made report to the Viceroy what he had done and how
far he had travelled, and that for certain he was informed that Captain
Drake was not to be heard of. To which the Viceroy replied and said
"Surely we shall have him shortly come into our hands, driven aland
through necessity in some one place or other, for he being now in these
seas of Sur it is not possible for him to get out of them again, so that if
he perish not at sea yet hunger will force him to land". And then again
I was commanded by the Viceroy that I should not depart the city of
Mexico, but always be at my master's house in a readiness at an hour's
warning whensoever I should be called. For that notwithstanding,
within one month after certain Spaniards going to Mecamecq, 18
leagues from Mexico, to send away certain hides and *cochinilla* that
they had there at their *estancias* or dairy-houses, and my master having
leave of the Secretary for me to go with them, I took my journey with
them being very well horsed and appointed, and coming thither, and
passing the time there at Mecamecq certain days till we had perfect
intelligence that the fleet was ready to depart, I, not being past 3 days'
journey from the port of Saint John de Ulua, thought it to be the
meetest time for me to make an escape; and I was the bolder presuming
upon my Spanish tongue which I spoke as naturally as any of them
all, thinking with myself that when I came to Saint John de Ulua I
would get to be entertained as a soldier, and so go home into Spain in
the same fleet. And therefore secretly one evening late I conveyed
myself away, and riding so for the space of two nights and two days,
sometimes in and sometimes out, resting very little all that time, upon
the second day at night I came to the town of Vera Cruz, distant from
the port of Saint John de Ulua, where the ships rode, but only 5
leagues.

And here purposing to rest myself a day or two, I was no sooner
alighted but within the space of one half hour after I was by ill hap
arrested and brought before justices there, being taken and sus-

pected to be a gentleman's son of Mexico that was run away from his father, who in truth was the man they sought for. So I being arrested and brought before the justices, there was a great hurly-burly about the matter, every man charging me that I was the son of such a man dwelling in Mexico, which I flatly denied, affirming that I knew not the man. Yet would they not believe me, but urged still upon me that I was he that they sought for, and so I was conveyed away to prison. And as I was thus going to prison, to the further increase of my grief it chanced that at that very instant there was a poor man in the press that was come to town to sell hens, who told the justices that they did me wrong, and that in truth he knew very well that I was an Englishman and no Spaniard. They then demanded of him how he knew that, and threatened him that he said so for that he was my companion and sought to convey me away from my father, so that he also was threatened to be laid in prison with me. He, for the discharge of himself, stood stiffly in it that I was an Englishman, and one of Captain Hawkins' men, and that he had known me wear the San Benito in the Black Friars at Mexico for 3 or 4 whole years together. Which when they heard, they forsook him, and began to examine me anew whether that speech of his were true, yea or no; which they perceived that I could not deny, and perceiving that I was run from Mexico and came thither of purpose to convey myself away with the fleet, I was presently committed to prison with a sorrowful heart, often wishing myself that that man which knew of me had at that time been further off. Howbeit, he in sincerity had compassion of my distressed estate, thinking by his speech, and knowing of me, to have set me free from that present danger which he saw me in, howbeit contrary to his expectation I was thereby brought into my extreme danger and to the hazard of my life; yet there was no remedy but patience perforce. And I was no sooner brought into prison but I had a great pair of bolts clapped on my legs, and thus I remained in that prison for the space of 3 weeks, where were also many other prisoners which were thither committed for sundry crimes and condemned to the galleys.

During which time of imprisonment there I found amongst those my prison-fellows some that had known me before in Mexico, and truly they had compassion of me, and would spare of their victuals and anything else that they had to do me good. Amongst whom there was one of them that told me that he understood by a secret friend of his, which often came to the prison to him, that I should be shortly sent back again to Mexico by wagon, so soon as the fleet was gone from Saint John de Ulua for Spain. This poor man my prison-fellow, of himself and without any request made by me, caused his said friend, which came often unto him to the grate of the prison to bring him wine and victuals, to buy for him 2 knives which had files in their backs, which files were so well made that they would serve and suffice any prisoner to file off his irons; and of those knives or files he brought one to me, and told me that he had caused it to be made for me, and let me have it at that very price it cost him, which was 2 pesos, the value of 8s. of our money. Which knife when I had it I was a joyful man, and conveyed the same into the foot of my boot, upon the inside of my left leg. And so, within 3 or 4 days after that I had thus received my knife, I was suddenly called for and brought before the head justice, which caused those my irons with the round bolt to be struck off and sent to a smith's in the town, where was a new pair of bolts made ready for me, of another fashion, which had a broad iron bar coming between the shackles, and caused my hands to be made fast with a pair of manacles; and so was I presently laid into a wagon all alone, which was there ready to depart with sundry other wagons, to the number of 60, towards Mexico, and they all were laden with sundry merchandise which came in the fleet out of Spain.

The wagon that I was in was foremost in all the company; and as we travelled I, being alone in the wagon, began to try if I could pluck my hands out of the manacles. And as God would, although it were somewhat painful for me, yet my hands were so slender that I could pull them out and put them in again; and ever as we went, when the wagon made most noise and the men were busiest, I would be working to file off my bolts. And travelling thus for the space of 8 leagues from Vera Cruz we came to a high hill, at the entering up of which (as God would) one of the wheels of the wagon wherein I was broke, so that by that means the other wagons went afore, and the wagon-man that had charge of me set an Indian carpenter awork to mend the wheel. And here at this place they baited at a hostelry that a negro-woman keeps; and at this place, for that the going up of the hill is very steep for the space of two leagues and better, they do always accustom to take the mules of 3 or 4 wagons and to place them all together for the drawing up of one wagon, and so to come down again and fetch up others in that order. All which came very well to pass: for as it drew towards night when most of the wagoners were gone to draw up their wagons, in this sort I being alone had quickly filed off my bolts, and so, espying my time in the dark of the evening before they returned down the hill again, I conveyed myself into the woods there adjoining, carrying my bolts and manacles with me, and a few biscuits and two small cheeses. And being come into the woods I threw my irons into a thick bush, and then covered them with moss and other things, and then shifted for myself as I might all that night. And thus by the good providence of Almighty God I was freed from my irons, all saving the collar that was about my neck, and so got my liberty a second time.

Chapter 7

Wherein is showed how I escaped to Guatemala upon the South Sea, and from thence to the Port of Caballos, where I got passage to go into Spain; and of our arrival at Havana, and our coming to Spain, where I was again like to have been committed prisoner; and how through the great mercy of God I escaped, and came home in safety into England in February 1582.

The next morning, daylight being come, I perceived by the sunrising what way to take to escape their hands, for when I fled I took the way into the woods upon the left hand; and having left that way that went to Mexico upon my right hand, I thought to keep my course as the woods and mountains lay, still direct south as near as I could, by means whereof I was sure to convey myself far enough from that way that went to Mexico. And as I was thus going in the woods I saw many great fires made to the north not past a league from the mountain where I was; and travelling thus in my boots with my iron collar about my neck, and my bread and cheese, the very same forenoon I met with a company of Indians which were hunting of deer for their sustenance. To whom I spoke in the Mexican tongue, and told them how that I had of a long time been kept in prison by the cruel Spaniards, and did desire them to help me to file off my iron collar, which they willingly did, rejoicing greatly with me that I was thus escaped out of the Spaniards' hands. Then I desired that I might have one of them to guide me out of those desert mountains towards the south, which they also most willingly did; and so they brought me to an Indian town 8 leagues distant from thence, named Jalapa, where I stayed three days, for that I was somewhat sickly. At which town, with the gold that I had quilted in my doublet I bought me a horse of one of the Indians, which cost me 6 pesos; and so travelling south within the space of 2 leagues I happened to overtake a grey friar, one that I had been familiar withal in Mexico, whom then I knew to be a zealous good man and one that did much lament the cruelty used against us by the Inquisitors, and truly he used me very courteously. And I, having confidence in him, did indeed tell him that I was minded to adventure to see if I could get out of the said country if I could find shipping, and did therefore pray him of his aid, direction, and advice herein. Which he faithfully did, not only in directing me which was my safest way to travel, but he also of himself kept me company for the space of three days, and ever as we came to the Indians' houses (who used and entertained us very well) he gathered among them in money to the value of 20 pesos, which at my departure from him he freely gave unto me.

So I came to the city of Guatemala upon the South Sea, which is distant from Mexico about 250 leagues, where I stayed 6 days, for that my horse was weak. And from thence I travelled still south and by east seven days' journey, passing by certain Indian towns, until I came to an Indian town distant from Mexico direct south 309 leagues; and here at this town enquiring to go to the Port of Caballos in the Northeast Sea, it was answered that in travelling thither I should not come to any town in 10 or 12 days' journey. So here I hired two Indians to be my guides, and I bought hens and bread to serve us so long time, and took with us things to kindle fire every night because of wild beasts and to dress our meat; and every night when we rested my Indian guides would make two great fires, between the which we placed ourselves, and my horse. And in the night time we should hear the lions roar, with tigers, ounces, and other beasts, and some of them we should see in the night which had eyes shining like fire. And travelling thus for the space of twelve days we came at last to the Port of Caballos upon the East Sea, distant from Guatemala south and by east two hundred leagues, and from Mexico 450 or thereabouts. This is a good harbour for ships, and is without either castle or bulwark.

I, having despatched away my guides, went down to the haven where I saw certain ships laden chiefly with Canary wines, where I spoke with one of the masters who asked me what countryman I was; and I told him that I was born in Granada, and he said that then I was his countryman. I required of him that I might pass home with him in his ship, paying for my passage; and he said yea, so that I had a safe conduct or letter testimonial to show, that he might incur no danger. "For," said he, "it may be that you have killed some man, or be indebted, and would therefore run away". To that I answered that there was not any such cause. Well, in the end we grew to a price, that for 60 pesos he would carry me into Spain. A glad man was I at this good hap, and I quickly sold my horse and made my provision of hens and bread to serve me in my passage. And thus within 2 days after we set sail, and never stayed until we came to Havana, which is distant from Puerto de Caballos by sea 500 leagues; where we found the whole fleet of Spain, which was bound home from the Indies. And here I was hired for a soldier to serve in the admiral ship of the same fleet, wherein the General himself went.

There landed while I was here 4 ships out of Spain, being all full of soldiers and ordnance, of which number there were 200 men landed here and 4 great brass pieces of ordnance, although the castle were before sufficiently provided, 200 men more were sent to Campeche and certain ordnance, 200 to Florida with ordnance, and 100 lastly to Saint John de Ulua. As for ordnance, there they have sufficient and of the very same which was ours, which we had in the *Jesus* and those others which we had planted in the place where the Viceroy betrayed Master Hawkins our General, as hath been declared. The sending of those soldiers to every of those ports, and the strengthening of them, was done by commandment from the King of Spain, who wrote also by them to the General of his fleet, giving him in charge so to do, as also directing him what course he should keep in his coming home into Spain; charging him in any hand not to come nigh to the isles of the Azores, but to keep his course more to the northward, advertising him withal what number and power of French ships of war, and other, Dom Antonio had at that time at Terceira and the isles aforesaid. Which the General of the fleet well considering, and what great store of riches he had to bring home with him into Spain, did in all very dutifully observe and obey. For in truth he had in his said fleet 37 sail of ships, and in every of them there was as good as 30 pipes of silver, one with another, besides great store of gold, *cochinilla*, sugars, hides, and *cana fistula*, with other apothecary drugs. This our General, who was called Don Pedro de Guzman, did providently take order for, for their most strength and defence if need should be, to the uttermost of his power, and commanded upon pain of death that neither passenger nor soldier should come aboard without his sword and arquebus, with shot and powder, to the end that they might be the better able to encounter the fleet of Dom Antonio if they should hap to meet with them, or any of them. And ever as the weather was fair, the said General would himself go aboard from one ship to another, to see that every man had his full provision according to the commandment given. Yet to speak truly what I think, two good tall ships of war would have made a foul spoil amongst them. For in all this fleet there were not any that were strong and warlike appointed saving only the admiral and vice-admiral. And again. over and besides the weakness and the ill furnishing of the rest, they were all so deeply laden that they had not been able, if they had been charged, to have held out any long fight.

Well, thus we set sail, and had a very ill passage home, the weather was so contrary. We kept our course in manner north-east, and beought ourselves to the height of 42 degrees of latitude to be sure not to meet with Dom Antonio's fleet, and were upon our voyage from the 4th of June until the 10th of September, and never saw land till we fell with the Arenas Gordas hard by San Lucar. And there was an order taken that none should go on shore until he had a licence. As for me, I was known by one in the ship, who told the master that I was an Englishman, which, as God would, it was my good hap to hear; for if I had not heard it, it had cost me my life. Notwithstanding, I would not take any knowledge of it, and seemed to be merry and pleasant that we were all come so well in safety. Presently after, licence came that we should go on shore, and I pressed to be gone with the first. Howbeit, the Master came unto me and said "Sirrah, you must go with me to Seville by water". I knew his meaning well enough, and that he meant there to offer me up as a sacrifice to the Holy House. For the ignorant zeal of a number of these superstitious Spaniards is such that they think that they have done God good service when they have brought a Lutheran heretic to the fire to be burnt; for so do they account of us.

Well, I perceiving all this took upon me not to suspect anything, but was still jocund and merry. Howbeit, I knew it stood upon me to shift for myself. And so waiting my time when the Master was in his cabin asleep, I conveyed myself secretly down by the shrouds into the ship's boat, and made no stay but cut the rope wherewithal she was moored, and so by the cable hauled on shore, where I leapt on land and let the boat go whither it would. Thus by the help of God I escaped that day, and then never stayed at San Lucar but went all night by the way that I had seen others take toward Seville. So that the next morning I came to Seville, and sought me out a workmaster that I might fall to my science which was weaving of taffetas. And being entertained, I set myself close to my work and durst not for my life once to stir abroad for fear of being known; and being thus at my work within 4 days after I heard one of my fellows say that he heard there was great enquiry made for an Englishman that came home in the fleet. "What! a heretic Lutheran", quoth I, "was it? I would to God I might know him; surely I would present him to the Holy House". And thus I kept still within doors at my work, and feigned my self not well at ease and that I would labour as I might to get me new clothes. And continuing thus for the space of 3 months I called for my wages, and bought me all things new, different from the apparel that I did wear at sea, and yet durst not be overbold to walk abroad. And after understanding that there were certain English ships at San Lucar bound for England, I took a boat and went aboard one of them and desired the master that I might have passage with him to go to England, and told him secretly that I was one of those which Captain Hawkins did set on shore in the Indies. He very courteously prayed me to have him excused for he durst not meddle with me, and prayed me therefore to return from whence I came. Which when I perceived, with a sorrowful heart, God knoweth, I took my leave of him, not without watery cheeks.

And then I went to Saint Mary Port, which is 3 leagues from San Lucar, where I put myself to be a soldier to go in the King of Spain's galleys which were bound for Majorca; and coming thither in the end of the Christmas holidays I found there two English ships, the one of London and the other of the west country, which were ready freighted and stayed but for a fair wind. To the master of the one which was of the west country went I, and told him that I had been 2 years in Spain to learn the language and that I was now desirous to go home and see my friends, for that I lacked maintenance; and so, having agreed with him for my passage, I took shipping. And thus through the providence of Almighty God, after 16 years' absence, having sustained many and sundry great troubles and miseries, as by this discourse appeareth, I came home to this my native country of England in the year 1582, in the month of February, in the ship called the *Landret*, and arrived at Poole.

The travails of Job Hortop, which Sir John Hawkins set on land within the Bay of Mexico, after his departure from the haven of St John de Ulua in Nueva España, the 8th of October, 1568.

NOT untruly nor without cause, said Job, the faithful servant of God (whom the sacred Scriptures tell us to have dwelt in the land of Hus) that man being born of a woman, living a short time, is replenished with many miseries: which some know by reading of histories, many by the view of others' calamities, and I by experience in myself, as this present treatise ensuing shall show.

It is not unknown unto many that I, Job Hortop, powder-maker, was born at Bourne, a town in Lincolnshire, from my age of twelve years brought up in Redriff, near London, with Master Francis Lee, who was the Queen's Majesty's powder-maker, whom I served until I was pressed to go on the 3rd voyage to the West Indies with the Right Worshipful Sir John Hawkins, who appointed me to be one of the gunners in Her Majesty's ship called the *Jesus of Lubeck*, who set sail from Plymouth in the month of October, 1567, having with him another ship of Her Majesty's called the *Minion*, and four ships of his own, namely the *Angel*, the *Swallow*, the *Judith* and the *William and John*. He directed his vice-admiral that if foul weather did separate them to meet at the island of Tenerife. After which by the space of seven days and seven nights we had such storms at sea that we lost our long boats and a pinnace, with some men. Coming to the isle of Tenerife there our General heard that his vice-admiral with the *Swallow* and the *William and John* were at the island called Gomera, where, finding his vice-admiral, he anchored, took in fresh water, and set sail for Cape Blank, where in the way we took a Portugal caravel laden with fish called mullets.

From thence we sailed to Cape Verde. In our course thither we met a Frenchman of Rochelle, called Captain Bland, who had taken a Portugal caravel, whom our vice-admiral chased and took. Captain Drake, now Sir Francis Drake, was made master and captain of the caravel, and so we kept our way till we came to Cape Verde, and there we anchored, took our boats and set soldiers on shore. Our General was the first that leapt on land and with him Captain Dudley. There we took certain negroes, but not without damage to ourselves, for our General, Captain Dudley, and eight other of our company were hurt with poisoned arrows. About nine days after, the eight that were wounded died. Our General was taught by a negro to draw the poison out of his wound with a clove of garlic, whereby he was cured. From thence we went to Sierra Leone, where be monstrous fishes called sharks which will devour men. I amongst others was sent in the *Angel* with two pinnaces into the river called Callousa to seek two caravels that were there trading with the negros; we took one of them with the negros and brought them away.

In this river in the night time we had one of our pinnaces bulged by a sea-horse so that our men swimming about the river were all taken into the other pinnaces, except two that took hold one of another and were carried away by the sea-horse. This monster hath the just proportion of a horse, saving that his legs be short, his teeth very great and a span in length. He useth in the night to go on land into the woods seeking at unawares to devour the negros in their cabins, whom they by their vigilance prevent and kill him in this manner. The negros keep watch and diligently attend their coming, and when they are gone into the woods they forthwith lay a great tree overthwart the way so that at their return, for that their legs be so short, they cannot go over it; then the negros set upon them with their bows, arrows, and darts, and so destroy them.

From thence we entered the river called the Casserroes, where there were other caravels trading with the negros, and them we took. In this island, betwixt the river and the main, trees grow with oysters upon them. There grow *palmito* trees, which be as high as a ship's mainmast and on their tops grow nuts, wine and oil, which they call palmito wine and palmito oil. The plantain tree also groweth in that country; the tree is as big as a man's thigh and as high as a fir pole, the leaves thereof be long and broad, and on the top grow the fruit which are called *plantanos*: they are crooked and a cubit long, and as big as a man's wrist; they grow on clusters. When they be ripe they be very good and dainty to eat; sugar is not more delicate in taste than they be.

From thence with the *Angel*, the *Judith*, and the two pinnaces we sailed to Sierra Leone, where our General at that time was, who with the captains and soldiers went up into the river called Tanguarim to take a town of the negroes, where he found three kings of that country with fifty thousand negroes besieging the same town, which they could not take in many years before when they had warred with it. Our General made a breach, entered and valiantly took the town, wherein were found five Portugals which yielded themselves to his mercy and he saved their lives. We took and carried thence for traffic to the West Indies 500 negroes. The three kings drove 7,000 negroes into the sea at low water at the point of the land, where they were all drowned in the ooze for that they could not take their canoes to save themselves. We returned back again in our pinnaces to the ships, and there took in fresh water and made ready sail towards Rio Grande. At our coming thither we entered with the *Angel*, the *Judith* and the two pinnaces, and found there seven Portugal caravels which made great fight with us. In the end by God's help we won the victory and drove them to the shore, from whence with the negroes they fled, and we fetched the caravels from the shore into the river. The next morning Master Francis Drake with his caravel, the *Swallow*, and the *William and John* came into the river with Captain Dudley and his soldiers, who landed being but a hundred soldiers, and fought with seven thousand negroes, burned the town, and returned to our General with the loss of one man.

In that place there by many musk-cats which breed in hollow trees. The negroes take them in a net and put them in a cage and nourish them very daintily, and take the musk from them with a spoon.

Now we directed our course from Guinea towards the West Indies; and by the way died Captain Dudley.

In sailing towards the Indies the first land that we escried was the island called Dominica, where at our coming we anchored and took in fresh water and wood for our provision; which done, we sailed towards the island called Margarita, where our General, in despite of the Spaniards, anchored, landed, and took in fresh victuals. A mile off the island there is a rock in the sea wherein do breed many fowls like unto barnacles; in the night we went out in our boats and with cudgels we killed many of them and brought them with many of their eggs aboard with us. Their eggs be as big as turkeys' eggs, and speckled like them. We did eat them and found them very good meat.

From thence we sailed to Borburata, which is in the mainland of the West Indies. There we came in, moored our ships, and tarried two months, trimming and dressing our ships, and in the meantime traded with certain Spaniards of that country. There our General sent us unto a town called Placentia (which stood on a high hill) to have entreated a bishop that dwelt there for his favour and friendship in their laws, who, hearing of our coming, for fear forsook the town.

On our way up the hill to Placentia we found a monstrous venomous worm with two heads; his body was as big as a man's arm and a yard long. Our Master, Robert Barrett, did cut him in sunder with his sword, and it made it as black as if it were coloured with ink.

Here be many tigers, monstrous and furious beasts, which by subtlety devour and destroy many men. They use the traded ways, and will show themselves twice or thrice to the travellers, and so depart secretly, lurking till they be past, then suddenly and at unawares they leap upon them and devour them. They had so used two of our company had not one of them looked behind. Our General sent three ships unto the island called Curaçao to make provision for the rest, where they remained until his coming. He sent from thence the *Angel* and the

Judith to Rio de Hacha, where we anchored before the town. The Spaniards shot three pieces at us from the shore, whom we requited with two of ours and shot through the Governor's house. We weighed anchor and anchored again without shot of the town, where we rode five days in despite of the Spaniards and their shot. In the mean space there came a caravel of advice from Santo Domingo, whom with the *Angel* and the *Judith* we chased and drove to the shore. We fetched him from thence in spite of 200 Spaniards' arquebus shot, and anchored again before the town and rode there with them till our General's coming, who anchored, landed his men, and valiantly took the town with the loss of one man whose name was Thomas Surgeon. We landed and planted on the shore for our safeties our field ordnance. We drove the Spaniards up into the country above two leagues, whereby they were enforced to trade with our General, to whom he sold most part of his negroes.

In this river we killed a monstrous *lagarto* or crocodile in this port at sunset. Seven of us went in the pinnace up into the river carrying with us a dog, unto whom with ropeyarn we bound a great hook of steel with a chain that had a swivel which we put under the dog's belly, the point of the hook coming over his back fast bound, as aforesaid. We put him overboard and veered out our rope by little and little, rowing away with our boat. The *lagarto* came and presently swallowed up the dog, then did we row hard till we had choked him; he plunged and made a wonderful stir in the water. We leapt on shore and hauled him on land. He was 23 foot by the rule, headed like a hog, in body like a serpent, full of scales as broad as a saucer; his tail long and full of knots as big as a falcon shot. He hath four legs, his feet have long nails like unto a dragon. We opened him, took out his guts, flayed him, dried his skin and stuffed it with straw, meaning to have brought it home had not the ship been cast away. This monster will carry away and devour both man and horse.

From hence we shaped our course to Santa Marta where we landed, traded, and sold certain negroes. There two of our company killed a monstrous adder going towards his cave with a coney in his mouth; his body was as big as any man's thigh and seven foot long. Upon his tail he had sixteen knots, every one as big as a great walnut, which they say do show his age; his colour was green and yellow. They opened him and found two coneys in his belly.

From thence we sailed to Cartagena, where we went in, moored our ships, and would have traded with them but they durst not for fear of the King. We brought up the *Minion* against the castle and shot at the castle and town. Then we landed in an island where were many gardens; there in a cave we found certain *botijos* of wine which we brought away with us, in recompense whereof our General commanded to be set on shore woollen and linen cloth to the value thereof.

From hence by foul weather we were forced to seek the port of Saint John de Ulua. In our way thwart of Campeche we met with a Spaniard, a small ship, who was bound for Santo Domingo. He had in him a Spaniard called Augustin de Villanueva, who was the man that betrayed all the noblemen in the Indies and caused them to be beheaded, wherefore he with two friars fled to Santo Domingo. Them we took and brought with us into the port of Saint John de Ulua. Our General made great account of him and used him like a nobleman; howbeit in the end he was one of them that betrayed us.

When we had moored our ships and landed we mounted the ordnance that we found there in the island, and for our safety kept watch and ward. The next day after we discovered the Spanish fleet, whereof Luçon, a Spaniard, was General; with him came a Spaniard called Don Martin Henriquez, whom the King of Spain sent to be his Viceroy of the Indies. He sent a pinnace with a flag of truce unto our General to know of what country those ships were that rode there in the King of Spain's port; who said, they were the Queen of England's ships, which came in there for victuals for their money: "Wherefore if your General will come in here he shall give me victuals and all other necessaries, and I will go out on the one side of the port and he shall come in on the other side." The Spaniard returned for answer that he was a Viceroy and had a thousand men, and therefore he would come in. Our General said, "If he be a Viceroy I represent my Queen's person and I am a Viceroy as well as he; and if he have a thousand men, my powder and shot will take the better place."

Then the Viceroy, after council among themselves, yielded to our General's demand, swearing by his King and his crown, by his commission and authority that he had from his King, that he would perform it, and thereupon pledges were given on both parts. Our General, bearing a godly and Christian mind void of fraud and deceit, judged the Spaniards to have done the like, delivered to them six gentlemen, not doubting to have received the like from them. But the faithless Spaniards in costly apparel gave of the basest of their company, as afterwards it was well known. These things finished, proclamation was made on both sides that on pain of death no occasion should be given whereby any quarrel should grow to the breach of the league, and then they peaceably entered the port with great triumph on both sides.

The Spaniards presently brought a great hulk, a ship of six hundred, and moored her by the side of the *Minion*, and they cut out ports in their other ships planting their ordnance towards us. In the night they filled the hulk with men to lay the *Minion* aboard, as the sequel did show, which made our General doubtful of their dealings. Wherefore, for that he could speak the Spanish tongue, he sent Robert Barrett aboard the Viceroy to know his meaning in those dealings, who willed him with his company to come in to him, whom he commanded presently to be set in the bilboes. And forthwith a cornet (for a watchword among the false Spaniards) was sounded for the enterprising of their pretended treason against our General, whom Augustine de Villanueva, sitting at dinner with him, should then presently have killed with a poniard which he had privily in his sleeve, which was espied and prevented by one, John Chamberlain, who took the poniard out of his sleeve. Our General hastily rose up and commanded him to be put prisoner in the steward's room and to be kept with two men. The faithless Spaniards, thinking all things to their desire had been finished, suddenly sounded a trumpet, and therewith three hundred Spaniards entered the *Minion*, whereat our General with a loud and fierce voice called unto us, saying, "God and Saint George, upon those traitorous villains and rescue the *Minion*. I trust in God the day shall be ours."

And with that the mariners and soldiers leapt out of the *Jesus of Lubeck* into the *Minion* and beat out the Spaniards, and with a shot out of her fired the Spaniards' vice-admiral, where the most part of 300 Spaniards were spoiled and blown overboard with powder. Their admiral also was on fire half an hour. We cut our cables, wound off our ships, and presently fought with them. They came upon us on every side and continued the fight from ten of the clock until it was night. They killed all our men that were on shore in the island, saving three, which by swimming got aboard the *Jesus of Lubeck*. (One of those three was Job Hortop, the reporter hereof.) They sunk the General's ship called the *Angel*, and took the *Swallow*. The Spaniards' admiral had above threescore shot through her; many of his men were spoiled; four other of their ships were sunk. There were in that fleet and that came from the shore to rescue them fifteen hundred. We slew of them five hundred and forty, as we were credibly informed by a note that came to Mexico. In this fight the *Jesus of Lubeck* had five shot through her mainmast; her foremast was struck in sunder under the hounds with a chain shot, and her hull was wonderfully pierced with shot, therefore it was impossible to bring her away. They set two of their own ships on fire intending therewith to have burnt the *Jesus of Lubeck*, which we prevented by cutting our cables in the hawse and winding off by our stern-fast.

The *Minion* was forced to set sail and stand off from us and come to an anchor without shot of the island. Our General courageously cheered up his soldiers and gunners and called to Samuel, his page, for a cup of beer, who brought it him in a silver cup, and he drinking to all men willed the gunners to stand by their ordnance lustily like men. He had no sooner set the cup out of his hand but a demi-culverin shot struck away the cup and a cooper's plane that stood by the mainmast, and ran out on the other side of the ship; which nothing dismayed our General, for he ceased not to encourage us, saying, "Fear nothing, for

God, who hath preserved me from this shot will also deliver us from these traitors and villains."

Then Captain Bland, meaning to have turned out of the port, had his mainmast struck overboard with a chain shot that came from the shore, wherefore he anchored, fired his ship, took his pinnace with all his men, and came aboard the *Jesus of Lubeck* to our General, who said unto him that he thought he would not have run away from him. He answered that he was not minded to have run away from him, but his intent was to have turned up and to have laid the weathermost ship of the Spanish fleet aboard and fired his ship in hope therewith to have set on fire the Spanish fleet. He said if he had done so he had done well. With this, night came on. Our General commanded the *Minion* for safeguard of her masts to be brought under the *Jesus of Lubeck*'s lee. He willed Master Francis Drake to come in with the *Judith*, and to lay the *Minion* aboard to take in men and other things needful and to go out, and so he did.

At night when the wind came off the shore we set sail and went out in despite of the Spaniards and their shot, where we anchored with two anchors under the island, the wind being northerly, which was wonderful dangerous and we feared every hour to be driven with the lee shore. In the end, when the wind came larger we weighed anchor and set sail, seeking the river of Panuco for water, whereof we had very little, and victuals were so scarce that we were driven to eat hides, cats, rats, parrots, monkeys, and dogs; wherefore our General was forced to divide his company into two parts, for there was a mutiny among them for want of victuals. And some said that they had rather be on the shore to shift for themselves amongst the enemies than to starve on shipboard. He asked them who would go on shore and who would tarry on shipboard; those that would go on shore he willed to go on foremast, and those that would tarry he willed to go on baft-mast. Fourscore and sixteen of us were willing to depart. Our General gave unto every one of us six yards of roan cloth, and money to them that demanded it. When we were landed he came unto us, where friendlily embracing every one of us he was greatly grieved that he was forced to leave us behind him. He counselled us to serve God and to love one another, and thus courteously he gave us a sorrowful farewell and promised if God sent him safe home he would do what he could that so many of us as lived should by some means be brought into England, and so he did.

Since my return into England I have heard that many misliked that he left us so behind him and brought away negroes; but the reason is this, for them he might have had victuals or any other thing needful, if by foul weather he had been driven upon the islands, which for gold nor silver he could not have had.

And thus our General departed to his ship and we remained on land, where for our safeties, fearing the wild Indians that were about us, we kept watch all night, and at sun rising we marched on our way, three and three in a rank, until that we came into a field under a grove, where the Indians came upon us, asking us what people we were and how we came there. Two of our company, namely Anthony Goddard and John Cornish, for that they could speak the Spanish tongue, went to them and said we were Englishmen that never came in that country before, and that we had fought with the Spaniards and for that we lacked victuals our General set us on shore. They asked us whither we intended to go; we said to Panuco. The captain of the Indians willed us to give unto them some of our clothes and shirts, which we did. Then he bade us give them all, but we would not so do, whereupon John Cornish was then slain with an arrow which an Indian boy that stood by the captain shot at him; wherefore he struck the boy on the neck with his bow that he lay for dead, and willed us to follow him, who brought us into a great field where we found fresh water. He bade us sit down about the pond and drink, and he with his company would go in the mean space to kill five or six deer and bring them us. We tarried there till three of the clock, but they came not. There one of our company, whose name was John Cooke, with four other departed from us into a grove to seek relief, where presently they were taken by the Indians and stripped as naked as ever they were born, and so returned to us.

Then we divided ourselves into two parts, half to Anthony Goddard and the rest to James Collier, and thus severally we sought for Panuco. Anthony Goddard with his company bid us farewell; they passed a river where the Indians robbed many of them of their clothes, and so passing on their way came to a stony hill where they stayed. James Collier with his company that day passed the same river and were also robbed, and one of them slain by chance. We came that night unto the hill where Anthony Goddard and his company rested; there we remained till morning, and then we marched all together from thence, entering between two groves, where the Indians robbed us of all our clothes and left us naked; they hurt many, and killed eight of us. Three days after we came to another river; there the Indians showed us the way to Panuco, and so left us. We passed the river into the wilderness where we made wreaths of green grass which we wound about our bodies, to keep us from the sun and gnats of that country.

We travelled there seven days and seven nights before we came to Panuco, feeding on nothing but roots and guavas, a fruit like figs. At our coming to the river of Panuco two Spanish horsemen came over unto us in a canoe. They asked us how long we had been in the wilderness, and where our General was, for they knew us to be of the company that had fought with their countrymen. We told them seven days and seven nights, and for lack of victuals our General set us on shore, and he was gone away with his ships. They returned to their Governor, who sent them with five canoes to bring us all over, which done they set us in array where a hundred horsemen with their lances came forcibly upon us, but did not hurt us. They carried us prisoners to Panuco, where we remained one night. In the river of Panuco there is a fish like a calf, the Spaniards call it a *mallatin*; he hath a stone in his head which the Indians use for the disease of the colic. In the night he cometh on land and eateth grass. I have eaten of it and it eateth not much unlike to bacon.

From thence we were sent to Mexico, which is 90 leagues from Panuco. In our way thither, 20 leagues from the sea side, I did see white crabs running up and down the sands; I have eaten of them and they be very good meat. There groweth a fruit which the Spaniards call avocados; it is proportioned like an egg and as black as a coal, having a stone in it, and it is an excellent good fruit. There also groweth a strange tree which they call *magueys*; it serveth them to many uses. Below by the root they make a hole whereat they do take out of it twice every day a certain kind of liquor which they seethe in a great kettle till the third part be consumed and that it wax thick; it is as sweet as any honey and they do eat it. Within twenty days after that they have taken all the liquor from it it withereth, and they cut it down and use it as we use our hemp here in England, which done, they convert it to many uses. Of some part they make mantles, ropes, and thread; of the ends they make needles to sew their saddles, panels, and other furniture for their horses; of the rest they make tiles to cover their houses, and they put it to many other purposes.

And thus we came to Mexico, which is seven or eight miles about, seated in a great fen, environed with 4 hills. It hath but two ways of entrance, and it is full of creeks in the which in their canoes they pass from place to place, and to the islands there within. In the Indies ordinarily three times a year be wonderful earthquakes which put the people in great fear and danger. During the time of two years that I was in Mexico I saw them six times. When they come they throw down trees, houses and churches. There is a city 25 leagues from Mexico called Tlaxcala which is inhabited with a hundred thousand Indians. They go in white shirts, linen breeches and long mantles, and the women wear about them a garment much like unto a flannel petticoat. The King's palace was the first place we were brought unto in Mexico, where without we were willed to sit down. Much people, men, women, and children came wandering about us, many lamented our misery, and some of their clergy asked us if we were Christians. We said, we praised God, we were as good Christians as they. They asked how they might know that; we said by our confessions. From thence we were carried in a canoe to a tanner's house which standeth a little from the city. The next morning two friars and two priests came thither to us, and willed us to bless ourselves, and say our prayers in the Latin tongue that they might understand us. Many of our company did so, whereupon they returned to the Viceroy and told him that we were good Christians and that they liked us well, and then they brought us much relief, with clothes. Our sick men were sent to their hospitals where many were cured, and many died. From the tanner's house we were led to a gentleman's place where upon pain of death we were charged to abide and not to come into the city; thither we had all things necessary brought us. On Sundays and holy days much people came and brought us great relief.

The Viceroy practised to hang us and caused a pair of new gallows to be set up to have executed us, whereunto the noblemen of that country would not consent but prayed him to stay until the ship of advice brought news from the King of Spain what should be done with us, for they said they could not find anything by us whereby they might lawfully put us to death.

The Viceroy then commanded us to be sent to an island thereby, and he sent for the Bishop of Mexico, who sent four priests to the island to examine and confess us, who said that the Viceroy would burn us when we were examined and confessed, according to the laws of the country. They returned to the Bishop and told him that we were very good Christians. The Bishop certified the Viceroy of our examinations and confessions, and said that we were good Christians, therefore he would not meddle with us. Then the Viceroy sent for our Master, R. Barrett, whom he kept prisoner in his palace until the fleet was departed for Spain. The rest of us he sent to a town seven leagues from Mexico, called Tezcoco, to card wool among the Indian slaves, which drudgery we disdained and concluded to beat our masters, and so we did. Wherefore they sent to the Viceroy, desiring him for God's sake and Our Lady's to send for us for they would not keep us any longer; they said that we were devils and no men.

The Viceroy sent for us and imprisoned us in a house in Mexico. From thence he sent Anthony Goddard and some other of our company with him into Spain with Luçon, the General that took us. The rest of us stayed in Mexico two years after, and then were sent prisoners into Spain, with Don Juan de Velasco de Varre, Admiral and General of the Spanish fleet, who carried with him in his ship to be presented to the King of Spain the anatomy of a giant, which was sent from China to Mexico to the Viceroy, Don Martin Henriquez, to be sent to the King of Spain for a great wonder. It did appear by the anatomy that he was of a monstrous size, the skull of his head was near as big as half a bushel, his neck-bones, shoulder-plates, arm-bones and all other lineaments of his other parts were huge and monstrous to behold, the shank of his leg from the ankle to the knee was as long as from any man's ankle up to his waist, and of bigness accordingly.

At this time and in this ship were also sent to be presented to the King of Spain two chests full of earth with ginger growing in them, which were also sent from China to be sent to the King of Spain. The ginger runneth in the ground like to liquorice, the blades grow out of it in length and proportion like unto the blades of wild garlic, which they cut every fifteen days. They use to water them twice a day, as we do our herbs here in England; they put the blades in their pottage and use them in their other meats, whose excellent savour and taste is very delightful and procureth a good appetite.

When we were shipped in the port of St John de Ulua the General called our Master, Robert Barrett, and us with him, into his cabin and asked us if we would fight against Englishmen if we met them at the sea. We said that we would not fight against our Crown, but if we met with any other we would do what we were able. He said if we had said otherwise he would not have believed us, and for that we should be the better used and have allowance as other men had; and he gave a charge to every one of us, according unto our knowledge. Robert Barrett was placed with the pilot, I was put in the gunners' room, William Cawse with the boatswain, John Beare with the quartermasters, Edward Rider and Geoffrey Giles with the ordinary mariners, Richard the Master's boy attended on him and the pilot. Shortly after we departed from the port of St John de Ulua with all the fleet of Spain for the port called Havana. We were 26 days sailing thither. There we came in, anchored, took in fresh water, and stayed 16 days for the fleet of Nombre de Dios, which is the fleet that brings the treasure from Peru.

The General of that fleet was called Diego Flores de Valdes. After his coming, when he had watered his ships, both the fleets joined in one, and Don Juan de Velasco de Varre was the first fifteen days General of both the fleets, who turning through the channel of Bahama his pilot had like to have cast away all the fleet upon the Cape called Canaveral, which was prevented by me, Job Hortop, and our Master, Robert Barrett; for I, being in the second watch, escried land and called to Robert Barrett, bidding him look overboard, for I saw land under the lee bow of the ship. He called to the boatswain and bid him let fly the foresail sheet, and lay the helm upon the lee and cast the ship about. When we were cast about we were but in seven fathom water. We shot off a piece, giving advice to the fleet to cast about, and so they did. For this we were beloved of the General and all the fleet.

The General was in a great rage and swore by the King that he would hang his pilot, for he said that twice before he had almost cast away the admiral. When it was day he commanded a piece to be shot off to call to council. The other Admiral in his ship came up to him and asked what the matter was. He said that his pilot had cast away his ship and all the fleet had it not been for two of the Englishmen, and therefore he would hang him. The other Admiral with many fair words persuaded him to the contrary.

When we came in the height of Bermuda we discovered a monster in the sea who showed himself three times unto us from the middle upwards, in which parts he was proportioned like a man, of the complexion of a mulatto or tawny Indian. The General did command one of his clerks to put it in writing, and he certified the King and his nobles thereof. Presently after this for the space of sixteen days we had wonderful foul weather, and then God sent us a fair wind until such time as we discovered the island called Fayal.

On St James' day we made rockets, wheels, and other fireworks to make pastime that night, as it is the order of the Spaniards. When we came near the land our Master, Robert Barrett, conferred with us to take the pinnace one night, when we came on the island called Terceira, to free ourselves from the danger and bondage that we were going into, whereunto we agreed. None had any pinnace astern then but our ship, which gave great courage to our enterprise. We prepared a bag of bread and a *botijo* of water which would have served us nine days, and provided ourselves to go. Our Master borrowed a small compass of the master gunner of the ship, who lent it him but suspected his intent and closely made the General privy to it, who for a time dissembled the matter. In the end seeing our pretence he called R. Barrett, commanding his head to be put in the stocks and a great pair of iron bolts on his legs, and the rest of us to be set in the stocks by the legs. Then he willed a piece to be shot off, and he sent the pinnace for the other Admiral and all the captains, masters and pilots of both fleets to come aboard of him. He commanded the mainyard to be struck down and to put two pulleys, on every yardarm one; the hangman was called, and we were willed to confess ourselves, for he swore by the King that he would hang us.

When the other Admiral and the rest were come aboard he called them into his council-chamber and told them that he would hang the Master of the Englishmen and all his company. The Admiral, whose name was Diego Flores de Valdes, asked him wherefore. He said that we had determined to rise in the night with the pinnace, and with a ball of firework to set the ship on fire and go our ways. "Therefore," said he, "I will have you, the Captains, Masters and Pilots, to set your hands unto that, for I swear by the King that I will hang them." Diego Flores de Valdes answered, "I, nor the Captains, Masters, and Pilots will not set our hands to that," for he said if he had been prisoner as we were he would have done the like himself. He counselled him to keep us fast in prison till he came into Spain, and then send us to the Contractation House in Seville, where if we had deserved death the law would pass on us, for he would not have it said that in such a fleet as that was, six men and a boy should take the pinnace and go away, and so he returned to his ship again.

When he was gone the General came to the mainmast to us and

swore by the King that we should not come out of the stocks till we came into Spain. Within sixteen days after we came over the bar of San Lucar, and came up to the *hurcados*; then he put us into a pinnace in the stocks and sent us prisoners to the Contractation House in Seville. From thence after one year we broke prison on St Stephen's day at night; 7 of our company escaped, Robert Barrett, I, Job Hortop, John Emery, Humphrey Roberts and John Gilbert were taken and brought back to the Contractation House, where we remained in the stocks till twelve tide was past. Then our keeper put up a petition to the Judge of the Contractation House that we might be sent to the great prison house in Seville, for that we broke prison; whereupon we were presently led thither, where we remained one month, and then from thence to the Castle of the Inquisition House in Triana, where we continued one year. Which expired, they brought us out in procession, every one of us having a candle in his hand and the coat with St Andrew's cross on our backs. They brought us up on a high scaffold that was set up in the place of St Francis, which is in the chief street of Seville. There they set us down upon benches, every one in his degree, and against us on another scaffold sat all the judges and the clergy on their benches. The people wondered and gazed on us, some pitying our cases, other said "burn those heretics". When we had sat there two hours we had a sermon made to us; after which one called Bresinia, Secretary to the Inquisition, went up into the pulpit with the process, and called Robert Barrett and John Gilbert, whom two familiars of the Inquisition brought from the scaffold before the judges, where the Secretary read the sentence, which was that they should be burnt, and so they returned to the scaffold and were burnt.

Then I, Job Hortop, and John Bone were called and brought to the place, as before, where we heard our sentence, which was that we should go to the galleys and there row at the oar's end ten years, and then to be brought back to the Inquisition House to have the coat with St Andrew's cross put on our backs, and from thence to go to the everlasting prison remediless, and so were returned from the scaffold from whence we came.

Thomas Marks and Thomas Ellis were called, and had sentence to serve in the galleys eight years, and Humphrey Roberts and John Emery to serve five years, and so were returned to the benches on the scaffold, where we sat till four of clock in the afternoon. Then we were led again to the Inquisition House from whence we were brought.

The next day, in the morning, Bresinia, the Treasurer, came thither to us and delivered to every one of us his sentence in writing. I with the rest were sent to the galleys, where we were chained four and four together. Every man's daily allowance was 26 ounces of coarse black biscuit, and water, our clothing for the whole year two shirts, two pair of breeches of coarse canvas, a red coat of coarse cloth, soon on and soon off, and a gown of hair with a friar's hood. Our lodging was on the bare boards and banks of the galleys, our heads and beards were shaven every month; hunger, thirst, cold and stripes we lacked none, till our several times expired.

And after the time of twelve years, for I served two years above my sentence, I was sent back to the Inquisition House in Seville, and there having put on the coat with St Andrew's cross I was sent to the everlasting prison remediless, where I wore the coat 4 years; and then upon great suit I had it taken off for 50 ducats, which Hernando de Soria, treasurer of the King's mint, lent me, whom I served for it as a drudge 7 years, and until the month of October last, 1590. And then I came from Seville to San Lucar, where I made means to come away in a flyboat that was laden with wines and salt, which were Flemings' goods, the King of Spain's subjects, dwelling in Seville, married to Spanish women and sworn to their King. In this month of October last, departing from San Lucar at sea, off the southernmost cape we met an English ship, called the galleon *Dudley*, who took the Fleming, and me out of him, and brought me to Portsmouth, where they set me on land the 2nd day of December last past, 1590. From thence I was sent by Master Muns, the Lieutenant of Portsmouth, with letters to the Right Honourable the Earl of Sussex, who commanded his secretary to take my name and examination, how long I had been out of England, and with whom I went, which he did. And on Christmas Even I took my leave of his honour and came to Redriff.

The Computation of My Imprisonment

I suffered imprisonment in Mexico, two years.
In the Contractation House in Seville, one year.
In the Inquisition House in Triana, one year.
I was in the galleys, twelve years.
In the everlasting prison remediless, with the coat with St Andrew's cross on my back, 4 years.
And at liberty I served as a drudge Hernando de Soria 3 years, which is the full complement of 23 years.
Since my departure from England until this time of my return I was five times in great danger of death, besides the many perils I was in in the galleys.
First, in the port of St John de Ulua, where being on shore with many other of our company, which were all slain saving I and two other that by swimming got aboard the *Jesus of Lubeck*.
Secondly, when we were robbed by the wild Indians.
Thirdly after we came to Mexico, the Viceroy would have hanged us.
Fourthly, because he could not have his mind to hang us he would have burnt us.

Fifthly, the General that brought us into Spain would have hanged us at sea.

Thus, having truly set down unto you my travails, misery and dangers, endured the space of 23 years, I end.

The first voyage made to the coasts of America, with two barks, wherein were captains Master Philip Amadas and Master Arthur Barlow, who discovered part of the country now called Virginia, anno 1584. Written by one of the said captains, and sent to Sir Walter Raleigh, knight, at whose charge and direction the said voyage was set forth.

THE 27th day of April, in the year of our redemption 1584, we departed the west of England with two barks well furnished with men and victuals, having received our last and perfect directions by your letters, confirming the former instructions and commandments delivered by yourself at our leaving the river of Thames. And I think it a matter both unnecessary, for the manifest discovery of the country, as also for tediousness' sake, to remember unto you the diurnal of our course, sailing thither and returning; only I have presumed to present unto you this brief discourse, by which you may judge how profitable this land is likely to succeed, as well to yourself, by whose direction and charge, and by whose servants, this our discovery hath been performed, as also to Her Highness and the commonwealth. In which we hope your wisdom will be satisfied, considering that as much by us hath been brought to light as by those small means and number of men we had could any way have been expected or hoped for.

The tenth of May we arrived at the Canaries, and the tenth of June in this present year we were fallen with the islands of the West Indies, keeping a more south-easterly course than was needful, because we doubted that the current of the Bay of Mexico, disboguing between the Cape of Florida and Havana, had been of greater force than afterwards we found it to be. At which islands we found the air very unwholesome, and our men grew for the most part ill-disposed; so that having refreshed ourselves with sweet water and fresh victual, we departed the twelfth day of our arrival there. These islands, with the rest adjoining, are so well known to yourself, and to many others, as I will not trouble you with the remembrance of them.

The second of July we found shoal water, where we smelt so sweet and so strong a smell, as if we had been in the midst of some delicate garden abounding with all kinds of odoriferous flowers; by which we were assured that the land could not be far distant. And keeping good watch and bearing but slack sail, the fourth of the same month we arrived upon the coast, which we supposed to be a continent and firm land, and we sailed along the same a hundred and twenty English miles before we could find any entrance, or river issuing into the sea.

The first that appeared unto us we entered, though not without some difficulty, and cast anchor about three arquebus-shot within the haven's mouth, on the left hand of the same; and after thanks given to God for our safe arrival thither, we manned our boats, and went to view the land next adjoining, and to take possession of the same in the right of the Queen's most excellent Majesty, as rightful queen and princess of the same, and after delivered the same over to your use, according to Her Majesty's grant and letters patents, under Her Highness' great seal. Which being performed according to the ceremonies used in such enterprises, we viewed the land about us, being, where as we first landed, very sandy and low towards the water's side, but so full of grapes as the very beating and surge of the sea overflowed them. Of which we found such plenty, as well there as in all places else, both on the sand and on the green soil on the hills, as in the plains, as well on every little shrub, as also climbing towards the tops of high cedars, that I think in all the world the like abundance is not to be found; and myself having seen those parts of Europe that most abound, find such difference as were incredible to be written.

We passed from the sea side towards the tops of those hills next adjoining, being but of mean height; and from thence we beheld the sea on both sides, to the north and to the south, finding no end any of both ways. This land lay stretching itself to the west, which after we found to be but an island of twenty miles long, and not above six miles broad. Under the bank or hill whereon we stood, we beheld the valleys replenished with goodly cedar trees, and having discharged our arquebus-shot, such a flock of cranes (the most part white) arose under us, with such a cry redoubled by many echoes, as if an army of men had shouted all together.

This island had many goodly woods full of deer, coneys, hares and fowl, even in the midst of summer, in incredible abundance. The woods are not such as you find in Bohemia, Moscovia, or Hercynia, barren and fruitless, but the highest and reddest cedars of the world, far bettering the cedars of the Azores, of the Indies, or Libanus; pines, cypress, sassafras, the lentisk, or the tree that beareth the mastic; the tree that beareth the rind of black cinnamon, of which Master Winter brought from the Straits of Magellan; and many other of excellent smell and quality.

We remained by the side of this island two whole days before we saw any people of the country. The third day we espied one small boat rowing towards us, having in it three persons. This boat came to the island side, four arquebus-shot from our ships; and there two of the people remaining, the third came along the shore side towards us, and we being then all within board, he walked up and down upon the point of the land next unto us. Then the Master and the Pilot of the admiral, Simon Ferdinando, and the Captain, Philip Amadas, myself, and others, rowed to the land; whose coming this fellow attended, never making any show of fear or doubt. And after he had spoken of many things not understood by us, we brought him, with his own good liking, aboard the ships, and gave him a shirt, a hat, and some other things, and made him taste of our wine and our meat, which he liked very well; and, after having viewed both barks, he departed, and went to his own boat again, which he had left in a little cove or creek adjoining. As soon as he was two bow-shot into the water he fell to fishing, and in less than half-an-hour he had laden his boat as deep as it could swim, with which he came again to the point of the land, and there he divided his fish into two parts, pointing one part to the ship and the other to the pinnace. Which, after he had, as much as he might, requited the former benefits received, departed out of our sight.

The next day there came unto us divers boats, and in one of them the King's brother, accompanied with forty or fifty men, very handsome and goodly people, and in their behaviour as mannerly and civil as any of Europe. His name was Granganimeo, and the King is called Wingina; the country, Wingandacoa, and now, by Her Majesty, Virginia. The manner of his coming was in this sort: he left his boats, altogether as the first man did, a little from the ships by the shore, and came along to the place over against the ships, followed with forty men. When he came to the place, his servants spread a long mat upon the ground, on which he sat down, and at the other end of the mat four others of his company did the like; the rest of his men stood round about him somewhat afar off. When we came to the shore to him, with our weapons, he never moved from his place, nor any of the other four, nor never mistrusted any harm to be offered from us; but, sitting still, he beckoned us to come and sit by him, which we performed; and, being set, he made all signs of joy and welcome, striking on his head and his breast and afterwards on ours, to show we were all one, smiling and making show the best he could of all love and familiarity. After he had made a long speech unto us we presented him with divers things, which he received very joyfully and thankfully. None of the company durst speak one word all the time; only the four which were at the other end spoke one in the other's ear very softly.

The King is greatly obeyed, and his brothers and children reverenced. The King himself in person was at our being there sore wounded in a fight which he had with the king of the next country, called Wingana, and was shot in two places through the body, and once clean through the thigh, but yet he recovered; by reason whereof, and for that he lay at the chief town of the country, being six days' journey off, we saw him not at all.

After we had presented this his brother with such things as we thought he liked, we likewise gave somewhat to the other that sat with him on the mat. But presently he arose and took all from them and put it into his own basket, making signs and tokens that all things ought to be delivered unto him, and the rest were but his servants and followers. A day or two after this we fell to trading with them, exchanging some things that we had for chamois, buff, and deer skins. When we shewed him all our packet of merchandise, of all things that he saw a bright tin dish most pleased him, which he presently took up and clapped it before his breast, and after made a hole in the brim thereof and hung it about his neck, making signs that it would defend him against his enemies' arrows. For those people maintain a deadly and terrible war with the people and king adjoining. We exchanged our tin dish for twenty skins, worth twenty crowns or twenty nobles; and a copper kettle for fifty skins, worth fifty crowns. They offered us good exchange for our hatchets and axes, and for knives, and would have given anything for swords; but we would not depart with any.

After two or three days the King's brother came aboard the ships and drank wine, and ate of our meat and of our bread, and liked exceedingly thereof. And after a few days overpassed, he brought his wife with him to the ships, his daughter, and two or three children. His wife was very well-favoured, of mean stature, and very bashful. She had on her back a long cloak of leather, with the fur side next to her body, and before her a piece of the same. About her forehead she had a band of white coral, and so had her husband many times. In her ears she had bracelets of pearls hanging down to her middle, whereof we delivered your worship a little bracelet, and those were of the bigness of good peas. The rest of her women of the better sort had pendants of copper hanging in either ear, and some of the children of the King's brother and other noblemen have five or six in either ear. He himself had upon his head a broad plate of gold, or copper; for, being un-polished, we knew not what metal it should be, neither would he by any means suffer us to take it off his head, but feeling it, it would bow very easily. His apparel was as his wife's, only the women wear their hair long on both sides, and the men but on one. They are of colour yellowish, and their hair black for the most part; and yet we saw children that had very fine auburn and chestnut-coloured hair.

After that these women had been there, there came down from all parts great store of people, bringing with them leather, coral, divers kinds of dyes very excellent, and exchanged with us. But when Gran-ganimeo, the King's brother, was present, none durst trade but himself, except such as wear red pieces of copper on their heads like himself; for that is the difference between the noblemen and the governors of countries, and the meaner sort. And we both noted there, and you have understood since by these men which we brought home, that no people in the world carry more respect to their king, nobility, and governors than these do. The King's brother's wife, when she came to us (as she did many times), was followed with forty or fifty women always. And when she came into the ship she left them all on land, saving her two daughters, her nurse, and one or two more. The King's brother always kept this order: as many boats as he would come withal to the ships, so many fires would he make on the shore afar off, to the end we might understand with what strength and company he approached. Their boats are made of one tree, either of pine, or of pitch-trees; a wood not commonly known to our people, nor found growing in England. They have no edge-tools to make them withal; if they have any they are very few, and those, it seems, they had twenty years since, which, as those two men declared, was out of a wreck, which happened upon their coast, of some Christian ship, being beaten that way by some storm and outrageous weather, whereof none of the people were saved, but only the ship, or some part of her, being cast upon the sand, out of whose sides they drew the nails and the spikes, and with those they made their best instruments. The manner of making their boats is thus: they burn down some great tree, or take such as are windfallen, and, putting gum and rosin upon one side thereof, they set fire into it, and when it hath burnt it hollow they cut out the coal with their shells, and ever where they would burn it deeper or wider they lay on gums, which burn away the timber, and by this means they fashion very fine boats, and such as will transport men. Their oars are like scoops, and many times they set with long poles, as the depth serveth.

The King's brother had great liking of our armour, a sword and divers other things which we had, and offered to lay a great box of pearl in gage for them; but we refused it for this time, because we would not make them know that we esteemed thereof, until we had understood in what places of the country the pearl grew, which now your worship doth very well understand. He was very just of his promise, for many times we delivered him merchandise upon his word, but ever he came within the day and performed his promise. He sent us every day a brace or two of fat bucks, coneys, hares, fish the best of the world. He sent us divers kinds of fruits, melons, walnuts, cucumbers, gourds, pease, and divers roots, and fruits very excellent good, and of their country corn, which is very white, fair, and well tasted, and groweth three times in five months: in May they sow, in July they reap; in June they sow, in August they reap; in July they sow, in September they reap. Only they cast the corn into the ground, breaking a little of the soft turf with a wooden mattock or pickaxe. Ourselves proved the soil, and put some of our peas in the ground, and in ten days they were of fourteen inches high. They have also beans very fair, of divers colours, and wonderful plenty, some growing naturally and some in their gardens; and so have they both wheat and oats. The soil is the most plentiful, sweet, fruitful, and wholesome of all the world. There are above fourteen several sweet-smelling timber-trees, and the most part of their underwoods are bays and suchlike. They have those oaks that we have, but far greater and better.

After they had been divers times aboard our ships, myself with seven more went twenty mile into the river that runneth toward the city of Skicoake, which river they call Occam; and the evening following we came to an island which they call Roanoke, distant from the harbour by which we entered seven leagues; and at the north end thereof was a village of nine houses built of cedar and fortified round about with sharp trees to keep out their enemies, and the entrance into it made like a turnpike very artificially. When we came towards it, standing near unto the water's side, the wife of Granganimeo, the King's brother, came running out to meet us very cheerfully and friendly. Her husband was not then in the village. Some of her people she commanded to draw our boat on shore, for the beating of the billow. Others she appointed to carry us on their backs to the dry ground, and others to bring our oars into the house for fear of stealing. When we were come into the outer room (having five rooms in her house) she caused us to sit down by a great fire, and after took off our clothes and washed them and dried them again. Some of the women plucked off our stockings and washed them, some washed our feet in warm water, and she herself took great pains to see all things ordered in the best manner she could, making great haste to dress some meat for us to eat.

After we had thus dried ourselves, she brought us into the inner room, where she set on the board standing along the house some wheat like furmenty, sodden venison and roasted, fish sodden, boiled, and roasted, melons raw and sodden, roots of divers kinds, and divers fruits. Their drink is commonly water, but while the grape lasteth they drink wine; and for want of casks to keep it, all the year after they drink water, but it is sodden with ginger in it, and black cinnamon, and sometimes sassafras, and divers other wholesome and medicinable herbs and trees. We were entertained with all love and kindness, and with as much bounty (after their manner) as they could possibly devise.

We found the people most gentle, loving, and faithful, void of all guile and treason, and such as live after the manner of the golden age. The people only care how to defend themselves from the cold in their short winter, and to feed themselves with such meat as the soil affordeth. Their meat is very well sodden, and they make broth very sweet and savoury. Their vessels are earthen pots, very large, white, and sweet; their dishes are wooden platters of sweet timber. Within the place where they feed was their lodging, and within that their idol which they worship, of whom they speak incredible things. While we were at meat, there came in at the gates two or three men with their bows and arrows from hunting, whom when we espied we began to look one towards another, and offered to reach our weapons; but as soon as she espied our mistrust, she was very much moved, and caused some of her men to run out, and take away their bows and arrows and break them, and withal beat the poor fellows out of the gate again. When we departed in the evening and would not tarry all night, she was very sorry, and gave us into our boat our supper half-dressed, pots and all, and brought us to our boat side, in which we lay all night, removing the same a pretty distance from the shore. She, perceiving our jealousy, was much grieved, and sent divers men and thirty women to sit all night on the bank-side by us, and sent us into our boats five mats to cover us from the rain, using very many words to entreat us to rest in their houses. But because we were few men, and if we had miscarried the voyage had been in very great danger, we durst not adventure anything, although there was no cause of doubt; for a more kind and loving people there cannot be found in the world, as far as we have hitherto had trial.

Beyond this island there is the mainland, and over against this island falleth into this spacious water the great river called Occam by the inhabitants, on which standeth a town called Pomeiook, and six days' journey from the same is situate their greatest city called Skicoake, which this people affirm to be very great; but the savages were never at it, only they speak of it by the report of their fathers and other men, whom they have heard affirm it to be above one hour's journey about. Into this river falleth another great river called Cipo, in which there is found great store of mussels in which there are pearls; likewise there descendeth into this Occam another river called Nomopano, on the one side whereof standeth a great town called Chawanook, and the lord of that town and country is called Pooneno. This Pooneno is not subject to the King of Wingandacoa, but is a free lord. Beyond this country is there another king, whom they call Menatonon, and these three kings are in league with each other. Towards the south-west four days' journey is situate a town called Secotan, which is the southernmost town of Wingandacoa, near unto which six-and-twenty years past there was a ship cast away, whereof some of the people were saved, and those were white people, whom the country people preserved. And after ten days remaining in an out island uninhabited, called Wococon, they, with the help of some of the dwellers of Secotan, fastened two boats of the country together, and made masts unto them, and sails of their shirts, and having taken into them such victuals as the country yielded, they departed after they had remained in this out island 3 weeks. But shortly after, it seemed, they were cast away, for the boats were found upon the coast, cast aland in another island adjoining. Other than these, there was never any people apparelled, or white of colour, either seen or heard of amongst these people, and these aforesaid were seen only of the inhabitants of Secotan; which appeared to be very true, for they wondered marvellously when we were amongst them at the whiteness of our skins, ever coveting to touch our breasts, and to view the same. Besides they had our ships in marvellous admiration, and all things else were so strange unto them, as it appeared that none of them had ever seen the like. When we discharged any piece, were it but an arquebus, they would tremble thereat for very fear, and for the strangeness of the same, for the weapons which themselves use are bows and arrows. The arrows are but of small canes, headed with a sharp shell or tooth of a fish sufficient enough to kill a naked man. Their swords be of wood hardened; likewise they use wooden breastplates for their defence. They have besides a kind of club, in the end whereof they fasten the sharp horns of a stag, or other beast. When they go to wars they carry about with them their idol, of whom they ask counsel, as the Romans were wont of the oracle of Apollo. They sing songs as they march towards the battle, instead of drums and trumpets. Their wars are very cruel and bloody, by reason whereof, and of their civil dissensions which have happened of late years amongst them, the people are marvellously wasted, and in some places the country left desolate.

Adjoining to this country aforesaid, called Secotan, beginneth a country called Ponouike, belonging to another king, whom they call Pimacum; and this king is in league with the next king adjoining towards the setting of the sun, and the country Neiosioke, situate upon a goodly river called Neuse. These kings have mortal war with Wingina, king of Wingandacoa; but about two years past there was a peace made between the King Pimacum and the lord of Secotan, as these men which we have brought with us to England have given us to understand; but there remaineth a mortal malice in the Secotans, for many injuries and slaughters done upon them by this Pimacum. They invited divers men, and thirty women of the best of his country, to their town to a feast, and when they were altogether merry, and praying before their idol (which is nothing else but a mere illusion of the devil) the captain or lord of the town came suddenly upon them, and slew them every one, reserving the women and children; and these two have oftentimes since persuaded us to surprise Pimacum's town, having promised and assured us that there will be found in it great store of commodities. But whether their persuasion be to the end they may be revenged of their enemies, or for the love they bear to us, we leave that to the trial hereafter.

Beyond this island called Roanoke are many islands very plentiful of fruits and other natural increases, together with many towns and villages along the side of the continent, some bounding upon the islands, and some stretching up further into the land.

When we first had sight of this country, some thought the first land we saw to be the continent; but after we entered into the haven we saw before us another mighty long sea, for there lieth along the coast a tract of islands two hundred miles in length, adjoining to the ocean sea, and between the islands two or three entrances. When you are entered between them, these islands become very narrow for the most part, as in most places six miles broad, in some places less, in few more, then there appeareth another great sea, containing in breadth in some places forty, and in some fifty, in some twenty miles over, before you come unto the continent; and in this enclosed sea there are above a hundred islands of divers bignesses, whereof one is sixteen miles long, at which we were, finding it a most pleasant and fertile ground, replenished with goodly cedars, and divers other sweet woods, full of currants, of flax, and many other notable commodities, which we at that time had no leisure to view. Besides this island there are many, as I have said, some of two, or three, of four, of five miles, some more, some less, most beautiful and pleasant to behold, replenished with deer, coneys, hares, and divers beasts, and about them the goodliest and best fish in the world, and in greatest abundance.

Thus, Sir, we have acquainted you with the particulars of our discovery made this present voyage, as far forth as the shortness of the time we there continued would afford us to take view of; and so contenting ourselves with this service at this time, which we hope hereafter to enlarge as occasion and assistance shall be given, we resolved to leave the country, and to apply ourselves to return for England, which we did accordingly, and arrived safely in the west of England about the midst of September.

And whereas we have above certified you of the country taken in possession by us to Her Majesty's use, and so to yours by Her Majesty's grant, we thought good for the better assurance thereof, to record some of the particular gentlemen, and men of account, who then were present, as witnesses of the same, that thereby all occasion of cavil to the title of the country, in Her Majesty's behalf, may be prevented, which otherwise such as like not the action may use and pretend. Whose names are, Master Philip Amadas, Master Arthur Barlow, Captains; William Grenville, John Wood, James Bromewich, Henry Greene, Benjamin Wood, Simon Ferdinando, Nicholas Petman, John Hughes, of the company.

We brought home also two of the savages, being lusty men, whose names were Wanchese and Manteo.

The discovery of the large, rich, and beautiful empire of Guiana, with a relation of the great and golden city of Manoa, which the Spaniards call El Dorado, and the provinces of Emeria, Aromaia, Amapaia, and other countries, with their rivers adjoining; performed in the year 1595 by Sir Walter Raleigh, knight, Captain of Her Majesty's Guard, Lord Warden of the Stanneries, and Her Highness' Lieutenant-General of the County of Cornwall. (Raleigh's dedicatory preface, to Lord Charles Howard, and that To the Reader, are here omitted as adding little to the narrative.)

O N Thursday the 6th of February, in the year 1595, we departed England, and the Sunday following had sight of the North Cape of Spain, the wind for the most part continuing prosperous; we passed in sight of the Burlings, and the Rock, and so onwards for the Canaries, and fell with Fuerteventura on the 17th of the same month, where we spent two or three days, and relieved our companies with some fresh meat. From thence we coasted by the Grand Canary, and so to Tenerife, and stayed there for the *Lion's Whelp*, your lordship's ship, and for Captain Amyas Preston and the rest. But when after 7 or 8 days we found them not, we departed and directed our course for Trinidad, with my own ship, and a small bark of Captain Cross's only (for we had before lost sight of a small galego on the coast of Spain, which came with us from Plymouth). We arrived at Trinidad the 22nd of March, casting anchor at Point Curiapan, which the Spaniards call Punta de Gallo, which is situate in 8 degrees or thereabouts. We abode there 4 or 5 days, and in all that time we came not to the speech of any Indian or Spaniard. On the coast we saw a fire, as we sailed from the Point Carao towards Curiapan, but for fear of the Spaniards none durst come to speak with us. I myself coasted it in my barge close aboard the shore and landed in every cove, the better to know the island, while the ships kept the channel. From Curiapan after a few days we turned up north-east to recover that place which the Spaniards call Puerto de los Españoles, and the inhabitants Conquerabia, and as before (revictualling my barge) I left the ships and kept by the shore, the better to come to speech with some of the inhabitants, and also to understand the rivers, watering-places, and ports of the island, which (as it is rudely done) my purpose is to send your lordship after a few days. From Curiapan I came to a port and seat of Indians called Parico, where we found a fresh water river, but saw no people. From thence I rowed to another port, called by the naturals Piche, and by the Spaniards Tierra de Brea. In the way between both were divers little brooks of fresh water and one salt river that had store of oysters upon the branches of the trees, and were very salt and well tasted. All their oysters grow upon those boughs and sprays, and not on the ground; the like is commonly seen in other places of the West Indies, and elsewhere. This tree is described by Andrew Thevet, in his *France Antarctique*, and the form figured in the book as a plant very strange, and by Pliny in his 12th book of his *Natural History*. But in this island, as also in Guiana, there are very many of them.

At this point, called Tierra de Brea or Piche, there is that abundance of stone pitch that all the ships of the world may be therewith laden from thence; and we made trial of it in trimming our ships to be most excellent good, and melteth not with the sun as the pitch of Norway, and therefore for ships trading the south parts very profitable. From thence we went to the mountain foot called Annaperima, and so passing the river Caroni on which the Spanish city was seated, we met with our ships at Puerto de los Españoles or Conquerabia.

This island of Trinidad hath the form of a sheephook, and is but narrow; the north part is very mountainous, the soil is very excellent and will bear sugar, ginger, or any other commodity that the Indies yield. It hath store of deer, wild porks, fruit, fish, and fowl; it hath also for bread sufficient maize, cassava, and of those roots and fruits which are common everywhere in the West Indies. It hath divers beasts which the Indies have not; the Spaniards confessed that they found grains of gold in some of the rivers, but they having a purpose to enter Guiana (the magazine of all rich metals) cared not to spend time in the search thereof any further. This island is called by the people thereof Cairi, and in it are divers nations; those about Parico are called Jajo, those at Punta de Carao are of the Arawaks, and between Carao and Curiapan they are called Salvajos, between Carao and Punta de Galera are the Nepoios, and those about the Spanish city term themselves Carinepagotes. Of the rest of the nations, and of other ports and rivers I leave to speak here, being impertinent to my purpose, and mean to describe them as they are situate in the particular plot and description of the island, three parts whereof I coasted with my barge, that I might the better describe it.

Meeting with the ships at Puerto de Los Españoles, we found at the landing-place a company of Spaniards who kept a guard at the descent; and they offering a sign of peace, I sent Captain Whiddon to speak with them, whom afterwards to my great grief I left buried in the said island after my return from Guiana, being a man most honest and valiant. The Spaniards seemed to be desirous to trade with us, and to enter into terms of peace, more for doubt of their own strength than for aught else, and in the end, upon pledge, some of them came aboard; the same evening there stole also aboard us in a small canoe two Indians, the one of them being a *cacique* or lord of the people called Cantyman, who had the year before been with Captain Whiddon, and was of his acquaintance. By this Cantyman we understood what strength the Spaniards had, how far it was to their city, and of Don Antonio de Berrio, the governor, who was said to be slain in his second attempt of Guiana, but was not.

While we remained at Puerto de los Españoles some Spaniards came aboard us to buy linen of the company, and such other things as they wanted, and also to view our ships and company, all which I entertained kindly and feasted after our manner; by means thereof I learned of one and another as much of the estate of Guiana as I could, or as they knew, for those poor soldiers having been many years without wine, a few draughts made them merry, in which mood they vaunted of Guiana and of the riches thereof, and all what they knew of the ways and passages, myself seeming to purpose nothing less than the entrance or discovery thereof, but bred in them an opinion that I was bound only for the relief of those English which I had planted in Virginia, whereof the bruit was come among them; which I had performed in my return, if extremity of weather had not forced me from the said coast.

I found occasions of staying in this place for two causes. The one was to be revenged of Berrio, who the year before, 1594, had betrayed eight of Captain Whiddon's men, and took them while he departed from them to seek the *Edward Bonaventure*, which arrived at Trinidad the day before from the East Indies: in whose absence Berrio sent a canoe aboard the pinnace only with Indians and dogs inviting the company to go with them into the woods to kill a deer. Who, like wise men, in the absence of their captain followed the Indians, but were no sooner one arquebus shot from the shore, but Berrio's soldiers lying in ambush had them all notwithstanding that he had given his word to Captain Whiddon that they should take water and wood safely. The other cause of my stay was, for that by discourse with the Spaniards I daily learned more and more of Guiana, of the rivers and passages, and of the enterprise of Berrio by what means or fault he failed, and how he meant to prosecute the same.

While we thus spent the time I was assured by another *cacique* of the north side of the island that Berrio had sent to Margarita and Cumana for soldiers, meaning to have given me a *cassado* at parting, if it had been possible. For although he had given order through all the island that no Indian should come aboard to trade with me upon pain of hanging and quartering (having executed two of them for the same, which I afterwards found), yet every night there came some with most lamentable complaints of his cruelty: how he had divided the island and given to every soldier a part; that he made the ancient *caciques* which were lords of the country to be their slaves; that he kept them in chains, and dropped their naked bodies with burning bacon, and such other torments, which I found afterwards to be true. For in the city, after I entered the same, there were 5 of the lords or little kings (which they call *caciques* in the West Indies) in one chain almost dead of famine, and wasted with torments. These are called in their own language Acarewana, and now of late since English, French, and Spanish are come among them they call themselves Captains, because they perceive that the chiefest of every ship is called by that name. Those five Captains in the chain were called Wannawanare, Carroaori, Maquarima, Tarroopanama, and Aterima. So as both to be revenged of the former wrong, as also considering that to enter Guiana by small boats, to depart 400 or 500 miles from my ships, and to leave a garrison in my back interested in the same enterprise, who also daily expected supplies out of Spain, I should have savoured very much of the ass; and therefore taking a time of most advantage, I set upon the *Corps du garde* in the evening, and having put them to the sword, sent Captain Calfield onwards with 60 soldiers, and myself followed with 40 more, and so took their new city, which they called St Joseph, by break of day. They abode not any fight after a few shot, and all being dismissed, but only Berrio and his companion, I brought them with me aboard, and at the instance of the Indians I set their new city of St Joseph on fire.

The same day arrived Captain George Gifford with your lordship's ship, and Captain Keymis, whom I lost on the coast of Spain, with the galego, and in them divers gentlemen and others, which to our little army was a great comfort and supply.

We then hasted away towards our purposed discovery, and first I called all the captains of the island together that were enemies to the Spaniards; for there were some which Berrio had brought out of other countries, and planted there to eat out and waste those that were natural of the place, and by my Indian interpreter, which I carried out of England, I made them understand that I was the servant of a Queen who was the great *cacique* of the north, and a virgin, and had more *caciqui* under her than there were trees in that island; that she was an enemy to the *Castellani* in respect of their tyranny and oppression, and that she delivered all such nations about her, as were by them oppressed, and having freed all the coast of the northern world from their servitude, had sent me to free them also, and withal to defend the country of Guiana from their invasion and conquest. I showed them Her Majesty's picture, which they so admired and honoured as it had been easy to have brought them idolatrous thereof.

The like and a more large discourse I made to the rest of the nations, both in my passing to Guiana and to those of the borders, so as in that part of the world Her Majesty is very famous and admirable, whom they now call Ezrabeta Cassipuna Acarewana, which is as much as "Elizabeth, the great princess or greatest commander." This done, we left Puerto de los Españoles, and returned to Curiapan, and having Berrio my prisoner, I gathered from him as much of Guiana as he knew.

This Berrio is a gentleman well descended, and had long served the Spanish king in Milan, Naples, the Low Countries, and elsewhere, very valiant and liberal, and a gentleman of great assuredness, and of a great heart. I used him according to his estate and worth in all things I could, according to the small means I had.

I sent Captain Whiddon the year before to get what knowledge he could of Guiana, and the end of my journey at this time was to discover and enter the same. But my intelligence was far from truth, for the country is situate above 600 English miles further from the sea than I was made believe it had been; which afterwards understanding to be true by Berrio, I kept it from the knowledge of my company, who else would never have been brought to attempt the same. Of which 600 miles I passed 400, leaving my ships so far from me at anchor in the sea, which was more of desire to perform that discovery than of reason, especially having such poor and weak vessels to transport ourselves in. For in the bottom of an old galego which I caused to be fashioned like a galley, and in one barge, two wherries, and a ship-boat of the *Lion's Whelp*, we carried 100 persons and their victuals for a month in the same, being all driven to lie in the rain and weather in the open air, in the burning sun, and upon the hard boards, and to dress our meat, and to carry all manner of furniture in them; wherewith they were so pestered and unsavory, that what with victuals being most fish, with wet clothes of so many men thrust together, and the heat of the sun, I will undertake there was never any prison in England that could be found more unsavoury and loathsome, especially to myself, who had for many years before been dieted and cared for in a sort far more differing.

If Captain Preston had not been persuaded that he should have come too late to Trinidad to have found us there (for the month was expired which I promised to tarry for him there ere he could recover the coast of Spain) but that it had pleased God he might have joined with us, and that we had entered the country but some ten days sooner ere the rivers were overflown, we had adventured either to have gone to the great city of Manoa, or at least taken so many of the other cities and towns nearer at hand as would have made a royal return. But it pleased not God so much to favour me at this time; if it shall be my lot to prosecute the same, I shall willingly spend my life therein, and if any else shall be enabled thereunto, and conquer the same, I assure him thus much, he shall perform more than ever was done in Mexico by Cortes, or in Peru by Pizarro, whereof the one conquered the Empire of Montezuma, the other of Huascar, and Atabalipa. And whatsoever prince shall possess it, that prince shall be lord of more gold, and of a more beautiful

13 *Raleigh captures Berrio.*

empire, and of more cities and people, than either the King of Spain or the Great Turk.

But because there may arise many doubts, and how this Empire of Guiana is become so populous, and adorned with so many great cities, towns, temples, and treasures, I thought good to make it known that the Emperor now reigning is descended from those magnificent princes of Peru, of whose large territories, of whose policies, conquests, edifices, and riches, Pedro de Cieza, Francisco Lopez, and others have written large discourses. For when Francisco Pizarro, Diego Almagra and others conquered the said Empire of Peru, and had put to death Atabalipa, son to Guaynacapa, which Atabalipa had formerly caused his eldest brother Huascar to be slain, one of the younger sons of Guaynacapa fled out of Peru, and took with him many thousands of those soldiers of the Empire called Orejones, and with those and many others that followed him, he vanquished all that tract and valley of America which is situate between the great river of Amazons and Baraguan, otherwise called Orinoco and Marañon.

The Empire of Guiana is directly east from Peru towards the sea, and lieth under the equinoctial line, and it hath more abundance of gold than any part of Peru, and as many or more great cities than ever Peru had when it flourished most. It is governed by the same laws, and the Emperor and people observe the same religion, and the same form and policies in government as were used in Peru, not differing in any part; and I have been assured by such of the Spaniards as have seen Manoa, the imperial city of Guiana, which the Spaniards call El Dorado, that for the greatness, for the riches, and for the excellent seat, it far exceedeth any of the world, at least of so much of the world as is known to the Spanish nation. It is founded upon a lake of salt water of 200 leagues long, like unto *Mare Caspium*. And if we compare it to that of Peru, and but read the report of Francisco Lopez and others, it will seem more than credible; and because we may judge of the one by the other, I thought good to insert part of the 120th chapter of Lopez in his general history of the Indies, wherein he describeth the Court and magnificence of Guaynacapa, ancestor to the Emperor of Guiana, whose very words are these:— "Todo el servicio de su casa, mesa y cocina era de oro y de plata, y cuando menos de plata y cobre, por mas recio. Tenia en su recamara estatuas huecas de oro, que parescian gigantes, y las figuras al propio, y tamaño de cuantos animales, aves, arboles, y yerbas produce la tierra, y de cuantos peces cria la mar y agua de sus reynos. Tenia asimesmo sogas, costales, cestas, y troxes de oro y plata; rimeros de palos de oro, que pareciesen leña rajada para quemar. En fin no avia cosa en su tierra, que no la tuviese de oro contrahecha; y aun dizen, que tenian los Ingas un verjel en una isla cerca de la Puna, donde se iban a holgar, quando querian mar, que tenia la hortaliza, las flores, y arboles de oro y plata, invencion y grandeza hasta entonces nunca vista. Allende de todo esto tenia infinitisima cantidad de plata y oro por labrar en el Cuzco, que se perdio por la muerte de Guascar; ca los Indios lo escondieron, viendo que los Españoles so lo tomavan, y embiavan a España." That is, "All the vessels of his house, table, and kitchen, were of gold and silver, and the meanest of silver and copper for strength and hardness of metal. He had in his wardrobe hollow statues of gold which seemed giants, and the figures in proportion and bigness of all the beasts, birds, trees, and herbs, that the earth bringeth forth; and of all the fishes that the sea or waters of his kingdom breedeth. He had also ropes, budgets, chests, and troughs of gold and silver, heaps of billets of gold, that seemed wood marked out to burn. Finally, there was nothing in his country whereof he had not the counterfeit in gold. Yea, and they say, the Incas had a garden of pleasure in an island near Puna, where they went to recreate themselves, when they would take the air of the sea, which had all kinds of garden-herbs, flowers, and trees of gold and silver, an invention and magnificence till then never seen. Besides all this, he had an infinite quantity of silver and gold unwrought in Cuzco, which was lost by the death of Huascar, for the Indians hid it, seeing that the Spaniards took it and sent it into Spain."

And in the 117th chapter, Francisco Pizarro caused the gold and silver of Atabalipa to be weighed after he had taken it, which Lopez setteth down in these words following:—"Hallaron cincuenta y dos mil marcos de buena plata, y un millon y trecientos y veinte y seis mil y quinientos pesos de oro." Which is, "They found fifty and two thousand marks of good silver, and one million and three hundred and twenty and six thousand and five hundred pezos of gold."

Now, although these reports may seem strange, yet, if we consider the many millions which are daily brought out of Peru into Spain, we may easily believe the same. For we find that by the abundant treasure of that country the Spanish King vexeth all the princes of Europe, and is become, in a few years, from a poor King of Castille, the greatest monarch of this part of the world, and likely every day to increase if other princes forslow the good occasions offered, and suffer him to add this empire to the rest, which by far exceedeth all the rest. If his gold now endanger us, he will then be unresistible. Such of the Spaniards as afterward endeavoured the conquest thereof (whereof there have been many, as shall be declared hereafter) thought that this Inca (of whom this Emperor now living is descended) took his way by the river of Amazons, by that branch which is called Papamene; for by that way followed Orellana (by the commandment of Gonzalo Pizarro, in the year 1542), whose name the river also beareth this day, which is also by others called Marañon, although Andrew Thevet doth affirm that between Marañon and Amazons there are 120 leagues; but sure it is that those rivers have one head and beginning, and the Marañon, which Thevet describes, is but a branch of Amazons or Orellana, of which I will speak more in another place. It was attempted by Ordaz; but it is now little less than 70 years since that Diego Ordaz, a Knight of the Order of Santiago, attempted the same; and it was in the year 1542 that Orellana discovered the river of Amazons; but the first that ever saw Manoa was Juan Martin, master of the munition to Ordaz. At a port called Morequito, in Guiana, there lieth at this day a great anchor of Ordaz's ship; and this port is some 300 miles within the land, upon the great river of Orinoco.

I rested at this port four days, twenty days after I left the ships at Curiapan. The relation of this Martin (who was the first that discovered Manoa), his success and end are to be seen in the Chancery of Saint Juan de Puerto Rico, whereof Berrio had a copy, which appeared to be the greatest encouragement as well to Berrio as to others that formerly attempted the discovery and conquest. Orellana, after he failed of the discovery of Guiana by the said river of Amazons, passed into Spain, and there obtained a patent of the King for the invasion and conquest, but died by sea about the islands, and his fleet severed by tempest, the action for that time proceeded not. Diego Ordaz followed the enterprise, and departed Spain with 600 soldiers and 30 horse, who arriving on the coast of Guiana was slain in a mutiny, with the most part of such as favoured him, as also of the rebellious part, insomuch as his ships perished and few or none returned, neither was it certainly known what became of the said Ordaz until Berrio found the anchor of his ship in the river of Orinoco; but it was supposed, and so it is written by Lopez, that he perished on the seas, and of other writers diversely conceived and reported. And hereof it came that Martin entered so far within the land, and arrived at that city of Inca the Emperor; for it chanced that while Ordaz with his army rested at the port of Morequito (who was either the first or second that attempted Guiana), by some negligence the whole store of powder provided for the service was set on fire, and Martin, having the chief charge, was condemned by the General Ordaz to be executed forthwith. Martin, being much favoured by the soldiers, had all the means possible procured for his life; but it could not be obtained in other sort than this: that he should be set into a canoe alone, without any victual, only with his arms, and so turned loose into the great river. But it pleased God that the canoe was carried down the stream, and certain of the Guianians met it the same evening, and, having not at any time seen any Christian nor any man of that colour, they carried Martin into the land to be wondered at, and so from town to town, until he came to the great city of Manoa, the seat and residence of Inca the Emperor. The Emperor, after he had beheld him, knew him to be a Christian (for it was not long before that his brethren Huascar and Atabalipa were vanquished by the Spaniards in Peru) and caused him to be lodged in his palace and well entertained. He lived seven months in Manoa, but was not suffered to wander into the country anywhere. He was also brought thither all the way blindfold, led by the Indians, until he came to the entrance of Manoa itself, and was fourteen or fifteen days in the passage. He avowed at his death that he entered the city at noon, and then they uncovered his face, and that he travelled all that day till night through the city, and the next day from sun rising to sun setting ere he came to the palace of Inca. After that Martin had lived seven months in Manoa, and began to understand the language of the country, Inca asked him whether he desired to return into his own country, or would willingly abide with him. But Martin, not desirous to stay, obtained the favour of Inca to depart, with whom he sent divers Guianians to conduct him to the river of Orinoco, all laden with as much gold as they could carry, which he gave to Martin at his departure. But when he was arrived near the river's side, the borderers, which are called the Orinocoponi, robbed him and his Guianians of all the treasure (the borderers being at that time at wars, which Inca had not conquered) save only of two great bottles of gourds, which were filled with beads of gold curiously wrought, which those Orinocoponi thought had been no other thing than his drink or meat, or grain for food, with which Martin had liberty to pass. And so in canoes he fell down from the river of Orinoco to Trinidad and from thence to Margarita, and also to Saint Juan de Puerto Rico, where, remaining a long time for passage into Spain, he died. In the time of his extreme sickness, and when he was without hope of life, receiving the sacrament at the hands of his confessor, he delivered these things, with the relation of his travels, and also called for his *calabazas* or gourds of the gold beads, which he gave to the church and friars to be prayed for. This Martin was he that christened the city of Manoa by the name of El Dorado, and, as Berrio informed me, upon this occasion, "Those Guianians, and also the borderers, and all other in that tract which I have seen, are marvellous great drunkards; in which vice I think no nation can compare with them. And at the times of their solemn feasts, when the Emperor carouseth with his captains, tributaries, and governors, the manner is thus. All those that pledge him are first stripped naked and their bodies anointed all over with a kind of white balsam (by them called *curca*), of which there is great plenty, and yet very dear amongst them, and it is of all other the most precious, whereof we have had good experience. When they are anointed all over, certain servants of the Emperor, having prepared gold made into fine powder, blow it through hollow canes upon their naked bodies, until they be all shining from the foot to the head; and in this sort they sit drinking by twenties and hundreds, and continue in drunkenness sometimes six or seven days together." The same is also confirmed by a letter written into Spain which was intercepted, which Master Robert Dudley told me he had seen. Upon this sight, and for the abundance of gold which he saw in the city, the images of gold in their temples, the plates, armours, and shields of gold which they use in the wars, he called it El Dorado.

After the death of Ordaz and Martin, and after Orellana, who was employed by Gonzalo Pizarro, one Pedro de Ursua, a knight of Navarre, attempted Guiana, taking his way into Peru, and built his brigantines upon a river called Oia, which rises to the southward of Quito, and is very great. This river falleth into Amazons, by which Ursua with his companies descended and came out of that province which is called Mutylonez; and it seemeth to me that this empire is reserved for Her Majesty and the English nation, by reason of the hard success which all these and other Spaniards found in attempting the same, whereof I will speak briefly, though impertinent in some sort to my purpose.

This Pedro de Ursua had among his troops a Biscayan called Aguirre, a man meanly born, who bore no other office than a sergeant or *alferez*; but after certain months, when the soldiers were grieved with travels and consumed with famine, and that no entrance could be found by the branches or body of Amazons, this Aguirre raised a mutiny, of which he made himself the head, and so prevailed as he put Ursua to the sword and all his followers, taking on him the whole charge and commandment, with a purpose not only to make himself Emperor of Guiana but also of Peru and of all that side of the West Indies. He had of his party seven hundred soldiers, and of those many promised to draw in other captains and companies, to deliver up towns and forts in Peru; but neither finding by the said river any passage into Guiana, nor any possibility to return towards Peru by the same Amazons, by reason that the descent of the river made so great a current, he was enforced to disembogue at the mouth of the said Amazons, which cannot be less than a thousand leagues from the place where they embarked. From thence he coasted the land till he arrived at Margarita to the north of Mompatar, which is at this day called Puerto de Tyranno for that he there slew Don Juan de Villa Andrando, Governor of Margarita, who was father to Don Juan Sarmiento, Governor of Margarita when Sir John Burgh landed there and attempted the island. Aguirre put to the sword all other in the island that refused to be of his party, and took with him certain Simerons and other desperate companions. From thence he went to Cumana and there slew the Governor, and dealt in all as at Margarita. He spoiled all the coast of Caracas and the province of Venezuela and of Rio de la Hacha; and, as I remember, it was the same year that Sir John Hawkins sailed to Saint Juan de Ulua in the *Jesus of Lubeck*; for himself told me that he met with such a one upon the coast that rebelled, and had sailed down all the river of Amazons. Aguirre from thence landed about Santa Marta and sacked it also, putting to death so many as refused to be his followers, purposing to invade Nuevo Reyno de Granada and to sack Pamplona, Merida, Lagrita, Tunxa, and the rest of the cities of Nuevo Reyno, and from thence again to enter Peru; but in a fight in the said Nuevo Reyno he was overthrown, and, finding no way to escape, he first put to the sword his own children, foretelling them that they should not live to be dcfamed or upbraided by the Spaniards after his death, who would have termed them the children of a traitor or tyrant; and that, since he could not make them princes, he would yet deliver them from shame and reproach. These were the ends and tragedies of Ordaz, Martin, Orellana, Ursua, and Aguirre.

Also soon after Ordaz followed Jeronimo Ortal de Saragosa with 130 soldiers, who failing his entrance by sea, was cast with the current on the coast of Paria, and peopled about San Miguel de Neveri. It was then attempted by Don Pedro de Silva, a Portuguese of the family of Ruy Gomes de Silva, and by the favour which Ruy Gomes had with the King he was set out. But he also shot wide of the mark; for being departed from Spain with his fleet, he entered by Marañon and Amazons, where by the nations of the river, and by the Amazons, he was utterly overthrown, and himself and all his army defeated; only seven escaped, and of those but two returned.

After him came Pedro Hernandez de Serpa, and landed at Cumana, in the West Indies, taking his journey by land towards Orinoco, which may be some 120 leagues; but ere he came to the borders of the said river, he was set upon by a nation of the Indians, called Wikiri, and overthrown in such sort, that of 300 soldiers, horsemen, many Indians, and negroes, there returned but 18. Others affirm that he was defeated in the very entrance of Guiana, at the first civil town of the empire called Macuraguara. Captain Preston, in taking Santiago de Leon (which was by him and his companies very resolutely performed, being a great town, and far within the land) held a gentleman prisoner, who died in his ship, that was one of the company of Hernandez de Serpa, and saved among those that escaped, who witnessed what opinion is held among the Spaniards thereabouts of the great riches of Guiana, and El Dorado, the city of Inca. Another Spaniard was brought aboard me by Captain Preston, who told me in the hearing of himself and divers other gentlemen, that he met with Berrio's camp-master at Caracas, when he came from the borders of Guiana, and that he saw with him forty most pure plates of gold, curiously wrought, and swords of Guiana decked and inlaid with gold, feathers garnished with gold, and divers rarities which he carried to the Spanish king.

After Hernandez de Serpa, it was undertaken by the Adelantado, Don Gonzales Ximenes de Quesada, who was one of the chiefest in the conquest of Nuevo Reyno, whose daughter and heir Don Antonio de Berrio married. Gonzales sought the passage also by the river called Papamene, which riseth by Quito in Peru, and runneth south-east 100 leagues, and then falleth into Amazons, but he also failing the entrance, returned with the loss of much labour and cost. I took one Captain George, a Spaniard, that followed Gonzales in this enterprise. Gonzales gave his daughter to Berrio, taking his oath and honour to follow the enterprise to the last of his substance and life; who since, as he hath sworn to me, hath spent 300,000 ducats in the same, and yet never could enter so far into the land as myself with that poor troop, or rather a handful of men, being in all about 100 gentlemen, soldiers, rowers, boat-keepers, boys, and of all sorts; neither could any of the forepassed undertakers, nor Berrio himself, discover the country, till now lately by conference with an ancient king, called Carapana, he got the true light thereof. For Berrio came about 1,500 miles ere he understood aught, or could find any passage or entrance into any part thereof, yet he had experience of all these forenamed, and divers others, and was persuaded of their errors and mistakings. Berrio sought it by the river Cacanare, which falleth into a great river called Pauto; Pauto falleth into Meta, and Meta into Baraguan, which is also called Orinoco.

He took his journey from Nuevo Reyno de Granada, where he dwelt, having the inheritance of Gonzales Ximenes in those parts; he was followed with 700 horse, he drove with him 1000 head of cattle, he had also many women, Indians, and slaves. How all these rivers cross and encounter, how the country lieth and is bordered, the passage of Ximenes and Berrio, my own discovery, and the way that I entered, with all the rest of the nations and rivers, your lordship shall receive in a large chart or map, which I have not yet finished, and which I shall most humbly pray your lordship to secrete, and not to suffer it to pass your own hands. For by a draught thereof all may be prevented by other nations; for I know it is this very year sought by the French, although by the way that they now take, I fear it not much. It was also told me ere I departed England, that Villiers, the Admiral, was in preparation for the planting of Amazons, to which river the French have made divers voyages, and returned much gold and other rarities. I spoke with a captain of a French ship that came from thence, his ship riding in Falmouth the same year that my ships came first from Virginia. There was another this year in Helford, that also came from thence, and had been fourteen months at an anchor in Amazons, which were both very rich. Although, as I am persuaded, Guiana cannot be entered that way, yet no doubt the trade of gold from thence passeth by branches of rivers into the rivers of Amazons, and so it doth on every hand far from the country itself; for those Indians of Trinidad have plates of gold from Guiana, and those cannibals of Dominica which dwell in the islands by which our ships pass yearly to the West Indies, also the Indians of Paria, those Indians called Tucaris, Choques, Apotomios, Cumanagotos, and all those other nations inhabiting near about the mountains that run from Paria through the province of Venezuela, and in Maracapana, and the cannibals of Guanipa, the Indians called Assawa, Coaca, Ajai, and the rest (all which shall be described in my description as they are situate) have plates of gold of Guiana. And upon the river of Amazons, Thevet writeth that the people wear croissants of gold, for of that form the Guianians most commonly make them; so as from Dominica to Amazons, which is above 250 leagues, all the chief Indians in all parts wear of those plates of Guiana. Undoubtedly those that trade Amazons return much gold, which (as is aforesaid) cometh by trade from Guiana, by some branch of a river that falleth from the country into Amazons, and either it is by the river which passeth by the nations called Tinados, or by Caripuna.

I made enquiry amongst the most ancient and best travelled of the Orinocoponi, and I had knowledge of all the rivers between Orinoco and Amazons, and was very desirous to understand the truth of those warlike women, because of some it is believed, of others not. And though I digress from my purpose, yet I will set down that which hath been delivered me for truth of those women, and I spoke with a *cacique*, or lord of people, that told me he had been in the river, and beyond it also. The nations of these women are on the south side of the river in the provinces of Topago, and their chiefest strengths and retreats are in the islands situate on the south side of the entrance some 60 leagues within the mouth of the said river. The memories of the like women are very ancient as well in Africa as in Asia: in Africa those that had Medusa for queen; others in Scythia, near the rivers of Tanais and Thermodon. We find, also, that Lampedo and Marthesia were queens of the Amazons. In many histories they are verified to have been, and in divers ages and provinces; but they which are not far from Guiana do accompany with men but once in a year, and for the time of one month, which I gather by their relation, to be in April; and that time all kings of the borders assemble, and queens of the Amazons; and after the queens have chosen, the rest cast lots for their valentines. This one month they feast, dance, and drink of their wines in abundance; and the moon being done they all depart to their own provinces. If they conceive, and be delivered of a son, they return him to the father; if of a daughter, they nourish it and retain it. And as many as have daughters send unto the begetters a present, all being desirous to increase their own sex and kind; but that they cut off the right dug of the breast I do not find to be true. It was further told me that if in these wars they took any prisoners, that they used to accompany with those also at what time soever, but in the end for certain they put them to death; for they are said to be very cruel and bloodthirsty, especially to such as offer to invade their territories. These Amazons have likewise great store of these plates of gold, which they recover by exchange chiefly for a kind of green stones, which the Spaniards call *piedras hijadas*, and we use for spleen stones; and for the disease of the stone we also esteem them. Of these I saw divers in Guiana, and commonly every king or *cacique* hath one, which their wives for the most part wear, and they esteem them as great jewels.

But to return to the enterprise of Berrio, who (as I have said) departed from Nuevo Reyno with 700 horse, besides the provisions above rehearsed; he descended by the river called Cacanare, which riseth in Nuevo Reyno out of the mountains by the city of Tunja, from which mountain also springeth Pauto; both which fall into the great river of Meta, and Meta riseth from a mountain joining to Pamplona, in the same Nuevo Reyno de Granada. These, as also Guaiare, which issueth out of the mountains by Timana, fall all into Baraguan, and are but of his heads; for at their coming together they lose their names, and Baraguan farther down is also rebaptized by the name of Orinoco. On the other side of the city and hills of Timana riseth Rio Grande, which falleth in the sea by Santa Marta. By Cacanare first, and so into Meta, Berrio passed, keeping his horsemen on the banks, where the country served them for to march; and where otherwise, he was driven to embark them in boats which he built for the purpose, and so came with the current down the river of Meta, and so into Baraguan. After he entered that great and mighty river, he began daily to lose of his companies both men and horse; for it is in many places violently swift, and hath forcible eddies, many sands, and divers islands sharp pointed with rocks. But after one whole year, journeying for the most part by river, and the rest by land, he grew daily to fewer numbers; for both by sickness, and by encountering with the people of those regions through which he travelled, his companies were much wasted, especially by divers encounters with the Amapaians. And in all this time he never could learn of any passage into Guiana, nor any news or fame thereof, until he came to a further border of the said Amapaia, eight days' journey from the river Caroni, which was the furthest river that he entered. Among those of Amapaia Guiana was famous, but few of these people accosted Berrio, or would trade with him the first three months of the six which he sojourned there. This Amapaia is also marvellous rich in gold (as both Berrio confessed and those of Guiana, with whom I had most conference) and is situate upon Orinoco also. In this country Berrio lost 60 of his best soldiers, and most of all his horse that remained in his former year's travel; but in the end, after divers encounters with those nations, they grew to peace, and they presented Berrio with ten images of fine gold among divers other plates and croissants, which, as he swore to me, and divers other gentlemen, were so curiously wrought, as he had not seen the like either in Italy, Spain, or the Low Countries; and he was resolved, that when they came to the hands of the Spanish king, to whom he had sent them by his campmaster, they would appear very admirable, especially being wrought by such a nation as had no iron instruments at all, nor any of those helps which our goldsmiths have to work withal. The particular name of the people in Amapaia which gave him these pieces, are called Anebas, and the river of Orinoco at that place is above 12 English miles broad, which may be from his outfall into the sea 700 or 800 miles.

This province of Amapaia is a very low and a marsh ground near the river; and by reason of the red water which issueth out in small branches through the fenny and boggy ground, there breed divers poisonful worms and serpents. And the Spaniards not suspecting, nor in any sort foreknowing the danger, were infected with a grievous kind of flux by drinking thereof; and even the very horses poisoned therewith, insomuch as at the end of the 6 months that they abode there of all their troops there were not left above 120 soldiers, and neither horse nor cattle. For Berrio hoped to have found Guiana by 1,000 miles nearer than it fell out to be in the end; by means whereof they sustained much want, and much hunger, oppressed with grievous diseases, and all the miseries that could be imagined.

I demanded of those in Guiana that had travelled Amapaia, how they lived with that tawny or red water when they travelled thither; and they told me that after the sun was near the middle of the sky they used to fill their pots and pitchers with that water, but either before that time or towards the setting of the sun it was dangerous to drink of, and in the night strong poison. I learned also of divers other rivers of that nature among them, which were also (while the sun was in the meridian) very safe to drink, and in the morning, evening, and night, wonderful dangerous and infective. From this province Berrio hasted away as soon as the spring and beginning of summer appeared, and sought his entrance on the borders of Orinoco on the south-side; but there ran a ledge of so high and impassable mountains as he was not able by any means to march over them, continuing from the east sea into which Orinoco falleth, even to Quito in Peru. Neither had he means to carry victual or munition over those craggy, high, and fast hills, being all woody, and those so thick and spiny, and so full of prickles, thorns, and briars, as it is impossible to creep through them. He had also neither friendship among the people, nor any interpreter to persuade or treat with them; and more, to his disadvantage, the *caciques* and kings of Amapaia had given knowledge of his purpose to the Guianians, and that he sought to sack and conquer the empire for the hope of their so great abundance and quantities of gold. He passed by the mouths of many great rivers which fell into Orinoco both from the north and south, which I forbear to name for tediousness, and because they are more pleasing in describing than reading.

Berrio affirmed that there fell a hundred rivers into Orinoco from the north and south, whereof the least was as big as Rio Grande that passed between Popayan and Nuevo Reyno de Granada (Rio Grande being esteemed one of the renowned rivers in all the West Indies, and numbered among the great rivers of the world); but he knew not the names of any of these but Caroni only, neither from what nations they descended, neither to what provinces they led. For he had no means to discourse with the inhabitants at any time; neither was he curious in these things, being utterly unlearned, and not knowing the east from the west. But of all these I got some knowledge, and of many more, partly by my own travel, and the rest by conference; of some one I learned one, of others the rest, having with me an Indian that spoke many languages, and that of Guiana naturally. I sought out all the aged men, and such as were greatest travellers, and by the one and the other I came to understand the situations, the rivers, the kingdoms from the east sea to the borders of Peru, and from Orinoco southward as far as Amazons or Marañon, and the regions of Maria Tamball, and of all the kings of provinces, and captains of towns and villages, how they stood in terms of peace or war, and which were friends or enemies the one with the other, without which there can be neither entrance nor conquest in those parts, nor elsewhere. For by the dissension between Huascar and Atabalipa Pizarro conquered Peru, and by the hatred that the Tlaxcallians bore to Montezuma Cortes was victorious over Mexico; without which both the one and the other had failed of their enterprise, and of the great honour and riches which they attained unto.

Now Berrio began to grow into despair, and looked for no other success than his predecessor in this enterprise, until such time as he arrived at the province of Emeria towards the east sea and mouth of the river, where he found a nation of people very favourable, and the country full of all manner of victual. The king of this land is called Carapana, a man very wise, subtle, and of great experience, being little less than a hundred years old. In his youth he was sent by his father into the island of Trinidad, by reason of civil war among themselves, and was bred at a village in that island, called Parico. At that place in his youth he had seen many Christians, both French and Spanish, and went divers times with the Indians of Trinidad to Margarita and Cumana, in the West Indies (for both those places have ever been relieved with victual from Trinidad) by reason whereof he grew of more understanding, and noted the difference of the nations, comparing the strength and arms of his country with those of the Christians, and ever after temporised so as whosoever else did amiss, or was wasted by contention, Carapana kept himself and his country in quiet and plenty. He also held peace with the Caribs or cannibals, his neighbours, and had free trade with all nations, whosoever else had war.

Berrio sojourned and rested his weak troop in the town of Carapana six weeks, and from him learned the way and passage to Guiana, and the riches and magnificence thereof; but being then utterly disable to proceed, he determined to try his fortune another year, when he had renewed his provisions and regathered more force, which he hoped for as well out of Spain as from Nuevo Reyno, where he had left his son Don Antonio Ximenes to second him upon the first notice given of his entrance; and so for the present embarked himself in canoes, and by the branches of Orinoco arrived at Trinidad, having from Carapana sufficient pilots to conduct him. From Trinidad he coasted Paria, and so recovered Margarita; and having made relation to Don Juan Sarmiento, the Governor, of his proceeding, and persuaded him of the riches of Guiana, he obtained from thence fifty soldiers, promising presently to return to Carapana, and so into Guiana. But Berrio meant nothing less at that time; for he wanted many provisions necessary for such an enterprise, and therefore departed from Margarita, seated himself in Trinidad, and from thence sent his camp-master and his sergeant-major back to the borders to discover the nearest passage into the empire, as also to treat with the borderers, and to draw them to his party and love; without which he knew he could neither pass safely, nor in any sort be relieved with victual or aught else. Carapana directed his company to a king called Morequito, assuring them that no man could deliver so much of Guiana as Morequito could, and that his dwelling was but five days journey from Macuraguara, the first civil town of Guiana.

Now your lordship shall understand that this Morequito, one of the greatest lords or kings of the borders of Guiana, had two or three years before been at Cumana and at Margarita, in the West Indies, with great store of plates of gold, which he carried to exchange for such other things as he wanted in his own country, and was daily feasted, and presented by the governors of those places, and held amongst them some two months, in which time one Vides, Governor of Cumana, won him to be his conductor into Guiana, being allured by those croissants and images of gold which he brought with him to trade, as also by the ancient fame and magnificence of El Dorado. Whereupon Vides sent into Spain for a patent to discover and conquer Guiana, not knowing of the precedence of Berrio's patent, which, as Berrio affirmeth, was signed before that of Vides. So as when Vides understood of Berrio, and that he had made entrance into that territory, and foregone his desire and hope, it was verily thought that Vides practised with Morequito to hinder and disturb Berrio in all he could, and not to suffer him to enter through his seignory, nor any of his companies; neither to victual, nor guide them in any sort. For Vides, Governor of Cumana, and Berrio, were become mortal enemies, as well for that Berrio had gotten Trinidad into his patent with Guiana, as also in that he was by Berrio prevented in the journey of Guiana itself. Howsoever it was, I know not, but Morequito for a time dissembled his disposition, suffered Spaniards and a friar (which Berrio had sent to discover Manoa) to travel through his country, gave them a guide for Macuraguara, the first town of civil and apparelled people, from whence they had other guides to bring them to Manoa, the great city of Inca; and being furnished with those things which they had learned of Carapana were of most price in Guiana, went onward, and in eleven days arrived at Manoa, as Berrio affirmeth for certain; although I could not be assured thereof by the lord which now governeth the province of Morequito, for he told me that they got all the gold they had in other towns on this side Manoa, there being many very great and rich, and (as he said) built like the towns of Christians, with many rooms.

When these ten Spaniards were returned, and ready to put out of the border of Aromaia, the people of Morequito set upon them, and slew them all but one that swam the river, and took from them to the value of forty thousand pesos of gold; and one of them only lived to bring the news to Berrio, that both his nine soldiers and holy father were benighted in the said province. I myself spoke with the captains of Morequito that slew them, and was at the place where it was executed. Berrio, enraged herewithal, sent all the strength he could make into Aromaia, to be revenged of him, his people, and country. But Morequito suspecting the same, fled over Orinoco, and through the territories of the Siama and Wikiri recovered Cumana, where he thought himself very safe with Vides the governor. But Berrio sending for him in the King's name, and his messengers finding him in the house of one Fashardo, on the sudden, ere he was suspected, so as he could not then be conveyed away, Vides durst not deny him, as well to avoid the suspicion of the practice as also for that a holy father was slain by him and his people. Morequito offered Fashardo the weight of three quintals in gold, to let him escape; but the poor Guianian, betrayed on all sides, was delivered to the camp-master of Berrio, and was presently executed.

After the death of this Morequito, the soldiers of Berrio spoiled his territory and took divers prisoners. Among others they took the uncle of Morequito, called Topiawari, who is now king of Aromaia (whose son I brought with me into England) and is a man of great understanding and policy; he is above a hundred years old, and yet of a very able body. The Spaniards led him in a chain seventeen days, and made him their guide from place to place between his country and Emeria, the province of Carapana aforesaid, and he was at last redeemed for a hundred plates of gold, and divers stones called *piedras hijadas*, or spleen-stones. Now Berrio, for executing of Morequito, and other cruelties, spoils, and slaughters done in Aromaia, hath lost the love of the Orinocoponi, and of all the borderers, and dare not send any of his soldiers any further into the land than to Carapana, which he called the port of Guiana; but from thence by the help of Carapana he had trade further into the country, and always appointed ten Spaniards to reside in Carapana's town, by whose favour, and by being conducted by his people, those ten searched the country thereabouts, as well for mines as for other trades and commodities.

They also have gotten a nephew of Morequito, whom they have christened and named Don Juan, of whom they have great hope, endeavouring by all means to establish him in the said province. Among many other trades, those Spaniards used canoes to pass to the rivers of Barima, Pawroma, and Dissequebe, which are on the south side of the mouth of Orinoco, and there buy women and children from the cannibals, which are of that barbarous nature as they will for three or four hatchets sell the sons and daughters of their own brethren and sisters, and for somewhat more, even their own daughters. Hereof the Spaniards make great profit; for buying a maid of twelve or thirteen years for three or four hatchets, they sell them again at Margarita in the West Indies for fifty and a hundred pesos, which is so many crowns.

The master of my ship, John Douglas, took one of the canoes which came laden from thence with people to be sold, and the most of them escaped; yet of those he brought, there was one as well favoured and as well shaped as ever I saw any in England; and afterwards I saw many of them, which but for their tawny colour may be compared to any in Europe. They also trade in those rivers for bread of cassava, of which they buy a hundred pound weight for a knife, and sell it at Margarita for ten pesos. They also recover great store of cotton, Brazil wood, and those beds which they call *hamacas* or Brazil beds, wherein in hot countries all the Spaniards use to lie commonly, and in no other, neither did we ourselves while we were there. By means of which trades, for ransom of divers of the Guianians, and for exchange of hatchets and knives, Berrio recovered some store of gold plates, eagles of gold, and images of men and divers birds, and despatched his camp-master for Spain, with all that he had gathered, therewith to levy soldiers, and by the show thereof to draw others to the love of the enterprise. And having sent divers images as well of men as beasts, birds, and fishes, so curiously wrought in gold, he doubted not but to persuade the King to yield to him some further help, especially for that this land hath never been sacked, the mines never wrought, and in the Indies their works were well spent, and the gold drawn out with great labour and charge. He also despatched messengers to his son in Nuevo Reyno to levy all the forces he could, and come down the river Orinoco to Emeria, the province of Carapana, to meet him; he had also sent to Santiago de Leon on the coast of the Caracas, to buy horses and mules.

After I had thus learned of his proceedings past and purposed, I told him that I had resolved to see Guiana, and that it was the end of my journey, and the cause of my coming to Trinidad, as it was indeed, and for that purpose I sent Jacob Whiddon the year before to get intelligence; with whom Berrio himself had speech at that time, and remembered how inquisitive Jacob Whiddon was of his proceedings, and of the country of Guiana. Berrio was stricken into a great melancholy and sadness, and used all the arguments he could to dissuade me, and also assured the gentlemen of my company that it would be labour lost, and that they should suffer many miseries if they proceeded. And first he delivered that I could not enter any of the rivers with any bark or pinnace, or hardly with any ship's boat, it was so low, sandy, and full of flats, and that his companies were daily grounded in their canoes, which drew but twelve inches water. He further said, that none of the country would come to speak with us, but would all fly; and if we followed them to their dwellings, they would burn their own towns. And besides that, the way was long, the winter at hand, and that the rivers beginning once to swell, it was impossible to stem the current, and that we could not in those small boats by any means carry victuals for half the time, and that (which indeed most discouraged my company) the kings and lords of all the borders of Guiana had decreed that none of them should trade with any Christians for gold, because the same would be their own overthrow, and that for the love of gold the Christians meant to conquer and dispossess them of all together.

Many and the most of these I found to be true, but yet I resolving to make trial of whatsoever happened directed Captain George Gifford, my Vice-Admiral, to take the *Lion's Whelp*, and Captain Calfield his bark, to turn to the eastward, against the mouth of a river called Capure, whose entrance I had before sent Captain Whiddon and John Douglas, the Master, to discover, who found some nine feet of water or better upon the flood, and five at low water; to whom I had given instructions that they should anchor at the edge of the shoal, and upon the best of the flood to thrust over, which shoal John Douglas buoyed and beaconed for them before. But they laboured in vain; for neither could they turn it up altogether so far to the east, neither did the flood continue so long but the water fell ere they could have passed the sands, as we after found by a second experience. So as now we must either give over our enterprise, or leaving our ships at adventure four hundred miles behind us, must run up in our ship's boats, one barge, and two wherries. But being doubtful how to carry victuals for so long a time in such baubles, or any strength of men, especially for that Berrio assured us that his son must be by that time come down with many soldiers, I sent away one King, master of the *Lion's Whelp*, with his ship's boat, to try another branch of the river in the bottom of the Bay of Guanipa, which was called Amana, to prove if there were water to be found for either of the small ships to enter. But when he came to the mouth of Amana, he found it as the rest, but stayed not to discover it thoroughly, because he was assured by an Indian, his guide, that the cannibals of Guanipa would assail them with many canoes, and that they shot poisoned arrows; so as if he hasted not back, they should all be lost.

In the meantime, fearing the worst, I caused all the carpenters we had to cut down a *galego* boat which we meant to cast off, and to fit her with banks to row on, and in all things to prepare her the best they could, so as she might be brought to draw but five foot; for so much we had on the bar of Capure at low water. And doubting of King's return, I sent John Douglas again in my long barge, as well to relieve him as also to make a perfect search in the bottom of that bay; for it hath been held for infallible, that whatsoever ship or boat shall fall therein can never disembogue again, by reason of the violent current which setteth into the said bay, as also for that the breeze and easterly wind bloweth directly into the same. Of which opinion I have heard John Hampton of Plymouth, one of the greatest experience of England, and divers other besides that have traded to Trinidad.

I sent with John Douglas an old *cacique* of Trinidad for a pilot, who told us that we could not return again by the bay or gulf, but that he knew a by-branch which ran within the land to the eastward, and he thought by it we might fall into Capure, and so return in four days. John Douglas searched those rivers, and found four goodly entrances, whereof the least was as big as the Thames at Woolwich; but in the bay thitherward it was shoal and but six feet water, so as we were now without hope of any ship or bark to pass over, and therefore resolved to go on with the boat and the bottom of the *galego*, in which we thrust sixty men. In the *Lion's Whelp*'s boat and wherry we carried twenty, Captain Caulfield in his wherry carried ten more, and in my barge other ten, which made up a hundred; we had no other means but to carry victuals for a month in the same, and also to lodge therein as we could, and to boil and dress our meat. Captain Gifford had with him Master Edward Porter, Captain Eynos, and eight more in his wherry, with all their victual, weapons, and provisions. Captain Calfield had with him my cousin Butshead Gorges, and eight more. In the galley, of gentlemen and officers myself had Captain Thyn, my cousin John Grenville, my nephew John Gilbert, Captain Whiddon, Captain Keymis, Edward Hancock, Captain Clarke, Lieutenant Hughes, Thomas Upton, Captain Facy, Jerome Ferrar, Anthony Welles, William Connock, and above fifty more.

We could not learn of Berrio any other way to enter but in branches so far to windward as it was impossible for us to recover; for we had as much sea to cross over in our wherries as between Dover and Calais, and in a great billow, the wind and current being both very strong, so as we were driven to go in those small boats directly before the wind into the bottom of the Bay of Guanipa, and from thence to enter the mouth of some one of those rivers which John Douglas had last discovered. We had with us for pilot an Indian of Barima, a river to the south of

Orinoco, between that and Amazons, whose canoes we had formerly taken as he was going from the said Barima laden with cassava bread to sell at Margarita. This Arawakan promised to bring me into the great river of Orinoco; but indeed of that which he entered he was utterly ignorant, for he had not seen it in twelve years before at which time he was very young, and of no judgment; and if God had not sent us another help, we might have wandered a whole year in that labyrinth of rivers ere we had found any way either out or in, especially after we were past ebbing and flowing, which was in four days. For I know all the earth doth not yield the like confluence of streams and branches, the one crossing the other so many times, and all so fair and large, and so like one to another, as no man can tell which to take: and if we went by the sun or compass, hoping thereby to go directly one way or other yet that way we were also carried in a circle amongst multitudes of islands, and every island so bordered with high trees as no man could see any further than the breadth of the river, or length of the breach. But this it chanced, that entering into a river (which because it had no name, we called the river of the Red Cross, ourselves being the first Christians that ever came therein) on the two and twentieth of May, as we were rowing up the same we espied a small canoe with three Indians, which (by the swiftness of my barge, rowing with eight oars) I overtook ere they could cross the river. The rest of the people on the banks, shadowed under the thick wood, gazed on with a doubtful conceit what might befall those three which we had taken. But when they perceived that we offered them no violence, neither entered their canoe with any of ours, nor took out of the canoe any of theirs, they then began to show themselves on the bank's side, and offered to traffic with us for such things as they had. And as we drew near, they all stayed, and we came with our barge to the mouth of a little creek which came from their town into the great river.

As we abode there awhile, our Indian pilot, called Ferdinando, would needs go ashore to their village to fetch some fruits and to drink of their artificial wines, and also to see the place and know the lord of it against another time, and took with him a brother of his which he had with him in the journey. When they came to the village of these people the lord of the island offered to lay hands on them, purposing to have slain them both, yielding for reason that this Indian of ours had brought a strange nation into their territory to spoil and destroy them. But the pilot, being quick and of a disposed body, slipped their fingers and ran into the woods, and his brother, being the better footman of the two, recovered the creek's mouth, where we stayed in our barge, crying out that his brother was slain. With that we set hands on one of them that was next us, a very old man, and brought him into the barge, assuring him that if we had not our pilot again we would presently cut off his head. This old man, being resolved that he should pay the loss of the other, cried out to those in the woods to save Ferdinando, our pilot; but they followed him notwithstanding, and hunted after him upon foot with the deer-dogs, and with so many a cry that all the woods echoed with the shout they made. But at the last this poor, chased Indian recovered the river side and got upon a tree, and, as we were coasting, leaped down and swam to the barge half dead with fear. But our good hap was that we kept the other old Indian, which we handfasted to redeem our pilot withal; for, being natural of those rivers, we assured ourselves that he knew the way better than any stranger could. And, indeed, but for this chance, I think we had never found the way either to Guiana or back to our ships; for Ferdinando after a few days knew nothing at all, nor which way to turn; yea, and many times the old man himself was in great doubt which river to take. Those people which dwell in these broken islands and drowned lands are generally called Tivitivas. There are of them two sorts, the one called Ciawani, and the other Waraweete.

The great river of Orinoco or Baraguan hath nine branches which fall out on the north side of his own main mouth. On the south side it hath seven other fallings into the sea, so it disembogueth by sixteen arms in all between islands and broken ground; but the islands are very great, many of them as big as the Isle of Wight, and bigger, and many less. From the first branch on the north to the last of the south it is at least 100 leagues, so as the river's mouth is 300 miles wide at his entrance into the sea, which I take to be far bigger than that of Amazons. All those that inhabit in the mouth of this river upon the several north branches are these Tivitivas, of which there are two chief lords which have continual wars one with the other. The islands which lie on the right hand are called Pallamos, and the land on the left, Hororotomaka, and the river by which John Douglas returned within the land from Amana to Capure they call Macuri.

These Tivitivas are a very goodly people and very valiant, and have the most manly speech and most deliberate that I ever heard of what nation soever. In the summer they have houses on the ground as in other places; in the winter they dwell upon the trees, where they build very artificial towns and villages, as it is written in the Spanish story of the West Indies that those people do in the low lands near the gulf of Uraba. For between May and September the river of Orinoco riseth thirty foot upright, and then are those islands overflowed twenty foot high above the level of the ground, saving some few raised grounds in the middle of them. And for this cause they are enforced to live in this manner. They never eat of anything that is set or sown; and as at home they use neither planting nor other manurance, so when they come abroad they refuse to feed of aught but of that which nature without labour bringeth forth. They use the tops of *palmitos* for bread, and kill deer, fish, and porks for the rest of their sustenance. They have also many sorts of fruits that grow in the woods, and great variety of birds and fowls. And if to speak of them were not tedious and vulgar, surely we saw in those passages of very rare colours and forms not elsewhere to be found, for as much as I have either seen or read.

Of these people those that dwell upon the branches of Orinoco, called Capure and Macureo, are for the most part carpenters of canoes, for they make the most and fairest canoes, and sell them into Guiana for gold and into Trinidad for tobacco, in the excessive taking whereof they exceed all nations. And notwithstanding the moistness of the air in which they live, the hardness of their diet, and the great labours they suffer to hunt fish and fowl for their living, in all my life, either in the Indies or in Europe, did I never behold a more goodly or better-favoured people or a more manly. They were wont to make war upon all nations, and especially on the cannibals, so as none durst without a good strength trade by those rivers; but of late they are at peace with their neighbours, all holding the Spaniards for a common enemy. When their commanders die they use great lamentation, and when they think the flesh of their bodies is putrified and fallen from their bones, then they take up the carcase again and hang it in the *cacique*'s house that died, and deck his skull with feathers of all colours, and hang all his gold plates about his arms, thighs, and legs. Those nations which are called Arawaks, which dwell on the south of Orinoco (of which place and nation our Indian pilot was), are dispersed in many other places, and do use to beat the bones of their lords into powder, and their wives and friends drink it all in their several sorts of drinks.

After we departed from the port of these Ciawani we passed up the river with the flood and anchored the ebb, and in this sort we went onward. The third day that we entered the river our galley came on ground, and stuck so fast as we thought that even there our discovery had ended, and that we must have left fourscore and ten of our men to have inhabited like rooks upon trees with those nations; but the next morning, after we had cast out all her ballast, with tugging and hauling to and fro we got her afloat and went on. At four days' end we fell into as goodly a river as ever I beheld, which was called the Great Amana, which ran more directly without windings and turnings than the other. But soon after the flood of the sea left us, and, being enforced either by main strength to row against a violent current, or to return as wise as we went out, we had then no shift but to persuade the companies that it was but two or three days' work, and therefore desired them to take pains, every gentleman and others taking their turns to row and to spell one the other at the hour's end. Every day we passed by goodly branches of rivers, some falling from the west, others from the east, into Amana; but those I leave to the description in the chart of discovery, where every one shall be named with his rising and descent. When three days more were overgone, our companies began to despair, the weather being extreme hot, the river bordered with very high trees that kept away the air, and the current against us every day stronger than other; but we evermore commanded our pilots to promise an end the next day, and used it so long as we were driven to assure them from four reaches of the river to three, and so to two, and so to the next reach. But so long we laboured that many days were spent and we driven to draw ourselves to harder allowance, our bread even at the last, and no drink at all, and our men and ourselves so wearied and scorched, and doubtful withal whether we should ever perform it or no, the heat increasing as we drew towards the line; for we were now in 5 degrees.

The further we went on (our victual decreasing and the air breeding great faintness) we grew weaker and weaker, when we had most need of strength and ability; for hourly the river ran more violently than other against us, and the barge, wherries, and ship's boat of Captain Gifford and Captain Calfield had spent all their provisions; so as we were brought into despair and discomfort, had we not persuaded all the company that it was but only one day's work more to attain the land where we should be relieved of all we wanted, and if we returned, that we were sure to starve by the way, and that the world would also laugh us to scorn. On the banks of these rivers were divers sorts of fruits good to eat, flowers and trees of such variety as were sufficient to make ten volumes of herbals; we relieved ourselves many times with the fruits of the country, and sometimes with fowl and fish. We saw birds of all colours, some carnation, some crimson, orange-tawny, purple, watchet, and of all other sorts, both simple and mixed, and it was unto us a great good passing of the time to behold them, besides the relief we found by killing some store of them with our fowling pieces; without which, having little or no bread, and less drink, but only the thick and troubled water of the river, we had been in a very hard case.

Our old pilot of the Ciawani (whom, as I said before, we took to redeem Ferdinando) told us, that if we would enter a branch of a river on the right hand with our barge and wherries, and leave the galley at anchor the while in the great river, he would bring us to a town of the Arawaks where we should find store of bread, hens, fish, and of the country wine; and persuaded us that departing from the galley at noon we might return ere night. I was very glad to hear this speech, and presently took my bark, with eight musketeers, Captain Gifford's wherry, with himself and four musketeers, and Captain Calfield with his wherry, and as many, and so we entered the mouth of this river; and because we were persuaded that it was so near, we took no victuals with us at all. When we had rowed three hours, we marvelled we saw no sign of any dwelling, and asked the pilot where the town was; he told us a little further. After three hours more, the sun being almost set, we began to suspect that he led us that way to betray us; for he confessed that those Spaniards which fled from Trinidad, and also those that remained with Carapana in Emeria, were joined together in some village upon that river. But when it grew towards night, and we demanded where the place was, he told us but four reaches more. When we had rowed four and four, we saw no sign; and our poor watermen, even heart-broken and tired, were ready to give up the ghost, for we had now come from the galley near forty miles.

At the last we determined to hang the pilot, and if we had well known the way back again by night, he had surely gone; but our own necessities pleaded sufficiently for his safety. For it was as dark as pitch, and the river began so to narrow itself, and the trees to hang over from side to side, as we were driven with arming swords to cut a passage through those branches that covered the water. We were very desirous to find this town, hoping of a feast, because we made but a short breakfast aboard the galley in the morning, and it was now eight o'clock at night, and our stomachs began to gnaw apace; but whether it was best to return or go on we began to doubt, suspecting treason in the pilot more and more; but the poor old Indian ever assured us that it was but a little further, but this one turning and that turning; and at the last about one o'clock after midnight we saw a light, and rowing towards it we heard the dogs of the village. When we landed we found few people; for the lord of that place was gone with divers canoes above four hundred miles off, upon a journey towards the head of Orinoco, to trade for gold, and to buy women of the cannibals, who afterward unfortunately passed by us as we rode at an anchor in the port of Morequito in the dark of the night, and yet came so near us as his canoes grated against our barges. He left one of his company at the port of Morequito, by whom we understood that he had brought thirty young women, divers plates of gold, and had great store of fine pieces of cotton cloth, and cotton beds. In his house we had good store of bread, fish, hens, and Indian drink, and so rested that night, and in the morning, after we had traded with such of his people as came down, we returned towards our galley, and brought with us some quantity of bread, fish, and hens.

On both sides of this river we passed the most beautiful country that ever mine eyes beheld; and whereas all that we had seen before was nothing but woods, prickles, bushes, and thorns, here we beheld plains of twenty miles in length, the grass short and green, and in divers parts groves of trees by themselves, as if they had been by all the art and labour in the world so made of purpose; and still as we rowed, the deer came down feeding by the water's side as if they had been used to a keeper's call. Upon this river there were great store of fowl, and of many sorts; we saw in it divers sorts of strange fishes, and of marvellous bigness; but for *lagartos* it exceeded, for there were thousands of those ugly serpents, and the people call it, for the abundance of them, the river of Lagartos in their language. I had a negro, a very proper young fellow, who leaping out of the galley to swim in the mouth of this river, was in all our sights taken and devoured with one of those *lagartos*. In the meanwhile our companies in the galley thought we had been all lost (for we promised to return before night), and sent the *Lion's Whelp*'s ship's boat with Captain Whiddon to follow us up the river. But the next day, after we had rowed up and down some fourscore miles, we returned, and went on our way up the great river; and when we were even at the last cast for want of victuals, Captain Gifford being before the galley and the rest of the boats, seeking out some place to land upon the banks to make fire, espied four canoes coming down the river, and with no small joy caused his men to try the uttermost of their strengths. And after a while two of the four gave over and ran themselves ashore, every man betaking himself to the fastness of the woods, the two other lesser got away, while he landed to lay hold on these; and so turned into some by-creek, we knew not whither. Those canoes that were taken were loaded with bread, and were bound for Margarita in the West Indies, which those Indians (called Arawaks) purposed to carry thither for exchange; but in the lesser there were three Spaniards, who having heard of the defeat of their Governor in Trinidad, and that we purposed to enter Guiana, came away in those canoes. One of them was a *cavallero*, as the captain of the Arawaks after told us, another a soldier, and the third a refiner.

In the meantime nothing on the earth could have been more welcome to us, next unto gold, than the great store of very excellent bread which we found in these canoes; for now our men cried, "Let us go on, we care not how far." After that Captain Gifford had brought the two canoes to the galley, I took my barge and went to the bank's side with a dozen shot, where the canoes first ran themselves ashore, and landed there, sending out Captain Gifford and Captain Thyn on one hand, and Captain Calfield on the other, to follow those that were fled into the woods. And as I was creeping through the bushes, I saw an Indian basket hidden, which was the refiner's basket; for I found in it his quicksilver, saltpetre, and divers things for the trial of metals, and also the dust of such ore as he had refined, but in those canoes which escaped there was a good quantity of ore and gold. I then landed more men, and offered five hundred pound to what soldier soever could take one of those three Spaniards that we thought were landed. But our labours were in vain in that behalf; for they put themselves into one of the small canoes, and so while the greater canoes were in taking, they escaped. But seeking after the Spaniards we found the Arawaks hidden in the woods, which were pilots for the Spaniards, and rowed their canoes; of which I kept the chiefest for a pilot, and carried him with me to Guiana, by whom I understood where and in what countries the Spaniards had laboured for gold, though I made not the same known to all. For when the springs began to break, and the rivers to raise

14 Walter Raleigh (c. 1585).

themselves so suddenly as by no means we could abide the digging of
any mine, especially for that the richest are defended with rocks of hard
stones, which we call the white spar, and that it required both time,
men, and instruments fit for such a work, I thought it best not to hover
thereabouts, lest if the same had been perceived by the company, there
would have been by this time many barks and ships set out, and
perchance other nations would also have gotten of ours for pilots; so as
both ourselves might have been prevented, and all our care taken for
good usage of the people been utterly lost, by those that only respect
present profit, and such violence or insolence offered as the nations

which are borderers would have changed their desire of our love and defence into hatred and violence. And for any longer stay to have brought a more quantity (which I hear hath been often objected) whosoever had seen or proved the fury of that river after it began to arise, and had been a month and odd days, as we were, from hearing aught from our ships, leaving them meanly manned 400 miles off, would perchance have turned somewhat sooner than we did, if all the mountains had been gold or rich stones. And to say the truth, all the branches and small rivers which fell into Orinoco were raised with such speed as if we waded them over the shoes in the morning outward we were covered to the shoulders homeward the very same day; and to stay to dig our gold with our nails, had been *opus laboris* but not *ingenii*. Such a quantity as would have served our turns we could not have had, but a discovery of the mines to our infinite disadvantage we had made, and that could have been the best profit of further search or stay. For those mines are not easily broken, nor opened in haste, and I could have returned a good quantity of gold ready cast if I had not shot at another mark than present profit.

This Arawakan pilot, with the rest, feared that we would have eaten them, or otherwise have put them to some cruel death, for the Spaniards, to the end that none of the people in the passage towards Guiana, or in Guiana itself, might come to speech with us, persuaded all the nations that we were men-eaters and cannibals. But when the poor men and women had seen us, and that we gave them meat, and to every one something or other, which was rare and strange to them, they began to conceive the deceit and purpose of the Spaniards, who indeed (as they confessed) took from them both their wives and daughters daily and used them for the satisfying of their own lusts, especially such as they took in this manner by strength. But I protest before the majesty of the living God, that I neither know nor believe that any of our company, one or other, by violence or otherwise ever knew any of their women, and yet we saw many hundreds, and had many in our power, and of those very young and excellently favoured, which came among us without deceit, stark naked.

Nothing got us more love amongst them than this usage. For I suffered not any man to take from any of the nations so much as a pine or a potato root without giving them contentment, nor any man so much as to offer to touch any of their wives or daughters; which course, so contrary to the Spaniards (who tyrannise over them in all things), drew them to admire Her Majesty, whose commandment I told them it was, and also wonderfully to honour our nation.

But I confess it was a very impatient work to keep the meaner sort from spoil and stealing when we came to their houses; which, because in all I could not prevent, I caused my Indian interpreter at every place when we departed, to know of the loss or wrong done, and if aught were stolen or taken by violence, either the same restored, and the party punished in their sight, or else was paid for to their uttermost demand.

They also much wondered at us, after they heard that we had slain the Spaniards at Trinidad, for they were before resolved that no nation of Christians durst abide their presence, and they wondered more when I had made them know of the great overthrow that Her Majesty's army and fleet had given them of late years in their own countries.

After we had taken in this supply of bread, with divers baskets of roots, which were excellent meat, I gave one of the canoes to the Arawaks which belonged to the Spaniards that were escaped, and when I had dismissed all but the captain (who by the Spaniards was christened Martin) I sent back in the same canoe the old Ciawani, and Ferdinando, my first pilot, and gave them both such things as they desired, with sufficient victual to carry them back, and by them wrote a letter to the ships, which they promised to deliver, and performed it; and then I went on, with my new hired pilot, Martin the Arawakan. But the next or second day after, we came aground again with our galley, and were like to cast her away with all our victuals and provisions, and so lay on the sand one whole night, and were far more in despair at this time to free her than before, because we had no tide of flood to help us, and therefore feared that all our hopes would have ended in mishaps. But we fastened an anchor upon the land, and with main strength drew her off; and so the fifteenth day we discovered afar off the mountains of Guiana, to our great joy, and towards the evening had a slant of a northerly wind that blew very strong, which brought us in sight of the great river Orinoco, out of which this river descended wherein we were. We descried afar off three other canoes as far as we could discern them, after whom we hastened with our barge and wherries, but two of them passed out of sight, and the third entered up the great river, on the right hand to the westward, and there stayed out of sight, thinking that we meant to take the way eastward towards the province of Carapana, for that way the Spaniards keep, not daring to go upwards to Guiana, the people in those parts being all their enemies, and those in the canoes thought us to have been those Spaniards that were fled from Trinidad, and escaped killing. And when we came so far down as the opening of that branch into which they slipped, being near them with our barge and wherries we made after them, and ere they could land came within call, and by our interpreter told them what we were, wherewith they came back willingly aboard us; and of such fish and *tortugas'* eggs as they had gathered they gave us, and promised in the morning to bring the lord of that part with them, and to do us all other services they could.

That night we came to an anchor at the parting of the three goodly rivers (the one was the river of Amana, by which we came from the north, and ran athwart towards the south, the other two were of Orinoco, which crossed from the west and ran to the sea towards the east) and landed upon a fair sand, where we found thousands of *tortugas'* eggs, which are very wholesome meat, and greatly restoring, so as our men were now well filled and highly contented both with the fare, and nearness of the land of Guiana which appeared in sight.

In the morning there came down, according to promise, the lord of that border, called Toparimaca, with some thirty or forty followers, and brought us divers sorts of fruits, and of his wine, bread, fish, and flesh, whom we also feasted as we could; at least we drank good Spanish wine (whereof we had a small quantity in bottles), which above all things they love. I conferred with this Toparimaca of the next way to Guiana, who conducted our galley and boats to his own port, and carried us from thence some mile and a half to his town, where some of our captains caroused of his wine till they were reasonable pleasant, for it is very strong with pepper and the juice of divers herbs and fruits digested and purged. They keep it in great earthen pots of ten or twelve gallons, very clean and sweet, and are themselves at their meetings and feasts the greatest carousers and drunkards of the world. When we came to his town we found two *caciques*, whereof one was a stranger that had been up the river in trade, and his boats, people, and wife encamped at the port where we anchored, and the other was of that country, a follower of Toparimaca. They lay each of them in a cotton *hamaca*, which we call Brazil beds, and two women attending them with six cups and a little ladle to fill them out of an earthen pitcher of wine; and so they drank each of them three of those cups at a time one to the other, and in this sort they drink drunk at their feasts and meetings.

That *cacique* that was a stranger had his wife staying at the port where we anchored, and in all my life I have seldom seen a better favoured woman. She was of good stature, with black eyes, fat of body, of an excellent countenance, her hair almost as long as herself, tied up again in pretty knots, and it seemed she stood not in that awe of her husband as the rest, for she spoke and discoursed, and drank among the gentlemen and captains, and was very pleasant, knowing her own comeliness, and taking great pride therein. I have seen a lady in England so like to her, as but for the difference of colour I would have sworn might have been the same.

The seat of this town of Toparimaca was very pleasant, standing on a little hill, in an excellent prospect, with goodly gardens a mile compass round about it, and two very fair and large ponds of excellent fish adjoining. This town is called Arowocai; the people are of the nation called Nepoios, and are followers of Carapana. In that place I saw very aged people, that we might perceive all their sinews and veins without any flesh, and but even as a case covered only with skin. The lord of this place gave me an old man for pilot who was of great experience and travel, and knew the river most perfectly both by day and night; and it shall be requisite for any man that passeth it to have such a pilot, for it is four, five, and six miles over in many places, and twenty miles in other places, with wonderful eddies and strong currents, many great islands, and divers shoals, and many dangerous rocks, and besides upon any increase of wind so great a billow as we were sometimes in great peril of drowning in the galley, for the small boats durst not come from the shore but when it was very fair.

The next day we hasted thence, and having an easterly wind to help us, we spared our arms from rowing; for after we entered Orinoco, the river lieth for the most part east and west, even from the sea unto Quito in Peru. This river is navigable with barks little less than a thousand miles, and from the place where we entered it may be sailed up in small pinnaces to many of the best parts of Nuevo Reyno de Granada and of Popayan; and from no place may the cities of these parts of the Indies be so easily taken and invaded as from hence. All that day we sailed up a branch of that river, having on the left hand a great island, which they call Assapana, which may contain some five-and-twenty miles in length and six miles in breadth, the great body of the river running on the other side of this island. Beyond that middle branch there is also another island in the river called Iwana, which is twice as big as the Isle of Wight, and beyond it, and between it and the main of Guiana, runneth a third branch of Orinoco, called Arraroopana; all three are goodly branches, and all navigable for great ships. I judge the river in this place to be at least thirty miles broad, reckoning the islands which divide the branches in it, for afterwards I sought also both the other branches.

After we reached to the head of the island called Assapana, a little to the westward on the right hand there opened a river which came from the north, called Europa, and fell into the great river, and beyond it on the same side we anchored for that night by another island, six miles long and two miles broad, which they call Ocaywita. From hence in the morning we landed two Guianians, which we found in the town of Toparimaca, that came with us, who went to give notice of our coming to the lord of that country called Putijma, a follower of Topiawari, chief lord of Aromaia, who succeeded Morequito, whom (as you have heard before) Berrio put to death; but his town being far within the land, he came not unto us that day so as we anchored again that night near the banks of another island of bigness much like the other, which they call Putapayma, over against which island, on the main land, was a very high mountain called Oecope. We coveted to anchor rather by these islands in the river than by the main, because of the *tortugas'* eggs, which our people found on them in great abundance, and also because the ground served better for us to cast our nets for fish, the main banks being for the most part stony and high and the rocks of a blue, metalline colour, like unto the best steel-ore, which I assuredly take it to be. Of the same blue stone are also divers great mountains which border this river in many places.

The next morning, towards nine of the clock, we weighed anchor, and the breeze increasing, we sailed always west up the river, and, after a while opening the land on the right side, the country appeared to be champaign and the banks showed very perfect red. I therefore sent two of the little barges with Captain Gifford, and with him Captain Thyn, Captain Calfield, my cousin Grenville, my nephew John Gilbert, Captain Eynos, Master Edward Porter, and my cousin Butshead Gorges, with some few soldiers, to march over the banks of that red land and to discover what manner of country it was on the other side; who at their return found it all a plain level as far as they went or could discern from the highest tree they could get upon. And my old pilot, a man of great travel, brother to the *cacique* Toparimaca, told me that those were called the Plains of the Chayma, and that the same level reached to Cumana and Caracas, in the West Indies, which are a hundred and twenty leagues to the north, and that there inhabited four principal nations. The first were the Chayma, the next Assawai, the third and greatest the Wikiri, by whom Pedro Hernandez de Serpa, before mentioned, was overthrown as he passed with three hundred horse from Cumana towards Orinoco in his enterprise of Guiana; the fourth are called Aroras, and are as black as negroes, but have smooth hair, and these are very valiant (or rather desperate) people, and have the most strong poison on their arrows, and most dangerous of all nations, of which I will speak somewhat, being a digression not unnecessary.

There was nothing whereof I was more curious than to find out the true remedies of these poisoned arrows; for besides the mortality of the wound they make, the party shot endureth the most insufferable torment in the world, and abideth a most ugly and lamentable death, sometimes dying stark mad, sometimes their bowels breaking out of their bellies, which are presently discoloured as black as pitch, and so unsavory as no man can endure to cure or to attend them. And it is more strange to know that in all this time there was never Spaniard, either by gift or torment, that could attain to the true knowledge of the cure, although they have martyred and put to invented torture I know not how many of them. But everyone of these Indians know it not, no, not one among thousands, but their soothsayers and priests, who do conceal it, and only teach it but from the father to the son.

Those medicines which are vulgar and serve for the ordinary poison are made of the juice of a root called *tupara*; the same also quencheth marvellously the heat of burning fevers, and healeth inward wounds and broken veins that bleed within the body. But I was more beholding to the Guianians than any other; for Antonio de Berrio told me that he could never attain to the knowledge thereof, and yet they taught me the best way of healing as well thereof as of all other poisons. Some of the Spaniards have been cured in ordinary wounds of common poisoned arrows with the juice of garlic. But this is a general rule for all men that shall hereafter travel the Indies where poisoned arrows are used, that they must abstain from drink; for if they take any liquor into their body, as they shall be marvellously provoked thereunto by drought, I say, if they drink before the wound be dressed, or soon upon it, there is no way with them but present death.

And so I will return again to our journey, which for this third day we finished, and cast anchor again near the continent on the left hand between two mountains, the one called Aroami and the other Aio. I made no stay here but till midnight; for I feared hourly lest any rain should fall, and then it had been impossible to have gone any further up, notwithstanding that there is every day a very strong breeze and easterly wind. I deferred the search of the country on Guiana side till my return down the river.

The next day we sailed by a great island in the middle of the river, called Manoripano, and, as we walked awhile on the island, while the galley got ahead of us, there came for us from the main a small canoe with seven or eight Guianians, to invite us to anchor in their port, but I deferred till my return. It was that *cacique* to whom those Nepoios went, which came with us from the town of Toparimaca. And so the fifth day we reached as high up as the province of Aromaia, the country of Morequito, whom Berrio executed, and anchored to the west of an island called Murrecotima, ten miles long and five broad. And that night the *cacique* Aramiary (to whose town we made our long and hungry voyage out of the river of Amana) passed by us.

The next day we arrived at the port of Morequito, and anchored there, sending away one of our pilots to seek the King of Aromaia, uncle to Morequito, slain by Berrio as aforesaid. The next day following, before noon, he came to us on foot from his house, which was fourteen English miles (himself being a hundred and ten years old), and returned on foot the same day, and with him many of the borderers, with many women and children, that came to wonder at our nation and to bring us down victual, which they did in their great plenty, as venison, pork, hens, chickens, fowl, fish, with divers sorts of excellent fruits and roots, and great abundance of pines, the princes of fruits that grow under the sun, especially those of Guiana. They brought us also store of bread and of their wine, and a sort of paraquitos no bigger than wrens, and of all other sorts both small and great. One of them gave me a beast called by the Spaniards armadillo, which they call *cassacam*, which seemeth to be all barred over with small plates somewhat like to a rhinoceros, with a white horn growing in his hinder parts as big as a great hunting-horn, which they use to wind instead of a trumpet.

Monardus writeth that a little of the powder of that horn put into the ear cureth deafness.

After this old King had rested awhile in a little tent that I caused to be set up, I began by my interpreter to discourse with him of the death of Morequito, his predecessor, and afterward of the Spaniards; and ere I went any farther I made him know the cause of my coming thither, whose servant I was, and that the Queen's pleasure was I should undertake the voyage for their defence and to deliver them from the tyranny of the Spaniards, dilating at large (as I had done before to those of Trinidad) Her Majesty's greatness, her justice, her charity to all oppressed nations, with as many of the rest of her beauties and virtues as either I could express or they conceive. All which being with great admiration attentively heard and marvellously admired, I began to sound the old man as touching Guiana and the state thereof, what sort of commonwealth it was, how governed, of what strength and policy, how far it extended, and what nations were friends or enemies adjoining, and finally of the distance and way to enter the same. He told me that himself and his people, with all those down the river towards the sea, as far as Emeria, the province of Carapana, were of Guiana, but that they called themselves Orinocoponi, and that all the nations between the river and those mountains in sight, called Wacarima, were of the same cast and appellation: and that on the other side of those mountains of Wacarima there was a large plain (which after I discovered in my return) called the Valley of Amariocapana. In all that valley the people were also of the ancient Guianians.

I asked what nations those were which inhabited on the further side of those mountains, beyond the Valley of Amariocapana. He answered with a great sigh (as a man which had inward feeling of the loss of his country and liberty, especially for that his eldest son was slain in a battle on that side of the mountains, whom he most entirely loved) that he remembered in his father's lifetime, when he was very old and himself a young man, that there came down into that large valley of Guiana a nation from so far off as the sun slept (for such were his own words), with so great a multitude as they could not be numbered nor resisted, and that they wore large coats, and hats of crimson colour, which colour he expressed by shewing a piece of red wood wherewith my tent was supported, and that they were called Orejones and Epuremei, those that had slain and rooted out so many of the ancient people as there were leaves in the wood upon all the trees, and had now made themselves lords of all, even to that mountain foot called Curaa, saving only of two nations, the one called Yguaracuyri and the other Cassipagotos, and that in the last battle fought between the Epuremei and the Yguaracuyri his eldest son was chosen to carry to the aid of the Yguaracuyri a great troop of the Orinocoponi, and was there slain with all his people and friends, and that he had now remaining but one son;

and farther told me that those Epuremei had built a great town called Macuraguara at the said mountain foot, at the beginning of the great plains of Guiana, which have no end; and that their houses have many rooms, one over the other, and that therein the great King of the Orejones and Epuremei kept three thousand men to defend the borders against them, and withal daily to invade and slay them; but that of late years, since the Christians offered to invade his territories and those frontiers, they were all at peace, and traded one with another, saving only the Yguaracuyri and those other nations upon the head of the river of Caroni called Cassipagotos, which we afterwards discovered, each one holding the Spaniard for a common enemy.

After he had answered thus far, he desired leave to depart, saying that he had far to go, that he was old and weak, and was every day called for by death, which was also his own phrase. I desired him to rest with us that night, but I could not entreat him, but he told me that at my return from the country above he would again come to us, and in the meantime provide for us the best he could, of all that his country yielded. The same night he returned to Orocotona, his own town; so as he went that day eight-and-twenty miles, the weather being very hot, the country being situate between 4 and 5 degrees of the equinoctial.

This Topiawari is held for the proudest and wisest of all the Orinocoponi, and so he behaved himself towards me in all his answers at my return as I marvelled to find a man of that gravity and judgment, and of so good discourse, that had no help of learning nor breed.

The next morning we also left the port, and sailed westward up to the river, to view the famous river called Caroni, as well because it was marvellous of itself, as also for that I understood it led to the strongest nations of all the frontiers, that were enemies to the Epuremei, which are subjects to Inca, Emperor of Guiana and Manoa; and that night we anchored at another island called Caiama, of some five or six miles in length, and the next day arrived at the mouth of Caroni. When we were short of it as low or further down as the port of Morequito, we heard the great roar and fall of the river; but when we came to enter with our barge and wherries, thinking to have gone up some forty miles to the nations of the Cassipagotos, we were not able with a barge of eight oars to row one stone's cast in an hour, and yet the river is as broad as the Thames at Woolwich, and we tried both sides, and the middle, and every part of the river, so as we encamped upon the banks adjoining, and sent off our Orinocopone (which came with us from Morequito) to give knowledge to the nations upon the river of our being there, and that we desired to see the Lords of Canuri, which dwelt within the province upon that river, making them know that we were enemies to the Spaniards (for it was on this river side that Morequito slew the friar, and those nine Spaniards which came from Manoa, the city of Inca, and took from them forty thousand pesos of gold) so as the next day there came down a lord or *cacique* called Wanuretona, with many people with him, and brought all store of provisions to entertain us, as the rest had done. And as I had before made my coming known to Topiawari, so did I acquaint this *cacique* therewith, and how I was sent by Her Majesty for the purpose aforesaid, and gathered also what I could of him touching the estate of Guiana; and I found that those also of Caroni were not only enemeies to the Spaniards, but most of all to the Epuremei, which abound in gold, and by this Wanuretona I had knowledge that on the head of this river were three mighty nations, which were seated on a great lake, from whence this river descended, and were called Cassipagotos, Eparegotos, and Arawagotos, and that all those either against the Spaniards or the Epuremei would join with us, and that if we entered the land over the mountains of Curaa we should satisfy ourselves with gold and all other good things. He told us farther of a nation called Yguaracuyri, before spoken of, that held daily war with the Epuremei that inhabited Macuraguara, the first civil town of Guiana, of the subjects of Inca, the Emperor.

Upon this river one Captain George, that I took with Berrio, told me that there was a great silver mine, and that it was near the banks of the said river. But by this time as well Orinoco, Caroni, as all the rest of the rivers were risen four or five foot in height, so as it was not possible by the strength of any men, or with any boat whatsoever, to row into the river against the stream. I therefore sent Captain Thyn, Captain Grenville, my nephew John Gilbert, my cousin Butshead Gorges, Captain Clarke, and some thirty shot more to coast the river by land, and to go to a town some twenty miles over the valley called Amnatapoi, and they found guides there to go farther towards the mountain foot to another great town called Capurepana, belonging to a *cacique* called Haharacoa (that was a nephew to old Topiawari, King of Aromaia, our chiefest friend), because this town and province of Capurepana adjoined to Macuraguara, which was a frontier town of the empire; and the meanwhile myself with Captain Gifford, Captain Calfield, Edward Hancock, and some half-a-dozen shot marched overland to view the strange overfalls of the river of Caroni, which roared so far off, and also to see the plains adjoining, and the rest of the province of Canuri. I sent also Captain Whiddon, William Connock, and some eight shot with them, to see if they could find any mineral stone alongst the river side. When we were come to the tops of the first hills of the plain adjoining to the river, we beheld that wonderful breach of waters, which ran down Caroni; and might from that mountain see the river how it ran in three parts, above twenty miles off, and there appeared some ten or twelve overfalls in sight, every one as high over the other as a church-tower, which fell with that fury that the rebound of water made it seem as if it had been all covered over with a great shower of rain, and in some places we took it at the first for a smoke that had risen over some great town.

For my own part I was well persuaded from thence to have returned, being a very ill footman, but the rest were all so desirous to go near the said strange thunder of waters as they drew me on by little and little, till we came into the next valley, where we might better discern the same. I never saw a more beautiful country, nor more lively prospects, hills so raised here and there over the valleys, the river winding into divers branches, the plains adjoining without bush or stubble, all fair green grass, the ground of hard sand, easy to march on, either for horse or foot, the deer crossing in every path, the birds towards the evening singing on every tree with a thousand several tunes, cranes and herons of white, crimson, and carnation perching in the river's side, the air fresh with a gentle casterly wind, and every stone that we stooped to take up promised either gold or silver by his complexion. Your lordship shall see of many sorts, and I hope some of them cannot be bettered under the sun; and yet we had no means but with our daggers and fingers to tear them out here and there, the rocks being most hard of that mineral spar aforesaid, which is like a flint, and is altogether as hard or harder, and besides the veins lie a fathom or two deep in the rocks. But we wanted all things requisite save only our desires and good will to have performed more if it had pleased God. To be short, when both our companies returned, each of them brought also several sorts of stones that appeared very fair, but were such as they found loose on the ground, and were for the most part but coloured, and had not any gold fixed in them; yet such as had no judgment or experience kept all that glittered, and would not be persuaded but it was rich because of the lustre, and brought of those, and of marquesite withal, from Trinidad, and have delivered of those stones to be tried in many places, and have thereby bred an opinion that all the rest is of the same. Yet some of these stones I showed afterwards to a Spaniard of the Caracas, who told me that it was *el madre del oro*, that is the mother of gold, and that the mine was farther in the ground.

But it shall be found a weak policy in me either to betray myself or my country with imaginations, neither am I so far in love with that lodging, watching, care, peril, diseases, ill savours, bad fare, and many other mischiefs that accompany these voyages, as to woo myself again into any of them were I not assured that the sun covereth not so much riches in any part of the earth. Captain Whiddon, and our surgeon, Nicholas Millechamp, brought me a kind of stones like sapphires; what they may prove I know not. I showed them to some of the Orinocoponi, and they promised to bring me to a mountain that had of them very large pieces growing diamond-wise; whether it be crystal of the mountain, Bristol diamond, or sapphire I do not yet know, but I hope the best; sure I am that the place is as likely as those from whence all the rich stones are brought, and in the same height or very near.

On the left hand of this river Caroni are seated those nations which I called Yguaracuyri before remembered, which are enemies to the Epuremei; and on the head of it, adjoining to the great lake Cassipa, are situate those other nations which also resist Inca and the Epuremei, called Cassipagotos, Eparegotos, and Arawagotos. I further understood that this lake of Cassipa is so large as it is above one day's journey for one of their canoes to cross, which may be some forty miles, and that thereinto fall divers rivers, and that great store of grains of gold are found in the summer time when the lake falleth by the banks, in those branches.

There is also another goodly river beyond Caroni which is called Arui, which also runneth through the lake Cassipa, and falleth into Orinoco farther west, making all that land between Caroni and Arui an island, which is likewise a most beautiful country. Next unto Arui there are two rivers Atoica and Caura, and on that branch which is called Caura are a nation of people whose heads appear not above their shoulders, which though it may be thought a mere fable, yet for my own part I am resolved it is true, because every child in the provinces of Aromaia and Canuri affirm the same. They are called Ewaipanoma. They are reported to have their eyes in their shoulders, and their mouths in the middle of their breasts, and that a long train of hair groweth backward between their shoulders. The son of Topiawari, which I brought with me into England, told me that they are the most mighty men of all the land, and use bows, arrows, and clubs, thrice as big as any of Guiana or of the Orinocoponi, and that one of the Yguaracuyri took a prisoner of them the year before our arrival there, and brought him into the borders of Aromaia, his father's country. And, further, when I seemed to doubt of it, he told me that it was no wonder among them, but that they were as great a nation and as common as any other in all the provinces, and had of late years slain many hundreds of his father's people, and of other nations their neighbours, but it was not my chance to hear of them till I was come away, and if I had but spoken one word of it while I was there I might have brought one of them with me to put the matter out of doubt. Such a nation was written of by Mandeville, whose reports were held for fables many years and yet, since the East Indies were discovered, we find his relations true of such things as heretofore were held incredible. Whether it be true or no, the matter is not great, neither can there be any profit in the imagination; for my own part I saw them not, but I am resolved that so many people did not all combine or forethink to make the report.

When I came to Cumana in the West Indies afterwards by chance I spoke with a Spaniard dwelling not far from thence, a man of great travel, and after he knew that I had been in Guiana, and so far directly west as Caroni, the first question he asked me was whether I had seen any of the Ewaipanoma, which are those without heads; who being esteemed a most honest man of his word, and in all things else, told me that he had seen many of them. I may not name him, because it may be for his disadvantage, but he is well known to Monsieur Mucheron's son of London, and to Peter Mucheron, merchant, of the Flemish ship that was there in trade, who also heard what he avowed to be true of those people.

The fourth river to the west of Caroni is Casnero, which falleth into the Orinoco on this side of Amapaia; and that river is greater than Danubius, or any of Europe. It riseth on the south of Guiana from the mountains which divide Guiana from Amazons, and I think it to be navigable many hundred miles. But we had no time, means, nor season of the year, to search those rivers, for the causes aforesaid, the winter being come upon us, although the winter and summer as touching cold and heat differ not, neither do the trees ever sensibly lose their leaves, but have always fruit either ripe or green, and most of them both blossom, leaves, ripe fruit, and green at one time. But their winter only consisteth of terrible rains, and overflowing of the rivers, with many great storms and gusts, thunder and lightnings, of which we had our fill ere we returned.

On the north side, the first river that falleth into the Orinoco is Cari. Beyond it on the same side is the river of Limo. Between these two is a great nation of cannibals, and their chief town beareth the name of the river, and is called Acamacari. At this town is a continual market of women for three or four hatchets apiece; they are bought by the Arawaks, and by them sold into the West Indies. To the west of Limo is the river Pao, beyond it Caturi, beyond that, Voari, and Capure which falleth out of the great river of Meta, by which Berrio descended from Nuevo Reyno de Granada. To the westward of Capure is the province of Amapaia, where Berrio wintered, and had so many of his people poisoned with the tawny water of the marshes of the Anebas. Above Amapaia, towards Nuevo Reyno, fall in Meta, Pauto and Cacanare. To the west of those, towards the provinces of the Ashaguas and Catetios, are the rivers of Beta, Dawney, and Ubarro, and toward the frontier of Peru are the provinces of Thomebamba, and Caxamalca. Adjoining to Quito in the north side of Peru are the rivers of Guiacar and Guaviare; and on the other side of the said mountains the river of Papamene which descendeth into Marañon or Amazons, passing through the province Mutylonez, where Don Pedro de Ursua, who was slain by the traitor Aguirre before rehearsed, built his brigantines, when he sought Guiana by the way of Amazons.

Between Dawney and Beta lieth a famous island in Orinoco (now called Baraguan, for above Meta is not known by the name of Orinoco) which is called Athule, beyond which ships of burden cannot pass by reason of a most forcible overfall, and current of waters; but in the eddy all smaller vessels may be drawn even to Peru itself. But to speak of more of these rivers without the description were but tedious, and therefore I will leave the rest to the description. This river of Orinoco is navigable for ships little less than 1,000 miles, and for lesser vessels near 2,000. By it (as aforesaid) Peru, Nuevo Reyno, and Popayan may be invaded. It also leadeth to the great empire of Inca, and to the province of Amapaia and Anebas, which abound in gold; his branches of Casnero, Manta, Caura descended from the middle land and valley which lieth between the eastern province of Peru and Guiana; and it falls into the sea between Marañon and Trinidad in 2 degrees and a half: all which your honours shall better perceive in the general description of Guiana, Peru, Nuevo Reyno, the kingdom of Popayan, and Roidas, with the province of Venezuela, to the Bay of Uraba, behind Cartagena westward, and to Amazons southward.

While we lay at anchor on the coast of Canuri, and had taken knowledge of all the nations upon the head and branches of this river, and had found out so many several people which were enemies to the Epuremei and the new conquerors, I thought it time lost to linger any longer in that place, especially for that the fury of Orinoco began daily to threaten us with dangers in our return: for no half day passed but the river began to rage and overflow very fearfully, and the rains came down in terrible showers and gusts in great abundance; and withal our men began to cry out for want of shift, for no man had place to bestow any other apparel than that which he wore on his back, and that was thoroughly washed on his body for the most part ten times in one day; and we had now been well near a month, every day passing to the westward farther and farther from our ships. We therefore turned towards the east, and spent the rest of the time in discovering the river towards the sea, which we had not viewed, and which was most material.

The next day following we left the mouth of Caroni, and arrived again at the port of Morequito where we were before; for passing down the stream we went without labour, and against the wind, little less than a hundred miles a day. As soon as I came to anchor, I sent away one for old Topiawari, with whom I much desired to have further conference, and also to deal with him for some one of his country to bring with us into England, as well to learn the language, as to confer withal by the way, the time being now spent of any longer stay there. Within three hours after my messenger came to him, he arrived also, and with him such a rabble of all sorts of people, and everyone laden with somewhat, as if it had been a great market or fair in England; and our hungry companies clustered thick and threefold among their baskets, every one laying hand on what he liked. After he had rested awhile in my tent, I shut out all but ourselves and my interpreter, and told him that I knew that both the Epuremei and the Spaniards were enemies to him, his country and nations, that the one had conquered Guiana already, and the other sought to regain the same from them both; and therefore I desired him to instruct me what he could, both of the passage into the golden parts of Guiana, and to the civil towns and apparelled people of Inca. He gave me an answer to this effect: first, that he could not perceive that I meant to go onward towards the city of Manoa, for neither the time of the year served neither could he perceive any sufficient numbers for such an enterprise: and if I did, I was sure with all my company to be buried there, for the Emperor was of that strength as that many times so many men more were too few. Besides he gave me this good council and advised me to hold it in mind (as for himself he knew he could not live till my return), that I should not offer by any means hereafter to invade the strong parts of Guiana without the help of all those nations which were also their enemies; for that it was impossible without those either to be conducted, to be victualled, or to have aught carried with us, our people not being able to endure the march in so great heat, and travail, unless the borderers gave them help to carry with them both their meat and furniture. For he remembered that in the plains of Macuraguara three hundred Spaniards were overthrown, who were tired out, and had none of the borderers to their friends; but meeting their enemies as they passed the frontier, were environed on all sides, and the people setting the long dry grass on fire, smothered them, so as they had no breath to fight nor could discern their enemies for the great smoke. He told me further that 4 days' journey from his town was Macuraguara, and that those were the next and nearest of the subjects of Inca and of the Epuremei, and the first town of apparelled and rich people, and that all those plates of gold which were scattered among the borderers and carried to other nations far and near came from the said Macuraguara and were there made; but that those of the land within were far finer, and were fashioned after the images of men, beasts, birds, and fishes. I asked him whether he thought that those companies that I had there with me were sufficient to take that town or no. He told me that he thought they were. I then asked him whether he would assist me with guides, and some companies of his people to join with us. He answered that he would go himself with all the borderers, if the rivers did remain fordable, upon this condition, that I would leave with him till my return again fifty soldiers, which he undertook to victual. I answered that I had not above fifty good men in all there; the rest were labourers and rowers, and that I had no provision to leave with them of powder, shot, apparel, or aught else, and that without those things necessary for their defence they should be in danger of the Spaniards in my absence, who I knew would use the same measures towards mine that I offered them at

Trinidad. And although upon the motion Captain Calfield, Captain Grenville, my nephew John Gilbert, and divers others were desirous to stay, yet I was resolved that they must needs have perished, for Berrio expected daily a supply out of Spain, and looked also hourly for his son to come down from Nuevo Reyno de Granada, with many horse and foot, and had also in Valencia in the Caracas two hundred horse ready to march, and I could not have spared above forty, and had not any store at all of powder, lead, or match to have left with them, nor any other provision, either spade, pickaxe, or aught else to have fortified withal.

When I had given him reason that I could not at this time leave him such a company, he then desired me to forbear him and his country for that time; for he assured me that I should be no sooner three days from the coast but those Epuremei would invade him and destroy all the remain of his people and friends if he should any way either guide us or assist us against them.

He further alleged that the Spaniards sought his death, and as they had already murdered his nephew Morequito, lord of that province, so they had him seventeen days in a chain before he was king of the country, and led him like a dog from place to place until he had paid a hundred plates of gold and divers chains of spleen-stones for his ransom; and now, since he became owner of that province, that they had many times laid wait to take him, and that they would be now more vehement when they should understand of his conference with the English. "And because," said he, "they would the better displant me if they cannot lay hands on me, they have gotten a nephew of mine called Eparacano, whom they have christened Don Juan, and his son Don Pedro, whom they have also apparelled and armed, by whom they seek to make a party against me in my own country. He also had taken to wife one Loviana, of a strong family, which are borderers and neighbours, and myself now being old and in the hands of death am not able to travel nor to shift as when I was of younger years." He therefore prayed us to defer it till the next year, when he would undertake to draw in all the borderers to serve us, and then, also, it would be more seasonable to travel; for at this time of the year we should not be able to pass any river, the waters were and would be so grown ere our return.

He further told me that I could not desire so much to invade Macuraguara and the rest of Guiana but that the borderers would be more vehement than I; for he yielded for a chief cause that in the wars with the Epuremei they were spoiled of their women, and that their wives and daughters were taken from them, so as for their own parts they desired nothing of the gold or treasure for their labours, but only to recover women from the Epuremei. For he further complained very sadly (as it had been a matter of great consequence) that whereas they were wont to have ten or twelve wives, they were now enforced to content themselves with three or four, and that the lords of the Epuremei had fifty or a hundred. And in truth they war more for women than either for gold or dominion. For the lords of countries desire many children of their own bodies to increase their races and kindreds, for in those consist their greatest trust and strength. Divers of his followers afterwards desired me to make haste again, that they might sack the Epuremei, and I asked them of what. They answered, "Of their women for us, and their gold for you." For the hope of those many of women they more desire the war than either for gold or for the recovery of their ancient territories. For what between the subjects of Inca and the Spaniards, those frontiers are grown thin of people, and also great numbers are fled to other nations farther off for fear of the Spaniards.

After I received this answer of the old man we fell into consideration whether it had been of better advice to have entered Macuraguara and to have begun a war upon Inca at this time, yea or no, if the time of the year and all things had sorted. For my own part, as we were not able to march it for the rivers, neither had any such strength as was requisite, and durst not abide the coming of the winter, or to tarry any longer from our ships, I thought it were evil counsel to have attempted it at that time, although the desire for gold will answer many objections; but it would have been, in my opinion, an utter overthrow to the enterprise if the same should be hereafter by Her Majesty attempted. For then (whereas now they have heard we were enemies to the Spaniards and were sent by Her Majesty to relieve them) they would as good cheap have joined with the Spaniards at our return as to have yielded unto us when they had proved that we came both for one errand, and that both sought but to sack and spoil them. But as yet our desire of gold, or our purpose of invasion, is not known to them of the empire. And it is likely that if Her Majesty undertake the enterprise they will rather submit themselves to her obedience than to the Spaniards, of whose cruelty both themselves and the borderers have already tasted; and therefore, till I had known Her Majesty's pleasure, I would rather have lost the sack of one or two towns (although they might have been very profitable) than to have defaced or endangered the future hope of so many millions, and the great good and rich trade which England may be possessed of thereby. I am assured now that they will all die, even to the last man, against the Spaniards in hope of our succour and return. Whereas, otherwise, if I had either laid hands on the borderers or ransomed the lords, as Berrio did, or invaded the subjects of Inca, I know all had been lost for hereafter.

After that I had resolved Topiawari, Lord of Aromaia, that I could not at this time leave with him the companies he desired, and that I was contented to forbear the enterprise against the Epuremei till the next year, he freely gave me his only son to take with me into England, and hoped that though he himself had but a short time to live, yet that by our means his son should be established after his death. And I left with him one Francis Sparrow, a servant of Captain Gifford (who was desirous to tarry, and could describe a country with his pen) and a boy of mine called Hugh Goodwin to learn the language. I after asked the manner how the Epuremei wrought those plates of gold, and how they could melt it out of the stone. He told me that the most of the gold which they made in plates and images was not severed from the stone, but that on the lake of Manoa, and in a multitude of other rivers, they gathered it in grains of perfect gold and in pieces as big as small stones, and that they put it to a part of copper, otherwise they could not work it; and that they used a great earthen pot with holes round about it, and when they had mingled the gold and copper together they fastened canes to the holes, and so with the breath of men they increased the fire till the metal ran, and then they cast it into moulds of stone and clay, and so make those plates and images. I have sent your honours of two sorts such as I could by chance recover, more to show the manner of them than for the value. For I did not in any sort make my desire of gold known, because I had neither time nor power to have a great quantity. I gave among them many more pieces of gold than I received, of the new money of 20 shillings with Her Majesty's picture to wear, with promise that they would become her servants thenceforth.

I have also sent your honours of the ore, whereof I know some is as rich as the earth yieldeth any, of which I know there is sufficient, if nothing else were to be hoped for. But besides that we were not able to tarry and search the hills, so we had neither pioneers, bars, sledges, nor wedges of iron to break the ground, without which there is no working in mines. But we saw all the hills with stones of the colour of gold and silver, and we tried them to be no marquesite, and therefore such as the Spaniards call *el madre del oro* or 'the mother of gold', which is an undoubted assurance of the general abundance; and myself saw the outside of many mines of the spar, which I know to be the same that all covet in this world, and of those more than I will speak of.

Having learned what I could in Canuri and Aromaia, and received a faithful promise of the principallest of those provinces to become servants to Her Majesty, and to resist the Spaniards if they made any attempt in our absence, and that they would draw in the nations about the Lake of Cassipa and those of Yguaracuyri, I then parted from old Topiawari, and received his son for a pledge between us, and left with him two of ours as aforesaid. To Francis Sparrow I gave instructions to travel to Marcuraguara with such merchandises as I left with them, thereby to learn the place, and if it were possible, to go on to the great city of Manoa; which being done, we weighed anchor and coasted the river on Guiana side, because we came upon the north side, by the lawns of the Chayma and Wikiri.

There came with us from Aromaia a *cacique* called Putijma, that commanded the province of Warapana (which Putijma slew the nine Spaniards upon Caroni before spoken of), who desired us to rest in the port of his country, promising to bring us unto a mountain adjoining to his town that had stones of the colour of gold, which he performed. And after we had rested there one night I went myself in the morning with most of the gentlemen of my company overland towards the said mountain, marching by a river's side called Mana, leaving on the right hand a town called Tuteritona, standing in the province of Tarracoa, of which Wariaaremagoto is principal. Beyond it lieth another town towards the south, in the valley of Amariocapana, which beareth the name of the said valley, whose plains stretch themselves some sixty miles in length, east and west, as fair ground and as beautiful fields as any man hath ever seen, with divers copses scattered here and there by the river's side, and all as full of deer as any forest or park in England, and in every lake and river the like abundance of fish and fowl, of which Irraparragota is lord.

From the river of Mana we crossed another river in the said beautiful valley called Oiana, and rested ourselves by a clear lake which lay in the middle of the said Oiana, and one of our guides kindling us fire with two sticks, we stayed awhile to dry our shirts, which with the heat hung very wet and heavy on our shoulders. Afterwards we sought the ford to pass over towards the mountain called Iconuri, where Putijma foretold us of the mine. In this lake we saw one of the great fishes, as big as a wine pipe, which they call manatee, being most excellent and wholesome meat. But after I perceived that to pass the said river would require half-a-day's march more, I was not able myself to endure it, and therefore I sent Captain Keymis with six shot to go on, and gave him order not to return to the port of Putijma, which is called Chiparepare, but to take leisure, and to march down the said valley as far as a river called Cumaca, where I promised to meet him again, Putijma himself promising also to be his guide; and as they marched, they left the towns of Emperapana and Capurepana on the right hand, and marched from Putijma's house, down the said valley of Amariocapana. And we returning the same day to the river's side, saw by the way many rocks like unto gold ore, and on the left hand a round mountain which consisted of mineral stone.

From hence we rowed down the stream, coasting the province of Parino. As for the branches of rivers which I overpass in this discourse, those shall be better expressed in the description, with the mountains of Aio, Ara, and the rest, which are situate in the provinces of Parino and Carricurrina. When we were come as far down as the land called Ariacoa (where Orinoco divideth itself into three great branches, each of them being most goodly rivers), I sent away Captain Henry Thyn, and Captain Grenville with the galley the nearest way, and took with me Captain Gifford, Captain Calfield, Edward Porter, and Captain Eynos with my own barge and the two wherries, and went down that branch of Orinoco which is called Carerupana, which leadeth towards Emeria, the province of Carapana, and towards the east sea, as well to find out Captain Keymis, whom I had sent overland, as also to acquaint myself with Carapana, who is one of the greatest of all the lords of the Orinocoponi; and when I came to the river of Cumaca (to which Putijma promised to conduct Captain Keymis), I left Captain Eynos and Master Porter in the said river to expect his coming, and the rest of us rowed down the stream towards Emeria.

In this branch called Carerupana were also many goodly islands, some of six miles long, some of ten, some of twenty. When it grew towards sunset, we entered a branch of a river that fell into Orinoco, called Winicapora, where I was informed of the mountain of crystal, to which in truth for the length of the way, and the evil season of the year, I was not able to march, nor abide any longer upon the journey. We saw it afar off, and it appeared like a white church-tower of an exceeding height. There falleth over it a mighty river which toucheth no part of the side of the mountain, but rusheth over the top of it, and falleth to the ground with so terrible a noise and clamour as if a thousand great bells were knocked one against another. I think there is not in the world so strange an overfall, nor so wonderful to behold. Berrio told me that there were diamonds and other precious stones on it, and that they shined very far off; but what it hath I know not, neither durst he or any of his men ascend to the top of the said mountain, those people adjoining being his enemies (as they were) and the way to it so impassable.

Upon this river of Winicapora we rested a while, and from thence marched into the country to a town called after the name of the river, whereof the captain was one Timitwara, who also offered to conduct me to the top of the said mountain called Wacarima. But when we came in first to the house of the said Timitwara, being upon one of their said feast days, we found them all as drunk as beggars, and the pots walking from one to another without rest. We that were weary and hot with marching were glad of the plenty, though a small quantity satisfied us, their drink being very strong and heady, and so rested ourselves awhile. After we had fed, we drew ourselves back to our boats upon the river, and there came to us all the lords of the country, with all such kind of victuals as the place yielded, and with their delicate wine of *pinas*, and with abundance of hens and other provisions, and of those stones which we call spleen-stones.

We understood by the chieftains of Winicapora, that their Lord, Carapana, was departed from Emeria, which was now in sight, and that he was fled to Cairamo, adjoining to the mountains of Guiana, over the valley called Amariocapana, being persuaded by those ten

Spaniards which lay at his house that we would destroy him and his country.

But after these *caciques* of Winicapora and Saporatona, his followers, perceived our purpose, and saw that we came as enemies to the Spaniards only, and had not so much as harmed any of those nations, no, though we found them to be of the Spaniards' own servants, they assured us that Carapana would be as ready to serve us as any of the lords of the provinces which we had passed; and that he durst do no other till this day but entertain the Spaniards, his country lying so directly in their way, and next of all other to any entrance that should be made in Guiana on that side.

And they further assured us that it was not for fear of our coming that he was removed, but to be acquitted of the Spaniards or any other that should come hereafter. For the province of Cairoma is situate at the mountain foot which divideth the plains of Guiana from the countries of the Orinocoponi; by means whereof if any should come in our absence into his towns, he would slip over the mountains into the plains of Guiana among the Epuremei, where the Spaniards durst not follow him without great force.

But in my opinion, or rather I assure myself, that Carapana (being a notable wise and subtle fellow, a man of one hundred years of age and therefore of great experience) is removed to look on, and if he find that we return strong he will be ours; if not, he will excuse his departure to the Spaniards, and say it was for fear of our coming.

We therefore thought it bootless to row so far down the stream, or to seek any further of this old fox; and therefore from the river of Waricapana (which lieth at the entrance of Emeria), we returned again, and left to the eastward those four rivers which fall from the mountains of Emeria into Orinoco, which are Waracayari, Coirama, Akaniri, and Iparoma. Below those four are also these branches and mouths of Orinoco, which fall into the east sea, whereof the first is Araturi, the next Amacura, the third Barima, the fourth Wana, the fifth Morooca, the sixth Paroma, the last Wijmi. Beyond them there fall out of the land between Orinoco and Amazons fourteen rivers which I forbear to name, inhabited by the Arawaks and cannibals.

It is now time to return towards the north, and we found it a wearisome way back from the borders of Emeria, to recover up again to the head of the river Carerupana, by which we descended, and where we parted from the galley, which I directed to take the next way to the port of Toparimaca by which we entered first.

All the night it was stormy and dark, and full of thunder and great showers, so as we were driven to keep close by the banks in our small boats, being all heartily afraid both of the billow and terrible current of the river. By the next morning we recovered the mouth of the river of Cumaca, where we left Captain Eynos and Edward Porter to attend the coming of Captain Keymis overland; but when we entered the same, they had heard no news of his arrival, which bred in us a great doubt what might become of him. I rowed up a league or two further into the river, shooting off pieces all the way, that he might know of our being there; and the next morning we heard them answer us also with a piece. We took them aboard us, and took our leave of Putijma, their guide, who of all others most lamented our departure, and offered to send his son with us into England, if we could have stayed till he had sent back to his town. But our hearts were cold to behold the great rage and increase of Orinoco, and therefore departed, and turned towards the west till we had recovered the parting of the three branches aforesaid, that we might put down the stream after the galley.

The next day we landed on the island of Assapana (which divideth the river from that branch by which we sent down to Emeria), and there feasted ourselves with that beast which is called armadillo, presented unto us before at Winicapora, and the day following we recovered the galley at anchor at the port of Toparimaca, and the same evening departed with very foul weather, and terrible thunder and showers, for the winter was come on very far. The best was, we went no less than one hundred miles a day down the river. But by the way we entered it was impossible to return, for that the river of Amana, being in the bottom of the bay of Guanipa, cannot be sailed back by any means, both the breeze and currents of the sea were so forcible; and therefore we followed a branch of Orinoco called Capure, which entered into the sea eastward of our ships, to the end we might bear with them before the wind. And it was not without need, for we had by that way as much to cross of the main sea after we came to the river's mouth as between Gravelines and Dover, in such boats as your honour hath heard.

To speak of what passed homeward were tedious, either to describe or name any of the rivers, islands, or villages of the Tivitivas, which dwell on trees. We will leave all those to the general map. And to be short, when we were arrived at the sea-side, then grew our greatest doubt and the bitterest of all our journey forepassed, for I protest before God, that we were in a most desperate estate: for the same night which we anchored in the mouth of the river of Capure, where it falleth into the sea, there arose a mighty storm, and the river's mouth was at least a league broad, so as we ran before night close under the land with our small boats, and brought the galley as near as we could; but she had as much ado to live as could be, and there wanted little of her sinking, and all those in her. For my own part, I confess I was very doubtful which way to take, either to go over in the pestered galley, there being but six foot water over the sands for two leagues together, and that also in the channel, and she drew five; or to adventure in so great a billow, and in so doubtful weather, to cross the seas in my barge. The longer we tarried the worse it was, and therefore I took Captain Gifford, Captain Calfield, and my cousin Grenville into my barge; and after it cleared up about midnight we put ourselves to God's keeping, and thrust out into the sea, leaving the galley at anchor, who durst not adventure but by daylight. And so being all very sober and melancholy, one faintly cheering another to show courage, it pleased God that the next day about nine of the clock we descried the island of Trinidad, and steering for the nearest part of it, we kept the shore till we came to Curiapan, where we found our ships at anchor, than which there was never to us a more joyful sight.

Now that it hath pleased God to send us safe to our ships, it is time to leave Guiana to the sun, whom they worship, and steer away towards the north. I will therefore in a few words finish the discovery thereof. Of the several nations which we found upon this discovery I will once again make repetition, and how they are affected. At our first entrance into Amana, which is one of the outlets of Orinoco, we left on the right hand of us in the bottom of the bay, lying directly against Trinidad, a nation of inhuman cannibals, which inhabit the rivers of Guanipa and Berreese. In the same bay there is also a third river, which is called Areo, which riseth on Paria side towards Cumana, and that river is inhabited with the Wikiri, whose chief town upon the said river is Chayma. In this bay there are no more rivers but these three before rehearsed and the four branches of Amana, all which in the winter thrust so great an abundance of water into the sea, as the same is taken up fresh two or three leagues from the land. In the passages towards Guiana (that is, in all those lands which the eight branches of Orinoco fashion into islands) there are but one sort of people, called Tivitivas, but of two castes, as they term them, the one called Ciawani, the other Waraweete, and those war one with another.

On the hithermost part of Orinoco, as at Toparimaca and Winicapora, those are of a nation called Nepoios, and are the followers of Carapana, Lord of Emeria. Between Winicapora and the port of Morequito, which standeth in Aromaia, and all those in the valley of Amariocapana, are called Orinocoponi, and did obey Morequito and are now followers of Topiawari. Upon the river of Caroni are the Canuri, which are governed by a woman (who is inheritrix of that province) who came far off to see our nation, and asked me divers questions of Her Majesty, being much delighted with the discourse of Her Majesty's greatness, and wondering at such reports as we truly made of Her Highness's many virtues. And upon the head of Caroni and on the lake of Cassipa are the three strong nations of the Cassipagotos. Right south into the land are the Capurepani and Emparepani, and beyond those adjoining to Macureguara (the first city of Inca) are the Yguaracuyri. All these are professed enemies to the Spaniards, and to the rich Epuremei also. To the west of Caroni are divers nations of cannibals and of those Ewaiponoma without heads. Directly west are the Amapaias and Anebas, which are also marvellous rich in gold. The rest towards Peru we will omit. On the north of Orinoco, between it and the West Indies, are the Wikiri, Chaymi, and the rest before spoken of, all mortal enemies to the Spaniards. On the south side of the main mouth of Orinoco are the Arawaks; and beyond them, the cannibals, and to the south of them the Amazons.

To make mention of the several beasts, birds, fishes, fruits, flowers, gums, sweet woods, and of their several religions and customs, would for the first require as many volumes as those of Gesnerus, and for the next another bundle of *Decades*. The religion of the Epuremei is the same which the Incas, Emperors of Peru used, which may be read in Cieza and other Spanish stories, how they believe the immortality of the soul, worship the sun, and bury with them alive their best beloved wives and treasure, as they likewise do in Pegu in the East Indies, and other places. The Orinocoponi bury not their wives with them, but their jewels, hoping to enjoy them again. The Arawaks dry the bones of their lords, and their wives and friends drink them in powder. In the graves of the Peruvians the Spaniards found their greatest abundance of treasure. The like also is to be found among these people in every province. They have all many wives, and the lords five-fold to the common sort. Their wives never eat with their husbands, nor among the men, but serve their husbands at meals and afterwards feed by themselves. Those that are past their younger years make all their bread and drink, and work their cotton-beds, and do all else of service and labour; for the men do nothing but hunt, fish, play, and drink when they are out of the wars.

I will enter no further into discourse of their manners, laws, and customs. And because I have not myself seen the cities of Inca I cannot avow on my credit what I have heard, although it be very likely that the Emperor Inca hath built and erected as magnificent palaces in Guiana as his ancestors did in Peru, which were for their riches and rareness most marvellous, and exceeding all in Europe, and, I think, of the world, China excepted; which also the Spaniards which I had assured me to be true, as also the nations of the borderers, who, being but savages to those of the inland, do cause much treasure to be buried with them. For I was informed of one of the *caciques* of the valley of Amariocapana, which had buried with him a little before our arrival a chair of gold most curiously wrought, which was made either in Macuraguara adjoining or in Manoa. But if we should have grieved them in their religion at the first, before they had been taught better, and have digged up their graves, we had lost them all; and therefore I held my first resolution, that Her Majesty should either accept or refuse the enterprise ere anything should be done that might in any sort hinder the same. And if Peru had so many heaps of gold, whereof those

Incas were princes, and that they delighted so much therein, no doubt but this which now liveth and reigneth in Manoa hath the same honour, and, I am assured, hath more abundance of gold within his territory than all Peru and the West Indies.

For the rest, which myself have seen, I will promise these things that follow, which I know to be true. Those that are desirous to discover and to see many nations may be satisfied within this river, which bringeth forth so many arms and branches leading to several countries and provinces, above 2,000 miles east and west and 800 miles south and north, and of these the most either rich in gold or in other merchandises. The common soldier shall here fight for gold, and pay himself, instead of pence, with plates of half-a-foot broad, whereas he breaketh his bones in other wars for provant and penury. Those commanders and chieftains that shoot at honour and abundance shall find there more rich and beautiful cities, more temples adorned with golden images, more sepulchres filled with treasure than either Cortes found in Mexico or Pizarro in Peru; and the shining glory of this conquest will eclipse all those so far-extended beams of the Spanish nation. There is no country which yieldeth more pleasure to the inhabitants, either for those common delights of hunting, hawking, fishing, fowling, or the rest, than Guiana doth. It hath so many plains, clear rivers, abundance of pheasants, partridges, quails, rails, cranes, herons, and all other fowl; deer of all sorts, porks, hares, lions, tigers, leopards, and divers other sorts of beasts, either for chase or food. It hath a kind of beast called *cama* or *anta*, as big as an English beef, and in great plenty.

To speak of the several sorts of every kind I fear would be troublesome to the reader, and therefore I will omit them, and conclude that both for health, good air, pleasure, and riches, I am resolved it cannot be equalled by any region either in the east or west. Moreover the country is so healthful, as of a hundred persons and more (which lay without shift most sluttishly, and were every day almost melted with heat in rowing and marching, and suddenly wet again with great showers, and did eat of all sorts of corrupt fruits, and made meals of fresh fish without seasoning, of *tortugas*, of *lagartos* or crocodiles, and of all sorts good and bad, without either order or measure, and besides lodged in the open air every night) we lost not any one, nor had one ill-disposed to my knowledge, nor found any calentura or other of those pestilent diseases which dwell in all hot regions, and so near the equinoctial line.

Where there is store of gold it is in effect needless to remember other commodities for trade; but it hath, towards the south part of the river, great quantities of brazil-wood and divers berries that dye a most perfect crimson and carnation; and for painting, all France, Italy, or the East Indies yield none such. For the more the skin is washed, the fairer the colour appeareth, and with which even those brown and tawny women spot themselves and colour their cheeks. All places yield abundance of cotton, of silk, of balsamum, and of those kinds most excellent and never known in Europe, of all sorts of gums, of Indian pepper; and what else the countries may afford within the land we know not, neither had we time to abide the trial and search. The soil besides is so excellent and so full of rivers, as it will carry sugar, ginger, and all those other commodities which the West Indies have.

The navigation is short, for it may be sailed with an ordinary wind in six weeks, and in the like time back again, and by the way neither lee-shore, enemies' coast, rocks, nor sands, all which in the voyages to the West Indies and all other places we are subject unto; as the channel of Bahama, coming from the West Indies, cannot well be passed in the winter, and when it is at the best it is a perilous and a fearful place, the rest of the Indies for calms, and diseases very troublesome, and the sea about the Bermudas a hellish sea for thunder, lightning, and storms.

This very year there were seventeen sail of Spanish ships lost in the channel of Bahama, and the great *Philip*, like to have sunk at the Bermudas, was put back to San Juan de Puerto Rico. And so it falleth out in that navigation every year for the most part, which in this voyage are not to be feared. For the time of year to leave England is best in July, and the summer in Guiana is in October, November, December, January, February, and March, and then the ships may depart thence in April, and so return again into England in June, so as they shall never be subject to winter weather, either coming, going, or staying there; which, for my part, I take to be one of the greatest comforts and encouragements that can be thought on, having (as I have done) tasted in this voyage by the West Indies so many calms, so much heat, such outrageous gusts, foul weather, and contrary winds.

To conclude, Guiana is a country that hath yet her maidenhead, never sacked, turned, nor wrought; the face of the earth hath not been torn, nor the virtue and salt of the soil spent by manurance; the graves have not been opened for gold, the mines not broken with sledges, nor their images pulled down out of their temples. It hath never been entered by any army of strength, and never conquered or possessed by any Christian prince. It is besides so defensible that if two forts be built in one of the provinces which I have seen, the flood setteth in so near the bank, where the channel also lieth, that no ship can pass up but within a pike's length of the artillery, first of the one, and afterwards of the other; which two forts will be a sufficient guard both to the Empire of Inca, and to a hundred other several kingdoms, lying within the said river, even to the city of Quito in Peru.

There is therefore great difference between the easiness of the conquest of Guiana, and the defence of it being conquered, and the West or East Indies. Guiana hath but one entrance by the sea (if it hath that) for any vessels of burden; so as whosoever shall first possess it, it shall be found unaccessible for any enemy, except he come in wherries, barges, or canoes, or else in flat-bottomed boats, and if he do offer to enter it in that manner, the woods are so thick two hundred miles together upon the rivers of such entrance, as a mouse cannot sit in a boat unhit from the bank. By land it is more impossible to approach, for it hath the strongest situation of any region under the sun, and is so environed with impassable mountains on every side as it is impossible to victual any company in the passage; which hath been well proved by the Spanish nation, who since the conquest of Peru have never left five years free from attempting this empire, or discovering some way into it, and yet of three-and-twenty several gentlemen, knights, and noblemen, there was never any that knew which way to lead an army by land, or to conduct ships by sea, anything near the said country. Orellana, of whom the river of Amazons taketh name, was the first, and Don Antonio de Berrio (whom we displanted) the last; and I doubt much whether he himself or any of his yet know the best way into the said Empire. It can therefore hardly be regained, if any strength be formerly set down, but in one or two places, and but two or three crumsters or galleys built, and furnished upon the river within. The West Indies have many ports, watering places, and landings, and nearer than three hundred miles to Guiana no man can harbour a ship, except he know one only place, which is not learned in haste, and which I will undertake there is not any one of my companies that knoweth, whosoever hearkened most after it.

Besides, by keeping one good fort, or building one town of strength, the whole Empire is guarded, and whatsoever companies shall be afterwards planted within the land, although in twenty several provinces, those shall be able all to reunite themselves upon any occasion either by the way of one river, or be able to march by land without either wood, bog, or mountain; whereas in the West Indies there are few towns or provinces that can succour or relieve one the other either by land or sea. By land the countries are either desert, mountainous, or strong enemies; by sea, if any man invade to the eastward, those to the west cannot in many months turn against the breeze and eastern wind. Besides, the Spaniards are therein so dispersed as they are nowhere strong but in Nueva España only. The sharp mountains, the thorns, and poisoned prickles, the sandy and deep ways in the valleys, the smothering heat and air, and want of water in other places, are their only and best defence, which (because those nations that invade them are not victualled or provided to stay, neither have any place to friend adjoining) do secure them instead of good arms and great multitudes.

The West Indies were first offered Her Majesty's grandfather by Columbus, a stranger, in whom there might be doubt of deceit; and besides it was then thought incredible that there were such and so many lands and regions never written of before. This Empire is made known to Her Majesty by her own vassal, and by him that oweth to her more duty than an ordinary subject, so that it shall ill sort with the many graces and benefits which I have received to abuse Her Highness, cither with fables or imaginations. The country is already discovered, many nations won to Her Majesty's love and obedience, and those Spaniards which have latest and longest laboured about the conquest, beaten out, discouraged, and disgraced, which among these nations were thought invincible. Her Majesty may in this enterprise employ all those soldiers and gentlemen that are younger brethren, and all captains and chieftains that want employment, and the charge will be only the first setting out in victualling and arming them; for after the first or second year I doubt not but to see in London a contractation house of more receipt for Guiana than there is now in Seville for the West Indies.

And I am resolved that if there were but a small army afoot in Guiana, marching towards Manoa, the chief city of Inca, he would yield to Her Majesty by composition so many hundred thousand pounds yearly as should both defend all enemies abroad and defray all expenses at home, and that he would besides pay a garrison of three or four thousand soldiers very royally to defend him against other nations. For he cannot but know how his predecessors, yea, how his own great uncles, Huascar and Atabalipa, sons to Guaynacapa, Emperor of Peru, were (while they contended for the Empire) beaten out by the Spaniards, and that both of late years and ever since the said conquest the Spaniards have sought the passages and entry of his country; and of their cruelties used to the borderers he cannot be ignorant. In which respects no doubt but he will be brought to tribute with great gladness; if not, he hath neither shot nor iron weapon in all his Empire, and therefore may easily be conquered.

And I further remember that Berrio confessed to me and others (which I protest before the majesty of God to be true) that there was found among the prophecies in Peru (at such time as the Empire was reduced to the Spanish obedience) in their chiefest temples, amongst divers others which foreshowed the loss of the said Empire, that from Inglatierra those Incas should be again in time to come restored, and delivered from the servitude of the said conquerors. And I hope, as we with these few hands have displanted the first garrison and driven them out of the said country, so Her Majesty will give order for the rest, and either defend it, and hold it as tributary, or conquer and keep it as Empress of the same. For whatsoever prince shall possess it, shall be greatest, and if the King of Spain enjoy it he will become unresistible. Her Majesty hereby shall confirm and strengthen the opinions of all nations as touching her great and princely actions. And where the south border of Guiana reacheth to the dominion and empire of the

Amazons, those women shall hereby hear the name of a virgin which is not only able to defend her own territories and her neighbours, but also to invade and conquer so great empires and so far removed.

To speak more at this time I fear would be but troublesome. I trust in God this, being true, will suffice, and that he which is King of all Kings and Lord of Lords, will put it into her heart which is Lady of Ladies to possess it; if not, I will judge those men worthy to be kings thereof that by her grace and leave will undertake it of themselves.

Part 6

THE STRAITS OF MAGELLAN
AND BEYOND

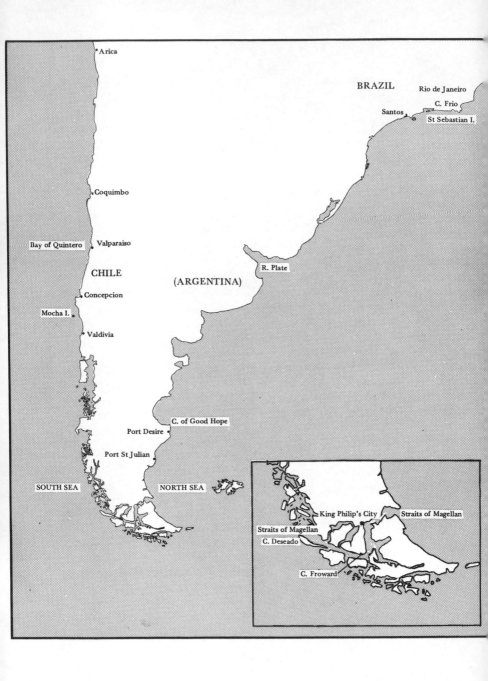

The only practical sea-route to the East Indies, apart from the one by the Cape of Good Hope which was watched by the Portuguese, was round the Horn, or rather through the straits discovered by the first circumnavigator of the globe, Magellan, and named after him. This route had an added attraction, for it gave direct access to the "soft underbelly" of the Spanish empire in America. The venture was, however, even more difficult and dangerous than the attempt on the north-east or north-west passage. From these one could, with luck, disengage; but winds and currents in Magellan's Straits were so unpredictable and at times so outrageous that often, in Macbeth's words, "returning were as tedious as go o'er". The natives of Patagonia were much wilder than the Eskimo and no commerce with them was possible. Watering and victualling were alike difficult. In addition the Spaniards in 1584 set up two forts in the Straits, although the near-impossibility of relieving or supplying the garrisons soon closed them down.

Nevertheless two English captains triumphantly followed Magellan. The first, in 1577, was Drake, though not without suffering a mutiny before he entered the Straits and permanent separation from his consort, Captain Winter's Elizabeth, as he left them. The second Englishman to pass the Straits was Thomas Cavendish or Candish in 1586. A third expedition, by John Chidley in 1589, was disastrous. Only one ship, the Delight, got anywhere near the Straits, and just what happened there is tantalisingly hard to decipher from William Magoths' discreet account and the pathetic petition of the ship's company.

In 1591 Cavendish rashly attempted to repeat his earlier success. For this second voyage the captain of one of the ships in Cavendish's fleet was John Davis, hero of the north-west passage. The account of the horrors that Davis and his crew endured is perhaps the most graphic in the whole of Hakluyt's collection, and amply confirms the evil reputation of the Straits. Cavendish himself fared if possible even worse. The letter that he wrote when dying at sea on his retreat (it is printed in Purchas His Pilgrims, the sequel to "Hakluyt") blames "that villain Davis" for all his troubles; but this would seem to be no more than a symptom of the paranoia from which he was evidently suffering throughout the voyage.

The famous voyage of Sir Francis Drake into the South Sea, and therehence about the whole globe of the earth, begun in the year of Our Lord 1577. (A composite narrative: the first part, as far as the Pacific, by John Cooke; the remainder possibly by William Legg.)

THE 15th day of November, in the year of our Lord 1577, Master Francis Drake, with a fleet of five ships and barks, and to the number of 164 men, gentlemen and sailors, departed from Plymouth, giving out his pretended voyage for Alexandria. But the wind falling contrary, he was forced the next morning to put into Falmouth Haven, in Cornwall, where such and so terrible a tempest took us as few men have seen the like, and was indeed so vehement that all our ships were like to have gone to wrack. But it pleased God to preserve us from that extremity, and to afflict us only for that present with these two particulars: the mast of our admiral, which was the *Pelican*, was cut overboard for the safeguard of the ship, and the *Marigold* was driven ashore, and somewhat bruised. For the repairing of which damages we returned again to Plymouth; and having recovered those harms, and brought the ships again to good state, we set forth the second time from Plymouth, and set sail the 13th day of December following.

The 25th day of the same month we fell with the Cape Cantino, upon the coast of Barbary; and coasting along, the 27th day we found an island called Mogador, lying one mile distant from the main, between which island and the main we found a very good and safe harbour for our ships to ride in, as also very good entrance, and void of any danger.

On this island our General erected a pinnace, whereof he brought out of England with him four already framed. While these things were in doing, there came to the water's side some of the inhabitants of the country, showing forth their flags of truce, which being seen of our General, he sent his ship's boat to the shore to know what they would. They being willing to come aboard, our men left there one man of our company for a pledge, and brought two of theirs aboard our ship; which by signs showed our General that the next day they would bring some provision, as sheep, capons, and hens, and suchlike. Whereupon our General bestowed amongst them some linen cloth and shoes, and a javelin, which they very joyfully received, and departed for that time.

The next morning they failed not to come again to the water's side; and our General again setting out our boat, one of our men leaping over-rashly ashore, and offering friendly to embrace them, they set violent hands on him, offering a dagger to his throat if he had made any resistance, and so laying him on a horse carried him away. So that a man cannot be too circumspect and wary of himself among such miscreants.

Our pinnace being finished, we departed from this place the 30th and last day of December, and coasting along the shore we did descry, not contrary to our expectation, certain *canters*, which were Spanish fishermen; to whom we gave chase and took three of them. And proceeding further we met with 3 caravels, and took them also.

The 17th day of January we arrived at Cape Blanco, where we found a ship riding at anchor, within the Cape, and but two simple mariners in her. Which ship we took and carried her further into the harbour, where we remained 4 days; and in that space our General mustered and trained his men on land in warlike manner, to make them fit for all occasions. In this place we took of the fishermen such necessaries as we wanted, and they could yield us; and leaving here one of our little barks, called the *Benedict*, we took with us one of theirs which they called *canters*, being of the burden of 40 tons or thereabouts.

All these things being finished we departed this harbour the 22nd of January, carrying along with us one of the Portugal caravels, which was bound to the islands of Cape Verde for salt, whereof good store is made in one of those islands. The master or pilot of that caravel did advertise our General that upon one of those islands, called Mayo, there was great store of dried *cabritos*, which a few inhabitants there dwelling did yearly make ready for such of the King's ships as did there touch, being bound for his country of Brazil or elsewhere. We fell with this island the 27th of January, but the inhabitants would in no case traffic with us, being thereof forbidden by the King's edict. Yet the next day our General sent to view the island, and the likelihoods that might be there of provision of victuals, about threescore and two men under the conduct and government of Master Winter and Master Doughty; and marching towards the chief place of habitation in this island (as by the Portugal we were informed), having travelled to the mountains the space of three miles, and arriving there somewhat before the daybreak, we arrested ourselves, to see day before us. Which appearing, we found the inhabitants to be fled; but the place, by reason that it was manured, we found to be more fruitful than the other part, especially the valleys among the hills.

Here we gave ourselves a little refreshing, as by very ripe and sweet grapes, which the fruitfulness of the earth at that season of the year yielded us; and that season being with us the depth of winter, it may seem strange that those fruits were then there growing. But the reason thereof is this, because they being between the tropic and the equinoctial, the sun passeth twice in the year through their zenith over their heads, by means whereof they have two summers; and being so near the heat of the line they never lose the heat of the sun so much but the fruits have their increase and continuance in the midst of winter. The island is wonderfully stored with goats and wild hens; and it hath salt also, without labour, save only that the people gather it into heaps; which continually in great quantity is increased upon the sands by the flowing of the sea, and the receiving heat of the sun kerning the same, so that of the increase thereof they keep a continual traffic with their neighbours.

Amongst other things we found here a kind of fruit called *cocos*, which because it is not commonly known with us in England, I thought good to make some description of it. The tree beareth no leaves nor branches, but at the very top the fruit groweth in clusters, hard at the top of the stem of the tree, as big every several fruit as a man's head; but having taken off the outermost bark, which you shall find to be very full of strings or sinews, as I may term them, you shall come to a hard shell, which may hold of quantity in liquor a pint commonly, or some quart, and some less. Within that shell, of the thickness of half-an-inch good, you shall have a kind of hard substance and very white, no less good and sweet than almonds; within that again, a certain clear liquor, which being drunk, you shall not only find it very delicate and sweet, but most comfortable and cordial.

After we had satisfied ourselves with some of these fruits, we marched further into the island, and saw great store of *cabritos* alive, which were so chased by the inhabitants that we could do no good towards our provision; but they had laid out, as it were to stop our mouths withal, certain old dried *cabritos*, which being but ill, and small and few, we made no account of.

Being returned to our ships, our General departed hence the 31st of this month, and sailed by the island of Santiago, but far enough from the danger of the inhabitants, who shot and discharged at us three pieces, but they all fell short of us, and did us no harm. The island is fair and large, and, as it seemeth, rich and fruitful, and inhabited by the Portugals; but the mountains and high places of the island are said to be possessed by the Moors, who having been slaves to the Portugals, to ease themselves made escape to the desert places of the island, where they abide with great strength. Being before this island, we espied two ships under sail, to the one of which we gave chase, and in the end boarded her with a ship-boat without resistance; which we found to be a good prize, and she yielded unto us good store of wine. Which prize our General committed to the custody of Master Doughty; and retaining the pilot, sent the rest away with his pinnace, giving them a butt of wine and some victuals, and their wearing clothes, and so they departed.

The same night we came with the island called by the Portugals Ilha do Fogo, that is, the burning island; in the north side whereof is a consuming fire. The matter is said to be of sulphur, but, notwithstanding, it is like to be a commodious island, because the Portugals have built, and do inhabit there. Upon the south side thereof lieth a most pleasant and sweet island, the trees whereof are always green and fair to look upon, in respect whereof they call it Ilha Brava, that is, the brave island. From the banks thereof into the sea do run in many places reasonable streams of fresh waters easy to come by, but there was no convenient road for our ships; for such was the depth that no ground could be had for anchoring. And it is reported that ground was never found in that place; so that the tops of Fogo burn not so high in the air, but the roots of Brava are quenched as low in the sea.

Being departed from these islands, we drew towards the line, where we were becalmed the space of 3 weeks, but yet subject to divers great storms, terrible lightnings and much thunder. But with this misery we had the commodity of great store of fish, as dolphins, bonitos, and flying-fishes, whereof some fell into our ships; wherehence they could not rise again for want of moisture, for when their wings are dry they cannot fly.

From the first day of our departure from the islands of Cape Verde, we sailed 54 days without sight of land. And the first land that we fell with was the coast of Brazil, which we saw the fifth of April in the height of 33 degrees towards the pole antarctic. And being discovered at sea by the inhabitants of the country, they made upon the coast great fires for a sacrifice (as we learned) to the devils; about which they use conjurations, making heaps of sand, and other ceremonies, that when any ship shall go about to stay upon their coast, not only sands may be gathered together in shoals in every place, but also that storms and tempests may arise, to the casting away of ships and men, whereof, as it is reported, there have been divers experiments.

The seventh day in a mighty great storm both of lightning, rain, and thunder we lost the *canter*, which we called the *Christopher*. But the eleventh day after, by our General's great care in dispersing his ships, we found her again; and the place where we met our General called the Cape of Joy, where every ship took in some water. Here we found a good temperature and sweet air, a very fair and pleasant country with an exceeding fruitful soil, where were great store of large and mighty deer, but we came not to the sight of any people; but travelling further into the country we perceived the footing of people in the clay ground, showing that they were men of great stature. Being returned to our ships we weighed anchor, and ran somewhat further, and harboured ourselves between the rock and the main; where by means of the rock that broke the force of the sea, we rode very safe. And upon this rock we killed for our provision certain sea-wolves, commonly called with us seals.

From hence we went our course to 36 degrees, and entered the great river of Plate, and ran into 54 and 55 fathoms and a half of fresh water, where we filled our water by the ship's side; but our General finding here no good harbour, as he thought he should, bore out again to sea the 27th of April, and in bearing out we lost sight of our flyboat, wherein Master Doughty was. But we, sailing along, found a fair and reasonable good bay, wherein were many, and the same profitable, islands; one whereof had so many seals as would at the least have laden all our ships, and the rest of the islands are, as it were, laden with fowls, which is wonderful to see, and they of divers sorts. It is a place very plentiful of victuals, and hath in it no want of fresh water. Our General, after certain days of his abode in this place, being on shore in an island, the people of the country showed themselves unto him, leaping and dancing, and entered into traffic with him; but they would not receive anything at any man's hands, but the same must be cast upon the ground. They are of clean, comely, and strong bodies, swift on foot, and seem to be very active.

The eighteenth day of May, our General thought it needful to have a care of such ships as were absent; and therefore endeavouring to seek the flyboat wherein Master Doughty was, we espied her again the next day. And whereas certain of our ships were sent to discover the coast and to search a harbour, the *Marigold* and the *canter* being employed in that business came unto us and gave us understanding of a safe harbour that they had found. Wherewith all our ships bore, and entered it; where we watered and made new provision of victuals, as by seals, whereof we slew to the number of 200 or 300 in the space of an hour.

Here our General in the admiral rode close aboard the flyboat, and took out of her all the provision of victuals and what else was in her, and hauling her to the land, set fire to her, and so burnt her to save the iron work. Which being a-doing, there came down of the country certain of the people naked, saving only about their waist the skin of some beast with the fur or hair on, and something also wreathed on their heads. Their faces were painted with divers colours, and some of them had on their heads the similitude of horns, every man his bow, which was an ell in length, and a couple of arrows. They were very agile people and quick to deliver, and seemed not to be ignorant in the feats of wars, as by their order of ranging a few men might appear. These people would not of a long time receive anything at our hands; yet at length our General being ashore, and they dancing after their accustomed manner about him, and he once turning his back towards them, one leaped suddenly to him, and took his cap with his gold band off his head, and ran a little distance from him, and shared it with his fellow, the cap to the one, and the band to the other.

15 Drake loses his cap. In the background the abandoned flyboat is being burned.

Having despatched all our business in this place, we departed and set sail. And immediately upon our setting forth we lost our *canter*, which was absent three or four days; but when our General had her again, he took out the necessaries, and so gave her over, near to the Cape of Good Hope.

The next day after, being the twentieth of June, we harboured ourselves again in a very good harbour, called by Magellan Port St Julian, where we found a gibbet standing upon the main; which we supposed to be the place where Magellan did execution upon some of his disobedient and rebellious company.

The two and twentieth day our General went ashore to the main, and in his company John Thomas, and Robert Winterhie, Oliver the master gunner, John Brewer, Thomas Hood, and Thomas Drake; and entering on land, they presently met with two or three of the country people, and Robert Winterhie having in his hands a bow and arrows, went about to make a shoot of pleasure, and in his draught his bowstring brake; which the rude savages taking as a token of war, began to bend the force of their bows against our company, and drove them to their shifts very narrowly.

In this port our General began to enquire diligently of the actions of Master Thomas Doughty, and found them not to be such as he looked for, but tending rather to contention or mutiny, or some other disorder, whereby, without redress, the success of the voyage might greatly have been hazarded. Whereupon the company was called together and made acquainted with the particulars of the cause, which were found, partly by Master Doughty's own confession, and partly by the evidence of the fact, to be true. Which when our General saw, although his private affection to Master Doughty, as he then in the presence of us all sacredly protested, was great, yet the care he had of the state of the voyage, of the expectation of Her Majesty, and of the honour of his country did more touch him, as indeed it ought, than the private respect of one man. So that the cause being thoroughly heard, and all things done in good order as near as might be to the course of our laws in England, it was concluded that Master Doughty should receive punishment according to the quality of the offence. And he, seeing no remedy but patience for himself, desired before his death to receive the communion, which he did at the hands of Master Fletcher, our minister, and our General himself accompanied him in that holy action. Which being done, and the place of execution made ready, he having embraced our General, and taken his leave of all the company, with prayers for the Queen's Majesty and our realm, in quiet sort laid his head to the block, where he ended his life.

This being done, our General made divers speeches to the whole company, persuading us to unity, obedience, love, and regard of our voyage; and for the better confirmation thereof, willed every man the next Sunday following to prepare himself to receive the communion, as Christian brethren and friends ought to do, which was done in very reverent sort; and so with good contentment every man went about his business.

The 17th day of August we departed the port of St Julian, and the 20th day we fell with the Strait or Fret of Magellan, going into the South Sea; at the cape or headland whereof we found the body of a dead man, whose flesh was clean consumed. The 21st day we entered the Strait, which we found to have many turnings, and as it were shuttings-up, as if there were no passage at all, by means whereof we had the wind often against us; so that some of the fleet recovering a cape or point of land, others should be forced to turn back again, and to come to an anchor where they could. In this Strait there be many fair harbours, with store of fresh water. But yet they lack their best commodity, for the water there is of such depth that no man shall find ground to anchor in, except it be in some narrow river or corner, or between some rocks, so that if any extreme blasts or contrary winds do come, whereunto the place is much subject, it carrieth with it no small danger.

The land on both sides is very huge and mountainous; the lower mountains whereof, although they be monstrous and wonderful to look upon for their height, yet there are others which in height exceed them in a strange manner, reaching themselves above their fellows so high, that between them did appear three regions of clouds. These mountains are covered with snow. At both the southerly and easterly parts of the Strait there are islands, among which the sea hath his indraught into the Straits, even as it hath in the main entrance of the fret. This Strait is extreme cold, with frost and snow continually; the trees seem to stoop with the burden of the weather, and yet are green continually, and many good and sweet herbs do very plentifully grow and increase under them. The breadth of the Strait is in some places a league, in some other places 2 leagues and three leagues, and in some other 4 leagues; but the narrowest place hath a league over.

The 24th of August we arrived at an island in the Straits, where we found great store of fowl which could not fly, of the bigness of geese; whereof we killed in less than one day 3,000, and victualled ourselves throughly therewith.

The 6th day of September we entered the South Sea at the cape or head shore. The 7th day we were driven by a great storm from the entering into the South Sea 200 leagues and odd in longitude, and one degree to the southward of the Strait; in which height, and so many leagues to the westward, the 15th day of September fell out the eclipse of the moon at the hour of six of the clock at night. But neither did the ecliptical conflict of the moon impair our state, nor her clearing again amend us a whit; but the accustomed eclipse of the sea continued in his force, we being darkened more than the moon sevenfold.

From the bay which we called the Bay of Severing of Friends we were driven back to the southward of the Straits in 57 degrees and a tierce; in which height we came to an anchor among the islands, having there fresh and very good water, with herbs of singular virtue. Not far from hence we entered another bay, where we found people, both men and women, in their canoes naked, and ranging from one island to another to seek their meat; who entered traffic with us for such things as they had. We returning hence northward again, found the 3rd of October three islands, in one of which was such plenty of birds as is scant credible to report. The 8th day of October we lost sight of one of our consorts, wherein Master Winter was; who, as then we supposed, was put by a storm into the Straits again, which at our return home we found to be true, and he not perished, as some of our company feared. Thus being come into the height of the Straits again, we ran, supposing the coast of Chile to lie as the general maps have described it, namely north-west; which we found to lie and trend to the north-east and eastwards. Whereby it appeareth that this part of Chile hath not been truly hitherto discovered, or at least not truly reported, for the space of 12 degrees at the least; being set down either of purpose to deceive, or of ignorant conjecture.

We continuing our course, fell the 29th of November with an island called La Mocha, where we cast anchor; and our General, hoisting out our boat, went with ten of our company to shore, where we found people whom the cruel and extreme dealings of the Spaniards have forced, for their own safety and liberty, to flee from the main, and to fortify themselves in this island. We being on land, the people came down to us to the water side with show of great courtesy, bringing to us potatoes, roots, and two very fat sheep, which our General received, and gave them other things for them, and had promise to have water there. But the next day repairing again to shore, and sending two men aland with barrels to fill water, the people taking them for Spaniards (to whom they use to show no favour if they take them) laid violent hands on them, and, as we think, slew them.

Our General seeing this, stayed here no longer, but weighed anchor, and set sail towards the coast of Chile. And drawing towards it, we met near to the shore an Indian in a canoe, who thinking us to have been Spaniards, came to us and told us, that at a place called Santiago there was a great Spanish ship laden from the kingdom of Peru; for which good news our General gave him divers trifles whereof he was glad, and went along with us and brought us to the place, which is called the port of Valparaiso.

When we came thither we found, indeed, the ship riding at anchor, having in her eight Spaniards and three negroes; who, thinking us to have been Spaniards, and their friends, welcomed us with a drum, and made ready a *botija* of wine of Chile to drink to us. But as soon as we were entered, one of our company called Thomas Moone began to lay about him, and struck one of the Spaniards, and said unto him, *Abaxo, perro!* that is in English, "Go down, dog!" One of these Spaniards, seeing persons of that quality in those seas, all to-crossed and blessed himself. But, to be short, we stowed them under hatches, all save one Spaniard, who suddenly and desperately leapt overboard into the sea, and swam ashore to the town of Santiago, to give them warning of our arrival.

They of the town, being not above 9 households, presently fled away and abandoned the town. Our General manned his boat and the Spanish ship's boat, and went to the town; and, being come to it, we rifled it, and came to a small chapel, which we entered, and found therein a silver chalice, two cruets, and one altar-cloth, the spoil whereof our General gave to Master Fletcher, his minister. We found also in this town a warehouse stored with wine of Chile and many boards of cedar-wood; all which wine we brought away with us, and certain of the boards to burn for firewood. And so, being come aboard, we departed the haven, having first set all the Spaniards on land, saving one John Griego, a Greek born, whom our General carried with him as pilot to bring him into the haven of Lima.

When we were at sea our General rifled the ship, and found in her good store of the wine of Chile, and 25,000 pesos of very pure and fine gold of Valdivia, amounting in value to 37,000 ducats of Spanish money, and above. So, going on our course, we arrived next at a place called Coquimbo, where our General sent 14 of his men on land to fetch water. But they were espied by the Spaniards, who came with 300 horsemen and 200 footmen, and slew one of our men with a piece. The rest came aboard in safety, and the Spaniards departed. We went on shore again and buried our man, and the Spaniards came down again with a flag of truce; but we set sail, and would not trust them.

From hence we went to a certain port called Tarapaca; where, being landed, we found by the sea side a Spaniard lying asleep, who had lying by him 13 bars of silver, which weighed 4,000 ducats Spanish. We took the silver and left the man. Not far from hence, going on land for fresh water, we met with a Spaniard and an Indian boy driving 8 llamas or sheep of Peru, which are as big as asses; every of which sheep had on his back 2 bags of leather, each bag containing 50 lb. weight of fine silver. So that, bringing both the sheep and their burthen to the ships, we found in all the bags 8 hundredweight of silver.

Herehence we sailed to a place called Arica; and, being entered the port, we found there three small barks, which we rifled, and found in one of them 57 wedges of silver, each of them weighing about 20 lb. weight, and every of these wedges were of the fashion and bigness of a brickbat. In all these 3 barks we found not one person. For they, mistrusting no strangers, were all gone aland to the town, which consisteth of about twenty houses, which we would have ransacked if our company had been better and more in number. But our General, contented with the spoil of the ships, left the town and put off again to sea, and set sail for Lima, and, by the way, met with a small bark, which he boarded, and found in her good store of linen cloth, whereof taking some quantity, he let her go.

To Lima we came the 13th day of February; and, being entered the haven, we found there about twelve sail of ships lying fast moored at an anchor, having all their sails carried on shore; for the masters and merchants were here most secure, having never been assaulted by enemies, and at this time feared the approach of none such as we were. Our General rifled these ships, and found in one of them a chest full of riyals of plate, and good store of silks and linen cloth; and took the chest into his own ship, and good store of the silks and linen. In which ship he had news of another ship called the *Cacafuego*, which was gone towards Paita, and that the same ship was laden with treasure. Whereupon we stayed no longer here, but, cutting all the cables of the ships in the haven, we let them drive whither they would either to sea or to the shore; and with all speed we followed the *Cacafuego* toward Paita, thinking there to have found her. But before we arrived there she was gone from thence towards Panama; whom our General still pursued, and by the way met with a bark laden with ropes and tackle for ships, which he boarded and searched, and found in her 80 lb weight of gold, and a crucifix of gold with goodly great emeralds set in it, which he took, and some of the cordage also for his own ship.

From hence we departed, still following the *Cacafuego*; and our General promised our company that whosoever could first descry her should have his chain of gold for his good news. It fortuned that John Drake, going up into the top, descried her about three of the clock. And about six of the clock we came to her and boarded her, and shot at her three pieces of ordnance, and struck down her mizen; and, being entered, we found in her great riches, as jewels and precious stones, thirteen chests full of riyals of plate, fourscore pound weight of gold, and six-and-twenty ton of silver. The place where we took this prize was called Cape de San Francisco, about 150 leagues from Panama.

The pilot's name of this ship was Francisco; and amongst other plate that our General found in this ship he found two very fair gilt bowls of silver, which were the pilot's. To whom our General said, "Señor Pilot, you have here two silver cups, but I must needs have one of them", which the pilot, because he could not otherwise choose, yielded unto, and gave the other to the steward of our General's ships. When this pilot departed from us, his boy said thus unto our General; "Captain, our ship shall be called no more the *Cacafuego*, but the *Cacaplata*, and your ship shall be called the *Cacafuego*." Which pretty speech of the pilot's boy ministered matter of laughter to us, both then and long after.

When our General had done what he would with this *Cacafuego*, he cast her off, and we went on our course still towards the west; and not long after met with a ship laden with linen cloth and fine China dishes of white earth, and great store of China silks, of all which things we took as we listed. The owner himself of this ship was in her, who was a Spanish gentleman from whom our General took a falcon of gold with a great emerald in the breast thereof; and the pilot of the ship he took also with him, and so cast the ship off.

This pilot brought us to the haven of Guatulco, the town whereof, as he told us, had but 17 Spaniards in it. As soon as we were entered this haven, we landed, and went presently to the town, and to the town-house where we found a judge sitting in judgment, being associate with three other officers, upon three negroes that had conspired the burning of the town. Both which judges and prisoners we took, and brought them a-shipboard, and caused the chief judge to write his letter to the town to command all the townsmen to avoid, that we might safely water there. Which being done, and they departed, we ransacked the town; and in one house we found a pot, of the quantity of a bushel, full of riyals of plate, which we brought to our ship. And here one Thomas Moone, one of our company, took a Spanish gentleman as he was flying out of the town; and, searching him, he found a chain of gold about him, and other jewels, which he took, and so let him go.

At this place our General, among other Spaniards, set ashore his Portugal pilot which he took at the islands of Cape Verde out of a ship of St Mary port, of Portugal. And having set them ashore we departed hence, and sailed to the island of Cano, where our General landed, and brought to shore his own ship, and discharged her, mended and graved her, and furnished our ship with water and wood sufficiently.

And while we were here we espied a ship and set sail after her, and took her, and found in her two pilots and a Spanish governor going for the islands of the Philippines. We searched the ship, and took some of her merchandises, and so let her go. Our General at this place and time, thinking himself, both in respect of his private injuries received from the Spaniards, as also of their contempts and indignities offered to our country and prince in general, sufficiently satisfied and revenged; and supposing that Her Majesty at his return would rest contented with this service, purposed to continue no longer upon the Spanish coasts, but began to consider and to consult of the best way for his country.

He thought it not good to return by the Straits, for two special causes: the one, lest the Spaniards should there wait and attend for him in great number and strength, whose hands he, being left but one ship, could not possibly escape. The other cause was the dangerous situation of the mouth of the Straits in the South Sea, where continual storms reigning and blustering, as he found by experience, besides the shoals and sands upon the coast, he thought it not a good course to adventure that way. He resolved, therefore, to avoid these hazards, to go forward to the islands of the Moluccas, and therehence to sail the course of the Portugals by the Cape of Buena Esperanza. Upon this resolution he began to think of his best way to the Moluccas, and finding himself, where he now was, becalmed, he saw that of necessity he must be forced to take a Spanish course; namely, to sail somewhat northerly to get a wind. We therefore set sail, and sailed 600 leagues at the least for a good wind; and thus much we sailed from the 16th of April till the 3rd of June.

The 5th day of June, being in 43 degrees towards the pole arctic, we found the air so cold that our men, being grievously pinched with the same, complained of the extremity thereof; and the further we went, the more the cold increased upon us. Whereupon we thought it best for that time to seek the land, and did so, finding it not mountainous, but low plain land, till we came within 38 degrees towards the line. In which height it pleased God to send us into a fair and good bay, with a good wind to enter the same. In this bay we anchored; and the people of the country, having their houses close by the water's side, showed themselves unto us, and sent a present to our General. When they came unto us, they greatly wondered at the things that we brought. But our General, according to his natural and accustomed humanity, courteously entreated them, and liberally bestowed on them necessary things to cover their nakedness; whereupon they supposed us to be gods, and would not be persuaded to the contrary. The presents which they sent to our General were feathers, and cauls of net-work.

Their houses are digged round about with earth, and have from the outermost brims of the circle clefts of wood set upon them, joining close together at the top like a spire steeple, which by reason of that closeness are very warm. Their beds is the ground with rushes strewed on it; and lying about the house, have the fire in the midst. The men go naked; the women take bulrushes, and comb them after the manner of hemp, and thereof make their loose garments, which being knit about their middles, hang down about their hips, having also about their shoulders a skin of deer with the hair upon it. These women are very obedient and serviceable to their husbands.

After they were departed from us, they came and visited us the second time, and brought with them feathers and bags of tobacco for presents. And when they came to the top of the hill, at the bottom whereof we had pitched our tents, they stayed themselves; where one appointed for speaker wearied himself with making a long oration, which done, they left their bows upon the hill, and came down with their presents. In the meantime the women, remaining upon the hill, tormented themselves lamentably, tearing their flesh from their cheeks, whereby we perceived that they were about a sacrifice. In the meantime our General with his company went to prayer, and to reading of the Scriptures, at which exercise they were attentive, and seemed greatly to be affected with it; but when they were come unto us, they restored again unto us those things which before we bestowed upon them.

The news of our being there being spread through the country, the people that inhabited round about came down, and amongst them the king himself, a man of a goodly stature and comely personage, with many other tall and warlike men; before whose coming were sent two ambassadors to our General, to signify that their king was coming, in doing of which message their speech was continued about half an hour. This ended, they by signs requested our General to send something by their hand to their king, as a token that his coming might be in peace. Wherein our General having satisfied them, they returned with glad tidings to their king, who marched to us with a princely majesty, the people crying continually after their manner; and as they drew near unto us, so did they strive to behave themselves in their actions with comeliness.

In the fore-front was a man of a goodly personage, who bore the sceptre or mace before the king, whereupon hanged two crowns, a less and a bigger, with three chains of a marvellous length. The crowns were made of knit work, wrought artificially with feathers of divers colours. The chains were made of a bony substance, and few be the persons among them that are admitted to wear them; and of that number also the persons are stinted, as some ten, some 12, etc. Next unto him which bore the sceptre was the king himself, with his guard about his person clad with coney skins, and other skins. After them followed the naked common sort of people, every one having his face painted, some with white, some with black, and other colours, and having in their hands one thing or another for a present, not so much as their children but they also brought their presents.

In the meantime our General gathered his men together, and marched within his fenced place, making against their approaching a very warlike show. They being trooped together in their order, and a general salutation being made, there was presently a general silence. Then he that bore the sceptre before the king, being informed by another whom they assigned to that office, with a manly and lofty voice proclaimed that which the other spoke to him in secret, continuing half an hour. Which ended, and a general Amen, as it were, given, the king with the whole number of men and women, the children excepted, came down without any weapon; who, descending to the foot of the hill, set themselves in order.

In coming towards our bulwarks and tents, the sceptre-bearer began a song, observing his measures in a dance, and that with a stately countenance; whom the king with his guard, and every degree of persons, following, did in like manner sing and dance, saving only the women, which danced and kept silence. The General permitted them to enter within our bulwark, where they continued their song and dance a reasonable time. When they had satisfied themselves, they made signs to our General to sit down; to whom the king and divers other made several orations, or rather supplications, that he would take their province and kingdom into his hand, and become their king, making signs that they would resign unto him their right and title of the whole land, and become his subjects. In which, to persuade us the better, the king and the rest, with one consent, and with great reverence, joyfully singing a song, did set the crown upon his head, enriched his neck with all their chains, and offered unto him many other things, honouring him by the name of *Hioh*, adding thereunto, as it seemed, a sign of triumph; which thing our General thought not meet to reject, because he knew not what honour and profit it might be to our country. Wherefore, in the name and to the use of Her Majesty, he took the sceptre, crown, and dignity of the said country into his hands, wishing that the riches and treasure thereof might so conveniently be transported to the enriching of her kingdom at home, as it aboundeth in the same.

The common sort of people, leaving the king and his guard with our General, scattered themselves together with their sacrifices among our people, taking a diligent view of every person: and such as pleased their fancy (which were the youngest), they enclosing them about offered their sacrifices unto them with lamentable weeping, scratching and tearing their flesh from their faces with their nails, whereof issued abundance of blood. But we used signs to them of disliking this, and stayed their hands from force, and directed them upwards to the living God, whom only they ought to worship. They showed unto us their wounds, and craved help of them at our hands; whereupon we gave them lotions, plasters, and ointments agreeing to the state of their griefs, beseeching God to cure their diseases. Every third day they brought their sacrifices unto us, until they understood our meaning, that we had no pleasure in them; yet they could not be long absent from us, but daily frequented our company to the hour of our departure, which departure seemed so grievous unto them, that their joy was turned into sorrow. They entreated us that being absent we would remember them, and by stealth provided a sacrifice, which we misliked.

Our necessary business being ended, our General with his company travelled up into the country to their villages, where we found herds of deer by 1000 in a company, being most large, and fat of body. We found the whole country to be a warren of a strange kind of coneys;

their bodies in bigness as be the Barbary coneys, their heads as the heads of ours, the feet of a want, and the tail of a rat, being of great length. Under her chin is on either side a bag, into the which she gathereth her meat, when she hath filled her belly abroad. The people eat their bodies, and make great account of their skins, for their king's coat was made of them.

Our General called this country Nova Albion, and that for two causes: the one in respect of the white banks and cliffs, which lie towards the sea, and the other, because it might have some affinity with our country in name, which sometime was so called. There is no part of earth here to be taken up, wherein there is not some probable show of gold or silver.

At our departure hence our General set up a monument of our being there, as also of Her Majesty's right and title to the same: namely a plate, nailed upon a fair great post, whereupon was engraved Her Majesty's name, the day and year of our arrival there, with the free giving up of the province and people into Her Majesty's hands, together with Her Highness' picture and arms, in a piece of six pence of current English money, under the plate, whereunder was also written the name of our General.

It seemeth that the Spaniards hitherto had never been in this part of the country, neither did ever discover the land by many degrees to the southwards of this place.

After we had set sail from hence, we continued without sight of land till the 13th day of October following, which day in the morning we fell with certain islands 8 degrees to the northward of the line, from which islands came a great number of canoes, having in some of them 4, in some 6, and in some also 14 men, bringing with them cocos and other fruits. Their canoes were hollow within, and cut with great art and cunning, being very smooth within and without, and bearing a gloss, as if it were a horn daintily burnished, having a prow and a stern of one sort, yielding inward circle-wise, being of a great height, and full of certain white shells for a bravery; and on each side of them lie out two pieces of timber about a yard and a half long, more or less, according to the smallness or bigness of the boat.

These people have the nether part of their ears cut into a round circle, hanging down very low upon their cheeks, whereon they hang things of a reasonable weight. The nails of their hands are an inch long, their teeth are as black as pitch, and they renew them often, by eating of a herb with a kind of powder, which they always carry about them in a cane for the same purpose.

Leaving this island the night after we fell with it, the 18th of October we lighted upon divers others, some whereof made a great show of inhabitants. We continued our course by the islands of Tagulada, Zelon, and Zewarra, being friends to the Portugals, the first whereof hath growing in it great store of cinnamon. The 14th of November we fell in with the islands of Moluccas. Which day at night (having directed our course to run with Tidore) in coasting along the island of Motir, belonging to the King of Ternate, his deputy or vice-king, seeing us at sea, came with his canoe to us without all fear, and came aboard; and after some conference with our General willed him in any wise to run in with Ternate, and not with Tidore, assuring him that the King would be glad of his coming, and would be ready to do what he would require, for which purpose he himself would that night be with the King, and tell him the news. With whom if he once dealt, we should find that as he was a king, so his word should stand; adding further, that if he went to Tidore before he came to Ternate, the King would have nothing to do with us, because he held the Portugal as his enemy. Whereupon our General resolved to run with Ternate, where the next morning early we came to anchor; at which time our General sent a messenger to the King, with a velvet cloak for a present and token of his coming to be in peace, and that he required nothing but traffic and exchange of merchandise, whereof he had good store, in such things as he wanted.

In the meantime the vice-king had been with the King according to his promise, signifying unto him what good things he might receive from us by traffic. Whereby the King was moved with great liking towards us, and sent to our General with special message, that he should have what things he needed, and would require with peace and friendship; and moreover that he would yield himself and the right of his island to be at the pleasure and commandment of so famous a prince as we served. In token whereof he sent to our General a signet, and within short time after came in his own person, with boats and canoes to our ship, to bring her into a better and safer road than she was in at present.

In the meantime our General's messenger, being come to the Court, was met by certain noble personages with great solemnity, and brought to the King, at whose hands he was most friendly and graciously entertained. The King, purposing to come to our ship, sent before 4 great and large canoes, in every one whereof were certain of his greatest states that were about him, attired in white lawn of cloth of Calicut, having over their heads, from the one end of the canoe to the other, a covering of thin perfumed mats, borne up with a frame made of reeds for the same use, under which every one did sit in his order according to his dignity, to keep him from the heat of the sun; divers of whom, being of good age and gravity, did make an ancient and fatherly show. There were also divers young and comely men attired in white, as were the others; the rest were soldiers, which stood in comely order round about on both sides. Without whom sat the rowers in certain galleries; which being three on a side all along the canoes, did lie off from the side thereof three or four yards, one being orderly built lower than another, in every of which galleries were the number of 4 score rowers. These canoes were furnished with warlike munition, every man for the most part having his sword and target, with his dagger, beside other weapons, as lances, calivers, darts, bows and arrows; also every canoc had a small cast base mounted at the least one full yard upon a stock set upright.

Thus coming near our ship, in order, they rowed about us one after another, and passing by, did their homage with great solemnity; the great personages beginning with great gravity and fatherly countenances, signifying that the King had sent them to conduct our ship into a better road. Soon after the King himself repaired, accompanied with 6 grave and ancient persons, who did their obeisance with marvellous humility. The King was a man of tall stature, and seemed to be much delighted with the sound of our music; to whom, as also to his nobility, our General gave presents, wherewith they were passing well contented.

At length the King craved leave of our General to depart, promising the next day to come aboard, and in the meantime to send us such victuals as were necessary for our provision. So that the same night we received of them meal, which they call *sagu*, made of the tops of certain trees, tasting in the mouth like sour curds, but melteth like sugar, whereof they make certain cakes, which may be kept the space of ten years, and yet then good to be eaten. We had of them store of rice, hens, unperfect and liquid sugar, sugar-canes, and a fruit which they call *figu*, with store of cloves.

The King having promised to come aboard, broke his promise, but sent his brother to make his excuse, and to entreat our General to come on shore, offering himself pawn aboard for his safe return. Whereunto our General consented not, upon mislike conceived of the breach of his promise; the whole company also utterly refusing it. But to satisfy him, our General sent certain of his gentlemen to the Court, to accompany the King's brother, reserving the vice-king for their safe return. They were received of another brother of the King's, and other states, and were conducted with great honour to the castle. The place that they were brought unto was a large and fair house, where were at least 1000 persons assembled.

The King being yet absent, there sat in their places 60 grave personages, all which were said to be of the King's council. There were besides 4 grave persons, apparelled all in red, down to the ground, and attired on their heads like the Turks; and these were said to be Romans and liegers there to keep continual traffic with the people of Ternate. There were also two Turks liegers in this place, and one Italian. The King at last came in guarded with 12 lances, covered over with a rich canopy with embossed gold. Our men, accompanied with one of their captains called Moro, rising to meet him, he graciously did welcome and entertain them. He was attired after the manner of the country, but more sumptuously than the rest. From his waist down to the ground was all cloth of gold, and the same very rich; his legs were bare, but on his feet were a pair of shoes, made of Cordovan skin. In the attire of his head were finely wreathed hooped rings of gold, and about his neck he had a chain of perfect gold, the links whereof were great, and one fold double. On his fingers he had six very fair jewels; and sitting in his chair of state, at his right hand stood a page with a fan in his hand, breathing and gathering the air to the King. The same was in length two foot, and in breadth one foot, set with 8 sapphires richly embroidered, and knit to a staff 3 foot in length, by the which the page did hold and move it. Our gentlemen having delivered their message and received order accordingly, were licensed to depart, being safely conducted back again by one of the King's council.

This island is the chief of all the islands of Moluccas, and the king hereof is king of 70 islands besides. The King with his people are Moors in religion, observing certain new moons, with fastings; during which fasts they neither eat nor drink in the day, but in the night.

After that our gentlemen were returned, and that we had here by the favour of the King received all necessary things that the place could yield us, our General considering the great distance, and how far he was yet off from his country, thought it not best here to linger the time any longer, but weighing his anchors, set out of the island, and sailed to a certain little island to the southwards of Celebes, where we graved our ship, and continued there, in that and other businesses, 26 days. This island is throughly grown with wood of a large and high growth, very straight, and without boughs save only in the head or top, whose leaves are not much differing from our broom in England. Amongst these trees night by night, through the whole land, did show themselves an infinite swarm of fiery worms flying in the air, whose bodies, being no bigger than our common English flies, make such a show and light as if every twig or tree had been a burning candle. In this place breedeth also wonderful store of bats, as big as large hens. Of cray-fishes also here wanted no plenty, and they of exceeding bigness, one whereof was sufficient for four hungry stomachs at a dinner, being also very good and restoring meat, whereof we had experience: and they dig themselves holes in the earth like coneys.

When we had ended our business here we weighed, and set sail to run for the Moluccas. But having at that time a bad wind, and being amongst the islands, with much difficulty we recovered to the northward of the island of Celebes; where by reason of contrary winds not able to continue our course to run westwards, we were enforced to alter the same to the southward again, finding that course also to be very hard and dangerous for us, by reason of infinite shoals which lie off and among the islands; whereof we had too much trial, to the hazard and danger of our ship and lives. For, of all other days, upon the 9th of January, in the year 1579 we ran suddenly upon a rock, where we stuck fast from 8 of the clock at night till 4 of the clock in the afternoon the next day, being indeed out of all hope to escape the danger. But our General, as he had always hitherto showed himself courageous and of a good confidence in the mercy and protection of God, so now he continued in the same, and lest he should seem to perish wilfully, both he and we did our best endeavour to save ourselves; which it pleased God so to bless, that in the end we cleared ourselves most happily of the danger.

We lighted our ship upon the rocks of 3 ton of cloves, 8 pieces of ordnance, and certain meal and beans; and then the wind, as it were in a moment by the special grace of God, changing from the starboard to the larboard of the ship, we hoisted our sails, and the happy gale drove our ship off the rock into the sea again, to the no little comfort of all our hearts, for which we gave God such praise and thanks as so great a benefit required.

The 8th of February following, we fell with the fruitful island of Barateve, having in the mean time suffered many dangers by winds and shoals. The people of this island are comely in body and stature, and of a civil behaviour, just in dealing, and courteous to strangers; whereof we had the experience sundry ways, they being most glad of our presence, and very ready to relieve our wants in those things which their country did yield. The men go naked, saving their heads and privities, every man having something or other hanging at their ears. Their women are covered from the middle down to the foot, wearing a great number of bracelets upon their arms; for some had 8 upon each arm, being made some of bone, some of horn, and some of brass, the lightest whereof, by our estimation, weighed two ounces apiece.

With this people linen-cloth is good merchandise, and of good request: whereof they make rolls for their heads, and girdles to wear about them. Their island is both rich and fruitful; rich in gold, silver, copper, and sulphur, wherein they seem skilful and expert, not only to try the same, but in working it also artificially into any form and fashion that pleaseth them. Their fruits be divers and plentiful; as nutmegs, ginger, long pepper, lemons, cucumbers, cocos, *figu*, *sagu*, with divers other sorts. And among all the rest we had one fruit, in bigness, form and husk, like a bay berry, hard of substance and pleasant of taste, which being sodden becometh soft, and is a most good and wholesome victual; whereof we took reasonable store, as we did also of the other fruits and spices. So that to confess a truth, since the time that we first set out of our own country of England, we happened upon no place, Ternate only excepted, wherein we found more comforts and better means of refreshing.

At our departure from Barateve, we set our course for Java Major;

where arriving, we found great courtesy, and honourable entertainment. This island is governed by five kings, whom they call Rajah; as Rajah Donaw, and Rajah Mang Bange, and Rajah Cabuccapollo, which live as having one spirit and one mind. Of these five we had four a-shipboard at once, and two or three often. They are wonderfully delighted in coloured clothes, as red and green; their upper parts of their bodies are naked, save their heads, whereupon they wear a Turkish roll as do the Moluccans. From the middle downward they wear a *pintado* of silk, trailing upon the ground, in colour as they best like.

The Moluccans hate that their women should be seen of strangers; but these offer them of high courtesy, yea, the kings themselves. The people are of goodly stature, and warlike, well provided of swords and targets, with daggers, all being of their own work, and most artificially done, both in tempering their metal, as also in the form; whereof we bought reasonable store.

They have a house in every village for their common assembly; every day they meet twice, men, women, and children, bringing with them such victuals as they think good, some fruits, some rice boiled, some hens roasted, some *sagu*, having a table made 3 foot from the ground, whereon they set their meat, that every person sitting at the table may eat, one rejoicing in the company of another.

They boil their rice in an earthen pot, made in form of a sugar loaf, being full of holes, as our pots which we water our gardens withal, and it is open at the great end, wherein they put their rice dry, without any moisture. In the mean time they have ready another great earthen pot, set fast in a furnace, boiling full of water, whereinto they put their pot with rice, by such measure that they swelling become soft at the first and, by their swelling stopping the holes of the pot, admit no more water to enter, but the more they are boiled, the harder and more firm substance they become. So that in the end they are a firm and good bread, of the which with oil, butter, sugar, and other spices, they make divers sorts of meats very pleasant of taste, and nourishing to nature.

The French pox is here very common to all, and they help themselves, sitting naked from ten to two in the sun, whereby the venomous humour is drawn out.

Not long before our departure they told us that not far off there were such great ships as ours, wishing us to beware; upon this our Captain would stay no longer. From Java Major we sailed for the Cape of Good Hope, which was the first land we fell withal; neither did we touch with it, or any other land, until we came to Sierra Leone, upon the coast of Guinea; notwithstanding we ran hard aboard the cape, finding the report of the Portugals to be most false, who affirm that it is the most dangerous cape of the world, never without intolerable storms and present danger to travellers which come near the same. This cape is a

16 Francis Drake (1581).

most stately thing, and the fairest cape we saw in the whole circumference of the earth, and we passed by it the 18th of June.

From thence we continued our course to Sierra Leone, on the coast of Guinea, where we arrived the 22nd of July, and found necessary provisions, great store of elephants, oysters upon trees of one kind, spawning and increasing infinitely, the oyster suffering no bud to grow. We departed thence the 24th day.

We arrived in England the third of November, 1580, being the third year of our departure.

The names of the kings or princes of Java at the time of our Englishmen's being there:

> Rajah Donaw   Rajah Tymbanton
> Rajah Rabacapala   Rajah Mawgbange
> Rajah Bacabatra   Rajah Patimara

Certain words of the natural language of Java, learned and observed by our men there:

Sabuck, silk	*Larnike*, drink
Sagu, bread of the country	*Paree*, rice in the husk
Braas, sodden rice	*Bebeck*, a duck
Calapa, cocos	*Anjange*, a deer
Cricke, a dagger	*Popran*, ointment
Catcha, a looking-glass	*Coar*, the head
Arbo, an ox	*Endam*, rain
Vados, a goat	*Jonge*, a ship
Cabo, gold	*Chay*, the sea
Gardange, a plantain	*Sapelo*, ten in number
Hiam, a hen	*Dopolo*, twenty
Sevit, linen cloth	*Treda*, no
Doduck, blue cloth	*Lau*, understand you
Totopps, one of their caps	*Bayer*, go
Gula, black sugar	*Adadizano*, I will fetch it
Tadon, a woman	*Suda*, enough

The admirable and prosperous voyage of the worshipful Master Thomas Candish, of Trimley in the county of Suffolk, Esquire, into the South Sea, and from thence round about the circumference of the whole earth, begun in the year of Our Lord 1586 and finished 1588. Written by Master Francis Pretty, lately of Eye in Suffolk, a gentleman employed in the same action.

WE departed out of Plymouth on Thursday, the 21st of July 1586, with 3 sails, to wit, the *Desire*, a ship of 120 tons, the *Content*, of 60 tons, and the *Hugh Gallant*, a bark of 40 tons, in which small fleet were 123 persons of all sorts, with all kind of furniture and victuals sufficient for the space of two years, at the charges of the worshipful Master Thomas Cavendish of Trimley in the county of Suffolk, Esquire, being our General. On Tuesday, the 26th of the same month, we were 45 leagues from Cape Finisterre, where we met with 5 sails of Biscayans coming from the Grand Bay in Newfoundland, as we supposed, which our admiral shot at, and fought with them 3 hours, but we took none of them by reason the night grew on. The first of August we came in sight of Fuerteventura, one of the Isles of the Canaries, about ten of the clock in the morning.

On Sunday, being the 7th of August, we were gotten as high as Rio do Ouro, on the coast of Barbary. On Monday, the 19th, we fell with

Cape Blanco; but the wind blew so much at the north, that we could not get up where the canters do use to ride and fish; therefore we lay off 6 hours west-south-west, because of the sand which lieth off the Cape south-west and by south. The 15th day of the same month we were in the height of Cape Verde, by estimation 50 leagues off the same. The 18th, Sierra Leone did bear east of us, being 45 leagues from us; and the same day the wind shifted to the north-west, so that by the 20th day of the said month we were in 6 degrees and a half to the northward from the equinoctial line. The 23rd we put room for Sierra Leone, and the 25th day we fell with the point on the south side of Sierra Leone, which Master Brewer knew very well, and went in before with the *Content*, which was vice-admiral; and we had no less than 5 fathoms water when we had least, and had for 14 leagues in south-west all the way running into the harbour of Sierra Leone, 16, 14, 12, 10, and 8 fathoms of water.

The 26th of the said month we put into the harbour, and in going in we had (by the southermost point, when we had least) 5 fathoms water fair by the rock as it lieth at the said point; and after we came 2 or 3 cables' lengths within the said rock, we never had less than 10 fathoms, until we came up to the road, which is about a league from the point, borrowing always on the south side until you come up to the watering-place, in which bay is the best road; but you must ride far into the bay because there run marvellous great tides in the offing, and it floweth into the road next of anything at a south-east and by east moon. It is out of England to this place 930 leagues, which we ran from the 21st of July to the 26th of this month of August.

On Saturday, being the 27th day, there came two negroes aboard our admiral from the shore, and made signs unto our General that there was a Portugal ship up within the harbour: so the *Hugh Gallant*, being the rear-admiral, went up 3 or 4 leagues, but for want of a pilot they sought no farther; for the harbour runneth 3 or 4 leagues up more, and is of a marvellous breadth and very dangerous, as we learned afterwards by a Portugal.

On Sunday the 28th, the General sent some of his company on shore, and there as they played and danced all the forenoon among the negroes, to the end to have heard some good news of the Portugal ship, toward their coming aboard they espied a Portugal which lay hid among the bushes, whom we took and brought away with us the same night, and he told us it was very dangerous going-up with our boats for to seek the ship that was at the town. Whereupon we went not to seek her, because we knew he told us the truth; for we bound him and made him fast, and so examined him. Also he told us that his ship was there cast away, and that there were two more of his company among the negroes. The Portugal's name was Emmanuel, and was by his occupation a caulker, belonging to the Port of Portugal.

On Monday morning, being the 29th day, our General landed with 70 men, or thereabouts, and went up to their town, where we burnt 2 or 3 houses, and took what spoil we would, which was but little; but all the people fled. And in our retiring aboard in a very little plain at their town's end they shot their arrows at us out of the woods, and hurt 3 or 4 of our men. Their arrows were poisoned, but yet none of our men miscarried at that time, thanked be God. Their town is marvellous artificially built with mud walls, and built round, with their yards paled in and kept very clean as well in their streets as in their houses. These negroes use good obedience to their king, as one of our men said, which was with them in pawn for the negroes which came first. There were in their town by estimation about one hundred houses.

The first of September there went many of our men on shore at the watering-place, and did wash shirts very quietly all the day, and the second day they went again, and the negroes were in ambush round about the place; and the carpenter of the admiral going into the wood to do some special business, espied them by good fortune. But the negroes rushed out upon our men so suddenly that in retiring to our boats many of them were hurt; among whom one William Pickman, a soldier, was shot into the thigh, who plucking the arrow out broke it, and left the head behind, and he told the surgeons that he plucked out all the arrow, because he would not have them lance his thigh; where-upon the poison wrought so that night that he was marvellously swollen, and the next morning he died, the piece of the arrow with the poison being plucked out of his thigh.

The third day of the said month divers of our fleet went up 4 miles within the harbour with our boat, and caught great store of fish, and went on shore and took lemons from the trees, and coming aboard again saw two buffs.

The 6th day we departed from Sierra Leone, and went out of the harbour, and stayed one tide 3 leagues from the point of the mouth of the harbour in 6 fathoms, and it floweth south-south-west. On Wednesday, being the 7th of the same month, we departed from one of the islands of Cape Verde, alias the islands of Madrabumba, which is 10 leagues distant from the point of Sierra Leone, and about five of the clock the same night we anchored 2 miles off the island in 6 fathoms water, and landed the same night, and found plantains only upon the island. The 8th day one of our boats went out and sounded round about the island, and they passed through a sound at the west end of the island, where they found 5 fathoms round about the island until they came into the very gut of the sound, and then for a cast or two they had but two fathoms, and presently after 6 fathoms, and so deeper and deeper. And at the east end of the island there was a town, where negroes do use at sometimes, as we perceived by their provision.

There is no fresh water on all the south side, as we could perceive, but on the north side three or four very good places of fresh water; and all the whole island is a wood, save certain little places where their houses stand, which are environed round about with plantain trees, whereof the fruit is excellent meat. This place is subject marvellous much to thunder, rain, and lightning in this month. I think the reason is, because the sun is so near the line equinoctial. On Saturday, the tenth, we departed from the said island, about 3 of the clock in the afternoon, the wind being at the south-west.

The last of October, running west-south-west, about 24 leagues from Cape Frio in Brazil, we fell with a great mountain which had a high round knob on the top of it, standing from it like a town, with two little islands from it.

The first of November we went in between the island of St Sebastian and the main land, and had our things on shore, and set up a forge, and had our cask on shore; our coopers made hoops, and so we remained there until the 23rd day of the same month in which time we fitted our things, built our pinnace, and filled our fresh water. And while our pinnace was in building, there came a canoe from the River of Janeiro, meaning to go to Saint Vincent, wherein were six naked slaves of the country people, which did row the canoe, and one Portugal. And the Portugal knew Christopher Hare, Master of the admiral, for that Master Hare had been at Saint Vincent, in the *Minion* of London, in the year 1581; and thinking to have John Whithall, the Englishman which dwelleth at Saint Vincent, come unto us, which is twenty leagues from this harbour, with some other, thereby to have had some fresh victuals, we suffered the Portugal to go with a letter unto him, who promised to return or send some answer within ten days, for that we told him we were merchants, and would traffic with them; but we never received answer from him any more. And seeing that he came not according to appointment, our business being despatched, we weighed anchor, and set sail from Saint Sebastian on the 23rd of November.

The 16th day of December we fell in with the coast of America in 47 degrees and a tierce, the land bearing west from us about 6 leagues off; from which place we ran along the shore until we came into 48 degrees. It is a steep beach all along. The 17th day of December, in the afternoon, we entered into a harbour, where our admiral went in first, wherefore our General named the said harbour Port Desire; in which harbour is an island or two, where there is wonderful great store of seals, and another island of birds, which are grey gulls. These seals are of a wonderful great bigness, huge, and monstrous of shape, and for the fore-part of their bodies cannot be compared to anything better than to a lion; their head, and neck, and fore-parts of their bodies are full of rough hair; their feet are in manner of a fin, and in form like unto a man's hand; they breed and cast every month, giving their young milk, yet continually get they their living in the sea, and live altogether upon fish. Their young are marvellous good meat, and being boiled or roasted are hardly to be known from lamb or mutton. The old ones be of such bigness and force that it is as much as four men are able to do to kill one of them with great cowl-staves; and he must be beaten down with striking on the head of him, for his body is of that bigness that four men could never kill him, but only on the head. For being shot through the body with an arquebus or a musket, yet he will go his way into the sea and never care for it at the present. Also the fowls that were there were very good meat, and great store of them. They have burrows in the ground like coneys, for they cannot fly. They have nothing but down upon their pinions; they also fish and feed in the sea for their living, and breed on shore.

This harbour is a very good place to trim ships in, and to bring them on ground, and grave them in; for there ebbeth and floweth much water. Therefore we graved and trimmed all our ships there.

The 24th of December, being Christmas Eve, a man and a boy of the rear-admiral went some forty score from our ships unto a very fair green valley at the foot of the mountains, where was a little pit or well which our men had digged and made some two or three days before to get fresh water, for there was none in all the harbour; and this was but brackish. Therefore this man and boy came thither to wash their linen; and being in washing at the said well, there were great store of Indians which were come down, and found the said man and boy in washing. These Indians being divided on each side of the rocks, shot at them with their arrows and hurt them both, but they fled presently, being about fifty or threescore, though our General followed them with but sixteen or twenty men. The man's name which was hurt was John Garge, the boy's name was Lutch. The man was shot clean through the knee, the boy into the shoulder, either of them having very sore wounds. Their arrows are made of little canes, and their heads are of a flint stone, set into the cane very artificially. They seldom or never see any Christians. They are as wild as ever was a buck or any other wild beast; for we followed them, and they ran from us as it had been the wildest thing in the world. We took the measure of one of their feet, and it was 18 inches long. Their use is, when any of them die, to bring him or them to the cliffs by the sea-side, and upon the top of them they bury them, and in their graves are buried with them their bows and arrows, and all their jewels which they have in their life-time, which are fine shells which they find by the sea-side, which they cut and square after an artificial manner; and all is laid under their heads. The grave is made all with great stones of great length and bigness, being set all along full of the dead man's darts which he used when he was living. And they colour both their darts and their graves with a red colour which they use in colouring of themselves.

The 28th of December we departed out of the Port of Desire, and went to an island which lieth 3 leagues to the southward of it; where we trimmed our saved penguins with salt for victual all that and the next day, and departed along the coast south-west and by south. The 30th day we fell with a rock which lieth about 5 leagues from the land, much like unto Eddystone, which lieth off the sound of Plymouth, and we sounded, and had 8 fathoms rocky ground within a mile thereof, the rock bearing west-south-west. We went coasting along south-south-west, and found great store of seals all along the coast. This rock standeth in 48 degrees and a half to the southward of the line.

The 2nd day of January we fell with a very fair white cape, which standeth in 51 degrees, and had 7 fathoms water a league off the land. The third day of the aforesaid month we fell with another great white cape, which standeth in 52 degrees and 45 minutes; from which cape there runneth a low beach about a league to the southward, and this beach reacheth to the opening of the dangerous Strait of Magellan, which is in divers places 5 or 6 leagues wide, and in two several places more narrow. Under this cape we anchored and lost an anchor, for it was a great storm of foul weather, and lasted three days very dangerous. The 6th day we put in for the Straits. The 7th day, between the mouth of the Straits and the narrowest place thereof, we took a Spaniard whose name was Hernando, who was there with 23 Spaniards more, which were all that remained of four hundred which were left there three years before in these Straits of Magellan, all the rest being dead with famine. And the same day we passed through the narrowest of the Straits, where the aforesaid Spaniard shewed us the hull of a small bark, which we judged to be a bark called the *John Thomas*. It is from the mouth of the Straits unto the narrowest of the Straits 14 leagues, and the course lieth west and by north. The mouth of the Straits standeth in 52 degrees. From the narrowest of the Straits unto Penguin Island is 10 leagues, and lieth west-south-west somewhat to the southward, where we anchored the 8th day, and killed and salted great store of penguins for victuals.

The 9th day we departed from Penguin Island, and ran south-south-west to King Philip's City, which the Spaniards had built; which town or city had four forts, and every fort had in it one cast piece, which pieces were buried in the ground. The carriages were standing in their places unburied; we digged for them and had them all. They had contrived their city very well, and seated it in the best place of the Straits for wood and water; they had built up their churches by themselves. They had laws very severe among themselves, for they had erected a gibbet, whereon they had done execution upon some of their company. It seemed unto us that their whole living for a great space was altogether upon mussels and limpets, for there was not anything else to be had, except some deer which came out of the mountains down to the fresh rivers to drink. These Spaniards which were there were only come to fortify the Straits, to the end that no other nation should have passage through into the South Sea, saving only their own; but as it appeared, it was not God's will so to have it. For during the time that they were there, which was two years at the least, they could never have anything to grow or in anywise prosper. And on the other side the Indians oftentimes preyed upon them, until their victuals grew so short (their store being spent which they had brought with them out of Spain, and having no means to renew the same) that they died like dogs in their houses, and in their clothes, wherein we found them still at our coming, until that in the end the town being wonderfully tainted with the smell and the savour of the dead people, the rest which remained alive were driven to bury such things as they had there in their town either for provision or for furniture, and so to forsake the town, and to go along the sea-side, and seek their victuals to preserve them from starving, taking nothing with them but every man his arquebus and his furniture that was able to carry it (for some were not able to carry them for weakness) and so lived for the space of a year and more with roots, leaves, and sometimes a fowl which they might kill with their piece. To conclude, they were determined to have travelled towards the River of Plate, only being left alive twenty-three persons, whereof two were women, which were the remainder of four hundred. In this place we watered and wooded well and quietly. Our General named this town Port Famine; it standeth in 53 degrees by observation to the southward.

The 14th day we departed from this place, and ran south-south-west, and from thence south-west unto Cape Froward, 5 leagues west-south-west, which cape is the southermost part of all the straits, and standeth in the latitude of 54 degrees. From which cape we ran west and by north 5 leagues, and put into a bay or cove on the south side, which we called Mussel Cove, because there were great store of them. We rode therein 6 days, the wind being still westerly.

The 21st day of January we departed from Mussel Cove, and went north-west and by west 10 leagues to a very fair sandy bay on the north side, which our General called Elizabeth Bay, and as we rode there that night, one of our men died which went in the *Hugh Gallant*, whose name was Grey, a carpenter by his occupation, and was buried there in that bay.

The 22nd we departed from Elizabeth Bay in the afternoon, and went about 2 leagues from that place, where there was a fresh water river, where our General went up with the ship-boat about three miles, which river hath very good and pleasant ground about it, and it is low and champaign soil, and so we saw none other ground else in all the straits but that was craggy rocks and monstrous high hills and mountains. In this river are great store of savages, which we saw and had conference with them. They were men-eaters, and fed altogether upon raw flesh and other filthy food; which people had preyed upon some of the Spaniards before spoken of. For they had gotten knives and pieces of rapiers to make darts of. They used all the means they could possibly to have allured us up farther into the river, of purpose to have betrayed us, which being espied by our General, he caused us to shoot at them with our arqucbuscs, whereby we killed many of them. So we sailed from this river to the Channel of Saint Jerome, which is two leagues off.

From the river of Saint Jerome about three or four leagues we ran west unto a cape which is on the north side; and from that cape into the mouth of the Straits the course lieth north-west and by west and north-west. Between which place and the mouth of the Straits to the southward we lay in harbour until the three and twentieth of February, by reason of contrary winds and most vile and filthy foul weather, with such rain and vehement stormy winds, which came down from the mountains and high hills, that they hazarded the best cables and anchors that we had for to hold, which if they had failed we had been in great danger to have been cast away, or at the least famished. For during this time, which was a full month, we fed almost altogether upon mussels, and limpets, and birds, or such as we could get on shore, seeking every day for them, as the fowls of the air do, where they can find food, in continual rainy weather. There is at every mile or two miles' end a harbour on both sides of the land. And there are, between the river of Saint Jerome and the mouth of the Straits going into the South Sea, about 34 leagues by estimation, so that the length of the whole Straits is about 90 leagues. And the said mouth of the Straits standeth in the same height that the entrance standeth in when we pass out of the North Sea, which is about 52 degrees and two tierces to the southward of the line.

The 24th day of February we entered into the South Sea; and on the south side of the going out of the Straits is a fair high cape with a low point adjoining unto it; and on the north side are 4 or 5 islands which lie 6 leagues off the main, and much broken and sunken ground about them. By noon the same day we had brought these islands east of us 5 leagues off, the wind being southerly. The first of March a storm took us at north, which night the ships lost the company of the *Hugh Gallant* being in 49 and a-half, and 45 leagues from the land. This storm continued 3 or 4 days, and for that time we in the *Hugh Gallant,* being separated from the other 2 ships, looked every hour to sink, or bark was so leaky and ourselves so dilvered and weakened with freeing it of water, that we slept not in three days and three nights.

The 15th of March, in the morning, the *Hugh Gallant* came in between the Island of St Mary and the main, where she met with the admiral and the *Content,* which had rid at the island called La Mocha 2 days, which standeth in the southerly latitude of 38 degrees; at which place some of our men went on shore with the vice-admiral's boat, where the Indians fought with them with their bows and arrows, and were marvellous wary of their calivers. These Indians were enemies to the Spaniards, and belonged to a great place called Arauco, and took us for Spaniards, as afterward we learned. This place which is called Arauco is wonderful rich and full of gold-mines, and yet could it not be subdued at any time by the Spaniards, but they always returned with the greatest loss of men. For these Indians are marvellous desperate and careless of their lives to live at their own liberty and freedom.

The 15th day aforesaid, in the afternoon, we weighed anchor and ran under the west side of St Mary Island, where we rode very well in 6 fathoms water and very fair ground all that night. The 16th day our General went on shore himself with 70 or 80 men, everyone with his furniture. There came down to us certain Indians with two which were the principals of the island to welcome us on shore, thinking we had been Spaniards, for it is subdued by them; who brought us up to a place where the Spaniards had erected a church with crosses and altars in it. And there were about this church 2 or 3 storehouses, which were full of wheat and barley ready threshed and made up in cades of straw to the quantity of a bushel of corn in every cade. The wheat and barley was as fair, as clean, and everyway as good as any we have in England. There were also the like cades full of potato roots, which were very good to eat, ready made up in the storehouses for the Spaniards against they should come for their tribute. This island also yieldeth many sorts of fruits, hogs, and hens. These Indians are held in such slavery by them that they dare not eat a hen or a hog themselves. But the Spaniards have made them all in that island Christians. Thus we fitted ourselves here with corn as much as we would have, and as many hogs as we had salt to powder them withal, and great store of hens, with a number of bags of potato roots, and about 500 dried dog-fishes, and Guinea wheat, which is called maize. And, having taken as much as we would have, yet we left marvellous great store behind us. Our General had the two principals of the island aboard our ship, and provided great cheer for them, and made them merry with wine; and they in the end perceiving us to be no Spaniards, made signs, as near as our General could perceive, that if we would go over unto the mainland unto Arauco, that there was much gold, making us signs that we should have great store of riches. But because we could not understand them our General made some haste, and within 2 or three days we furnished ourselves.

The 18th day, in the morning, we departed from this place, and ran all that day north-north-east about 10 leagues, and at night lay with a short sail off and on the coast. The 19th we ran in east-north-east with the land, and bore in with a place called The Conception, where we anchored under an island, and departed the next morning without going on land. The 20th we departed from The Conception, and went into a little bay which was sandy, where we saw fresh water and cattle, but we stayed not there.

The 30th day we came into the Bay of Quintero, which standeth in 33 degrees and 50 minutes. The said day, presently after we were come to an anchor in the bay, there was a neatherd, or one that kept cattle, which lay upon the point of the hill asleep, which, when he awaked and had espied three ships which were come into the bay, before we could get on shore he had caught a horse which was feeding by and rode his way as fast as ever he might; and our General, with 30 shot with him, went on shore. He had not been on land one hour but there came 3 horsemen with bright swords towards us so hard as they might ride, until they came within some twenty or thirty score of us, and so stayed, and would come no nearer unto us. So our General sent unto them a couple of our men with their shot, and one Fernando, which was the Spaniard that we had taken up at the mouth of the Straits, which was one of the 400 that were starved there. But the Spaniards would not suffer our men to come near with their shot, but made signs that one of our men should come alone unto them; so the said Fernando, the Spaniard, went unto them, and our two men stood not far from them. They had great conference, and in the end Fernando came back from them and told our General that he had parleyed with them for some victuals, who had promised as much as we would have. Our General sent him back again with another message and another shot with him; and, being come near unto them, they would not suffer any more than one to approach them; whereupon our men let the Spaniard go unto them alone himself, who, being some good distance from them, they stayed but a small time together but that the said Fernando leaped up behind one of them and rode away with them, for all his deep and damnable oaths which he had made continually to our General and all his company never to forsake him, but to die on his side before he would be false. Our General, seeing how he was dealt withal, filled water all that day with good watch and carried it aboard; and, night being come, he determined the next day to send into the country to find their town, and to have taken the spoil of it, and to have fired it if they could have found it.

The last of March Captain Havers went up into the country with 50 or 60 men with their shot and furniture with them, and we travelled 7 or 8 miles into the land; and as we were marching along we espied a number of herds of cattle, of kine and bullocks, which were wonderful wild. We saw also great store of horses, mares, and colts, which were very wild and unhandled. There is also great store of hares and coneys, and plenty of partridges and other wild fowls. The country is very fruitful, with fair fresh rivers all along full of wild fowl of all sorts. Having travelled so far that we could go no further for the monstrous high mountains, we rested ourselves at a very fair fresh river running in and along fair low meadows at the foot of the mountains, where every man drank of the river and refreshed themselves. Having so done, we returned to our ships the likest way that we thought their town should be. So we travelled all the day long, not seeing any man, but we met with many wild dogs. Yet there were two hundred horsemen abroad that same day by means of the Spaniard which they had taken the day before from us, who had told them that our force was but small, and that we were wonderfully weak; who, though they did espy us that day, yet durst they not give the onset upon us. For we marched along in array, and observed good order, whereby we seemed a great number more than we were, until we came unto our ships that night again.

The next day, being the first of April, 1587, our men went on shore to fill water at a pit which was a quarter of a mile from the water's side; and being early hard at their business were in no readiness. In which meanwhile there came pouring down from the hills almost 200 horsemen, and before our people could return to the rocks from the watering-place, twelve of them were cut off, part killed and part taken prisoners, the rest were rescued by our soldiers, which came from the rocks to meet with them, who being but fifteen of us that had any weapons on shore, yet we made the enemy retire in the end with loss of some twenty-four of their men, after we had skirmished with them an hour.

The names of our men that were slain were these:—Thomas Lucas, of London, soldier; Richard Wheeler, of London; Robert Pitcher, of Norfolk, soldier; John Langston, of Gloucestershire; William Kingman, of Dorsetshire, soldier; William Hilles, of Cornwall, out of the admiral. William Byet of Weymouth; Laurence Gamesby, of Newcastle, killed out of the vice-admiral. Henry Blackenals, of Weymouth; William Stevens, of Plymouth, gunner; William Pitt, of Sherborne, in Dorsetshire; Humphrey Derrick, of London, killed out of the *Hugh Gallant.* After the loss of these men we rode in the road, and watered in despite of them with good watch and ward, until the fifth of the said month.

The fifth day we departed out of this bay of Quintero, and off from the bay there lieth a little island about a league distant, whereon there are great store of penguins and other fowls; whereof we took to serve our turns, and sailed away north, and north and by west: for so lieth the coast along in this place.

The fifteenth we came thwart of a place which is called Moro Moreno, which standeth in 23 degrees and a half, and is an excellent good harbour; and there is an island which maketh it a harbour, and a ship may go in at either end of the island. Here we went with our General on shore to the number of 30 men; and at our going on shore upon our landing, the Indians of the place came down from the rocks to meet with us, with fresh water and wood on their backs. They are in marvellous awe of the Spaniards, and very simple people, and live marvellous savagely; for they brought us to their bidings about two miles from the harbour, where we saw their women and lodging, which is nothing but the skin of some beast laid upon the ground; and over them, instead of houses, is nothing but five or six sticks laid across, which stand upon two forks with sticks on the ground, and a few boughs laid on it. Their diet is raw fish, which stinketh most vilely; and when any of them die, they bury their bows and arrows with them, with their canoe and all that they have; for we opened one of their graves, and saw the order of them. Their canoes or boats are marvellous artificially made of two skins like unto bladders, and are blown full at one end with quills. They have two of these bladders blown full, which are sewn together and made fast with a sinew of some wild beast, which when they are in the water swell, so that they are as tight as may be. They go to sea in these boats, and catch very much fish with them, and pay much of it for tribute unto the Spaniards; but they use it marvellous beastly.

The 23rd in the morning we took a small bark which came out of Arica road, which we kept and called the *George*; the men forsook it, and went away with their boat. Our admiral's pinnace followed the boat, and the *Hugh Gallant*'s boat took the bark. Our admiral's pinnace could not recover the boat before it got on shore, but went along into the road of Arica, and laid aboard a great ship of a hundred tons, riding in the road right afore the town, but all the men and goods were gone out of it, only the bare ship was left alone. They made three or four very fair shots at the pinnace as she was coming in, but missed her very narrowly with a minion shot which they had in the fort. Whereupon we came into the road with the admiral and the *Hugh Gallant*; but the *Content*, which was vice-admiral, was behind out of sight, by means whereof, and for want of her boat to land men withal, we landed not; otherwise if we had been together our General with the company would resolutely have landed to take the town, whatsoever had come of it. The cause why the *Content* stayed behind was that she had found about 14 leagues to the southward of Arica, in a place where the Spaniards had landed, a whole ship's lading of *botijas* of wine of Castile, whereof the said *Content* took into her as many as she could conveniently carry, and came after us into the road of Arica the same day. By this time we perceived that the town had gathered all their power together, and also had conveyed all their treasure away, and buried it before we were come near the town, for they had heard of us. Now because it was very populous with the aid of one or two places up in the land, our General saw there was no landing without the loss of many men, wherefore he gave over that enterprise. While we rode in the road they shot at us, and our ships shot at them again for every shot two. Moreover our pinnace went in hard almost to the shore, and fetched out another bark which rode there in despite of all their forts though they shot still at the pinnace, which they could never hit. After these things our General sent a boat on shore with a flag of truce to know if they would redeem their great ship or no; but they would not, for they had received special commandment from the Viceroy from Lima, not to buy any ship, nor to ransom any man upon pain of death. Our General did this in hope to have redeemed some of our men which were taken prisoners on shore by the horsemen at Quintero, otherwise he would have made them no offer of parley.

The 25th, riding still in the said road, we espied a sail coming from the southward, and our General sent out his pinnace to meet her, with all our boats. But the town made such signs from the hill with fires and tokens out of the watch-house that, before our pinnace could get to them, they ran the bark on shore two miles to the southward of the town; but they had small leisure to carry anything with them, but all the men escaped, among whom were certain friars, for we saw them in their friar's weeds as they ran on shore. Many horsemen came from the town to rescue them, and to carry them away, otherwise we had landed and taken or killed them. So we went aboard the bark as she lay sunk, and fetched out the pillage, but there was nothing in it of any value; and came aboard our ships again the same night, and the next morning we set the great ship on fire in the road, and sunk one of the barks, and carried the other along with us, and so departed from thence and went away north-west.

The 27th day we took a small bark, which came from Santiago, near unto Quintero, where we lost our men first. In this bark was one George, a Greek, a reasonable pilot for all the coast of Chile. They were sent to the city of Lima with letters of advice of us, and of the loss of our men. There were also in the said bark one Fleming and three Spaniards, and they were all sworn and received the sacrament before they came to sea, by three or four friars, that if we should chance to meet them they should throw those letters overboard, which (as we were giving them chase with our pinnace) before we could fetch them up they had accordingly thrown away. Yet our General wrought so with them that they did confess it; but he was fain to cause them to be tormented with their thumbs in a wrench, and to continue them at several times with extreme pain. Also he made the old Fleming believe that he would hang him, and the rope being about his neck he was pulled up a little from the hatches, and yet he would not confess, choosing rather to die, than he would be perjured. In the end it was confessed by one of the Spaniards, whereupon we burnt the bark, and carried the men with us.

The third of May we came into a bay where are three little towns, which are called Paracas, Chincha, and Pisca, where some of us landed and took certain houses, wherein was bread, wine, figs, and hens; but the sea went so high that we could not land at the best of the towns without sinking of our boats and great hazard of us all. This place standeth in thirteen degrees and 2 tierces to the southward of the line. The fifth of May we departed from this harbour, leaving the *Content,* our vicc-admiral, within at an island of seals, by which means at that time we lost her company. The ninth we gave chase to a sail, namely, our admiral, the *Hugh Gallant,* and the *George* which we had taken before coming out of the road of Arica, the *Content,* which was our vice-admiral, being still lost; but we could not fetch it. The *George* made after it, but lost it that night. The tenth day the *Hugh Gallant* (in which bark I, Francis Pretty, was) left company of our admiral.

The eleventh we which were in the *Hugh Gallant* put into a bay which standeth in 12 degrees and two tierces, in which bay we found a river of fresh water about eight of the clock at night, and though we were but of small force, and no more but one bark and 18 men in it, yet we went on shore to fill water; where, having filled one boat's lading, while our boat was in going aboard, two or three of our company which were on shore, as they were going a little from the watering-place with their furniture about them, espied where there were four or five hundred bags of meal on a heap covered with a few reeds. So that night we filled water and took as much meal as we thought good; which fell out well for us that were then lost and stood in need of victuals, and by break of day in the morning we came aboard, and there stayed and rode until the afternoon. In which mean time the town seeing us ride there still, brought down much cattle to the sea-side to have enticed us to come on shore; but we saw their intent, and weighed anchor and departed the twelfth day.

The 13th day at night we put into a bay which standeth in 9 degrees and a tierce, where we saw horsemen; and that night we landed, namely, Master Brewer, captain, myself Francis Pretty, Arthur Warford, John Way, preacher, John Newman, Andrew Wight, William Gargefield, and Henry Hilliard. And we 8 only, having every man his arquebus and his furniture about him, marched three-quarters of a mile along the sea-side, where we found a boat of five or six tons hauled up dry on the shore about a cable's length from the water; and with extreme labour we launched the bark. When it was on float, Captain Brewer and I went in, while the rest of our company were fetching their things; but suddenly it was ready to sink. And the Captain and I stood up to the knees lading out water with our targets, but it sunk down faster than we were able to free it, insomuch as in the end we had much ado to save ourselves from drowning. When we were out, we stood in great fear that our own boat wherein we came on shore was sunk; for we could nowhere see it. Howbeit the Captain commanded them to keep it off, for fear of the great surge that went by the shore. Yet in the end we spied it, and went aboard by two and two, and were driven to wade up to the arm-holes 60 paces into the sea before we could get into the boat, by reason of the shoalness; and then departed the fourteenth day in the morning.

The 16th we took with the *Hugh Gallant*, being but sixteen men of us in it, a great ship which came from Guayaquil, which was called the *Lewis*, and was of the burden of three hundred tons, having four-and-twenty men in it, wherein was pilot one Gonsalvo de Ribas, whom we carried along with us, and a negro called Emmanuel. The ship was laden with nothing but timber and victuals; wherefore we left her seven leagues from the land, very leaky and ready to sink in 7 degrees to the southward of the line. We sunk her boat and took away her foresail and certain victuals.

The 17th of May we met with our admiral again, and all the rest of our fleet. They had taken two ships, the one laden with sugar, molasses, maize, Cordovan skins, *montego de porco*, many packs of *pintados*, many Indian coats, and some marmalade, and 1000 hens; and the other ship was laden with wheat-meal and boxes of marmalade. One of these ships, which had the chief merchandise in it, was worth twenty thousand pounds if it had been in England or in any other place of Christendom where we might have sold it. We filled all our ships with as much as we could bestow of these goods; the rest we burnt and the ships also, and set the men and women that were not killed on shore.

The 20th day in the morning we came into the road of Paita, and being at an anchor, our General landed with sixty or seventy men, skirmished with them of the town, and drove them all to flight to the top of the hill which is over the town, except a few slaves and some other which were of the meaner sort, who were commanded by the governors to stay below in the town at a place which is in building for a fort, having with them a bloody ensign, being in number about one hundred men. Now as we were rowing between the ships and the shore, our gunner shot off a great piece out of one of the barks, and the shot fell among them, and drove them to fly from the fort as fast as they might run, who got them up upon a hill, and from thence shot among us with their small shot. After we were landed and had taken the town, we ran upon them, and chased them so fiercely up the hills for the space of an hour that we drove them in the end away perforce, and being got up the hills, we found where they had laid all their stuff which they had brought out of the town, and had hidden it there upon the mountains. We also found the quantity of 25 pounds weight in silver in pieces of eight riyals, and abundance of household stuff and storehouses full of all kinds of wares; but our General would not suffer any man to carry much cloth or apparel away, because they should not cloy themselves with burdens. For he knew not whether our enemies were provided with furniture according to the number of their men; for they were five men to one of us, and we had an English mile and a half to our ships. Thus we came down in safety to the town, which was very well built, and marvellous clean kept in every street, with a town-house or Guild-hall in the midst, and had to the number of two hundred houses at the least in it. We set it on fire to the ground, and goods to the value of five or six thousand pounds; there was also a bark riding in the road which we set on fire, and departed, directing our course to the Island of Puna.

The 25th day of May we arrived at the Island of Puna, where is a very good harbour, where we found a great ship of the burden of 250 tons riding at an anchor with all her furniture, which was ready to be hauled on ground; for there is a special good place for that purpose. We sunk it, and went on shore where the lord of the island dwelt, which was by the waterside, who had a sumptuous house, marvellous well contrived, with very many singular good rooms and chambers in it; and out of every chamber was framed a gallery with a stately prospect into the sea on the one side, and into the island on the other side, with a marvellous great hall below, and a very great storehouse at the one end of the hall, which was filled with *botijas* of pitch, and bass to make cables withal, for the most part of the cables of the South Sea are made upon that island. This great *cacique* doth make all the Indians upon the island to work and to drudge for him; and he himself is an Indian born, but is married to a marvellous fair woman which is a Spaniard, by reason of his pleasant habitation and of his great wealth.

This Spanish woman his wife is honoured as a queen in the island, and never goeth on the ground upon her feet, but holdeth it too base a thing for her. But when her pleasure is to take the air, or to go abroad, she is always carried in a shadow like unto a horse-litter upon four men's shoulders, with a veil or canopy over her for the sun or the wind, having her gentlewomen still attending about her, with a great troop of the best men of the island with her. But both she and the lord of the island with all the Indians in the town were newly fled out of the island before we could get to an anchor, by reason we were becalmed before we could get in, and were gone over unto the mainland, having carried away with them to the sum of 100,000 crowns, which we knew by a captain of the island, an Indian, which was left there with some other upon the island under him, whom we had taken at sea as we were coming into the road, being in a *balsa* or canoe for a spy to see what we were.

The 27th our General himself with certain shot and some targeteers went over into the main unto the place where this aforesaid Indian captain which we had taken had told us that the *cacique*, which was the lord of all the island, was gone unto, and had carried all his treasure with him; but at our coming to the place which we went to land at, we found newly arrived there four or five great *balsas*, which were laden with plantains, bags of meal, and many other kinds of victuals. Our General marvelled what they were and what they meant, asking the

Indian guide and commanding him to speak the truth upon his life. Being then bound fast, he answered being very much abashed, as well as our company were, that he neither knew from whence they should come, nor who they should be; for there was never a man in any one of the *balsas*; and because he had told our General before, that it was an easy matter to take the said *cacique* and all his treasure, and that there were but three or four houses standing in a desert place and no resistance, and that if he found it not so he should hang him. Again being demanded to speak upon his life what he thought these *balsas* should be, he answered that he could not say from whence they should come, except it were to bring 60 soldiers, which he did hear were to go to a place called Guayaquil, which was about 6 leagues from the said island, where two or three of the King's ships were on the stocks in building, where are continually a hundred soldiers in garrisons, who had heard of us and had sent for sixty more for fear of burning of the ships and town. Our General, not any whit discouraged either at the sight of the *balsas* unlooked for, or for hearing of the threescore soldiers not until then spoken of, with a brave courage animating his company in the exploit, went presently forward, being in the night in a most desert path in the woods, until such time as he came to the place; where, as it seemed, they had kept watch either at the waterside, or at the houses, or else at both, and were newly gone out of the houses, having so short warning that they left their meat both boiling and roasting at the fire and were fled with their treasure with them, or else buried it where it could not be found, being also in the night. Our company took hens and such things as we thought good, and came away.

The 29th day of May our General went in the ship's-boat into a little island thereby, whereas the said *cacique* which was the lord of Puna had caused all the hangings of his chambers, which were of Cordovan leather all gilded over and painted very fair and rich, with all his household stuff, and all the ship's tackling which was riding in the road at our coming in, with great store of nails, spikes of iron, and very many other things to be conveyed; all of which we found, and brought away what our General thought requisite for the ship's business.

This island is very pleasant for all things requisite, and fruitful; but there are no mines of gold nor silver in it. There are at the least 200 houses in the town about the *cacique*'s palace, and as many in one or two towns more upon the island, which is almost as big as the Isle of Wight in England. There is planted on the one side of the *cacique*'s house a fair garden, with all herbs growing in it, and at the lower end a well of fresh water, and round about it are trees set, whereon bombasine cotton groweth after this manner. The tops of the trees grow full of cods, out of which the cotton groweth, and in the cotton is a seed of the bigness of a pea, and in every cod there are seven or eight of these seeds; and if the cotton be not gathered when it is ripe, then these seeds fall from it, and spring again. There are also in this garden fig-trees which bear continually, also pumpkins, melons, cucumbers, radishes, rosemary, and thyme, with many other herbs and fruits. At the other end of the house there is also another orchard, where grow oranges sweet and sour, lemons, pomegranates, and limes, with divers other fruits.

There is very good pasture ground in this island; and withal many horses, oxen, bullocks, sheep very fat and fair, great store of goats, which be very tame, and are used continually to be milked. They have moreover abundance of pigeons, turkeys, and ducks of a marvellous bigness. There was also a very large and great church hard by the *cacique*'s house, whither he caused all the Indians in the island to come and hear mass. For he himself was made a Christian when he was married to the Spanish woman before spoken of, and upon his conversion he caused the rest of his subjects to be christened. In this church was a high altar with a crucifix, and five bells hanging in the nether end thereof. We burnt the church and brought the bells away.

By this time we had hauled on ground our admiral, and had made her clean, burnt her keel, pitched and tarred her, and had hauled her on float again; and in the meanwhile continually kept watch and ward in the great house both night and day.

The second day of June in the morning, by-and-by after break of day, every one of the watch being gone abroad to seek to fetch in victuals, some one way, some another, some for hens, some for sheep, some for goats, upon the sudden there came down upon us a hundred Spanish soldiers with muskets and an ensign, which were landed on the other side of the island that night, and all the Indians of the island with them, everyone with weapons and their baggage after them; which was by means of a negro, whose name was Emmanuel, which fled from us at our first landing there. Thus being taken at advantage we had the worst; for our company was not past sixteen or twenty, whereof they had slain one or two before they were come to the houses. Yet we skirmished with them an hour and a half; at the last being sore overcharged with multitudes, we were driven down from the hill to the water-side, and there kept them play awhile, until in the end Zachary Saxie, who with his halbered had kept the way of the hill, and slain a couple of them, as he breathed himself, being somewhat tired, had an honourable death and a short. For a shot struck him to the heart; who feeling himself mortally wounded, cried to God for mercy, and fell down presently dead. But soon after the enemy was driven somewhat to retire from the bank's side to the green; and in the end our boat came and carried as many of our men away as could go in her, which was in hazard of sinking while they hastened into it. And one of our men, whose name was Robert Maddock, was shot through the head with his own piece, being a snap-hance, as he was hastening into the boat. But four of us were left behind, which the boat could not carry: to wit, myself Francis Pretty, Thomas Andrewes, Steven Gunner, and Richard Rose, which had our shot ready and retired ourselves unto a cliff, until the boat came again, which was presently after they had carried the rest aboard. There were six and forty of the enemy slain by us, whereof they had dragged some into bushes, and some into old houses, which we found afterwards. We lost twelve men in manner following:—Zachary Saxie, Neales Johnson, William Gargefield, Nicholas Hendy, Henry Cooper, slain by the enemy; Robert Maddock, killed with his piece; Henry Mawdley, burnt; Edward, the gunner's-man, Ambrose, the musician, drowned; Walter Tilliard, Edward Smith, Henry Aselye, taken prisoners.

The self-same day, being the second of June, we went on shore again with seventy men, and had a fresh skirmish with the enemies, and drove them to retire, being a hundred Spaniards serving with muskets, and two hundred Indians with bows, arrows, and darts. This done, we set fire on the town and burnt it to the ground, having in it to the number of three hundred houses; and shortly after made havoc of their fields, orchards, and gardens, and burnt four great ships more which were in building on the stocks.

The third of June, the *Content*, which was our vice-admiral, was hauled on ground to grave at the same place in despite of the Spaniards, and also our pinnace, which the Spaniards had burnt, was new trimmed. The fifth day of June we departed out of the road of Puna, where we had remained eleven days, and turned up for a place which is called Rio Dolce, where we watered; at which place also we sunk our rear-admiral called the *Hugh Gallant*, for want of men, being a bark of forty tons. The tenth day of the same month we set the Indians on shore which we had taken before in a *balsa* as we were coming into the road of Puna. The eleventh day we departed with the said Rio Dolce. The twelfth of June we doubled the equinoctial line, and continued our course northward all that month.

The first of July we had sight of the coast of Nueva España, being four leagues distant from land in the latitude of 10 degrees to the northward of the line. The ninth of July we took a new ship of the burden of 120 tons, wherein was one Michael Sancius, whom our General took to serve his turn to water along the coast; for he was one of the best coasters in the South Sea. This Michael Sancius was a Provençal, born in Marseilles, and was the first man that told us news of the great ship called the *Santa Anna*, which we afterward took coming from the Philippines. There were six men more in this new ship; we took her sails, her ropes, and fire-wood to serve our turn, set her on fire, and kept the men. The tenth day we took another bark which was going with advice of us and our ships all along the coast, as Michael Sancius told us; but all the company that were in the bark were fled on shore. None of both these ships had any goods in them. For they came both from Sonsonate, in the province of Guatemala, the new ship for fear we should have taken her in the road, and the bark, to carry news of us along the coast; which bark also we set on fire.

The 26th day of July we came to an anchor at 10 fathoms in the river of Copalita, where we made account to water. And the same night we departed with 30 men in the pinnace, and rowed to Guatulco, which is but two leagues from the aforesaid river and standeth in 15 degrees 40 minutes to the northward of the equinoctial line.

The 27th, in the morning by the break of day, we came into the road of Guatulco, where we found a bark of 50 tons, which was come from Sonsonate laden with cocoas and anil, which they had there landed; and the men were all fled on shore. We landed there and burnt their town, with the church and custom-house, which was very fair and large; in which house were 600 bags of anil to dye cloth, every bag whereof was worth 40 crowns, and 400 bags of cocoas, every bag whereof is worth ten crowns. These cocoas go among them for meat and money; for 150 of them are in value one riyal of plate in ready payment. They are very like unto an almond, but are nothing so pleasant in taste; they eat them and make drink of them. This the owner of the ship told us. I found in this town, before we burnt it, a flasket full of boxes of balm. After we had spoilt and burnt the town, wherein there were some hundred houses, the owner of the ship came down out of the hills with a flag of truce unto us, which before with the rest of all the townsmen was run away at our first coming, and at length came aboard our pinnace upon Captain Havers' word of safe return. We carried him to the river of Copalita where our ships rode; and when he came to our General he caused him to be set on shore in safety the same night, because he came upon the captain's word.

The 28th day we set sail from Copalita, because the sea was so great there that we could not fill water, and ran the same night into the road of Guatulco. The 29th our General landed and went on shore with thirty men two miles into the woods, where we took a *mestizo*, whose name was Michael de Truxillo, who was customer of that town, and we found with him two chambers full of his stuff; we brought him and his stuff aboard. And whereas I say he was a *mestizo*, it is to be understood that a *mestizo* is one which hath a Spaniard to his father and an Indian to his mother.

The second day of August we had watered and examined the said mestizo, and set him on shore again, and departed from the port of Guatulco the same night, which standeth, as I said before, in 15 degrees and 40 minutes to the northward of the line.

Here we overslipped the haven of Acapulco, from whence the ships are set forth for the Philippines. The four and twentieth day of August our General, with 30 of us, went with the pinnace unto a haven called Puerto de Natividad, where we had intelligence by Michael Sancius that there should be a pinnace; but before we could get thither the said pinnace was gone to fish for pearls 12 leagues further, as we were informed by certain Indians which we found there. We took a mulatto in this place in his bed, which was sent with letters of advice concerning us along the coast of Nueva Galicia, whose horse we killed, took his letters, left him behind, set fire on the houses, and burnt two new ships of 200 tons the piece which were in building there on the stocks, and came aboard of our ships again. The six and twentieth day of August we came into the bay of Santiago, where we watered at a fresh river, along which river many plantains are growing. Here is great abundance of fresh fish. Here, also, certain of our company dragged for pearls and caught some quantity.

The second of September we departed from Santiago at four of the clock in the evening. This bay of Santiago standeth in 19 degrees and 18 minutes to the northward of the line. The 3rd of September we arrived in a little bay, a league to the westward of Port de Natividad, called Malacca, which is a very good place to ride in. And the same day, about twelve of the clock, our General landed with thirty men or thereabout, and went up to a town of Indians which was two leagues from the road, which town is called Acatlan. There were in it about 20 or 30 houses and a church, which we defaced, and came aboard again the same night. All the people were fled out of the town at the sight of us. The fourth of September we departed from the road of Malacca and sailed along the coast.

The 8th we came to the road of Chaccalla, in which bay there are two little houses by the water's side. This bay is eighteen leagues from the Cape de los Corrientes. The 9th, in the morning, our General sent up Captain Havers with forty men of us before day, and, Michael Sancius being our guide, we went unto a place about two leagues up into the country in a most villainous desert path through the woods and wilderness, and in the end we came to a place where we took three householders with their wives and children and some Indians, one carpenter, which was a Spaniard, and a Portugal; we bound them all and made them to come to the seaside with us. Our General made their wives to fetch us plantains, lemons, and oranges, pineapples, and other fruits, whereof they had abundance, and so let their husbands depart, except Sembrano, the Spanish carpenter, and Diego, the Portugal; and the tenth day we departed the road.

The 12th day we arrived at a little island called the Isle of Saint Andrew, on which there is great store of fowl and wood, where we dried and salted as many of the fowls as we thought good. We also killed there abundance of seals and iguanos, which are a kind of serpents, with four feet, and a long, sharp tail, strange to them which have not seen them; but they are very good meat. We rode here until the seventeenth day, at which time we departed.

The 24th day we arrived in the road of Massadan, which standeth in 23 and a half degrees, just under the Tropic of Cancer. It is a very great river within, but it is barred at the mouth; and upon the north side of the bar without is good fresh water, but there is very evil filling of it, because at a low water it is shoaled half a mile off the shore. There is great store of fresh fish in that bay, and good fruits up into the country, whereof we had some, though not without danger.

The seven and twentieth day of September we departed from the road of Massadan, and ran to an island which is a league to the northward the said Massadan, where we trimmed our ships and new built our pinnace; and there is a little island a quarter of a league from it, on which are seals, where a Spanish prisoner, whose name was Domingo, being sent to wash shirts with one of our men to keep him, made a scape and swam to the main, which was an English mile distant, at which place we had seen 30 or 40 Spaniards and Indians, which were horsemen and kept watch there, which came from a town called Ciametlan, which was 11 leagues up into the country, as Michael Sancius told us. We found upon the island where we trimmed our pinnace fresh water, by the assistance of God in that our great need, by digging two or three foot deep in the sand, where no water nor sign of water was before to be perceived. Otherwise we had gone back 20 or 30 leagues to water, which might have been occasion that we might have missed our prey we had long waited for. But God raised one Flores, a Spaniard, which was also a prisoner with us, to make a motion to dig in the sands. Now our General, having had experience once before of the like, commanded to put his motion in practice, and in digging three foot deep we found very good and fresh water. So we watered our ships, and might have filled a thousand tuns more if we had would. We stayed in this island until the 9th day of October, at which time we departed at night for the Cape of St Lucar, which is on the west side of the point of California.

The 14th of October we fell with the Cape of St Lucar, which cape is very like the Needles at the Isle of Wight; and within the said cape is a great bay, called by the Spaniards Aguada Segura, into which bay falleth a fair fresh river, about which many Indians use to keep. We watered in the river, and lay off and on from the said Cape of St Lucar until the fourth of November, and had the winds hanging still westerly.

The 4th of November the *Desire* and the *Content*, wherein were the number of [blank] Englishmen only living, beating up and down upon the headland of California, which standeth 23 degrees and two tierces to the northward, between seven and 8 of the clock in the morning one of the company of our admiral, which was the trumpeter of the ship, going up into the top, espied a sail bearing in from the sea with the cape; whereupon he cried out, with no small joy to himself and the whole company, "A sail! a sail!" With which cheerful word the master of the ship and divers others of the company went also up into the maintop, who, perceiving the speech to be very true, gave information unto our General of these happy news, who was no less glad than the cause required; whereupon he gave in charge presently unto the whole company to put all things in readiness, which being performed, we gave them chase some 3 or 4 hours, standing with our best advantage and working for the wind. In the afternoon we got up unto them, giving them the broadside with our great ordnance and a volley of small shot, and presently laid the ship aboard, whereof the King of Spain was owner, which was admiral of the South Sea, called the *Santa Anna*, and thought to be 700 tons in burthen. Now, as we were ready on their ship's side to enter her, being not past 50 or 60 men at the uttermost in our ship, we perceived that the captain of the said ship had made fights fore and aft, and laid their sails close on their poop, their midship, with their forecastle, and having not one man to be seen, stood close under their fights, with lances, javelins, rapiers, and targets, and an innumerable sort of great stones, which they threw overboard upon our heads and into our ship so fast, and being so many of them, that they put us off the ship again with the loss of 2 of our men, which were slain, and with the hurting of 4 or 5. But for all this we new trimmed our sails, and fitted every man his furniture, and gave them a fresh encounter with our great ordnance and also with our small shot, raking them through and through, to the killing and maiming of many of their men. Their captain still, like a valiant man, with his company, stood very stoutly unto his close fights, not yielding as yet. Our General, encouraging his men afresh with the whole noise of trumpets, gave them the third encounter with our great ordnance and all our small shot, to the great discomforting of our enemies, raking them through in divers places, killing and spoiling many of their men. They being thus discomforted and spoiled, and their ship being in hazard of sinking by reason of the great shot which were made, whereof some were under water, within 5 or 6 hours' fight set out a flag of truce and parleyed for mercy, desiring our General to save their lives and to take their goods, and they would presently yield. Our General, of his goodness, promised them mercy, and willed them to strike their sails, and to hoist out their boat and to come aboard, which news they were full glad to hear of, and presently struck their sails, hoisted their boat out, and one of their chief merchants came aboard unto our General, and, falling down upon his knees, offered to have kissed our General's feet, and craved mercy. Our General most graciously pardoned both him and the rest upon the promise of their true dealing with him and his company concerning such riches as were in the ship; and sent for the captain and their pilot, who, at their coming, used the like duty and reverence as the former did. The General, of his great mercy and humanity, promised their lives and good usage. The said captain and pilot presently certified the General what goods they had within board, to wit, a hundred and twenty-two thousand pesos of gold; and the rest of the riches that the ship was laden with was in silks, satins, damasks, with musk and divers other merchandise, and great store of all manner of victuals, with the choice of many conserves of all sorts for to eat, and sundry sorts of very good wines. These things being made known to the General by the aforesaid captain and pilot, they were commanded to stay aboard the *Desire*, and on the 6th day of November following we went into a harbour which is called by the Spaniards Aguada Segura or Puerto Seguro.

Here the whole company of the Spaniards, both of men and women to the number of 190 persons, were set on shore, where they had a fair river of fresh water, with great store of fresh fish, fowl, and wood, and also many hares and coneys upon the main land. Our General also gave them great store of victuals, of *garbanzos*, pease, and some wine. Also they had all the sails of their ship to make them tents on shore, with licence to take such store of planks as should be sufficient to make them a bark. Then we fell to hoisting in of our goods, sharing of the treasure, and allotting to every man his portion. In division whereof, the eighth of this month, many of the company fell into a mutiny against our General, especially those which were in the *Content*, which nevertheless were after a sort pacified for the time.

On the 17th day of November, which is the day of the happy Coronation of Her Majesty, our General commanded all his ordnance to be shot off, with the small shot both in his own ship where himself went, and also in the *Content*, which was our vice-admiral. This being done, the same night we had many fireworks and more ordnance discharged, to the great admiration of all the Spaniards which were there; for the most part of them had never seen the like before.

This ended, our General discharged the captain, gave him a royal reward, with provision for his defence against the Indians, and his company, both of swords, targets, pieces, shot, and powder to his great contentment; but before his departure, he took out of this great ship two young lads born in Japan, which could both write and read their own language, the eldest being about 20 years old was named Christopher, the other was called Cosmus, about 17 years of age, both of very good capacity. He took also with him out of their ship 3 boys born in the islands of Manilla, the one about 15, the other about 13, and the youngest about 9 years old. The name of the eldest was Alphonso, the second Anthony de Dasi, the third remaineth with the Right Honourable the Countess of Essex. He also took from them one Nicholas Roderigo, a Portugal, who hath not only been in Canton and other parts of China, but also in the islands of Japan, being a country most rich in silver mines, and hath also been in the Philippines.

He took also from them a Spaniard, whose name was Thomas de Ersola, which was a very good pilot from Acapulco and the coast of Nueva España unto the islands of Ladrones, where the Spaniards do put in to water sailing between Acapulco and the Philippines; in which isles of Ladrones they find fresh water, plantains, and potato roots; howbeit the people be very rude and heathens. The 19th day of November aforesaid, about 3 of the clock in the afternoon, our General caused the King's ship to be set on fire, which having to the quantity of 500 tons of goods in her, we saw burnt unto the water, and then gave them a piece of ordnance and set sail joyfully homewards towards England with a fair wind, which by this time was come about to east-north-east, and night growing near we left the *Content* astern of us, which was not as yet come out of the road. And here, thinking she would have overtaken us, we lost her company and never saw her after. We were sailing from this haven of Aguada Segura, in California, unto the islands of Ladrones, the rest of November and all December, and so forth until the 3rd of January, 1588, with a fair wind for the space of 45 days; and we esteemed it to be between 17 and 18 hundred leagues. The 3rd day of January by six of the clock in the morning we had sight of one of the islands of Ladrones called the island of Guana, standing in 13 degrees and two tierces towards the north, and sailing with a gentle gale before the wind, by 1 or 2 of the clock in the afternoon we were come up within 2 leagues of the island, where we met with 60 or 70 sail of canoes full of savages, who came off to sea unto us, and brought with them in their boats plantains, cocos, potato-roots, and fresh fish which they had caught at sea, and held them up unto us for to truck or exchange with us; which when we perceived we made fast little pieces of old iron upon small cords and fishing-lines, and so veered the iron into their canoes, and they caught hold of them and took off the iron, and in exchange of it they would make fast unto the same line either a potato root or a bundle of plantains, which we hauled in, and thus our company exchanged with them until they had satisfied themselves with as much as did content them; yet we could not be rid of them. For afterward they were so thick about the ship that it stemmed and broke 1 or 2 of their canoes; but the men saved themselves, being in every canoe 4, 6, or 8 persons all naked and excellent swimmers and divers. They are of a tawny colour and marvellous fat, and bigger ordinarily of stature than the most part of our men in England, wearing their hair marvellous long; yet some of them have it made up and tied with a knot on the crown, and some with 2 knots, much like unto their images which we saw them have carved in wood and standing in the head of their boats like unto the images of the devil. Their canoes were as artificially made as any that ever we had seen, considering they were made and contrived without any edge-tool. They are not above half-a-yard in breadth, and in length some seven or eight yards, and their heads and sterns are both alike; they are made out with rafts of canes and reeds on the starboard side, with mast and sail. Their sail is made of mats of sedges, square or triangle-wise, and they sail as well right against the wind as before the wind. These savages followed us so long, that we could not be rid of them, until in the end our General commanded some half-a-dozen arquebuses to be made ready, and himself struck one of them and and the rest shot at them; but they were so yare and nimble, that we could not discern whether they were killed or no, because they could fall backward into the sea, and prevent us by diving.

The 14th day of January lying at hull with our ship all the middle watch from 12 at night until four in the morning, by the break of day we fell with a headland of the islands of the Philippines which is called Cabo del Spirito Santo, which is of very great bigness and length, high land in the midst of it, and very low land as the Cape lieth east and west, trending far into the sea to the westward. This cape or island is distant from the island of Guana, one of the Ladrones, 310 leagues. We were in sailing of this course eleven days with scant winds and some foul weather, bearing no sail two or three nights. This island standeth in 13 degrees, and is a place much peopled with heathen people, and all woody through the whole land; and it is short of the chiefest island of the Philippines, called Manilla, about 60 leagues. Manilla is well planted and inhabited with Spaniards to the number of six or seven hundred persons, which dwell in a town unwalled, which hath 3 or 4 small block-houses, part made of wood and part of stone, being indeed of no great strength; they have one or two small galleys belonging to the town. It is a very rich place of gold and many other commodities; and they have yearly traffic from Acapulco in Nueva España, and also 20 or 30 ships from China and from the Sanguelos, which bring them many sorts of merchandise. The merchants of China and the Sanguelos are part Moors and part heathen people. They bring great store of gold with them, which they traffic and exchange for silver, and give weight for weight. These Sanguelos are men of marvellous capacity in devising and making all manner of things, especially in all handicrafts and sciences, and every one is so expert, perfect, and skilful in his faculty as few or no Christians are able to go beyond them in that which they take in hand. For drawing and embroidering upon satin, silk, or lawn, either beast, fowl, fish, or worm for liveliness and perfectness, both in silk, silver, gold and pearl, they excel. Also the 14th day at night we entered the straits between the island of Luzon and the island of Camlaia.

The fifteenth of January we fell with an island called Capul, and had betwixt the said island and another island but a narrow passage, and a marvellous rippling of a very great tide with a ledge of rocks lying off the point of the island of Capul; and no danger, but water enough a fair breadth off, and within the point a fair bay and a very good harbour in four fathoms water hard aboard the shore within a cable's length. About ten of the clock in the morning we came to an anchor.

Our ship was no sooner come to an anchor but presently there came a canoe rowing aboard us, wherein was one of the chief *caciques* of the island, whereof there be seven, who, supposing that we were Spaniards, brought us potato-roots, which they call *camotas*, and green cocos, in exchange whereof we gave his company pieces of linen, to the quantity of a yard, for four cocos, and as much linen for a basket of potato-roots of a quart in quantity, which roots are very good meat, and excellent sweet either roasted or boiled.

This *cacique's* skin was carved and cut with sundry and many streaks and devices all over his body. We kept him still aboard, and caused him to send those men which brought him aboard back to the island to cause the rest of the principals to come aboard; who were no sooner gone on shore but presently the people of the island came down with their cocos and potato-roots, and the rest of the principals likewise came aboard and brought with them hens and hogs, and they used the same order with us which they do with the Spaniards. For they took for every hog (which they call *balboye*), eight riyals of plate, and for every hen or cock one riyal of plate. Thus we rode at anchor all that day, doing nothing but buying roots, cocos, hens, hogs, and such things as they brought, refreshing ourselves marvellously well.

The same day at night, being the fifteenth of January, 1588, Nicolas Roderigo, the Portugal, whom we took out of the great *Santa Anna*, at the Cape of California, desired to speak with our General in secret; which when our General understood he sent for him, and asked him what he had to say unto him. The Portugal made him this answer, that although he had offended his worship heretofore, yet now he had vowed his faith and true service unto him, and in respect thereof he neither could nor would conceal such treason as was in working against him and his company, and that was this: that the Spaniard which was taken out of the great *Santa Anna* for a pilot, whose name was Thomas de Ersola, had written a letter, and secretly sealed it and locked it up in his chest, meaning to convey it by the inhabitants of this island to Manilla, the contents whereof were that there had been two English ships along the coast of Chile, Peru, Nueva España, and Nueva Galicia, and that they had taken many ships and merchandise in them, and burnt divers towns, and spoiled all that ever they could come unto, and that they had taken the King's ship which came from Manilla and all his treasure, with all the merchandise that was therein, and had set all the people on shore, taking himself away perforce. Therefore he willed them that they should make strong their bulwarks with their two galleys, and all such provision as they could possibly make. He further signified that we were riding at an island called Capul, which was at the end of the island of Manilla, being one ship with small force in it, and that the other ship, as he supposed, was gone for the north-west passage, standing in 55 degrees; and that if they could use any means to surprise us, being there at an anchor, they should despatch it; for our force was but small, and our men but weak, and that the place where we rode was but 50 leagues from them. Otherwise, if they let us escape, within few years they must make account to have their town besieged and sacked with an army of English. This information being given, our General called for him, and charged him with these things, which at the first he utterly denied; but in the end, the matter being made manifest, and known of certainty by especial trial and proofs, the next morning our General willed that he should be hanged; which was accordingly performed the 16th of January.

We rode for the space of nine days about this island of Capul, where we had divers kinds of fresh victuals, with excellent fresh water in every bay, and great store of wood. The people of this island go almost all naked and are tawny of colour. The men wear only a strap about their waists, of some kind of linen of their own weaving, which is made of plantain leaves, and another strap coming from their back under their twists, which covereth their privy parts and is made fast to their girdles at their navels.

These people use a strange kind of order among them, which is this. Every man and man-child among them hath a nail of tin thrust quite through the head of his privy part, being split in the lower end and riveted, and on the head of the nail is as it were a crown; which is driven through their privities when they be young, and the place groweth up again without any great pain to the child; and they take this nail out and in as occasion serveth. And for the truth thereof we ourselves have taken one of these nails from a son of one of the kings which was of the age of 10 years, who did wear the same in his privy member. This custom was granted at the request of the women of the country who, finding their men to be given to the foul sin of sodomy, desired some remedy against that mischief, and obtained this before-named of the magistrates. Moreover all the males are circumcised, having the foreskin of their flesh cut away. These people wholly worship the devil, and often times have conference with him, which appeareth unto them in most ugly and monstrous shape.

On the 23rd day of January, our General, Master Thomas Candish, caused all the principals of this island, and of an hundred islands more which he had made to pay tribute unto him (which tribute was in hogs, hens, potatoes, and cocos), to appear before him, and made himself and his company known unto them, that they were Englishmen, and enemies to the Spaniards; and thereupon spread his ensign and sounded up the drums, which they much marvelled at. To conclude, they promised both themselves and all the islands thereabout to aid him, whensoever he should come again to overcome the Spaniards. Also our General gave them, in token that we were enemies to the Spaniards, money back again for all their tribute which they had paid; which they took marvellous friendly, and rowed about our ships to show us pleasure marvellous swiftly. At the last our General caused a saker to be shot off, whereat they wondered, and with great contentment took their leaves of us.

The next day being the twenty-fourth of January, we set sail about six of the clock in the morning, and ran along the coast of the Island of Manilla, shaping our course northwest between the Isle of Manilla and the Isle of Masbate.

The 28th day in the morning about 7 of the clock, riding at an anchor betwixt 2 islands, we spied a frigate under her two courses, coming out between 2 other islands, which as we imagined came from Manilla, sailing close aboard the shore along the main island of Panuma. We chased this frigate along the shore, and got very fast upon it, until in the end we came so near that it stood into the shore close by a wind, until she was becalmed and was driven to strike her sail, and banked up with her oars; whereupon we came unto an anchor with our ship, a league and a half from the place where the frigate rowed in, and manned our boat with half-a-dozen shot and as many men with swords, which did row the boat. Thus we made after the frigate which had hoisted sail and ran into a river, which we could not find. But as we rowed along the shore, our boat came into very shallow water, where many weirs and sticks were set up in divers places in the sea, from whence two or three canoes came forth, whereof one made somewhat near unto us, with three or four Indians in it. We called unto them, but they would not come nearer unto us, but rowed from us, whom we durst not follow too far for fear of bringing ourselves too much to the leeward of our ship. Here, as we looked about us, we espied another *balsa* or canoe of a great bigness, which they which were in her did set along as we do usually set a barge with long staves or poles, which was built up with great canes, and below hard by the water made to row with oars; wherein were about five or six Indians and one Spaniard. Now as we were come almost at the *balsa*, we ran aground with our boat; but one or two of our men leaped overboard and freed it again presently, and keeping thwart her head, we laid her aboard and took into us the Spaniard, but the Indians leaped into the sea and dived and rose far off again from us. Presently upon the taking of this canoe, there showed upon the sand a band of soldiers marching with an ensign having a red cross like the flag of England, which were about 50 or 60 Spaniards, which were lately come from Manilla to that town which is called Ragaun in a bark to fetch a new ship of the King's, which was building in a river within the bay, and stayed there but for certain irons that did serve for the rudder of the said ship, which they looked for every day.

This band of men shot at us from the shore with their muskets, but hit none of us, and we shot at them again. They also manned a frigate and sent it out after our boat to have taken us, but we with sail and oars went from them; and when they perceived that they could not fetch us but that they must come within danger of the ordnance of our ship, they stood in with the shore again and landed their men, and presently sent their frigate about the point, but whither we knew not. So we came aboard with this one Spaniard, which was neither soldier nor sailor but one that was come among the rest from Manilla, and had been in the hospital there a long time before, and was a very simple soul, and such a one as could answer to very little that he was asked concerning the state of the country. Here we rode at anchor all that night, and perceived that the Spaniards had dispersed their band into 2 or 3 parts, and kept great watch in several steads with fires and shooting off their pieces. This island hath much plain ground in it in many places, and many fair and straight trees do grow upon it, fit for to make excellent good masts for all sorts of ships. There are also mines of very fine gold in it which are in the custody of the Indians. And to the southward of this place there is another very great island, which is not subdued by the Spaniards, nor any other nation. The people which inhabit it are all negroes; and the island is called the Island of Negroes and is almost as big as England, standing in 9 degrees. The most part of it seemeth to be very low land, and by all likelihood is very fruitful.

The 29th day of January, about six of the clock in the morning, we set sail, sending our boat before until it was two of the clock in the afternoon, passing all this time as it were through a strait betwixt the said two Islands of Panuma and the Island of Negroes, and about 16 leagues off we espied a fair opening, tending south-west and by south, at which time our boat came aboard, and our General sent commendations to the Spanish captain which we came from the evening before by the Spaniard which we took, and willed him to provide good store of gold. For he meant for to see him with his company at Manilla within few years, and that he did but want a bigger boat to have landed his men, or else he would have seen him then. And so caused him to be set on shore. The 8th day of February by eight of the clock in the morning we espied an island near Gilolo, called Batochina, which standeth in one degree from the equinoctial line northward. The 14th day of February we fell in with eleven or twelve very small islands, lying very low and flat, full of trees, and passed by some islands which be sunk and have the dry sands lying in the main sea. These islands near the Moluccas stand in 3 degrees and 10 minutes to the southward of the line.

On the 17th day, one John Gameford, a cooper, died, which had been sick of an old disease a long time. The 20th day we fell with certain other islands which had many small islands among them, standing 4 degrees to the southward of the line. On the 21st day of February, being Ash Wednesday, Captain Havers died of a most severe and pestilent ague which held him furiously some 7 or 8 days, to the no small grief of our General and of all the rest of the company, who caused two falcons and one saker to be shot off, with all the small shot in the ship; who, after he was shrouded in a sheet and a prayer said, was heaved overboard with great lamentation of us all. Moreover, presently after his death myself with divers others in the ship fell marvellously sick, and so continued in very great pain for the space of three weeks or a month by reason of the extreme heat and intemperateness of the climate.

The first of March, having passed through the straits of Java Minor and Java Major, we came to an anchor under the south-west parts of Java Major where we espied certain of the people which were fishing by the sea-side in a bay which was under the Island. Then our General taking into the ship-boat certain of his company, and a negro which could speak the Morisco tongue, which he had taken out of the great *Santa Anna*, made towards those fishers, which having espied our boat ran on shore into the wood for fear of our men; but our General caused his negro to call unto them who no sooner heard him call but presently one of them came out to the shore-side and made answer. Our General by the negro enquired of him for fresh water, which they found, and caused the fisher to go to the king and to certify him of a ship that was come to have traffic for victuals, and for diamonds, pearls, or any other rich jewels that he had; for which he should have either gold or other merchandise in exchange. The fisher answered that we should have all manner of victuals that we would request. Thus the boat came aboard again. Within a while after we went about to furnish our ship thoroughly with wood and water.

About the eighth of March two or three canoes came from the town unto us with eggs, hens, fresh fish, oranges and limes, and brought word we should have had victuals more plentifully, but that they were so far to be brought to us where we rode. Which when our General heard he weighed anchor and stood in nearer for the town; and as we were under sail we met with one of the king's canoes coming towards us, whereupon we shook the ship in the wind and stayed for the canoe until it came aboard of us, and stood into the bay which was hard by and came to an anchor. In this canoe was the king's secretary, who had on his head a piece of dyed linen cloth folded up like unto a Turk's turban. He was all naked saving about his waist; his breast was carved with the broad arrow upon it; he went barefooted. He had an interpreter with him, which was a *mestizo*, that is, half Indian, and half a Portugal, who could speak very good Portuguese. This secretary signified unto our

General that he had brought him a hog, hens, eggs, fresh fish, sugar-canes, and wine (which wine was as strong as any aquavitæ, and as clear as any rock water). He told him further that he would bring victuals so sufficiently for him as he and his company would request, and that within the space of four days. Our General used him singularly well, banqueted him most royally with the choice of many and sundry conserves, wines both sweet and other, and caused his musicians to make him music. This done our General told him that he and his company were Englishmen, and that we had been at China and had had traffic there with them, and that we were come thither to discover, and purposed to go to Malacca. The people of Java told our General that there were certain Portugals in the island, which lay there as factors continually to traffic with them, to buy negroes, cloves, pepper, sugar, and many other commodities. This secretary of the king with his interpreter lay one night aboard our ship. The same night because they lay aboard in the evening at the setting of the watch, our General commanded every man in the ship to provide his arquebus and his shot, and so with shooting off 40 or 50 small shot and one saker, himself set the watch with them. This was no small marvel unto these heathen people, who had not commonly seen any ship so furbished with men and ordnance. The next morning we dismissed the secretary and his interpreter with all humanity.

The fourth day after, which was the 12th of March, according to their appointment came the king's canoes; but the wind being somewhat scant they could not get aboard that night, but put into a bay under the island until the next day, and presently after the break of day there came to the number of 9 or 10 of the king's canoes so deeply laden with victuals as they could swim, with two great live oxen, half a score of wonderful great and fat hogs, a number of hens which were alive, drakes, geese, eggs, plantains, sugar-canes, sugar in plates, cocos, sweet oranges and sour, limes, great store of wine and aquavitæ, salt to season victuals withal, and almost all manner of victuals else, with divers of the king's officers which were there. Among all the rest of the people, in one of these canoes came two Portugals, which were of middle stature, and men of marvellous proper personage. They were each of them in a loose jerkin, and hose which came down from the waist to the ankle, because of the use of the country, and partly because it was Lent, and a time for doing of their penance (for they account it as a thing of great dislike among these heathens to wear either hose or shoes on their feet). They had on each of them a very fair and a white lawn shirt, with falling bands on the same, very decently, only their bare legs excepted. These Portugals were no small joy unto our General and all the rest of our company, for we had not seen any Christian, that was our friend, of a year and a half before. Our General used and entreated them singularly well, with banquets and music.

They told us that they were no less glad to see us than we to see them, and enquired of the state of their country, and what was become of Dom Antonio, their King, and whether he were living or no; for that they had not of long time been in Portugal, and that the Spaniards had always brought them word that he was dead. Then our General satisfied them in every demand; assuring them that their King was alive, and in England, and had honourable allowance of our Queen, and that there was war between Spain and England, and that we were come under the King of Portugal into the South Sea, and had warred upon the Spaniards there, and had fired, spoiled, and sunk all the ships along the coast that we could meet withal, to the number of eighteen or twenty sails. With this report they were sufficiently satisfied.

On the other side they declared unto us the state of the island of Java. First the plentifulness and great choice and store of victuals of all sorts, and of all manner of fruits as before is set down. Then the great and rich merchandise which are there to be had. Then they described the properties and nature of the people as followeth. The name of the king of that part of the island was Raja Bolamboam, who was a man had in great majesty and fear among them. The common people may not bargain, sell, or exchange anything with any other nation without special licence from their king; and if any so do, it is present death for him. The king himself is a man of great years, and hath a hundred wives; his son hath fifty. The custom of the country is, that whensoever the king doth die they take the body so dead and burn it, and preserve the ashes of him, and within five days next after, the wives of the said king so dead, according to the custom and use of their country, everyone of them go together to a place appointed, and the chief of the women, which was nearest unto him in account, hath a ball in her hand, and throweth it from her, and to the place where the ball resteth thither they go all, and turn their faces to the eastward, and everyone with a dagger in their hand (which dagger they call a creese, and is as sharp as a razor) stab themselves to the heart, and with their hands all to-bebathe themselves in their own blood, and falling grovelling on their faces so end their days. This thing is as true as it seemeth to any hearer to be strange.

The men of themselves be very politic and subtle, and singularly valiant, being naked men, in any action they undertake, and wonderfully at commandment and fear of their king. For example, if their king command them to undertake any exploit, be it never so dangerous or desperate, they dare not nor will not refuse it, though they die every man in the execution of the same. For he will cut off the heads of every one of them which return alive without bringing of their purpose to pass; which is such a thing among them, as it maketh them the most valiant people in all the south-east parts of the world, for they never fear any death. For being in fight with any nation, if any of them feeleth himself hurt with lance or sword, he will willingly run himself upon the weapon quite through his body to procure his death the more speedily, and in this desperate sort end his days, or overcome his enemy. Moreover, although the men be tawny of colour and go continually naked, yet their women be fair of complexion and go more apparelled.

After they had thus described the state of the island, and the orders and fashions of the people, they told us further, that if their King Dom Antonio would come unto them they would warrant him to have all the Moluccas at commandment, besides China, Sangles, and the isles of the Philippines, and that he might be assured to have all the Indians on his side that are in the country. After we had fully contented these Portugals, and the people of Java which brought us victuals in their canoes, they took their leaves of us with promise of all good entertainment at our returns, and our General gave them three great pieces of ordnance at their departing. Thus the next day, being the 16th of March, we set sail towards the Cape of Good Hope, called by the Portuguese Cabo de Buena Esperança, on the southermost coast of Africa.

The rest of March and all the month of April we spent in traversing that mighty and vast sea, between the Isle of Java and the main of Africa, observing the heavens, the Crosiers or Southpole, the other stars, the fowls, which are marks unto the seamen of fair weather, foul weather, approaching of lands or islands, the winds, the tempests, the rains and thunders, with the alteration of tides and currents.

The 10th day of May we had a storm at the west, and it blew so hard that it was as much as the ship could stir close by under the wind; and the storm continued all that day and all that night. The next day, being the 11th of May, in the morning one of the company went into the top, and espied land bearing north and north and by west of us, and about noon we espied land to bear west of us, which, as we did imagine, was the Cape of Buena Esperança, whereof, indeed, we were short some 40 or 50 leagues. And by reason of the scantness of the wind we stood along to the south-east until midnight, at which time the wind came fair, and we hauled along westward. The 12th and 13th days we were becalmed, and the sky was very hazy and thick until the 14th day at three of the clock in the afternoon, at which time the sky cleared, and we espied the land again which was the cape called Cabo Falso, which is short of the Cape de Buena Esperança 40 or 50 leagues. This cape is very easy to be known; for there are right over it three very high hills standing but a small way one off another, and the highest standeth in the midst, and the ground is much lower by the seaside. The Cape of Good Hope beareth west and by south from the said Cabo Falso.

The 16th day of May, about 4 of the clock in the afternoon, the wind came up at east a very stiff gale, which held until it was Saturday, with as much wind as ever the ship could go before, at which time, by six of the clock in the morning, we espied the promontory or headland called the Cape de Buena Esperança, which is a reasonable high land, and at the westernmost point, a little off the main, do show two hummocks, the one upon the other, and three other hummocks lying further off into the sea, yet low land between and adjoining unto the sea. This Cape of Buena Esperança is set down and accounted for two thousand leagues from the island of Java in the Portugal sea-charts; but it is not so much almost by a hundred and fifty leagues, as we found by the running of our ship. We were in running of these eighteen hundred and fifty leagues just nine weeks.

The eighth day of June, by break of day, we fell in sight of the island of St Helena, seven or eight leagues short of it, having but a small gale of wind, or almost none at all, insomuch as we could not get into it that day, but stood off and on all that night. The next day, being the 9th of June, having a pretty easy gale of wind, we stood in with the shore, our boat being sent away before to make the harbour; and about one of the clock in the afternoon we came unto an anchor in 12 fathoms water, two or three cables' length from the shore, in a very fair and smooth bay under the north-west side of the island. This island is very high land, and lieth in the main sea, standing as it were in the midst of the sea between the mainland of Africa and the main of Brazil and the coast of Guinea, and is in 15 degrees and 48 minutes to the southward of the equinoctial line, and is distant from the Cape of Buena Esperança between 5 and 6 hundred leagues.

The same day, about two or three of the clock in the afternoon, we went on shore, where we found a marvellous fair and pleasant valley, wherein divers handsome buildings and houses were set up, especially one which was a church, which was tiled and whited on the outside very fair and made with a porch, and within the church at the upper end was set an altar, whereon stood a very large table set in a frame having in it the picture of our Saviour Christ upon the cross and the image of Our Lady praying, with divers other histories curiously painted in the same. The sides of the church were all hung with stained cloths having many devices drawn in them. There are two houses adjoining to the church, on each side one, which serve for kitchens to dress meat in, with necessary rooms and houses of office. The coverings of the said houses are made flat, whereon is planted a very fair vine, and through both the said houses runneth a very good and wholesome stream of fresh water. There is also, right over against the said church, a fair causeway made up with stones reaching unto a valley by the sea-side, in which valley is planted a garden wherein grow great store of pumpkins and melons. And upon the said causeway is a frame erected whereon hang two bells wherewith they ring to Mass; and hard unto it is a cross set up, which is squared, framed, and made very artificially of freestone, whereon is carved in ciphers what time it was built, which was in the year of our Lord 1571.

This valley is the fairest and largest low plot in all the island, and it is marvellous sweet and pleasant, and planted in every place either with fruit-trees or with herbs. There are fig-trees, which bear fruit continually and marvellous plentifully; for on every tree you shall have blossoms, green figs, and ripe figs all at once, and it is so all the year long. The reason is that the island standeth so near the sun. There be also great store of lemon-trees, orange-trees, pomegranate-trees, pomecitron-trees, date-trees, which bear fruit as the fig-trees do, and are planted carefully and very artificially with very pleasant walks under and between them, and the said walks be overshadowed with the leaves of the trees; and in every void place is planted parsley, sorrel, basil, fennel, anise-seed, mustard-seed, radishes, and many special good herbs; and the fresh water brook runneth through divers places of this orchard, and may with very small pains be made to water any one tree in the valley.

This fresh water stream cometh from the tops of the mountains, and falleth from the cliff into the valley the height of a cable, and hath many arms out of it, which refresh the whole island and almost every tree in it. The island is altogether high mountains and steep valleys, except it be in the tops of some hills and down below in some of the valleys, where marvellous store of all these kinds of fruits before spoken of do grow. There is greater store growing in the tops of the mountains than below in the valleys; but it is wonderful laboursome and also dangerous travelling up unto them and down again, by reason of the height and steepness of the hills.

There is also upon this island great store of partridges, which are very tame, not making any great haste to fly away though one come very near them, but only to run away and get up into the steep cliffs. We killed some of them with a fowling piece. They differ very much from our partridges which are in England both in bigness and also in colour; for they be within a little as big as a hen, and are of an ash colour, and live in coveys twelve, sixteen, and twenty together. You cannot go ten or twelve score but you shall see or spring one or two coveys at the least.

There are likewise no less store of pheasants in the island, which are also marvellous big and fat, surpassing those which are in our country in bigness and in numbers of a company. They differ not very much in colour from the partridges before spoken of.

We found moreover in this place a great store of Guinea cocks, which we call turkeys, of colour black and white, with red heads. They are much about the same bigness which ours be of in England. Their eggs be white, and as big as a turkey's egg.

There are in this island thousands of goats, which the Spaniards call *cabritos*, which are very wild. You shall see one or two hundred of them together, and sometimes you may behold them going in a flock almost a mile long. Some of them (whether it be the nature of the breed of them or of the country I wot not) are as big as an ass, with a mane like a horse and a beard hanging down to the very ground. They will climb up the cliffs, which are so steep that a man would think it a thing impossible for any living thing to go there. We took and killed many of them, for all their swiftness; for there be thousands of them upon the mountains.

Here are in like manner great store of swine, which be very wild and very fat, and of a marvellous bigness. They keep altogether upon the mountains, and will very seldom abide any man to come near them, except it be by mere chance when they be found asleep, or otherwise, according to their kind, be taken laid in the mire.

We found in the houses at our coming 3 slaves which were negroes and one which was born in the island of Java, which told us that the East Indian fleet, which were in number 5 sails, the least whereof were in burden 800 or 900 tons, all laden with spices and Calicut cloth, with store of treasure and very rich stones and pearls, were gone from the said island of St Helena but twenty days before we came thither.

This island hath been found of long time by the Portugals, and hath been altogether planted by them for their refreshing as they come from the East Indies. And when they come they have all things plentiful for their relief, by reason that they suffer none to inhabit there that might spend up the fruit of the island, except some very few sick persons in their company, which they stand in doubt will not live until they come home, whom they leave there to refresh themselves, and take away the year following with the other fleet if they live so long. They touch here rather in their coming from the East Indies than at their going thither, because they are thoroughly furnished with corn when they set out of Portugal, but are but meanly victualled at their coming from the Indies, where there groweth little corn.

The 20th day of June, having taken in wood and water, and refreshed ourselves with such things as we found there, and made clean our ship, we set sail about eight of the clock in the night toward England. At our setting sail we had the wind at south-east, and we hauled away north-west and by west. The wind is commonly off the shore at this island of St Helena. On Wednesday, being the third day of July, we went away north-west, the wind being still at south-east; at which time we were in 1 degree and 48 minutes to the southward of the equinoctial line. The twelfth day of the said month of July it was very little wind, and toward night it was calm and blew no wind at all, and so continued until it was Monday, being the 15th day of July. On Wednesday, the 17th day of the abovesaid month, we had the wind scant at west-north-west. We found the wind continually to blow at east, and north-east, and east-north-east after we were in 3 or 4 degrees to the northward; and it altered not until we came between 30 and 40 degrees to the northward of the equinoctial line.

On Wednesday, the 21st day of August, the wind came up at south-west a fair gale, by which day at noon we were in 38 degrees of northerly latitude. On Friday, in the morning, being the 23rd day of August, at four of the clock, we hauled east, and east and by south for the northermost islands of the Azores. On Saturday, the 24th day of the said month, by five of the clock in the morning, we fell in sight of the two islands of Flores and Corvo, standing in 39 and a half degrees and sailed away north-east. The third day of September we met with a Flemish hulk, which came from Lisbon, and declared unto us the overthrowing of the Spanish Fleet, to the singular rejoicing and comfort of us all. The 9th of September, after a terrible tempest which carried away most part of our sails, by the merciful favour of the Almighty we recovered our long-wished port of Plymouth in England, from whence we set forth at the beginning of our voyage.

A brief relation of a voyage of the *Delight*, a ship of Bristol, one of the consorts of Master John Chidley, Esquire, and Master Paul Wheele, made unto the Strait of Magellan: with divers accidents that happened unto the company during their 6 weeks abode there. Begun in the year 1589. Written by W. Magoths.

THE fifth of August, 1589, the worshipful Master John Chidley, of Chidley in the county of Devon, Esquire, with Master Paul Wheele and Captain Andrew Merick, set forth from Plymouth with three tall ships, the one called *The Wild Man*, of three hundred tons, wherein went for General the aforesaid Master John Chidley and Benjamin Wood as master, the other called *The White Lion*, whereof Master Paul Wheele was captain and John Ellis master, of the burden of 340 tons; the third, *The Delight of Bristol*, wherein went Master Andrew Merick as captain and Robert Burnet master, with two pinnaces of 14 or 15 tons apiece. The General in his ship had 180 persons; Master Paul Wheele had 140; in our own ship we were 91 men and boys.

Our voyage was intended by the Strait of Magellan for the South Sea, and chiefly for the famous province of Arauco on the coast of Chile. We kept company together to the Isles of the Canaries, and so forward to Cape Blanco, standing near the northerly latitude of 20 degrees on the coast of Barbary, where some of our people went on shore, finding nothing to their content. Within twelve days after our departure from this place the *Delight*, wherein I, William Magoths, was, lost the company of the other two great ships and the two small pinnaces. Howbeit, we constantly kept our course according to our directions along the coast of Brazil, and by the River of Plate, without touching anywhere on land until we came to Port Desire in the latitude of 48 degrees to the southward of the equinoctial.

Before we arrived at this place there died of our company by God's visitation of sundry diseases 16 persons. We stayed in this harbour 17 days to grave our ship and refresh our wearied people, hoping here to have met with our consorts; which fell out contrary to our expectations. During our abode in this place we found two little springs of fresh water, which were upon the north-westerly part of the land, and lighted upon good store of seals, both old and young. From hence we sailed toward the Strait of Magellan, and entered the same about the first of January. And coming to Penguin Island within the Strait we took and salted certain hogsheads of penguins, which must be eaten with speed, for we found them to be of no long continuance; we also furnished ourselves with fresh water. And here at the last sending off our boat to the island for the rest of our provision we lost her and 15 men in her by force of foul weather; but what became of them we could not tell. Here also in this storm we lost two anchors.

From hence we passed farther into the Strait, and by Port Famine we spoke with a Spaniard, who told us that he had lived in those parts 6 years, and that he was one of the 400 men that were sent thither by the King of Spain in the year 1582 to fortify and inhabit there, to hinder the passage of all strangers that way into the South Sea. But that and the other Spanish colony being both destroyed by famine, he said he had lived in a house by himself a long time, and relieved himself with his caliver until our coming thither.

Here we made a boat of the boards of our chests; which being finished, we sent armed men in the same on land on the north shore, being wafted on land by the savages with certain white skins; who as soon as they came on shore were presently killed by a hundred of the wild people in the sight of 2 of our men which rowed them on shore, which two only escaped back again to us with the boat.

After this traitorous slaughter of our men we fell back again with our ship to the north-eastward of Port Famine to a certain road, where we refreshed ourselves with mussels, and took in water and wood. At this time we took in the Spaniard aforesaid, and so sailed forward again into the Strait. We passed 7 or 8 times 10 leagues westward beyond Cape Froward, being still encountered with mighty north-west winds. These winds and the current were so vehement against us that they forced us back as much in two hours as we were getting up in 8 hours.

Thus after we had spent 6 weeks in the Strait striving against the fury of the elements, and having at sundry times, partly by casualty and partly by sickness, lost 38 of our best men and 3 anchors, and now having but one anchor left us and small store of victuals, and, which was not the least mischief, divers of our company raising dangerous mutinies, we consulted, though somewhat with the latest, for the safeguard of our lives, to return while there was some small hope remaining; and so set sail out of the Strait homeward about the 14th of February, 1590.

We returned back again by the River of Plate. And sailing near the coast of Brazil we met with a Portugal ship of 80 tons, which rode at an anchor upon the coast, who as soon as she descried us to chase her incontinently weighed and ran herself on ground between the island of St Sebastian and the mainland. But we, for want of a good boat and by reason of the foul weather, were neither able to board her nor to go on shore. Thence in extreme misery we shaped our course for the isles of Cape Verde, and so passing to the isles of the Azores, the Canaries being something out of our course.

The first land that we met withal in our narrow sea was the Isle of Alderney. And having now but six men of all our company left alive, the Master and his two mates and chief mariners being dead, we ran in with Monville de Hague, eight miles to the west of Cherbourg in Normandy, where the next day after our coming to an anchor, having but one in all left, being the last of August, 1590, by the foul weather that rose the anchor came home and our ship drove on the rocks. And the Normans, which were commanded by the Governor of Cherbourg (who came down to us that night) to have laid out another anchor for her, neglecting his commandment, suffered her miserably to be splitted, with desire to enrich themselves by her wreck.

Within few days after this last mischance four of us, being Englishmen, departed from Cherbourg, and passed home for England in a bark of Weymouth, leaving the two strangers there behind us.

The names of us six that returned of all our company were these: 1, William Magoths of Bristol; 2, Richard Bush; 3, John Read; 4, Richard Hodgkins of Westbury near Bristol; the two strangers: 5, Gabriel Valerosa, a Portugal; 6, Peter, a Breton.

A petition made by certain of the company of the *Delight* of Bristol unto the Master of the said ship, Robert Burnet, one of the consorts of Master Chidley, being in the Straits of Magellan the 12th of February 1589.

WE have thought good to show unto you, being our Master, our whole minds and griefs in writing. That whereas our Captain, Matthew Hawlse, and Walter Street do begin to take into the Captain's cabin this 12th of February both bread and butter, such as was put in for the provision of the ship and company, only to feed themselves and a few others which are of their mess, meaning thereby rather to starve us than to keep us strong and in health; and likewise upon the same he hath taken into his cabin certain furniture, as swords, calivers, and muskets; we, therefore, not well knowing their intents herein, except by certain words cast out unawares we may conjecture that your death, which God forbid, by them hath been determined, do all most humbly desire you, being our Master, and having charge of the ship and us this present voyage committed to you, to consider:

First, that by God's visitation we have lost 16 men, and that so much the rather because they were not allotted such necessary provision as was in the ship to be had. Also to consider the great loss of 15 of our men with our boat at Penguin Island within the Straits of Magellan, and of 7 good and serviceable men besides near Port Famine, and of three anchors, and our carpenter. Over and besides all these calamities to consider how you have, without all reason and conscience, been over-thwarted, disgraced, and out-countenanced by your mate, Street, and Matthew Hawlse; also what danger you now are subject unto, your death having been so often conspired, and what danger we should be in if it were (which God forbid) effected. Furthermore, to weigh with yourself the great want of many necessaries in our ship, namely, that we have but 6 sailors (besides yourself, and your mate, Street, whom we dare not trust), also that we have but one anchor, likewise the lack of our boat and a carpenter, of ropes, of pitch, tree-nails, bolts, and planks, and the want of a skilful surgeon. And whereas, a view being taken of our provision, there was found but five months' victuals of bread, meal, grits, and pease, and also but three months' victuals of beef, penguins, and pork, three hogsheads of wine, ten gallons of aquavitae (whereof the sick men could not get any to relieve them), four hogsheads of cider, and 18 flitches of bacon, etc., the company hath but three flitches. Also the said Captain Hawlse and Street have taken and seized upon 17 pots of butter, with certain cheese, and a hogshead of bread at a time, and have been thereof possessed to their own private uses; and have not only immoderately spent the company's provision in butter, cheese, aquavitae, etc., but have also consumed those sweetmeats which were laid up in the ship only for the relief of sick persons (themselves being healthy and sound, and withholding the said meats from others in their sickness); and even at this time also, by reason of the small store of our provision we being enforced to come to a shorter allowance, they, the said Captain Hawlse and your mate, Street, do find themselves aggrieved at the very same allowance wherewith other men are well contented. And although, besides our ordinary allowance, and more than all the rest of the company, they only have their breakfasts permitted to them, yet they complain that the company goeth about to famish them, whereas indeed they do what lieth in them to famish the company by feeding themselves fat which do no labour at all.

These things being well weighed, you ought likewise to consider the long time that we have lain here in these Straits of Magellan, having been at, and seven or eight times ten leagues beyond, Cape Froward; we have had but a small gale of wind with us, neither could we come to an anchor, the water being so deep; and, you know, the place is so dangerous that we were once embayed and could scarce get out again. And likewise, what fogs and mists are here already! Much more here will be, the winter and dark nights being at hand, and we having not so much as a boat to seek out any road to ride in saving a small, weak boat made of men's chests, in which it is not convenient to go on shore in a foreign country, where we must go with force; and having but one anchor left us, there is but little hope of life in us, as you may sufficiently judge, if we should lose either the said anchor or our boat, and therefore we dare not put the same in danger for fear of losing them. Also, we having lain here these six weeks and upward, the wind hath continued in the north-west directly against our course, so that we can no way hope to get through the Straits into the South Sea this year, and if we could, yet our provision is not sufficient, having spent so much thereof in this our lingering abode. Nay, we have scarcely victuals enough to carry us home into England, if they be not used sparingly, and with very good government.

Therefore we do again most humbly desire you to consider and have regard unto the premises, as you tender your own safety and the safety of us which remain alive, that we may, by God's help, return back into England rather than die here among wild and savage people. For if we make any longer abode in this place, it will be, without all doubt, to the utter decay and loss both of ourselves and of the ship; and, in returning back, it may please God that we may find our fifteen men and our boat at Penguin Island (although this be contrary to the minds of Matthew Hawlse and your mate, Street), and having found them we do not despair in God's mercy but that in our return homeward he will send us purchase sufficient, if we would join ourselves together in prayer and love one another. And thus doing, as we shall be bound, even so we will also heartily pray for the continuance of your good estate and welfare and for the length of your days, to the pleasure of Almighty God.

Lastly, we do most humbly beseech you to consider that, after the loss of so many men and all the casualties aforesaid, as we were taking in of water by Port Famine, our boatswain, the hooper, and William Magoths being on shore, Matthew Hawlse did halloo to have them in all the haste come on board, saying therewithal these words, "He that will come in this voyage must not make any reckoning to leave two or three men on shore behind him"; whereas we had so lately lost all the foresaid men, having then but six sailors left us on board. Also the said Matthew Hawlse did carry a pistol for the space of two days secretly under his gown, intending therewithal to have murdered Andrew Stoning and William Combe, as by confession of Hawlse's man, William Martin, it is manifest. For the said William Martin reported unto two of his friends, viz. Richard Hungate and Emmanuel Dornel, that he kneeled upon his knees one whole hour before Matthew Hawlse in his own cabin, desiring him, for God's cause, not to kill either of them, especially because the said Stoning and Martin came both out of one town. Also the said Hawlse, at our second time of watering in the place aforesaid, came into the gunners' room to speak with you (yourself with the Master Gunner, Thomas Browne, and his mate, William Frier, being then present), demanding of you if he should send certain men to Port Famine being two leagues from the ship by land. Thomas Browne answered him presently that he should send none, for fear lest the wind might arise, and by that means we should lose so many of our men more. To whom Matthew Hawlse replied that it was not material, for that he had made choice of a company for the very same purpose, whose names were Emmanuel Dornel, Richard Hungate, Paul Cary, John Davis, Gabriel Valerosa, a Portugal, and Peter, a Breton, and the Spaniard which we had taken in at the same place at our first time of watering.

And thus we end, desiring God to send us well into our native country.

In witness whereof we have subscribed our names,

Thomas Browne, Gunner
John Morrice, etc.

The last voyage of the worshipful Master Thomas Candish, Esquire, intended for the South Sea, the Philippines, and the coast of China, with 3 tall ships and two barks. Written by Master John Janes, a man of good observation, employed in the same and many other voyages.

THE 26th of August, 1591, we departed from Plymouth with three tall ships and two barks, the *Galleon*, wherein Master Candish went himself, being admiral, the *Roebuck*, vice-admiral, whereof Master Cocke was captain, the *Desire*, rear-admiral, whereof was captain Master John Davis (with whom and for whose sake I went this voyage), the *Black Pinnace*, and a bark of Master Adrian Gilbert, whereof Master Randolph Cotton was captain.

The 29th of November we fell in with the Bay of Salvador, upon the coast of Brazil, 12 leagues on this side Cabo Frio, where we were becalmed until the second of December, at which time we took a small bark bound for the River of Plate with sugar, haberdashery wares, and negroes. The master of this bark brought us unto an isle called Placentia, 30 leagues west from Cabo Frio, where we arrived the fifth of December, and rifled six or seven houses inhabited by Portugals. The 11th we departed from this place, and the 14th we arrived at the Isle of Saint Sebastian, from whence Master Cocke and Captain Davis presently departed with the *Desire* and the *Black Pinnace*, for the taking of the town of Santos. The 15th at evening we anchored at the bar of Santos, from whence we departed with our boats to the town; and the next morning about nine of the clock we came to Santos, where, being discovered, we were enforced to land with 24 gentlemen, our long boat being far astern, by which expedition we took all the people of the town at mass, both men and women, whom we kept all that day in the church as prisoners. The cause why Master Candish desired to take this town was to supply his great wants; for being in Santos, and having it in quiet possession, we stood in assurance to supply all our needs in great abundance. But such was the negligence of our governor, Master Cocke, that the Indians were suffered to carry out of the town whatsoever they would in open view, and no man did control them; and the next day after we had won the town our prisoners were all set at liberty, only four poor old men were kept as pawns to supply our wants. Thus in three days the town that was able to furnish such another fleet with all kind of necessaries was left unto us nakedly bare, without people and provision.

Eight or ten days after, Master Candish himself came thither, where he remained until the 22nd of January, seeking by entreaty to have that whereof we were once possessed. But in conclusion we departed out of the town through extreme want of victual, not being able any longer to live there, and were glad to receive a few canisters or baskets of cassava meal; so that in every condition we went worse furnished from the town than when we came unto it. The 22nd of January we departed from Santos, and burnt St Vincent to the ground. The 24th we set sail, shaping our course for the Straits of Magellan.

The seventh of February we had a very great storm, and the 8th our fleet was separated by the fury of the tempest. Then our Captain called unto him the Master of our ship, whom he found to be a very honest and sufficient man, and conferring with him he concluded to go for Port Desire, which is in the southerly latitude of 48 degrees; hoping that the General would come thither, because that in his first voyage he had found great relief there. For our Captain could never get any direction what course to take in any such extremities, though many times he had entreated for it, as often I have heard him with grief report. In sailing to this port by good chance we met with the *Roebuck*, wherein Master Cocke had endured great extremities, and had lost his boat, and therefore desired our Captain to keep him company, for he was in very desperate case. Our Captain hoisted out his boat and went aboard him to know his estate, and returning told us the hardness thereof, and desired the Master and all the company to be careful in all their watches not to lose the *Roebuck*, and so we both arrived at Port Desire the sixth of March.

The 16th of March the *Black Pinnace* came unto us, but Master Gilbert's bark came not, but returned home to England, having their captain aboard the *Roebuck* without any provision more than the apparel that he wore, who came from thence aboard our ship to remain with our Captain, by reason of the great friendship between them. The 18th the *Galleon* came into the road, and Master Candish came into the harbour in a boat which he had made at sea; for his long-boat and light-horseman were lost at sea, as also a pinnace which he had built at Santos; and being aboard the *Desire* he told our Captain of all his extremities, and spoke most hardly of his company, and of divers gentlemen that were with him, purposing no more to go aboard his own ship, but to stay in the *Desire*. We all sorrowed to hear such hard speeches of our good friends; but having spoken with the gentlemen of the *Galleon* we found them faithful, honest, and resolute in proceeding, although it pleased our General otherwise to conceive of them.

The 20th of March we departed from Port Desire, Master Candish being in the *Desire* with us. The eighth of April, 1592, we fell with the Straits of Magellan, enduring many furious storms between Port Desire and the Straits. The 14th we passed through the first strait. The 16th we passed the second strait, being 10 leagues distant from the first. The 18th we doubled Cape Froward, which cape lieth in 53 degrees and a half. The 21st we were enforced by the fury of the weather to put into a small cove with our ships, 4 leagues from the said cape, upon the south shore, where we remained until the 15th of May. In the which time we endured extreme storms, with perpetual snow, where many of our men died with cursed famine and miserable cold, not having wherewith to cover their bodies nor to fill their bellies, but living by mussels, water, and weeds of the sea, with a small relief of the ship's store in meal sometimes. And all the sick men in the *Galleon* were most uncharitably put ashore into the woods in the snow, rain, and cold, when men of good health could scarcely endure it, where they ended their lives in the highest degree of misery, Master Candish all this while being aboard the *Desire*. In these great extremities of snow and cold, doubting what the end would be, he asked our Captain's opinion, because he was a man that had good experience of the north-west parts, in his 3 several discoveries that way, employed by the merchants of London. Our Captain told him that this snow was a matter of no long continuance, and gave him sufficient reason for it, and that thereby he could not much be prejudiced or hindered in his proceeding. Notwithstanding, he called together all the company, and told them that he purposed not to stay in the Straits, but to depart upon some other voyage, or else to return again for Brazil. But his resolution was to go for the Cape of Buena Esperança. The company answered that, if it pleased him, they did desire to stay God's favour for a wind, and to endure all hardness whatsoever rather than to give over the voyage, considering they had been here but a small time, and because they were within 40 leagues of the South Sea, it grieved them now to return; notwithstanding what he purposed that they would perform. So he concluded to go for the Cape of Buena Esperança, and to give over this voyage. Then our Captain, after Master Candish was come aboard the *Desire* from talking with the company, told him that if it pleased him to consider the great extremity of his estate, the slenderness of his provisions, with the weakness of his men, it was no course for him to proceed in that new enterprise. "For if the rest of your ships", said he, "be furnished answerable to this, it is impossible to perform your determination. For we have no more sails than masts, no victuals, no ground-tackling, no cordage more than is over head, and among seventy and five persons there is but the Master alone that can order the ship, and but fourteen sailors. The rest are gentlemen, serving-men, and artificers. Therefore it will be a desperate case to take so hard an enterprise in hand". These persuasions did our Captain not only use to Master Candish, but also to Master Cocke. In fine, upon a petition delivered in writing by the chief of the whole company, the General determined to depart out of the Straits of Magellan, and to return again for Santos, in Brazil.

So the 15th of May we set sail, the General then being in the *Galleon*. The eighteenth we were free of the Straits, but at Cape Froward it was our hard hap to have our boat sunk at our stern in the night, and to be split and sore spoiled, and to lose all our oars.

The twentieth of May, being thwart of Port Desire, in the night the General altered course, as we suppose, by which occasion we lost him; for in the evening he stood close by a wind to seaward, having the wind at north-north-east, and we standing the same way, the wind not altering, could not the next day see him; so that we then persuaded ourselves that he was gone for Port Desire to relieve himself, or that he had sustained some mischance at sea, and was gone thither to remedy it. Whereupon our Captain called the General's men unto him, with the rest, and asked their opinion what was to be done. Everyone said that they thought that the General was gone for Port Desire. Then the Master, being the General's man, and careful of his master's service, as also of good judgment in sea matters, told the company how dangerous it was to go for Port Desire, if we should there miss the General. "For", said he, "we have no boat to land ourselves, nor any cables nor anchors that I dare trust in so quick streams as are there". Yet in all likelihood concluding that the General was gone thither, we stayed our course for Port Desire, and by chance met with the *Black Pinnace*, which had likewise lost the fleet, being in very miserable case; so we both concluded to seek the General at Port Desire.

The six and twentieth of May we came to Port Desire, where not finding our General as we hoped, being most slenderly victualled, without sails, boat, oars, nails, cordage, and all other necessaries for our relief, we were stricken into a deadly sorrow. But referring all to the providence and fatherly protection of the Almighty, we entered the harbour, and by God's favour found a place of quiet road, which before we knew not. Having moored our ship with the pinnace's boat, we landed upon the south shore, where we found a standing pool of fresh water, which by estimation might hold some ten tuns, whereby we were greatly comforted. From this pool we fetched more than forty tuns of water, and yet we left the pool as full as we found it. And because at our first being in this harbour we were at this place and found no water, we persuaded ourselves that God had sent it for our relief. Also there were such extraordinary low ebbs as we had never seen, whereby we got mussels in great plenty. Likewise God sent about our ships great abundance of smelts, so that with hooks made of pins every man caught as many as he could eat; by which means we preserved our ship's victuals, and spent not any during the time of our abode here.

Our Captain and Master falling into the consideration of our estate and despatch to go to the General, found our wants so great as that in a month we could not fit our ship to set sail. For we must needs set up a smith's forge, to make bolts, spikes, and nails, besides the repairing of our other wants. Whereupon they concluded it to be their best course to take the pinnace, and to furnish her with the best of the company, and to go to the General with all expedition, leaving the ship and the rest of the company until the General's return; for he had vowed to our Captain that he would return again for the Straits, as he had told us. The Captain and Master of the pinnace being the General's men were well contented with the motion.

But the General having in our ship two most pestilent fellows, when they heard of this determination they utterly misliked it, and in secret dealt with the company of both ships, vehemently persuading them that our Captain and Master would leave them in the country to be devoured of the cannibals, and that they were merciless and without charity; whereupon the whole company joined in secret with them in a night to murder our Captain and Master, with myself, and all those which they thought were their friends. There were marks taken in his cabin how to kill him with muskets through the ship's side, and bullets made of silver for the execution if their other purposes should fail. All agreed hereunto, except it were the boatswain of our ship, who, when he knew the matter and the slender ground thereof, revealed it unto our Master, and so to the Captain. Then the matter being called in question, those two most murderous fellows were found out, whose names were Charles Parker and Edward Smith.

The Captain being thus hardly beset, in peril of famine, and in danger of murdering, was constrained to use lenity, and by courteous means to pacify this fury; showing, that to do the General service, unto whom he had vowed faith in this action, was the cause why he purposed to go unto him in the pinnace, considering that the pinnace was so necessary a thing for him, as that he could not be without her, because he was fearful of the shore in so great ships. Whereupon all cried out, with cursing and swearing, that the pinnace should not go unless the ship went. Then the Captain desired them to show themselves Christians, and not so blasphemously to behave themselves, without regard or thanksgiving to God for their great deliverance and present sustenance bestowed upon them, alleging many examples of God's sharp punishment for such ingratitude; and withal promised to do anything that might stand with their good liking. By which gentle speeches the matter was pacified, and the Captain and Master, at the request of the company, were content to forgive this great treachery of Parker and Smith, who after many admonitions concluded in these words: "The Lord judge between you and me;" which after came to a most sharp revenge even by the punishment of the Almighty. Thus by a general consent it was concluded not to depart, but there to stay for the General's return. Then our Captain and Master, seeing that they could not do the General that service which they desired, made a motion to the company that they would lay down under their hands the losing of the General, with the extremities wherein we then stood; whereunto they consented, and wrote unto their hands as followeth:

The Testimonial of the Company of the Desire, *touching their losing of their General, which appeareth to have been utterly against their meanings.*

The 26th of August, 1591, we whose names be hereunder written, with divers others departed from Plymouth under Master Thomas Candish, our General, with 4 ships of his, to wit, the *Galleon*, the *Roebuck*, the *Desire*, and the *Black Pinnace* for the performance of a voyage into the South Sea. The 19th of November we fell with the bay of Salvador, in Brazil. The 16th of December we took the town of Santos, hoping there to revictual ourselves, but it fell not out to our contentment. The 24th of January we set sail from Santos, shaping our course for the Straits of Magellan. The 8th of February by violent storms the said fleet was parted; the *Roebuck* and the *Desire* arrived in Port Desire the 6th of March. The 16th of March the *Black Pinnace* arrived there also, and the 18th of the same our admiral came into the road, with whom we departed the 20th of March in poor and weak estate.

The 8th of April, 1592, we entered the Straits of Magellan. The 21st of April we anchored beyond Cape Froward, within 40 leagues of the South Sea, where we rode until the 15th of May, in which time we had great store of snow, with some gusty weather, the wind continuing still at west-north-west against us. In this time we were enforced, for the preserving of our victuals, to live for the most part upon mussels, our provision was so slender, so that many of our men died in this hard extremity. Then our General returned for Brazil there to winter, and to procure victuals for this voyage against the next year. So we departed the Straits the 15th of May.

The 21st, being thwart of Port Desire, 30 leagues off the shore, the wind then at north-east and by north, at five of the clock at night, lying north-east, we suddenly cast about lying south-east and by south, and sometimes south-east, the whole fleet following the admiral. Our ship coming under his lee shot ahead of him, and so framed sail fit to keep company. This night we were severed, by what occasion we protest we know not, whether we lost them or they us. In the morning we only saw the *Black Pinnace*, then supposing that the admiral had overshot us.

All this day we stood to the eastwards, hoping to find him, because it was not likely that he would stand to the shore again so suddenly. But missing him towards night, we stood to the shoreward, hoping by that course to find him. The 22nd of May at night we had a violent storm, with the wind at north-west, and we were enforced to hull, not being able to bear sail, and this night we perished our main trestle-trees, so that we could no more use our main-topsail, lying most dangerously in the sea. The pinnace likewise received a great leak, so that we were forced to seek the next shore for our relief. And because famine was like to be the best end, we desired to go for Port Desire, hoping with seals and penguins to relieve ourselves, and so to make shift to follow the General, or there to stay his coming from Brazil. The 24th of May we had much wind at north. The 25th was calm, and the sea very lofty, so that our ship had dangerous foul weather. The 26th our fore-shrouds broke, so that if we had not been near the shore it had been impossible for us to get out of the sea.

And now being here moored in Port Desire, our shrouds are all rotten, not having a running rope whereto we may trust, and being provided only of one shift of sails all worn, our top-sails not able to abide any stress of weather; neither have we any pitch, tar, or nails, nor any store for the supplying of these wants, and we live only upon seals and mussels, having but five hogsheads of pork within board, and meal three ounces for a man a day, with water for to drink. And forasmuch as it hath pleased God to separate our fleet, and to bring us into such hard extremities, that only now by His mere mercy we expect relief, though otherwise we are hopeless of comfort; yet because the wonderful works of God in His exceeding great favour towards us His creatures are far beyond the scope of man's capacity, therefore by Him we hope to have deliverance in this our deep distress. Also forasmuch as those upon whom God will bestow the favour of life, with return home to their country, may not only themselves remain blameless, but also manifest the truth of our actions, we have thought good in Christian charity to lay down under our hands the truth of all our proceedings, even till the time of this our distress.

Given in Port Desire the 2nd of June, 1592. Beseeching the Almighty God of His mercy to deliver us from this misery, how or when it shall please His Divine Majesty.

John Davis (Captain), Randolph Cotton, John Pery, William Maber (gunner), Charles Parker, Rowland Miller, Edward Smith, Thomas Purpet, Matthew Stubbes, John Jenkinson, Thomas Edwards, Edward Granger, John Lewis, William Hayman, George Straker, Thomas Walbie, William Wyeth, Richard Alard, Stpehen Popham, Alexander Cole, Thomas Watkins, George Cunington, John Whiting, James Ling, the Boatswain, Francis Smith, John Layes, the Boatswain's Mate,—Fisher, John Austin, Francis Copstone, Richard Garet, James Eversby, Nicolas Parker,—Leonard, John Pick,—Benjamin, William Maber, James Not, Christopher Hauser.

After they had delivered this relation unto our Captain under their hands, then we began to travail for our lives, and we built up a smith's forge, and made a coal-pit, and burnt coals, and there we made nails, bolts, and spikes, others made ropes of a piece of our cable, and the rest gathered mussels, and took smelts for the whole company. Three leagues from this harbour there is an isle with four small isles about it, where there are great abundance of seals, and at the time of the year the penguins come thither in great plenty to breed. We concluded with the pinnace that she should sometimes go thither to fetch seals for us, upon which condition we would share our victuals with her man for man; whereunto the whole company agreed. So we parted our poor store, and she laboured to fetch us seals to eat, wherewith we lived when smelts and mussels failed: for in the neap streams we could get no mussels. Thus in most miserable calamity we remained until the sixth of August, still keeping watch upon the hills to look for our General, and so great was our vexation and anguish of soul, as I think never flesh and blood endured more. Thus our misery daily increasing, time passing, and our hope of the General being very cold, our Captain and Master were fully persuaded that the General might perhaps go directly for the Straits, and not come to this harbour; whereupon they thought no course more convenient than to go presently for the Straits, and there to stay his coming, for in that place he could not pass, but of force we must see him. Whereunto the company most willingly consented, as also the Captain and Master of the pinnace; so that upon this determination we made all possible speed to depart.

The sixth of August we set sail, and went to Penguin Island, and the next day we salted twenty hogsheads of seals, which was as much as our salt could possibly do; and so we departed for the Straits the poorest wretches that ever were created. The seventh of August toward night we departed from Penguin Island, shaping our course for the Straits, where we had full confidence to meet with our General. The ninth we had a sore storm, so that we were constrained to hull, for our sails were not to endure any force. The 14th we were driven in among certain islands never before discovered by any known relation, lying fifty leagues or better from the shore east and northerly from the Straits; in which place, unless it had pleased God of his wonderful mercy to have ceased the wind, we must of necessity have perished. But the wind shifting to the east, we directed our course for the Straits, and the 18th of August we fell with the Cape in a very thick fog, and the same night we anchored ten leagues within the Cape. The 19th day we passed the first and the second Straits. The 21st we doubled Cape Froward. The 22nd we anchored in Savage Cove, so named because we found many savages there; notwithstanding the extreme cold of this place, yet do all these wild people go naked, and live in the woods like satyrs, painted and disguised, and fly from you like wild deer. They are very strong, and threw stones at us of three or four pound weight an incredible distance. The 24th in the morning we departed from this cove, and the same day we came into the north-west reach, which is the last reach of the Straits. The 25th we anchored in a good cove, within fourteen leagues of the South Sea: in this place we purposed to stay for the General, for the Strait in this place is scarce three miles broad, so that he could not pass but we must see him.

After we had stayed here a fortnight in the depth of winter, our victuals consuming (for our seals stunk most vilely, and our men died pitifully through cold and famine, for the greatest part of them had not clothes to defend the extremity of the winter's cold), being in this heavy distress, our Captain and Master thought it the best course to depart from the Straits into the South Sea, and to go for the Isle of Santa Maria, which is to the northward of Valdivia, in 37 degrees and a quarter, where we might have relief, and be in a temperate clime, and there stay for the General, for of necessity he must come by that Isle. So we departed the 13th of September, and came in sight of the South Sea. The 14th we were forced back again, and recovered a cove 3 leagues within the Straits from the South Sea. Again we put forth, and being 8 or 10 leagues free of the land, the wind rising furiously at west-north-west, we were enforced again into the Straits only for want of sails; for we never durst bear sail in any stress of weather, they were so weak. So again we recovered the cove three leagues within the Straits, where we endured most furious weather, so that one of our two cables broke, whereby we were hopeless of life. Yet it pleased God to calm the storm, and we unrove our sheets, tacks, halyards, and other ropes, and moored our ship to the trees close by the rocks. We laboured to recover our anchor again, but could not by any means, it lay so deep in the water, and, as we think, clean covered with ooze. Now had we but one anchor which had but one whole fluke, a cable spliced in two places, and a piece of an old cable. In the midst of these our troubles it pleased God that the wind came fair the first of October; whereupon with all expedition we loosed our moorings, and weighed our anchor, and so towed off into the channel, for we had mended our boat in Port Desire, and had five oars of the pinnace. When we had weighed our anchor, we found our cable broken, only one strand held. Then we praised God; for we saw apparently His mercies in preserving us.

Being in the channel, we rove our ropes, and again rigged our ship; no man's hand was idle, but all laboured even for the last gasp of life. Here our company was divided; some desired to go again to Port Desire, and there to be set on shore, where they might travail for their lives, and some stood with the Captain and Master to proceed. Where- upon the Captain said to the Master: "Master, you see the wonderful extremity of our estate, and the great doubts among our company of the truth of your reports, as touching relief to be had in the South Sea. Some say in secret, as I am informed, that we undertake these desper- ate attempts through blind affection that we bear to the General. For my own part I plainly make known unto you that the love which I bear to the General caused me first to enter into this action, whereby I have not only heaped upon my head this bitter calamity now present, but also have in some sort procured the dislike of my best friends in England, as it is not unknown to some in this company. But now being thus entangled by the providence of God for my former offences (no doubt), I desire that it may please His Divine Majesty to show us such merciful favour that we may rather proceed, than otherwise; or if it be His will that our mortal being shall now take an end, I rather desire that it may be in proceeding than in returning. And because I see in reason that the limits of our time are now drawing to an end, I do in Christian charity entreat you all, first to forgive me in whatsoever I have been grievous unto you; secondly, that you will rather pray for our General than use hard speeches of him; and let us be fully persuaded, that not for his cause or negligence, but for our own offences against the Divine Majesty, we are presently punished. Lastly, let us forgive one another and be reconciled as children in love and charity, and not think upon the vanities of this life; so shall we in leaving this life live with our glorious Redeemer, or abiding in this life, find favour with God. And now, good Master, forasmuch as you have been in this voyage once before with your master the General, satisfy the comapny of such truths as are to you best known; and you, the rest of the General's men, which likewise have been with him in his first voyage, if you hear anything contrary to the truth, spare not to reprove it, I pray you. And so I beseech the Lord to bestow His mercy upon us." Then the Master began in these speeches: "Captain, your request is very reasonable, and I refer to your judgment my honest care, and great pains taken in the General's service, my love towards him, and in what sort I have discharged my duty from the first day to this hour. I was commanded by the General to follow your directions, which hitherto I have performed. You all know that when I was extremely sick, the General was lost in my mate's watch, as you have well examined; since which time in what anguish and grief of mind I have lived God only knoweth, and you are in some part a witness. And now if you think good to return, I will not gainsay it; but this I assure you, if life may be preserved by any means, it is in proceeding. For at the Isle of Santa Maria I do assure you of wheat, pork, and roots enough. Also I will bring you to an isle where pelicans be in great abundance, and at Santos we shall have meal in great plenty, besides all our possibility of intercepting some ships upon the coast of Chile and Peru. But if we return there is nothing but death to be hoped for. Therefore do as you like, I am ready; but my desire is to proceed." These his speeches being confirmed by others that were in the former voyage, there was a general consent of proceeding; and so on the second of October we put into the South Sea, and were free of all land.

This night the wind began to blow very much at west-north-west, and still increaseṡd in fury, so that we were in great doubts what course to take: to put into the Straits we durst not for lack of ground-tackle; to bear sail we doubted, the tempest was so furious and our sails so bad. The pinnace came room with us, and told us that she had received many grievous seas, and that her ropes did every hour fail her, so as they could not tell what shift to make. We, being unable in any sort to help them, stood under our courses in view of the lee-shore, still expecting our ruinous end.

The fourth of October, the storm growing beyond all reason furious, the pinnace, being in the wind of us, struck suddenly a-hull, so that we thought she had received some grievous sea, or sprung a leak, or that her sails failed her, because she came not with us; but we durst not hull in that unmerciful storm, but sometimes tried under our main course, sometimes with a haddock of our sail, for our ship was very leeward, and most laboursome in the sea. This night we lost the pinnace, and never saw her again.

The fifth, our foresail was split, and all to-torn. Then our Master took the mizen and brought it to the foremast, to make our ship work, and with our spritsail we mended our foresail, the storm continuing without reason in fury, with hail, snow, rain, and wind, such and so mighty as that in nature it could not possibly be more, the seas such and so lofty, with continual breach, that many times we were doubtful whether our ship did sink or swim.

The tenth of October being by the account of our Captain and Master very near the shore, the weather dark, the storm furious, and most of our men having given over to travail, we yielded ourselves to death, without further hope of succour. Our Captain sitting in the gallery very pensive, I came and brought him some *rosa solis* to comfort him; for he was so cold that he was scarce able to move a joint. After he had drunk, and was comforted in heart, he began for the ease of his conscience to make a large repetition of his forepassed time, and with many grievous sighs he concluded in these words: "Oh, most glorious God, with whose power the mightiest things among men are matters of no moment, I most humbly beseech Thee, that the intolerable burden of my sins may, through the blood of Jesus Christ, be taken from me; and end our days with speed, or show us some merciful sign of Thy love and our preservation." Having thus ended, he desired me not to make known to any of the company his intolerable grief and anguish of mind, because they should not thereby be dismayed. And so suddenly, before I went from him, the sun shone clear so that he and the master both observed the true elevation of the pole, whereby they knew by what course to recover the Straits. Wherewithal our Captain and Master were so revived, and gave such comfortable speeches to the company, that every man rejoiced, as though we had received a present deliverance.

The next day, being the 11th of October, we saw Cabo Deseado, being the Cape on the south shore (the north shore is nothing but a company of dangerous rocks, isles, and shoals). This cape being within two leagues to leeward of us, our Master greatly doubted that we could not double the same; whereupon the Captain told him, "You see there is no remedy; either we must double it, or before noon we must die; therefore loose your sails, and let us put it to God's mercy." The Master, being a man of good spirit, resolutely made quick despatch and set sail. Our sails had not been half an hour aboard but the footrope of our foresail broke, so that nothing held but the eyelet holes. The seas continually broke over the ship's poop, and flew into the sails with such violence that we still expected the tearing of our sails or oversetting of the ship, and withal, to our utter discomfort, we perceived that we fell still more and more to leeward, so that we could not double the cape. We were now come within half a mile of the cape, and so near the shore, that the counter-surf of the sea would rebound against the ship's side, so that we were much dismayed with the horror of our present end. Being thus at the very pinch of death, the wind and seas raging beyond measure, our Master veered some of the main sheet; and whither it was by that occasion, or by some current, or by the wonderful power of God, as we verily think it was, the ship quickened her way, and shot past that rock where we thought she would have shored. Then between the cape and the point there was a little bay, so that we were somewhat farther from the shore, and when we were come so far as the cape, we yielded to death. Yet our good God, the Father of all mercies, delivered us, and we doubled the cape about the length of our ship, or very little more. Being shot past the cape, we presently took in our sails, which only God had preserved unto us; and when we were shot in between the highlands, the wind blowing trade, without any inch of sail we spooned before the sea, three men being not able to guide the helm, and in six hours we were put five-and-twenty leagues within the Straits, where we found a sea answerable to the ocean.

In this time we freed our ship from water, and after we had rested a little our men were not able to move; their sinews were stiff and their flesh dead, and many of them (which is most lamentable to be reported) were so eaten with lice as that in their flesh did lie clusters of lice as big as peas, yea, and some as big as beans. Being in this misery, we were constrained to put into a cove for the refreshing our men. Our Master, knowing the shore and every cove very perfectly, put in with the shore and moored to the trees as beforetime we had done, laying our anchor to the seaward. Here we continued until the twentieth of October; but not being able any longer to stay through extremity of famine, the one and twentieth we put off into the channel, the weather being reasonable calm; but before night it blew most extremely at west-north-west. The storm growing outrageous, our men could scarcely stand by their labour; and, the Straits being full of turning reaches, we were constrained by discretion of the Captain and Master in their accounts to guide the ship in the hell-dark night, when we could not see any shore, the channel being in some places scarce three miles broad. But our Captain, as we first passed through the Straits, drew such an exquisite plat of the same as I am assured it cannot in any sort be bettered, which plat he and the Master so often perused, and so carefully regarded, as that in memory they had every turning and creek; and in the deep dark night, without any doubting, they conveyed the ship through that crooked channel. So that I conclude the world hath not any so skilful pilots for that place as they are; for otherwise we could never have passed in such sort as we did.

The 25th we came to an island in the Straits named Penguin Isle, whither we sent our boat to seek relief; for there were great abundance of birds, and the weather was very calm. So we came to an anchor by the island in seven fathoms. While our boat was at shore, and we had great store of penguins, there arose a sudden storm, so that our ship did drive over a breach, and our boat sank at the shore. Captain Cotton and the Lieutenant, being on shore, leapt into the boat and freed the same, and threw away all the birds, and with great difficulty recovered the ship. Myself also was in the boat the same time, where for my life I laboured to the best of my power. The ship all this while driving upon the lee-shore, when we came aboard we helped to set sail and weighed the anchor; for before our coming they could scarce hoist up their yards, yet with much ado they set their fore-course. Thus, in a mighty fret of weather, the seven and twentieth day of October, we were free of the Straits, and the thirtieth of October we came to Penguin Isle, being three leagues from Port Desire, the place which we purposed to seek for our relief.

When we came to this isle we sent our boat on shore, which returned laden with birds and eggs; and our men said that the penguins were so thick upon the isle that ships might be laden with them, for they could not go without treading upon the birds, whereat we greatly rejoiced. Then the Captain appointed Charles Parker and Edward Smith, with twenty others, to go on shore and to stay upon the isle for the killing and drying of those penguins, and promised after the ship was in harbour to send the rest, not only for expedition, but also to save the small store of victuals in the ship. But Parker, Smith, and the rest of their faction suspected that this was a device of the Captain to leave his men on shore, that by these means there might be victuals for the rest to recover their country. And when they remembered that this was the place where they would have slain their Captain and Master, surely (thought they) for revenge hereof will they leave us on shore. Which, when our Captain understood, he used these speeches unto them: "I understand that you are doubtful of your security through the perverseness of your own guilty consciences. It is an extreme grief unto me that you should judge me bloodthirsty, in whom you have seen nothing but kind conversation. If you have found otherwise, speak boldly, and accuse me of the wrongs that I have done; if not, why do you then measure me by your own uncharitable consciences? All the company knoweth, indeed, that in this place you practised to the utmost of your powers to murder me and the Master causeless, as God knoweth, which evil in this place we did remit you. And now I may conceive, without doing you wrong, that you again purpose some evil in bringing these matters to repetition. But God hath so shortened your confederacy as that I nothing doubt you. It is for your master's sake that I have forborne you in your unchristian practices. And here I protest before God that for his sake alone I will yet endure this injury, and you shall in no sort be prejudiced, or in anything be by me commanded. But when we come into England (if God so favour us) your master shall know your honesties. In the mean space be void of your suspicions, for, God I call to witness, revenge is no part of my thought." They gave him thanks, desiring to go into the harbour with the ship, which he granted. So there were ten left upon the isle, and on the last of October we entered the harbour. Our Master, at our last being here, having taken careful notice of every creek in the river, in a very convenient place, upon sandy ooze, ran the ship on ground, laying our anchor to seaward, and with our running ropes moored her to stakes upon the shore which he had fastened for that purpose, where the ship remained till our departure.

The third of November our boat, with water, wood, and as many as she could carry, went for the Isle of Penguins; but, being deep, she durst not proceed, but returned again the same night. Then Parker, Smith, Townesend, Purpet, with five others, desired that they might go by land, and that the boat might fetch them when they were against the isle, it being scarce a mile from the shore. The Captain bade them do what they thought best, advising them to take weapons with them. "For," said he, "although we have not at any time seen people in this place, yet in the country there may be savages." They answered that here were great store of deer and ostriches; but if there were savages they would devour them. Notwithstanding, the Captain caused them to carry weapons, calivers, swords, and targets. So the sixth of November they departed by land, and the boat by sea; but from that day to this day we never heard of our men. The 11th, while most of our men were at the isle, only the Captain and Master with six others being left in the ship, there came a great multitude of savages to the ship, throwing dust in the air, leaping and running like brute beasts, having vizards on their faces like dog's faces, or else their faces are dog's faces indeed. We greatly feared lest they would set our ship on fire, for they would suddenly make fire, whereat we much marvelled. They came to windward of our ship and set the bushes on fire, so that we were in a very stinking smoke. But as soon as they came within our shot, we shot at them, and, striking one of them in the thigh, they all presently fled, so that we never heard nor saw more of them. Hereby we judged that these cannibals had slain our nine men. When we considered what they were that thus were slain, and found that they were the principal men that would have murdered our Captain and Master, with the rest of their friends, we saw the just judgment of God, and made supplication to His Divine Majesty to be merciful unto us.

While we were in this harbour our Captain and Master went with the boat to discover how far this river did run, that, if need should enforce us to leave our ship, we might know how far we might go by water. So they found that farther than 20 miles they could not go with the boat. At their return they sent the boat to the Isle of Penguins, whereby we understood that the penguins dried to our heart's content, and that the multitude of them was infinite. This penguin hath the shape of a bird, but hath no wings, only two stumps in the place of wings, by which he swimmeth under water with as great swiftness as any fish. They live upon smelts, whereof there is great abundance upon this coast. In eating they be neither fish nor flesh. They lay great eggs, and the bird is of a reasonable bigness, very near twice so big as a duck. All the time that we were in this place we fared passing well with eggs, penguins, young seals, young gulls, besides other birds such as I know not; of all which we had great abundance. In this place we found a herb called scurvy-grass, which we fried with eggs, using train oil instead of butter. This herb did so purge the blood that it took away all kind of swellings, of which many died, and restored us to perfect health of body, so that we were in as good case as when we came first out of England. We stayed in this harbour until the 22nd of December, in which time we had dried 20,000 penguins; and the Captain, the Master, and myself had made some salt by laying salt water upon the rocks in holes, which in 6 days would be kerned. Thus God did feed us even as it were with manna from heaven.

The 22nd of December we departed with our ship for the isle, where with great difficulty, by the skilful industry of our Master, we got 14,000 of our birds, and had almost lost our Captain in labouring to bring our birds aboard; and had not our Master been very expert in the set of those wicked tides, which run after many fashions, we had also lost our ship in the same place. But God of His goodness hath in all our extremities been our protector. So the 22nd, at night, we departed with 14,000 dried penguins, not being able to fetch the rest, and shaped our course for Brazil. Now our Captain rated our victuals, and brought us to such allowance as that our victuals might last six months; for our hope was that within six months we might recover our country, though our sails were very bad. So the allowance was two ounces and a-half of meal for a man a-day, and to have so twice a week, so that 5 ounces did serve for a week. Three days a week we had oil, three spoonfuls for a man a day; and 2 days in a week pease, a pint between 4 men a day, and every day 5 penguins for 4 men, and 6 quarts of water for 4 men a day.

This was our allowance, wherewith (we praise God) we lived, though weakly and very feeble.

The 30th of January we arrived at the island of Placentia, in Brazil, the first place that outward bound we were at; and having made the shoal, our ship lying off at sea, the Captain with 24 of the company went with the boat on shore, being a whole night before they could recover it. The last of January at sun-rising they suddenly landed, hoping to take the Portugals in their houses, and by that means to recover some cassava-meal, or other victuals for our relief; but when they came to the houses they were all razed and burnt to the ground, so that we thought no man had remained on the island. Then the Captain went to the gardens, and brought from thence fruits and roots for the company, and came aboard the ship, and brought her into a fine creek which he had found out, where we might moor her by the trees, and where there was water and hoops to trim our cask. Our case being very desperate, we presently laboured for despatch away; some cut hoops, which the coopers made, others laboured upon the sails and ship, every man travailing for his life, and still a guard was kept on shore to defend those that laboured, every man having his weapon likewise by him. The 3rd of February our men with 23 shot went again to the gardens, being 3 miles from us upon the north shore, and fetched cassava-roots out of the ground, to relieve our company instead of bread, for we spent not of our meal whilst we stayed here.

The 5th of February, being Monday, our Captain and Master hasted the company to their labour; so some went with the coopers to gather hoops, and the rest laboured aboard. This night many of our men in the ship dreamed of murder and slaughter. In the morning they reported their dreams, one saying to another, this night I dreamt that thou wert slain; another answered, and I dreamed that thou wert slain; and this was general through the ship. The Captain hearing this, who likewise had dreamed very strangely himself, gave very strait charge that those which went on shore should take weapons with them, and saw them himself delivered into the boat, and sent some of purpose to guard the labourers. All the forenoon they laboured in quietness, and when it was ten of the clock, the heat being extreme, they came to a rock near the wood's side (for all this country is nothing but thick woods), and there they boiled cassava-roots, and dined. After dinner some slept, some washed themselves in the sea, all being stripped to their shirts, and no man keeping watch, no match lighted, not a piece charged. Suddenly as they were thus sleeping and sporting, having gotten themselves into a corner out of sight of the ship, there came a multitude of Indians and Portugals upon them, and slew them sleeping; only two escaped, one very sore hurt, the other not touched, by whom we understood of this miserable massacre. With all speed we manned our boat, and landed to succour our men, but we found them slain, and laid naked on a rank one by another, with their faces upward, and a cross set by them; and withal we saw two very great pinnaces come from the river Janeiro very full of men, whom we mistrusted came from thence to take us, because there came from Janeiro soldiers to Santos, when the General had taken the town, and was strong in it. Of 76 persons which departed in our ship out of England, we were now left but 27, having lost 13 in this place, with their chief furniture, as muskets, calivers, powder, and shot. Our cask was all in decay, so that we could not take in more water than was in our ship for want of cask, and that which we had was marvellous ill-conditioned; and being there moored by trees, for want of cables and anchors, we still expected the cutting of our moorings, to be beaten from our decks with our own furniture, and to be assailed by them of Janeiro. What distress we were now driven into I am not able to express. To depart with 8 tuns of water in such bad cask was to starve at sea, and in staying our case was ruinous. These were hard choices; but being thus perplexed, we made choice rather to fall into the hands of the Lord than into the hands of men, for His exceeding mercies we had tasted, and of the others' cruelty we were not ignorant.

So concluding to depart, the 6th of February we were off in the channel, with our ordnance and small shot in a readiness for any assault that should come, and having a small gale of wind we recovered the sea in most deep distress. Then bemoaning our estate one to another, and recounting over all our extremities, nothing grieved us more than the loss of our men twice, first by the slaughter of the cannibals at Port Desire, and at this isle of Placentia by the Indians and Portugals. And considering what they were that were lost, we found that all those that conspired the murdering of our Captain and Master were now slain by savages, the Gunner only excepted. Being thus at sea, when we came to Cape Frio the wind was contrary; so that for 3 weeks we were grievously vexed with cross winds, and our water consuming, our hope of life was very small. Some desired to go to Bahia, and to submit themselves to the Portugals, rather than to die for thirst, but the Captain with fair persuasions altered their purpose of yielding to the Portugals. In this distress it pleased God to send us rain in such plenty as that we were well watered, and in good comfort to return. But after we came near unto the sun, our dried penguins began to corrupt, and there bred in them a most loathsome and ugly worm of an inch long. This worm did so mightily increase and devour our victuals that there was in reason no hope how we should avoid famine, but be devoured of these wicked creatures; there was nothing that they did not devour, only iron excepted. Our clothes, boots, shoes, hats, shirts, stockings; and for the ship they did so eat the timbers, as that we greatly feared they would undo us by gnawing through the ship's side. Great was the care and diligence of our Captain, Master, and company to consume these vermin, but the more we laboured to kill them the more they increased, so that at the last we could not sleep for them, but they would eat our flesh, and bite like mosquitos. In this woeful case, after we had passed the equinoctial toward the north, our men began to fall sick of such a monstrous disease, as I think the like was never heard of. For in their ankles it began to swell, from thence in two days it would be in their breasts, so that they could not draw their breath, and then fell into their cods; and their cods and yards did swell most grievously, and most dreadfully to behold, so that they could neither stand, lie, nor go. Whereupon our men grew mad with grief. Our Captain with extreme anguish of his soul was in such woeful case that he desired only a speedy end; and though he were scarce able to speak for sorrow, yet he persuaded them to patience, and to give God thanks, and like dutiful children to accept of His chastisement. For all this divers grew raging mad, and some died in most loathsome and furious pain. It were incredible to write our misery as it was; there was no man in perfect health, but the Captain and one boy. The Master, being a man of good spirit, with extreme labour bore out his grief, so that it grew not upon him.

To be short, all our men died except 16, of which there were but 5 able to move. The Captain was in good health, the Master indifferent, Captain Cotton and myself swollen and short-winded, yet better than the rest that were sick, and one boy in health; upon us 5 only the labour of the ship did stand. The Captain and Master, as occasion served, would take in and heave out the top-sails, the Master only attended on the sprit-sail, and all of us at the capstan without sheets and tacks. In fine, our misery and weakness was so great, that we could not take in nor heave out a sail; so our top-sail and sprit-sails were torn all in pieces by the weather. The Master and Captain, taking their turns at the helm, were mightily distressed and monstrously grieved with the most woeful lamentation of our sick men. Thus, as lost wanderers upon the sea, the 11th of June 1593 it pleased God that we arrived at Berehaven, in Ireland, and there ran the ship on shore, where the Irish men helped us to take in our sails, and to moor our ship for floating; which slender pains of theirs cost the Captain some ten pounds before he could have the ship in safety. Thus without victuals, sails, men, or any furniture, God only guided us into Ireland, where the Captain left the Master and three or four of the company to keep the ship, and within 5 days after he and certain others had passage in an English fisher-boat to Padstow in Cornwall. In this manner our small remnant by God's only mercy were preserved and restored to our country, to Whom be all honour and glory, world without end.

Glossary

Glossary of obsolete phrases and of technical terms not explained in the text.

abide (past participle abidden), to endure
abroad, out of one's house
admiral, (1) a flagship, (2) the commander of a fleet
adventure, (1) to take a chance, (2) to have a financial stake in an enterprise
agree with, to do well with e.g. a certain food or climate
almade, a Guinean canoe
almain, a French type of ship's boat
aloof, at a distance
amarodina, a fruit (currant) used to flavour a liqueur
amend, to better e.g. workmanship
anatomy, a skeleton
angel, a gold coin also used as a measure of weight
anil, a shrub (*Indigofera*) and the dark blue dye (indigo) made from it
anta, a tapir
antic work, figured or highly decorated embroidery
arecas, betel-nut
areshine, a Persian measure of cloth
argomack, a thoroughbred horse
arming sword, a sword as part of regular military equipment
arquebus, a general term for hand guns including musket and caliver
arquebusier, a soldier armed with an arquebus
arquebus-shot, probably no more than 50 yards. Although early fire-arms inspired more fear and inflicted more dangerous wounds than the bow, their range was less
arrest, to come or bring to a stop
artificial, craftsmanlike or skilfully made
a-seaboard, on the seaward side
avoid, to withdraw or depart from
a-weather, on the windward side

babe, a doll
balsa, a South American raft or fishing platform
bank, (1) a row e.g. of targets, (b) a rowers' bench in a galley; bank up, to get out the oars and take to rowing
bark, a small (less than 100 tons) usually 3-masted merchant vessel
barrico, a wooden keg
base, the smallest (1-pounder) cannon, which could be carried in the arms; base-shot, 40 yards or less
basilisk, the largest size of cannon ($8\frac{3}{4}$ inch)

bass, vegetable fibre
bear with, to sail towards
because, in order that
bedstaff, a wooden rod used to support bedding
behoof, benefit
bend, to aim
benjamin, gum benzoin used in perfumery
bigg, four-rowed barley
bilboes, leg-shackles
billow, waves ("sea", caused by local wind, as supposed to "swell"
    resulting from a distant disturbance)
board, (1) a tack, (b) a table, (3) the surface on which a picture is
    painted
bolt, to move rapidly
bombasine cotton, raw cotton
bonnet, additional canvas laced to the foot of a course
borrow, to sail near the shore
bound (of a ship), strengthened with applied timbers
bow-shot, 80 to 100 yards
brage, bragget, an alcoholic drink made from honey and ale
branched, decorated with figured embroidery
brand-iron, a grid-iron
brave, splendid or showy
bravery, a show or an act of bravado
brazil, a wood (*Caesalpinia*) producing a red dye
breach, breaking seas
brigantine, a small ship easily manoeuvrable with sail or oars
broadcloth, fine plain-wove double-width cloth
bruit, a report or rumour
brustling, rushing and splashing
buff, bison or buffalo
but, unless

cabie, a cabaya or muslin tunic
cable's length, 200 yards
cabrito, a wild goat
cacique, an American Indian chieftain
cade, a basket
calentura, a tropical fever
caliver, a light musket usually fired without a rest
cameline, a garment made of camel hair
cana fistula, cassia-bark, an inferior kind of cinnamon
cape, to head or point (of a ship)
capelin, a small fish like a smelt
capule, a Mexican stone-fruit

caramoussal, the Turkish or Moorish term for a brigantine, q.v.

caravel, (1) a fast Portuguese lateen-rigged ship, (2) a light Turkish frigate using both sail and oars

carbuse, a water-melon

card, a map or chart

carmosant, unexplained but probably a form of carmesi or cramoisi (crimson)

carnation, flesh-coloured

carrack, a very large merchant vessel

cassado, unexplained, possibly a misprint for *passado*, an attacking lunge in fencing

cast about, to put the ship on the opposite tack

catter, a mule

caul, a cap

chamber, the charge-piece or cartridge for breech-loading guns

champaign, level open country

charge, (1) weight or draught (of ships), (2) expense

charter-party, the contract between the owners of a ship and a consigner of goods to be carried in it

cheap, a bargain; good cheap, cheap; better cheap, cheaper

cheapen, to bargain

chekin or *chikino*, a gold coin of Venice

cimarron, a maroon, i.e. escaped negro slave

cleft, a piece of split wood

cock, (1) a ship's boat, (2) a spout or tap

cod, (1) a pod, (2) the scrotum, (3) a fish

common, to associate with

compass, to pass round

confine, to have a common boundary with

conversation, social intercourse

copped, with a rounded peak

Cordovan skin, cordwain or leather of Cordova

corselet, a steel breastplate

corsive, corrosive

cotton-wool, raw cotton

countervail, to provide an equivalent in exchange

course, (1) a direction steered, (2) the larger, lower square-sail on fore and main masts

cowl-staff, a pole for carrying a tub or basket

crasko, a material (linen-crash)

crayer or crare, a small trading vessel

Crosiers, the constellation of the Southern Cross

crusado, a Portuguese coin, also used as a weight

crumster, a squat boat or hoy

culverin, a large (18-pounder) cannon

customer, a customs-officer
cut (a sail), to unfurl it

dainty, fine, of a high standard, or agreeable (the modern English
    "nice")
deliverly, deftly
demi-culverin, the largest cannon (9-pounder) generally acceptable on
    shipboard; demi-culverin shot, about 350 yards. This estimate is
    based on the belief that, at sea, guns were normally used at point
    blank range, i.e. with the centre of the barrel level
depart with, to part with
devise, to chat
disable, to weaken or damage; to declare invalid
disembogue, to come out of a river into the sea
displease, to take offensive action against
dilvered, shaken (a term from sieving tin-ore)
double cannon, a large (60-pounder) cannon, the same as a cannon-
    royal
dreary, grievous
dress, to prepare (e.g. food) or set in order
dure, to last or persist
dynie, a musk-melon

earnestly, seriously, in truth
eland, the European elk or the Canadian elk (wapiti)
ell, a measure of length (in England 45 inches)
engine, any mechanical contrivance
enter, to undertake
entertain, to receive as a guest
entreat, (1) to beg, (2) to treat or deal with
evet, an eft or newt
expedition, speed
experiment, experience

factor, a merchants' selling agent
falchion, a curved sword
falcon, a 2¼ to 2½ inch 3-pounder cannon; falcon-shot, about 250 yards
    (but see note on demi-culverin shot)
falconet, a 1½ to 2 inch 2-pounder cannon
fall with, to come to or light upon
fancy, something pleasing or entertaining
fear, to frighten
feats of war, military exercises
fetch, a trick

fight, a screen concealing and protecting the crew in a naval engagement

fighting sails, the principal sails (the others being furled to reduce the need for handling during a naval engagement)

figu, the fruit of the plantain

finding, keep or maintenance

fizgig, a kind of harpoon

flasket, a shallow basket

flaw, a sudden squall of wind

flesh, meat

flight, a light arrow for long-distance shooting; flight-shot, 200 to 240 yards (the "clout", or ultimate limit, was set at 240 yards)

flow (of the tide), to reach high-water

flown sheet, the sheet eased off so that the sail is more nearly square across the ship

flux, dysentery

flyboat, a small fast-sailing vessel

foist, a light galley moved either by sail or oars

footings, the junctions in a ship's timbers

footrope, the rope stitched along the foot or bottom of a sail to strengthen it

forslow, to be slow about or to neglect

for that, because

frame, (1) to cope with, (2) to shape (of carpenter's work)

frank, to pen and feed up animals

fret, a squall of wind

frieze, coarse woollen cloth

frigate, a very light vessel (smaller than a foist) moved by sail or oars

fuff, fusee, or spindle-full, a measure of thread in a length of cloth

full sea, the 'top' of spring tides, i.e. High Water Full & Change

furmenty (frumenty), wheat boiled in milk

furniture, accoutrements

gage, a hostage

gale, a breeze, not necessarily a strong one

galego, unexplained but evidently a boat of shallow draught and yet capable of making the sea-passage from England to Trinidad under sail

galley, a low single-decked vessel propelled by oars, with auxiliary sails

galliot, a small galley, easily manoeuvrable by sail or oars

garboil, a disturbance or brawl

garbanzos, chick-peas

gaunt (sea-bird), a gannet

gear, "stuff", in this case a powder

gentile, a pagan

glass, a ½-hour glass for measuring time; a bell was rung when the glass
  was turned (hence "eight bells" marks the end of a four-hour watch)
goosewing, a sail with one side brailed up to reduce the sail-area
gossip, a godparent
grains, grains of paradise, i.e. pepper
grapnel, a small anchor
grave, to clean a ship's bottom
green fowl, young birds or chicks
gripe, (1) the piece of timber at the forward end of the keel, (2) a
  vulture
grits, coarse oatmeal
guard, a stripe or band of colour
guiacco, probably the date-plum
gulf, a whirlpool

haddock (hullock), a storm-sail of very small area
hail-shot, multiple shot in a single cartridge
half-hake, a small arquebus or hand-gun
halyard, a vertical rope for hoisting a sail
handfast, to handcuff or manacle
haul, to sail on a certain course
hawse, the hole or slot through which the anchor-cable runs
headfast, the rope securing the ship's head to the shore
height, latitude
high (of the tide), to reach high water
hing, the drug asafoetida
hold, a fortress or stronghold
Hollantide, All Hallows or All Saints' Day
hounds, wooden projections either side of the masthead
hull, to drift with sails furled; a-hull describes a ship in this condition
hurcados, the harbour-bar at San Lucar in Andalusia
hurts, whortleberries or blueberries

iegur, a cereal (sorghum)
in case that, a possibility that
indurate, harden
in fine, eventually or in conclusion

janissary, a soldier of the Turkish standing army
junk, old or inferior rope

kedge, a small anchor
keep, to dwell
keep about, to continue changing direction
ken, to con or pilot a ship by observing marks

kern, to crystallise e.g. salt by exposure to the air
kersey, coarse woollen cloth
knot, an intricate pattern

lagarto, an alligator
landfang, shelter (given by the land) from the wind
large, (1) broad, (2) (of wind) broad on the beam i.e. not a head-wind
lay, (1) to aim the ship's head, (2) to set guard over
lee, (1) shelter from the wind, (2) the sheltered side away from the
    wind; upon the lee, with sails aback i.e. not drawing; leeward,
    inclined to drift away from the wind
let, to hinder or prevent; an obstacle
lewd, wicked
lieger, a resident agent
licerous, greedy
light-horseman, a light ship's-boat, later called a gig
lodia, a Russian coasting vessel
luff, to turn the ship's head towards the wind

magueys, agave
main, (1) the mainland, (2) the open sea
main force, fully exerted strength
maine, to lower (a sail)
making, shape or appearance, and so within the making of the land,
    within sight of it
malieno, a fruit (raspberry) used to flavour a liqueur
manilla, a bracelet
manurance, cultivation; manure, to cultivate
margarite, a bead
mean, an instrument or agent
means, by the means that, because
meat, food (not necessarily flesh)
medine, Levant currency
meetly, fitly or suitably
mete, to measure
mill, the cereal millet
minion, a 3 to $3\frac{1}{4}$ inch 3-pounder cannon; minion-shot, about 275 yards
    (but see note on demi-culverin shot)
montego de porco, lard
Morian, a Moor
morion, a steel helmet
morse, a walrus
mortar-piece, a large-bore cannon for lofting projectiles on a high
    trajectory
motion, (1) a motive or intention, (2) a suggestion

move, to urge or persuade
mure, a wall
Muscovy glass, mica
musket, the heavier kind of hand-gun, usually supported on a forked
    strutt or "rest" when firing

nail, a cloth measure of 1/16 of a yard
neat, cattle
nochole, a Mexican fruit
nurse, a kind of dogfish

occupation, profession; men of occupation, professional men
occupy, to work at or with, or to use
of force, necessarily
olens (eland), an elk, see eland above
ooze, mud
open, in full view
outligger, a spar projecting horizontally from the side of a ship, e.g. to
    extend a sail
overblow (of wind), to blow with great violence
overfall, an area of turbulent water
overseen, deluded

painful, taking pains or industrious
pargo, a species of sea-bream
partisan, a spear with cutting projections on the blade
passing, surpassingly or in the highest degree
pawn, (1) a colonnade or cloister, (2) a hostage
peppered, dotted or speckled
perry, a gust of wind
persuaded, determined
pester, to clog or encumber; an encumbrance
piece, a fire-arm (musket or cannon)
pike, (1) a long spear, (2) a peak; piked, peaked or pointed
pill, to plunder
pine, a pine-apple
pine-apple, a pine-cone or pine-tree
pintado, painted cotton cloth
piscary, a fishing-ground
pistolet, a gold coin
plant, (1) to mount (artillery), (2) to colonise
plat, a plot or chart
ply, to manoeuvre
point, a piece of lace
poise, weight

pomecitron, a fruit, the true citron
post, with speed
pot-gun, a short cannon of large bore, a mortar
powder, to salt or pickle
presently, instantly
press, a crowd
prest, ready and in good order
pretence, an expressed intention
pretend, to express an intention (not a false one)
prevent, to go ahead of or anticipate in action
privy, hidden
proportion, a rationing schedule
proportionally, perhaps in symmetrical or geometrical patterns
proportioned, shaped
provant, a provision or allowance of food
puke, a blue-black colour
purchase, advantage

race, to scratch or cut
rear, to raise, i.e. bring above the horizon by approaching it
reeve (past tense rove), to thread a rope through a block or ring
regiment, government
reis, a Portuguese coin
relation, a report
riyal, a silver coin
roader, a ship riding at anchor
roan cloth, linen from Rouen
room (come or go), to turn the ship's head away from the wind (the
    opposite to luff); go room with, to turn to leeward of a point of land
    (the opposite to weather)
rout, a band or troop
royal cannon, a large 60-pounder cannon, the same as a double cannon
rummage, to clear out the bilges of a ship in order to disinfect them or
    to search for a leak
running-glass, an hour or more usually a half-hour glass, turned each
    time the sand has *run* through
rush in on, to move a boat by short heaves on head- or anchor-rope
rut, breaking waves

sad, serious; (of colour) sober
sagu, the cereal sago
saker, a medium-size (5-pounder) cannon; saker-shot, about 300 yards
    (but see note on demi-culverin shot)
saline, a salt-pan

sanguis draconis, a drug compounded of mercury and brimstone
saved, preserved by drying or pickling
scant, scarcely; (of wind) to alter direction to more nearly ahead
scantling, a limited target
scarf, the overlap of ship's timbers at a joint
sea-crow, probably a skua
sea-gate, a sea or swell
sea-pie, an oystercatcher
seethe (past tense sod), to boil or stew
seize, to reach or arrive at
serviceable, ready or willing to serve
servitor, a serviceman
shadow, a sunshade
shall-lines, unexplained, but presumably an item of ships' gear
shear-hook, a sickle-shaped hook mounted on the yard-arm to tear the
    rigging of an enemy ship approaching too close
sheet, a horizontal rope controlling the angle of a sail to the wind
shift, a change of clothing or of sails
shore, to run ashore
short upon, to haul in on a rope
shrink (of wind), to alter direction to more nearly ahead
shrouds, (1) fixed rigging bracing the mast to the side of the ship, (2)
    the chapel of St Faith in St Paul's Cathedral, London
sign, to communicate with by signs
similitude, likelihood
sinisterly, maliciously
sith, because
skiff, a ship's boat
slant, a suddenly arising breeze
sleeveless, useless or unsuccessful
sleight, a ruse
slight, small (e.g. bells)
snaphance, a flintlock
sod, see seethe
sort, a collection or crowd
spar, crystalline mineral
spent, worn out or used up
spinel, a precious stone (inferior ruby)
spodium, tutty, i.e. zinc oxide used as an ointment
spoil, (1) to despoil or plunder, (2) to hurt or wound, (3) damage
stagne, a pond
stang, a pole or beam
states, city magnates or governors
stay, to stop or prevent
sternfast, the rope securing a ship's stern to the shore

stickle, rapid
stint, to restrict
store, plenty
suavle, meaning obscure, possibly "swirling" (from the dialect swavel, a swirl)
sucket, a sweetmeat, candy
sun (north, south etc.), time calculated by the position of the sun, e.g. in the northern hemisphere south sun is noon, north sun is midnight
sun (land), low-lying

table, a picture
tangomangoes, renegade Portuguese in Guinea
target, a small shield
tell, to count
tender, to cherish or take care of
threaden point, a piece of lace made of linen thread
tide-gate, a channel where the tide runs strongly
timber, a measure of furs (forty skins)
tisik, the headman of a Persian village
toll, to entice
tolmach, Tartar word for interpreter
top, the platform or look-out post at the head of the mast
topgallant, the platform at the head of the topmast
topnet, a basket made of rushes
toy, a pretty trifle
traffic, trade or commerce
trail, a train or trailing garment
train-oil, whale-oil
traverse, to swing across
trestle-trees, pieces of timber supporting the top at the masthead
trim, (1) to fit out or repair, (2) to prepare food
truck, to barter or exchange
try, to ride out a gale by riding more or less head to wind with reduced sails; a-try, a ship in this situation; out of try, unbalanced or listing
twist, the fork or groin

unconvenient, unseemly or impolite
utter, to offer for sale; little utterance, little market for

vail, to drop downstream
vent, a trade outlet
Visitor, an inspector from the Spanish Inquisition
visnova, a fruit (cherry) used to flavour a liqueur

waist, the open part of the upper or main deck

wales, horizontal timbers strengthening the sides of a ship
want, a mole
warp, to move a ship by pulling on a rope or warp
watch, the period, usually four hours, when one part of the crew is on
    duty
watchet, light blue
waterworks, strengthening timbers (see wales)
way, the wake of a ship
weather, to pass to windward of; in the weather of, to windward of
wildfire, a ball of highly inflammable substance ignited and tossed from
    a mortar into an enemy ship or fort
without, outside

yard, (1) the spar at the head of a sail (2) the penis
yaw, to make a sudden change in the direction of a ship's head

INDEX OF PERSONS, PLACES, SHIPS, AND BOOKS QUOTED

NOTE: The entries for principal persons include (in brackets) some important biographical details which do not appear in the narratives selected. Where modern place-names differ markedly from those used by the Elizabethans, they are appended (in brackets).

INDEX

631